EFFECTIVE ENFORCEMENT OF EU LABOUR LAW

This book by the ETUI Transnational Trade Union Rights Expert Network analyses enforcement as a key element making EU labour law effective or ineffective.

Enforcement is the key ingredient that makes rights effective and ensures compliance. It can make or break a legal system. Despite this, enforcement of EU labour law has received little scholarly attention in recent decades and has rarely been examined in a comprehensive way. This book aims to fill this gap.

Intended for academics and practitioners alike, the book adopts a threefold approach to examine this issue. First of all, it explores the idea of effective enforcement and sets out the wider context in which EU labour law enforcement takes place. Secondly, it analyses how enforcement operates in particular areas, including non-discrimination, health and safety, information and consultation rights, and the rights of migrating workers. Thirdly, it critically assesses the role of specific actors (in particular collective actors like trade unions, as well as whistle-blowers and the European Labour Authority) and settings (public procurement, economic and monetary policy) regulated by EU law. Drawing on the insights produced by these analyses, the book concludes by proposing a comprehensive Draft for a Model Directive on 'Effective Enforcement of EU Labour Law' as an inspiration for policy development and scholarly debate in this area.

Effective Enforcement of EU Labour Law

Edited by
Zane Rasnača
Aristea Koukiadaki
Niklas Bruun
and
Klaus Lörcher

•HART•
OXFORD • LONDON • NEW YORK • NEW DELHI • SYDNEY

HART PUBLISHING

Bloomsbury Publishing Plc

Kemp House, Chawley Park, Cumnor Hill, Oxford, OX2 9PH, UK

1385 Broadway, New York, NY 10018, USA

29 Earlsfort Terrace, Dublin 2, Ireland

HART PUBLISHING, the Hart/Stag logo, BLOOMSBURY and the Diana logo are trademarks of Bloomsbury Publishing Plc

First published in Great Britain 2022

A catalogue record for this book is available from the British Library.

A catalogue record for this book is available from the Library of Congress.

Library of Congress Control Number: 2022935332

ISBN: HB: 978-1-50994-441-5
ePDF: 978-1-50994-443-9
ePub: 978-1-50994-442-2

Typeset by Compuscript Ltd, Shannon

FOREWORD

There was a time, not so long ago, when questions of enforcement of EU labour law could easily be brushed under the carpet of the principle of 'national procedural autonomy', with the occasional nonchalant reference to rather abstract, if not anodyne, concepts such as 'effectiveness' and 'equivalence'. The bulk of the enforcement questions pertaining to EU labour and social law Directives were effectively shifted into, no doubt descriptively accurate and conceptually sophisticated, constructs such as 'decentralised enforcement', 'two parent' theories, reflexivity, and the creative – and often complicit – use of the preliminary references procedure.

But all these interesting theoretical elaborations could barely mask the lack of a suitable response to a fundamental question that was on everybody's lips, and that sits at the heart of the enquiry of the present book. Given the growing fragmentation and polycentricity of what we understand as EU (and European) labour law and regulation, what are the most effective enforcement responses 'either in a particular area of EU labour law or to enable a particular actor to make a change and to contribute to achieving justice'?

The present book – another quality product of the ETUI's Transnational Trade Union Rights (TTUR) Network – therefore explores the question of enforcement of EU labour law from a strategic perspective, as also noted in the opening pages of the first introductory chapter written by the editors, Zane Rasnača, Aristea Koukiadaki, Klaus Lörcher and Niklas Bruun. This is an unabashedly 'worker-centric' enquiry, that is performed in an admirably coherent and systematic fashion by all the chapters in the publication. Perhaps inevitably, the rigour through which this analysis is carried out, leads the authors of this work to identify a number of 'enforcement gaps', to which some of the chapters seek to provide remedial suggestions. Ultimately it falls on the editors of the book to bring together these contributions, as well as their own findings, into a proposal for a Directive on Effective Enforcement, whose main purpose is, at the same time, to fill in these' enforcement gaps' but also to bring some strategic coherence in the way the solutions identified in the earlier parts of the book are presented and could be operationalised.

Indeed, there was a time when questions of enforcement of EU labour law could easily be brushed under the carpet. With this book, this is no longer the case.

Nicola Countouris
Director of the Research Department
ETUI

CONTENTS

PART II
ENFORCEMENT IN SPECIFIC AREAS OF EU LABOUR LAW

PART III
MECHANISMS AND SPECIFIC ACTORS FOR ENFORCING EU LABOUR LAW

LIST OF CONTRIBUTORS

Bhumika Billa is a PhD scholar in law and researcher at the University of Cambridge. She has previously worked for the Indian government in trade policy and is currently looking at issues in law and technology

Niklas Bruun is Professor (Emeritus) of Law at Hanken School of Economics, Helsinki, Finland. He is also a guest professor (part-time) at the Faculty of Law, Stockholm University and a member of the research project group 'An inclusive and sustainable Swedish labour law – the ways ahead' (led by Professor Petra Herzfeld-Olsson and funded by the Swedish Research Council). He is a former member of the Freedom of Association Committee (ILO) and the CEDAW Committee (UN).

Aude Cefaliello is a legal researcher at the ETUI in the Occupational Health and Safety & Working Conditions Unit, with a PhD from the University of Glasgow on how to improve the legal framework for occupational safety and health in the European Union.

Eliot Cobbaut is currently working as a research and teaching assistant and PhD student at the Law Faculty of the Catholic University of Louvain (Belgium) under the supervision of Professors Filip Dorssemont, Simon Deakin, Auriane Lamine and Marc Maesschalck. In his PhD research, he analyses how, in the light of the pragmatic sociology of the risk, the existing alert laws can contribute to a better corporate risk management for a better protection of the health and environment. Beyond the topic of alert law, his scientific interest concern all the legal issues related to the information's management in private entities

Olivier De Schutter teaches at UC Louvain and SciencesPo. He is since 2020 the UN Special Rapporteur on extreme poverty and human rights. He was a member of the UN Committee on Economic, Social and Cultural Rights (2015–20) and the UN Special Rapporteur on the right to food (2008–14). He was chair of the EU Network of Independent Experts on Fundamental Rights (2002–07) and member of the Scientific Committee of the EU Fundamental Rights Agency (2012–17).

Simon Deakin is a Professor of Law and director of the Centre for Business Research at the University of Cambridge.

Filip Dorssemont is Full Professor of Labour Law at the UC Louvain and Guest Professor at the Université Libre de Bruxelles.

Mijke Houwerzijl is a Professor of Labour Law at Tilburg University, the Netherlands.

Antoine Jacobs is Emeritus Professor of Law at the University of Tilburg, the Netherlands.

Csilla Kollonay-Lehoczky is Professor Emerita of the Central European University (Legal Studies Department), former member of the European Committee of Social Rights and of the European Gender Equality Network operated by the Commission of the European Union.

Aristea Koukiadaki is Professor of Labour Law and Industrial Relations at the University of Manchester (Department of Law). Her most recent work focuses on precarious work, public procurement and social clauses and collective bargaining and Covid-19.

Barbara Kresal is Professor of Labour Law and Social Security at the University of Ljubljana, Slovenia.

Klaus Lörcher is former Legal/Human Rights Adviser to the European Trade Union Confederation (ETUC) and former Legal Secretary to the Civil Service Tribunal of the European Union, Germany.

Giovanni Orlandini is Professor of Labour Law and Social Security Law at the University of Siena (Italy).

Silvia Rainone is a researcher at the ETUI and is affiliated with the Institute of Labour Law at KU Leuven. Her work focuses on the EU approach to labour policies and on how labour rights could preserve their relevance. In her PhD dissertation, written jointly under Tilburg University and KU Leuven, Silvia addressed the EU approach to workers' rights in case of business restructurings.

Zane Rasnača is a senior researcher at the European Trade Union Institute and affiliated member at the Institute for European Law, KU Leuven.

Marco Rocca is a permanent researcher at the French National Centre for Scientific Research (CNRS). He is a member of the DRES (*Droit, religion, entreprise et société*) research unit of the University of Strasbourg.

Mélanie Schmitt is Professor of Labour Law at the University of Strasbourg (Faculty of Law) and deputy head of the research centre UMR 7354 Law, Religion, Business and Society (DRES).

Joanna Unterschütz is an Associated Professor at the University of Business and Administration in Gdynia (Department of Law). Her recent research focuses on the intersection of labour law and criminal law, as well as labour law in the digital economy.

Piet Van Nuffel is senior expert at the Legal Service of the European Commission and Professor of European law (part-time), Institute for European Law, KU Leuven.

TABLE OF CASES

Case Law

Court of Justice of the European Union

Other International Courts

European Court of Human Rights

European Committee of Social Rights

ILO Committee on Freedom of Association

National Courts

TABLE OF LEGISLATION

European Union

International Law

National legislation

Introduction

Effective Enforcement of EU Labour Law

ZANE RASNAČA, ARISTEA KOUKIADAKI,
KLAUS LÖRCHER AND NIKLAS BRUUN

In the study of law, enforcement often comes as an afterthought. Even legal judgments, which in fact are snapshots of an enforcement process, are seen primarily as sources explaining substantive law. Nevertheless, the study of enforcement does have a significant, albeit inconspicuous role at the national level, and recently it has been receiving more and more attention globally.[1] The EU has also recently moved from enhancing national enforcement rules in order to make EU law more effective, towards improving its own enforcement-oriented landscape by developing EU-level enforcement mechanisms and institutions. This is visible both beyond[2] and within the area of EU labour law.[3]

With some notable but not very recent exceptions,[4] however, the enforcement of EU labour law has received little scholarly attention in recent decades and has rarely been examined comprehensively. This book attempts to fill this gap in order not only to enrich but also trigger further discussion. We approach enforcement as the key element in determining the effectiveness of EU labour law. The book takes a threefold approach. First, it explores the idea of effective enforcement and the classic enforcement typology from the perspective of EU labour law. It then analyses how enforcement operates in certain contexts, including non-discrimination, health and safety, information and consultation rights, and the rights of migrant workers. Finally, it turns to specific actors (whistleblowers, the European Labour Authority) and settings (European Pillar of Social Rights, public procurement, economic and monetary policy) regulated by EU law. It is primarily a collective work about how enforcement operates in the context of EU labour law, but also a research endeavour that necessarily adds to the general understanding of enforcement.

[1] See T Hardy and S Ariyawansa, 'Literature Review on the Governance of Work', ILO, October 2021.

[2] For example, the recent Directive (EU) 2020/1828 of the European Parliament and of the Council of 25 November 2020 on representative actions for the protection of the collective interests of consumers and repealing Directive 2009/22/EC.

[3] For example, the establishment of the European Labour Authority.

[4] See J Malmberg and M Gotthardt (eds), *Effective Enforcement of EC Labour Law* (Kluwer, 2003).

In the broad sense, enforcement comprises, on one hand, requirements for the full effectiveness of rights deriving from EU law, and on the other, remedies for breaches of EU law. For a long time, the main idea has been that EU law enforcement should and could be left mainly to national level and regulated principally by using ordinary national judicial remedies in cases of violation. Although the Court of Justice of the European Union (CJEU) has requested that Member States put effective remedies in place to ensure that substantive provisions of EU law are followed, there has been much less focus on detecting violations once they have been committed and on applying appropriate methods of redress than on substantive law. Although the European Commission has always been charged with overseeing the effective application, implementation and enforcement of EU law (Article 17(1) TEU), it has rarely (and even less so systematically) acted in this regard. The contribution of the European Commission to enforcement of EU labour law has been sporadic at best. Furthermore, the issue of effective enforcement of EU labour law has largely been neglected at the regulatory level. While the EU legislator has certainly approached the topic of enforcement in some of the legislative initiatives in the field, what has been lacking is a systematic and holistic approach to making sure that EU labour is enforced effectively.

This book aims to take stock of the enforcement of EU labour law. Some horizontal questions, however, should be explored before diving deeper into the study. We have to ask how do we conceptualise EU labour law, whose enforcement we are exploring here. What do we mean by 'effective enforcement', and how can we make sure that we keep workers in the centre of the enforcement debate? Finally, why is this book structured the way it is, and how should the reader approach it?

1. Scope of EU Labour Law

There are various ways of looking at the EU labour law *acquis* and its enforcement. While there is an identifiable body of law that could be described as 'labour law' or 'social policy', its coverage is far from comprehensive.[5] To define 'EU labour law' one could take a very narrow approach and look only at the part of the Treaty titled 'Social policy' and secondary measures adopted on the legal basis that can be found there. Or one could take a very broad approach, covering everything that seeks to promote the common interest by protecting and assisting weaker members of society (workers, the unemployed, people with disabilities, the elderly, migrants and so on) at the EU level. EU labour and social policy law often spills over into other areas of EU law (especially the internal market) and potentially represents a wide range of scenarios for enforcement.

Because of the very wide range of matters which one could gather under the notion of 'EU labour law', we needed to make some choices when it came to the

[5] C Barnard, *EU Employment Law*, 4th edn (Oxford, Oxford University Press, 2012) 641.

scope of this book. This was guided both by an attempt to capture as wide a variety of scenarios as possible in our exploration of enforcement, and by the need to remain concrete and concise in our approach.

In the book we therefore approach the scope of EU labour law from three standpoints. In the first part we focus on EU labour law broadly conceived, as embodied not only in the Social Policy title of the Treaty on the Functioning of the European Union (TFEU), but also internal market rules and even association and free trade agreements. We also venture beyond 'hard law' into the realm of 'soft law'. In contrast, in the second part of the book the authors have explored how enforcement works within specific areas of EU labour law covered by either free movement of workers or the Social Policy title. One aspect missing there, but perhaps worth a separate study in the future, is social security and protection. Although they are discussed to some extent in various contributions here, they are largely beyond the scope of the book. In the third and final part of the book we again approach labour law in a broad sense by trying to capture the roles of certain actors and mechanisms in enforcing EU labour law. Finally, the rather wide and comprehensive approach to the scope of EU labour law comes very much to the forefront in the last chapter of the book, in which a Model Directive on enforcement is proposed.

Our aim in this book is to portray EU labour law in terms of its ability to cover a wide variety of actors and to look into many EU law settings that are typically excluded from the area of labour law narrowly construed.

2. Effective Enforcement – A Contextualised Approach

The question of what kind of enforcement is effective is certainly not new. In fact, in the context of international criminal law it has even been asked whether enforcement really is necessary to make law effective?[6] In an ideal world, in which law is known, understood, applied and complied with without a second thought, we may be able to live without enforcement mechanisms. In reality, however, there is always some distance between rights 'on paper' and rights 'in practice', and, to achieve at least some justice, enforcement is necessary in any situation in which law is not applied or complied with correctly or at all. This situation is even more exacerbated in labour law because of the unbalanced relationship between workers and employers, and increasingly so also due to the sheer complexity of the employment, organisation and liability structures in today's labour market. Thus, effective enforcement is vital to successful implementation of labour law, and labour law that is not enforced rarely fulfils its social objectives.[7]

[6] MJ Gilligan, 'Is enforcement necessary for effectiveness? A model of the international Criminal Regime' (2006) 60(4) *International Organisation*, 935–67.

[7] N Gunningham, 'Enforcement and Compliance Strategies' in R Baldwin, M Cave and M Lodge (eds), *The Oxford Handbook of Regulation* (Oxford, OUP, 2010), ch 7.

An activity is effective if it is successful in attaining a desired or intended result. In the case of enforcement, one might thus assume that enforcement is effective if, say, law has reached its addressees after initially being ignored and has led to the effective realisation of rights. Namely, enforcement is the activity that, through various mechanisms, happens after (substantive) law has not been complied[8] with, and is effective if it brings about the situation that should have prevailed if there had been compliance in the first place, or at least if the victim of non-compliance is duly compensated.

Making sure that enforcement mechanisms and tools are effective is in the interest of everyone. All enforcement systems create costs, and nobody wants to spend money on a system that does not work. It is also vital that the enforcement system is effective because workers are disadvantaged in terms of both time and resources. Moreover, who should ultimately be responsible for pursuing enforcement and achieving justice for individual workers? Is it the state? Do workers' organisations such as trade unions also bear responsibility? Or maybe individual workers should be tasked with enforcing their rights and also paying for their enforcement? Clear chains of accountability might be lost in multi-actor enforcement regimes, and the accountability of state enforcement agencies can also suffer, if narrow measures of administrative performance take precedence over their accountability to the public for upholding employment standards legislation.[9] This may be even more complicated in EU law because of its multi-level and polycentric nature.

In this book particular attention is certainly paid to the role of workers' representatives and trade unions when it comes to enforcement of EU labour law (see Chapter 11 by Rainone and Chapter 16 by Dorssemont). The idea of co-enforcement, where state enforcement agencies (such as labour inspectorates) engage in sustained partnerships with workers' centres, trade unions, legal advocacy organisations, and other-community based organisations,[10] is central to developing any effective enforcement structure in the EU regulatory environment. Here labour is regulated in different ways and by different actors in each of the 27 Member States, and on top of that, the EU multilevel reality comes with additional challenges for effective enforcement. Any effective response has to be nuanced and take into account the necessity of cooperation in terms of both actors in pursuit of the enforcement of EU labour law and the applicable regulatory regimes.

[8] It is important to keep in mind that the term 'compliance' has been associated with soft law and voluntary compliance and used in a broader sense (LF Vosko et al, 'The Compliance Model of Employment Standards Enforcement: An Evidence-Based Assessment of Its Efficacy in Instances of Wage Theft' (2017) 48(3) *Industrial Relations Journal* 256–73).

[9] L Vosko, J Grundy and M Thomas, 'Challenging New Governance: Evaluating New Approaches to Employment Standards Enforcement in Common Law Jurisdictions' (2016) 37(2) *Economic and Industrial Democracy* 373–98, 381.

[10] There is an interesting discussion in the United States about this; see J Fine, 'Strategic enforcement and co-enforcement of U.S. labour standards are needed to protect workers through the coronavirus recession', 14 January 2021, https://equitablegrowth.org/strategic-enforcement-and-co-enforcement-of-u-s-labor-standards-are-needed-to-protect-workers-through-the-coronavirus-recession/.

Indeed, the 'effectiveness' of enforcement is especially relevant for complex settings like that of EU labour law, in which national rules interact with EU law. Even though the relationship between parties to employment contracts comes under private law, it is inherently unbalanced, with one party (the employer) having much more control than the other (the worker). This aspect poses challenges in terms of enforcement. Nevertheless, workers' situations and employers' approaches can vary greatly. Some workers are in a more vulnerable situation than others, and some employers are geared towards exploiting any competitive advantage they can possibly gain via labour law or its avoidance. Finally, employment relationships nowadays are rarely straightforward. For example, determining whether we are in fact dealing with labour law can sometimes be difficult because determining whether a 'worker' is indeed a worker and finding out who is their employer is becoming increasingly complex. This adds a layer of complexity to the issue of effective enforcement because when the subjects to whom enforcement is geared are not clearly definable, it is disputable whether application of the law can be effective. The dissipation of the employment relationship can increase the incentives for non-compliance, for example, at the bottom of several levels of subcontractors or between small undertakings who face fierce competition. It can also complicate efforts to define who is responsible for compliance.[11]

How can the task of enforcement be conducted in a way that achieves outcomes that are both effective (reducing the incidence of social harm) and efficient (done at the least cost to both obligation holder and regulator) while maintaining confidence in the system?[12]

Should enforcement – in order to be effective – be based on the idea of deterrence or persuasion? These are two underlying approaches that exist in the enforcement literature. The deterrence-based model assumes that employers act in a calculated manner and will take costly measures to comply with the law only when they are required to do so and believe that non-compliance is likely to be detected and severely punished.[13] According to this approach the severity and certainty of penalties must be such as to make it not economically rational to defy the law.[14] At the same time, there are studies that show that deterrence in the form of penalties does not always work and perception of risk might be more important than objective likelihood of legal sanctions.[15] Even in that case, empirical research

[11] D Weil, 'Creating a Strategic Enforcement Approach to Address Wage Theft: One Academic's Journey in Organizational Change' (2018) 60(3) *Journal of Industrial Relations* 437–60, 437; see also M Ji and D Weil, 'The Impact of Franchising on Labor Standards Compliance' (2015) 68(5) *ILR Review* 977–1006, 977.

[12] Gunningham, n 7 above, at 122.

[13] GS Becker, 'Crime and Punishment: An Economic Approach' (1968) 76(2) *Journal of Political Economy* 169–217; GJ Stigler, 'The theory of economic regulation' (1971) 2(1) *The Bell Journal of Economics and Management Science* 3–21.

[14] Gunningham, n 7 above, at 123–24.

[15] S Simpson, *Corporate Crime, Law and Social Control* (Cambridge, Cambridge University Press, 2002) ch 2.

has shown that sometimes there is no correlation between regulatory compliance and perceptions of the certainty and severity of punishment for violations.[16]

On the other hand, over-reliance in enforcement on an approach based on advice and persuasion (compliance-oriented) may also deteriorate into intolerable laxity and fail to deter those that simply have no interest in complying voluntarily.[17] There is even evidence that cooperative approaches may discourage improved regulatory performance if lawbreakers are allowed to go unpunished.[18] Most specialists now argue for a mix of both approaches, but how such a mix might best be achieved and what the ideal combination between cooperation and punishment might be, remains open. In this book we take as the starting point the need to have a minimum level of strict enforcement requirements in place in the area of labour law.[19] Such requirements do not exclude enforcement via 'soft law', however, and have to be complemented by coordination and 'co-enforcement' by multiple actors operating at multiple levels including for example, courts, the national enforcement authorities, EU-level bodies, workers' representatives – such as works councils and trade unions – among other actors.

When seeking effective enforcement it is worth starting by referring to the seminal contribution by Ian Ayres and John Braithwaite, in which they make the argument for 'responsive regulation'.[20] They approach enforcement from the angle of a dialogic regulatory culture in which regulators signal to business their commitment to escalate their enforcement response whenever a lower level of intervention fails.[21] According to Braithwaite's notion of a pyramid of enforcement strategy, the state is the enforcer and the response to any infraction should be scaled up if the lower-level approaches do not work. The first level is self-regulation, the second enforced self-regulation, the third command regulation with discretionary punishment, and the final level is command regulation with non-discretionary punishment (eg criminal sanctions).[22]

This approach considers only the 'state' to be the primary enforcer, however, and has a number of other limits for the purposes of our study. It is not created with multi-level governance in mind and could be difficult to apply in the EU context, where responsibility for enforcement of EU labour law is partly divided between the EU and national levels. It is also not enough for studying enforcement beyond the public sphere. In this context the so-called smart regulation approach

[16] J Braithwaite and T Makkai, 'Testing an Expected Utility Model of Corporate Deterrence' (1991) 25(1) *Law & Society Review* 7–40, 35.

[17] N Gunningham, 'Negotiated Non-Compliance: A Case Study of Regulatory Failure' (1987) 9(1) *Law & Policy* 69–95.

[18] SA Shapiro and RS Rabinowitz, 'Punishment versus Cooperation in Regulatory Enforcement: A Case Study of OSHA' (1997) 49 *Administrative Law Review* 714–62.

[19] I Ayres and J Braithwaite, Responsive Regulation: Transcending the Deregulation Debate (Oxford, Oxford University Press, 1992); M Wright, S Marsden and A Antonelli, *Building an Evidence Base for the Health and Safety Commission Strategy to 2010 and Beyond* (Sudbury, HSE Books, 2004).

[20] Ayres and Braithwaite, n 19 above.

[21] Ibid.

[22] This is the pyramid as explained by Ayres and Braithwaite, n 19 above.

to enforcement might be more useful because it conceives of enforcement in a multi-level and multi-actor setting, where escalation to higher levels of coercion is possible across several instruments and across different faces of the pyramid in a context-based way.[23] A more recent variant of this approach is the 'strategic enforcement' approach developed by Weil, which also permits an enforcement response in a polycentric multilevel environment. It is typically targeted at specific instances of non-compliance rather than approaching enforcement horizontally, however.

At the same time, these pyramid-based approaches have their limits. First, 'in situations which involve serious risk of irreversible loss or catastrophic damage' a graduated response might be inadequate because the risks are too high (eg in some situations pertaining to health and safety at work). Second, a graduated response to breaches is appropriate only where the parties have continuing interactions because only then one can possibly start with a low interventionist response and escalate it according to need. Where there is only one chance to influence behaviour – for example, because of the scarcity of inspections or the risk that the employer will cease to operate – a more interventionist initial response is necessary.[24] Because of these limits in labour law, a common floor seems necessary, and not only in terms of substantive procedural enforcement rules.

A further recent method that allows a more horizontal approach is based on 'protective gaps' that, among other things, focuses on identifying different types of enforcement gaps. Grimshaw et al (2016) have distinguished between four 'types' of enforcement gaps: gaps in awareness, power, mechanism and coverage. A comprehensive response and study of enforcement-related deficiencies has to take all these into account. For example, if workers or their representatives are not aware of a breach, there is no chance of enforcement; if resources are lacking in terms of time or increased dependency of the worker on the employer, enforcement is further frustrated. Furthermore, there must be (adequate) enforcement mechanisms to allow and foster a possibility of redress (for example, courts or extra-judicial opportunities). Finally, some workers might still be excluded if they are not covered by protection at all (eg in the case of undocumented employment). Hence enforcement gaps, even though they and their extent might differ in particular settings, have to be accounted for in order for enforcement mechanisms to be effective. In this book, however, we adapt this idea of enforcement gaps in two ways. First, we focus on the role of regulatory framework, the structural determinants of enforcement gaps.[25] Second, we consider these in a multi-level system, namely the EU.

[23] Gunningham, n 7 above, at 133.

[24] Ibid, at 135.

[25] V Mantouvalou, 'Legal Construction of Structures of Exploitation' in H Collins, G Lester and V Mantouvalou (eds), *Philosophical Foundations of Labour Law* (Oxford, OUP, 2018); Hardy and Ariyawansa, n 1 above; and D Grimshaw et al (eds), *Reducing Precarious Work. Protective gaps and the roles of social dialogue in Europe*, report for the European Commission, November 2016.

But there are no magic responses in terms of enforcement and no single approach that will function both efficiently and effectively for all workers and all employers. Nevertheless, one might reasonably expect that in certain settings some enforcement tools and responses will work better than others. This is the approach taken by this book: beyond studying enforcement in the context of EU labour law we also try to identify what kinds of enforcement responses are already effective or where enforcement has so far failed. We explore what kinds of enforcement would be necessary either in a particular area of EU labour law or to enable a particular actor to make a change and to contribute to achieving justice. In that sense, the authors of this book are 'strategising' about enforcement. Weil has described this approach as seeking 'to use the limited enforcement resources available to a regulatory agency to protect workers as prescribed by laws by changing employer behaviour in a sustainable way'.[26]

3. Putting the Worker at the Centre of Enforcement

Before diving into the structure of the book, one further clarification is needed to highlight the context of our study. An important starting point is that human rights (should) play a significant role for and in the European labour market and in particular in protecting both individual workers and collective actors active in defence of workers, such as trade unions and workers' representatives.

Indeed, labour rights are human rights, and therefore enforcement of labour rights is very often also enforcement of human rights and brings with it the same challenges. The Charter of Fundamental Rights of the European Union (CFREU) thus plays a significant role also in this book and helps in locating the worker at the centre of the whole endeavour. Indeed, the prime objective of enforcement is to achieve, if possible, restorative justice for individual workers or at least to duly compensate them. It is not for the purpose of punishing or compensating the state for missed taxes, for example. While other objectives arise in the enforcement discussion, it is extremely important to maintain a bird's eye view of the whole process and to make sure that the underlying objective is achievement of justice for workers rather than anything else.

Indeed, the effective enforcement of fundamental social rights enshrined in the CFREU is a specific challenge. To cope, however, the CFREU itself provides an important set of rights.[27] In the first place, as a core provision of Title VI, Article 47 CFREU guarantees the right 'to an effective remedy and to a fair trial', thus forming the foundation of minimum requirements for the whole judicial system. Evidently, this is the heart of enforcement. The current struggle between

[26] Weil, n 11 above, at 437.

[27] See eg F Dorssemont, K Lörcher, S Clauwaert and M Schmitt (eds), *The Charter of Fundamental Rights of the European Union and the Employment Relation* (Oxford, Hart Publishing, 2019).

the Polish Constitutional Court and the CJEU on the necessity for an independent judicial system is of crucial importance.[28] Secondly, several rights contained in Title V – Citizens' Rights – provide for administrative means of enforcement, such as the right to good administration (Article 41), the right of access to documents (Article 42), the European Ombudsman (Article 43) and the right to petition (Article 44).

The procedure for a preliminary reference to the CJEU remains for the time being probably the most important avenue for the CJEU to strengthen the enforcement of fundamental rights in general and social rights in particular. Practice especially in labour law, however, shows the need for a right to a 'constitutional complaint' for securing the rights enshrined in the CFREU, which could be addressed directly to the CJEU. Endeavours in this direction have not been successful to date. While not denying the need for certain admissibility criteria, this should nevertheless be an important demand for improvement in the next Treaty revision process. In any event, the EU's speedy accession to the European Convention on Human Rights (ECHR) is both necessary and important. This would at least make it possible to address the European Human Rights Court. Specifically for social rights, this first step should be followed by the EU's accession to the European Social Charter (ESC) and the Collective Complaints Procedure Protocol. These three measures would help to make fundamental (social) rights much more accessible and thus enforceable via judicial means.

4. Approach and Structure of the Book

This volume offers a comprehensive and updated account of enforcement as it functions in the context of EU labour law. The book, first, engages with the idea of 'effective enforcement' adequate for labour law and what it means in various settings. Second, it offers topical case studies, covering several areas of EU labour law and provides information about the actors, avenues and strategic choices relevant for enforcement.

As already indicated, the book is structured in three – or one could even argue three plus one – parts. In the first part of the book the authors engage with enforcement as such, and how it could and should be understood in the area of EU labour law. Part I starts with contributions by Jacobs (Chapter 1) and Koukiadaki (Chapter 2) that tackle, respectively, the fundamental issues of enforcement structure and remedies and sanctions in EU labour law. Further, Lörcher explores the special role of courts in enforcement in his contribution on access to justice, followed by Unterschütz, who tackles enforcement of EU labour law in both

[28] See Chapter 3 by K Lörcher; for the latest developments in relation to the CJEU: Order 27 October 2021, C-204/21 R *Commission v Poland*; for the ECtHR: 8 November 2021, nos 49868/19 and 57511/19, *Dolińska-Ficek and Ozimek v Poland*.

administrative law and criminal law settings (Chapters 4 and 5). After that, Kollonay-Lehoczky (Chapter 6) engages with the fascinating idea of soft methods as enforcement tools for European labour law standards. Finally, three specific and highly topical matters are tackled. First, strategic enforcement by Lörcher (Chapter 7). Second, enforcement of EU labour law in transnational context by Houwerzijl (Chapter 8), and finally the EU's role in the extra-territorial enforcement of labour laws (Deakin and Billa, Chapter 9).

In the second part of the book several authors explore enforcement in specific areas of EU labour law. These areas were chosen to capture a diverse set of enforcement examples, ranging from areas in which the EU legislator has done little or almost nothing in facilitating enforcement (see Chapter 11 on information and consultation rights by Rainone), to areas in which the legislator's attempts have not been particularly successful so far (see Chapter 12 on migrant and mobile workers' rights by Rasnača and Chapter 10 on enforcing non-discrimination by Kollonay-Lehoczky), as well as areas in which prevention rather than classical enforcement plays a key role (Chapter 14 on occupational health and safety by Cefaliello), and areas in which work is still under way to respond to the fast-changing world of work from an enforcement perspective (Chapter 13 on enforcing rights of non-standard workers by Kresal).

In the third part of the book the objective is threefold. First, to tackle specific actors that play a significant role in enforcing EU labour law (Chapter 16 on collective actors enforcing EU labour law by Dorssemont and Chapter 17 on the European Labour Authority by Van Nuffel). Second, to analyse certain settings or mechanisms that might be especially conducive for enforcing labour law (Chapter 15 on enforcing EU law via collective action by Orlandini, Chapter 18 on whistleblowing in light of enforcement of EU labour law by Cobbaut, and Chapter 20 on the European Pillar of Social Rights by de Schutter). Third, to examine some EU law settings that potentially constrain the enforcement of EU labour law (see Chapter 19 on enforcing labour law via public procurement by Bruun and Chapter 21 on enforcing EU labour law in the context of Economic and Monetary Union by Schmitt and Rocca).

Last but certainly not least, building upon all the contributions of the book, we propose a draft model Directive on effective enforcement of EU labour and social law, meant as a starting point for discussing ways in which we could improve the enforcement of workers' rights in the European Union in a systemic and strategically harmonised way.

All in all, this is primarily a book about enforcement within the broad area of EU labour law rather than about enforcement as such. In the process of exploring enforcement in this area, however, several authors also raise points relevant to a more general analysis of enforcement structure and its role in the European Union.

PART I

Understanding Enforcement

1

The Enforcement Structure for EU Labour Law

ANTOINE JACOBS

1. The Legal Shape of EU Labour Law

Laws are senseless if they are not enforced. Effective enforcement of the laws is served if the law is known by most of the people affected by it. Unfortunately, tomes on labour law are not exactly on the bookshelves of most workers in Europe. They certainly are on the desks of trade union officials, human resources staff at enterprises and lawyers and judges, but that is national labour law – French, German, Polish and so on. EU labour law, by contrast, is hardly known even by labour law experts. Partly this is irrelevant because much of EU labour law is, as a sponge absorbs water, implemented by national rules of the EU Member States. Sometimes, however, one needs to refer to the origin of such rules and then one is confronted with a bunch of extraordinary sources, which require clarification.

National labour law is – apart from what is created by the social partners – commonly laid down in acts of parliament and administrative regulations and orders. Questions rarely arise about their binding force and supremacy in the legal hierarchy of sources. All this is a bit different with EU law.

In the EU, some labour law is contained in a number of provisions of the Treaties of the EU and the EU Charter of Fundamental Rights. Some have direct binding effect and even indirect horizontal effect for workers.[1] Beyond doubt, the most elaborate EU labour law is to be found in Regulations and Directives.

Regulations are the strongest of the two as they are directly applicable in all Member States, in any sort of litigation, and override any national provision that runs counter to them. No further legislative measures by the Member States are needed to implement them. In the labour law field, however, Regulations are used almost exclusively to realise the free movement of workers, provided for in Articles 45–48 TFEU, to unify social conditions in the transport business

[1] K Lorcher in F Dorssemont et al (eds), *The Charter of Fundamental Rights of the European Union and the Employment Relation* (Oxford, Hart, 2019) 620.

(Article 91 TFEU), to establish the rules of the conflict of laws and to establish EU-level institutions.

For EU labour law, the most used act is the *Directive* as it does not aim to 'unify' national laws; it only aims to 'harmonise' them to a certain extent. This means that the Member States are only bound to achieve certain results in their national law, but they are given freedom in the way they do so. Very often, in the social field, Directives contain only minimum norms, which means that Member States may maintain/issue provisions more favourable to workers. Not every provision of a Directive has direct effect, however, and horizontal effect (effect in cases between private parties) is also often missing.

Besides these classic instruments of national and of EU labour law there is an upcoming trend, in both national and EU labour law, to formulate standards in the guise of 'soft' law. As for EU labour law, one might recall the fruits of the Open Method of Coordination, the European Employment Strategy, the European Semester, the new Economic Governance, the European Pillar of Social Rights and so on. (For its dangers and potentials for enforcement of EU labour law, see Chapter 20 by De Schutter, Chapter 21 by Schmitt and Rocca and Chapter 6 by Kollonay-Lehoczky.)

2. The Institutional Arrangements for the Enforcement of EU Labour Law

In every Member State of the EU the national constitution has made various arrangements to ensure that its laws are respected.

The progenitors of the EU Treaties opted to give the EU institutions only a secondary role in the enforcement of EU law. In principle, it is the institutions and functions for enforcement that the Member States have created for their own domestic law that should be used to enforce European labour law. Then, behind that, various EU institutions are entrusted with the task of supervising the enforcement of EU labour law in the Member States.

2.1. National Arrangements for Enforcing Labour Law

Let us look at all these national arrangements made by the various Member States to enforce labour law from a comparative point of view.

In all European countries some parts of labour law are subject to criminal sanctions. In most EU Member States the duty of monitoring the implementation of this type of labour laws has been assigned to a special branch of the police, the labour inspectorate. This organisation is responsible for the supervision and control of labour law compliance. In their work, labour inspectors may cooperate with trade unions, employers' organisations, self-governing staff bodies, works councils, the state administration and local authorities. What differs is the severity of criminal sanctions and the powers of supervision. In all European countries it is primarily the legislation on health and safety which is subject to criminal sanctions and supervised by the labour inspectorate. The same often applies to other parts of statutory labour law, such as working times, minimum wages, child labour, work performed by foreigners and human trafficking. In Belgium and France even the terms of generally binding collective agreements are sanctioned under criminal law. In practice, only serious violations or violations with severe consequences are criminally prosecuted, however. The majority of violations nowadays are dealt with by means of administrative fines (see Chapter 5 by Unterschütz and Chapter 14 by Cefaliello).

Those parts of labour law that are neither subject to criminal sanctions nor monitored by the labour inspectorate must be enforced in courts of civil or administrative law. It is up to the parties to a contract of employment or their mandates to bring an issue of labour law before the court. This is indeed the dominant practice in the field of labour law.

The various rights and obligations of labour law require a well functioning system of labour law litigation and fair trial (see Chapter 7 by Lörcher).[2]

In many EU Member States employment cases are dealt with by a special branch of the judiciary. In a few countries there is a labour court besides the ordinary courts. In a minority of EU Member States there is no specialised branch of the judiciary dealing with labour law cases. The ordinary courts of civil and administrative law are competent instead.

In a number of countries, if labour cases contain one or more aspects of constitutional law, a further appeal may be possible to a Constitutional Court.

Whether a country has special courts for employment matters or not, it is important to take into account whether there are enough facilities for workers if they go to court to invoke their rights. Very important for the enforceability of labour law are the various arrangements that may facilitate access to the court. The rules in various EU Member States include items such as the following:

- no mandatory legal representation;
- low court fees;
- moderate process risk;
- simplified rules of procedure;
- quick procedures;
- possibilities for injunctive release;
- vicinity of courts

[2] S van Drooghenbroeck, 'Labour Law Litigation and Fair Trial under Article 6 ECHR' in F Dorssemont et al (eds), *The European Convention on Human Rights and the Employment Relationship* (Oxford, Hart, 2013) 159–82; K Lörcher, 'Article 47 – Right to an Effective Remedy and to a Fair Trial' in F Dorssemont et al (eds), *The Charter of Fundamental Rights of the European Union and the Employment Relation* (Oxford, Hart, 2019) 609–31.

In most EU Member States trade unions may act in court on behalf of all employees or at least on behalf of their own members, or they may at least assist employees. In some states they have access to the courts in their own name ('collective redress') (see Chapter 16 by Dorssemont).

In many countries legal assistance is available to employees with low incomes for litigation purposes.

Employees generally do not relish the prospect of having to sue their employer and employment cases are rarely brought by workers who still have an employment contract. Most labour cases are related to dismissal.

This problem is notably strong with regard to migrant workers. They for several reasons are subject to a wide 'justice gap' (see Chapter 12 by Rasnača). Transborder workers may experience extra hurdles because of the complexity of international private law arrangements (see Chapter 8 by Houwerzijl).

For all these reasons less adversarial forms of dispute resolution have long been tried and tested in labour law, such as grievance procedures within the company, collective dispute committees of the parties to the collective agreement, or mediation and arbitration bodies, such as an easily accessible equal treatment body ('early settlement mechanism').

In several Member States, out-of-court mechanisms are important in labour law, but in other countries there are almost no official permanent ADR mechanisms in force, or they are of relatively little importance. Except for the last-mentioned mechanism, all the abovementioned forms of national labour law enforcement are the typical 'judicial' ways. Certainly in the field of labour law, however, one should not neglect the out-of-court ways of enforcing the law. Mention should be made here of collective action, such as strikes, sit-institutions or boycotts, often supported by trade unions (see Chapter 15 by Orlandini and Chapter 16 by Dorssemont). In addition, workers' representatives have information, consultation and participation rights (trade unions, works councils and so on) (see Chapter 11 by Rainone, Chapter 14 by Cefaliello and Chapter 16 by Dorssemont), the phenomenon of the alert (see Chapter 18 by Cobbaut and Chapter 19 by Bruun) and finally the role of the media.

For the moment my presumption concerning all the abovementioned facilities is that the situations in the various Member States seem to vary so much that one may seriously question whether there is a real 'level playing field' between the Member States regarding the enforcement of EU labour law.

I shall return to that point in section 6 of this chapter.

2.2. EU Arrangements for Enforcing EU Labour Law

As already mentioned, a number of EU institutions have been given a 'back-seat role' in supervising the enforcement of EU labour law in the various Member States.

2.2.1. European Commission

Over the years, the EU Commission has always been very active in making sure that Member States implement EU rules properly. If in doubt, it will first try to reconcile differences in an amicable procedure. If the difference nevertheless persists, the Commission will bring the case to court, as upon the application of the EU Commission or of a Member State, the Court of Justice of the European Union (CJEU) has the power to determine whether a Member State has failed to fulfil an obligation under the Treaty (Articles 258–59 TFEU) (see Chapter 5 by Unterschütz).

If the Court finds that a Member State has failed to fulfil an obligation under the EU Treaties, the state shall be required to take the necessary steps to comply with the judgment of the Court. If the state fails to comply with the judgment, the Court may impose a lump sum penalty on it (Article 260 TFEU).

All Member States have been the subject of infraction proceedings in the field of labour law, some more frequently than others.[3]

2.2.2. Court of Justice of the European Union

There is a special Court of Justice of the European Union, with its seat in Luxembourg, tasked with supervising all business of the European institutions and the correct behaviour of the Member States as regards European law. The Court has the important task of ensuring that 'in the interpretation and application of the Treaties the law is observed' (Article 19 TEU).

Many cases are handled directly by the CJEU itself. Some cases are handled by the so-called General Court (formerly the Court of First Instance).[4] The decisions handed down by the General Court may only to a limited extent be subject to a right of appeal to the CJEU (see Article 256 TFEU). Finally, decisions can also be taken by the so-called specialised courts. There is, for instance, a specialised court for European civil servants' cases.

At the instance of the EU Commission or a Member State or the Council of Ministers or any natural or legal person directly and individually concerned, the Court also has the power to review the legality of acts carried out by the Council or the Commission (Article 263 TFEU). If such an action is well founded, the CJEU shall annul the act concerned (Article 264 TFEU).[5]

[3] See the annual reports of the Commission on the application of EU law. The United Kingdom seems to have been the most assiduous EU Member State as far as the implementation of Directives is concerned!

[4] The General Court handles, among other things, cases concerning the European Social Fund and state aid.

[5] See Case 45/86 *Commission v Council* [1987] ECR 1493; Case C-300/89 *Commission v Council* [1991] ECR I-2867.

The European Parliament may also bring an action for annulment before the Court against an Act of the Council or of the Commission, provided that such an action seeks only to defend the Parliament's powers and that it is based exclusively on arguments concerning the infringement of those powers.[6] National courts do not have jurisdiction to determine for themselves whether acts of the EU institutions are invalid or not.[7] An as yet unresolved question concerns whether the European social partners could bring such an action before the Court when their prerogatives are violated by the Council or the Commission.

Natural and legal persons can also invoke the Court's review, but only in relation to acts that affect them directly and individually. This means that they can almost never invoke the Court's review of Directives or Regulations.

Finally, the Court has the power to issue preliminary rulings at the request of national courts concerning the interpretation of the Treaty and of Acts of the EU (Article 267 TFEU).[8] This last possibility is often invoked – including in the field of labour law – in the course of a domestic lawsuit if the domestic judge wants to see the national law tested under EU law.

However, the parties in a domestic lawsuit cannot themselves turn to the CJEU for preliminary rulings; they can only encourage the domestic judge to put questions to the CJEU.

In itself it is rather strange that this set-up, which perhaps can be explained by the cautious beginnings of the EC in the 1950s, has not been modernised and brought to the level of direct access by the interested parties within the framework of the Convention on a Constitution for Europe and the subsequent Treaty of Lisbon. Such a change was discussed at the said Convention, but it has not been adopted.[9]

Not only may the highest judge put preliminary questions to the CJEU, all judges *may* do so, and sometimes even *must* do so.[10] However, the highest judge must seek the opinion of the Court, except if the European provision has already been interpreted by the Court ('*acte éclairé*') or if there is no reasonable doubt about how the question should be answered ('*acte clair*').[11] Quite remarkably, it was the European Court of Human Rights (ECtHR) that ruled that a court in a EU Member State that without motivation fails to put preliminary questions to the CJEU has violated Article 6 ECHR![12]

[6] Case C-70/88 *European Parliament v Council* [1990] ECR I-2067; see also Case C-295/90 *European Parliament v Council* [1992] ECR I 4193, and Case C-65/90 *European Parliament v Council*, 16 July 1992 [1992] ECR I-4593.

[7] Case 314/85 *Foto-Frost* [1987] ECR 4225.

[8] See for hints on the formulation of preliminary questions the weekly bulletin of the EC Court of Justice of 18–22 November 1996, 31/96.

[9] ATJM Jacobs, *The European Constitution* (Nijmegen, Wolf Legal Publishers, 2005) 70.

[10] CJEU 10 September 2015, C-160/14 *Ferreira da Silva*.

[11] The Court may refuse to answer; see Case C-415/93 *Bosman* [1995] ECR I-4921.

[12] ECtHR 8 April 2014, Case 17120/09 *Dhahbi v Italy*, in which this court considers that if EU law is at stake the judge must show why he is not putting a question for a preliminary ruling. See also ECtHR 21 July 2015 Case 38369/09 and ECtHR 20 September 2011, *Ullens v Belgium*. Also interesting is a

Anyway, this possibility of presenting preliminary questions to the CJEU has become the major source of interpretation for European labour law.

Often European labour law leaves it to the Member States to determine sanctions on violations of the implemented EU rule. However, the CJEU requires that the sanctions be 'effective, proportionate and dissuasive' (see Chapter 2 by Koukiadaki). The CJEU has further determined that the system of the EU Treaties requires the Member States to afford reparation of damages caused to individuals as a result of breaches of EU law for which they are responsible, whichever authority of the Member State is responsible for the damage. This includes infringements attributable to national courts adjudicating a case at last instance. This is the so-called Francovich doctrine.[13] State responsibility is deemed to exist if the following three conditions are met: (i) the rule of law infringed must be intended to confer rights on individuals; (ii) the breach must be manifest and sufficiently serious; and (iii) there has to be a direct causal relationship between the breach of the obligation incumbent on the state and the loss or damage sustained.[14] It is in principle for the national courts to determine whether the criteria for establishing this liability of the Member State are satisfied[15] (see Chapter 2 by Koukiadaki).

2.2.3. European Labour Authority

Recently, the European Labour Authority (ELA) was established to enhance the enforcement of European labour and social security law in a cross-border context, for example in a situation of workers posted abroad.[16] This institution should, among other things, support compliance and cooperation between Member States in the application and enforcement of the EU law related to labour mobility across the Union. The actual scope of action of this European Labour Authority is a minimal political compromise (see Chapter 5 by Unterschütz and Chapter 17 by Van Nuffel). It could have much wider powers.

2.2.4. European Ombudsman

The European Ombudsman was instituted to investigate complaints about maladministration of the European institutions and bodies. It also proactively promotes good administration at EU level (see Chapter 5 by Unterschütz). Even if the interventions of the Ombudsman do not create binding law, it may nevertheless serve

Dutch court case (Court of Appeal The Hague, 25 October 2016 KLM ECLI:NL:GHDHA:2016:2984) about the possibilities of claiming damages if the Supreme Court has not put forward preliminary questions to the CJEU.

[13] Joined Cases C-6/90 and C-9/90 *Francovich and Bonifaci* [1991] ECR I-5357; see D Curtin in ILJ (1992) 81; T Hervey in ILJ (1997) 74 et seq; see also CJEU 10 September 2015, C-160/14 *Ferreira da Silva*.

[14] ECJ 5 March 1996, Cases C-46/93 and C-48/93 *Brasserie du Pecheur and Factortame*; ECJ 30 September 2003, C-224/01 *Köbler*.

[15] See the Dutch Supreme Court in a case reproduced in ILLR 2017.

[16] See Regulation (EU) 2019/1149.

the proper enforcement of EU labour law by every worker in the EU in general and by the workers at the EU institutions and bodies in particular.

3. EU Requirements Concerning Enforcement

In the foregoing we have seen that the EU has certainly not created a simple layer of administration. It has developed its own series of legislative instruments that are in a complicated relationship with national law. At the same time, it has developed a complicated entanglement of enforcement tracks, at both domestic and at EU level, to ensure the effective enforcement of EU rules.

It is certainly marvellous to see how well, in the 70 years of the EC/EU, its rules have been applied in numerous cases in which national administrations and courts, organisations and individuals have spontaneously applied them without any incitement to do so.

However, EU rules have not always found their bed made for them, and enforcement had to be carried out in tougher areas. On these occasions the EU bodies have shown themselves not indifferent to enforcement. The Commission, the European Parliament, the Council and the CJEU have frequently shown concern for the effective enforcement of EU rules. The Commission has started procedures against Member States under Article 258 TFEU in numerous cases. Many were subsequently interrupted because the state in question reviewed its legislation, but several have led to CJEU judgments to bring national law into agreement with EU law. Many of these actions by the Commission have been launched under pressure from the European Parliament. It may be argued that the Commission should be more active in this field, and not put up with a formal fulfilment of EU obligations by Member States, but insist on material fulfilment (see Chapter 3 by Lörcher).

The EU legislator has from time to time played its own role in framing the EU rules in such a way that their effectiveness is ensured. For instance the new generation of Equality Directives already contain provisions that open up some space for Member States to expand national rules on collective redress and injunctive relieve for trade unions in this area (see Chapter 10 by Kollonay-Lehoczky).

The CJEU has, at the invitation of national judges, clarified various legal aspects of EU rules, thereby enabling national courts to enforce them in complicated legal situations. It has used its power to issue preliminary rulings at the request of national courts concerning the interpretation of the Treaty and of EU Acts (Article 267 TFEU). This last possibility is often invoked – including in the field of labour law – in the course of domestic lawsuits if the domestic judge wants to see national law tested against EU law. In fact, the CJEU ought to play this role because of Article 47 CFREU, which ensures the right to effective judicial protection (see Chapter 3 by Lörcher and Chapter 2 by Koukiadaki).[17] These experiences

[17] CJEU, C-414/16 *Egenberger*, 17 April 2018.

highlight a number of problems in the enforcement of EU labour law rules and offer us a number of wise lessons for solving them.

Many of these experiences have been in the area of anti-discrimination law (see Chapter 10 by Kollonay-Lehoczky).[18] When a German court sanctioned an employer in a vacancy procedure for discriminating against a woman merely by imposing restitution of a train ticket, the CJEU corrected it: sanctions ought to be 'effective, proportionate and dissuasive'. However, the Court denied that the Directive provisions require 'punitive damages'[19] (see Chapter 2 by Koukiadaki). Notably in two anti-discrimination Directives the EU legislator has taken over CJEU case law to the effect that

> Member States shall lay down the rules on sanctions applicable to infringements of the national provisions adopted pursuant to this Directive and shall take all measures necessary to ensure that they are applied. The sanctions which may comprise the payment of compensation to the victim must be effective, proportionate and dissuasive.[20]

In the Directive on temporary agency work, a further sentence is added to these rules: 'They shall, in particular, ensure that workers and/or their representatives have adequate means of enforcing the obligations under this Directive.'[21] To counter discriminatory practices, pecuniary sanctions alone are insufficient; also the procedural rules must be oriented to accommodate claims against the abuse: first the CJEU[22] and then the EU lawmakers[23] have ordered a fair division of the burden of proof in discrimination cases (see Chapter 10 by Kollonay-Lehoczky).

When discriminatory practices persisted despite a long list of regulatory measures, the legislator established the European Institute for Gender Equality in Vilnius to assist the Member States in banning such practices. In the same vein, the EU has established the European Foundation for the Improvement of Living and Working Conditions in Dublin, the European Agency for Safety and Health at Work in Bilbao, and the European Centre for the Development of Vocational Training and the EU Agency for Fundamental Rights in Vienna (see Chapter 5 by Unterschütz).

In 2022 the Written Information Directive will be replaced by the Transparency Directive. This Directive, besides the usual provision on penalties, contains the innovative provision that Member States must, in cases of violation, offer the

[18] R Iordanache and I Ionescu, 'Discrimination and its sanctions – Symbolic vs Effective remedies' (2014) 19 *European Anti-discrimination Law Review*.

[19] CJEU, C-407/14 *Arjona Camacho*, 17 December 2015; L Meurkens, 'The punitive damages debate in continental Europe: food for thought', Maastricht European Private Law Institute, Working Paper No 2014/01.

[20] Art 15 Directive 2000/43/EC (race discrimination); Art 25 Directive 2006/54/EC (sex discrimination); there is now a comparable provision also in the Work–Life Balance Directive, Art 13 Directive 2019/1158/EU.

[21] Art 10 Directive 2008/104/EC.

[22] ECJ, C-109/88 *Danfoss*, 17 October 1989; and others.

[23] Directive 97/80 of 15 December 1997, [1998] OJ L 14/6.

workers either a legal assumption or an early settlement mechanism.[24] When the EU rules on banning illegal migrant labour were apparently applied too leniently, the EU legislator reacted by toughening its rules against this undesirable phenomenon.[25] In this Directive even specific sanctions are mentioned explicitly: Member States shall adopt sanctions of both criminal and non-criminal nature and involving liability of the legal person. Moreover, this Directive sets standards on financial sanctions, back-payments, subcontracting and inspections.[26] Something similar was done by the EU legislator when the Posted Workers Directive was not applied in such a way as to curb social dumping using this type of worker. The EU adopted a specific Enforcement Directive. In this Directive one finds even more extensively formulated comparable provisions as regards control measures, inspections, facilitation of complaints, back-payments and subcontracting liability (see Chapter 8 by Houwerzijl).[27]

Effective enforcement of EU rules may sometimes also require the introduction and ordering of functional registration practices, as can be learned from a recent Spanish case on the application of the Working Time Directive.[28]

Also very useful for the enforcement of labour law are 'Francovich' claims against Member States that allow practices to persist that are in contravention of EU rules, even when these rules are laid down in Directives that have no horizontal effect. The CJEU has imposed numerous restrictions on the use of this facility, however (see above). As already mentioned, the effective enforcement of EU labour law is promoted by the Court's preparedness to give indirect horizontal effect to some Articles of the CFREU.[29]

In the newest proposal for a Directive on adequate minimum wages in the EU[30] the European Commission introduced the requirement of 'effective access of workers to statutory minimum wages', which would notably consist of reinforcing controls and field inspection systems (Article 8). Moreover there is a requirement that in the performance of public procurement and concession contracts, economic operators respect the applicable collectively agreed wages and statutory minimum wages (Article 9).

Finally, the newest proposal for a Directive for Equal Pay (m/f)[31] contains an almost revolutionary catalogue of workers' rights in both court and out of court litigation.

[24] Art 15-19 Directive 2019/1152/EU.

[25] Directive 2009/52, [2009] OJ L 168.

[26] Art 9-14 Directive 2009/52/EC.

[27] Art 9-12 Directive 2014/67/EU.

[28] Case C-55/18 *Federación de Servisios de Comisiones Obreras v Deutsche Bank SAE* [2019] ECLI:EU:C:2019:402.

[29] CJEU, C-414/16 *Egenberger*, 17 April 2018.

[30] COM (2020) 682 final.

[31] COM (2021) 93 final.

Article 12 – Defence of Rights

Member States shall ensure that, after possible recourse to conciliation, judicial procedures for the enforcement of rights and obligations related to the principle of equal pay between men and women for equal work or work of equal value are available to all workers who consider themselves wronged by a failure to apply the principle of equal pay for equal work or work of equal value. Such procedures shall be easily accessible to workers and to those who act on their behalf, even after the labour relationship in which the discrimination is alleged to have occurred has ended.

Article 13 – Procedures on Behalf or in Support of Workers

Member States shall ensure that associations, organisations, equality bodies and workers' representatives or other legal entities which have, in accordance with the criteria laid down by national law, a legitimate interest in ensuring equality between men and women, may engage in any judicial or administrative procedure to enforce any of the rights or obligations related to the principle of equal pay between men and women for equal work or work of equal value. They may act on behalf or in support of a worker who is a victim of an infringement of any right or obligation related to the principle of equal pay between men and women for equal work or work of equal value, with the latter's approval. Equality bodies and workers' representatives shall also have the right to act on behalf or in support of several workers, with the latter's approval.

Article 14 – Right to Compensation

Member States shall ensure that any worker who has suffered harm as a result of an infringement of any right or obligation related to the principle of equal pay between men and women for equal work or work of equal value shall have the right to claim and to obtain full compensation or reparation, as determined by the Member State, for that harm. The compensation or reparation referred to in paragraph 1 shall ensure real and effective compensation for the loss and damage sustained, in a way which is dissuasive and proportionate to the damage suffered. The compensation shall place the worker who has suffered harm in the position in which that person would have been if he or she had not been discriminated against based on sex, or if no infringement of any of the rights or obligations relating to equal pay between men and women for equal work or work of equal value had occurred. It shall include full recovery of back pay and related bonuses or payments in kind, compensation for lost opportunities and moral prejudice. It shall also include the right to interest on arrears. The compensation or reparation may not be restricted by the fixing of a prior upper limit.

Article 15 – Other Remedies

Member States shall ensure that, in legal proceedings aimed at ensuring the enforcement of any right or obligation related to the principle of equal pay between men and women for equal work or work of equal value, the courts or other competent authorities may order, at the request of the claimant and at the expense of the defendant: (a) an injunction order establishing an infringement of any right or obligation related to the principle of equal pay between men and women for equal work or work of equal value and stopping the infringement; (b) an injunction order ordering the defendant to take structural or organisational measures to comply with any right or obligation related to the principle of equal pay between men and women for equal work or work of equal value or to stop an infringement thereof. Non-compliance with any of these orders shall, where appropriate, be subject to a recurring penalty payment, with a view to ensuring compliance.

Article 16 – Shift of Burden of Proof

Member States shall take the appropriate measures, in accordance with their national judicial systems, to ensure, when workers who consider themselves wronged because the principle of equal pay has not been applied to them, or establish before a court or other competent authority facts from which it may be presumed that there has been direct or indirect discrimination, that it shall be for the defendant to prove that there has been no direct or indirect discrimination in relation to pay. Member States shall ensure that, in any legal or administrative proceedings concerning direct or indirect discrimination, where an employer failed to comply with any of the rights or obligations related to pay transparency set out in Articles 5 to 9 of this Directive, it shall be for the employer to prove that there has been no such discrimination. The claimant shall benefit from any doubt that might remain. This Directive does not prevent Member States from introducing evidential rules that are more favourable to the claimant in proceedings instituted to enforce any of the rights or obligations related to equal pay between men and women for equal work or work of equal value. Member States need not apply paragraph 1 to proceedings in which it is for the court or competent body to investigate the facts of the case. This Article shall not apply to criminal procedures, unless otherwise provided by national law.

Article 17 – Access to Evidence

Member States shall ensure that in proceedings concerning a claim regarding equal pay between men and women for equal work or work of equal value, national courts or competent authorities are able to order the defendant to disclose any relevant evidence which lies in their control. Member States shall ensure that national courts have the power to order the disclosure of evidence containing confidential information where they consider it relevant to the claim. They shall ensure that, when ordering the disclosure of such information, national courts have at their disposal effective measures to protect such information. This Article shall not prevent Member States from maintaining or introducing rules that are more favourable to claimants.

Article 18 – Limitation Periods

Member States shall lay down rules applicable to limitation periods for bringing claims regarding equal pay between men and women for equal work, or work of equal value. Those rules shall determine when the limitation period begins to run, the duration thereof and the circumstances under which it is interrupted or suspended. Limitation periods shall not begin to run before the violation of the principle of equal pay between men and women for equal work or for work of equal value or infringement of the rights or obligations under this Directive has ceased and the claimant knows, or can reasonably be expected to know, about the violation or infringement. Member States shall ensure that the limitation periods for bringing claims are set at three years at least. Member States shall ensure that a limitation period is suspended or, depending on national law, interrupted, as soon as a claimant undertakes action by lodging a claim or bringing the claim to the attention of the employer, workers' representatives, labour inspectorate or equality body.

Article 19 – Legal and Judicial Costs

Claimants who prevail on a pay discrimination claim shall have the right to recover from the defendant, in addition to any other damages, reasonable legal and experts' fees and costs. Defendants who prevail on a pay discrimination claim shall not have the right to recover any legal and experts' fees from the claimant(s) and costs, unless the claim was brought in bad faith, was clearly frivolous or where such non-recovery is considered manifestly unreasonable under the specific circumstances of the case.

Article 20 – Penalties

Member States shall lay down the rules on penalties applicable to infringements of national provisions adopted pursuant to this Directive and shall take all measures necessary to ensure that they are implemented. The penalties provided for shall be effective, proportionate and dissuasive. Member States shall, without delay, notify the Commission of those rules and of those measures and of any subsequent amendment affecting them. Member States shall ensure that fines are applied to infringements of the rights and obligations relating to equal pay for the same work or work of equal value. They shall set a minimum level for such fines ensuring real deterrent effect. The level of the fines shall take into account: (a) the gravity and duration of the infringement; (b) any intent or serious negligence on the part of the employer; (c) any other aggravating or mitigating factor applicable to the circumstances of the case. Member States shall establish specific penalties to be imposed in case of repeated infringements of the rights and obligations relating to equal pay between men and women, such as the revocation of public benefits or the exclusion, for a certain period of time, from any award of financial inducements. Member States shall take all measures necessary to ensure that the penalties provided for are effectively applied in practice.

Article 21 – Equal Pay Matters in Public Contracts and Concessions

The appropriate measures that the Member States take in accordance with Article 30(3) of Directive 2014/23/EU, Article 18(2) of Directive 2014/24/EU and Article 36(2) of Directive 2014/25/EU, shall include measures to ensure that, in the performance of public contracts or concessions, economic operators comply with the obligations relating to equal pay between men and women for equal work or work of equal value. Member States shall consider for contracting authorities to introduce, as appropriate, penalties and termination conditions ensuring compliance with the principle of equal pay in the performance of public contracts and concessions. Where Member States' authorities act in accordance with Article 38(7)(a) of Directive 2014/23/EU, Article 57(4)(a) of Directive 2014/24/EU, or Article 80(1) of Directive 2014/25/EU in conjunction with Article 57(4)(a) of Directive 2014/24/EU, they may exclude or may be required by Member States to exclude any economic operator from participation in a public procurement procedure where they can demonstrate by any appropriate means the infringement of the obligations referred to in paragraph 1, related either to a failure to comply with pay transparency obligations or a pay gap of more than 5 per cent in any category of workers which is not justified by the employer on the basis of objective, gender-neutral criteria. This is without prejudice to any other rights or obligations set out in Directive 2014/23/EU, Directive 2014/24/EU or Directive 2014/25/EU.

4. Strengths and Weaknesses of Various Tools of Enforcement

All this looks like a Shangri-La for worker's rights. This breathtaking summary of the tools of enforcement of workers' rights, proposed on the issue of equal pay for men and women may inspire us to reflect somewhat further on the strengths and weaknesses of the various tools of enforcement. Is this summary comprehensive or should we take even more tools of enforcement in consideration? Moreover, the question may arise: why such a far-reaching approach to the issue of claims for equal pay for men and women? Should it not be applied in other sorts of workers' claims? What should be the grounds for applying certain tools of enforcement as regards one labour standard and not concerning another standard?

4.1. Civil Law Enforcement

It is often supposed that employees in all EU Member States have sufficient access to courts that can enforce EU labour law. Time and again, however, exceptions appear. Several cases have shown that such courts do not always exist, that they are not available for judging a labour law suit, or that they are not independent or impartial, or do not respect the principle of equality of arms or the right to a hearing, or do not give judgment within a reasonable time, or their judgments are not well-founded.[32] It is not unreasonable that the EU should unceasingly call out these imperfections and put pressure on the Member States to deal with them (see Chapter 3 by Lörcher).

This is only a first step. If one approaches this problem from the point of view of the individual worker (and leaving aside the well-paid), it is clear that most workers are not in a position to easily launch lawsuits to invoke their EU labour law rights. Lawsuits are expensive (in the Netherlands, for example, registry costs run to hundreds of euros, as do lawyers' hourly fees, on top of the risk of losing the case and having to pay the costs of the other party). Many workers may take out insurance against such costs, and many may be members of trade unions that may support their claim financially. But commercial insurers are reluctant to finance doubtful lawsuits and many trade unions do not have enough resources for generous legal assistance, or do not act because of strategic considerations (see Chapter 7 by Lörcher). Sometimes free legal aid may be available, such as students' legal clinics. But even if such things do exist, they are not a real option for many workers. Poorly educated workers, flexible workers (see Chapter 13 by Kresal) and migrant workers (see Chapter 12 by Rasnača) are especially disadvantaged in this way. In addition to this there is the fact that a lawsuit, however it turns out, will almost certainly spoil the relationship with the employer. Consequently, most claims do not lead to lawsuits during the period of employment. At best they are filed in

[32] Lörcher, n 2 above, at 622–28.

dismissal cases, but then they may have become irreparable (health damages) or extinguished by the statute of limitations. The admissibility of limitation clauses has come into play in some EU labour law cases.[33] Not all these problems are typical of EU labour law, but they may be more onerous because of the complicated relationship between EU rules and national rules, certainly when there are constitutional and transborder aspects at issue (see Chapter 8 by Houwerzijl). There are solutions for such problems: 'early settlement mechanism'/low-threshold bodies, such as the Human Rights Board in the Netherlands) (see Chapter 10 by Kollonay-Lehoczky), ADR and the possibility for trade unions to bring forward collective and individual claims under their own name (see Chapter 16 by Dorssemont). It is, however, doubtful whether such solutions exist at a sufficient level in all Member States.

An alternative is the public enforcement of labour law.

4.2. Criminal Law Enforcement

EU labour law only exceptionally requires the Member States to enforce it by means of criminal law. Indeed, in most Member States criminal law may only exceptionally be applied to violations of EU labour law, perhaps only in relation to the worst violations, such as slavery, forced labour, human trafficking or death caused by bad safety conditions. Nowadays there may be a tendency to extend this list of 'worst violations' to odious discrimination cases, but in general a strong expansion of criminal law is out of fashion (see Chapter 5 by Unterschütz). Public prosecutors have no time and do not consider most labour law violations as a priority (this may be different in case of alleged mass social security fraud, however). Moreover the burden of proof is heavier in criminal procedures than in civil law proceedings.

4.3. Administrative Law Enforcement

Against this background, many countries have brought violations of several aspects of labour law into the domain of administrative law. Here, violations can be sanctioned by fines, which in the first instance are imposed by administrative agencies and only come before an administrative law judge if they are challenged. In labour law, in most Member States the administrative agency is the labour inspectorate, which therefore plays a major role in the enforcement of EU labour law. These labour inspectorates are often still very underdeveloped, however. Usually, their competences are restricted to a small number of labour laws that have an administrative law character and/or are sanctioned under criminal law. Working time and health and safety have traditionally been fields of operation. In recent years also the influx of illegal migrant labour, anti-discrimination laws and minimum wage legislation have been brought under their activities. In some countries (such as

[33] CJEU, C-429/12 *Pöhl*, 16 January 2014.

France) they also control the application of extended collective agreements. In most Member States, however, labour inspectorates are still far from covering all labour laws, and certainly do not cover all EU labour laws (see Chapter 4 by Unterschütz).

Moreover, insofar as labour inspectorates cover labour laws, the fact remains that most simply do not have the resources to effectuate sufficient controls (see Chapter 14 by Cefaliello). In an era in which the tasks of labour inspectorates have greatly expanded, governments have often cut their financial resources. Most enterprises have only a one in a hundred thousand or even a one in a million chance of receiving a visit from the labour inspectorate once a year. Moreover it is doubtful whether the inspectors have sufficient qualifications to detect complicated risks to workers, such as in the engineering and chemical industries. In any case, they are likely to lack sufficient powers to intervene and even to stop illegal practices. In a few EU Member States individual workers may solicit inquiries by the labour inspectorate, but in many Member States not even works councils and trade union representatives have the right to call for intervention by the labour inspectorate (see Chapter 16 by Dorssemont).

As maintaining well-equipped labour inspectorates is costly, in several EU Member States governments and social partners have experimented with cheaper alternatives in recent years. In the Netherlands, for example, two alternatives have been applied.

The first was privately organised control bodies, set up by the social partners, in order to monitor and to fine non-observance of collective agreements. This has happened in some of the sectors most vulnerable to violations, such as road transport, temporary agency work, closed bus transport, the taxi business and supermarkets. As these control bodies must be financed by the enterprises in the various sectors one must assume that they are suffering from similar shortcomings to the labour inspectorates.

A second alternative is certification. The idea behind this is that in the sector concerned the social partners create their own standard of good behaviour and set up a certification system. Companies in possession of such a certificate are visited by the labour inspectorate less frequently. If these standards embrace EU law rules as well, this alternative may promote a certain compliance, but how reliable is this alternative for the butcher who tests his own meat?

4.4. Company Law Enforcement

The enforcement of most of the obligations on information and consultation of workers' representatives contained in various directives[34] is badly specified (see Chapter 11 by Rainone). The texts used in these provisions are often vague and

[34] Art 6 of Directive 98/59 (Collective redundancies), Art 9 of Directive 2001/23/EC (Transfer of enterprises), Art 11(2) of Directive 2009/38/EC (EWC Directive, Art 12 (2) of Directive 2001/86/EC (Societas Europea) and Art 8 of Directive 2002/14/EC.

not supported by concrete sanctions. Only a few contain the provision that sanctions must be effective, proportional and dissuasive. Employees of the company are often insufficiently protected by the usual anti-victimisation clauses in the Directives (see Chapter 16 by Dorssemont). If works councils or trade unions do not have locus standi or do not have the money to invoke these Directives in court, what are such rules worth?

If courts can only issue soft declarations on these issues, what is the point of them? The best sanctions lie in company law, as, once again, in the Netherlands. Both works councils and trade unions have full access to the courts to invoke these rights. Courts will halt the implementation of managerial decisions that are contrary to codetermination rules, even in summary procedures. Courts may hold managing directors personally responsible or deprive citizens of the right to lead companies if they have committed mismanagement, for instance in cases of fraudulent bankruptcy. I doubt whether many other Member States have comparably forceful enforcement instruments. Even in the Netherlands, however, the courts are reluctant to become involved in tackling the economic rationale of managerial decision-making. Their investigations are only procedural.

4.5. Other Tools of Enforcement

Finally, this book will show that a number of other enforcement tools are already operational in certain Member States and are apt for all EU use. They include the following:

- naming and shaming may sometimes be useful as a tool of enforcement, but on other occasions it is simply too weak;
- administrative orders with a penalty are only sufficient to counteract violations of obligations if the financial penalty is a deterrent;
- public procurement provisions (labour rights as a condition of obtaining public orders, concessions, permits) only make sense in sectors of the economy that are highly dependent on government orders and concessions/permits and are enforced by fines and the exclusion of companies from such advantages for certain periods (see Chapter 19 by Bruun);
- whistleblowers are already recognised in some aspects of labour law in the Member States. They can certainly play a valuable role in the enforcement of EU labour law. Unfortunately – and inexplicably – labour law is excluded from the subject matters covered in EU Directive 2019/1937 on whistleblowers (see Chapter 19 by Bruun and Chapter 18 by Cobbaut);
- collective action (such as strikes) should not be so restricted by the national law of EU Member States that they make this tool impracticable for enforcing EU labour law in cases in which other enforcement tools are not adequate (see Chapter 15 by Orlandini);

- traditionally, 'soft' law is not easy to enforce, although there are often quasi courts for complaints, such as ILO Committees and the tools of the European Committee for Social Rights. Inside the EU there is now the European Semester, which results in Country Specific Recommendations and the Annual Growth Survey, in which increasing attention has been paid to social desiderata, such as binding targets for the reduction of poverty and inequality. Since 2002 the European Commission has published impact assessments for legislative measures in fundamental social rights, which have gradually come to play a greater role. Proposals have been made to match the Macroeconomic Imbalances Procedure with a Social Imbalances Procedure, for instance in relation to health care. The European Commission has created a so-called Scoreboard, which includes an increasing number of social indicators (see Chapter 21 by Schmitt and Rocca). This progress is sometimes positively evaluated as a 'socialisation of New Economic Governance', and they may eventually acquire teeth if they acquire a financial component. Every seven years the EU legislator sets its Multi-annual Financial Framework (MFF) (see Article 312 TFEU), which amounts to about a trillion euros. The current MFF amounts to 1.8 trillion euros, as an extra 800 billion has been set aside for the Covid-19 Recovery Fund. The criteria for spending all this money are laid down in the yearly Budget and in the rules of the various EU Funds (for labour law, notably the European Social Funds and the Globalisation Funds). Given that all this money is not disbursed to the Member States unconditionally, but only if they use it for objectives that comply with EU social goals, these Guidelines and Recommendations are becoming rather hard law than soft law (see Chapter 6 by Kollonay-Lehoczky and Chapter 21 by Schmitt and Rocca).

Many people feel that the observance of EU labour law should not end at Europe's borders. They may be inspired by the altruistic idea that European labour standards are so beneficial to the working population that the whole world should be able to enjoy them. Less charitably, European labour standards can survive only if they are not threatened by social dumping from countries with lower standards.

One tool suitable for pursuing this ambition is the policy of systematically including clauses in EU trade agreements with third countries ensuring that they adopt European labour standards if they want to have preferential treatment for their products in European markets (see Chapter 9 by Deakin and Billa). This tool of enforcement should not be underestimated (but also not overestimated). Strong formulation and enforcement of such clauses is difficult to achieve in relation to powerful third countries such as the United States, China and Russia, but also the UK, not to mention third countries on which the EU economy is heavily dependent for imports of materials and/or export of its products.

As an alternative tool one might think of the international movement for codes of conduct in global supply chains. Since the 1990s thousands of companies have adopted voluntary regulatory measures to strengthen the application of international labour standards in their supply chains. Companies with global business activities based in Europe must also assume responsibility for rights-holders in their supply chains and at production sites outside Europe. The European Commission plans to table a legislative proposal on due diligence requirements to protect human rights and the environment in the supply chains. The European Parliament and the European Council have welcomed these plans.

5. Structural Problems Hampering Effective Enforcement

One should also be aware of more structural problems affecting proper enforcement of EU labour law.

5.1. Network Enterprises

Over recent decades the concept of 'employer' has changed significantly. Enterprises are less and less monolithic structures. Nowadays they may cooperate closely with other enterprises in groups of companies (*Konzern*), or in producing a product or service. Enterprises may outsource various of their activities, engage workers of other employers and independent workers, or act in structures with franchises.

It has therefore become increasingly difficult to enforce labour law, as it has become harder to attribute responsibility for violations to a specific employer. To take one striking example, in the case of Romanian children performing in the Netherlands at a concert by André Rieu, according to the Dutch Council of State responsibility for the violation of the rules on child labour (also of EU origin) did not pertain to the concert organiser (André Rieu) but the leader of the participating Romanian children's band.

Some legal techniques have been developed to overcome such problems, as in the case of chain responsibility for wage payments (see Chapter 8 by Houwerzijl). Or the law may attribute shared responsibility between two employers (for instance, between the temporary work agency and the user firm). Unfortunately, group (*Konzern*) responsibility for affiliates and network responsibility for connected enterprises is still very underdeveloped.

5.2. Homework, Telework, Moonlighting, Job-Sharing, Platform Work

Recent decades have seen further differentiation on the labour market, with moonlighting, job-sharing and platform work on the increase. Homeworking and teleworking already existed, but have grown enormously during the Covid-19 pandemic. They can make it very hard for inspectors, lawyers and judges to establish whether labour laws are being observed properly. Now that the European Commission has started to consult the social partners on an instrument for tackling platform work,[35] moonlighting has been brought under the Transparency Directive and the EU Agreement on Telework is being reconsidered, enforcement should be a priority (see Chapter 13 by Kresal).

5.3. An Old Enemy of Labour Law Enforcement: 'Patriotism'

There are certainly political dividends in highlighting labour law enforcement. Shocking examples of labour law violations are bound to grab the headlines. When it comes to a strict application of labour law rules, however, workers sometimes become pig-headed (obligatory helmets or construction workers forced to wear a shirt). And when strict application of labour law rules threatens the economic viability of a certain company or an entire sector, employers and workers may unite in opposition. Then there may be strong pressure on the authorities and labour inspectors to turn a blind eye to labour law compliance, for the sake of retaining jobs.

5.4. The 'Proportionality Principle'

For most labour lawyers it is evident that employers should shoulder more of the burden when it comes to labour law enforcement. It should be observed, however, that the vast majority of employers in the Member States are SMEs, often start-ups. They can easily succumb if they are heavily sanctioned because of violations of EU labour law. Sanctions must always respect the principle of proportionality and contain hardship clauses. This may mean that the level of sanctions should take into account the bearing-capacity of the perpetrator (see Chapter 4 by Unterschütz).

6. Towards a General Labour Law Enforcement Measure?

It has been suggested that the EU should build a new structure to promote the enforcement of its labour law rules. This idea is prominent in the ETUC's Action Programme 2019–23. The ETUC is in favour of an enforcement measure (most likely a directive) to set minimum enforcement standards across the area of EU social policy and labour law.

[35] COM(2021) 1127 final dd 24.2.2021.

As shown in section 3 of this chapter the various EU labour directives do not provide consistent formulations of the requirements of enforcement, remedies, penalties and sanctions in relation to their various substantive rules. This may raise questions as to why certain forms of enforcement should be applied in one case and not in another.

In general, it is not clear why violations of certain workers' rights require other and, in particular, lighter forms of enforcement than violations of other rights. Grounds for differentiation in this respect must be provided in the recitals of the relevant Directive.

In principle, all Member States should apply equal weight to sanctions on violations of an EU obligation. Otherwise there will be no level playing field for business in the various Member States and this will distort competition.

A general Directive might be drawn up that sets out minimum rules for enforcement in the Member States. The closing chapter of this book outlines such a Directive.

7. Conclusions

The entire system of enforcement is outdated for EU law in general. The Conference on the Future of Europe, which started in 2021, should question whether the existing set up can be modernised and simplified.

In the early years of the EEC many scholars believed that it had no power to intervene in the enforcement of its rules. This had to be left to the Member States.[36] This is obviously no longer the case. The EU certainly has the competency to issue minimum rules about the quality and intensity of its Member States' enforcement measures. The CJEU has shown this in a number of cases mentioned in this chapter.

EU labour law has a variable impact in the workplace in the 27 Member States. Variation is not a bad thing in itself. The European Treaties confirm the diversity between the Member States of the EU (Article 153(2) TFEU). Too much diversity, however, may easily lead to social dumping on an open market, which is unacceptable.

[36] W Voermans, 'De communautarisering van toezicht en handhaving' in T Barkhuyzen, W den Ouden and JEM Polak (eds), *Recht realiseren* (Deventer, Kluwer, 2005) 69–87.

2

Remedies and Sanctions in EU Labour Law

ARISTEA KOUKIADAKI

1. Introduction

In ordinary language, a remedy is a cure for something nasty.[1] In legal theory, however, various conceptual understandings have been put forward to define the concept of remedies.[2] A pure remedies analysis, often found in common law systems, suggests that it is the potency of a remedy and its availability that determine the nature of a legal right and, indeed, its very existence. Consequently, the presence of a remedy points to the existence of a legal right, reflected in the dictum *ubi remedium ibi ius*.[3] By contrast, the primacy of the rights model, typical of continental legal systems, is premised on the idea that legal rights have an independent existence and it is possible to conceive of legal rights unsupported by legal remedies.[4] While the concept of remedies has recently been elaborated in legal theory, to date no such debate has taken place in labour law and regulation scholarship.[5] In rare cases where research in labour law and regulation has dealt with the issue, it has done so in an incomplete way. One approach, found predominantly in common law systems, has been to focus on enforcement as a means to ensure the effectiveness of labour rights. However, the remedial nature of the legal/institutional framework tends to be concealed in such cases and emphasis is laid on access to justice. A second approach, particularly prevalent in continental legal systems, does not distinguish the concept of remedies from the concept

[1] P Birk, 'Wrongs, and Remedies' (2000) 20 *Oxford Journal of Legal Studies* 1, 9.

[2] See, among others, Birk, n 1 above, H Dedek, 'From Norms to Facts: The Realization of Rights in Common and Civil Private Law' (2010) 56 *McGill Law Journal* 77.

[3] D Friedmann, 'Rights and Remedies' in N Cohen and E McKendrick (eds), *Comparative Remedies for Breach of Contract* (Oxford, Hart Publishing, 2005).

[4] On this, see, among others, JF Hoffman, 'Remedies in Private Law from a German Perspective' in F Hoffmann and F Kurz (eds), *Law of Remedies: A European Perspective* (Cambridge, Intersentia, 2019).

[5] For examples, see S Smith, *Rights, Wrongs and Injustices* (Oxford, Oxford University Press, 2019) and F Hoffmann and F Kurz (eds), *Law of Remedies: A European Perspective* (Cambridge, Intersentia, 2019).

of procedure as a distinctive part of a legal claim. Remedies are thus approached as an addendum, a mere 'legal by-product' to the 'primary' rights provided to individuals.[6] While there is significant commentary on remedies in European Union (EU) law,[7] the issue has not been addressed systematically in EU labour law either, with most contributions focusing so far on specific areas, eg discrimination, or more recently on the significance of the Charter of Fundamental Rights of the European Union (CFREU).[8]

Against this context, this chapter explores the EU's approach to the question of remedies and sanctions in EU labour law. In doing so, the analysis adopts a remedial rights approach that has the potential to 'infuse subtlety into the rights domain' itself.[9] It will consider not only the case of remedies, as the means of redress and enforcement of an EU labour right in the event that it is violated, but also that of sanctions, which penalise or punish unlawful conduct, as a distinct but interrelated aspect of the remedial framework of the EU labour law system. In this respect, choosing between different remedies but also sanctions may be seen as a way for law to accommodate qualitative and normatively attractive distinctions between different types of rights.[10] This is particularly important in the area of labour law, where these concepts remain largely unexplored. What is more, the analysis attempts to treat the issue of remedies and sanctions in EU labour law in a comprehensive way. This has the advantage of enabling the similarities and differences between different types of remedies and sanctions and their governing principles, if any, to be fully appreciated. Attention here is paid to the functions of the concepts,[11] but also the substantive areas in which these are regulated, as well as the levels selected as the appropriate response, as these also set the boundaries of the process of their legal characterisation in the EU legal system.[12] Finally, an understanding of remedies and sanctions should not be static. In EU labour law, this involves examining the evolution of the concepts across different periods, including on the basis of the distinction between the nature of enforcement

[6] F Hoffmann and F Kurz, 'Introduction to the "Law of Remedies"' in F Hoffmann and F Kurz (eds), *Law of Remedies: A European Perspective* (Cambridge, Intersentia, 2019) 5.

[7] For a recent example, see Part V: Judicial Protection in the EU, in R Schutze and T Tridimas (eds), *Oxford Principles of European Union Law*, Vol I: *The European Legal Order* (Oxford, Oxford University Press, 2018).

[8] See K Lörcher, 'Article 47 – Right to an Effective Remedy and to a Fair Trial' in F Dorssemont, K Lörcher, S Clauwaert, M Schmitt (eds), *The Charter of Fundamental Rights of the European Union and the Employment Relation* (Oxford, Hart Publishing, 2019). J Adams-Prassl, 'Article 47 CFR and the Effective Enforcement of EU Labour Law: Teeth for Paper Tigers?' (2020) 11 *European Labour Law Journal* 391.

[9] H Dagan, *Reconstructing American Legal Realism & Rethinking Private Law Theory* (Oxford, Oxford University Press, 2013) 144.

[10] Ibid.

[11] Hofmann and Kurz, n 7 above at 24.

[12] On this, see J Fudge, 'Modern Slavery, Unfree Labour and the Labour Market: The Social Dynamics of Legal Characterization' (2018) 27 *Social & Legal Studies* 414 at 416; C Kilpatrick, 'The Future of Remedies in Europe' in C Kilpatrick, T Novitz and P Skidmore (eds), *The Future of Remedies in Europe* (Oxford, Hart Publishing, 2000).

(ie public and/or private), level of regulation (ie EU or national) and range of available mechanisms for redress against violations of labour rights.[13]

Before proceeding further, it is useful to distinguish here the concepts of remedies and sanctions. Drawing broadly on insights from legal theory and EU law, it is possible to do this on the basis of the following dimensions. The first is the level at which these are located. Here, there is a twofold distinction between remedies and sanctions in national courts for breaches of EU law and those that are available in EU courts for breaches of EU law. In respect of the former, these may include, among others, claims for damages, injunctions against private parties and interim relief in actions involving the state, restitution and judicial reviews. Regarding the latter, ie in EU courts, these include proceedings against EU Member States for breach of EU law,[14] judicial review of EU acts,[15] plea of illegality,[16] judicial review of failure to act,[17] suing the EU in damages[18] and interim relief.[19]

The second dimension is in respect of the nature of the remedies and sanctions, ie private or public. Private enforcement takes place through actions brought by private parties before the courts of the Member States or the EU courts (eg through actions for damages and contractual remedies). In contrast, public enforcement is based on a set of rules that establish a competent authority and define its investigating and sanctioning powers.[20] The advantages in pursuing private or public enforcement are quite distinct. On one hand, private enforcement relies on making use of private information about infringements and as such takes advantage of the claimants' ability to identify breaches of the law efficiently, while on the other hand, public enforcement may enable more effective allocation of enforcement resources.[21]

The third dimension is concerned with underlying theories and concepts of justice which may be used to justify the regulatory choices made in respect of redress. Existing approaches tend to emphasise primarily the remedial, compensatory, punitive and preventive justice aspects of specific remedies and sanctions. Remedial mechanisms include here primarily compensation[22] and reinstatement rights. Remedies and sanctions with a punitive character usually comprise

[13] See section 2 below.
[14] Articles 258 and 259 TFEU.
[15] Article 263 TFEU.
[16] Article 277 TFEU.
[17] Article 265 TFEU.
[18] Article 340 TFEU.
[19] Article 278 and 279 TFEU. See also Articles 104 to 110 of the Rules of Procedure of the Court of Justice.
[20] See JU Franck, 'Private Enforcement versus Public Enforcement' in F Hoffmann and F Kurz (eds), *Law of Remedies: A European Perspective* (Intersentia, 2019) 109.
[21] Franck, n 36 above at 128.
[22] Compensation is considered a remedy and not a sanction (cf this with the approach adopted by the Court of Justice of the European Union (CJEU) regarding the remedy of compensation as a 'is', eg see Case 14/83 *Sabine von Colson and Elisabeth Kamann v Land Nordrhein-Westfalen* [1984] ECR 1891, para 27 and discussion below).

criminal/administrative fines and publication of decision. In contrast, sanctions and remedies that adopt a preventive justice approach may include, for example, suspension of licence or business activities and the exclusion of contractors from tendering for public procurement contracts. A distinction may also exist in terms of whether such mechanisms are premised on an individual or a group justice mode, with this being reflected in the identity of the addressees (individuals or collectives) of the remedies and recipients of sanctions.[23]

Bearing these issues in mind, the analysis will go on to highlight the following issues. First of all, it will be argued that the predominant responses in EU labour law have been characterised by either an express recognition of labour rights at EU level but with no explicit reference to remedies/sanctions or by deferring these issues to the national level. Where explicit provisions are made on remedies and sanctions at EU level, their definition has predominantly reflected the common law definition, ie rights and remedies/sanctions as two distinct issues.[24] Secondly, there is some evidence of evolution of the EU labour remedial framework that relies not only on private but also public enforcement and combining this with a variety of remedies and sanctions that may serve different objectives. This has been accompanied and prompted by the development of a range of principles led primarily by the CJEU and culminating recently in Article 47 CFREU. Finally but equally importantly, the remedial approach in EU labour law seems to be differentiated on the basis of the underlying conceptualisation of labour rights. The latter have been traditionally conceived as human rights, as mechanisms to promote social justice or to deal with issues related to economic development. In the context of EU labour law, an additional dimension has to be considered, ie that of labour rights as a mechanism to respond to the transnational regulatory problems emerging from the EU project.[25] The analysis illustrates that, with the exception of equality rights, the development of remedies and sanctions in EU labour law has traditionally been influenced by considerations of transnational regulatory gaps rather than labour rights protection per se. This may be considered problematic as it fails to consider the distinctive elements of the employment relationship and is prone to considerable discrepancies at national level, contributing ultimately to the horizontal and vertical fragmentation of the regulatory framework relevant to the effective enforcement of EU labour law.[26]

[23] At present, EU law contains no 'federal' legal framework for Member States' collective action regimes (see CI Nagy, *Collective Actions in Europe: A Comparative, Economic and Transsystemic Analysis* (Springer, 2019)).

[24] The EU notion of remedies has substantive, as well as procedural elements. The primary focus of this chapter is on the substantive right to adequate redress. The issue of the procedural right of effective access to justice is dealt with in chapter 3 by K Lörcher in this book.

[25] B Ryan, 'The Private Enforcement of European Union Labour Laws' in C Kilpatrick, T Novitz and P Skidmore (eds), *The Future of Remedies in Europe* (Oxford, Hart Publishing, 2000).

[26] For a similar argument made in respect of damages in EU private law, see C Heinze, 'Common Principles of Damages in EU Private Law?' in F Hoffmann and F Kurz (eds), *Law of Remedies: A European Perspective* (Intersentia, 2019).

The chapter is structured as follows. Section 2 goes on to examine how the concept of remedies and sanctions has evolved in EU law with a particular emphasis on general principles and fundamental rights, including, among others, that of effective judicial protection. Section 3 then focuses on the way these concepts have been articulated in the particular context of EU labour law. The section will provide a breakdown of the different mechanisms used in EU primary and secondary law and will evaluate the evolution of these concepts across different areas and periods. Section 4 concludes with a summary assessment.

2. Principles of Effective Judicial Protection, Effectiveness and Equivalence and the Role of Article 47 CFREU

2.1. The Principle of Effective Judicial Protection and the Role of Article 47 CFREU

In EU primary law, the word 'remedies' is mentioned only once, ie in Article 19(1) TEU.[27] Article 19(1) TEU explicitly provides that it is for the Member States, and therefore in principle not for the EU, to provide 'remedies sufficient to ensure effective legal protection in the fields covered by EU law'.[28] The principle of effective judicial protection, referred to in Article 19(1) TEU,[29] is a general principle of EU law stemming from the constitutional traditions common to the Member States. It has been enshrined in Articles 6 and 13 of the European Convention on Human Rights.[30] It is also linked to the rule of law within the EU,[31] when Member States are acting within the scope of EU law and thus transposing its provisions into national law.[32] The CJEU first relied on the principle of effective judicial protection to assure the right to an effective remedy in a labour law case, *von Colson and Kamann*.[33]

[27] P. Komninos, *EC Private Antitrust Enforcement: Decentralised Application of EC Competition Law by National Courts* (Oxford, Hart Publishing, 2008) 149. No definition of remedies is provided in the case law of regional human rights bodies (eg by the ECthR). The term 'sanctions' appears in Article 83 TEU and Protocol 4 on the Statute of the European System of Central Banks and of the European Central Bank (Article 19).

[28] See also judgments in C-64/16 *Associação Sindical dos Juízes Portugueses v Tribunal de Contas* [2018] 3 CMLR 16 para 34 and the case law cited, and C-619/18 *European Commission v Poland* [2020] 1 CMLR 6, para 48.

[29] The provision refers to the 'fields covered by Union law', irrespective of whether the Member States are implementing Union law within the meaning of Article 51(1) of the Charter (*Associação Sindical dos Juízes Portugueses*, ibid, para 29, and *Commission v Poland*, ibid, para 50).

[30] *Associação Sindical dos Juízes Portugueses*, ibid, *Commission v Poland*, ibid, and Lörcher, n 9 above.

[31] Article 2 TEU.

[32] Article 51(1) CFREU. See A Koukiadaki, 'Application (Article 51) and Limitations (Article 52(1))' in F Dorssemont, K Lörcher, S Clauwaert, M Schmitt (eds), *The Charter of Fundamental Rights of the European Union and the Employment Relation* (Oxford, Hart Publishing, 2019).

[33] *Von Colson and Kamann*, n 23 above.

Addressing the issue of whether a specific national remedy was sufficient to ensure an adequate level of protection under Directive 76/207/EEC, the Court held that the national remedies at issue had to 'guarantee real and effective judicial protection'.[34] Importantly from an EU labour law perspective, national remedies and procedures must be able to accord effective judicial protection, irrespective of whether the substantive right to be guaranteed derives from the direct effect of clear, precise and unconditional EU rules or from an interpretation of national law consistent with the purpose of EU law or from state liability for a failure to transpose EU law.[35]

The principle of effective judicial protection has now been reaffirmed by Article 47 CFREU, which establishes a right to an effective remedy.[36] Article 47 CFREU consolidates the pre-Lisbon CJEU case law regarding public law remedies, eg in respect of state liability, but also requires a remedy against private parties.[37] The essence of the provision, as established in the Court's case law,[38] lies in ensuring that a legal remedy exists to ensure respect for EU rights. The interaction of Articles 47 CFREU and 19(1)(2) TEU has meant, according to Safian, that the 'composite legal order as a Union of effective judicial protection [is] characterised by a unique, common and autonomous standard of protection'.[39] In this respect, Article 47 CREU is seen as articulating a 'thick' conception of rights.[40] The right is to be found in the 'law of the Union', meaning that rules of EU law at all levels, and on any subject matter, can create rights.[41] The rule must 'guarantee' the right and 'everyone' is the bearer of the right to judicial protection.[42]

From the perspective of labour law, it was anticipated that the incorporation of the CFREU into EU primary law had the potential to improve substantially the effectiveness of EU labour law enforcement.[43] A reading of Article 47 CFREU confirms its inclusive coverage, thus overcoming the challenge of the contractual status of claimants, usually encountered in labour law.[44] Article 47 is also one

[34] Ibid, para 23.

[35] See A Lo Faro, Judicial Enforcement of EC Labour Law: Time Limits, Burden of Proof, ex Officio Application of EC Law, WP CSDLE "Massimo d'Antona" No 3/2002, 6.

[36] No corresponding right has been explicitly recognised by the ILO or by the International Covenant on Economic, Social and Cultural Rights.

[37] K Lenaerts, 'Exploring the limits of the EU Charter of Fundamental Rights' (2012) 8 *European Constitutional Law Revue* 375.

[38] Case C-432/05 *Unibet (London) Ltd v Justitiekanslern* [2007] ECR I-2271.

[39] M Safian, 'A Union of Effective Judicial Protection: Addressing a Multi-level Challenge through the Lens of Article 47 CFREU', King's College London, February 2014, 1.

[40] V Roeben, 'Judicial Protection as the Meta-norm in the EU Judicial Architecture' (2020) 12 *Hague Journal on the Rule of Law* 29, 34.

[41] Explanations, 2007 OJ C 303/17, 29. In contrast, ECHR Art 6 only protects private rights in national law, see ECtHR, *Coorplan-Jenni GmbH and Hascic v Austria*, No 10523/02, 27 July 2006, para 56.

[42] Roeben, n 56 above at 35. However, while 'every individual whose rights have been breached' can invoke Article 47 CFREU, a third party may not (see C-403/16 *Soufiane El Hassani v Minister Spraw Zagranicznych*, [2017] ECLI:EU:C:2017:960 Opinion of Advocate General Bobek).

[43] Adams-Prassl, n 9 above and Lörcher, n 9 above.

[44] See Lörcher, n 9 above.

of the few Charter rights that have been found by the CJEU to be horizontally directly effective, including between workers and employers.[45] The cases of *Schüth* and *IR* exemplify the impact of the CFREU in terms of not only influencing procedural law, but also leading to an increase of judicial reviews of substantive law.[46] But while Article 47 CFREU has been described as 'perhaps the most important provision of the Charter',[47] it has to date been of limited use to claimants of labour rights.[48] As discussed by Adams-Prassl, this can be attributed firstly to the significant deference in assessing Member States' choices when it comes to different areas of EU labour law and secondly the difficulty of mandating the creation of specific, positive duties to be imposed on employers.[49]

2.2. The Principles of Equivalence and Effectiveness

In its 1976 decision in *Rewe*, the CJEU held that, based on the principle of sincere cooperation set out in Article 4(3) TEU (as it is now), 'it is the national courts which are entrusted with ensuring the legal protection which citizens derive from the direct effect of the provisions of [EU] law'.[50] The Court further stated that

> it is for the domestic legal systems of each Member State to designate the courts having jurisdiction and to determine the procedural conditions governing actions at law intended to ensure the protection of the rights which citizens have from the direct effect of [EU] law.[51]

This principle of national procedural autonomy, as it is generally known, is restricted in two ways. First, it must not be more difficult to enforce EU rights than similar domestic rights (principle of equivalence). Second, the relevant rules must not render it virtually impossible or exceedingly difficult to exercise EU rights (principle of effectiveness). Both principles enable the development and operation of different models of remedies and sanctions at national level. This may also

[45] Article 47 is sufficient in itself and does not need to be made more specific by provisions of EU or national law to confer on individuals a right which they may rely on as such (see C-414/16 *Egenberger v Evangelisches Werk fur Diakonie und Entwicklung eV* [2019] 1 CMLR 9 para 78, and C-924/19 PPU and C-925/19 PPU *FMS v Országos Idegenrendézeti Főigazgatóság Dél-alföldi Regionális Igazgatóság*, [2020] 5 WLUK 176, para 140).

[46] M Gotthardt, 'Effective Enforcement of EU Labour Law: A Comparative Example' (2020) 11(4) *European Labour Law Journal* 403.

[47] Together with Article 51 CFREU. See also P Aalto, HCH Hofmann, L Solopainen, E Paunio, L Pech, D Sayers, D Shelton and A Ward, 'Article 47 – Right to an Effective Remedy and to a Fair Trial' in S Peers, T Harvey, J Kenner and A Ward (eds), *The EU Charter of Fundamental Rights – A Commentary* (Oxford, Hart, 2014).

[48] Lörcher, n 9 above.

[49] See discussion in Adams-Prassl, n 9 above.

[50] Case 33/76 *Rewe-Zentralfinanz eG and Rewe-Zentral AG v Landwirtschaftskammer für das Saarland* [1976] ECR 1989, para 5.

[51] Ibid.

include differences in the understanding of legal concepts involved (eg restitution) and the mix between redress and preventative measures.[52]

Concerning the principle of equivalence, it is settled case law that observance of that principle requires that the national rule at issue be applied without distinction, where the purpose and cause of action are similar. It is for the national court, which has direct knowledge of the detailed procedural rules applicable, to ascertain whether the actions concerned are similar as regards their purpose, cause of action and essential characteristics.[53] Nevertheless, the concern to give the national court a helpful answer sometimes prompts the CJEU to make more specific observations regarding possible criteria for comparison. Thus, in *Palmisani*,[54] a case concerning state liability for the late transposition of Directive 80/987/EEC, the CJEU helped the national court to identify, in its national law, the internal remedies that might be comparable to actions to secure redress for damages deriving from the belated transposition of a directive.

The principle of effectiveness is complemented by the principle of consistent interpretation[55] and the duty owed by Member States to ensure that Directives are fully effective within their legal system,[56] entailing effective remedies with a real deterrent effect.[57] CJEU case law moved from an initial position where the principle was considered to be satisfied provided only that the action for the protection of the EU right did not prove virtually impossible,[58] to a formulation later on requiring that the remedies provided by the national legislature should not have made the exercise of rights deriving from Union law 'virtually impossible or excessively difficult'.[59] Reflecting a growing judicial activism on the part of the CJEU, the concept was later interpreted in a positive and substantive way, meaning that it implies 'that a remedy should not only compensate the victim for a potential loss or injury to a right, but also deter potential wrongdoers for violating it in the first place'.[60] Since then, the CJEU approach has been defined as 'contextual, as it is directed at identifying a point of balance and dynamic equilibrium between the principles of effectiveness and procedural autonomy of Member States in the individual specific cases'.[61]

[52] T Tridimas, 'Remedies as an EU Law Concept', 14th Annual Conference of the GCLC (Brussels, 2019), www.coleurope.eu/system/tdf/uploads/event/gclc_-_t._tridimas_-_31.01.2019.pdf?file=1&type=node&id=47689&force=.

[53] C-326/96 *Levez v T H Jennings (Harlow Pools) Ltd* [1998] ECR I-7835, para 39.

[54] Case C-261/95 *Palmisani v INPS* [1997] ECR I-4025, paras 33 to 38.

[55] Case C-441/14 *Dansk Industri, acting on behalf of Ajos A/S v Estate of Karsten Eigil Rasmussen*, EU:C:2016:278 paras 41–42.

[56] Article 288 TFEU.

[57] Article 19 TEU, *Von Colson* n 23 above, paras 15, 23. The same holds true in terms of sanctions, see Joined Cases C 870/19 *Prefettura Ufficio territoriale del governo di Firenze v MI*, C 871/19 *TB* ECLI:EU:C:2021:233.

[58] C-45/76 *Comet BV v Produktschap voor Siergewassen*, EU:C:1976:191.

[59] C-199/82 *Amministrazione delle Finanze dello Stato v SpA San Giorgio*, EU:C:1983:318.

[60] N. Reich, 'Judicial Protection in the EU' (2005) 1 *Revista Direito GV* 111, 112. See, among others, C-271/91 *Marshall II*, EU:C:1993:335.

[61] S Giubboni and S Robin-Oliver, Analytical Report 2016 Effective judicial protection in the framework of Directive 2014/54/EU (European Commission, 2016), https://ec.europa.eu/social/BlobServlet?docId=16856&langId=en 20.

Although there is some overlap between the principle of effective judicial protection and the so-called 'Rewe mantra',[62] ie the principles of equivalence and effectiveness, they 'serve different purposes and are driven by different rationales'.[63] This is illustrated in CJEU case law, where the principles have been applied by the CJEU in a separate, yet complementary manner.[64] The CJEU has tended to rely on the equivalence/effectiveness test to outline the boundaries of national discretion to promote remedies for the enforcement of EU law. In contrast, the principle of effective judicial protection has been used to safeguard the right to an effective remedy as a crucial human right in a rule of law system.[65]

3. Remedies and Sanctions in EU Labour Law

3.1. The Regulatory Framework in EU Labour Law

This section considers in detail the nature and extent of remedies and sanctions found in EU labour law and assesses how these have evolved in different areas and levels. The analysis is divided in two parts. The first part draws on the typology developed by Tridimas[66] in the wider context of EU law and applies this in the specific field of EU labour law with a view of identifying the main regulatory responses when it comes to remedies and sanctions relating to labour rights. The second part focuses on two particular mechanisms that are of crucial important in EU law, including in respect of labour rights, ie damage claims and state liability.

3.1.1. Express Recognition of Rights at EU Level But No Reference to Remedies or Sanctions

A number of EU labour law instruments include an express recognition of rights but with no reference to remedies. In primary EU law, Article 18 TFEU, for instance, prescribes that any discrimination on grounds of nationality should be prohibited. In the absence of a reference to remedies, the principles of effectiveness and equivalence apply. In, for instance, *Raccanelli*,[67] the Court explained that

> 'EU law does not prescribe any specific measure to be taken by the Member States […] in the event of a breach of the prohibition of discrimination, but leaves them free to

[62] *Rewe*, n 74 above.

[63] S Prechal and R Widdershoven, 'Redefining the Relationship between "Rewe-effectiveness" and Effective Judicial Protection' (2011) 4(2) *Review of European Administrative Law* 31, 47.

[64] Eg Case C-12/08 *Mono Car Styling*, EU:C:2009:466, para 49.

[65] SB Lahuerta, 'Enforcing EU Equality Law through Collective Redress: Lagging Behind?' (2018) 55 *Common Market Law Review* 783, 799.

[66] Tridimas, n 77 above.

[67] Case C-94/07 *Andrea Raccanelli v Max-Planck-Gesellschaft zur Förderung der Wissenschaften eV* [2008] ECR I-05939.

> choose between the different solutions suitable for achieving the objective of those respective provisions, depending on the different situations which may arise'.[68]

In EU secondary law, a number of EU labour law directives tend to prescribe how an employer shall treat employees but do not specify what is to happen if the employer does not follow these rules (see, among others, Directive 2008/94/EC on the protection of employees in the event of the insolvency of their employer and Directive 2003/88/EC on certain aspects of the organisation of working time).[69] This regulatory silence is contrary to other areas of EU substantive law, where Directives are also used as instruments of regulation (eg consumer protection).[70]

In the absence of EU rules on remedies and procedures, domestic procedures are to be applied in compliance with the general principles of equivalence and effectiveness.[71] For instance, in *Syndicat des cadres de la sécurité intérieure v Premier ministre and Others*, the CJEU relied on the principle of effectiveness to find that the referring court must

> 'examine the effectiveness of the remedies available to the workers concerned under national law in order to bring promptly to an end, where appropriate by accelerated procedures or interlocutory proceedings, any practice which does not comply with the requirements of the Working Time Directive'.[72]

A particular case here concerns EU Directives that contain a right to 'request'. While, for example, Directive 2019/1158 extends the right to request flexible working arrangements to all working parents with children up to the age of eight, as well as to carers, this is not interpreted as an enforceable legal entitlement, as the Directive only provides for a right to 'request' flexible working arrangements.[73]

3.1.2. *Establishment of Requirements or Standards at EU Level without Reference to Remedies*

EU law may impose a requirement or prescribe a standard without making any reference whatsoever to remedies.[74] The most obvious example in the area of labour law concerns Regulation (EU) 2019/1149 establishing a European Labour

[68] Ibid, para 50.

[69] J Malmberg, 'Effective Enforcement of EC Labour Law: A Comparative Analysis of Community Law Requirements' (2004) 10 *European Journal of Industrial Relations* 219.

[70] See, for instance, the Consumer Injunctions Directive (Directive 2009/22/EC of the European Parliament and of the Council of 23 April 2009 on injunctions for the protection of consumers' interests (OJ L 110, 1.5.2009, p. 30).

[71] See analysis in section 2 above.

[72] Case C-254/18 *Syndicat des cadres de la sécurité intérieure v Premier ministre and Others* ECLI:EU:C:2019:318, para 47.

[73] In a similar vein, Article 12 of Directive 2019/1152 also provides a right to request employment with more predictable and secure working conditions. See E Chieregato, 'A Work-Life Balance for All? Assessing the Inclusiveness of EU Directive 2019/1158' (2020) 36 *International Journal of Comparative Labour Law and Industrial Relations* 59.

[74] Tridimas, n 77 above.

Authority (ELA).[75] While the Regulation does not make reference to remedies as such, it does provide that if irregularities are detected in checks, the Executive Director is responsible for 'recovering amounts wrongly paid and, where appropriate, by imposing effective, proportionate and dissuasive administrative, including financial, penalties'. The question that arises here is whether there is an implied right to enforce any of the requirements or standards included in such instruments, and if so, what the remedy might be.[76] While not dealing with EU labour rights, the CJEU's approach in *Muñoz*[77] and more recently *L'Oreal*[78] seems to suggest that Regulations may confer rights against infringing private parties. According to the Court in *Muñoz*, the full effectiveness of the rules in the Regulation implied that it must be possible to enforce that obligation by means of civil proceedings instituted by a private party against another, the rationale being that this would strengthen the practical working of the EU rules.[79]

3.1.3. General Reference to National Remedies and Sanctions

The third possibility is for EU law to make general reference to national remedies and sanctions.[80] A number of labour law directives set out the principles that Member States have to follow in respect of their enforcement regimes. In respect of remedies, one example here is Article 9 of Directive (EU) 2018/958 concerning a proportionality test before adoption of new regulation of professions. According to this, Member States shall ensure that an effective remedy is available with regard to the matters covered by this Directive, in accordance with procedures laid down in national law.[81] In this respect, the issue of whether it is necessary to modify the national procedural system so as to include a completely new remedy in order to comply with the EU principle of effective judicial protection has been addressed in the CJEU case-law. It is only where that is the only way to ensure that an EU law right can be protected that EU law may require a new remedy.[82] In *Heylens*, dealing with free movement of workers, the CJEU held that since free access to employment is a fundamental right, 'the existence of a remedy of a judicial nature against any decision of a national authority refusing the benefit of that right is essential in order to secure for the individual effective protection for his right'.[83]

[75] For a discussion of the role of ELA in enforcement, see the relevant chapter in the present volume.

[76] Tridimas, n 77 above.

[77] Case C-253/00 *Antonio Muñoz y Cia SA, Superior Fruiticola SA and Frumar Ltd, Redbridge Produce Marketing Ltd* [2002] ECR 7312.

[78] Case C-324/09 *L'Oréal SA and Others v eBay International AG and Others* [2011] ECR I-6011, 142.

[79] *Muñoz*, n 105 above, para 31.

[80] Tridimas, n 77 above.

[81] Directive (EU) 2018/958 on a proportionality test before adoption of new regulation of professions, OJ L 173, 9.7.2018, p. 25–34.

[82] Case C-432/05 *Unibet (London) Ltd Unibet (International) Ltd v Justitiekanslern*, Opinion of Advocate General Sharpston ECLI:EU:C:2006:755, para 35.

[83] Case 222/86 *Union nationale des entraîneurs et cadres techniques professionnels du football (Unectef) v Georges Heylens and others* [1987] ECR-04097, para 14.

General reference to national law in EU secondary law tends to be more commonly found in respect of sanctions. For example. Article 17 of Directive 2000/78 confers on Member States responsibility for determining the rules on sanctions applicable to infringements of the national provisions adopted pursuant to that directive and for taking all measures necessary to ensure that they are applied. Although it does not call for the adoption of specific sanctions, Article 17 requires that the sanctions applicable to infringements of the national provisions pursuant to that directive must be effective, proportional and dissuasive. The CJEU case-law has not dealt explicitly with the way the notions of effectiveness, proportionality and dissuasiveness should be interpreted. The only instance where a more detailed definition was provided, albeit by Advocate General Kokkott regarding the application of directives in criminal proceedings, was in *Berlusconi and Others*:[84]

> "A penalty is dissuasive where it prevents an individual from infringing the objectives pursued and rules laid down by Community law. What is decisive in this regard is not only the nature and level of the penalty but also the likelihood of its being imposed. Anyone who commits an infringement must fear that the penalty will in fact be imposed on him. There is an overlap here between the criterion of dissuasiveness and that of effectiveness. A penalty is proportionate where it is appropriate (that is to say, in particular, effective and dissuasive) for attaining the legitimate objectives pursued by it, and also necessary. Where there is a choice between several (equally) appropriate penalties, recourse must be had to the least onerous. Moreover, the effects of the penalty on the person concerned must be proportionate to the aims pursued. The question whether a provision of national law contains a penalty which is effective, proportionate and dissuasive within the meaning defined above must be analysed by reference to the role of that provision in the legislation as a whole, including the progress and special features of the procedure before the various national authorities, in each case in which that question arises."[85]

In the labour law sphere, the CJEU has dealt with these concepts more comprehensively in cases dealing with equality and anti-discrimination. According to CJEU case law, the rules on sanctions in such cases must in particular ensure "real and effective legal protection".[86] The severity of the sanctions must be commensurate to the seriousness of the breaches for which they are imposed, in particular by ensuring a genuinely dissuasive effect[87] while respecting the general principle of proportionality.[88] In this respect, it has been held that a purely symbolic sanction cannot be regarded as being compatible with the correct and effective

[84] Joined Cases C-387/02, C-391/02 and C-403/02 *Criminal proceedings against Silvio Berlusconi (C-387/02), Sergio Adelchi (C-391/02)* and *Marcello Dell'Utri and Others (C-403/02)* [2005] ECR I-03565.

[85] Ibid, paras 90–92.

[86] Case C-81/12 *Asociația Accept v Consiliul Național pentru Combaterea Discriminării* EU:C:2013:275, para 63.

[87] Case C-383/92 *Commission v United Kingdom* [1994] ECR I-2479, para 42.

[88] Case C-101/01 *Lindqvist* [2003] ECR I-12971, paras 87 and 88.

implementation of Directive 2000/78".[89] The Court's ruling in *Feryn*, made in the context of Directive 2000/43, also confirmed that the rules on sanctions (ie effective, proportionate and dissuasive) apply even though there may be no identifiable victim.[90]

3.1.4. Provision of Specific Remedies and Sanctions

An examination across different areas of EU labour law suggests that the extent to which EU law has provided explicitly for remedies and sanctions has been broadly determined by the rationale behind the legislative initiative. The incorporation of specific remedies and/or sanctions was, hitherto, traditionally found in EU legislation that sought to provide a degree of harmonisation of labour standards in transnational settings. Such provisions have usually been incorporated in Regulations rather than Directives.[91] These have been complemented in certain instances by the provision of leeway to EU Member States to introduce, for instance, more specific rules on certain aspects of remedies and sanctions.[92] Similarly, provisions on mutual assistance and recognition have been common in cases in which the regulatory instruments address issues with a transnational dimension. For instance, Directive 2014/67/EU on the enforcement of Directive 96/71/EC concerning the posting of workers provides this in the case of administrative penalties and/or fines.[93]

While it is true that the provision of specific remedies and sanctions has traditionally been found in regulatory instruments that address transnational issues, there is some evidence of evolution in the approach adopted to the explicit incorporation of these mechanisms in EU secondary law. The most prominent example here is in respect of equality rights. Directive 2006/54 (Gender Equality Directive), which dates from 1976, was recast in 2006.[94] Initially it contained only a single provision requiring Member States to enable 'all persons who considered themselves wronged by failure to apply to them the principle of equal treatment [set out elsewhere in that Directive] to pursue their claims by judicial process'.[95]

[89] *Asociaţia Accept*, see n 116 above, para 64.

[90] Case C-54/07 *Centrum voor gelijkheid van kansen en voor racismebestrijding v Firma Feryn NY*, [2008] ECR I-5187.

[91] See, for instance, Article 10(3)(3) and Preamble (recital 27) of Regulation (EC) No 561/2006 on the harmonisation of certain social legislation relating to road transport, OJ L 102, 11.4.2006, p. 1–14.

[92] Eg Regulation (EC) No 561/2006, ibid, provides that Member States may make the liability referred to above conditional on the undertaking's infringement of paras 1 and 2 of Article 10.

[93] See also Article 40 of Regulation (EU) No 165/2014 on tachographs in road transport, OJ L 60, 28.2.2014, 1–33.

[94] Directive 2006/54/EC on the implementation of the principle of equal opportunities and equal treatment of men and women in matters of employment and occupation (recast), OJ L 204, 26.7.2006, 23–36.

[95] Art 6 Directive 76/207/EEC on the implementation of the principle of equal treatment for men and women as regards access to employment, vocational training and promotion, and working conditions, OJ 1976, L 39/40. See also Directive 97/80/EC on the burden of proof in cases of discrimination based on sex, 0.1 1980, L 14/6.

This later evolved – in part as a codification of CJEU case law[96] – into a self-standing chapter on remedies and enforcement.[97] That chapter regulates issues such as the possibility for interested third parties to take legal action, compensation in damages and the burden of proof.[98] More recent EU secondary legislation includes specific rights to remedies, even though the substantive rights recognised in these instruments do not have a transnational dimension, nor are they concerned with equality rights. Among others, Directive (EU) 2019/1158 on work–life balance for parents and carers specifies that where workers who consider that they have been dismissed on the grounds that they have applied for, or have taken, leave, it shall be for the employer to prove that the dismissal was based on other grounds.[99] While this indicates an evolution in terms of the approach adopted regarding remedies, it still falls short of a comprehensive sectoral approach towards a remedial framework regarding EU labour rights (as is the case, for instance, in consumer law).

Still in the context of explicit remedies and sanctions, different approaches may be detected in respect of the extent and nature of these, as provided for in EU law. A first approach consists of determining the consequences of illegality (eg this may be in respect of nullity).[100] For instance, Article 7(4) of Regulation 492/11 provides for the nullity of collective or individual labour agreements, which lay down or authorise discriminatory conditions in respect of workers who are nationals of other EU Member States. EU Equality Directives also provide that States shall ensure that all provisions of laws, regulations, contracts, collective agreements, internal company regulations, statutes of the independent professions which are contrary to principles set out in EU Directives be abolished or declared void.[101] Compliance is also sought in respect of national courts owing to the direct vertical effect of a Directive's provisions, which, from the standpoint of their content, are unconditional and sufficiently precise.[102]

A second approach consists of a right to compensation.[103] While a number of EU labour law directives refer to compensation, this usually takes place in the context of effective, proportionate and dissuasive penalties.[104] As AG Mengozzi

[96] Eg Case C-271/91 *Marshall v. Southampton and South West Hampshire Area Health Authority* ['Marshall II'] [1994] QB 126 paras 25–26; Case 109/88 *Handels-og Kontorfunktionaerernes Forbund I Danmark v Dansk Arbejdsgiverforening, acting on behalf of Danfoss* [1989], ECR 3199 para 13; *Von Colson*, n 23 above, para 23.

[97] Ch 1 of Title III of Directive 2006/54, n 124 above.

[98] For a more recent example, see the EC proposal for a new directive on pay transparency, COM(2021) 93 final, 2021/0050 (COD).

[99] Article 12(3) and Preamble, recital 44, n 110 above. See similarly recital 20 to the Preamble and Article 7 of Directive 2000/43/EC implementing the principle of equal treatment between persons irrespective of racial or ethnic origin, OJ L 180, 19.7.2000, 22–26.

[100] Tridimas, n 77 above.

[101] Eg Article 16 of Directive 2000/78/EC establishing a general framework for equal treatment in employment and occupation OJ L 303, 2.12.2000, 16–22. See also Article 14 of Directive 2000/43, n 129 above.

[102] C-595/12 *Loredana Napoli v Ministero della Giustizia – Dipartimento dell'Amministrazione penitenziaria*, ECLI:EU:C:2014:128.

[103] For a more detailed discussion, see section 3.2 below.

[104] See, for instance, Article 25(3) Directive 2006/54/EC, n 124 above.

argued in C-407/14, the origins of the reference to compensation as a type of penalty were to be found in *von Colson* and in *Harz*.[105] The requirement of dissuasion seems to be satisfied if the compensation envisaged is 'adequate', in terms of guaranteeing real and effective judicial protection of the rights conferred, and must, therefore, amount to more than purely nominal compensation.[106] However, it does not extend to punitive damages.[107]

A third approach includes stipulating a more or less specific obligation to provide for effective remedies and sanctions. This may incorporate a variety of options, ranging from very specific obligations to identifying a band of possible mechanisms for redress, relying on private or public enforcement or employing a combination of both. An example of very specific mechanisms is Article 21 of Regulation (EC) No 561/2006 on driving times, breaks and rest periods, as it allows the competent authority to proceed with immobilisation of a vehicle until such time as the cause of the infringement of the Regulation has been rectified. A more recent example concerns the rules concerning posting of workers. Going further than Directive 96/71/EC, which was concerned with the substantive rights afforded to posted workers, Directive 2014/67/EU addresses in a comprehensive way the specific issue of enforcement.[108] Following explicit reference to the CFREU fundamental rights and principles (Articles 47, 48 and 50) in the preamble,[109] the Directive goes on to provide specific rights in terms of facilitating complaints by individual workers,[110] but also trade unions and other third parties.[111] On top of a requirement on EU Member States to provide for effective, dissuasive and proportionate penalties for any breaches of the obligations under this Directive,[112] Articles 11 and 12 impose specific rules in terms of the liability of the employer of the posted worker and in respect of subcontracting, respectively.[113]

Finally, EU law may explicitly incorporate procedural rights.[114] While the Framework Directive on Equality constituted the most comprehensive attempt, hitherto, to introduce rights related to access to justice[115] there is evidence to suggest increasing acknowledgement of the importance of such rights in more recent EU policy initiatives. Most prominent of all, arguably, is Article 18 of Directive (EU) 2019/1152 on transparent and predictable working conditions providing protection from dismissal and a reversal of the burden of proof.

[105] Case C-407/14 *María Auxiliadora Arjona Camacho v Securitas Seguridad España, SA*, Opinion of Advocate General Mengozzi, ECLI:EU:C:2015:534, para 31.

[106] *Von Colson*, n 23 above.

[107] *María Auxiliadora Arjona Camacho*, n 135 above.

[108] Directive 2014/67/EU on the enforcement of Directive 96/71/EC concerning the posting of workers in the framework of the provision of services, OJ L 159, 28.5.2014, 11–31.

[109] Article 20.

[110] Article 11(1).

[111] Article 11(3).

[112] Recital 47 to the Preamble.

[113] See also, among others, Article 3 of Directive 2014/54/EU on measures facilitating the exercise of rights conferred on workers in the context of freedom of movement for workers, OJ 2014, L 128/8.

[114] Tridimas, n 77 above.

[115] Article 10. See also Article 19 of Directive 2006/54/EC, n 124 above.

3.2. Damage Claims in EU Labour Law[116]

There are three potential categories of damage claims in EU law.[117] The first concerns an action for damages that results from the application of the principle of effectiveness in the absence or incompleteness of remedies or sanctions for the infringements of EU rights.[118] The second concerns the case of EU directives explicitly requiring the existence of a right to damages but implemented at national level.[119] The final category consists of a directly applicable EU right to damages in an EU Regulation.[120] Most damage claims in EU labour law tend to fall within the first and second sources. Again, it is in the sphere of equality rights, as interpreted this time in CJEU case law, where the EU law approach to damages has been most developed. The CJEU has long established, among other things, that in order to be effective, the principle of equal treatment implies that the compensation awarded for any breach must be adequate in relation to the damage sustained.[121] Considerations of equality of opportunity played a role in the CJEU decision in *Marshall* that reparation of the loss and damage sustained by a person injured as a result of discriminatory dismissal may not be limited to an upper limit fixed a priori.[122] However, subsequent case law,[123] now reflected in Article 18 of Directive 2006/54, eroded the 'no upper limit rule', where the employer can prove that the only damage suffered by an application as a result of discrimination is the refusal to take their job application into consideration.

Outside the area of equality rights, there is some evidence to suggest that the CJEU has been sensitive to the nature of the employment relationship. Reiterating previous case law to the effect that workers must be regarded as the weaker party in the employment relationship, and it is therefore necessary to prevent the employer being in a position to impose a restriction of their rights on them,[124] the Court held recently that it cannot be reasonable to require a worker who has suffered loss or damage as a result of the infringement by their employer of the maximum weekly working time limits under Directive 2003/88, to make a prior application to that employer in order to be entitled to reparation for that loss or damage.[125] Further, the CJEU found in *Levez* that temporal limits on damage claims may be

[116] For reasons of space, the analysis does not consider the case of a right in damages for the direct liability of the EU as represented through its institutions and as a derived liability of the Union as an employer.

[117] Heinze, n 47 above.

[118] See the analysis in section 2.

[119] See above for a discussion of this.

[120] Heinze, n 47 above.

[121] *Von Colson*, 23 above.

[122] *Marshall*, n 126 above.

[123] See eg Case C-180/95 *Nils Draehmpaehl v Urania Immobilienservice OHG* [1997] ECR-I 2195.

[124] See, to that effect, C-397/01 *Bernhard Pfeiffer*, C-398/01 *Wilhelm Roith*, C-399/01 *Albert Süß*, C-400/01 *Michael Winter*, C-401/01 *Klaus Nestvogel*, C-402/01 *Roswitha Zeller* and C-403/01 *Matthias Döbele v Deutsches Rotes Kreuz, Kreisverband Waldshut eV*, EU:C:2004:584, para 82.

[125] Case C-429/09 *Günter Fuß v Stadt Halle* [2010] ECR I-12167, para 86.

contrary to EU law, even when another remedy is available, if the latter is likely to entail procedural rules or other conditions that are less favourable than those applicable to similar domestic actions.[126] A related issue here concerns the extent to which, in cases where the employer has acted in accordance with national law but where that national law is considered contrary to the CFREU (read in combination with EU Directives), said employer is liable for providing a remedy. In his Opinion in *AMS*, AG Cruz Villalón considered that it was 'reasonable that the burden of an action for damages should fall on the person who has benefited from the unlawful conduct, and not on the holder of the right arising from the specific expression of the content of the principle'.[127] The employer that is held liable could then turn against the State. The Court did not address this issue directly but the decision in *DI* could be read as imposing such a requirement.[128]

The case law in respect of clause 5 of the Framework Agreement on fixed-term work, which obliges Member States to adopt measures to prevent the abuse of successive fixed-term contracts, is also instructive in terms of redress for individuals faced with abusive successive fixed-term contracts. In *Santoro*,[129] the CJEU was required to consider whether the measures in Italy in case of abuse, notably a flat-rate sum and payment for damages for the loss of favourable opportunities, can be considered 'equivalent and effective measures' for the purpose of compensating abusive successions of fixed-term contracts under the Fixed Term Directive. In its decision, the CJEU held that, while these workers may not be entitled to compensation for lack of conversion to which the private sector employees are entitled, they should be entitled to compensation for the loss of opportunity. The calculation of this compensation was left to the national court, but the CJEU indicated through its reference to the difficulties inherent in demonstrating the existence of a loss of opportunity that the burden of proof as regards establishing that this loss of opportunity did not exist should not be on the employee.

More recently, there is some evidence of reconsideration at EU level regarding the effectiveness of damages in the context of the employment relationship. In the area of equality, the limits in terms of enforcement have been repeatedly emphasised in research[130] and recently acknowledged by the European Commission.[131]

[126] Case C-326/96 *BS Levez v TH Jennings (Harlow Pools) Ltd* [1998] ECR I-07835.

[127] Case C-176/12, *Association de médiation sociale v Union locale des syndicats CGT, Hichem Laboubi, Union départementale CGT des Bouches-du-Rhône Confédération générale du travail (CGT)*, Opinion of Advocate General Cruz Villalón, ECLI:EU:C:2013:491, para 79.

[128] Case C-441/14, n 80 above, para 42.

[129] Case C-494/16 *Giuseppa Santoro v Comune di Valderice and Presidenza del Consiglio dei Ministri*, EU:C:2018:166.

[130] See, among others, M Dawson and E Muir, 'Individual, Institutional and Collective Vigilance in Protecting Fundamental Rights in the EU: Lessons from the Roma' (2011) 48(3) *Common Market Law Revue*.

[131] Joint Report on the application of Council Directive 2000/43/EC of 29 June 2000 implementing the principle of equal treatment between persons irrespective of racial or ethnic origin ('Racial Equality Directive') and of Council Directive 2000/78/EC of 27 November 2000 establishing a general framework for equal treatment in employment and occupation ('Employment Equality Directive').

These include that the sanctions foreseen are very low; that judges are relatively hesitant in applying sanctions at all, specifically in 'first time cases' and/or tend to issue sanctions close to the minimum amount rather than trying to establish adequate amounts to the problem; and that in many cases sanctions lack effectiveness as they are either not complied with or they cannot encourage a change of attitude.[132] There is also evidence that EU law has failed to deliver concrete remedies for vulnerable groups (eg in respect of Roma communities).[133] Outside the area of equality legislation and more recently, EU Directive 2019/1152 on transparent and predictable working conditions made direct reference in the preamble to the limits of systems centred on damage claims: 'redress systems based solely on claims for damages are less effective than systems that also provide for penalties, such as lump sums or loss of permits, for employers who fail to issue written statements'.[134] Disappointingly, the Directive stopped short of introducing explicit sanctions along these lines and reference is made instead to the requirement that the penalties provided for by Member States shall be effective, proportionate and dissuasive.[135]

3.3. The Principle of State Liability as a Functional Equivalent of Employer Liability?

As is generally accepted, a Directive cannot be relied upon as such against an individual (such as a private sector employer).[136] In such cases, the victim's remedy primarily takes the form of a damages action against the State.[137] The principle of state liability was first applied in *Francovich* and has been developed in subsequent case law.[138] According to this, a Member State may be liable for loss and damage caused to individuals as a result of breaches of EU law. Individuals harmed have a right to damages when three conditions are met: the rule of EU law breached is intended to confer rights upon individuals; the breach is sufficiently serious;

[132] Equinet Report (2015) The Sanctions Regime in Discrimination Cases and its Effects, 4, https://www.archive.equineteurope.org/IMG/pdf/sanctions_regime_discrimination_-_final_for_web.pdf. Note that sanctions here refer to compensation for damages.

[133] See n 164 above.

[134] Recital 49 in the preamble.

[135] See also 3.1.3 above.

[136] Case C-91/92 *Paola Faccini Dori v Recreb Srl* EU:C:1994:292, para 20; *Pfeiffer and Others*, n 158 above, para 108; Case C-555/07 *Kücükdeveci v Swedex GmbH & Co KG*, EU:C:2010:21, para 46.

[137] Joined cases C-6/90 and C-9/90 *Andrea Francovich and Danila Bonifaci and others v Italian Republic* [1991] ECR I-5357. Two other mechanisms are relevant here but are not discussed in depth due to lack of space. The first involves the broad interpretation of the notion of state bodies against which directives may be directly effective and the second involves requiring national courts to interpret national law so as to give effect to a Member State's obligations under EU law.

[138] *Francovich*, n 171 above. See also Case C-46/93 and C-48/93 *Brasserie du Pêcheur SA v Bundesrepublik Deutschland and The Queen v Secretary of State for Transport, ex parte: Factortame Ltd and others* [1996] ECR I-1029, Case C-224/01 *Gerhard Köbler v Republik Österreich* [2003] ECR I-10239, and Case C-445/06 *Danske Slagterier v Bundesrepublik Deutschland* [2009] ECR I-2119.

and there is a direct causal link between the breach of EU law and the damage sustained by any individual.[139] In *Köbler*[140] and *Traghetti del Mediterraneo*,[141] this case law was applied to situations of breach of EU law attributable to a court or tribunal against whose decisions there was no judicial remedy under national law.[142] Where the conditions for a State to incur liability are satisfied, it is on the basis of the rules of national law concerning liability that the State must make reparation for the consequences of the loss or damage caused, provided that the conditions laid down by national law respect both the principles of equivalence and effectiveness. In broad terms, the case law in this area suggests that the CJEU subscribes to the opinion that, where there is a right to reparation, there must also be a remedy to seek reparation before a court of law.[143] While, however, the CJEU has offered relatively clear guidance as to how to define the first two conditions,[144] it has not provided much clarification in terms of the issue of causality. Instead, it is typically left to competent national courts to determine how this condition is to be understood and applied in individual cases.[145]

From a labour law perspective, a number of issues are worth considering here. The first is whether state liability should be considered an adequate substitute for employer liability.[146] State liability provides damages for economic losses incurred by the claimant, but does not give the claimant direct access to the EU rights conferred through the law. Instead, what it does is to grant such access indirectly as the Member State, having been found in breach of its EU law obligations and ordered to compensate the affected claimant, will proceed to the amendment/clarification of the legislation to avoid any further claims. Following the finding of state liability, the state invariably grants access to individuals through remedial action.[147] On one hand, it can be argued that state liability provides an appropriate mechanism for the effectiveness of EU law and complete judicial protection, including in the context of labour law.[148] It essentially functions to fill in the significant regulatory gap left from the lack of direct effect of Directives vis-à-vis

139 These are the so-called *Brasserie du Pêcheur* conditions.

140 *Köbler*, n 172 above.

141 Case C-173/03 *Traghetti del Mediterraneo SpA v Repubblica italiana* [2006] ECR I-5177.

142 For criticism, see M Dougan, 'Addressing Issues of Protective Scope within the Francovich Right to Reparation' (2017) 13 *European Constitutional Law Review* 124.

143 T Eilmansberger, 'The Relationship between Rights and Remedies in EC Law: In Search of the Missing Link' (2004) 41 *Common Market Law Review* 1999.

144 See recently, among others, Case C-160/14, *João Filipe Ferreira da Silva e Brito and Others v Portuguese State*, ECLI:EU:C:2015:565.

145 T Lock, 'Is Private Enforcement of EU Law through State Liability a Myth? An Assessment of 20 Years of Francovich' (2012) 49 *Common Market Law Revue* 1697–1699; A Biondi and M Farley *The Right to Damages in EU Law* (The Hague, Kluwer, 2009) 55–57.

146 On this, see Ryan, n 46 above at 141–63.

147 J Marson and K Ferris, *Collective Redress: Broadening EU Enforcement through State Liability?* http://eprints.hud.ac.uk/id/eprint/24667/1/Marson_and_Ferris_-_Collective_Redress_in_the_EU_-_FINAL.pdf.

148 See *Brasserie du Pêcheur* and *Factortame*, Opinion of Advocate General Tesauro, n 172 above, para 32.

employers in the private sector.[149] Despite the CJEU's increasing reliance, as it seems, on the CFREU to hold certain provisions as directly effective in the context of private parties,[150] there are still questions regarding the extent to which such an approach will be adopted in disputes involving labour rights.[151] As labour claimants may not be able to rely on Article 47 CFREU to enforce their rights, state liability may offer an alternative avenue for redress.

On the other hand, various limitations may operate to dampen claimants' ability to successfully seek redress on the basis of state liability claims. The first relates to possible areas in which the liability rule may not be applicable. This may be where, for instance, a directive may be found to have a meaning that the Member State could not have anticipated, so that state liability does not arise.[152] A second limitation relates to more practical issues related to the resources needed for claims to be brought before courts. For instance, in the United Kingdom before its government took it out of the EU ('Brexit'), trade unions and some public bodies did fund state liability claims, but these were relatively rare.[153] The fact that state liability has been used to serve commercial interests confirms the challenges associated with such claims on behalf of labour claimants.[154] Thirdly, state liability may not be effective where a legal entitlement cannot be readily provided with a monetary value, eg when it concerns limitations on working time and information and consultation rights.[155] Fourthly, the claimants may not have an 'identifiable right' within the meaning of *Francovich*.[156] Finally, state liability for damages may have perverse effects in terms of private actors' liability to pay damages for breaches of EU law. The *Laval* case illustrates the implications of this for trade unions particularly. When the case returned to Sweden, the Swedish Labour Court relied on an interpretation of *Courage, Manfredi* and *Raccanelli* as cases that constituted expressions of a general principle of horizontal liability and went on to find that liability for damages can be extended to horizontal relations.[157] These issues have led authors such as Reich to conclude that '*Francovich* liability cannot substitute for absent enforcement actions by the Commission or Member States when they

[149] Case C-193/17, *Cresco Investigation GmbH v Markus Achatzi*, Opinion of Advocate General Bobek AG Opinion, ECLI:EU:C:2018:614 para 153.

[150] Ibid.

[151] See Koukiadaki, n 53 above.

[152] See Ryan, n 46 above at 150–151 for a discussion.

[153] See Marson and Ferris, n 181 above.

[154] T Tridimas, 'State Liability in Damages: Vingt Ans Après', paper presented at conference 'Celebrating 20 Years of Francovich in the EU', British Institute of International and Comparative Law, London, 17 November 2011. See discussion in N Reich, 'Francovich enforcement analysed and illustrated by German (and English) law' in A Jakab and D Kochenov (eds), *The Enforcement of EU Law and Values* (Oxford University Press, 2017) 112.

[155] See Ryan, n 46 above at 155.

[156] Reich, n 46 above at 114.

[157] J Malmberg, 'Trade Union Liability for "EU-Unlawful" Collective Action' (2012) 3(1) *European Labour Law Journal*.

are competent and required to act'.[158] This is even truer in the case of labour law, in respect of which infringement proceedings by the European Commission have been scarce.[159]

4. Conclusion

The objective of this chapter was to provide a systematic and comprehensive analysis of the regulatory approach in EU labour law towards remedies and sanctions and assess its relevance for the effective enforcement of EU labour rights. The analysis was largely premised on the idea that one can understand the meaning and content of a right by looking at how it is protected. In the EU law literature, remedies have been insightfully described by Tridimas as a corollary to rights and as means of enforcement, providing "contrasting aspects of EU law as a force empowering the citizen and as an authority exercising imperium".[160] Pre-Lisbon, it was the CJEU that invoked the rule of law for the 'complete system of remedies'[161] or the rule of law and fundamental rights,[162] to supplement the Treaty provision on remedies before the EU courts that the Treaties provided.[163] Post-Lisbon, the incorporation of the CFREU into EU primary law has provided considerable impetus for the development of the principle of effective judicial protection.

In this context, the central argument of the chapter is that the remedial approach in EU labour law has been traditionally characterised by horizontal and vertical fragmentation.[164] In terms of horizontal fragmentation, the current approach comprises of a patchwork of rules and principles that do not reflect a sectoral approach to enforcement but are guided instead by an overarching objective of EU law effectiveness, developed to address primarily issues of transnational nature. This is not attentive to the particularities of the employment relationship, however, and as a result, it fails to provide a basis for the development of a fully-fledged regulatory framework to provide adequate redress in cases of violations of EU labour law. This is compounded by the fact that, because of the traditional reliance on Directives in this area, the scope to rely on EU law against a private sector employer is significantly curtailed. In terms of its vertical fragmentation, the

[158] Reich, 188 above at 127.

[159] See analysis by K Lörcher in this volume.

[160] T Tridimas, *The General Principles of EU Law* (Oxford, OUP, 2006).

[161] 'The rule of law, inasmuch as neither its Member States nor its institutions can avoid review of the conformity of their acts with the basic constitutional charter, the EC Treaty, which established a complete system of legal remedies and procedures designed to enable the Court of Justice to review the legality of acts of the institutions', Case 294/83 *Les Verts v Parliament* [1986] ECR 1339, para 23.

[162] Joined Cases C-402/05 P and C-415/05 P *Yassin Abdullah Kadi and Al Barakaat International Foundation v Council and Commission (Kadi I)* [2008] ECR I-6351, paras 281 and 283.

[163] See Roeben, n 56 above.

[164] See also Heinze, n 47 above, for a similar argument in respect of damage claims in European private law.

EU approach to remedies and sanctions in labour law has historically depended on the procedural autonomy of Member States. While this autonomy allows Member States to define the procedural rules of judicial actions designed to ensure the protection of the rights which individuals derive from EU law, there is some evidence to suggest that the effectiveness of this approach may be constrained due to, among others, uncertainty concerning the way the scope of procedural autonomy should be interpreted. In turn, this has negative implications for the judicial protection of private parties but also for the regulation of these issues across the EU.

In order to overcome these challenges, consideration should be given to the development of a sectoral, ie EU labour law, approach to remedies and sanctions that is sensitive above all to the nature of the employment relationship.[165] Such an approach can build on what is already available, not only in EU labour law (especially in the context of equality rights), but also in other areas (eg consumer protection) to establish a more comprehensive framework, ultimately putting rules aimed at enforcing rights on an equal footing with rules allocating them.

[165] Cf with the proposal developed by Heinze regarding a sector-specific approach to damages (n 47 above). See the chapter in the book including a proposal for an EU Labour Law Enforcement Directive (chapter 22).

3

Access to Justice

KLAUS LÖRCHER

1. Introduction: Access to Justice as a Precondition of Effective Enforcement

Throughout modern history, justice has been considered as being inextricably linked to courts of law. 'When a right is violated or damage is caused, access to justice is of fundamental importance for the injured individual and it is an essential component of the rule of law.'[1] Accordingly, it is the very heart of enforcement. Obviously, the main component of 'access to justice' is access to courts, although it is not limited to that. This appears to be a common understanding shared by, among others, the EU's Fundamental Rights Agency (FRA) and the Council of Europe (CoE).[2]

For the CJEU the cornerstone is the 'principle of effective judicial protection of the rights which individuals derive from EU law'. Reaffirmed by Article 47 CFREU it comprises 'in particular, the rights of the defence, the principle of equality of arms, the right of access to a court or tribunal and the right to be advised, defended and represented'.[3]

Whereas 'access to justice' in general is indispensable, it is particularly important in the employment relationship. In this area, 'justice' also has to perform a specific compensatory function: as workers are structurally at a disadvantage vis-à-vis their employer, they have to be better protected by the judicial system. Obstacles that might restrict access to justice have to be evaluated against this background.

[1] F Francioni, 'Access to Justice as a Human Right' in *Collected Courses of the Academy of European Law*, XVI/4 (Academy of European Law, European University Institute, 2007; published to Oxford Scholarship Online, 2012), https://oxford.universitypressscholarship.com/view/10.1093/acprof:oso/9780199233083.001.0001/acprof-9780199233083?rskey=2YSYtl&result=6.

[2] Fundamental Rights Agency, Council of Europe (eds), *Handbook on European Law Relating to Access to Justice* (Luxembourg, Publications Office of the European Union, 2016), www.echr.coe.int/documents/handbook_access_justice_eng.pdf.

[3] Case C-662/17 *EG v Republic of Slovenia* [2018], ECLI:EU:C:2018:847, paras 47 and 48.

But part and parcel of 'access to justice' is the procedure that follows. In particular, a right cannot be 'enforced' (particularly in labour law) unless a fair trial is also guaranteed.

In any event, the benchmark is 'effectiveness'. In this chapter the term 'effectiveness' will be understood as including 'efficiency'.[4]

2. Access to Justice

> Access to justice is a basic principle of the rule of law. In the absence of access to justice, people are unable to have their voice heard, exercise their rights … or hold decision-makers accountable.[5]

Set against this fundamental approach, systems of judicial protection have to be assessed in terms of their enforcement of EU labour law,[6] both at EU level (see 2.1 below)[7] and – insofar as national judges are to be considered to be 'EU judges'[8] – also at domestic level (see 2.2 below). This duplicity is connected with the very limited direct access to EU courts and the 'compensation' for that available at national level.

As for the legal framework it should be noted that access to justice encompasses a number of core human rights, such as the right to a fair trial under Article 6 ECHR, and the right to an effective remedy under Article 13 ECHR, both included in Article 47 CFREU.[9] This legal framework is to be contrasted, however, with the

[4] For the differences see the following explanations:

Effective (adjective): adequate to accomplish a purpose; producing the intended or expected result.

Efficient (adjective): performing or functioning in the best possible manner with the least waste of time and effort.

The difference between effectiveness and efficiency can be summed up succinctly as follows: being effective is about doing the right things, while being efficient is about doing things right; www.insightsquared.com/blog/effectiveness-vs-efficiency-whats-the-difference/.

[5] See www.un.org/ruleoflaw/thematic-areas/access-to-justice-and-rule-of-law-institutions/access-to-justice/.

[6] EU labour law has a wider understanding and cross-over into (normal) civil, administrative and criminal law.

[7] Z Rasnača, 'Procedure – Litigating before EU Courts in the Light to the Charter' in F Dorssemont, K Lörcher, S Clauwaert and M Schmitt (eds), *The Charter of Fundamental Rights of the European Union and the Employment Relation* (Oxford, Hart, 2019) 163–88.

[8] See eg: N Fennelly, 'The National Judge as Judge of the European Union' in A Rosas, E Levits and Y Bot (eds), *The Court of Justice of the European Union – Analyses and Perspectives on Sixty Years of Case-law* (The Hague, Asser Press, 2013) 61ff.

[9] K Lörcher, 'Article 47 – Right to an Effective Remedy and to a Fair Trial' in F Dorssemont et al, see above n 7 at 610–631. A number of important elements will be taken from this contribution and further developed in this chapter; FRA and CoE (eds), *Handbook on European Law Relating to Access to Justice* (Luxembourg, Publications Office of the European Union, 2016) n 2, but in the third indent the role of Art 52(3) CFREU is not sufficiently taken into account. Accordingly, the words 'may correspond' have been changed to 'correspond' according also to the respective Explanations to Article 47 CFREU. Moreover, the words 'thus guaranteeing a minimum level of protection' have been added; see also for specific recommendations to improve access to justice, N Rass-Masson and V Rouas, 'Effective Access to Justice', Study for the European Parliament, PETI Committee, November 2017.

CJEU's general approach to 'effective judicial protection', which is restrictive in the sense

> that, as shown by well-established case-law, the Treaty, in Articles 263 TFEU and 277 TFEU, on the one hand, and Article 267 TFEU, on the other, established a complete system of legal remedies and procedures designed to enable the European Union Courts to review the legality of acts of the institutions. Under that system, where natural or legal persons cannot, by reason of the conditions for admissibility laid down in the fourth paragraph of Article 263 TFEU, directly challenge Community measures of general application, they are able to plead the invalidity of such acts before the national courts and ask them, since they have no jurisdiction themselves to declare those measures invalid, to make a reference to the Court of Justice for a preliminary ruling in that regard.[10]

Nevertheless, whether this interpretation sufficiently takes account of the legal requirement of 'effectiveness' remains to be seen.

Finally, non-judicial avenues might also contribute to ensure justice (see 2.3 below).

2.1. Access to EU Courts

EU law has many characteristic features. This is also illustrated by its judicial architecture, which is defined in general by Article 19 TEU and more specifically in section 5 (of Part six, Title I, Chapter 1 of the TFEU) 'The Court of Justice of the European Union'. Although it might initially sound simple, it is complex. It has to deal, among other things, with different forms of access (institutions/individuals) and with different layers (EU/national). According to Article 19(1) TEU the CJEU 'shall ensure that in the interpretation and application of the Treaties the law is observed'. On the other hand, the following sentence (second subparagraph) provides that 'Member States shall provide remedies sufficient to ensure effective legal protection in the fields covered by Union law'. This puts a strong emphasis on the level of the Member States.[11]

At EU level, access for individuals is very limited for direct action (Article 263(4) TFEU): the main judicial avenues of indirect involvement are foreseen for the Commission in instituting infringement procedures (Article 258 TFEU) and for domestic courts in the form of preliminary reference (Article 267 TFEU).

[10] T-541/10 *ADEDY* [2012], para 64, referring to Case C-50/00 P *Unión de Pequeños Agricultores v Council* [2002] ECR I-6677, para 40; Case C-263/02 P *Commission v Jégo-Quéré* [2004] ECR I-3425, para 30; and Case C-362/06 P *Sahlstedt and Others v Commission* [2009] ECR I-2903, para 43.

[11] In trying to cope with the challenges caused by digitalisation, the Council has adopted Conclusions 'Access to justice – seizing the opportunities of digitalisation' [2020] OJ CI 342/1. For the specific problem which women face wishing to access justice, see a recent report by the CoE (ed), 'Framework to Measure Access to Justice Including Specific Challenges Facing Women', July 2021, https://rm.coe.int/report-of-the-online-roundtable-on-framework-to-measure-access-to-just/1680a33bc0.

2.1.1. Direct Action Proceedings (Article 263(4) TFEU)

Direct action against EU acts is possible. But individuals can 'only institute proceedings against an act addressed to that person or which is of direct and individual concern to them' (Article 263(4) TFEU). Individuals can address their action in the first instance to the General Court (Article 256(1) TFEU).[12] The former provision is interpreted narrowly, however.[13]

It might be worth recalling that this limited access was originally based, among other things, on the assumption of the need to avoid overloading the CJEU (a malady also affecting the ECtHR in recent years). But this problem has long been recognised.[14] For example, this issue was discussed in the (second) Convention on the 'Future of Europe'. Indeed, in Working Group II 'Incorporation of the Charter/ accession to the ECHR', several proposals were aimed at facilitating this access.[15] Pointing out that this was a transversal question and not only specific to the enjoyment of fundamental rights, however, the Working Group did not propose an amendment to (the then) Article 230(4) TEC. Instead, it suggested that the Plenary should take care of this transversal problem.[16] The final outcome was a tiny amendment making it possible to challenge certain acts more easily.[17]

In future, Treaty amendments should ensure that – under certain conditions (such as exhaustion of domestic remedies) – individuals have the right to bring a case before the (General) Court. Moreover, in order to be prepared to adjudicate employment cases it would additionally require a specific chamber for labour issues.

On the basis of the existing legal framework, there are (rare) examples of admissible direct actions in the field of EU labour law. Concerning the first alternative in Article 263(4) TFEU of a direct action against an act 'addressed' to individuals, it is easier to determine the 'addressee'. One might refer to the *EPSU* case in which the General Court accepted the admissibility of the branch trade union federation at EU level for the public service to challenge the Commission's refusal to transmit a social partner agreement to the Council for a decision on whether it should

[12] 'The General Court shall have jurisdiction to hear and determine at first instance actions or proceedings referred to in Articles 263, 265, 268, 270 and 272'.

[13] A recent example might be Case C-352/19 P *Région de Bruxelles-Capitale* [2020], ECLI:EU:C:2020:978, in which the CJEU stated that this regional body was 'directly concerned' with the renewal of the approval of the active substance glyphosate.

[14] See, for example, J Sedemund and K Heinemann, 'Rechtsschutzdefizite in der EG' [Judicial Deficits in the EC] (1995) *Der Betrieb*, 1161ff.

[15] See, for example, Meyer (Einklagbarkeit der Charta-Grundrechte und Verbesserung des Individualrechtsschutzes) suggesting that ex-Art 230(4) TEC (now Art 263(4) TFEU) should be changed from cumulative ('direct *and* individual concern') to alternative ('direct *or* individual concern') conditions, see Working Document (WD) 17, 13.9.2002.

[16] Final report of Working Group II, CONV 354/02 (WG II 16), 22.10.2002, 15–16.

[17] See the addition in Art 263(4) TFEU: 'and against a regulatory act which is of direct concern to them and does not entail implementing measures'.

become a Directive or not.[18] A similar action had previously been filed by the employers' association UEAPME, but it had been declared inadmissible because of the lack of 'individual' concern.[19]

In relation to the second alternative ('direct and individual concern') the matter is much more complicated and disputed. This issue will be discussed later under the section dealing with the 'locus standi' (see section 4 below).

2.1.2. *Indirect Involvement*

If there is practically no direct access to EU courts the question arises whether other avenues provide at least for a certain 'compensation'.[20]

(a) Infringement Procedures (Article 258 TFEU)[21]

One cornerstone of the effectiveness of EU (labour) law is – or at least should be – the infringement proceedings to be initiated by the Commission as 'guardian of the Treaties' (Article 17(1) 2nd sentence TEU). In particular, it shall ensure the application of the Treaties, and of measures adopted by the institutions pursuant to them. Moreover, it shall oversee the application of Union law under the control of the CJEU (3rd sentence). Thus, it has to ensure not only the proper implementation of legislation, but also the application of EU law by Member States.[22] The avenue of infringement proceedings is not accessible directly for individuals, however.

Complaints to the Commission

The sole direct possibility for individuals to (perhaps) motivate the Commission to start an infringement procedure is to submit a complaint to the Commission.[23]

Based on its experience, one NGO describes the shortcomings of this as follows: it is not an easy and quick procedure to provide redress for citizens going

[18] GC (Ninth Chamber, Extended Composition), 24.10.2019, T–310/18 *European Federation of Public Service Unions (EPSU)* and *Jan Goudriaan v European Commission*, ECLI:EU:T:2019:757, para 39; in this respect implicitly confirmed by the CJEU (Grand Chamber), 2.9.2021, C-928/19 P, ECLI:EU:C:2021:656.

[19] T-135/96 *UEAPME v Council* [1998], EU:T:1998:128.

[20] For the possible 'compensation' in terms of Member State liability for EU law infringements, see Chapter 2 (in this volume).

[21] Although politically even less probable, particularly in the field of social policy, it should nevertheless be noted that also Member States have the possibility to introduce infringement procedures (Art 259 TFEU).

[22] The most recent example of control of the application of EU law is the formal notice according to Art 258 TFEU against the judgment of the German Constitutional Court concerning the joined constitutional complaints 2 BvR 859/15 ea INFR(2021)2114, 9 June 2021, against the actions of the European Central Bank in the form of its Secondary Markets Public Sector Asset Purchase Programme (PSPP).

[23] For more details (and links) see: https://ec.europa.eu/info/about-european-commission/contact/problems-and-complaints/complaints-about-breaches-eu-law/how-make-complaint-eu-level_en.

through hurdles; it requires the support of a legal expert in order to address all issues properly and the procedure is unclear regarding follow-up actions with national authorities.[24]

A brief analysis of the Commission's information on its Decision on multiple complaints shows that many issues concern competition, consumer protection or migration. But a substantial number also address labour law issues. Moreover, it shows that the Commission deals with these complaints in different ways. Taking the example of labour law issues the Commission either refers to recent CJEU judgments (working conditions of honorary judges),[25] or – additionally – to national initiatives (fixed-term contracts in Spain)[26] or indeed starting an infringement procedure (fixed-term contracts in Italy).[27] In this context, the follow-up of the complaints on the insufficient enforcement of the German Minimum Wage Act in the international transport sector is unclear,[28] in any event, the CJEU judgments in relation to working conditions of truck drivers clarified the applicability of Directive 96/71/EEC.[29] It seems to confirm that the procedures are lengthy and that there is not (always) a clear follow-up.

Commission's Framework for Infringement Procedures

As guardian of the Treaties (Article 17 TEU: 'It shall ensure the application of the Treaties') one should assume that the Commission would use the means of an infringement procedure in each case in which a Member State 'infringes' EU law. This impression is confirmed by the wording of Article 258(1) TFEU: 'If the Commission considers that a Member State has failed to fulfil an obligation under the Treaties, it shall deliver a reasoned opinion on the matter after giving the State concerned the opportunity to submit its observations'. However, the examples referred to above indicate that this is the case only under certain conditions.

After finding a violation of EU (labour) law the Commission will start any infringement procedure with a 'letter of formal notice' to the Government concerned. If the reply is insufficient, the next step will be a 'reasoned opinion' ('shall deliver'), to which the Government is supposed to reply. At this

[24] ILGA Europe, 'Bringing cases before the European Commission', https://ilga-europe.org/what-we-do/our-strategic-litigation-work/cases-before-european-commission.

[25] CHAP(2015)1071, referring to Case C-658/18, *UX v Governo della Repubblica italiana* [2020], ECLI:EU:C:2020:572, https://ec.europa.eu/info/sites/info/files/chap201501071_update_24_11_2020_en.pdf.

[26] CHAP(2013)01917, referring to 9 March 2020 on joined Cases C-103/18 *Sanchez Ruiz*, and C-429/18 *Fernandez Alvarez*, ECLI:EU:C:2020:219, https://ec.europa.eu/info/sites/info/files/reply_pm_es_public_sector_ftwd_20201006_en_0.pdf.

[27] See: https://ec.europa.eu/info/sites/info/files/file_import/information-complaint-update-chap-2013-02870_en_0.pdf, referring to a letter of formal notice (25 July 2019) which was followed 18 months later only by an 'additional' letter for formal notice, https://ec.europa.eu/commission/presscorner/detail/en/inf_20_2142.

[28] The Commission announced an infringement procedure (OJ [2015] C 233/7), but it is unknown whether it brought an action to the CJEU against Germany for failure to fulfil its obligations.

[29] C-815/18 *Federatie Nederlandse Vakbeweging* [2020] ECLI:EU:C:2020:976 and C-428/19 *Rapidsped* [2021] ECLI:EU:C:2021:548.

'first stage', problems can be solved. The Commission emphasises its will to engage in a 'dialogue' and possible negotiations, which should lead to good results. But this is not always the case.

The general problem, however, lies in the 'second stage'. The Commission is not obliged to refer cases to the CJEU. According to Article 258(2) TFEU it (only) 'may' bring the case to the CJEU. The latter accepts a wide margin of appreciation for the Commission.

> [A]ccording to settled case law, notably in the judgment … *Star Fruit v Commission* …,[30] an action for failure to act brought by a natural or legal person is inadmissible if it seeks a declaration that, by not bringing infringement proceedings against a Member State, the Commission has failed to act, in breach of the Treaty.[31]

The Commission should have only a limited margin of appreciation for rejecting a reference to the Court, however. First, this would better comply with the role of 'Guardian of the Treaties'. Moreover, it would compensate (at least to a certain extent) the very direct limited access to the Court. Furthermore, it would better follow the idea of an 'effective remedy' provided for in Article 47 CFREU. Finally, the principle of effectiveness would be better ensured if (at least indirect) judicial control were guaranteed.

Looking at the databases of the CJEU and the Commission we find the following statistical information: during the past 25 years (1995–2020) the Commission's Employment, Social Affairs and Equal Opportunities Directorate General has started about 300 infringement procedures (292 of which have been closed, 12 are still active). Of the 'closed' cases the Commission has referred 51 cases to the CJEU.[32] This means that only about a quarter of the cases launched by the Commission have led to court proceedings.

Looking in more detail at the specific areas of the 55 closed cases referred to the CJEU, only 31 relate to EU labour law.[33] In two areas (each accounting for roughly 40 per cent), 12 cases deal with anti-discrimination (based mainly on

[30] Case 247/87 *Star Fruit v Commission* [1989] ECR 291 (EU:C:1989:58). In para 13 it additionally justified its view by referring to the limited access to the Court provided for by Art 263(4) TFEU (ex-Art 173(2) EEC): 'It must also be observed that in requesting the Commission to commence proceedings pursuant to Article 169 the applicant is in fact seeking the adoption of acts which are not of direct and individual concern to it within the meaning of the second paragraph of Article 173 and which it could not therefore challenge by means of an action for annulment in any event.' Possibly, one could have argued the other way round (see above).

[31] Case C-284/19 P *Clarke v Commission* [2019], ECLI:EU:C:2020:285, para 34.

[32] Based on Art 258 TFEU including two cases based on Art 260 TFEU. Contrasting the 51 cases with the data available from the CJEU's website with the 71 infringement procedures filed by the Commission in the area of social policy there is, at first glance, an important difference. This difference can be explained to a large extent by taking into account two elements. The first relates to the periods covered: whereas the Commission database is limited to the past 25 years (from 1995) the Court's database includes 11 cases from 1978–95). Moreover, at least five cases probably do not originate from DG EMPL but from other DGs (as in the cases of 'Approximation of laws' or 'Principles, objectives and tasks of the Treaties').

[33] The other 24 cases are related mainly to social security. The single 'active' case which has been so far (3.12.2020) referred to the CJEU also deals with social security.

nationality) and 13 cases with occupational safety and health, and working time (four and nine cases, respectively). Only about 20 per cent represent cases from the other areas on EU labour law, however: fixed-term contracts (two), redundancies (one), transfer of undertakings (one), posting of workers (one), or mergers (one).

In conclusion, this means that in 25 years in relation to all Member States[34] and to all EU labour law Directives the Commission has referred only two dozen cases concerning anti-discrimination and occupational safety and health, including working time, and only half a dozen cases to the CJEU for failure to fulfil obligations under other EU labour law directives. Comparing these with the number of preliminary rulings in the 'social policy' field during the same period shows a clear disproportion: about 470 judgments were delivered by the CJEU overall.[35]

(b) Preliminary Proceedings (Article 267 TFEU)

From the outset, it should be recalled that these proceedings do not allow for direct access to EU courts. As for indirect access, Article 267 TFEU provides for two main avenues: any court can, and the court of last resort in a given case must, refer a case to the CJEU for interpretation of EU law unless a solution for this case is to be clearly found in the CJEU's case law.

Currently, this is the core of the judicial system of supervision of EU (labour) law. An important factor is the possibility for any (labour) court to ask preliminary questions in relation to the interpretation of EU law. About 130[36] preliminary reference rulings[37] have been delivered by the CJEU during the past five years in the 'social policy' field, about two-thirds of which came from four countries: Spain 32, Germany 25, Italy 15 and Austria 11.[38] Priority areas[39] were the Equality Framework Directive (2000/78/EG) with 34 cases, the Fixed-Term Contract Directive (1999/70/EC) with 21, the Working Time Directive (2003/88/EC) with 18 and the Transfer of Undertakings Directive (2001/23/EC) with 11, which again cover about two-thirds of the cases.

General Possibility (Para 2)

Any court or tribunal of a Member State 'may' refer a question on the interpretation of EU law to the CJEU. This avenue is probably most relevant in labour law matters. This is confirmed in quantitative terms: of the roughly 130 preliminary reference rulings nearly two-thirds were sought by lower courts.

[34] From EC15 (in 1995) to EU28 (2019).

[35] To which one could add the 17 orders (according to Art 99 of the Rules of Procedure of the Court).

[36] To be exact: 131 rulings, two of which were joined cases, ie 133 rulings; they were counted differently because in one case there was a preliminary reference from a lower court and one from the highest court.

[37] In principle, all were judgments; only six were delivered in the form of orders.

[38] It is interesting to note that about two-thirds of the cases came from only four countries.

[39] They are defined by the CJEU's characterisation in the headwords of each ruling.

Specific Obligation (Para 3)
In a case concerning the interpretation of EU law pending before a court or tribunal of a Member State, against whose decisions there is no judicial remedy under national law, that court or tribunal shall bring the matter before the CJEU. The figure of less than 50 preliminary references in five years raises serious doubts concerning whether Article 263(3) TFEU is applied fully. One avenue for correcting non-references lies in Article 6 ECHR. In the case of *Dhahbi v Italy* the ECtHR for the first time found a violation on account of the lack of reasons given by a domestic court for refusing to refer a question to the CJEU for a preliminary ruling. The Court of Cassation had made no reference to the applicant's request for a preliminary ruling or to the reasons why it had considered that the question raised did not warrant referral to the CJEU, or reference to the CJEU's case law. It was therefore unclear from the reasoning of the impugned judgment whether that question had been considered not to be relevant or to be related to a provision that was clear or had already been interpreted by the CJEU, or whether it had simply been ignored.[40]

2.1.3. Interim Conclusions

Neither the very limited possibility of accessing the EU Courts directly via Article 263(4) TFEU nor the (compensatory) possibilities of indirect involvement (Articles 258 and 263 TFEU) can be considered to ensure 'effective access to justice' by any stretch of the imagination.

2.2. Access to National Courts as EU Judges

Enforcement of EU (labour) law very much depends on national rules[41] and their application by judges. If there are substantial restrictions at national level on launching an action before a court such enforcement would be undermined. For example, the possibility of review by preliminary proceedings would be endangered. From an EU perspective, it is therefore very important that the right of access to a court is fully guaranteed in law and practice also at national level.

In the words of the CJEU,

> every Member State must, under the second subparagraph of Article 19(1) TEU, in particular ensure that the bodies which, as 'courts or tribunals' within the meaning of EU law, come within its judicial system in the fields covered by EU law and which,

[40] *Dhahbi v Italy* No 17120/09 (ECtHR, 8 April 2014), paras 32–34.

[41] For example, insofar as national rules allow the involvement of third parties they are also considered to be parties to the respective preliminary procedure before the CJEU (see Art 97(1) of the Rules of Procedure).

therefore, are liable to rule, in that capacity, on the application or interpretation of EU law, meet the requirements of effective judicial protection.[42]

Concerning secondary law, several anti-discrimination directives contain provisions requiring access to courts or at least to judicial and/or administrative procedures.[43] Even the new Directives do not expressly require the right of access to court, only a more general 'right to redress'.[44] This lack of a mandatory possibility of access to court cannot be considered to be in conformity with the requirements of Article 47 CFREU.

Some examples might demonstrate its impact in practice. If a disadvantaged person cannot challenge any discriminatory effects of, say, their remuneration, they will not be in a position to enforce all rights deriving from the principle of equal treatment, in breach of Article 47 of the Charter.[45] In the case of a certain assertion by an employer 'it must be possible for such an assertion to be the subject, if need be, of effective judicial review by which it can be ensured that the criteria set out in the Directive are satisfied in the particular case'.[46] Even if a Directive contains no provisions on judicial remedies available to the worker, in the case of a dispute with their employer, to enforce their right under that directive, the Member States must, in such a context, ensure compliance with the right to an effective remedy, as enshrined in Article 47 CFREU.[47]

The procedural guarantees are enshrined in Article 47 CFREU providing for effective remedy and fair trial. This provision is commonly characterised by the CJEU as a 'principle of effective judicial protection'.[48] In line with Article 6(1), 1st sentence ECHR para 2 foresees first that '[e]veryone is entitled to a fair and public hearing within a reasonable time by an independent and impartial tribunal previously established by law'. It adds in its 2nd sentence 'Everyone shall have the possibility of being advised, defended and represented.'

Based on Article 52(3) CFREU at least the minimum protection provided for by the ECHR must be ensured. According to the case law of the ECtHR at least the following elements have to be guaranteed.[49]

[42] Case C-192/18 *Commission v Poland (Independence of ordinary courts)* [2019], ECLI:EU:C:2019:924, para 103, referring to the judgment of 24 June 2019, *Commission v Poland (Independence of the Supreme Court)*, C-619/18, ECLI:EU:C:2019:531, para 55 and the case law cited; see also Case C-487/19 *WŻ* ECLI:EU:C:2021:798, para 102.

[43] Art 7(1) Directive 2000/43/EC on racial or ethnic origin; see also Art 9(1) Directive 2000/78/EC of 27 November 2000 on a general framework; Art 17(1) Directive 2006/54/EC on gender (recast) (strengthening access to judicial procedures: Member States shall ensure that, after possible recourse to other competent authorities including where they deem it appropriate conciliation procedures, judicial procedures for the enforcement of obligations under this Directive are available to all persons).

[44] Art 16 Directive 2019/1152/EU on transparent and predictable working conditions.

[45] Case C-396/17 *Leitner* [2019], ECLI:EU:C:2019:375, para 64.

[46] Case C-414/16 *Egenberger* [2018], ECLI:EU:C:2018:257, para 59.

[47] Case C-214/16 *King* [2017], ECLI:EU:C:2017:914, para 41 referring to the judgment of 15 September 2016, *Star Storage and Others*, C-439/14 and C-488/14, EU:C:2016:688, para 46.

[48] See, for example, Case C-223/19 *YS (Occupational pensions of managerial staff)* [2020], ECLI:EU:C:2020:753, para 96.

[49] Lörcher, Article 47, above n 9 at 622 ff.

2.2.1. *Right of Access to Court*

Without being mentioned explicitly in Article 47 CFREU, it is obvious that the main part of 'fair trial' requires access to a court. According to the ECtHR's case law the right of access to a court must be 'practical and effective'. For the right of access to be effective, an individual must 'have a clear, practical opportunity to challenge an act that is an interference with his rights'.[50] As an example, one might refer to a particular applicant who wished to acquire shares in the state company for which she was working at the time, which was to be privatised. Together with other employees of the company, the person in question brought court proceedings contesting the legality of the government decree concerning the privatisation, which stipulated that the shares were to be sold to a certain third party. The ECtHR found a violation of Article 6(1) ECHR, as she had been deprived of the right to challenge the legality of the decree before the competent courts, which had refused to examine the claim on the merits.[51]

However, this (in any event, much criticised)[52] judgment can no longer be considered to have a (negative) impact in the EU Member States. Indeed, the CJEU has thus taken a different view from the ECtHR (see section 3.1 below). Nevertheless, this contradiction does not create a problem under the CFREU because the second sentence of Article 52(3) provides that '[t]his provision shall not prevent Union law providing more extensive protection'. Accordingly, the CJEU would have to ensure effective access to the Court also in this case. Moreover, it should nevertheless be noted that the ECtHR provides for procedural rights also in relation to substantive rights, such as freedom of association. Indeed, it found a violation of Article 11 ECHR in a case in which a trade union (of military personnel) was denied the right of *locus standi*.[53]

In the CJEU's view, Article 47 does not, however, require it to be possible, as such, to bring a free-standing action that seeks primarily to dispute the compatibility of national provisions with EU law, provided one or more legal remedies exist, which make it possible to ensure, indirectly, respect for an individual's rights under EU law.[54]

2.2.2. *Possibility to be Advised and Represented (Para 2, 2nd Sentence)*

This element is explicitly enshrined in Article 47(2) 2nd sentence CFREU and is important particularly with regard to the employment relationship. In this context,

[50] ECtHR (ed), *Guide on Article 6 of the European Convention on Human Rights – Right to a fair trial (civil limb)*, updated (currently to 31 December 2021), www.echr.coe.int/Documents/Guide_Art_6_ENG.pdf (hereinafter the 'Guide'), para 91.

[51] *Melikyan v Armenia* No 9737/06 (ECtHR, 19 February 2013).

[52] Already several dissenting judges (out of the 10:7 minority) severely criticised this very restrictive approach ('Such an understanding of the case-law not only encourages domestic arbitrariness, but may also deprive many people who enter into ecclesiastical service of the protection of due process.').

[53] *ADEFDROMIL v France* No 32191/09 (ECtHR, 2 October 2014), paras 56–58.

[54] See, for example, Case C-223/19, *YS (Occupational pensions of managerial staff)* [2020], ECLI:EU:C:2020:753, para 96.

trade unions play an important role in terms of legal advice and representation before courts.

2.2.3. Legal Aid (Para 3)

Article 47 also has a financial dimension. Although related to environmental matters the CJEU linked the requirement that the cost should be 'not prohibitively expensive' to the observance of the right to an effective remedy enshrined in Article 47, while at the same time connecting it to 'the principle of effectiveness, in accordance with which detailed procedural rules governing actions for safeguarding an individual's rights under European Union law must not make it in practice impossible or excessively difficult to exercise rights conferred by European Union law'.[55]

2.2.4. Right to Know Reasons for the Alleged Measure

An element that is not commonly linked to access to court is the right to know the reasons for the alleged measure. If the specific reasons are not known to the person concerned, however, it will not be possible to assess whether there is a basis for challenging the measure before a court. For example, the ECtHR found that it was impossible to contest a civil servant's dismissal without explanation in court. This amounted to depriving the impugned right of action of all substance. Indeed, it was 'inconceivable for the applicant to have brought a meaningful action, for want of any known position of the respondent employer'. It concluded that such a limited review could not be considered to be an effective judicial review under Article 6(1) ECHR. Therefore, it found a violation of the applicant's right of access to a court.[56]

2.3. Non-judicial Avenues

Non-judicial avenues are increasingly being taken into account when looking at enforcement. Usually they are described as 'alternative dispute resolution' mechanisms. They will be dealt with only briefly here.

[55] Case C-260/11 *Edwards* [2013], ECLI:EU:C:2013:221, para 33; see also *Kreuz v Poland* No 28249/95 (ECtHR, 29 June 2001), para 59; see for more details: S Van Drooghenbroek, 'Labour Law Litigation and Fair Trial under Article 6 ECHR' in F Dorssemont, K Lörcher and I Schömann (eds), *The European Convention on Human Rights and the Employment Relation* (Oxford, Hart Publishing, 2013) 180; *Coşkun v Turkey* No 22443/05 (ECtHR, 27 January 2015), para 25 ('The court fees that the applicant was required to pay amounted to approximately EUR 20,600, while the monthly minimum wage was approximately EUR 260 at the time'.

[56] *KMC v Hungary* No 19554/11 (ECtHR, 10 July 2012), paras 34f.

2.3.1. At EU Level

Two means are explicitly recognised by rights enshrined in the Charter of Fundamental Rights of the European Union. First, Article 43 (European Ombudsman) guarantees that

> [a]ny citizen of the Union and any natural or legal person residing or having its registered office in a Member State has the right to refer to the European Ombudsman cases of maladministration in the activities of the institutions, bodies, offices or agencies of the Union, with the exception of the Court of Justice of the European Union acting in its judicial role.

It offers the possibility to complain to the Ombudsman if the person concerned is dissatisfied with an EU institution, body, office or agency because of alleged maladministration. However, the complaint must be made within two years of the date on which the person became aware of the problem.[57] For example, the ITUC and other NGOs have lodged a complaint against the Commission for failing to uphold fundamental human rights in trade policy.[58] The ETUC complained about the Commission's actions in relation to restructuring and the anticipation of change.[59] In relation to the public consultation on the composition of European Commission expert groups the ETUC provided information[60] that led to the Decision of the European Ombudsman in her strategic inquiry concerning the composition and transparency of European Commission expert groups.[61] Of course, substantive labour law matters will be possible only in relation to the EU public service.[62]

Second, in relation to the Parliament, Article 44 CFREU (Right to petition) acknowledges that '[a]ny citizen of the Union and any natural or legal person residing or having its registered office in a Member State has the right to petition the European Parliament.'

The FRA could be envisaged as a further non-judicial avenue. However, it is not empowered to investigate (individual complaints about) fundamental rights violations.[63]

[57] For more details see: www.ombudsman.europa.eu/en/home.

[58] Alleging maladministration by the European Commission in its failure to investigate the status of Bangladesh under the GSP, www.ituc-csi.org/IMG/pdf/bangladesh_ombudsman_complaint_final_2018_06_06_clean.pdf.

[59] See: www.etuc.org/sites/default/files/ETUC_complaint_to_EU_Ombudsman_on_European_Commission_1.pdf.

[60] See: www.ombudsman.europa.eu/pdf/en/59619.

[61] Case OI/6/2014/NF, Decision 14 November 2017, www.ombudsman.europa.eu/en/decision/en/86030#_ftn8.

[62] See as examples: 'Ombudsman welcomes EU decision to pay trainees in EU foreign delegations, in response to her recommendation', Press release, 30 November 2017; 'Ombudsman suggests further anti-harassment measures for EU institutions', Press release No 9/2018, 19 December 2018, www.ombudsman.europa.eu/en/press-release/en/107801.

[63] See: https://fra.europa.eu/en/about-fra/what-we-do.

2.3.2. At National Level

Mainly in collective labour law, voluntary arbitration might become an important means for effective enforcement. EU labour law will rarely (if ever) be an issue, however. The same might apply to mediation.[64]

3. Fair Trial

Access to justice is of no avail if it is not coupled with a 'fair trial'. Although a fair trial has to be ensured at both European and national levels, the following discussion will focus mainly on the latter. If there is only limited access to EU courts the main question remains how a fair trial is ensured at national level. This is even more true in relation to the procedures related to labour law matters. A 'fair trial' requires particular attention to the specificities of the employment relationship.

3.1. Right to an Independent and Impartial Judicial Body

As the CJEU recently stated, in order to ensure that ordinary courts are in a position to offer effective judicial protection, it is essential to maintain their independence, as confirmed by the second paragraph of Article 47 of the Charter, which refers to access to an 'independent' tribunal as one of the requirements linked to the fundamental right to an effective remedy.[65] Accordingly, it is for the Member States to establish a system of legal remedies and procedures ensuring for individuals compliance with their right to effective judicial protection in the fields covered by EU law.[66] It is necessary that judges be protected from external intervention or pressure liable to jeopardise their independence. The rules applicable to the status of judges and the performance of their duties must, in particular, be such as to preclude not only any direct influence, in the form of instructions, but also more indirect types of influence, which are liable to affect the decisions of the judges concerned, and thus preclude independence or impartiality on their part, which is likely to prejudice the trust that justice must inspire in people in a democratic

[64] The EU promotes methods of alternative dispute resolution ('ADR'), such as mediation. The Mediation Directive Directive 2008/52/EC applies only in civil and commercial matters (for more details see: https://e-justice.europa.eu/content_eu_overview_on_mediation-63-en.do. An attempt by the Belgian Government to transpose its model (The Social Conciliation and Mediation Procedure in Belgium, https://ec.europa.eu/social/BlobServlet?docId=2462&langId=en) to the EU was not successful.

[65] Case C-192/18 *Commission v Poland (Independence of ordinary courts)* [2019], ECLI:EU:C:2019:924, para 105, referring to judgments C-216/18 PPU *Minister for Justice and Equality (Deficiencies in the system of justice)* [2018], EU:C:2018:586, para 53 and the case law cited, and C-619/18 *Commission v Poland (Independence of the Supreme Court)* [2019], ECLI:EU:C:2019:531, para 57.

[66] Joined Cases C-83/19, C-127/19, C-195-19, C-291/19, C-355/19, and C-397/19 *Asociația "Forumul Judecătorilor din România" and Others v Inspecția Judiciară and Others* [2021], ECLI:EU:C:2021:393, para 190.

society governed by the rule of law.[67] These principles are particularly relevant in countries in which the independence of judges is particularly in jeopardy, such as Hungary[68] and Poland.[69]

In more concrete terms, the CJEU defined this principle as including, among other things, the receipt of a 'level of remuneration commensurate with the importance of the functions they carry out constitutes a guarantee essential to judicial independence'.[70]

In employment tribunals, the impartiality of lay judges from both the employers' and the workers' sides has been questioned. The ECtHR has, however, accepted the concept of collegial impartiality 'by balance of interests', also in the field of labour, in particular because of special knowledge and experience of the labour market.[71]

3.2. Right to a Fair Hearing

From the outset, it should be noted that, under the first and second paragraphs of Article 47 of the Charter, anyone whose rights and freedoms – guaranteed by the law of the European Union – have been violated has the right to an effective remedy before a tribunal in compliance with the conditions laid down in that article and, among other things, is entitled to a fair hearing.[72]

3.2.1. Right to Equality of Arms

According to ECtHR case law the principle of 'equality of arms' is inherent in the broader concept of a fair trial and is closely linked to the adversarial principle. The requirement of 'equality of arms', in the sense of a 'fair balance' between the parties, applies in principle to civil, as well as to criminal cases. The concept means maintaining a 'fair balance' between the parties. Equality of arms implies that each party must be afforded a reasonable opportunity to present their case – including evidence – under conditions that do not place them at a substantial disadvantage vis-à-vis the other party. The principle, which covers all aspects of procedural law

[67] Ibid, para 197.

[68] Indirectly, Case C-650/18 *Hungary v Parliament* [2021], ECLI:EU:C:2021:426.

[69] See eg: Case C-619/18 *Commission v Poland* [2019], ECLI:EU:C:2019:531; Case C-204/21 R *Commission v Poland* [2021], ECLI:EU:C:2021:593; Case C-791/19 *Commission v Poland* [2021], ECLI:EU:C:2021:596.

[70] Case C-64/16 *Associação Sindical dos Juízes Portugueses* [2018], ECLI:EU:C:2018:117, paras 44 and 45.

[71] *AB Kurt Kellermann v Sweden* No 41579/98 (ECtHR, 26 October 2004), para 60; see also *Luka v Romania* No 34197/02 (ECtHR, 21 June 2009), paras 41–42, and already *Langborger v Sweden* No 11179/84 (22 June 1989), paras 34–35; see for more details: S Van Drooghenbroek, above n 55 at 174ff.

[72] Case C-393/19 *Okrazhna prokuratura – Haskovo* [2021], ECLI:EU:C:2021:8, para 62; see also Case C-585/18 ea *AK* [2019], ECLI:EU:C:2019:982, para 119.

in the Contracting States,[73] also entails that applicants have the opportunity to express their views on every document in the file.[74]

While not calling 'into question the use of accelerated proceedings in certain disputes such as the one at issue seeking to address the demands of efficiency and economy', but attaching 'great importance to that objective' the ECtHR rejected the idea that it could 'justify disregarding such a fundamental principle as the right to adversarial proceedings'. Consequently, it falls within the responsibility of the domestic authorities to ensure that the standards set by Article 6(1) ECHR, and in particular, the protection of equality of arms, are respected.[75]

Concerning the use of evidence, the ECtHR stated that the Convention does not lay down rules on evidence as such. The admissibility of evidence and the way it should be assessed are primarily matters for regulation by national law and the national courts. The same applies to the probative value of evidence and the burden of proof. It is also for the national courts to assess the relevance of proposed evidence. However, the Court's task under the Convention is to ascertain whether the proceedings as a whole were fair, including the way in which evidence was collected. It must therefore establish whether the evidence was presented in such a way as to guarantee a fair trial.[76]

It is in this vein that the ECtHR found a violation of Article 6(1) ECHR in a case in which only one of the two participants in the events at issue was allowed to give evidence.[77] Such an equality requirement is particularly important in the employment relationship as workers claiming their rights are often the sole witness, for example, in relation to the (disputed) content of meetings with an employer's representative.

This is particularly important in relation to the burden of proof, given the unequal situation of the employee vis-à-vis the employer. The equality of arms requires that this situation has to be compensated by procedural law mechanisms in order to ensure a 'procedural balance'.[78]

In secondary law, there are examples that illustrate this necessity in terms of different levels of protection. The strongest procedural protection is the presumption in favour of the worker, which can be rebutted (and proved) by the employer, for example, in the Whistleblowers Directive 2019/1937[79] and the Transparent and Predictable Working Conditions Directive.[80] A lower level of protection but still a useful instrument for workers is provided by a reversal of the burden of proof in

[73] For more details see ECtHR, *Guide*, above n 50 at para 347, and specific examples of failure to observe the equality of arms principle in para 348.

[74] *Özgür Keskin v Turkey* No 12305/09 (ECtHR, 17 October 2017), para 32.

[75] Ibid, para 33.

[76] For more details see ECtHR, *Guide*, n 50, paras 354–55.

[77] *Dombo Beheer BV v the Netherlands* No 14448/88 (ECtHR, 27 October 1993), para 35.

[78] This is in principle recognised by the CJEU as stemming from the principle of 'effective judicial protection'; see: Case C-189/18 *Glencore Agriculture Hungary* [2019], ECLI:EU:C:2019:861, para 62.

[79] Art 21(5).

[80] Art 15(1) Directive 2019/1152/EU on transparent and predictable working conditions.

the Anti-Discrimination Directives.[81] In order to compensate the worker for their dependent situation this should be the minimal standard procedurally.

Although shifting the burden of proof directly onto the employer (at least in cases about working time), the CJEU's approach appears to be different. It looks more at the 'mandatory nature' of the respective provision and the *effet-utile* principle to justify that the employer has to bear the burden of proof.[82] In the same vein, the *CCOO* judgment offers a good example of the creation of specific means (the obligation of employers to measure all working hours) available for workers aimed at facilitating the acquisition of proof that an employer has violated (working time) provisions. This is even more important as the CJEU stresses the link to the respective material fundamental right enshrined in the CFREU.[83] In the abundant jurisprudence on the reversal of the burden of proof in anti-discrimination cases the CJEU refers to the respective provisions in the abovementioned Directives.[84]

3.2.2. Right to a Fair Trial within a Reasonable Time

In some areas of litigation of Article 6 ECHR the ECtHR recognises a more 'structural' approach, taking into account the specificities of the employment relationship.[85] Such is the case concerning the guarantee of 'reasonable time' for a given procedure. The ECtHR, in a dismissal case, stated that employment disputes by their very nature call for expeditious decision-making, in view of what is at stake for the person concerned, for example, the fact that dismissal deprives them of their means of subsistence.[86] This is also accepted in applications concerning suspension,[87] transfer[88] or reinstatement,[89] or where the amount claimed is of vital significance to the applicant.[90] This right to an expeditious decision has been enhanced in cases in which national legislation already requires a speedy procedure. The Court recalled 'that special diligence is necessary in employment disputes and this requirement is *reinforced additionally* in respect of states where the domestic law provides that such cases must be resolved with particular urgency'.[91]

[81] Art 8 Directive 2000/43/EC on racial or ethnic origin; Art 10 Directive 2000/78/EC on general framework; Art 19 Directive 2006/54/Econ gender (recast).

[82] Case C-131/04 *Robinson-Steele* [2006], ECLI:EU:C:2006:177, para 68 ('in the light of the mandatory nature of the entitlement to annual leave and in order to ensure the practical effect of [the provision concerned]'); see also case C-684/16 *Max-Planck-Gesellschaft* [CJEU 2018,], ECLI:EU:C:2018:874, paras 45–46.

[83] Case C-55/18 *CCOO* [2019], ECLI:EU:C:2019:402, para 56.

[84] Case C-531/15 *Otero Ramos* [2017], ECLI:EU:C:2017:789, paras 52 seq on the relationship between the provision on the burden of proof in the Gender Directive 2006/54/EC (Art 19) and the protection of the safety and health of a breastfeeding worker in Directive 92/85/EEC.

[85] See for more details: Van Drooghenbroek, above n 55 at 181f.

[86] *Mishgjoni v Albania* No 18381/05 (ECtHR, 7 December 2010), para 59; see also *Buchholz v Germany* No 7759/77 (ECtHR, 6 May 1981), para 52.

[87] *Obermeier v Austria* No 11761/85 (ECtHR, 28 June 1990), para 72.

[88] *Sartory v France* No 40589/07 (ECtHR, 24 September 2009), para 34.

[89] *Ruotolo v Italy* No 12460/86 (ECtHR, 27 February 1992), para 117.

[90] *Doustaly v France* No 26256/95 (ECtHR, 23 April 1998), para 48.

[91] *Vilotijević v Serbia* No 26042/06 (ECtHR, 10 December 2013), para 53; emphasis added.

If there are periods of conciliation, they form part of the assessment of the overall period. The ECtHR has made it clear that a period of one year and five months as 'duration of the conciliatory stage … seems manifestly excessive since it aimed at a possible agreement between the parties'.[92]

3.3. Right to Legal Aid and to Legal Assistance

According to the Explanations to Article 47 CFREU the right to legal aid is based on the ECtHR's case law on Article 6(1) ECHR in relation to the right of access to court.[93] However, any limitations that might derive from the wording of Article 6 ECHR[94] are not applicable to Article 47(3), as there are only two main conditions: (1) the 'lack of sufficient resources' and (2) legal aid 'is necessary to ensure effective access to justice'. Legal assistance can be provided by assigning a lawyer to represent a party. But this does not in itself guarantee effective assistance. The lawyer appointed for legal aid purposes may be prevented for a protracted period from acting or may shirk their duties. If they are notified of the situation, the competent national authorities must replace them; should they fail to do so, the litigant would be deprived of effective assistance in practice, despite the provision of free legal aid.[95]

In any event, it should be noted that the CJEU has admitted that financial problems, even in relation to the charging of VAT on the services supplied by lawyers, might create, by themselves, an insurmountable obstacle to access to justice or make it in practice impossible or excessively difficult to exercise the rights conferred by the EU legal order, and account would have to be taken of this by framing the right to legal aid appropriately, in accordance with the third paragraph of Article 47 of the Charter.[96]

In relation to employment issues trade unions might offer legal aid coupled with legal assistance for their members. But non-members will very much depend on a legal aid system.

4. *Locus Standi* of Workers, Trade Unions and Works Councils

The recognition of *locus standi* is crucial for the realisation of access to court and hence to effective enforcement. Whereas (individual) workers will, in principle,

[92] *Mendes v Portugal* No 49185/13 (ECtHR, 30 October 2014), para 23.
[93] ECtHR, *Guide*, above n 50, paras 130 ff.
[94] See for the (other) factors to be taken into account whether Art 6 implies a requirement to provide legal aid, above n 50, para 133.
[95] Ibid above n 50, para 138.
[96] Case C-543/14 *Ordre des barreaux francophones et germanophones* [2016], ECLI:EU:C:2016:605, para 37.

have no problems filing complaints on their own behalf, this is controversial in relation to trade unions (or workers' representatives) on individual workers' behalf. Several (mainly anti-discrimination) Directives recognise the role of trade unions in relation to enforcement. However, they might not – as far as is known – require national systems to provide for a general recognition of trade unions in their own name (but in the interest of the workers concerned).

4.1. Individual (Worker)s

4.1.1. EU Level

Without any doubt all persons employed by an EU institution will have legal standing before the EU Courts (subject still to further admissibility requirements). The long history of staff cases illustrates this access to court. For all other workers Article 263(4) TFEU limits to a very large extent access to justice at EU level (see above).

4.1.2. National Level

Against this background, it becomes crucial to be able to challenge EU law before national courts and tribunals and to be able to prevail upon the latter to request a preliminary ruling from the EU Court of Justice, at least when the case concerns implementing measures on the part of the EU Member States.[97] Usually, no problems should arise for a worker's locus *standi* to claim their rights either directly (as in the public service) or indirectly in light of the respective EU law, and the Courts will (under Article 267 TFEU) either implement the provisions directly in case of clear CJEU jurisprudence or ask for preliminary rulings.

Usually, national law provides for the possibility to be advised and represented by trade unions. The role of trade unions can be strengthened if the members assign their claims to the trade union concerned in order to be better protected.[98]

4.2. Trade Unions

Obviously, trade unions will have *locus standi* to claim their own rights. However, this standing is less clear if they claim the right on behalf of their members.

[97] See, for example, N Daminova, 'Access to Justice and the Development of the van Gend en Loos Doctrine: The Role of Courts and of the Individual In EU Law' (2017) 10(2) *Baltic Journal of Law & Politics* 133–53.

[98] Case C-396/13 *Sähköalojen ammattiliitto* [2015], ECLI:EU:C:2015:86, para 20 ('[T]he standing of the Sähköalojen ammattiliitto to bring proceedings before the referring court is governed by Finnish procedural law, which is applicable according to the principle of *lex fori*. Nor is it disputed that, under Finnish law, the applicant has standing to bring proceedings on behalf of the posted workers.')

Nothing like a 'Directive on representative actions for the protection of collective interests'[99] is in sight for trade unions.

4.2.1. EU Level

Locus standi for direct access depends on the fulfilment of one of the two alternatives of Article 263(4) TFEU (see above). For the first alternative, the General Court's judgments in the *EPSU* case[100] might serve as an illustrative example of alleged violations of rights conferred on the European Social Partners by Article 155 TFEU. However, this access has been denied for a similar action by the employers' association UEAPME for lack of individual concern (2nd alternative).[101]

In the context of the EU civil service the respective trade unions enjoy rights of their own. Two cases may be referred to. In the *IPSO* case the General Court[102] approved legal standing because the facts in the case were capable of distinguishing it from all other trade unions representing persons employed by or working for the employer concerned. Moreover, it was considered to be directly concerned by the contested act, inasmuch as the act had the immediate effect of affecting its position as social interlocutor in the discussions on agency staff issues.[103] The *TAO-AFI and SFIE-EP* case on the failure to consult trade unions led to a differentiated conclusion: whereas the General Court judgment accepted that SFIE-PE had *locus standi* under Article 263 TFEU to seek annulment of the contested regulations, it declared the action inadmissible insofar as it was brought by TAO-AFI, as the applicants had failed to prove how it had *locus standi* to act on its behalf in the present case.[104]

The voice of trade unions could be heard at least by third-party interventions. This is, however, is excluded for preliminary proceedings.[105] However, if national law provides for participation in the proceedings the respective position remains the same before the CJEU.[106] In direct action cases, even when trade unions aimed at third party interventions their requests were mostly dismissed.[107]

[99] Council Document: 'Directive on representative actions for the protection of the collective interests of consumers, and repealing Directive 2009/22/EC, Brussels, 30 June 2020, 9223/20 (in the meantime approved by the European Parliament, but not yet published.

[100] See n 19.

[101] Case T-135/96 *UEAPME* [1998] ECR II-2335.

[102] Case T-713/14 *IPSO v ECB* [2016], ECLI:EU:T:2016:727, paras 42–60.

[103] Ibid, paras 55 and 59 respectively.

[104] Case T-456/14 *TAO-AFI and SFIE-EP* [2016], ECLI:EU:T:2016:493, para 145.

[105] Art 23(2) of the Statute of the Court provides that 'the parties, the Member States, the Commission and, where appropriate, the institution, body, office or agency which adopted the act the validity or interpretation of which is in dispute, shall be entitled to submit statements of case or written observations to the Court'. This is interpreted by the CJEU as being an exclusive list (ever since CJEU, Order 3 June 1964, Case 6/64, *Costa/ENEL*).

[106] See, for example, Case C-270/05 *Athinaiki Chartopoiia* [2007], ECLI:EU:C:2007:101, with the Greek Confederation (Geniki Sinomospondia Ergaton Elladas (GSEE)) as third party (in a case on collective redundancies).

[107] Granting a third-party intervention: GC, Order of 26.1.2005 in respect of the IFJ (International Federation of Journalists) in the *Tillack* case (T-193/04); refusing a third-party intervention request for

These means are not sufficient for effective enforcement of EU labour law. This is even more true in relation to the lack of access to the Court for trade unions as EU social partners. Besides the Commission's obligation to consult social partners in CJEU cases on EU Framework Agreements turned into Directives,[108] there is a need for direct access to the CJEU as privileged applicants at least in cases dealing with framework agreements.[109]

Historically, the limitations on trade unions might be (at least to a certain extent) understandable, taking into account the context of the original EEC Treaty in which there were nearly no competences for labour law. However, the whole structure of the Treaties (including the fundamental social rights enshrined in the CFREU and the provisions for social partners in Articles 154 and 155 TFEU, and subsequent labour law in secondary legislation) has changed the architecture to a large extent and would accordingly require recognition of their role also in procedural terms, that is, the privileged role of applicants.

4.2.2. National Level

For national trade unions it is even more difficult to obtain direct access to an EU court. In an 'austerity' case in which a trade union had filed an action for annulment against decisions addressed to the Member State concerned with a view to remedying a situation of excessive deficit, the General Court denied direct concern and declared the action inadmissible.[110]

In preliminary proceedings, trade unions' legal standing in the EU judicial order is defined by their legal standing at domestic level:[111] Several EU Member States recognise the legal standing of trade unions, for example Belgium and France.[112] From the CJEU's practice further examples are known from Austria,[113]

'No interest in the result of a case': GC, Order 13 December 2018 (ECLI:EU:T:2018:1018) in respect of the European Transport Federation (ETF) in the *EPSU* case (T–310/18; see above n 19); Order of 20 October 2014, ECLI:EU:T:2014:951, para 68, in respect of the UNAF in the *Bayer CropScience* case (T-429/13), Order of 8 April 1981 in respect of the Food, Beverages and Catering Union (NGG) in the *Walzmühle* case (197 to 200, 243, 245 and 247/80), ECLI:EU:C:1981:311.

[108] See, as an example, Case C-149/10 *Chatzi* [2010], ECLI:EU:C:2010:534 (Framework agreement on parental leave).

[109] See to this effect: B Bercusson, *European Labour Law*, 2nd edn (Cambridge University Press, 2009) 502ff; A Jacobs, 'The European Court of Justice, Social Law and the European Social Partners' in R Blanpain (ed), *Labour Law, Human Rights and Social Justice (Liber Amicorum R Ben-Israel)* (Deventer, 2001) 145ff.

[110] Case T-541/10 *ADEDY* [2012], ECLI:EU:T:2012:626, para 88 (without the need to examine whether the contested acts were of individual concern to the applicants).

[111] M Eliantonio et al, 'Standing up for your right(s) in Europe – A Comparative study on Legal Standing (Locus Standi) before the EU and Member States' Courts', European Parliament (Brussels, 2012) Collective interest litigation and locus standi, 57ff. http://publications.europa.eu/resource/cellar/ba305f3b-cfc4-11e5-a4b5-01aa75ed71a1.0001.01/DOC_1.

[112] Ibid, 64: 'In France, trade unions may bring an action to protect the individual interests of a worker, even without the worker's approval'. As an example of a general action: Case C-176/12 *Association de médiation sociale v Union locale des syndicats CGT* [2014], ECLI:EU:C:2014:2 (Subjecting the setting up of bodies representing staff to certain thresholds of employees).

[113] As a recent example: Case C-24/17 *Österreichischer Gewerkschaftsbund* [2019], ECLI:EU:C:2019:373.

Finland[114] even in a cross-border context,[115] the Netherlands,[116] Romania,[117] Spain,[118] Sweden[119] and the United Kingdom.[120] An interesting case developed from a request for a preliminary ruling by the German Federal Labour Court to the CJEU, with two national trade union federations as applicants, aiming at nullifying a provision in an agreement concluded between the employer and the special negotiating body on the involvement of employees in a *Societas Europaea* which would limit the trade union's exclusive right of nomination for a certain number of supervisory board members representing the employees.[121] Certain Member States allow trade unions to act on behalf of their members.[122]

4.3. Works Councils

Cases in relation to competition (state aid) offered the CJEU an opportunity to examine a works council request for intervention. The Court stated:

> the Works Council represents the collective interests of all the employees of SNCM. Since the Commission, in its assessment of the compatibility of State aid in the maritime transport sector, takes account of numerous considerations of various kinds, linked in particular to the protection of competition, the Union's maritime policy, the promotion of Union maritime transport and the promotion of employment, the possibility cannot be excluded that the Works Council might submit to the Commission observations on considerations of a social nature which might possibly be taken into account by the Commission in the course of the formal investigation procedure provided for in Article 108(2) TFEU.[123]

It concluded that the Works Council was an 'interested party within the meaning of Article 108(2) TFEU' for the purpose of submitting to the European Commission observations on social considerations. However, it denied the right to shareholder-employees to intervene in the absence of a sufficiently direct interest in the outcome of the dispute.[124]

[114] Case C-533/13 *Auto- ja Kuljetusalan Työntekijäliitto AKT ry* [2015], ECLI:EU:C:2015:173.

[115] The *locus standi* of a trade union with its seat in the host Member State has been confirmed by Case C-396/13 *Sähköalojen ammattiliitto* [2015], para 21 ('the rules set out in the Polish Labour Code ... are irrelevant with regard to the *locus standi* of the Sähköalojen ammattiliitto before the referring court and do not prevent that trade union from bringing an action before the [Finnish Court]').

[116] As a recent example: Case C-815/18 *Federatie Nederlandse Vakbeweging* [2020], ECLI:EU:C:2020:976.

[117] Case C-147/17 *Sindicatul Familia Constanţa* [2018], ECLI:EU:C:2018:926.

[118] As a recent example: Case C-55/18 *CCOO* [2019], ECLI:EU:C:2019:402.

[119] Case C-336/15 *Unionen* [2017], ECLI:EU:C:2017:276.

[120] Case C-80/14 *Union of Shop, Distributive and Allied Workers (USDAW)* [2015], ECLI:EU:C:2015:291.

[121] C-677/20 *IG Metall and ver.di* (SAP case) [2020].

[122] For Denmark: Cases C-335/11 and C-337/11 *HK Danmark (acting on behalf of X)* [2013], ECLI:EU:C:2013:222; for France: Case C-463/19 *Syndicat CFTC* [2020], ECLI:EU:C:2020:932.

[123] CJEU, Order, 6 October 2015, Case C-410/15 P(I) *Comité d'entreprise de la Société nationale maritime Corse Méditerranée (SNCM)*, ECLI:EU:C:2015:669, para 12.

[124] Case C-362/15 P(I) *AEMMELL/Commission* [2015], ECLI:EU:C:2015:682; Case C-410/15 P(I) *Comité d'entreprise SNCM/Commission* [2015], ECLI:EU:C:2015:669; Case C-418/15 P(I) *Cap Actions SNCM/Commission* [2015], ECLI:EU:C:2015:671.

If national law opens the possibility for direct access for works councils to the (national) court and if this court refers a preliminary question to the CJEU the works council will remain in the same situation as in the main proceeding. As examples one can refer to cases from Germany[125] and Austria.[126]

5. Conclusions

This overview has shown that the architecture of the EU judicial system is still far from providing 'effective access to justice'. In particular, the specificities of the employment relationship are not sufficiently taken into account as long as direct access to EU Courts is still practically non-existent, especially for trade unions. For the time being, however, strategic litigation will be necessary.[127]

[125] Case C-216/15 *Betriebsrat der Ruhrlandklinik* [2016], ECLI:EU:C:2016:883 (temporary agency work – nursing staff who do not have a contract of employment assigned to a health care institution by a not-for-profit association).

[126] Case C-486/08 *Zentralbetriebsrat der Landeskrankenhäuser Tirols* [2010], ECLI:EU:C:2010:215 (disadvantageous provisions provided for by national legislation for contractual public servants working part-time).

[127] For more details, see Chapter 7.

4

Enforcing EU Labour Law by Means of Administrative Law

JOANNA UNTERSCHÜTZ

1. Introduction: General Framework of Implementation

The last stage of transposing European law into a national legal order is assessing its compliance with European law. The application of sanctions for non-compliance with this law is thus an important part of the enforcement of EU law. This chapter deals with enforcement measures applied in the field of administrative law. It is divided into two main parts: the first is dedicated to the European Commission and agencies operating at the EU level. Besides the role of the Commission as 'guardian of the Treaties', according to Article 17(1) TEU, scrutiny of compliance with the law is exercised by courts and extrajudicial bodies as stipulated by national law, according to the principle of institutional and procedural autonomy of the Member States. The constitutional foundations for the implementation of EU law are contained in the Treaty on European Union (TEU) and the Treaty on the Functioning of the European Union (TFEU). Other agencies – including the newly established European Labour Authority – have been created to guide and coordinate the activities of national bodies, without powers to issue decisions binding the Member States or their institutions. The European Ombudsman's role is to scrutinise the EU administration.

The second part of this chapter is dedicated to the institutions and measures applied by the Member States while implementing EU labour law. According to Article 197 paragraphs 1 and 2 TFEU, Member States are responsible for effective implementation of EU law in the common interest. In order to carry this out they must use all necessary measures of national law. The national bodies are obliged to take into account requirements resulting from the general principles of EU law (the principle of effectiveness, the principle of equivalence), as well as EU freedoms and fundamental rights. The main role here is played by national labour inspectorates.

Before presenting conclusions, some attention is devoted to sanctions applied for labour law infringements. While Chapter 2 of this volume provides a more general analysis of remedies and sanctions, this chapter concentrates on specific sanctions that can be applied by labour inspectors. Criminal sanctions are dealt with in Chapter 5. Member States may define and impose administrative sanctions, criminal sanctions and private law sanctions for non-compliance with EU law and law transposing EU law. The choice of sanction should take into account the specific circumstances. Should the sanction be preventive, repressive or restitutive, possibly redistributive?[1] Sanctions must be 'effective, proportionate and dissuasive'. This formula is fairly general and unless EU legislation explicitly provides for specific measures, the CJEU leaves the decision concerning sanctions to the Member State, as long as they are 'sufficiently effective to achieve the aim of that Directive and to ensure that they may be effectively relied upon before the national courts in order that judicial protection will be real and effective'.[2] This means that in the European Union the executive function belongs not only to its institutions, bodies or organisational units, but also, taking into account the wording of the TFEU, and primarily to the Member States.

2. At EU Level

2.1. Specific Role of the Commission as 'Guardian of the Treaties'

Although EU law does not contain any general procedural rules governing proceedings before the European administration, the CJEU referred to good administration as a 'fundamental principle of law' back in the 1990s.[3] This principle is reflected in Article 41 of the Charter of Fundamental Rights (CFR) (concerning the right to good administration in proceedings before the institutions, bodies, offices and agencies of the Union) and Article 42 CFR related to citizens' right of access to documents. The executive functions of the European Commission result

[1] D Miąsik and A Wrobel, 'Europeizacja prawa administracyjnego – pojęcie i konteksty' in R Hauser, A Wróbel and Z Niewiadomski (eds), *Europeizacja prawa administracyjnego*, Vol 3, *System Prawa Administracyjnego* (Warszawa, CH Beck, 2014) 119.

[2] Case C-54/07 *Centrum voor Gelijkheid van Kansen en voor Racismebestrijding v Firma Feryn NV*, para 36. See further Chapter 2 in this volume.

[3] Cf CJEU judgment of 18.3.1997, CC-282/95 *P Guérin automobiles v Commission of the European Communities*, ECLI:EU:C:1997:159. T Tridimas states that, although references to good administration can be found in the earlier case law of the CJ (eg CJ judgments: of 14.7.1977, C-61/76 *Jean-Jacques Geist v Commission of the European Communities*, ECLI:EU:C:1977:127, para 44; of 29.2.1984, C-270/82 *Estel NV v Commission of the European Communities*, ECLI:EU:C:1984:84, para 15).The development of this principle is attributed to the fact that EU law does not contain any general procedural rules governing proceedings before European administrative authorities (T Tridimas, *The general principles of EU juries* (Oxford, OUP, 2006) 411.

from Article 17 TEU, which underlines three basic functions of the Commission: as a lawmaker, as the guardian of the treaties, and as the executive. It thus ensures that EU law is implemented effectively. The Commission is referred to as being the 'guardian of the treaties' by virtue of its composition and the independence of its members and as such it is obliged to ensure that the Member States respect EU law. As regards private actors, the Commission has the possibility to react with administrative sanctions only in well-defined areas, such as competition law, but lacks such an express prerogative in labour law. But again, according to Article 4(3) TEU, it is ultimately up to the Member States to ensure compliance with EU law by private parties, if necessary with appropriate sanctions.[4]

The infringement procedure provided for in Articles 258–60 TFEU (ex 226–28 EC) is an essential tool of EU law enforcement against Member States.[5] According to Article 258 TFEU there are two stages of the procedure: (i) explanatory proceedings before the Commission and (ii) court proceedings before the European Court of Justice (ECJ). As the procedure may lead to court proceedings it is explained in more detail in Chapter 3 of this volume.

The general scheme of action against a Member State begins with an informal phase, in which the Commission becomes aware of an alleged breach of EU law by a Member State. The political dialogue that is the essence of the pre-litigation stage of the procedure allows the subjects involved (EU administration and national administrations) to identify and encourage practices of good administration for which judicial proceedings are ill-suited, and to sort out problems that are more political than legal.[6]

In principle, a Member State may also be held liable for failing to react to the actions of private actors that result in a violation of Treaty principles, including those contained in the Charter of Fundamental Rights.[7] If the Member State takes appropriate measures to prevent private infringements of EU law, however, and an infringement occurs nevertheless, there are no grounds for attributing liability to that state.[8] This can render difficult the enforcement of labour law provisions that were implemented properly by the law but abused or misused in practice.

The Commission has identified four main types of potential infringement case:

(i) Member States' failure to notify the Commission within a deadline concerning measures taken to transpose a Directive into national legislation;
(ii) non-conformity or non-compliance of Member State legislation with the requirements of an EU Directive;

[4] CJEU Judgment of 21.9.1989 r, 68/88, *Commission v Greece*, ECLI:EU:C:1989:339. K Kowalik-Bańczyk, 'Instytucje Unii Europejskiej' in S Biernat (ed), *Podstawy i źródła prawa Unii Europejskiej* (Warszawa, 2020) 488.

[5] L Prete and B Smulders, 'The coming of age of infringement proceedings' (2010) 1 *CML Rev* 9–61.

[6] Ibid.

[7] CJEU judgment C-265/95 *Commission v Republic of France*, §65.

[8] Cf C-132/05 *Commission v Federal Republic of Germany*.

(iii) infringement of the Treaties, regulations and decisions, where Member States' legislation is not in line with the requirements of the Treaties, regulations and decisions;
(iv) incorrect or non-application of EU law by a Member State.[9]

Since 2012 nearly 800 cases in the area of employment, social affairs and inclusion have been taken up by the Commission, and about 10 per cent of them concern OSH Directives, working time, equal treatment or the coordination of social security systems.[10]

Annual Commission reports on monitoring the application of EU law provide an overview of activities undertaken by the Commission in different policy areas, including working conditions across the EU. The reports highlight the Commission's priorities regarding law enforcement. In the recent reports of 2019 and 2018 the Commission refers to the European Pillar of Social Rights in order to demonstrate its political commitment to strengthening social rights, as well as economic ones. This did not result in major changes in the structure of the report nor in the proportion of cases.[11]

The reports refer to the policy sectors of infringement cases (working conditions, health and safety, labour mobility, anti-discrimination, social security), which vary from one year to another. Sometimes health and safety cases are prevalent (2015), sometimes working conditions (2017) while in other years cases are more diverse.

The Commission's own-initiative infringement cases are launched in different areas. Over the past five years they have concerned the following issues:[12]

- breach of the rules on the free movement of workers and social security;
- incompatibility of national rules on paid annual leave with EU labour legislation;
- insufficient protection of public sector workers against abusive successive fixed-term contracts and discrimination, as required under EU rules;
- discrimination on the grounds of nationality between workers from EU Member States;
- less favourable treatment of fixed-term staff in the public sector; this raises concerns under the Fixed-Term Work Directive;

[9] European Court of Auditors, *Putting EU law into practice: The European Commission's oversight responsibilities under Article 17(1) of the Treaty on European Union* (2018) 8, www.eca.europa.eu/Lists/ECADocuments/LR_EU_LAW/LR_EU_LAW_EN.pdf.

[10] This covers about 10 per cent of cases in all policy areas, including cases of non-communication.

[11] European Commission, *Monitoring the Application of European Union Law 2019. Annual Report*, 3, https://ec.europa.eu/info/sites/default/files/file_import/report-2019-annual-report-monitoring-application-eu-law_en.pdf; European Commission, *Monitoring the Application of European Union Law 2018. Annual Report*, 3, https://ec.europa.eu/info/sites/default/files/report-2018-annual-report-monitoring-application-eu-law.pdf.

[12] European Commission, *Annual reports on monitoring the application of EU law.*

- national provisions contrary to the Directive on information and consultation of employees, as it makes it less likely that staff representation bodies can be set up;
- ensuring the principle of unity in applying the social security contribution on income from the real estate of EU officials outside the national social security system;
- non-conformity with the Working Time Directive by applying a 12-month reference period for limiting average weekly working time to 48 hours for civil servants;
- failure to communicate national measures transposing the Directive on the organisation of working time in inland waterway transport;
- failure to communicate national measures transposing the EU rules which ensure the right of seafarers to fair and just working conditions, as well as their right to information and consultation;
- failure to provide notification of national measures transposing the Directive on the alignment of several EU health and safety at work Directives to the Regulation on classification, labelling and packaging of substances and mixtures.

There are also reported cases of late transposition of various EU Directives by the Member States and cases closed without a judgment.

Bearing in mind that the procedure provided for in Articles 258–60 is the primary possibility for the EU institutions to scrutinise Member States' compliance with their obligations, it should be pointed out that, in terms of efficiency, this procedure has significant drawbacks. First of all, it is an ex post control, initiated when a state has already failed to fulfil its obligations towards the EU; secondly, it is lengthy and formalistic; thirdly, it is insufficient from the point of view of the interests of individuals, as private entities may not initiate it, and a judgment establishing a failure under this procedure has no direct impact on individual rights.[13] Besides these general problems, the Commission appears to be very reluctant to use this instrument in the field of social policy.

2.2. Specific Role of Agencies and Other Relevant Bodies: 'From Collecting Information to Enforcement Action'

The Commission cooperates also with various agencies. Both the TFEU and the TEU, in addition to the EU institutions and bodies, also mention EU organisational units, which are usually referred to as 'European agencies' (see eg Article 298(1) TFEU). Agencies are expected to contribute to the better implementation of EU

[13] N Półtorak, 'Komentarz do art. 258' in D Kornobis-Romanowska, J Łacny and A Wróbel (eds), *Traktat o funkcjonowaniu Unii Europejskiej. Komentarz. Tom III (art. 223-358)* (Warszawa, 2012).

law. European agencies can be defined as structurally separate bodies. They are not formally part of treaty institutions or bodies, however, but are established on the basis of secondary legislation. They have legal personality and their own administration. They are also equipped with their own competences, are financially independent (they have their own budget) and are entrusted with the performance of tasks falling within the competence of the EU.[14]

They are seen as an important element in the multi-level governance structure of the European Union. From the point of view of EU law, European agencies are decentralised units in the sense that they are entrusted with the tasks of the EU institutions. From the point of view of the Member States, however, the implementation of EU law by the agencies is an expression of centralised administrative law enforcement at the EU level. Sometimes agencies are set up to manage the exchange of information between national authorities or to collect information from national authorities organised as a European network, in which the agency plays a coordinating role. In the area of labour law, relevant agencies include the European Agency for Safety and Health at Work (EU-OSHA), the European Centre for the Development of Vocational Training (CEDEFOP), the European Foundation for the Improvement of Living and Working Conditions (EUROFOUND), the Fundamental Rights Agency (FRA) and the European Labour Authority (ELA). The recently created Chief Trade Enforcement Officer (CTEO) is responsible for the implementation and enforcement of trade rules. This can be especially relevant insofar as agreements affect employment rights.[15]

Most European agencies are responsible for collecting and exchanging information, coordinating the activities of Member State authorities, providing the necessary knowledge and scientific support. Some agencies have been set up to coordinate the actions of the Member States when implementing EU law, and to monitor compliance by Member State authorities, as well as private entities with the rules and common principles in a given field laid down in EU secondary legislation. The role of an agency is not decisive in this regard. They do not have executive powers and are not empowered to address (legally binding) decisions to either individuals or Member States.

Both aspects of their activity (collecting and exchanging information and coordination of national activities) are also aimed at improving enforcement of EU labour law by national authorities. Expert opinions, studies and reports, or various types of conferences and scientific meetings are of interest to both the EU institutions and the relevant national authorities of the Member States and social partners. Disseminating knowledge in the field of social policy and labour policy can undoubtedly help to ensure better living and working conditions and

[14] D Miąsik and A. Wrobel, 'Europeizacja prawa administracyjnego – pojęcie i konteksty' in R Hauser, A Wróbel and Z Niewiadomski (eds), *Europeizacja prawa administracyjnego*, Vol 3, *System Prawa Administracyjnego* (Warszawa, CH Beck, 2014) 118.

[15] See section 3.3 in Chapter 7 of this volume.

the conduct of a more conscious policy aimed at achieving their convergence in individual Member States. Joint debate and exchange of information contribute to the promotion and support of cooperation between Member States in the field of occupational safety and health, which is undeniably important from the standpoint of protection of workers' social rights in cross-border conditions.[16]

2.2.1. *Eurofound*

The main task of Eurofound[17] is to disseminate knowledge on social and labour policy, and thus to contribute to the development and provision of better living and working conditions.[18]

In the 2017–2020 programming document, the strategic goal is to provide high-quality, impartial and relevant knowledge that will contribute to more informed policymaking, aimed at convergence (upwards) of living and working conditions in Europe.[19] Debate and information exchange are essential elements of Eurofound activities, and through its conferences and seminars, governments and civil society engage in an open discussion on the future of European social policy. The research, including pan-European surveys (the European Working Conditions Survey, the European Quality of Life Survey and the European Company Survey) makes it possible to monitor changes in living and working conditions, as a result of which it is able to provide governments and social partners with the necessary analyses and information.

2.2.2. *EU-OSHA*

EU-OSHA's[20] primary task is to provide EU authorities, Member States, social partners and all actors involved in safety and health at work with the appropriate technical, scientific and economic information they need in this area. Their work contributes to the European Commission's Strategic Framework for Safety and Health at work 2014–20.

The activities of EU-OSHA cover all issues related to safety and health at work, mainstreaming occupational safety and health (OSH) into education,

[16] J Ryszka, *Prawa społeczne pracowników a prawa pracodawców-przedsiębiorców na rynku wewnętrznym Unii Europejskiej* (Warszawa, CH Beck, 2018) 41–42.

[17] Regulation (EU) 2019/127 of the European Parliament and of the Council of 16 January 2019 establishing the European Foundation for the improvement of living and working conditions (Eurofound), and repealing Council Regulation (EEC) No 1365/75, PE/63/2018/REV/1, [2019] OJ L 30/4–89.

[18] www.eurofound.europa.eu/about-eurofound/what-we-do.

[19] Eurofound, *Programming document* 2017–2020, 6, www.eurofound.europa.eu/sites/default/files/ef_publication/field_ef_document/ef1659en.pdf.

[20] Regulation (EU) 2019/126 of the European Parliament and of the Council of 16 January 2019 establishing the European Agency for Safety and Health at Work (EU-OSHA), and repealing Council Regulation (EC) No 2062/94 PE/62/2018/REV/1 [2019] OJ L 30/58–73.

and the benefits of OSH. It carries out information campaigns for workers and employers The 2020–2022 campaign focuses on the prevention of work-related musculoskeletal disorders (MSDs). The 2018–2019 Healthy Workplaces Manage Dangerous Substances campaign aimed to raise awareness of dangerous substances in the workplace and the risks they pose, and to create a culture of prevention by disseminating campaign materials and carrying out promotional and engagement activities. The Healthy Workplaces for All Ages campaign promoted the importance of sustainable work – that is, safe and healthy working conditions from the start to the end of a person's life. And in 2014–2015 the Healthy Workplaces Manage Stress campaign concentrated on poor psychosocial work environments that can have significant negative effects on workers' health.[21]

At the EU level, the Senior Labour Inspectors' Committee (SLIC) was also called to express their opinion on matters related to the enforcement by the Member States of EU legislation on health and safety at work. It also plays a role in facilitating cooperation between labour inspectorates in the Member States.[22]

2.2.3. *Fundamental Rights Agency*

The Fundamental Rights Agency (FRA)[23] aims to provide expertise on fundamental rights to the relevant EU institutions and the Member States when implementing EU law. This is primarily to ensure that these rights are fully respected. To that end, it, in particular, collects, records, analyses and disseminates relevant, objective, reliable and comparable information and data, conducts research and surveys, publishes thematic reports and annual reports on fundamental rights. The FRA advises EU institutions and Member States mainly in the areas of: discrimination, access to justice, racism and xenophobia, data protection, rights of crime victims and children's rights.

As can be seen, issues pertaining to the protection of social rights have hitherto been only indirectly the subject of the FRA's activities, and they are undoubtedly closer to the work carried out within Eurofound and EU-OSHA. It can be concluded that the material scope of their work is in some ways complementary, thanks to which we have a comprehensive picture of a number of issues related to the social aspects of European integration.[24]

[21] See: https://osha.europa.eu/en/healthy-workplaces-campaigns.

[22] European Commission, Health and Safety at Work – Senior Labour Inspectors Committee, https://ec.europa.eu/social/main.jsp?catId=148&intPageId=685. The Committee gained its formal status on the basis of the Commission Decision of 22 October 2008, 2008/823/EC amending Decision 95/319/EC setting up a Committee of Senior Labour Inspectors (Text with EEA relevance), [2008] OJ L 288/5–6, ELI, http://data.europa.eu/eli/dec/2008/823/oj.

[23] Council Regulation (EC) No 168/2007 of 15 February 2007 establishing a European Union Agency for Fundamental Rights, [2007] OJ L 53/1–14, [2008] OJ L 4M/117–30 (MT).

[24] J Ryszka, above n 16 at 42.

2.2.4. European Labour Authority

The European Labour Authority was created in 2019,[25] primarily to address challenges in the area of exchange of information, cooperation between Member States and especially joint enforcement.[26] According to the Regulation, the Authority's overall objective is to support the Member States and the Commission in the effective application and enforcement of EU law related to the posting of workers, the free movement of workers, the coordination of social security, the social aspects of road transport and cooperation between Member States in the fight against undeclared work (Article 1(2) and 4). This catalogue remains closed, but it may be extended by any future act that confers tasks on the Authority.

It also incorporates some currently functioning bodies: the Expert Group on Posting, the EURES European Coordination Office, the Technical Committee on the Free Movement of Workers and the Committee of Experts on Posting of Workers (recitals 11, 22, 42, 43, 44; Articles 6, 12, 14) and the European Platform Tackling Undeclared Work. Before that the platform activities included information campaigns, staff learning, visits, joint actions and mutual assistance, as well as seminars, studies presenting problems specific to different countries and sectors, collecting data and information, and sharing best practices through a virtual library and Toolkits designed mainly for labour inspectors.

In March 2020, the European Platform tackling undeclared work launched #EU4FairWork, the first EU campaign about the benefits of declared work, with the participation of the European Labour Authority.[27] The main goals of the campaign included:

- raising awareness among workers about their rights, the negative impact of undeclared work and how to make the transition into declared work;
- making companies aware of the benefits of and their obligations to declare workers, as well as of the risk of sanctions in case of undeclared work;
- encouraging policymakers to better tackle undeclared work, through policy and legislation;
- increasing cooperation among platform members by implementing the campaign together.

One of the advantages of creating the Authority is that it will simplify cooperation by integrating the many existing committees and networks across the Member States, which should lead to the elimination of structural fragmentation in this field.[28]

[25] Regulation (EU) No 2019/1149 of 20.6.2019 establishing a European Labour Authority, amending Regulations (EC) No 883/2004, (EU) No 492/2011 and (EU) 2016/589 and repealing Decision (EU) 2016/344 (OJ EU L No. 186, 21–56).

[26] Proposal for a Regulation of the European Parliament and of the Council establishing the European Labour Authority, COM(2018) 131 final. Detailed analysis of the ELA's role in enforcement of European Labour law is presented in Chapter 18 of this volume.

[27] See: https://ec.europa.eu/social/main.jsp?catId=1496&langId=en.

[28] B Bednarowicz, 'Europejski Urząd ds. Pracy. Rola i uprawnienia nowej unijnej agencji' (2020) 7 *Monitor Prawa Pracy*.

The social partners have seats on the Management Board of the ELA.[29] The recitals also mention the social partners' role in the Stakeholders Group, the Advisory Committee for the Coordination of Social Security Systems and the Advisory Committee on the Free Movement of Workers. According to Article 8.1 of Regulation (EU) 2019/1149, social partner organisations at national level may bring cases to the attention of the Authority. Recital 19 also states that where trade unions are in charge of inspections at national level, concerted and joint inspections should take place following the agreement of, and in cooperation with, the relevant social partners. This does not mean, however, that the social partners can effectively request the Authority's intervention, which should be considered a weakness of the Regulation.[30]

Effective enforcement is the primary source of abuses of labour law, rather than the content of the law itself.[31] Furthermore, national authorities and labour inspectorates simply do not have the resources they need to investigate cross-border cases. In this context, the Authority acts as a large platform that can help Member States to enforce EU rules more effectively and easily.[32] National liaison officers seconded to the ELA will be fully responsible for cases which have been very difficult to handle so far, mainly due to lack of technical and logistical resources.[33]

Although the original proposal for the creation of the Authority envisaged a genuine European control and enforcement authority, the resulting configuration in fact seems to represent a much softer and more modest version of it. In its current legal position, the Authority will focus primarily on assisting and supporting national administrations. Moreover, Member States will participate in the activities of the Authority only on a voluntary basis. The very establishment of the Authority implies the establishment of a permanent structure providing support to national authorities, however, which in itself already has great potential to coordinate inspections at supranational level, as well as to facilitate access to information, mediation and resolution of cross-border disputes.[34]

[29] www.ela.europa.eu/en/governance.

[30] J Cremers, *The European Labour Authority and Enhanced Enforcement, Briefing requested by the EMPL committee*, www.europarl.europa.eu/RegData/etudes/BRIE/2018/619003/IPOL_BRI(2018)619003_EN.pdf.

[31] J Cremers, 'The European Labour Authority and rights-based labour mobility' (2020) 21(1) *ERA Forum* 10.

[32] J Cremers, above n 30 at 5.

[33] M Čaněk, K Kall, N Lillie, A Wallace and B Haidinger, *Transnational Cooperation among Labour Regulation Enforcement Agencies in Europe: Challenges and Opportunities Related to the Posting of Workers* (SOLIDAR, 2018) 3, https://inicjatywa.eu/wp-content/uploads/2018/07/TNC_Report_-_Challenges_and_Opportunities_Related_to_the_Posting_of_Workers___Attachements.pdf.

[34] A Garcia-Munoz Alhambra, B Ter Haar and A Kun, 'Harnessing Public Institutions for Labour Law Enforcement: Embedding a Transnational Labour Inspectorate within the ILO' (2020) 17 *International Organizations Law Review* 245.

2.3. Role of the European Ombudsman: 'The Control of Administration'

The European Ombudsman acts on the basis of Article 228 TFEU and Article 43 CFREU. Its main role is to receive complaints (also directly from natural and legal persons) concerning instances of maladministration[35] in the activities of EU institutions, bodies, offices or agencies, with the exception of the Court of Justice of the European Union acting in its judicial role. The ombudsman examines such complaints and reports on them.[36]

It is interesting to note that, according to Article 2.9 of the regulations and general conditions governing the performance of the Ombudsman's duties, if there is a complaint concerning work relationships between Community institutions and bodies and their officials and others, all options for the submission of internal administrative requests and complaints, in particular the procedures referred to in Article 90(1) and (2) of the Staff Regulations, must first be exhausted by the person concerned and the time limits for replies from the authorities thus petitioned must have expired before the Ombudsman may be approached.

The annual reports to the European Parliament do not show all cases concerning employment and social security issues. A review of the complaints for 2020, however, indicates that the vast majority of them are connected to the selection procedure for recruiting EU civil servants. There are also (far fewer) cases concerning alleged harassment, non-renewal of the complainant's employment contract and pension schemes. Maladministration was not upheld in all cases.[37]

One successful procedure concerned unpaid traineeships. The Ombudsman inquired into the European External Action Service's (EEAS) practice of offering only unpaid traineeships in EU Delegations. The inquiry arose from a complaint by a young EU citizen who had completed an unpaid traineeship. She argued that the EEAS's practice discriminates against young people from less well-off backgrounds.[38]

3. At Member State Level

EU law is generally implemented in four stages: transposition, operationalisation, application and enforcement. Member States are responsible for the effective

[35] Cf the remarks on Art 41 CFREU in section 2.

[36] An example of social partner involvement in proceedings is the Response to the public consultation from ETUC, UNI Europa and EPSU, as well as from major trade unions from Austria, Belgium, Denmark, Spain, Sweden and the United Kingdom in Case OI/6/2014/NF concerning the composition and transparency of European Commission expert groups (www.ombudsman.europa.eu/en/case/en/43789).

[37] www.ombudsman.europa.eu/en/search-inquiries?keys5=731.

[38] www.ombudsman.europa.eu/en/decision/en/83909. Decision in Case 454/2014/PMC concerning the European External Action Service's practice of offering unpaid traineeships in EU Delegations.

implementation of EU law, that is, the result in the form of achieving the legal and factual state required by EU law in a Member State. Enforcement of EU law, as well as national law transposing EU law rests with the judicial authorities, as well as non-judicial authorities with the power to monitor compliance and administrative enforcement bodies. The latter are of particular importance for enforcement of (EU) labour law.

National procedural regulations are subject to the Europeanisation process; in other words, they can be shaped under the influence of EU law. In the case of European labour law, one obstacle to effective enforcement might occur in the course of transposition of Directives to the national legal system, if, instead of adapting the regulations to the nomenclature and institutions already existing in a Member State, the legislator chooses to rewrite the Directive verbatim. Instead of the unification of labour law in all Member States, this would instead create confusion, especially if the terms in the Directive vary from those applied in other national legal acts. In other cases the clauses in national law would be too broad and as such open to too wide a margin of appreciation, especially by administrative and judicial bodies. Another important aspect is the transnational character of some employment relations; in such instances, as in the case of posting of workers, cooperation between Member States is crucial for effective enforcement.

In the Member States, administrative decisions are issued in principle in accordance with national procedural regulations (principle of procedural autonomy). This principle is limited by the obligation to ensure full effectiveness of EU law. The rules of conduct in cases aimed at ensuring the protection of rights of legal entities under EU law may not be less favourable than in the case of similar internal procedures (principle of equivalence). The use of national procedural solutions may not, in practice, make the exercise of EU law impossible or excessively difficult (principle of effectiveness).[39] In practice, the activities of labour inspectors will be guided by the same rules and procedures regardless of whether a given workers' right is regulated by EU law or not. Cross-border cases, such as the enforcement of the rights of posted workers, may be an exception as they usually require cooperation between institutions in the sending and the receiving country.

According to the principle of sincere cooperation, strengthened in the Lisbon Treaty, EU law is applied not only by the individual national authorities, but as a result of cooperation between the administrative authorities of the Member States and EU bodies or the administrative bodies of different Member States. Horizontal cooperation may consist in the exchange of information necessary to issue an administrative act, carried out by an authority of another Member State (for example, posting of workers).[40] Another aspect of cooperation is recognising

[39] M Niedźwiedź, 'Administracyjne wykonywanie prawa Unii Europejskiej' in R Hauser, Z Niewiadomski and A Wróbel (eds), *Europeizacja prawa administracyjnego*, Vol 3, *System Prawa Administracyjnego* (Warszawa, CH Beck, 2014) 167.

[40] Ibid at 170.

the legal effects of an administrative act of a Member State. This is an obligation under primary and secondary EU law (principle of mutual recognition).[41]

3.1. Role of Labour Inspections in the Member States

Labour inspection has always been a major issue for the International Labour Organization (ILO). Labour Inspection Convention No 81 (1947), with 128 ratifications (including all EU Member States) is one of the most widely accepted instruments of the ILO and confirms the importance of this issue.[42] It has a crucial role in enforcing workers' rights, as labour inspectors work directly with employers who need support or do not follow labour law provisions. The specific role of labour inspection in the enforcement of occupational safety and health provisions is discussed in Chapter 15.

Labour inspection is not a 'monolithic concept, let alone a single organization'.[43] Labour inspection systems have traditionally been categorised as either 'generalist' or 'specialist' (or a mixture of the two). The scope of competence of a general labour inspectorate covers, among other things, the following issues: occupational safety and health, working time, wages and salaries, equal treatment between men and women, legality of employment and undeclared work, migrant workers, and other areas, such as restructuring measures (only in some countries, Spain, Belgium and France) and social security (only in some countries, such as Italy and Spain).[44] The generalist pattern is followed also by Portugal, Czechia and Poland.[45]

In dual-system countries (such as Estonia, Finland, Germany, the Netherlands and Norway), they also cover a range of matters related to working conditions, including wages.[46]

The term 'specialist' would tend to describe systems dealing in the main with only one of these major labour inspection functions – usually occupational safety, health and the working environment. The pattern followed in Scandinavian countries is that inspectorates have a mandate mainly for the enforcement of compliance with occupational health, safety and welfare, plus certain general conditions of work regulations (though usually excluding wages). Similar solutions are found in Austria. Finland and Norway lie somewhere in between, with the main focus on

[41] See C-120/78 *Rewe-Zentral v Bundesmonopolverwaltung für Branntwein ('Cassis de Dijon')*, EU:C:1979:42, [1979] ECR 649.

[42] P De Baets, 'The labour inspection of Belgium, the United Kingdom and Sweden in a comparative perspective' (2003) 31 *International Journal of the Sociology of Law* 38.

[43] M Čaněk et al, above n 33 at 10.

[44] W von Richthofen, *Labour Inspection: A Guide to the Profession*, 38–39; Syndex, *A Mapping Report on Labour Inspection Services in 15 European countries*. A SYNDEX report for the European Federation of Public Service Unions (EPSU, 2012) 10.

[45] D Walters, 'Labour inspection and health and safety in the EU' (2016) 14 *HesaMag* 13.

[46] M Čaněk et al, above n 33 at 10.

occupational safety and health, but also covering some additional broader tasks in which they address, for example, undocumented or undeclared work.[47]

In many countries, in addition to a main labour inspectorate there may also be smaller specialist and associated inspectorates with responsibility for securing compliance in relation to particular economic sectors or technologies. Typically, there are separate inspectorates for seafaring, fire safety, railways and mines.[48]

Labour inspectorates can also be categorised by looking at the general pattern of intervention policies characteristic of different labour inspection services. In sanctioning systems the inspectors concentrate on punishable contraventions or violations of rules and regulations. In compliance systems even if the imposition of criminal or administrative penalties or fines is available as a 'last resort' measure, inspectors are concerned with securing conformity with the law without necessarily using formal methods of enforcement, such as prosecution or punishment.

Regardless of the type of labour inspectorate, the ILO proposes a functional approach, based on particular areas of labour protection, which allows for comparison of the resources allocated to different functions, and assessment of how effective a system is in accomplishing its mandate in different areas of functional competence:[49]

- occupational safety and health (and possibly 'welfare');
- general conditions of work (and possibly wage issues);
- industrial relations (including conciliation, but as a rule excluding arbitration);
- employment-related matters (from illegal employment to employment promotion, including vocational training programmes); and
- social security issues (though this is usually limited to controlling remittances and other workers' compensation matters, as in Spain).[50]

Taking these things into consideration, multi-functional systems are found in, for example, France, Belgium and Spain, while the United Kingdom's Health and Safety Executive (HSE) is an example of a single-function labour inspectorate.

3.2. Sanctions and Other Measures in the Case of Labour Law Infringements

A labour inspection system has a dual role: it provides information, training and advisory services to workers, employers and their representatives, and also it supervises the enforcement of legal provisions, especially in the field of occupational

[47] D Walters, above n 45 at 13.
[48] Ibid at 13.
[49] W von Richthofen, above n 44 at 41.
[50] Ibid at 41.

safety and health.[51] The sanctions complement other measures aimed at compliance with labour law. Article 13 of ILO Convention No 81 states (like Article 18 of Convention No 129 (1969)) '[labour] inspectors shall be empowered to take steps with a view to remedying defects observed in plant, layout or working methods which they may have reasonable cause to believe constitute a threat to the health or safety of the workers'.

Labour inspectors' powers of injunction vary from one country to the other. Usually, labour inspectors have a discretionary power to decide whether to launch an administrative procedure or just use their preventive power to issue a warning allowing the employer a specified period in which to rectify matters (according to the labour inspectors' prevention role).[52] In the event of imminent danger to the safety and health of workers, labour inspectors can require immediate measures to be taken, including an order to cease all activities deemed dangerous.

As far as the imposition of sanctions is concerned, two basic systems can be found: an administrative system in which labour inspectors are entitled to initiate an administrative procedure leading to the imposition of a fine (that is the case in almost all countries apart from France and the United Kingdom); and a legal prosecution system in which labour inspectors draft a report to be sent to the competent courts in order to instigate a legal prosecution process (in France). In most countries the two systems co-exist and the decision as to whether to start an administrative procedure or a criminal one depends mainly on the gravity of the violation.[53]

The ILO report summarising sanctions[54] imposed by labour inspectors presents the following types of sanctions, starting from the most severe (and rarely applied) to the most benign:

- criminal penalties;
- civil penalties;
- closure of operations;
- revocation of licences;
- suspension of operations;
- monetary fines.[55]

Not all countries have the whole spectrum of sanctions, and even if they have, not all of them can be imposed by labour inspectors when they visit enterprises. In particular, criminal sanctions may be reserved for the police, the prosecutor's office and the criminal courts.

[51] Ibid at 29.
[52] Syndex, *A Mapping Report*, above n 44 at 13.
[53] Ibid, 13.
[54] For specific issues concerning types of sanctions in general, as well as distinctions between sanctions and remedies see Chapter 2 of this volume.
[55] ML Vega and R Robert, *Labour Inspection Sanctions: Law and practice of national labour inspection systems* (Geneva, ILO, 2013) 6.

Monetary sanctions (fines) are one of the basic means available to many labour inspectors to compel compliance with labour legislation or to sanction violators.[56] The range of fines or maximum fines, and the procedures involved in imposing and enforcing fines – including whether inspectors may impose fines for infractions detected during an inspection visit – vary from one country to another.[57]

Whether or not a fine is an effective means of compelling compliance with the law or deterring violations depends on many factors. For example, fines that are too low will not be dissuasive, but too onerous fines might jeopardise an enterprise's very viability and threaten jobs.[58] Fines should therefore be flexible. Some countries, for example, allow adaptation of the amount of the fine to company size, number of workers employed or number of workers affected by the infringement. In many countries, labour inspectors, before imposing a fine, issue a warning; only if the employer fails to act and, in particular, to halt or reverse the effects of the infringement within a given time is the fine imposed.[59]

Work stoppages are a standard penalty in many countries for non-compliance with occupational safety and health provisions. They may take a form of a suspension of operations, closure of the establishment, or revocation of an employer's operating licence.[60]

Most countries have provisions (accompanied by sanctions) forbidding the obstruction of labour inspectors in the course of their duties, as provided for by Article 18 of Convention No 81.[61]

In the Polish legal system, for example, the following sanctions are applied.

Notice is the mildest legal measure used by labour inspectors. The labour inspector imposes an obligation on the employer to remedy the deficiencies found during the inspection or to draw consequences in relation to the persons responsible for their occurrence.

For example, a notice can be issued in cases of:

- failure to register employees in social insurance authority;
- failure to specify the type of employment contract concluded with a given employee;
- unreliable keeping of records on working time;
- no fixed date for payment of wages is specified in the work regulations.

Injunctions are issued by inspectors in the event of an employer's breach of labour law provisions. Orders and prohibitions may have the status of an administrative decision.

[56] Ibid, 14.
[57] Ibid, 47.
[58] Ibid, 47.
[59] Ibid, 17–20.
[60] Ibid, 25.
[61] Ibid, 27.

An injunction may provide for, among other things:

- an order to cease the identified breaches of occupational safety and health rules and provisions;
- an order to stop work or activity;
- an order to pay the remuneration due for work, as well as other benefits to which the employee is entitled.

Orders regarding the payment of due remuneration for work and other benefits are enforceable immediately.

Labour inspectors may also bring cases to a labour court to establish that an employment contract exists between the parties.

Criminal mandates can be issued by the labour inspector to the person responsible for the irregularities found during the control visit. The perpetrator is obliged to pay a fine, which at present ranges between €220 and €430, and in the case of repeat offences, between €430 and €1,100. If the employer refuses to accept the penalty notice, the labour inspector who imposed the fine may apply to a court to impose a penalty.

A request for sanctions, filed with the criminal court, is made when it is justified by the number or scale of violations of the law found during the inspection. Criminal courts may impose fines in the amount of €220 to €6,500 (Article 283 §1 Labour Code), or even higher (up to €22,000 in case of the illegal employment of migrant workers).

If there is a suspicion that the employer has committed a crime, the labour inspector is obliged to notify the police or the prosecutor's office. This concerns every identified offence, in particular offences against the rights of persons performing paid work or illegal employment of third-country migrants, as well as human trafficking.

In Sweden, the Work Environment Authority (Arbetsmiljöverket – SWEA[62]) is the authority mandated by the government and the Riksdag to see that companies and organisations comply with laws on the working environment and working hours. The SWEA's supervisory activities include carrying out inspections in order to strengthen workplaces' own ability to prevent risks. At the same time, the employer receives a notification about what shortcomings need to be fixed. The SWEA itself underlines the advisory role of the inspection and the role of safety representatives in the company, who can be advised about work environment shortcomings that may exist in the organisation, explain what the risks are and which rules apply.

If a problem with the work environment is found during the visit, the employer receives a written report after the inspection containing a description of the shortcomings and applicable rules. Inspectors usually ask that the employer informs

[62] www.av.se/en/.

them about what has been done or what will be done to remove the risks. Another visit may be planned to verify whether the demand was followed. If the employer does not fix the shortcomings voluntarily, the labour inspector may decide upon an injunction or a ban; in other words, to coerce the employer in different ways to comply with the work environment legislation. Inspectors can combine injunctions and bans with a penalty sum; money that the employer has to pay if the injunction or ban is not followed. Their decisions can be appealed by both the employer and the safety representative.

According to Chapter 7 section 7 Working Environment Act[63] inspectors may issue orders or prohibitions as needed to secure compliance with the Working Environment Act or Regulation (EC) No 1907/2006, which fall within the supervisory responsibility of the Swedish Work Environment Authority. The provision also stipulates that the decision to issue an order or prohibition may be accompanied by a conditional financial penalty both for private and state employers. If the order is not followed, the SWEA may order that remedial measures be taken at the employer's expense. Under section 10, to ensure compliance with a prohibition, the inspector may order that a facility, space or equipment be sealed or otherwise made inaccessible.

Chapter 8 of the Work Environment Act provides for fines and financial penalties. As the SWEA explains, a sanction fee is a fee, while fines are a penalty imposed by a court. To contravene a stipulation that carries a fine is considered to be a criminal act. Such work environment cases are therefore dealt with by the police and are later passed on to the prosecutor and the court.[64]

Fines or imprisonment for up to one year for intentional or negligent failure to comply with an order or prohibition described above. Fines can be applied for specific contraventions, especially those concerning minor workers, removal of safety equipment and failure to provide adequate information to supervisory bodies or violations of the obligation to report accidents and serious incidents. Moreover Chapter 20, section 3 of the Penal Code contains provisions concerning liability for OSH infringements. If any equipment or substance has been used in connection with an offence or prohibition stipulated in the Work Environment Act it can be confiscated.

Other measures include financial penalties for infringements by natural or legal persons of OSH regulations issued by the government (regardless of whether it was committed intentionally or negligently). A regulation may also indicate the manner in which the penalty is to be calculated for different kinds of infringement. It may be either a fixed fee or differentiated in accordance with company size (employer). The amount of the sanction is calculated according to the number of employees at the company or organisation. Both full-time and part-time employees

[63] www.government.se/4ac754/contentassets/86e9091526644e90b78d2ff937318530/sfs-19771160-work-environment-act.

[64] SWEA, Fines, penalties and sanction fees, www.av.se/en/work-environment-work-and-inspections/fines-penalties-and-sanction-fees.

are taken into account. Financial penalties in Sweden range from SEK 1,000 to SEK 1,000,000. Employers with 500 or more employees pay the maximum fee, irrespective of how many are active.[65] If the penalty order has not been accepted within the specified time, the Swedish Work Environment Authority may apply to the administrative court within whose jurisdiction the penalty order was issued for a financial penalty.

4. Conclusions

Administrative law plays a significant role in the enforcement of EU labour law. At the European level various bodies are involved, which may cause overlaps, but also gaps in their areas of competence and activities. First of all, the European Commission, as the guardian of the Treaties, is obliged to ensure application of the Treaties and EU law (Article 17 TEU). However, it seems that infringement proceedings are rare in the area of labour law. Moreover, the Commission concentrates on the wording of laws being transposed, not on practical implementation. In the case of labour law evading and circumventing provisions may adversely affect workers' situation (for example, when an employment contract is replaced with bogus self-employment).

The EU agencies usually play an advisory role and conduct research in their respective areas. Even though these activities are useful for national bodies (such as the guidelines issued by EU-OSHA), if EU labour law is not respected they do not have the power to issue binding decisions. The creation of the ELA has raised high expectations in relation to enforcement in general, as well as in particular to overcoming problems in the area of cooperation between national labour inspectorates. This especially concerns such problems as a lack of national networking between all relevant compliance offices and authorities, given that information may be diffused in various places, and demarcation and limitations of competences, which differ in every Member State. The power to conduct inspections in its own right would certainly strengthen the ELA's position as an enforcement body.

As far as labour exploitation is concerned, not all labour inspectorates and similar institutions have an explicit mandate to tackle labour exploitation or the labour rights violations of migrant workers. Moreover, their competences often stop at the border. Control of the regular collection of evidence and supporting documents has been hindered by fragmented competences and the lack of a mandate in the host country.

Cooperation between the EU and national bodies, as well as national bodies in different Member States should be guided by the principle of effectiveness, sincere cooperation and mutual recognition. However, civil servants who typically

[65] Above n 64.

carry out administrative enforcement often do not receive specialised training in CJEU case law and how to apply general principles of EU law in practice. Hence the impact such principles have on administrative enforcement in the Member States can be questioned, if they are not guaranteed by appropriate institutional procedures.

The main burden in the enforcement of EU labour law is still on the national labour inspectorates. Their competences and operational models vary from one country to another, but the majority have at their disposal measures that effectively allow them to prevent and/or punish infringements. The most effective enforcement approach seems to be a combination of compliance – that is, supporting compliance by employers and promoting rights and the awareness of rights – and deterrence.[66] Unfortunately, the responsible national institutions and offices lack staff and competences are too dispersed to guarantee effective control.

Another area in which an EU initiative would be necessary is sanctions. As indicated in Chapter 5 of this volume there are possibilities to further harmonise EU criminal law in terms of sanctions for breaches of workers' rights, including the harmonisation of infringements of OSH regulations, since double (or dual) criminality is a common precondition for mutual assistance and mutual recognition in the execution of financial fines. The experience of inspectors is that fines are weak in an extra-territorial context. Lack of effective penalties is especially visible in cross-border cases, as social fraud is still not regarded a major offence justifying a Europe-wide sanction.[67]

The last two areas – national labour inspectorates' lack of resources and less effective sanctions – weaken the efficiency of enforcement of national and European labour law alike.

Given the specificity of EU labour law it is recommended that general operational rules be established for labour inspections in the EU (and perhaps cooperation between them). Even though all EU Member States have ratified ILO Convention No 81 its potential has not been fully realised. It could therefore be argued that a Directive regulating the role of national labour inspectorates or other relevant bodies in the enforcement of EU labour law, especially as far as their competences and cooperation are concerned, could help to create more effective enforcement mechanisms also at the national level.

[66] D Cabrelli, 'Using Criminal Law to Enforce Statutory Employment Rights' in A Bogg, J Collins, M Freedland and J Herring (eds), *Criminality at Work* (Oxford, Oxford University Press, 2020) 93.

[67] Project Cibeles, *An Overview. Main Findings, Conclusions And Proposals*, 14–15. www.mites.gob.es/ITSS/ITSS/ITSS_Descargas/Sala_de_comunicaciones/Noticias/2011/Adj_not_20111122_6.pdf.

5

Enforcement by Means of Criminal Law

JOANNA UNTERSCHÜTZ

1. Introduction: Criminal Law and Criminal Sanctions

Criminal law, unlike labour law, does not regulate exhaustively any section of social life, but instead sets boundaries to human behaviour.[1] The reason for interfering with social life and establishing punitive sanctions is to protect certain values considered most important for the functioning of society.[2] Where certain rights are fundamental or reflect a community's collective goals or shared values, there is an argument that more symbolic forms of enforcement and remedies are needed.[3]

A criminal sanction always includes a message that is relevant from the societal point of view about important values and unacceptable behaviour, and the 'price' for violating the adopted legal order.[4] In this way, criminal sanctions can in the long run function as an instrument for internalising norms and values. This also concerns protection of workers' rights: introducing a criminal offence indicates that certain behaviour is not acceptable in society. Nevertheless, in the absence of a civil alternative, the criminalisation of certain labour law breaches may be more a distraction from the more fundamental question of how to achieve compliance than an effective means of enforcement.[5]

Criminal sanction is defined as a 'conscious, active, reaction of a human or a human group to the behaviour of a human or animal, assessed negatively by the subject of this reaction, and directed against the real or alleged subject of this behaviour or against a person associated with this subject'.[6] It is imposed on behalf

[1] W Wolter, 'Granice i zakres prawa karania' (1957) 2 *Państwo i Prawo* 243.

[2] M Cieślak, *Kara: istota, cel, uzasadnienie* (Arche, Sopot, 2010).

[3] D Cabrelli, 'Using Criminal Law to Enforce Statutory Employment Rights' in A Bogg, J Collins, M Freedland, J Herring (eds), *Criminality at Work* (Oxford University Press, 2020) 55.

[4] T Kaczmarek and W Zalewski, 'Kara kryminalna i jej racjonalizacja' in T Kaczmarek (ed), *Nauka o karze. sądowy wymiar kary. System prawa karnego tom 5* (Warszawa, CH Beck, 2017) 12.

[5] C Barnard and S Fraser Butlin, 'Where Criminal Law Meets Labour Law: The Effectiveness of Criminal Sanctions to Enforce Labour Rights' in *Criminality at Work*, above n 3 at 71.

[6] M Cieślak, above n 2.

of the state by competent courts against individuals who have committed crimes (or misdemeanours).[7] This definition covers the most general concept of a punitive reaction, including measures that are not commonly referred to as punishment in the strict sense.

Enforcement by means of criminal law should be considered an *ultima ratio* measure, applied only if no other avenues are effective or sufficient. Only when restorative justice procedures fail or prove insufficient, should traditional measures based on criminal law be resorted to, from the mildest, grading sanctions, up to full isolation.[8]

Many authors, opposing general prevention, narrowly understood, in the sense of deterring other people from committing crimes, also emphasise that the social impact of punishment is not due to severity alone, but above all to its inevitability.[9] From this point of view, for the overall preventive effect of the punishment the crime detection rate, the speed of punishment and the breadth of informing the public about the sentence will be important.

The success of criminalisation in the area covered in the present volume is to be measured most of all by whether employers change their behaviour. This will not happen if the risk of enforcement, whether actual or potential, is limited. Only if employers are likely to be caught might that prompt a change their behaviour.[10]

Criminal labour law on the European or national level is a broad subject. The aim of this chapter is to present the most crucial issues relevant to enforcement of European labour law. This introductory section includes general remarks on the nature of criminal law and its functions. The second section goes further, to present links between labour law and criminal law, which have existed for centuries, even though only in the twentieth century did the focus of criminal provisions in this area become protecting workers' rights. The Lisbon Treaty conferred new powers on the EU in the field of criminal law and section 3 briefly presents the EU Directives that include elements of crimes and penalties for human trafficking and employment of third-country nationals residing illegally in the EU. In the other labour law Directives the enforcement clauses are broad and general, usually allowing the Member States to choose between civil, administrative or criminal sanctions. Section 5 focuses on two specific instruments of procedural criminal law: the European Arrest Warrant and the European Investigation Order. Finally, before the conclusions (section 7), perspectives on the development of EU provisions on criminal labour law are considered (section 6), showing the potential for development of this group of provisions, but also the limitations connected to the specificity of criminal law and Member State autonomy in this area.

[7] M Cieślak, above n 2.

[8] Above n 4 at 128.

[9] W Świda, *Prawo karne. Część ogólna* (Warszawa, PWN, 1970) 265–66; M Szerer, *Karanie a humanizm* (Warszawa, PWN, 1964) 145; L Lernell, *Podstawy nauki polityki kryminalnej. Studia z zagadnień przestępstwa, odpowiedzialności i kary* (Warszawa, PWN, 1967) 458.

[10] C Barnard and S Fraser Butlin, above n 5 at 88.

2. Criminal Law and Labour Law

Historically, criminal provisions associated with performance of work can be traced back to guild regulations or even earlier. In modern times the criminal law has often been used for regulating labour markets. There have also been criminal laws targeted more specifically at the confederacy of organised trade union action as such.[11] Therefore, the good being protected was not the rights of the people performing work, but the employer's benefit, for example, by setting maximum wages for workers and, especially in the nineteenth and the beginning of the twentieth century, to prohibit strikes. Criminal social law – or more specifically, criminal labour law – is a relatively new phenomenon. Over the course of the nineteenth century there was a significant expansion of the administrative state in various spheres of social and economic life, and this was often reflected in criminalisation facilitated by public inspectorates.[12] Both Kahn-Freund and Wedderburn were very sceptical of the criminal law's value as an enforcement tool, because of the low levels of prosecution, its ineffectiveness and the practice of using criminal law against workers' rights by penalising striking workers.[13]

Nowadays, criminal law forms of intervention range from the prescription of more traditional forms of offences carrying the sanctions of imprisonment or fines, to quasi-criminal public agency (for example, withdrawing a licence or prohibition from participating in public tenders).[14] Criminal law might provide a substitute for civil enforcement. Or it might operate as an auxiliary mode of enforcement of labour standards, in parallel with individual rights of enforcement. Or the criminal law might be reserved for certain outstanding breaches of labour standards.[15]

Therefore it must be considered in what circumstances the law should intervene in work relationships to correct inequalities of bargaining power, subordination to managerial power, abuses of civil or social rights, or potential harm to workers' welfare.[16] The deterrence approach typical of criminal law is well aligned with the work and employment context because, particularly in relation to lower-level violations, the economics involved and the relative power between worker and employer play a more significant role.[17] One example of successful action in this domain was cooperation between the public prosecutor's office, local police and

[11] A Bogg, KD Ewing and A Moretta, 'The Persistence of Criminal Law and Police in Collective Labour Relations' in *Criminality at Work*, above n 3 at 362–64.

[12] Horder, 'Bureaucratic "Criminal" Law: Too Much of a Bad Thing?', in RA Duff, L Farmer, SE Marshall, M Renzo and V Tadros (eds), *Criminalization: The Political Morality of the Criminal Law* (Oxford, OUP, 2014) 101.

[13] A Bogg and M Freedland, 'Criminality at Work: A Framework for Discussion' in *Criminality at Work*, above n 3 at 4–5; PL Davies and M Freedland (eds), *Kahn-Freund's Labour and the Law* (Stevens, 1983) 50–51; Lord Wedderburn, *The Worker and the Law* (Penguin, 1986) 91–93, 139.

[14] D Cabrelli, above n 3 at 55.

[15] A Bogg and M Freedland, above n 13 at 6.

[16] M Ford, 'The Criminalization of Health and Safety at Work' in *Criminality at Work*, above n 3 at 410.

[17] C Barnard and Fraser Butlin, above n 5 at 87.

the labour inspectorate in Milan in 2019–20. Following a number of road accidents involving bicycle couriers ('riders'), the prosecutors office and the police set out to verify, after assessing their work status using questionnaires and road checks, compliance with accident prevention legislation for this new category of workers, whose number had been increasing significantly. As a result, it was established that couriers should be classified as workers and that occupational safety and health (OSH) provisions should apply. As a consequence, the prosecutors' office ordered the requalification of the contracts of 60,000 riders, the payment of due fees and adherence to OSH obligations towards them.[18]

There are also examples that show how the criminal law can be used to meet political goals. Germany's Minimum Wage Act of 2014 obliged posting companies to notify the German customs authorities about their workers' wages via specific forms. Severe penalties of between €30,000 and €500,000 applied if the remuneration paid does not comply with German law. This led to an infringement procedure as the Commission considered that the fines were too high.[19]

The perspective of the European Court of Human Rights (ECtHR) is interesting in this context. The ECtHR has often ruled that the Convention imposes positive obligations to criminalise conduct, mainly because of the deterrent effect of criminalisation and its ability to influence human behaviour: Convention rights have to be practical and effective, a duty to enact criminal laws aims to achieve exactly that by deterring people from engaging in the conduct in question.[20] The positive obligation to criminalise Article 4 violations was reiterated in subsequent case law, especially *Rantsev v Cyprus and Russia*, the first case that examined trafficking for sexual exploitation under the ECHR.[21] In addition, the Convention also imposes an obligation to investigate effectively when there is a suspicion that someone is a victim of treatment contrary to Article 4.[22] The *Siliadin* judgment also considered the definition of the prohibited conduct. It stated that slavery should be defined in light of the Slavery Convention of 1927. The severe exploitation of migrant domestic workers was rightly presented as a systemic wrong in France and elsewhere, which criminal law could deter.[23]

It is important to emphasise that criminalisation is not sufficient for a state to be deemed to be in compliance with Article 4 ECHR obligations. In *Rantsev*, the Court ruled that the state also has to take positive operational measures to

[18] Ispettorato Nazionale del Lavoro, 'Assicurate tutele del lavoro subordinato per 60.000 Riders', 24 February 2021, www.ispettorato.gov.it/it-it/notizie/Pagine/ASSICURATE-TUTELE-DEL-LAVORO-SUBORDINATO-PER-60-000-RIDERS-240202021.aspx.

[19] European Commission, 'Transport: Commission takes legal action against the systematic application of the French and German minimum wage legislation to the transport sector', https://ec.europa.eu/commission/presscorner/detail/en/IP_16_2101.

[20] V Mantouvalou, 'Human Rights, Labour Rights, and Criminal Wrongs' in *Criminality at Work*, above n 3 at 210.

[21] V Mantouvalou, above n 20 at 215; ECtHR judgment, *Siliadin v France* App no 73316/01 (2005); ECtHR judgment, *Rantsev v Cyprus and Russia* App No 25965/04 (2010) §29.

[22] *Rantsev v Cyprus and Russia*, §288; ECtHR (Grand Chamber) judgment, *SM v Croatia* App No 60561/14 (2020).

[23] *Siliadin v France* §49, 143–44. V Mantouvalou, above n 20 at 215.

protect victims or potential victims from violations.[24] For instance, it explicitly ruled that criminalisation of violations of collective labour rights is not sufficient in *Danilenkov v Russia*.[25]

3. Enforcement by Means of European Criminal Law

The Treaty of Lisbon brought about fundamental changes in the functioning of the criminal policy of the European Union. Currently, EU criminal law aims to establish common standards in a cross-border (or transnational) context for substantive and procedural criminal law alike. Article 83(1) 1 TFEU contains a closed list of cases in which the Council and the European Parliament may adopt Directives under the ordinary legislative procedure. These include trafficking in human beings and the sexual exploitation of women and children.

The criminal law of the European Union plays an important role in complementing the national criminal law systems of the Member States by adopting minimum standards of procedural rights in criminal proceedings. It also leads to the approximation of Member State national legislation, which, on one hand, strengthens mutual trust between their judicial and law enforcement authorities and, on the other, prevents the emergence of potential 'safe havens' in which perpetrators of many serious crimes have impunity.[26]

As a rule, criminal law per se reflects the fundamental values, customs and choices of a given society. The Treaty of Lisbon fully recognises this diversity, which is based on tradition and individual countries' legal cultures. Nevertheless, the cooperation of EU countries in criminal matters depends strongly on the harmonisation of national laws by adopting identical or similar legal regulations, as well as the principle of mutual recognition.

Enforcement by means of criminal law will largely depend on the relevant national criminal law system and the requirements established by the European legislator in labour law Directives.

The obligation of timely, proper and effective implementation of Directives rests with the Member States. It includes both the necessity to take appropriate legislative actions and the guarantee of the effectiveness of these standards under national law.[27] Union norms do not themselves contain sanctions for non-application of implemented norms, and compliance with properly implemented European law is based primarily on domestic law. Directives usually do not specify what kind of measures a Member State is to take for this purpose.[28]

[24] V Mantouvalou, above n 20 at 216.

[25] V Mantouvalou, above n 20 at 226.

[26] Commission Communication, 'Towards an EU Criminal Policy: Ensuring the Effective Implementation of EU Policy Through Criminal Law' of 2011.

[27] L Mitrus, *Wpływ regulacji wspólnotowych na poskie prawo pracy* (Zakamycze, 2006) 376.

[28] L Florek, 'Gwarancje stosowania europejskiego prawa pracy', in A Piontek (ed), *Prawo polskie a prawo Unii Europejskiej* (Warszawa, Lieber, 2000) 248.

Even before the Maastricht Treaty, the CJEU confirmed the relationship between Community law and criminal law. This is indicated by a group of judgments in which the CJEU encouraged the use of national criminal law to ensure the effectiveness of Community law, in particular in the case of imposing sanctions on individuals for failure to comply with obligations under Community law.[29]

The harmonisation of criminal definitions in the Member States is subject to a number of systemic limitations. One of the most important is the lack of a common general part of substantive criminal law, and thus a common 'conceptual framework'. Member States are also not constrained in adopting a broader scope for criminalising given categories of behaviour. A number of EU legal instruments harmonising the definitions of crimes include provisions requiring the penalisation of their phenomenal and stage forms.[30] The liability of legal persons for 'harmonised' crimes has also become standard in the EU. The important thing is that the choice of the type of responsibility is left to the Member States. This was and remains indispensable because of the variety of positions taken by the Member States regarding the criminal liability of legal persons.[31]

CJEU case law has evolved from the assertion that, where Community law does not provide for an obligation to impose specific sanctions on private entities infringing EU law, Member States are entitled to adopt such sanctions, as they deem appropriate.[32] Then, Case 68/88, *Commission v Greece* specified that the sanctions introduced must be effective, proportionate and dissuasive, and applied on the basis of the principle of equivalence with regard to infringements of national law. This also applies to criminal labour law provisions, which should not be more lenient than other norms protecting comparable values. In subsequent rulings, the CJEU added that the Member States are entitled to introduce criminal sanctions even when the Community law act provided for administrative or civil sanctions,[33] based on the principle of sincere cooperation.

Regarding the level of penalties, minimum standards may imply that certain types of sanctions should be imposed, or that the level of sanctions must be defined, or what are to be considered aggravating or mitigating circumstances at EU level. Full harmonisation is not possible in this respect. Thus, the Member States are entitled to specify in their national regulations higher levels of sanctions or other, more severe ones (apart from those provided for in the EU act), and are

[29] See Cases C-50/76 *Amsterdam Bulb*; C-68/88 *Commission v Greece*; C-186/98 *Nunes and de Matos*; A Grzelak, 'Commentary to Article 83' in D Miąsik, N Półtorak A Wróbel (eds), *Traktat o funkcjonowaniu Unii Europejskiej*, Vol I (art 1-89) (Komentarz, LEX online).

[30] A Grzelak, 'Współpraca w obszarze prawa karnego materialnego w ramach Rady Europy i Unii Europejskiej' in A Grzelak, M Królikowski and A Sakowicz (eds), *Europejskie prawo karne* (Warszawa, CH Beck, 2012) 298.

[31] B Namysłowska-Gabrysiak, *Odpowiedzialnośc karna osób prawnych* (Warsaw, CH Beck, 2003); J Warylewski and J Potulski, *Odpowiedzialność podmiotów zbiorowych w prawie polskim* (Bydgoszcz-Gdańsk, Komentarz. Oficyna Wydawnicza Branta, 2007); P Almond, 'Workplace Safety and Criminalization A Double-edged Sword' in *Criminality at Work*, above n 3 at 408.

[32] Case C-50/76 *Amsterdam Bulb*.

[33] Case C-186/98 *Nunes and de Matos*.

obliged to introduce the minimum specified in the EU legal act. The right to define sanctions will strengthen the effectiveness of EU policies, and this is the purpose of Article 83 section 2.

4. EU Labour Law

4.1. General Approach

Most labour law Directives introduce a general obligation to establish a redress mechanism in the event of a breach of their standards. Formulations used in the Directives differ, however. Some of them refer to 'appropriate measures in the event of failure to comply with the Directive' (Directive 96/71/EC, Directive 2008/104/EC, Council Directive 2003/72/EC, Directive 2002/14/EC); most add a phrase on making available adequate administrative or judicial procedures. Directive 2009/38/EC is even more specific, mentioning administrative or judicial appeal procedures available to employees' representatives. The concrete nature of these measures is to be decided by the Member States.

There is also a group of Directives that oblige Member States to lay down provisions on sanctions in case of non-compliance with laws that implement the Directive. In some Directives (Directive 2014/67/EU, Directive 2008/104/EC, Directive 2006/54/EC) the expression 'penalties' or 'rules on penalties' was used instead of 'sanctions'; this could indicate that the measures are in some ways different, but this distinction is absent in other language versions, which consistently use the national equivalent – usually derived from Latin – of 'sanctions'. 'Penalties' and 'sanctions' should be treated as equivalent. Neither specifies the character of the sanctions, be it civil, administrative or penal.

Most of them clearly indicate the need to introduce sanctions that should be 'effective, proportionate and dissuasive' (Directive 2014/67/EU, Directive 2008/104/EC, Council Directive 2000/78/EC, Directive 2006/54/EC, Council Directive 2000/43/EC), with the exception of Directive 2004/38/EC, which refers to 'effective and proportionate' sanctions. Directive 2002/14/EC is more specific as it refers to sanctions for non-compliance by the employer or employees' representatives.

A Member State is therefore free to choose between civil, administrative and criminal sanctions, or any combination of these. Nor does the EU impose procedural rules in force in the Member States on workers who wish to pursue claims arising from EU law in order to ensure the application of its provisions.[34] In *R (URTU) v Secretary of State for Transport* the Court of Appeal held that criminal penalties alone were a sufficient remedy for breach of the regulations on drivers' hours, in part because in some circumstances a civil remedy would not work, such

[34] Zob sprawa 14/83 *Von Colson i E Kamman przeciwko Land Nordrhein-Westfalen*, Zb Orz 1984, 1891.

as where an individual driver acted contrary to the instructions of their employer or no recoverable loss was suffered.[35]

Enforcement of health and safety provisions will be discussed at length in Chapter 15. It is sufficient to note that the majority of Member States have provisions introducing criminal sanctions for breach of OSH rules and regulations. Their aim is usually to achieve higher standards to promote general improvements in health and safety before accidents happen.[36] Unfortunately, the effects of criminalisation tend to be rather limited, as usually criminal courts deal with events after they have happened.[37]

Only the Seasonal Workers Directive 2014/36/EU is more specific as to the character of the sanctions, namely the exclusion of employers who are in serious breach of their obligations under this Directive from employing seasonal workers (Article 17.1). In the following paragraph it requires the creation of an obligation for employers to pay compensation to seasonal workers if the authorisation for the purpose of seasonal work is withdrawn, and paragraph 3 stipulates liability for subcontractors and main contractor.

It is argued that EU law cannot constitute a *lex imperfecta*, and therefore it is necessary to introduce ailments for breach of Community law, and it is worthwhile for the legislator to take into account methods that previously served to guarantee the effectiveness of national law in relation to similar institutions when establishing sanctions.[38]

4.2. Directive 2009/52/EC (Sanctions Directive)

It should not come as a surprise that only a few Directives explicitly require the introduction of criminal offences and draw up the necessary elements of these crimes. This is the case for Directive 2009/52/EC (Sanctions Directive) and Directive 2011/36/EU (HT Directive), which include provisions on criminal offences, specifying at least some elements of the crimes, penalties, liability of legal persons and penalties for legal persons, as well as criminal liability for incitement, aiding and abetting, and attempt (Article 3 Directive 2011/36/EU).

The main purpose of the Sanctions Directive is to limit the scale of illegal emigration to EU territory by reducing the attractiveness of employing third-country nationals residing illegally, and thus reducing the scope of the so-called 'shadow economy'. According to Recital 21 of Directive 2009/52/EC,

> experience has shown that the existing systems of sanctions have not been sufficient to achieve complete compliance with prohibitions against the employment of illegally

[35] *R (URTU) v Secretary of State for Transport* (n 138) § 44–57.

[36] P Almond, above n 31 at 418.

[37] Ibid, J Unterschütz, *Karnoprawna ochrona praw osób wykonujących pracę zarobkową* (Wolters Kluwer, 2010).

[38] L Mitrus, above n 27 at 379–80.

> staying third-country nationals. One of the reasons is that administrative sanctions alone are likely not to be enough to deter certain unscrupulous employers. Compliance can and should be strengthened by the application of criminal penalties.

This confirms the main purpose of the Directive: combating illegal employment of third-country nationals, while providing those who are already working with decent employment conditions.

The Directive did not and does not apply to third-country nationals legally residing in a Member State of the European Union, whether or not they have a permit to work in that country, or to workers posted under the Community's freedom to provide services. Ensuring workers the right to payment of any outstanding wages; establishing the presumption of at least the minimum wage (Article 6.1a) and a duration of at least three months for the working relationship in the absence of evidence (Article 6.3); and establishing the subcontractor's liability to pay any financial compensation and/or any back-payments (Article 8.1); all these things only complement employers' administrative obligations in terms of verifying the worker's legal status before employing a third-country national and notifying the competent authorities of the commencement of the working relationship (Article 4(1)).

It is not common, however, for employment Directives to contain an explicit statement on the need to introduce criminal measures.

In Article 9 the Directive provides for basic elements of the crimes. Employment of illegally resident third-country nationals constitutes a criminal offence when committed intentionally, in each of the following circumstances, as defined by national law:

(a) the infringement continues or is persistently repeated;
(b) the infringement is in respect of the simultaneous employment of a significant number of illegally resident third-country nationals;
(c) the infringement is accompanied by particularly exploitative working conditions;
(d) the infringement is committed by an employer who, while not having been charged with or convicted of an offence established pursuant to Framework Decision 2002/629/JHA, uses work or services exacted from an illegally staying third-country national in the knowledge that he or she is a victim of trafficking in human beings;
(e) the infringement relates to the illegal employment of a minor.

Additionally, inciting, aiding and abetting the intentional conduct referred to in paragraph 1 is punishable as a criminal offence.

Article 11 also establishes liability for an offence for legal persons if the crime was committed by persons acting on their behalf.

The Directive does not specify the character of criminal penalties, referring to the formula of 'effective, proportionate and dissuasive' sanctions (Article 10.1) for natural persons. The same formula is applied for sanctions on legal persons (Article 12), also allowing the Member States to decide that a list of employers who are legal persons and who have been held liable for the criminal offence be made public.

Furthermore, Articles 5 and 8 stipulate financial (non-criminal) sanctions against direct employers and subcontractors and an obligation to cover the costs of return of illegally employed workers to their country of origin.

A report on the implementation of the Sanctions Directive in Czechia, Hungary, Poland, Romania and Slovakia indicates huge differences because sanctions for offences, ranging from a minimum €2,000 in Slovakia to a mere €5 in Poland, with maximums of €1,200 in Poland and €373,000 in Czechia. This does not necessarily reflect differences between these states' minimum wages, but should be viewed rather as the result of different understandings of what constitutes a 'deterring sanction'.[39]

Organisations advocating for workers' rights criticise the Directive as implemented by the Member States because 'repercussions for employers remain very limited and facilitation of complaints insufficient, indicating that the directive does not deter employers from employing undocumented workers and cases of exploitation are not being reported'.[40] They also note that barriers to workers for lodging complaints still inhibit effective enforcement. For example, in EU countries, contrary to the provisions of the Directive, no specific provisions enabling complaints mechanisms have been laid down.[41] Also without a separation between immigration enforcement and labour rights protection, undocumented workers are not in a position to denounce exploitative employers and so exploitative practices are allowed to continue. As filing a complaint against their employer entails great risks for employees, the mechanism is not effective; agencies responsible for reviewing such complaints closely cooperate with immigration police, formally or informally.[42] The report also points to the lack of effective mechanisms to facilitate claiming due wages or other claims from the employer.

4.3. Directive 2011/36/EU (Human Trafficking Directive)

Directive 2011/36/EU in Article 2 formulates a definition of human trafficking largely based on the Palermo Protocol:[43] the recruitment, transportation, transfer, harbouring or reception of persons, including the exchange or transfer of

[39] K Słubik (ed), *Unprotected Migrant Workers in an Irregular Situation in Central Europe* (Warszawa, Stowarzyszenie Interwencji Prawnej, 2014) 43, https://interwencjaprawna.pl/wp-content/uploads/2020/04/unprotected.pdf.

[40] PICUM, 'Employers' Sanctions: Impacts on Undocumented Migrant Workers' Rights in Four EU Countries', April 2015, 11, https://picum.org/Documents/Publi/2015/EmployerSanctions.pdf.

[41] K Słubik, above n 39 at 46.

[42] Ibid at 46.

[43] Protocol to Prevent, Suppress and Punish Trafficking in Persons Especially Women and Children, supplementing the United Nations Convention against Transnational Organized Crime. Adopted and opened for signature, ratification and accession by General Assembly resolution 55/25 of 15 November 2000, www.ohchr.org/EN/ProfessionalInterest/Pages/ProtocolTraffickingInPersons.aspx.

control over those persons, by means of the threat or use of force or other forms of coercion, of abduction, of fraud, of deception, of the abuse of power or of a position of vulnerability (a situation in which the person concerned has no real or acceptable alternative but to submit to the abuse involved), or of the giving or receiving of payments or benefits to achieve the consent of a person having control over another person, for the purpose of exploitation. The Directive also explicitly mentions, among other things, forced labour as well as services, including begging, exploitation of the prostitution of others or other forms of sexual exploitation as well as practices similar to slavery or servitude.

There are three crucial elements of the definition: the action (recruitment, transportation etc), the means (threat or use of force etc) and the purpose (exploitation),[44] all of which have to be fulfilled at the same time. If any of the prohibited means were applied, the consent of the victim is irrelevant.[45] In many jurisdictions these means would make a declaration of worker status defective. The Directive also establishes a catalogue of sanctions to be applied to legal persons, without prejudging whether they have criminal, civil or administrative character.

As far as victims of human trafficking are concerned there are measures for assistance, support and protection for victims of human trafficking, including children, as well as an obligation to ensure a system of compensation. Moreover it prohibits prosecuting or imposing penalties on the victims if they committed a crime as a direct consequence of being subjected to human trafficking.

Surprisingly, the Directive does not contain any explicit reference to the principle of non-refoulement, which is a *jus cogens* principle of international law, providing for a prohibition of expelling and deporting a person to a country where they may be subject to torture or other serious human rights violations. Nevertheless EU Member States are bound to respect the principle[46] even though it is not specifically mentioned in this Directive.[47]

5. EU Procedural Criminal Law

Minimum common standards established on the basis of Article 82.1 TFEU must take into account the differences between the legal traditions and systems of the Member States. They concern mutual admissibility of evidence between Member States, the rights of individuals in criminal proceedings, the rights of victims of crime and other specific aspects of criminal proceedings.

[44] P Daniluk in RA Stefański (ed), *Kodeks karny* (Warszawa, CH Beck, Komentarz, 2017) SIP Legalis.

[45] Directive 2009/52/EC of the European Parliament and of the Council of 18 June 2009 providing for minimum standards on sanctions and measures against employers of illegally staying third-country nationals, [2009] OJ L 168/24.

[46] The principle of non-refoulement is recognised in Art 19(2) of CFREU.

[47] S Scarpa, *Trafficking in Human Beings: Modern Slavery* (Oxford, Oxford University Press, 2008) 192.

5.1. Framework Decision on the European Arrest Warrant (EAW)

According to Article 1 of the Framework Decision, the European Arrest Warrant (EAW) is a judicial decision issued by a Member State for the purpose of arresting and surrendering the requested person by another Member State for the purpose of criminal prosecution or execution of a custodial sentence or detention order. The EAW is based on mutual recognition of judgments and a high degree of trust in relations between Member States. It is considered an independent cooperation mechanism distinct from extradition. The procedure is also simpler and quicker.

Article 2(2) provides a list of 32 categories of criminal offences that give rise to surrender without verification of double criminality under certain conditions. The list includes trafficking in human beings, as well as facilitation of unauthorised entry and residence. While there are differences because the definitions of human trafficking in various Member States, they should not prevent the application of the EAW in such cases. Whether or not providing work for illegal migrant can be qualified as facilitation of illegal residence in a Member State will depend strongly on the interpretation of elements of this offence by the Member State in question. The principle of double criminality applies. In Case C-289/15 *Grundza*[48] the ECJ held that

> when assessing double criminality, the competent authority of the executing State is required to verify whether the factual elements underlying the offence, as reflected in the judgment handed down by the competent authority of the issuing State, would also, per se, be subject to a criminal penalty in the executing State if they were present there.[49]

The EAW could be applied for crimes stipulated in the national laws implementing the Sanctions Directive. As far as other crimes against workers' rights are concerned, the tool will be available only if provisions in Member States involved in the procedure are similar. For example, in Polish law, criminal provisions on discrimination are very inconsistent. Discrimination based on being or refusal to be a trade union member constitute a criminal offence (Article 35 of the Polish Trade Union Law), while discrimination against a member of a European works council (EWC), special negotiating body (SNB) or works council is a misdemeanour. At the same time, discrimination on other grounds such as sex, disability or nationality, as well as harassment, are not criminalised at all. In France, discrimination on certain grounds – including sex, nationality, disability, trade union participation or non-participation – is prohibited under Article 225-1 of the Penal Code; and discrimination based on trade union activity or sex is also a misdemeanour, enumerated in the Labour Code (Articles 2141-5 and 1142). In Sweden Article 9 of Chapter 16 of the Criminal Code also provides for penalties for discrimination

[48] CJEU, Case C-289/15 *Joszef Grundza v Krajská prokuratúra Prešov* (2017), ECLI:EU:C:2017:4.
[49] Case C-289/15 *Grundza*, §47.

on various grounds. This shows that, even in such a seemingly simple case, the efficiency of the EAW depends to a large extent on the respective national system.

The data collated by the European Commission on EAWs is based on questionnaires submitted by Member States since 2014. For example, in 2018 the Member States issued around 17,500 EAWs.[50] Some 137 of them were issued in human trafficking cases, with the largest number from France (55) and Hungary (24).[51] The reports allow us only to estimate the number of EAWs, as not all countries sent a response. Nevertheless, it is clear that in practice the EAW tends to be used in human trafficking cases. The data is not detailed enough to show whether the warrants concerned human trafficking for the purpose of work or for other purposes.

5.2. European Investigation Order

The European Investigation Order (EIO),[52] in line with Article 1 clause 1 of the Directive, is a 'judicial decision issued or approved by a judicial authority of one Member State to request another Member State to carry out one or more specific investigative measures in order to obtain evidence in accordance with this Directive'. The definition only shows that the EIO is a request for an investigative measure and its purpose is to obtain evidence. The Directive provides for numerous exceptions to the obligation to execute an EIO. However, it does not lay down any limitations on the seriousness of the offence under investigation. An order can therefore also be issued for offences punishable by a low penalty. It is also used in proceedings related to the liability of legal persons for crimes or violations of the law.

The Directive permits the issue of orders also by the police or other investigating authorities. The body in question must act as an investigative body in the criminal proceedings of the case and be competent to order the gathering of evidence. In such cases a warrant must receive approval from a judicial authority. The approval condition is intended to prevent abuses of the EIO.

It seems that the possibilities of applying this measure in case of a breach of workers' rights are much wider. According to Article 4 of the Directive, EIOs may be issued within the framework of both criminal proceedings and administrative proceedings, where the decision of the administrative body may give rise to proceedings before a court having jurisdiction, in particular, in criminal matters. Again citing the Polish legal system as an example, an EIO could be issued by the

[50] European Commission, Commission Staff Working Document, Replies to questionnaire on quantitative information on the practical operation of the European arrest warrant – Year 2018, SWD(2020) 127 final, https://ec.europa.eu/info/sites/info/files/swd_2020_127_f1_v1_en.pdf.

[51] Ibid.

[52] Because of the narrow scope of application and the small number of implementations, the EEW Framework Decision was repealed by Regulation 2016/95 of the European Parliament and the EU Council of 20 January 2016 on the repeal of certain acts in the field of police and judicial cooperation in criminal matters.

police, the prosecutor's office or the labour inspectorate in cases against workers' rights described in the Criminal Code. Similarly, the police can issue an EIO when investigating crimes related to the law implementing the Sanctions Directive concerning employment of third-country immigrants.

In contrast to the EAW, however, an Investigation Order may also be issued in minor cases, qualified in the Polish legal system as misdemeanours, such as all cases of non-payment of wages, infringements of OSH provisions, or provisions protecting parents at work, working time provisions, misdemeanours stipulated in temporary employment law and many others (the list including misdemeanours against workers' rights includes dozens of legal acts). This could be a useful tool, especially in investigations covering the employment conditions of posted workers or transport workers. Even though the list of evidence that can be obtained is limited, excluding for example, hearing witnesses, it could facilitate trans-border cooperation of the police or courts.

In accordance with Article 4 of the EIO decision, the order may be issued in order to obtain from the executing state objects, documents or data needed in the issuing state for the purposes of criminal proceedings.

In principle, no double criminality is required in relation to the EIO (except for Germany, which explicitly stipulates the double criminality condition in its declaration on the EIO Decision[53]).

6. Perspectives on EU-level Criminal Labour Law Legislation

At the EU level the Lisbon Treaty has opened up two possibilities for harmonising criminal measures. The first is the possibility to establish minimum rules concerning the definition of criminal offences and sanctions by means of Directives adopted in accordance with the ordinary legislative procedure (Article 83.1 TFEU) in case of, for instance, human trafficking.

This article also allows the Council to adopt a decision identifying other areas of crime that meet the criteria of particularly serious crime with a cross-border dimension, resulting from the nature or impact of such offences or from a special need to combat them on a common basis. This could include child labour and forced labour.

Another possibility is provided by Article 83.2 TFEU, which allows for the approximation of criminal laws and regulations of the Member States, if it proves essential to ensure the effective implementation of an EU policy in an area which has been subject to harmonisation measures, such as regulations or Directives based on harmonisation provisions, such as Article 19 TFEU. In such cases, a first Directive is adopted by ordinary or special legislative procedure, and then the

[53] A Serzysko, *Europejski nakaz dowodowy – kwestie implementacyjne (cz 1)* (Palestra, 2011) nos 3–4.

Directives establishing minimum rules with regard to the definition of criminal offences and sanctions. Without any doubt, employment conditions constitute an element of EU policy, so this avenue can also be considered.

Undertaking new initiatives should be preceded by a thorough analysis of current measures implemented by the Member States and their efficiency. The latter might be more difficult in practice, especially because the qualification of the measure as criminal does not necessarily mean that it is more severe or dissuasive. In this regard, the solution adopted to guarantee efficient implementation of the EWC Directive in Polish law could serve as a negative example. Article 39.1 of the law on EWCs stipulates a type of misdemeanour described as preventing the establishment of an EWC or an SNB or inhibiting the operation of these bodies, as well as inhibiting information and consultation procedures. These acts are punished by a fine of 20–5,000 PLN (approximately €4.50–€1,111). Even if the fine can be adjusted within this scope to the size of the enterprise and/or the number of workers affected, it can by no means be qualified as an efficient or dissuasive sanction. The effectiveness, proportionality and dissuasive character of criminal sanctions introduced by other Member States was also questioned, even though in some countries they constitute a criminal offence,[54] especially financial penalties. Even at the higher end, they are unlikely to deter companies from breaching the law and their own agreements.[55]

Given the lack of success of proper implementation illustrated above, it should be considered whether a certain level of harmonisation is possible. First of all, not all breaches of labour law should be qualified as a criminal offence or misdemeanour, and above all pecuniary penalties may be more effective than imprisonment, especially in micro or small enterprises, where without the owner, the functioning of the company could be endangered.

The level of fines should also reflect the size or income of the company and/or the number of workers affected. Otherwise, ostensibly low fines will not have an effect, but rather bring the system into disrepute. On the other hand, approximation of criminal provisions in the employment area allows for the use of EU criminal procedures, such as the European Investigation Order.

Another issue to consider is the responsibility of legal persons, even given the large disparities between Member States in this area. This is particularly important for labour law, as infringements may have a systemic character, stemming from company policy (for example, cost-saving and inefficient occupational safety and health measures) or management practice (avoiding direct employment in favour of subcontracting).

[54] R Jagodziński and P Lorber, 'Enforcement frameworks and employees' rights of access to enforcement' in R Jagodziński (ed), *Variations on a theme? The implementation of the EWC Recast Directive* (Brussels, ETUI, 2015) 156.

[55] R Jagodziński, 'Conclusions', in Jagodziński, above n 54 at 189–90. The book also provides detailed analysis of the enforcement measures applied.

7. Conclusions

At the national level, criminal measures can be applied to enforce workers' rights. The extent to which national criminal law penalises acts against workers' rights will differ from one Member State to another. Some Member States have well-developed criminal labour law systems (such as Belgium or France), while in others criminal sanctions will be applied only in the most severe cases, such as forced labour or human trafficking. To the extent that criminal law assists the weaker party, regulations are likely to have presumptive legitimacy from a labour law perspective. Perhaps even further expansion of the criminal law might be valuable in certain contexts, as with accessory liability for lead companies in supply chains, a new offence of wage fraud, criminal liability for blacklisting and other human rights abuses.[56] At present, the data on prosecutions appears to show that the degree of criminal enforcement is very low.[57]

There are also arguments against criminalisation of labour law. The costs of criminal enforcement may be too high and criminalisation may be disproportionate in light of the magnitude and extent of the wrong.[58] Criminalisation may also be used as a distraction from the more fundamental question of how to achieve compliance.[59] From the workers' perspective, devolution of control over enforcement to the state also carries the risk that the relevant prosecution officials decide not to take action, for one reason or another.[60]

It should be taken into account that establishing criminal sanctions should not be an aim in itself; as long as other (civil, administrative) measures are sufficient, criminal sanctions should remain the *ultima ratio* solution. The legislator should also be very diligent while establishing elements of the crime: if they are too narrow or specific, their use may be limited. But if they are too broadly set or too general, it may infringe the *nulla poena sine lege scripta* principle, which is a basic human right.

Another aspect that must be considered is the execution of sanctions and the role of labour inspection in criminal proceedings.[61] Solutions applied by Member States will differ significantly, depending on the role and character of labour inspection, as well as criminal procedure. If the police or prosecutor's offices are to deal with acts against workers' rights they need to receive appropriate and thorough training; in particular, application of criminal law in this area usually requires proficient knowledge of labour law. Labour inspectors, by the nature of their profession, are well qualified in the area and aware of the specificity of

[56] A Bogg and M Freedland, above n 13 at 29, 30.

[57] C Barnard and S Fraser Butlin, above n 5 at 90. This conclusion is true for the UK but also for Poland; J Unterschütz, above n 37.

[58] D Cabrelli, above n 3 at 64.

[59] C Barnard and S Fraser Butlin, above n 5 at 71.

[60] D Cabrelli, above n 3 at 64.

[61] The role of labour inspection in the enforcement of OSH provisions is further discussed in Chapter 15.

employment conditions in different types of companies and sectors, but they do not always have the competence to prosecute even misdemeanours. In any case, both labour inspectors and the prosecutor's office need adequate financial and human resources.

Where regulatory criminalisation is supported through adequate public resourcing of enforcement agencies, and where this leads to higher levels of employer compliance, it can be an important tool of enforcement in the field of labour regulation.[62]

[62] A Bogg and M Freedland, above n 13 at 29.

6

Soft Methods of Enforcement of European Labour Law Standards

CSILLA KOLLONAY-LEHOCZKY

1. Introduction

In customary legal thinking the term 'enforcement' is associated with coercion. That being so, 'soft enforcement' is something of an oxymoron. This chapter attempts to explain and demonstrate that this is not the case. Indeed, so-called 'soft' methods may achieve more stable results than traditional forms of enforcement, such as civil litigation, administrative or criminal sanctions.

The concepts of 'force' and 'soft' might seem to be opposites. However, if 'effective enforcement' is identified predominantly with compliance with existing norms, and the desired outcome is that labour law standards prevail in everyday employment relationships, the concept of 'enforcement' need not have a hard-coercive content.

In order to justify the place of 'soft enforcement' of labour standards in the legal world this chapter addresses enforcement in a broader sense. Achieving compliance with standards, implementation or application, if achieved, might be considered to constitute enforcement.[1] Methods are regarded as 'soft' if compliance is achieved through ways and methods different from reactive sanctions, such as remedial or penal procedures initiated before judicial or administrative organs in response to infringements of rights, violations. Soft measures are based rather on prevention, persuasion or establishing compliance as a social norm, perhaps supported by incentives for voluntary compliance, collaborative forms of dispute settlement or cooperative restitution, if necessary.

[1] In the literature 'application', 'implementation' and 'enforcement' are repeatedly used interchangeably, not incorrectly. At the same time, the separation of the two, with special regard to the distinction from national-level 'implementation' of EU-level norms may justify the distinction.

Labour rights and duties are laid down by both hard and soft law instruments. The term 'soft law enforcement' may have a double meaning. It is understood generally as meaning soft procedures for enforcing hard regulations, on one hand, and setting and fulfilling soft standards, on the other. The two types of procedures (norm-setting and norm-enforcing) are closely interrelated, and it is difficult and barely even worth trying to separate them. 'Soft mechanisms' of enforcement are able to achieve compliance not only with soft, but also hard laws, in some cases more effectively in the long term than judicial forms of enforcement. For this reason, even if the emphasis is on soft law implementation, the subject matter of 'soft' enforcement relates to the achievement of compliance with standards included in either hard or soft legal regulations.

One of the difficulties involved in presenting the problem is that effective enforcement, when achieved in a soft way, happens without noticeable signs or symptoms at individual level, especially in the short term.[2] It is noticeable in the long term, however, at statistical level. Successful enforcement through litigation or administrative sanction is noticeable in individual cases, when a procedure restores the standard and grants a remedy. However, effective enforcement in its broadest meaning would mean long-term, effective group realisation and compliance. Successful cure of a disease is visible, successful prevention and maintenance of health is not spectacular.

2. Concepts – Soft Law and Soft Enforcement

2.1. The Term 'Soft Law'

In international law, the broad term 'soft law' was first used in the 1980s.[3] In European law, however, the phenomenon even if not under this name – can be traced back to 1962.[4] The term indicates in part the content (soft obligations), in part the form (resolutions, recommendations, codes of conduct) and also the ways of enforcement (various follow-up agencies and monitoring bodies, negotiations and other alternative ways of settling disputes). The Vienna Convention on the Law of Treaties defines the term 'treaty' (ie its scope) without any right or obligation between states;[5] nevertheless the 'binding' nature of treaties is implied. The

[2] A simile might be mentioned here: successful medication is held to be 'effective enforcement' of health. Healthy ways of living or successful prevention of sickness are not regarded as 'successful medication'.

[3] RR Baxter, 'International Law in "Her Infinite Variety"' (1980) 29(4) *International and Comparative Law Quarterly* 549–66.

[4] So-called 'Christmas notices' in commercial law are referred to as the first soft law sources. L Senden and S Prechal, 'Differentiation in and through European Soft Law' in B de Witte, D Hanf and E Vos (eds), *The Many Faces of Differentiaton in European Law* (Intersentia, 2001) 181.

[5] See Art 2 VCLT.

rich literature on soft law[6] reflects non-abating disputes rather than consensus on the meaning or a coherent definition. Besides labelling the concept as heterogeneous, multi-layered and highly mixed, it is defined in the negative, by its missing attributes: lack of clear-cut normative content, lack of binding power and lack of enforcement mechanisms.[7]

Soft law is repeatedly seen as one end of a continuum either in a temporal or a substantive sense. The 'pre-law' approach considers that soft law is in the process of becoming hard law, although it is preceded by a process of 'incubation' in developing towards the state of hard law.[8] The various 'hybridity' approaches comprise a substantive mix of soft and hard law in European governance, in particular in the context of the Europe 2020 strategy and the European Semester.[9]

While acknowledging that 'there is no black-and-white contrast but rather manifold transitions both from hard law to soft law and from soft law to hard law',[10] traditional legal theory qualifies soft law as non-law, which nevertheless may have practical effects or may lead to legal effects. In international law (the birthplace of soft law), doubts and sharp categorisation call into question the power of soft law (documents issued by treaty-bodies), to the point of considering these declarations and 'far-reaching requirements' as 'wishful thinking', on the basis of the reactions of governments.[11]

The term is now used widely, in business, company and banking law, as well as labour and social law, consumer law and environmental law. We see an extraordinary abundance of broadly formulated norms, expressing policy requirements and guiding principles, located between law and ethics influencing compliance in correspondence to these 'locations'.

[6] To mention a few recent pieces referred to in the writing of this chapter: S Lagouette, *UN Guiding Principles on Business and Human Rights*; KW Abbott and D Snidal, 'Hard and Soft Law in International Governance' (2000) 54(3) *International Organization* 412–56; CM Chinkin, *The Challenge of Soft Law: Development and Change in International Law* (Cambridge University Press, 2008); E Pariotti, 'International Soft Law, Human Rights and Non-state Actors: Towards the Accountability of Transnational Corporations' (2009) 10 *Human Rights Revue* 139–55; AT Guzman and TL Meyer, 'International Soft Law' (Spring 2010) 2 *Journal of Legal Analysis* 171.

[7] Pariotti, n 6 above, 145; Lagouette, *UN Guiding Principles on Business and Human Rights*. It must be added at the outset that there are 'realist' opinions in international law that do not see, in the absence of a genuinely independent judiciary with supporting enforcement powers, a sharp difference between instruments labelled 'hard' and 'soft'. See Abbott and Snidal, n 6 at 422.

[8] J Cerone, 'A taxonomy of soft law' in S Lagoutte, T Gammeltoft-Hansen and J Cerone (eds), *Tracing the Roles of Soft Law in Human Rights* (Oxford University Press, 2017).

[9] B Vanhercke, 'From the Lisbon strategy to the European Pillar of Social Rights: the many lives of the Social Open Method of Coordination' in B Vanhercke, D Ghailani and S Spaso, with P Pochet (eds), *Social Policy in the European Union 1999–2019: the long and winding road* (Brussels, ETUI–OSE, 2020), referring to DM Trubek and LG Trubek, 'New Governance and Legal Regulation: Complementarity, Rivalry and Transformation' (2007) 13 *Columbia Journal of European Law* 539, 543; see also: O Stefan, 'Hybridity before the Court: A Hard Look at Soft Law in the EU Competition and State Aid Case Law' (2012) 37(49) *European Law Reports* 62–64.

[10] A Nussberger, 'Hard Law or Soft Law – Does it Matter? Distinction Between Different Sources of International Law in the Jurisprudence of the ECtHR' in A van Aaken and I Motoc (eds), *The European Convention on Human Rights and General International Law* (Oxford University Press, 2018) 42–43.

[11] Ibid, 47.

The connection with international law (international private law) is attributed to its origin in *'lex mercatoria'* – a form of custom, unwritten law, produced and enforced on a voluntary basis. It is something 'transnational', separate from the power of national states, that gradually crystallised into formal rules with different legal force. This ancient, historical predecessor has relevance here for two reasons. First, because of the value of looking at those non-state-made forms of industry norms and guidelines, model contracts, standard clauses guaranteed by custom and community commitment, realised and observed without formal state power or state intervention. Second, the intertwining of labour and entrepreneurial relations behind the operation of those ancient forms of '*societas*' – one historical precursor of labour law – can also offer ideas for new, interim models of work and its relations to property and the market.

The recent rapid spread of regulatory methods labelled 'soft' is a natural consequence of the challenges imposed by globalisation: competition for investment, social dumping and consequent regulatory competition.[12]

Another phenomenon, also connected to globalisation, namely the growing presence of non-state actors, has been mentioned as a driving force behind the growing emergence of soft law. Both factors – globalisation and the presence of non-state actors – have significance for labour law. The distorted competition brought about by globalisation, the pressure on governments for deregulation, leading to a 'race to the bottom' in labour law (together with other fields of law, importantly with company law, even environmental law to some extent, which seemed to be immune to regulatory competition[13]) are associated with the emergence of multinational companies as non-state actors and their increasing control over labour standards. The idea of a 'new *lex mercatoria*' has emerged, abandoning the idea of the state as 'the exclusive horizon for law-making and law legitimation', changing governments' attitudes toward 'self-organised institutions of society'.[14] The need for a parallel increasing role for 'non-state actors' on the opposite side – civil organisations (NGOs) and organisations of industrial parties (trade unions and employers' associations) – led to moves for non-traditional forms and applications of regulation.

2.2. Meanings of Enforcement: Effective Enforcement, Soft Enforcement

The concept of enforcement (disputed in broad terms, similar to the concept of soft law) is not separable from realisation of the goals of regulatory instruments; that

[12] O Ştefan, 'Soft Law and the Enforcement of EU Law' in A Jakab and D Kochenov (eds), *The Enforcement of EU Law and Values. Ensuring Member States' Compliance* (Oxford University Press, 2017) 200.

[13] FW Scharpf, *Governing in Europe – Effective and Democratic* (Oxford University Press, 1998) 98, 106–08. Here EU integration has had an effect.

[14] Pariotti, 141, quoting H-J Mertens, 'Lex mercatoria: A self-applying system beyond national law?' in G Teubner (ed), *Global law without a state* (Aldershot, Dartmouth, 1997) 40.

is, compliance with the standards laid down in a regulation. This brings into focus two elements: first, the distinction between the substantive and procedural side or meaning of 'enforcement', and second, the distinction between the imminent and the more distant goals of regulation.

From a procedural point of view, some theories locate enforcement 'between compliance and deterrence',[15] along a scale of possible attitudes and available instruments. Views in the literature on compliance (particularly in the EU context) claim that 'compliance is the more generic term', compared to 'enforcement', with more specific, coercive content.[16] This distinction also reflects the separation of the procedural and the substantive elements, similar to the notional overlap and difference between 'implementation' and 'enforcement'.[17]

Thus, in substantive terms enforcement means compliance with the standards, realisation of the goals behind the regulatory instruments, regardless of the process – soft or coercive – to achieving compliance.

The substantive question 'with what must compliance be secured?'[18] takes us further to the distinction between 'mere' compliance with concrete norms, and compliance 'with the collective goals underpinning a regulatory scheme'.[19] Looking from this more substantive and more distant point of view at the concept of 'effective enforcement', its 'goals' and results, the distinction shows its importance. Single successful cases of litigation or other procedures do not necessarily lead to the realisation of higher, collective goals.[20] When this is the case, what do we mean by 'effective enforcement'?

In summary: implementation and compliance is the goal, and the ways and means to it (soft or coercive) are 'effective', if and when the goal is achieved. Compliance not only in successful individual cases, but at collective level as a stable floor of daily operations, creating relations at the workplace based on justice and democracy.

2.2.1. Approach to 'Effectiveness': Group-wide and Effective over Time

Access to court, successful litigation achieving restoration, full remedies, or punitive procedures are held to be the primary category of 'effective enforcement'.[21] If effective enforcement is identified with stable compliance, it is not yet guaranteed in these primary forms.

[15] Ştefan, n 12 at 203.

[16] M Cremona (ed), *Compliance and Enforcement of EU Law* (Oxford University Press, 2012), Introduction, iv.

[17] S Andersen, *The Functional Overlap of Enforcement and Implementation Tools.*

[18] K Yeung, *Securing Compliance – A Principled Approach* (Hart, 2004) 11.

[19] Ibid.

[20] Yeung, n 18; Stefan, n 12 at 203.

[21] See among others: B Philine ter Haar and P Copeland, 'What are the Future Prospects for the European Social Model? An Analysis of EU Equal Opportunities and Employment Policy' (May 2010) 16(3) *European Law Journal* 284.

First, 'courts are reactive institutions': other actors have to bring their problems to them.[22] These are frequently weaker parties. Second, successful individual cases leave open the probability that the rights of many others will be violated. True, such cases may have an impact toward effective enforcement by the preventive power of the successful procedures. The deterrent impact of 'litigation risk' is stronger in the case of wide social publicity of the judgments, but at least among the relevant groups of rights-holders and those obliged.[23] Enforcement therefore can be deemed 'effective' if it goes beyond individual cases, and if observation of the standard is long-term and a collective reality for those entitled to have labour conditions corresponding to the standard.

Evidently such an enforcement goal needs a complex and long way, gradual progress and a technique comprising hard and soft law norms and enforcement methods. The 'hybridity' of regulation, especially in European law, is reflected in the hybrid mechanism of enforcement in procedural terms.[24]

The opinion suggesting that 'instead of focusing on enforcement a better perspective will be obtained by looking at the wider compliance picture … including normative and social motivations and rules awareness'[25] reflects this broader approach. The view of the different aspects of the European Social Model, featured as 'a mixture of hard law, soft law and underlying norms and values' emphasises that soft instruments – such as persuasion through public pressure by 'naming, shaming and blaming' – although less strong, legally 'are not necessarily less effective', underlining that 'it makes more sense' to assess the impact of the instruments 'over time than at one single moment'.[26]

From these approaches it might be concluded that effective enforcement – meaning prevalent or full compliance with labour law standards – is a collective, social concept, a result of progress that can be achieved by a combination of soft and hard methods alternating their parallel and sequential application.

2.2.2. Softness and Effectiveness

The advantages and contribution of non-constraining, non-judiciable mechanisms to the goal of progressing toward effective enforcement demonstrate the need for the dual method – soft and hard – to achieve compliance.

Yeung sees the enforcement mechanism as a pyramid, in a hierarchical fashion, involving even a cost/benefit trade-off in regulatory compliance. Starting with soft methods, the most numerous, timely and least costly mechanisms are at the

[22] L Conant, 'Compliance and What EU Member States Make of It' in Cremona (2012), n 11 at 11.

[23] This 'enforcement effect' is prevented by a general lack of publicity, and attention to the rulings of other domestic courts impedes prompt resolution of claims and results in similar cases being decided differently. Ibid, 28.

[24] Stefan, n 12 at 203.

[25] Ibid at 204.

[26] Ter Haar and Copeland, n 21 at 284. Referring also to D Shelton (ed), *Commitment and compliance: the role of non-binding norms in the international legal system* (Oxford University Press, 2000).

base of the pyramid. 'As the pyramid ascends the sanctions become increasingly severe in terms of their legal coercive and deterrent effect on the regulated and the cost involved to both the regulator and regulated.'[27]

The participatory forms of soft law-making have a significant informative role, implying values (such as transparency, legal certainty).[28] The forms of common discourse, meetings, networks and partnership forms can have broader sociological functions,[29] all potentially contributing to compliance without coercion. Participation of marginalised groups may also contribute to the sociological impact, letting them achieve results otherwise (especially through hard law) not available for them.[30]

Such forms can couple with morally, politically or socially binding force; furthermore, emotional factors are also mentioned by related research,[31] which can promote or ensure compliance with the law. Such factors can be effective either as negative (fear of shame or court procedures, or losing an advantage) or positive motivation (respect for authority, pleasure in compliance, empathy or public approval); the common result is compliance without coercive measures.[32]

The benefits of the proactive and collective (group) or social nature of soft methods (in contrast to the reactive and individual ways of administrative or court procedures), as well as the goal of long-term, stable compliance make soft methods and the dual approach to enforcement useful and even indispensable.

3. Multilevel and Historical Context of Soft Enforcement of Labour Law

3.1. Multilevel Context

Soft methods of enforcement of labour standards have a multilevel context: global, regional, national and company levels of origin and enforcement of labour law norms. This simple hierarchical view is complicated by the horizontal relations between actors, as well as by the distinct nature of norms: international human rights norms, on one hand, and national or supranational legislative acts, on the other. This complex web underlines the need and implies the space for soft methods of converting norms into practice.

[27] Yeung, n 18 at 161.

[28] For a comprehensive elaboration of such advantages see: L Senden, *Soft Law in European Community Law* (Oxford, Hart Publishing, 2004), ch 5 'Categories and Functions of Soft law', esp section 5.6.3, pp 224–28.

[29] J Zeitlin and B Vanhercke, 'Socializing the European Semester? Economic Governance and Social Policy Coordination in Europe 2020' (2014) 7 *Swedish Institute for European Policy Studies* 58–60.

[30] Stefan, n 12 at 206.

[31] Stefan, ibid.

[32] Stefan, n 12 at 205.

The arms or branches of EU labour law reach upward in living connection to its global framework at EU level, and reach downward when implemented at national and sectoral level, in the system of vertical and horizontal relations between the EU, the Member States' national legal systems and the social partners. It is put into reality at the ground level of individual employers, an important domain for the role of soft methods. In the process of globalisation, the changing web of actors and regulatory instruments offers a broadening variety of implementation schemes, connecting global norms with company-level application of EU standards, as well as increasing the role of soft methods in the process of transposition. The tripartite regulations of the ILO, as developed, and the considerable amount of soft law jurisprudence built up by supervisory bodies,[33] lays down the basis for labour standards for the world, including Europe. Compliance with these standards creates a favourable background for the fulfilment of EU labour law goals.

For our subject, the EU–ILO relationship represents a strategic partnership of active cooperation, resulting in the promotion of compliance with labour law norms in a soft and progressive way. This partnership has contributed, among other things, to the ratification not only of the eight core ILO conventions, but also a number of other priority or major documents.[34] The evident mutual interest in the Member States' compliance with ILO standards, and in promoting the strategic objectives of the Decent Work agenda has already resulted in a number of initiatives, work projects, and cooperation activities, including active EU participation in the adoption of new international labour standards and their implementation, promoted in the Member States.[35]

The EU also acts by supporting transnational projects aimed at strengthening the capacity of social partner organisations in Europe (with special attention to new and candidate Member States[36]), in relation to projects aimed at enhancing the capacity of tripartite constituents and other stakeholders in underdeveloped countries to advocate for the promotion and implementation of international labour standards.

At European level there are two regional systems for setting and enforcing labour standards: the international instruments of the Council of Europe (the European Social Charter first, but also the European Human Rights Convention),[37] and the supranational legal order of the EU. A distinction might also be drawn between the 'human rights system' and the 'economic integration system'.

[33] Expressing the returning scepticism in international law concerning the legal nature of these bodies and documents, according to A Nussberger, n 10 at 45, these are 'addressed as "jurisprudence"'.

[34] Such as the Convention on Labour Inspection (ratified by all Member States), and the maritime and fishing industry documents still to be mentioned.

[35] See: www.ilo.org/wcmsp5/groups/public/---ed_dialogue/---dialogue/documents/meetingdocument/wcms_663780.pdf.

[36] ILO, *The ILO and the EU, partners for decent work and social justice. Impact of ten years of cooperation* (ILO, 2012), www.ilo.org/wcmsp5/groups/public/---europe/---ro-geneva/---ilo-brussels/documents/publication/wcms_195135.pdf, 12.

[37] ECHR, Convention on the Protection of Human Rights and Fundamental Freedoms.

Cooperation between the Council of Europe and the EU could not reach the level of the EU–ILO partnership, although there is no difference between the global and regional-level international human rights systems regarding legal nature and status. Nonetheless, and despite the EU's reserved stance, there is an apparent and gradually increasing interaction between the 'two Europes' in terms of the impact of Council of Europe standards on the enforcement of EU labour law. (For more on this, see below, in section 6 on the European Social Charter.)

Capacity-building at international, European and national level potentially influences national-level implementation. The regulatory power of the state has been joined or replaced by that of the industrial parties on the basis of horizontal subsidiarity, depending on the social partners' power. These hard rules, implementing EU labour law and adopted by agreement, are enforced predominantly through soft means and procedures.

At institutional and enterprise level a combination of the increasing impact of global competition, and regional and national policies frame the available methods of promoting compliance. This tendency has established a specific connection between the global and company levels when it comes to respect for labour standards. The existence of cross-border production chains provoked the abovementioned EU-ILO cooperation efforts, whose aims included, beyond international goals, preserving fair and decent working conditions in the EU, among other things by making it harder for multinational companies to engage in a race to the bottom in Europe.

The recent Commission document on the promotion of decent work[38] is a clear declaration of EU–UN (ILO) partnership and a readiness to promote a resilient recovery from the Covid-19 crisis worldwide through flexible and soft measures.

3.2. Historical Context

Soft law has enjoyed elevated significance in the context of European labour law from its foundations. It is rooted in the inherently soft idea of the 'harmonisation' and 'approximation' of social systems under Articles 117 and 118 of the Rome Treaty, foreseen as taking place essentially without direct intervention in Member State legal systems.

Soft methods have a prominent role in the progressive shaping of national regulations and 'keeping the flock together', but also in achieving hard forms of European rules. The legislative steps – importantly, Treaty amendments – started when it became clear that the expectation that market freedom and free movement would automatically lead to upward harmonisation of working and living

[38] SWD (2020) 235 final Promote Decent Work Worldwide Responsible Global Value Chains for a Fair, Sustainable and Resilient Recovery from the COVID-19 Crisis (Brussels, 20.10.2020).

conditions was misplaced. This was coupled with the mid-1970s recession that led to the first labour law Directives.[39] Two features might be mentioned here: first, their direct aim was to protect fair competition, one basis for establishing an EU competence to regulate; second, their implementation required strong employee participation, which boosted soft methods.

The goals of the European Social Model[40] – the promotion of employment, improved living and working conditions, social security and social protection, dialogue between management and labour – gained impetus with the 1992 Maastricht Treaty (and its Social Protocol) and generated further legislative and governmental steps to construct today's European labour law.

Looking into the history of this process, three phases can be distinguished in the development of the European Social Model (and European labour law within it). Each of them are hybrids of hard and soft methods of governance. This was necessitated by the limited regulatory power and continuing uncertainties about the competences of the EU in social and employment matters, especially labour standards.

The three phases comprise roughly one decade each.

3.2.1. *The European Employment Strategy – the 1990s*

The 1990s were defined by the SEA innovations (1986) and post-Maastricht efforts, interwoven with post-1989 enthusiasm over the reunification of Europe. The moves in this decade – relying on extended legislative power in labour and social matters – initiated the European Social Model (ESM) and also the European Employment Strategy (EES).[41]

The aim of coordinating labour market policy put the emphasis on the role of dialogue between social partners and political actors. Guidance in achieving strategic labour market goals was provided by quantified targets, detailed timetables, monitoring and evaluating the effectiveness of employment policies in accordance with common statistical indicators and benchmarks. Without mentioning 'soft' methods, the goal was to achieve the adjustment of national employment policies by consultation, dialogue and cooperation, and a commitment on the part of the Member States.

[39] Council Directive 75/129/EEC on the approximation of the laws of the Member States relating to collective redundancies, Council Directive 77/187/EEC on the approximation of the laws of the Member States relating to the safeguarding of employees' rights in the event of transfers of undertakings, businesses or parts of businesses, and to some extent Council Directive 80/987/EEC on the approximation of the laws of the Member States relating to the protection of employees in the event of the insolvency of their employer.

[40] The beginning of the European Social Model is dated to the early 1990s (by some, even earlier, to the 1986 Single European Act), which is surely inseparable from the progressive Delors Commission. The White Paper on European Social Policy (COM (94) 333) is usually highlighted, and opinions diverge regarding its origin and nature. See ter Haar and Copeland, n 21 at 274.

[41] Based on the recommendations of the European Council Meeting in Essen 1994, introduced by the 1997 Luxemburg Summit issuing the first Employment Guidelines for national employment policies.

3.2.2. *The 'Lisbon Strategy' (2000–10)*

Building on earlier experience of the EES, the institutionalised turn of the European Union to 'soft governance' was launched by the introduction and political approval of the Open Method of Coordination (OMC) in 2000 as part of the Lisbon Strategy. Its declared goal was to promote social protection and social inclusion through effective social policies, including employment policies. The implementation of that goal rendered applicable a host of so-called 'soft' methods of achieving convergence towards EU goals in the relevant area. These (besides guidelines with timetables and NAPs) established indicators and benchmarks, and now relied on best practices as a means of comparison, setting specific targets, periodic monitoring, evaluation and peer review, organised as mutual learning processes.

Despite criticisms of the OMC – in part because of its 'non-legal' (non-binding) nature, emphasising persuasion rather than coercion, and also its supposed lack of efficiency – its results were acknowledged. It was recognised that methods of new governance and soft law can result in transformations in the behaviour and practices of the Member States and the institutions: 'formally non-binding agreements can gradually become politically, socially, and morally binding for the actors involved'.[42]

3.2.3. *The EU-2020 Strategy (2010–20)*

The decade of the EU-2020 Strategy – labelled the period of the 'European Semester' and 'country specific reports' – is the third of the three stages of the emergence of soft instruments of social and employment policy. To achieve its targets – among others, the setting and application of established standards in employment and labour relations – it combined mandatory regulation with dialogue and cooperation. It did not abandon the soft methods of open coordination, but rather reactivated them within the framework of the European Semester, country reports and Country Specific Recommendations, together with a number of earlier techniques for influencing activity towards common goals.

The three periods have built on each other, advancing and extending the methods developed in the previous period. If some slight differentiation could be made, then the stronger employment orientation of the EES might be mentioned, the experimental-cooperative feature of the OMC, and the more hierarchical system of the EU-2020 strategy.

Results of the three decades can be detected from various sources, accidentally or through systematic research. A clear account at EU level is missing, however. Regular 'Reviews of Progress' provide significant information, although on planned targets and intentions rather than on concrete results or progress. Further and

[42] Stefan, n 12 at 205.

more detailed data and information on outcomes, verifying the beneficial impact of the predominantly soft methods, may promote progress in the next steps.

The 2017 adoption of the European Pillar of Social Rights (EPSR) opened a new period in social and employment strategies, while at the same time representing an organic continuation of the EU-2020 strategy. Its 20 principles aim to set up a balance between 'fair working conditions' (included in Chapter II) and the other two branches (labour market and social protection) of a just and inclusive social policy. The 4 March 2021 European Pillar of Social Rights Action Plan of the Council and the Commission[43] confirms such potential for labour law standards in the next phase of development.[44]

4. Development of Soft Methods in Successive Periods of European Governance

In this section we shall provide an overview of the expansion of soft methods during the abovementioned three phases of development of social Europe. Remarkably, this development has taken place in parallel with the extension of EU legislative competence in employment matters, confirming that the two are not in an either/or relationship, but rather interact toward common goals.

4.1. Parallel Growth of Legal Competence and Soft Methods

Both European labour law and soft law have grown from the 'seed' of Articles 117–18 of the Rome Treaty. Article 118 delineated the subject area of the 'social field' as an intended area of integration, equalisation and upward harmonisation. Reading the list of 'social' matters, we see almost exclusively labour law issues: employment, labour legislation and working conditions, occupational and continuation training, social security, protection against occupational accidents and diseases, industrial hygiene, the law on trade unions, and collective bargaining between employers and workers.

The words of the Treaty clearly anticipated soft approximation (even if it was not termed as such): upward harmonisation almost automatically through 'collaboration' of the Member States, promoted by the Commission through 'close contact with Member States by means of studies, the issuing of opinions, and the organising of consultations'.[45]

[43] See: https://ec.europa.eu/commission/presscorner/detail/en/ip_21_820.
[44] See: Pillar_factsheet_4Mar_EN.pdf, 18–20.
[45] Art 118.

What followed afterwards is reminiscent of a *pas de deux* between soft and hard methods, shifting and mixing their steps, helping and holding each other, while moving ahead continuously, arriving at today's complex toolbox of 'European social law'. This comprises extended legislative competences in labour law, while turning the focus of 'governance' towards social (employment, poverty, social security) matters, establishing close interaction between them. Because some taboos remain (hopefully not for ever), therefore leaving serious gaps in legislative competence, this has maintained the strong significance of 'governance' methods and soft instruments in achieving the regulation and adequate protection of European labour standards in the Member States.

The doors to using binding legal instruments were opened by the 1986 Single European Act, taken over by the Maastricht Treaty that extended legislative power to the 'working environment', permitting the mandatory adoption of minimal requirements.[46]

The goals attached to the European Social Model – promotion of employment, improved living and working conditions, social security and social protection, dialogue between management and labour, development of human resources, combating exclusion – required not only the smart extension of EU regulatory power, but also the use of a variety of soft methods to realise the proclaimed policy goals. These methods – presented in more detail below – can be summarised as various forms of guided vertical and horizontal communication: rounds of exchanges of goals/plans, reports, evaluations (vertical, between the EU and Member States), exchanges of information, peer reviews and spreading best practices (horizontal, between Member States or their institutions). The principles and main procedures, although launched in different phases of the development of the European Social Model, have remained constant in the EU and now constitute part of the European Semester.

The European Employment Guidelines have to be mentioned as the main strategic instrument, issued regularly from the advent of the European Employment Strategy,[47] a permanent element of social coordination up to the present time. Its gradually changing focus is an indicator of changes in the concept of a 'social field'. The Guidelines aimed strongly at a favourable workplace environment in terms of stable employment (also a market balance issue), but labour conditions as such were handled separately from the strategic targets.

The Amsterdam Treaty has achieved the needed broadening of regulatory mandates in employment and social policy, including the labour law targets.[48] The new regulatory framework, coupled with the policy and government potential

[46] Treaty of Rome (amended), Art 118a(1).

[47] Based on the recommendations of the European Council Meeting in Essen, 1994, introduced by the 1997 Luxemburg Summit, issuing the first Employment Guidelines for national employment policies.

[48] Equal treatment and the health and safety agenda might be mentioned, with an impact on further labour conditions.

developing within the European Employment Strategy, became part of the building of the Lisbon Strategy.

The Open Method of Coordination was adopted at the March 2000 Lisbon European Council meeting as a new policy and coordination tool for achieving common policy targets. It was identified by (and celebrated for) its 'soft' methods of governance and coordination of the relevant activities of the Member States. Its primary target area remained the European Employment Strategy, joined by a number of others, including social inclusion and pensions, indirectly connected to labour standards, either as causes or results, although not directly in the focus of the common European objectives.

The OMC has come to be identified with various forms of guided communications between EU and national actors, recorded as the main forms of 'soft law'. The idea of peer review of national reports was aimed at fostering mutual learning toward common goals. Similarly, sharing data, comparisons and discussion of each other's good practices supposedly promotes learning and transmission of experiences. While not denying the potential advantages, the low impact on national practices was disappointing. Another novelty of the Lisbon Strategy, flexicurity – adopted as a 'crucial element in modernising the EU's labour market' – was part of the 2007 Employment Strategy.[49] Promising 'reliable and flexible' working conditions, it led to a decline in job security without adequate compensating security measures. Running into the 2008–09 financial and economic crisis, it contributed to disappointment with the novelties of the Lisbon programme.

4.2. 'Europe 2020 Strategy': The European Semester and Country Specific Recommendations

This new governance strategy, introduced in 2010, has not abandoned the soft methods of open coordination, but has rather reactivated them. As a means of achieving its goals a new form of communication was invented, the system of the European Semester and the Country Specific Recommendations (CSRs), all based on non-legal means. The application of a scoreboard of economic indicators and in-depth country reviews, as well as recommendations helped to keep cooperation between national and EU actors on an organised track. Financial sanctions for repeated non-compliance are possible,[50] but the Commission turned rather to incentives.

It marked employment and social issues as a subject of coordination and cooperation. The strategic goals included under the heading of 'employment' as a

[49] Council conclusions on the common principles of flexicurity (November 2007), https://ec.europa.eu/social/main.jsp?catId=102&langId=en.

[50] A Verdun and J Zeitlin, 'The European Semester – Country Specific Recommendations address important issues but need better implementation' (ND) 25 *Journal of European Public Policy* 137.

key target[51] were aimed primarily at increasing employment, with accompanying measures.

The detailed information available on the content of the CSRs in the 2011–14 period[52] shows that the recommendations on labour and employment were related almost exclusively to labour market matters, especially increasing employment. Surveillance of labour standards was not in focus. The statistics of the CSR recommendations reflect the same result. Efforts with 'employment' as a key target were made almost exclusively through labour market policies, employment services and the unemployment benefit system. The recommendation 'to combat labour market segmentation by revising employment protection legislation and contractual arrangements' sounds promising for labour standards, particularly those at the margins of the labour market. However, these recommendations under the headings 'combating segmentation' and 'aimed at increasing labour market flexibility', with little emphasis on transition to permanent employment,[53] decreased rather than increased job security.

A change in the text of the Guidelines (on the functioning of labour markets and social dialogue) in 2018 and even more in 2020 (nos 5 and 7) shows a positive change, emphasising the general requirement to foster a transition towards open-ended forms of employment, an appropriate level of job security, and healthy, safe and well-adapted working environments for workers.[54]

Looking at the methods for guiding national systems towards the set goals, it has been found that the European Semester and the CSRs on employment became more prescriptive, abandoning the earlier focus of new economic governance on experimental policy learning between states.[55] While several actors see the procedure rather as enforcement of compliance than as 'learning',[56] it was also confirmed that cooperative methods and mutual learning were more efficient. The socialisation function of surveillance of the CSRs' practical implementation was also confirmed by the research on practical experience. Despite critiques of the Member States' limited response, the Commission found an increase in the cumulative rate of implementation, with two-thirds of CSRs showing at least 'some progress' by 2016.[57]

The European Semester now combines the different instruments, introducing the method of 'integrated multilateral surveillance' of economic, budgetary,

[51] The five key targets of the EU-2020 to be translated into national targets were: 1. employment; 2. research and innovation; 3. climate change and energy; 4. education; and 5. combating poverty.

[52] J Zeitlin and B Vanhercke, 'Socializing the European Semester: EU social and economic policy co-ordination in crisis and beyond' (2018) 25(2) *Journal of European Public Policy*. Online Appendix.

[53] Ibid, Online Appendix, Section 2: The Expanding Social Orientation of the CSRs, 2011–2014. A. The CSRs for 2012 and 2013.

[54] Council Decision 2020/1512 of 13 October 2020.

[55] M Dawson, 'New Governance in the EU after the Euro Crisis – Retired or Reborn?' in M Cremona and C Kilpatrick (eds), *EU Legal Acts: Challenges and Transformations* (Oxford, Oxford University Press, 2018) 124.

[56] Zeitlin and Vanhercke, n 52 at 87.

[57] Verdun and Zeitlin, n 52 at 140.

employment and social policies. It aims to realise the Europe 2020 targets.[58] The comparative survey confirms the social partners' interest in such an examination, and the different systems are becoming more comparable, regarding both direction and the need to change.[59]

The system has been beset by criticisms from different sides from the beginning: inserting the social dimension in the process of economic integration has been seen to contradict the original Community goals, while on the other hand the prioritisation of economic goals as against social ones has caused dissatisfaction, and also claims about limited effectiveness. The criticism never questions the need for these instruments, especially in light of the need for progress in the social area, as well as the limited political and legal competence of EU governance in this field.

Despite the lack of progress, the techniques developed during the three decades can serve to further implementation of the European Pillar of Social Rights (EPSR), including its labour law provisions in Chapter II. The EPSR Action Plan[60] declared the intention of continuing to monitor through the European Semester and to use the toolbox developed so far, while of course revising the Scoreboard and the headline indicators.

In summary, the Europe 2020 strategy – in particular the CSR reports – may have long-term relevance for societal-level compliance with European labour standards. The shift of attention to working conditions and job security among the labour market and social targets is definitely coupled with good practice and regular feedback on the effective application of the proposed improvements. On the whole the repeated rounds of communication, the incentivising effect of mutual learning and the comparison of practices have contributed to the development of the abovementioned 'compliance culture'[61] in the area of labour law.

These processes are based on and necessarily involve the processes of social dialogue.

5. The Role of Social Dialogue in the Application and Effective Enforcement of Labour Standards

The role of social dialogue in the Treaties has grown with the development of the EU's social aspects, with its transformation from an economic community to a social and constitutional entity. Not even mentioned in the Treaty of Rome,

[58] Preamble of 2018 July Employment Guidelines. Recital (5).

[59] Joint Employment Report 2019, as adopted by the EPSCO Council.

[60] See: https://ec.europa.eu/commission/presscorner/detail/en/ip_21_820.

[61] T Prosser, 'Accounting for national and sectoral variance in the implementation of European Social Partner "Soft" Law: the cases of the implementation of the telework and work-related stress agreements' (2015) 53(2) *British Journal of Industrial Relations*.

and given a limited role in the Maastricht Treaty (Article 118b), it has grown to become a decisive instrument of labour law, both as a goal promoting the right to be involved (Article 151 TFEU) and as an instrument of making and enforcing European labour law norms (Articles 154 and 155 TFEU). It has followed more or less the same road as the development of the European Social Model itself through ups and downs, from its emergence in the Single European Act to the completion of the Europe 2020 strategy.

The concept of 'social dialogue' has a variety of meanings. Taken in its broadest sense – activities at different levels, by different actors and with different outcomes – it can help us to find niches in which the outcome of any form of dialogue might promote compliance with European labour standards.

'European social dialogue' refers primarily to European-level bipartite or tripartite interactions between European social partners (trade unions and employers' associations) and European institutions for the purpose of setting labour standards, economic and social policies. This raises the question of the connection between negotiated regulation and soft enforcement: when regulation is accomplished through negotiation, does it make enforcement easier, smoother or softer?

Arguably, it does. The manner and quality of norm-setting are linked inseparably with enforcement. Norms that are 'internalised' are followed most easily, without sanctions.[62] The closer the law-maker and the subject of the norm are to each other in the regulatory process, the more the norm is likely to be internalised, conflict-free enforcement of the norm being more assured, and its stable and voluntary observance more expected. The manner of norm-setting and also the internalisation of norms are strongly dependent on balancing interests at different levels.

For this reason, the involvement of social partners and stakeholders has become a strong requirement in the treaties[63] and a precondition of the legitimacy of legislative and governing acts. These can take the form of discussions and consultations, resulting in opinions or recommendations[64] submitted by the parties, as prescribed by the Treaty, and numerous other forms that have developed in the course of the time as optional actions. The result of the basic process might be either policy decisions or EU regulatory action (Directives) setting labour standards. Bipartite dialogue between social partners may lead to binding agreements at European level (sectoral or cross-sectoral agreements), which may become, if preconditions are fulfilled, Directives.

[62] Hart's much quoted theory on law's obligation-generating 'internal point of view' supports the practical requirement of the involvement of those affected as evident. HLA Hart, *The Concept of Law*, 2nd edn (Oxford University Press, 1997).

[63] Amsterdam Treaty Arts 138(1) and 139(1), requiring first of all the promotion of dialogue between the social parties, then, in TFEU Arts 154 and 155 making it a regular part of legislation.

[64] TFEU Art 154(2) and (3).

In the early 2000s the positive economic and political developments, the enthusiasm accompanying the Amsterdam Treaty process and expectations connected to the role of social dialogue made it a main part of the 'social dimension' agenda. Various solutions were developed to spread and channel EU measures to initiate actions at the national and sectoral levels.

The Lisbon Strategy gave formal status to the OMC, a flexible way of coordinating national social and employment policies. These flexible forms provided an opportunity to extend consultations and negotiations beyond formal procedures under the Treaty to various informal, technical forms of concertation, influencing the adoption of economic and social policies. The Lisbon Treaty and the European Semester process assigned the European Commission the task of increasing the social partners' involvement in social and labour law programmes. While there has been tension at the European level of social dialogue (on issues of transposition of framework agreements into legislation), for our purposes a look at the role of social dialogue in promoting the application of existing norms and other documents at national level also offers positive developments.

The sectoral social dialogue committees,[65] operating since 1998, consist of delegates of organisations acknowledged as representative in the sector. They have become the main forum for concertation on the Commission's sectoral policies, particularly on their effects on jobs and working conditions.[66] These negotiations result mainly in joint opinions and declarations, but also take the form of decisions and agreements.[67] In 2019, negotiations by 43 sectoral committees covered more than 80 per cent of employees in Europe.[68] The effectiveness of sectoral dialogue in improving working conditions depends, of course, on the effective implementation of standards in the workplace. On the part of the Commission support and close monitoring, as well as attention to organisational capacity at national level, strong relations and interaction between the committees and the national affiliates could bring results in various sectors.[69]

The European Semester process and discussion of the CSRs have increased cooperation and consultation between the social partners and national

[65] Committees promoting the dialogue between the social partners in the sectors at European level established by Commission decision in 1998 (98/500/EC).

[66] J-P Tricart, 'Once upon a time there was the European social dialogue', ch 4, in B Vanhercke, D Ghailani and S Spasova (with P Pochet) (eds), *Social policy in the European Union 1999–2019: the long and winding road* (Brussels, ETUI-OSE, 2020) 79.

[67] Commission SWD on the functioning and potential of European sectoral social dialogue, Brussels, 22.7.2010, SEC(2010) 964 final, 5–6, and 25, Annex 4.

[68] Tricart, ibid.

[69] B Larsson, M Galetto, S Weber, B Bechter and T Prosser, 'What's the point of European Sectoral Social Dialogue? Effectiveness and polycontexturality in the hospital and metal sectors' (September 2020) *Industrial Relations Journal*. For example, the role of the Sectoral Social Dialogue Committee for the Hospital and Healthcare Sector (SSDC HS) in the adoption and implementation of the project 'Promotion and support of the implementation of Directive 2010/32/EU on the prevention of sharps injuries in the hospital'.

institutions. The 2018 CSRs mentioned as a notable change that its content concerned the results of surveillance of social dialogue for the first time and would be repeated in the next conclusions.[70]

In addition to the two sides of industry as 'privileged stakeholders',[71] increasingly 'other stakeholders' (civil society organisations) are involved in European-level dialogue, not independently of the broadening scale of non-labour related issues in EU governance and policymaking. This process of advancing social dialogue has been further energised by the proclamation of the EPSR, which has also given special emphasis to the importance of social dialogue in designing employment and social policies. As a clear signal of such intentions, the 2021 March Action Plan on the implementation of the EPSR is built on a broad public consultation conducted between January and November 2020.

The results of social dialogue mainly end in non-binding outcomes, such as joint declarations and statements, joint websites, handbooks or other forms. These can serve as guidance, inspiration or support action in a certain field. Their impact on practice can be supported by the trust-building role of social dialogue, resulting, among other things, in a continuity of persons. If the same people meet in working groups, they get to know each other's views, outcomes tend to improve and it is less comfortable to retreat from agreements.[72]

Reports from experienced actors mention a number of hindering and supporting factors, such as the advantage of the role of European Semester Officers,[73] although also the difficulties with their availability outside capitals in major countries, or the role of primary social partners in Semester activities, not to mention the need for full clarity for processes, especially for smaller trade unions, in order to achieve productive involvement and results.[74]

Another significant point is the changing content of social dialogue. This includes changes in the labour market, as well as in European social policy, extending it to problems and groups outside the employment relationship (including independent contractors and platform work), while keeping working conditions at the top of the agenda. The fact that the concepts of 'worker' and 'self-employed' have become blurred in the digital economy led to the European Commission starting a consultation process to ensure that working conditions can be improved through collective agreements, not only for employees but also for vulnerable

[70] See: https://data.consilium.europa.eu/doc/document/ST-9931-2018-INIT/en/pdf, 5.

[71] A van Hoek, 'The social dialogue as a source of EU legal acts – past performance and future perspectives' in Cremona and Kilpatrick, n 55 at 129.

[72] Stakeholders' Views on and Experiences with the Articulation of Social Dialogue and its Effectiveness, 37.

[73] On ESOs see: M Munta, 'Building national ownership of the European Semester: the role of European Semester officers' (2020) 21(1) *European Politics and Society* 36–52. European Semester officers (ESOs) were sent to the Commission's representations in Member States to reinforce policy dialogue. See: Stakeholders' Views, n 72 at 8, 52.

[74] Ibid, 35.

self-employed, particularly platform workers.[75] While such issues might be raised also as a fair competition question, the interrelatedness between labour law in a narrow sense and social issues (employment, education, vulnerable persons) clearly governs social dialogue participation on the side of both trade unions and employers' organisations.

6. The European Social Charter – A Soft and Strong Instrument for Protecting Labour Standards

The European Social Charter[76] (the Charter) is a Council of Europe human rights convention guaranteeing economic and social rights, a counterpart of the European Convention on Human Rights (ECHR). All EU Member States have ratified either the 1961 or the 1996 Charter. It is an element of the European constitutional system, together with the Lisbon Treaty and the ECHR.

It is a binding treaty enforced through soft methods and for this reason a requisite instrument for analysing the soft enforcement of European labour law. The broad overlap between the contents of the two norm systems calls attention also to the procedural aspect, the historically developed, elaborate set of methods for promoting compliance with national obligations under the Charter.

The case law developed by the European Committee of Social Rights (ECSR), the Charter's supervisory body, provides excellent examples of the implementation of social rights through gradual, instructive, as well as institutional processes. Seemingly vague, programmatic 'soft' rights and obligations are turned into clear and accountable targets through systematic requirements and analysis of information and data. The application of a system of indicators and thresholds make compliance with and the progress of the Contracting Parties comparable and measurable.

The enforcement mechanism is based on parallel systems of monitoring and collective complaints. Although the system of collective complaints is considered more decisive for the legal nature of the Charter and its implementation mechanism, for our subject the reporting system offers potentially transferable experiences.

Three examples below may demonstrate the utility of the 60-year experience under the Charter for achieving the EU employment and policy targets.

Article 1§1 of the Charter lays down the obligation of the States Parties with regard to 'the achievement and maintenance of as high and stable a level of

[75] KM Anderson and E Heins, 'After the European elections and the first wave of Covid-19: prospects for EU social policymaking', ch 1 in B Vanhercke, S Spasova and B Fronteddu (eds), *Social policy in the European Union – state of play 2020* (Brussels, ETUI, 2021) 22.

[76] Adopted in 1961, its expanded and updated version, the Revised Social Charter was adopted in 1996.

employment as possible'. Over the course of time the ECSR has converted this vague text into measurable requirements through the elaboration of a complex evaluation system.

Lowering unemployment, a part of the EES, is included in the OMC, and is also part of the Semester system. These EU systems of monitoring and recommendations might be helped by the results of the ECSR's thorough scrutiny of the relevant steps taken by national governments under the Charter. The assessment rests on a number of economic and social indicators linked to the results achieved by states in transforming economic growth into employment, data related to the national economic situation (eg GDP growth, inflation, job growth), patterns of employment (eg the employment rate, part-time and fixed-term employment, regional disparities), as well as assistance to unemployed people with special regard to vulnerable groups such as young people, the long-term unemployed, ethnic minorities and persons with disabilities. The Committee also watches the amount of resources devoted to the goals, in terms of share of GDP, the balance between active and passive measures as well as the effects of different active measures (training, guidance, subsidised jobs) in terms of creating lasting employment. The Committee takes account of the economic situation of the state, as well as benchmarks and indicators that make the reporting states comparable.

The protection of health and safety is an essential part of the EU employment agenda and it is a principal issue under the Charter (Art 3 and 11) as well. The dangers to economic and social rights brought about by globalisation and the waves of economic and financial crisis are manifested in part by the dramatically rising number of atypical workers. The ECSR has paid more and more attention to the protection of their health and safety, as well as social security. The Committee pointed out that for the situation to be in conformity with Article 3§2 of the Revised Charter, states must take the necessary measures to provide non-permanent workers (temporary agency workers and fixed-term workers) with information, training and medical surveillance adapted to their employment status (frequent changes of employer) in order to avoid any discrimination in respect of their health and safety in the workplace. Also, in light of the growth in self-employment, the Committee repeatedly seeks information on the coverage of the self-employed with regard to all social security schemes under Article 12§1. The result of the regular checks shows that in most countries applicable regulations cover all workers, regardless of the nature of their contracts.

The difficulties involved in ensuring equal pay for women and men are as old as its regulation in the Rome Treaty. Despite the many successful ECJ cases – also under the 'Recast' gender equality Directive[77] – there has been no breakthrough

[77] Directive 2006/54/EC.

concerning the unequal position of women and men at work. The power of the soft method, with its collective (societal) approach, is well reflected in issues of gender equality and the pay gap under the Charter.[78] The prohibition of discrimination and equal treatment is legally guaranteed, and individual litigation is available in almost all States Parties. The ECSR goes further, however, requiring national rules to ensure the alignment of male and female wages through a broad (sectoral) comparison, especially when occupational segregation results in underpayment of women. The positive obligation of the state to achieve progress is assessed in terms of job statistics. The measures taken are also examined. The evaluation is based on efforts made, as well as results. This is indispensable for achieving equality not only in law but also in fact, as emphasised by the Committee already in the first Conclusions.[79]

These few examples may illustrate the urgent necessity of establishing a living connection between the Charter and the EU's policy instruments, and of relying on methods and conclusions under the Charter in EU institutions' monitoring and consultative activities.

7. Conclusion

Empirical findings on soft methods reflect the theoretical diversity to a substantial extent, in part because of the variable operationalisation of 'compliance'. Different scholars 'test' propositions with different types of evidence. Much of the empirical record remains inconclusive (because of the contradictory results) and there are many remaining 'black holes' where little knowledge exists.

The three decades of development and application of soft-law instruments under the New Economic Governance could not improve existing labour standards, as had been expected, together with achieving employment-policy goals. The reasons might be found in part in the substantive divergence of policy goals, while accomplishing noticeable development in methodology and mechanisms. This contrast and duality nevertheless might be encouraging for the expected next phases in the implementation of the European Pillar of Social Rights, with special regard to Chapter II, once the Member States and the Union emerge from the Covid-19 crisis.

Even if the original hopes could not be met, developments may justify the statement that the state of European labour standards in 2021 is not the same as 30 years ago The progress in skill, practice and capacities built up in the course of cooperation and participation also guarantee the irreversibility of the progressive results of increased dialogue.

[78] Arts 4§3 and 20.
[79] Conclusions I, Statement of Interpretation, Art 4§3.

7.1. The Role of Social and Cultural Factors

The main methods connected to various policy instruments and soft enforcement build on almost natural human activities, such as socialising and mutual learning, an eternal element of human society. Indeed, from a long-term point of view the 'socialising' and transformative effect can be considered the most valuable result of these steered exercises. Formally non-binding rules and agreements can gradually become accepted as binding in the process of communication and negotiation, and the persuasive effect of repetitive and multi-layered, multi-sided forms of communication.

Beyond achieved compliance with the actual soft law rules the major socialising impact can be seen in the chance to develop a common 'culture of compliance'.[80] Although different approaches in terms of (self- or related group) interests[81] and human emotions (such as pleasure, sympathy, shame and so on)[82] may lead to different assessments,[83] the gradual, even if slow effects of these soft forms of pressure have an evident integrating function, with special regard to the differences among the Member States (particularly taking into consideration the remaining differences between 'old' and 'new' Member States).[84]

Lack of tight surveillance is not, as such, an advantage in itself, but it might have a beneficial impact on the development of soft methods and the 'culture of compliance'. As for compliance with EU standards, in countries with an ingrained 'compliance culture', timely and complete compliance is the dominant pattern,[85] although further research into the application of social partner agreements at EU level might find a less convincing impact.[86] There is academic research demonstrating that trust in national institutions might promote stronger compliance with norms than strict binding provisions.[87]

7.2. Combination with the Social Charter?

Last but not least, regarding the connection between European labour law and the protection of labour standards under the European Social Charter, the

[80] Conant, n 22 at 8.
[81] Ibid, 4–5.
[82] Stefan, n 12 at 205.
[83] Prosser, n 61.
[84] Conant, n 22 at 28. Similar, though only an implicit reference: J Zeitlin and B Vanhercke, 'Economic Governance in Europe 2020. Socializing the European Semester Against the Odds?' in Vanhercke, Spasova and Fronteddu, n 75 at 88–89.
[85] Ibid, 8.
[86] Prosser, n 61 at 273.
[87] A Mouriki, 'Flexibility and Security: an asymmetrical relationship?', AIAS Working Paper 09-74 (November 2009).

examination of soft methods under EU policy suggests an exchange of supervision experiences under the Charter. Methodology, communication and means of gradual development are very similar to each other.

The analysis of improvements and progress among reporting states may make it worthwhile to make it more visible and use it as a practical tool for the effective realisation of labour rights in Europe. Serious reconsideration of the repeated proposal that the EU should accede to the Charter[88] would represent a major step forward for the soft enforcement of European labour law.

[88] O De Schutter, 'The European Social Charter as the Social Constitution of Europe' in N Bruun, I Schömann, K Lörcher and S Clauwaert (eds), *The European Social Charter and the Employment Relationship* (Bloomsbury, 2017) 37–42.

7

Strategic Enforcement of EU Labour Law

KLAUS LÖRCHER

1. Introduction: Strategic Enforcement of EU Labour Law

From description to action: this might be seen as the underlying 'motto' for this chapter. Without (strategic) activities, enforcement will not take place (sufficiently) or might even go in the wrong direction. Such action is aimed at helping to empower trade unions and workers in exercising the rights provided for by EU labour law, to protect them in case of violations and even to improve them. Strategic enforcement is therefore key to the realisation of human, trade union and workers' rights.[1]

As a general approach, it should be carefully assessed whether the strategy chosen is appropriate to effectively remedy a situation that is in violation of legal obligations (ex post) or to prevent such violations (ex ante), while both approaches have a 'strong connection'.[2] In particular, advantages and disadvantages will have to be weighed carefully. The following contribution aims at providing elements for such an assessment. Section 2 looks mainly at strategic litigation before judicial bodies, while the section 3 deals with enforcement beyond litigation in court.

As trade unions have a specific role to play in the strategic enforcement of EU labour law, by their very mission, such strategies are becoming increasingly relevant in their defence and promotion of social and labour rights, in particular

[1] See G Davidov, 'Compliance with an Enforcement of Labour Laws: An Overview and Some Timely Challenges' (2021) *Soziales Recht* 111, 126: 'Strategic enforcement' in a more limited way as only one 'factor in raising the cost of violations' (among 13 different methods of ensuring compliance). See, in general, A Weiss, 'The Essence of Strategic Litigation' in A Graser and C Helmrich (eds), *Strategic Litigation: Begriff und Praxis*, 1st edn (Baden-Baden, Nomos, 2019). Also see: https://doi.org/10.5771/9783845298276-27

[2] Davidov, above n 1 at 113.

at EU level. This contribution will therefore focus to a significant extent on trade union experiences, in particular those of the ETUC.[3]

2. Strategic Litigation before Judicial Bodies (Mainly Courts)

From the outset, it should be recalled that the main focus of this publication is the effective enforcement of EU labour law. Accordingly, other avenues at European or international level – such as the Council of Europe or the ILO and UN – will not be dealt with here. Nevertheless, in each case it should be carefully examined whether the problem at national level is EU-related or whether it should rather be addressed via other channels.[4] Even in the former case it should be borne in mind that the CJEU is not primarily a human rights or a labour law court.

The legal framework for strategic litigation in relation to labour law has been described elsewhere in this volume.[5] The aim of this section is therefore to analyse how best to litigate strategically within this framework. Before doing so, the starting point of what 'strategic litigation' could or should mean will be described.

2.1. Definitions

To date, it seems that no commonly accepted definition of 'strategic litigation' has become established. Often only a 'self-description' (*Selbstbeschreibung*)[6] is provided, depending much on the experiences and capabilities of the relevant organisation. To give examples from NGOs:

> Strategic litigation is the identification and pursuit of legal cases as part of a strategy to promote human rights. It focuses on an individual case in order to bring about broader social change. These cases set important legal precedents by publicly exposing injustices, raising awareness and bringing about changes in legislation, policy and practice. Strategic litigation can have a lasting impact on a large number of people at the national, regional or international level.[7]

[3] See ETUC Resolution on ETUC human rights, legal and strategic litigation network: ETUCLEX, adopted at the Executive Committee of 28–29 October 2020, www.etuc.org/en/document/resolution-etuc-human-rights-legal-and-strategic-litigation-etuclex

[4] The table at the end of this chapter will offer a broader picture, making it easier to assess the best avenue.

[5] See Chapter 3 in this volume.

[6] A Graser, 'Strategic Litigation – oder: Was man mit der Dritten Gewalt sonst noch so anfangen kann' (2019) 10(3) *Rechtswissenschaft* 317–53 at 319.

[7] TRIAL International takes an innovative approach to the law, paving the way to justice for survivors of unspeakable suffering. The organisation provides legal assistance, litigates cases, develops local capacity and pushes the human rights agenda forward; see also Helsinki Foundation for Human Rights, *Strategic Litigation in the Area of Human Rights proceedings – Before The Court of Justice of the European*

> The overall purpose of our strategic litigation work is to support victims of human rights violations and human rights defenders, and to achieve systemic change … In human rights, litigation is 'strategic' when it is consciously designed to advance the clarification, respect, protection and fulfilment of rights. The idea is to change laws, policies and practice, and to secure remedies or relief following violations. Strategic litigation is also often about raising public awareness of an injustice.[8]

> Strategic litigation is understood by ECRE to have a broad definition encompassing direct engagement with cases, third party interventions, support to lawyers (both formal and informal), training, capacity development, exchange of legal information, knowledge sharing, guidance and statements of supporting evidence.[9]

It may also be more thematically oriented, such as 'strategic litigation in EU gender equality law':

> This report examines strategic litigation (SL) in the area of sex discrimination law, both at the national and at the EU level. 'Strategic litigation' describes the employment of litigation strategies to elicit social, legal or policy change and is often carried out by civil society organisations and/or lawyers as a form of activism.[10]

More specifically, in relation to EU labour law there has been a long debate, which is still ongoing. For trade unions, strategic litigation involves defending and promoting workers' and trade union rights. Litigation may be used as a means of tackling injustices that have not (sufficiently/adequately) been addressed by law or politics, through the active development of (quasi-)judicial strategies to advance the protection, respect and enforcement of human rights in general, and of trade union and workers' rights in particular. In a complementary way it is also a policy-making-oriented strategy. It can also be used to put certain issues in the spotlight to create momentum without actually setting the aim of winning the case.

Within the European trade union movement, a litigation approach was first developed in the aftermath of the CJEU's *Viking* and *Laval* judgments,[11] which trade unions and a substantial number of authors regard as severely limiting collective rights.[12] The negative outcome of these judgments increased discussions in the trade union movement on how to best deal with CJEU case law in a strategic

Union, A guidebook for non-governmental organizations and human rights defenders (Warsaw, 2019), https://trialinternational.org/topics-post/strategic-litigation/.

[8] www.amnesty.org/en/strategic-litigation/.

[9] www.ecre.org/our-work/strategic-litigation/.

[10] M Guerrero for the Directorate-General for Justice and Consumers, European Commission (2020), https://op.europa.eu/en/publication-detail/-/publication/beaa7c36-90d1-11ea-aac4-01aa75ed71a1; in a wider sense, see Equal Rights Trust (ed), *Economic and Social Rights in the Courtroom – A Litigator's Guide to Using Equality and Non-Discrimination Strategies to Advance Economic and Social Rights* (London, 2014).

[11] Case C-438/05 *ITF and FSU v Viking Line* [2007], ECLI:EU:C:2007:772; Case C-341/05 *Laval un Partneri* [2007], ECLI:EU:C:2007:809.

[12] See for a recent overview: M Höpner and K Schmidt, *Can We Make the European Fundamental Freedoms Less Constraining? A Literature Review*, online publication (Cambridge University Press, 2020) note 27.

way, possibly with a long-term dimension. But this debate on the necessity of strategic litigation had already been relevant in the *Laval* case itself. Different opinions within the trade unions concerned led to a problematic approach before the CJEU.[13] In any event, these experiences have brought into being a new dimension in the work of the ETUC, the creation of a specific Working Group devoted to litigation (now called the Fundamental Rights and Litigation Advisory Group).

2.2. Objectives

While acknowledging that enforcement may be just one of several objectives that strategic litigation can serve, in the current context we are focusing on enforcement, which understands strategic litigation more as landmark litigation and empowerment, aimed at the overall objective of effectively improving the protection of workers' rights and interests via EU labour law.

Trade unions may pursue individual or collective cases with the objective of achieving a specific result as part of promoting labour rights more generally. By selecting and bringing suitable cases before courts and monitoring bodies, a positive outcome may stimulate developments in terms of jurisprudence and legislation, as well as policy and practice. Strategic litigation has the potential to expose clear-cut violations and injustices, as well as raising awareness, while at the same time bringing about systemic and societal change at national, European or international level, beyond the specific case at hand. These aims can all be relevant and complementary in a given situation, but in other situations only one might be topical, such as awareness-raising with the aim of bringing about political change.

For the purpose of identifying and selecting suitable cases at national level (possibly resulting in a procedure at European or international level) for strategic litigation, a number of indicative (but non-exhaustive) objectives and criteria may be used as guidance.

Beyond strategic considerations related to the choice of the appropriate approach, the following elements may help to define legal and trade union objectives, select the appropriate avenue for achieving the desired outcome, identify the relevant opportunities and challenges, as well as ensure a proper follow-up, whether the outcome of the litigation be positive or negative. More generally, the possible narrative might also be an important element for selecting a case: can the underlying 'story' be easily communicated to favourable forums, the press, the media in general? Furthermore, can the problem behind the envisaged case be integrated into other activities aiming at social transformation?

[13] See J Louis, 'La Confédération Européenne des Syndicats à l'épreuve du droit et de la justice – Genèse, usages et limites d'un mode d'action syndicale en faveur de l'Europe sociale' (thesis defended on 12 December 2019), 393ff. ('Un conflit entre juristes sur la conduite stratégique du litige'.)

Two perspectives may be distinguished. The first relates to a given judgment that is considered to be particularly problematic and therefore requires a strategic reaction ('reactive approach'). The second deals with the realisation of a specific objective, best achieved by strategic litigation ('proactive approach').

2.2.1. Legal Objectives

At national level, the starting point will be to increase compliance with the labour law provisions by ensuring that existing laws are correctly interpreted, applied and enforced. This includes filling a gap, clarifying a point of law, or the meaning, scope or applicability of a legal provision in a particular situation. Moreover, it might be important to overturn previous damaging case law.

While these objectives are more related to the existing legislation further objectives can be to advance national law through application of international and European standards by testing whether national law or practice complies with international or European human rights standards, potentially setting aside or annulling non-compliant legislation.

Similar objectives can be developed at EU level, namely to advance EU standards, by establishing progressive or innovative legal precedents, thus also enabling others to confidently enforce their rights.

2.2.2. Trade Union Objectives and Priorities

From a trade union point of view, the more general legal objectives already mentioned might be complemented by some more specific objectives. The exemplary character of a case can be shown by highlighting a particular problem or a widespread infringement with regard to its nature or scale, shedding light on problematic policies or practices with negative effects on many workers or triggering human rights-based reforms of national laws, policies and practices.[14]

The objectives in proceedings should align with trade union priorities more broadly. The claims in the case could be framed as part of a broader set of trade union demands. In some cases, trade union action through legal proceedings may be the most appropriate or even sole means to raise awareness, address the problem and achieve legal and/or political objectives beyond the individual case at hand.

2.3. Levels of Action

The objectives will have to be achieved primarily at EU level. However, because of their relationship to and impact on further dimensions the extra-EU dimension will also have to be taken into account.

[14] For practical approaches see among others A Allamprese and L Fassina, *Vademecum for Europe – A Practical Guide for Union Legal Bureau Offices* (Rome, Ediesse, 2015).

2.3.1. The Intra-EU Dimension

Obviously, the focus of this contribution lies at EU level. The main avenues have been described elsewhere in this volume.[15] Direct access to EU courts is very limited. Therefore, the indirect avenues become relevant. In principle, infringement procedures should play an important role in ensuring the proper application of EU law. In the social policy field, however, the Commission (as sole institution permitted to instigate such proceedings) rarely uses this instrument. The other avenue is characterised by preliminary ruling proceedings. They have the greatest impact in EU labour law. Accordingly, this avenue has to be analysed more deeply.

2.3.2. The Extra-EU Dimension

Another dimension of strategic litigation is the possible combination of different avenues to achieve better EU labour law enforcement because of the interdependence of international standards and EU labour law. The most important relationship exists regarding Council of Europe standards. Although containing few provisions directly related to labour law, the European Charter of Human Rights (ECHR) provides certain elements, the most important being freedom of association and (by expanding the scope to individual labour law) also respect for private life (Articles 11 and 8 ECHR, respectively).[16] All the human rights enshrined therein are directly related to the EU law via Article 6(3) TEU and Articles 52(3) and 53 CFREU, as well as the references in the Explanations to the Charter of Fundamental Rights of the European Union (CFREU)[17] and, accordingly, to ECtHR case law. EU (labour) law is also particularly linked to the European Social Charter (ESC) via direct references in EU primary law (recital 5 of the Preamble of the TEU and Article 151(1) TFEU, recital 5 of the Preamble of the CFREU and the Explanations to the relevant provisions in the CFREU). ILO standards also play a role (via the general reference in the Preamble of the Community Charter of Fundamental Social Rights of Workers (Article 151(1) TFEU) or specific references in EU Directives[18]). Even the UN Covenant on Economic, Social and Cultural Rights (ICESCR) can become relevant for EU labour law because all EU Member States have ratified it (Article 53 CFREU).

Accordingly, the avenues made available by these organisations also have to be considered for strategic litigation purposes. As regards the ECHR, applications may be filed to the ECtHR. In relation to the ESC, certain EU Member States

[15] See Chapter 2 in this volume.

[16] See in general F Dorssemont, K Lörcher and I Schömann (eds), *The European Convention on Human Rights and the Employment Relation* (Oxford, Hart Publishing, 2013) and the specific contributions on Arts 8 and 11 therein.

[17] See ch 7 in Dorssemont et al, n 16 at 150–53.

[18] Like the Working Time Directive.

have ratified the Protocol offering representative trade unions and certain NGOs the possibility to file collective complaints to the European Committee of Social Rights (ECSR). Finally, the ILO offers trade unions the possibility to file representations (Articles 24 and 25 of the ILO Constitution) and, under limited conditions, also complaints (Articles 26 et seq ILO Constitution). However, the most relevant avenue is the complaints procedure to the Committee on Freedom of Association (CFA). As regards the International Covenant on Economic, Social and Cultural Rights (ICESCR), certain EU Member States have ratified the Optional Protocol opening a path for individual communications to the Committee on Economic, Social and Cultural Rights (CESCR).

2.4. Possible Actors

For EU litigation purposes it is, first, important to identify the potential actors and their possibilities for access to court. In relation to labour law, the main actors are the individual workers concerned, the respective trade unions and/or workers' representatives, in particular works councils. All those main actors can be interrelated.[19] As a trade union member, an individual worker might wish to obtain legal assistance from their trade union. The trade union might be empowered to initiate court proceedings – depending on the national legal situation – in labour law matters, on behalf of its membership or on behalf of individual members. Other domestic systems only foresee trade unions as providing legal assistance to their members without themselves being engaged as parties of the proceedings.[20]

As already indicated, trade unions have specific access to other international (quasi-)judicial proceedings. In the social human rights field, individuals may become possible actors only in relation to the ECtHR and the CESCR.

It should be noted, however, that employers and their organisations also have an interest in strategic litigation. An interesting example is the *Laval* preliminary ruling proceeding, which may serve as a good illustration of strategic litigation from the employers' side. The Confederation of Swedish Industry sought to use the ruling to put pressure on the unions.[21]

[19] See for more details Chapter 3, under section 4.

[20] For an example in relation to the representation of (German) trade union members before the CJEU, see N Colneric [former CJEU judge], 'Der gewerkschaftliche Rechtsschutz vor dem EuGH' ['Legal protection by trade unions in proceedings before the CJEU'] (2018) *Arbeit und Recht* 323–28; see also B Brackelmann, 'Strategisch geführte Gerichtsverfahren des Gewerkschaftlichen Centrums für Revision und Europäisches Recht' ['Strategic Litigation by the Trade Union Center for Appeals on points of law and European Law'], in A Graser and C Helmrich (eds), *Strategic Litigation: Begriff und Praxis* (Baden-Baden, Nomos, 2019), https://doi.org/10.5771/9783845298276-27.

[21] M Höpner and SK Schmidt, *Can We Make the European Fundamental Freedoms Less Constraining? A Literature Review,* online publication (Cambridge University Press, 2020).

2.5. Criteria for Strategic Litigation

Each national trade union will have its own general approach and practical experiences in relation to judicial litigation. They might not necessarily consider this a 'strategic' approach. Nevertheless, for all trade unions it is essential to assist their members in securing application of their rights.

Developing general criteria will therefore always have to be checked against the legal, political and social realities in the country concerned. However, it also appears necessary to look at the European dimension. As there might be less experience within national trade unions the following criteria try to take specific account of it.

2.5.1. Identifying the Appropriate Avenue for Achieving the Objective

Achieving the objectives defined above very much depends on fulfilling the criteria in relation to finding the 'right' case and the appropriate procedure. For the latter, Table 1 below provides an overview of the main national, European and international avenues that could be used. It is important to note that several of the avenues mentioned are (legally) mutually exclusive.[22]

2.5.2. Criteria for Identifying Possible Opportunities

Besides identifying the strategic objectives and available avenues for litigation in the dispute at hand, the selection of potentially successful cases also necessitates an assessment of the risks and opportunities linked to the proceedings and the possible outcome.

All cases that either deal with a serious violation and/or affect a large number of victims will always be at the forefront of potential cases apt for strategic litigation.

Access to Justice

One of the main criteria is whether there is an appropriate avenue for seeking access to justice.[23] Actors such as trade unions should be provided with legal standing or at least be offered the possibility of a third-party intervention. Trade unions that have direct access to justice in other than own-interest cases have a

[22] See in particular: Art 35(2)(b) ECHR.

[23] See Chapter 3 in this volume. In order to improve access to justice throughout the EU the European Commission has set up a European e-justice portal (https://e-justice.europa.eu/sitenewslist?plang=en&pageNumber=7&itemsPerPage=10). It is not specifically related to (EU) labour law, however.

strategic advantage, in particular in relation to possible references for a preliminary ruling of the CJEU.[24] Concerning third-party interventions, the ETUC has rich experiences vis-à-vis the ECSR but also the ECtHR.[25]

Admissibility criteria should be easily fulfilled, otherwise procedural 'battles' will hide the substantive problem for which the litigation was initiated.

Probability of a Positive Outcome

One essential element for consideration is the possible outcome of any envisaged proceedings. In principle, there should be a fair chance of winning the case, and thus (effective) remedies should be provided for any harm suffered, unless other objectives prevail, such as building up a competing doctrinal narrative step by step.

In most cases this will require that the facts and arguments of the case are clear, strong and convincing. Accordingly, fact-finding and the evidence base should be easily made operational or accessible. This will be easier in cases in which trade unions are involved because of their more strategic knowledge beyond individual situations. Moreover, it would be particularly helpful if the existing line of case law has developed in a favourable direction and if relevant precedents in other jurisdictions support the claim (upward harmonisation by means of cross-fertilisation).

For a 'positive' outcome of preliminary ruling proceedings, the question(s) to be asked by the referring court is/are of specific importance. Influencing the wording of the question will be possible only to a limited extent, perhaps best in the courts of first instance, which might even be interested in suggestions in this respect. In any event, similar questions that have already been answered by the CJEU should be avoided. If the aim was to try to change existing case law, however, the difference from the case at hand should be clearly elaborated, thus giving the CJEU the opportunity to justify the desired deviation.

Moreover, it should be taken into account that even 'positive' outcomes may be combined with difficult or even dangerous motivations. For example, even if the *Achbita* judgment[26] might be considered 'positive', the Court's reference to Article 16 CFREU (freedom to conduct a business) justified the employer's right to determine the clothing of the worker concerned, with important limitative implications

[24] See for specific areas: E Muir, C Kilpatrick, J Miller and B de Witte (eds), 'How EU Law Shapes Opportunities for Preliminary References on Fundamental Rights: Discrimination, Data Protection and Asylum', EUI Working Paper LAW 2017/17 (European University Institute, Department of Law, 2017).

[25] K Lörcher and S Clauwaert, 'Activities by the European Trade Union Confederation in proceedings before the European Committee of Social Rights and the European Court of Human Rights' in B Brackelmann and R Buschmann (eds), *Völker, hört die Centrale für Revision und Europäisches Recht* (Kassel, 2017) 50–59.

[26] Case C-157/15 *G4S Secure Solutions G4S v Achbita* [2017], ECLI:EU:C:2017:203.

also for other areas of the employment relationship. Therefore, it should be recalled that if a fundamental right applies, all others might also apply, even those that, on their own, would not meet the requirements of Article 51(1) CFREU.[27]

Legal Impact and Transferability

The legally binding nature of the outcome and in particular the respective sanctions[28] are important elements for assessing whether to initiate strategic litigation as it is a precondition for enforcement (ie depending on the nature of the decision, more legal (strict) or only political (soft) enforcement mechanisms might be attached to it).

But it is not sufficient to look at the direct legal impact of a judgment. Conversely, if the potential impact of a positive outcome might go beyond the individual case at hand this would all the more call for strategic litigation in order to ensure transferability.

Supportive Context

Strategic litigation should not be developed in a legal 'ivory tower'. Positive results can be sustainably successful only if there is at least some support from the political, social or economic environment. Such support might have to be developed, for example, by acting in partnership or by creating synergies among legal/policy actors concerned with the case, benefitting from the pooled resources or experiences of repeated/recurrent players in legal fora.

2.5.3. *Criteria for Identifying Potential Challenges*

In addition to assessing the opportunities, the potential challenges linked to proceedings also should be considered. This should include taking into account the risk of losing and its consequences. At the same time, it should be borne in mind that sometimes even a 'bad' case with little prospect of winning may necessitate an action in order to highlight a fundamental problem (while at the same time trying to mitigate a negative outcome or its wider impact).

Legal and Political Risks of Bringing a Case

An examination of the possible prospects of a procedure might reveal that a positive outcome is not probable. Such a finding should not in itself necessarily cause

[27] See conversely: Case C-201/15 *AGET Iraklis* [2016], ECLI:EU:C:2016:972, where para 89 refers positively to Art 30 CFREU.

[28] For more details see Chapter 2 in this volume.

one to refrain from an action. In particular, in cases dealing with fundamental or new problems the specific aim could be that they become part of the political agenda. Instead, it should be carefully considered how the risks or consequences could be minimised or mitigated, eg by using an alternative avenue. Moreover, as strategic litigation not only aims to remedy the injustice in the case at hand but also to stimulate change, a negative outcome may imply a legal or political backlash beyond the individual lost case.

Length of the Procedure

The time dimension – which is often underestimated in decisions on strategic litigation – should be considered an important element from the very beginning because it may have dangerous repercussions.

Strategic litigation can be both lengthy and time-consuming as it usually provokes a strategic response from the defendant, which may result in a legal battle to the very end. In particular, the litigation process might require appeal(s) up to the highest national instance and even the European Courts, in particular the ECtHR, which especially requires the exhaustion of domestic remedies. Moreover, especially for trade unions a combination of different procedural avenues (such as representations or complaints to ECSR or ILO supervisory bodies such as the CFA) might turn out to be desirable. This could lead to a further prolongation of the overall process, however.

In any event, it should be considered to what extent potential negative consequences of lengthy procedures may possibly be mitigated by:

- injunction procedures or requests for interim/immediate measures;
- identifying several applicants at an early stage or joining similar cases (in order to avoid 'losing' the applicant during the procedure also as a result of a friendly settlement, withdrawal or lack of legal standing);
- choosing employers who are not on the verge of insolvency (in order to avoid 'losing' the defendant during the proceedings).

Also as a result of lengthy proceedings, a final decision may run the risk of becoming outdated, thus losing its added value, even before delivery.

Required Resources and Potential Costs

In principle, strategic litigation requires substantial financial and human resources; the risks and costs involved should thus be proportionate to the expected results and potential legal or policy gains. In particular, a lengthy procedure may result in considerable costs or even an obligation to reimburse the legal costs of the adversary as a result of a lost case. Nevertheless, any shortfall might be overcome by resort to external resources. In terms of financial means several resources that might not be obvious should be taken into account.[29] Concerning 'human resources', external support might be necessary. The experience of 'law clinics' developed in other areas than labour law but transferable (in particular in the case of human rights[30] and anti-discrimination) might turn out to be of added value in terms of specific support.

Possible or Probable Counter-strategies

Any labour law activity from the workers' or trade union side will probably trigger reactions from the employer's side,[31] especially in cases of strategic importance. Depending on the interests involved these activities might result in actions at different levels and dimensions. 'Usual' reactions include paying any sums claimed just before a strategic ruling that might favour the worker concerned; or gaining time by, for example, trying to introduce new facts or seek new forms of orders. Besides the purely procedural paths, other measures, whether of a legal or a political nature, might be used. 'Union busting' strategies can provide some illustrations in this respect.[32]

It will be important to take those possible or probable counter-strategies into account from the very beginning of any strategic case.

2.5.4. Follow-up Strategies on the Outcome of a Case

Strategic litigation is not limited to achieving a final result. The 'investments' in terms of time and resources during the proceedings require a proper follow-up in order to effectively extrapolate on a positive result or limit any damage that may be caused by a negative outcome.

Promoting the Spillover Effects of a Positive Outcome

First of all, it will be obvious to mobilise all available communicational means to raise awareness of the decision or precedent among the persons concerned,

[29] M Lipson and P Noorlander, 'Feasibility Study for financial support for litigating cases relating to violations of democracy, rule of law and fundamental rights', 29 June 2020, https://ec.europa.eu/info/sites/info/files/feasibility_study_for_financial_support_for_litigating_cases_relating_to_violations_of_democracy_rule_of_law_and_fundamental_rights.pdf.

[30] See eg: International Human Rights Clinic – Significant Achievements for 2019-20, 25 August 2020 www.law.uchicago.edu/news/international-human-rights-clinic-significant-achievements-2019-20.

[31] As a recent example in the digital economy, 'The Legal Armoury: "Gig Economy" Corporate Strategies to Avoid Obligations' are well analysed in: International Lawyers Assisting Workers (ILAW) Network (ed), 'Taken for a Ride – Litigating the Digital Platform Model', March 2021, 10–18. See for the important initiative aiming to protect journalists and human rights defenders in strategic lawsuits against public participation (SLAPP): https://ec.europa.eu/info/law/better-regulation/have-your-say/initiatives/13192-EU-action-against-abusive-litigation-SLAPP-targeting-journalists-and-rights-defenders_en.

[32] For example, the Burke Group (one of the most renowned agencies in this respect) advertises its strategic capacities for 'Union-free workplaces', www.tbglabor.com/.

policymakers and the public in order to promote its standard-setting impact for the purpose of advancing workers' and human rights.

Perhaps less obvious but nevertheless crucial will be to develop advocacy strategies on how to best extrapolate on the positive impacts of the precedent and frame it in the context of wider (possibly trade union) demands, making sure that human rights standards permeate national legal orders and are consolidated in future case law and legislation.

Finally, a proper follow-up will ensure documentation of positive and negative experiences and lessons learnt, sharing them with other decision-makers (in particular, in trade unions) and legal experts for future cases and litigation.

Managing the Implications of a (Possible) Negative Outcome

As already mentioned, the possibility of a negative outcome should never be excluded. Therefore, during the process of preparing a decision on strategic litigation it might be helpful to consider any possibility of appeal or alternative avenues for further action in other international human rights fora with more prospect of success.

In the event of a negative ruling, it will be important to ensure a coordinated and coherent communication strategy in order to effectively discredit, minimise and/or isolate it. The main approach could be to focus on understanding and explaining the circumstances of the case, in order to highlight the weaknesses and gaps in the (case) law in general and in the specific ruling in particular, thus triggering a discussion on the injustices illustrated by the case. Moreover, by situating the injustice confirmed by the ruling in the broader context of general political or more specifically trade union demands one consequence might be to call for legislative action to overturn the case law.

2.6. Examples

From the endless list of examples it is difficult but necessary to pick out only a few. Nevertheless, the following examples may highlight certain problems.

2.6.1. Union Activities

Trade unions have specific experiences in litigation. The most prominent examples are related to individual cases in which they have assisted their members. There are also important cases in which trade unions are involved themselves. With regard to individual cases, trade unions have to decide on legal assistance in cases which might have a positive impact not only for the individual worker but also for the objectives of the trade union itself. There are many examples.

In an early period of litigation (such as the 1980s) the judicial fight against discrimination against women as part-time workers was an important issue that the CJEU had to deal with. Trade unions were also involved, in particular in relation to occupational pension schemes. The respective CJEU judgments were in principle very successful.[33] However, EU governments were extremely worried by the enormous financial implications and reacted in the strongest possible way through a treaty revision, the so-called Barber Protocol limiting the application of the equal treatment principle to periods of work after the *Barber* judgment.[34]

Litigation in general and strategic litigation in particular might be more difficult if the issue at stake does not align with overall trade union objectives (for example, if an employer dismisses a worker for sexual harassment and this person as a trade union member applies for legal assistance). At an institutional level, a trade union official who is not content with their working conditions might apply for legal assistance from their union against this same union. Moreover, a trade union member might want to institute proceedings against a collective agreement concluded by their own union.[35] At a more thematic level, if a trade union member is dismissed for (alleged) sexual harassment or racist activities, this might become (very) problematic.

Concerning direct trade union involvement, the following examples might be highlighted.

Recent exemplary proceedings leading to the CJEU's *CCOO* judgment[36] might serve as a good illustration of a successful litigation strategy. This judgment was achieved by a trade union litigating against restrictive jurisprudence of the highest national court, according to which it was not necessary for companies to record working hours in order to delimit the difference between ordinary working hours and overtime. The CJEU stated that an obligation to set up an objective, reliable and accessible system that would make it possible to measure time worked each day is necessary more generally for all workers in order to ensure the effectiveness of the respective EU law.[37] Thus, the long judicial process culminated in a judgment supporting the workers and unequivocally defending their rights, making it clear that the previous national legal framework (the one in place when CCOO Services brought the case) and the respective case law was not in line with

[33] See N Colneric, n 20 at 325–26, referring in particular to the CJEU judgments C-170/84 *Bilka* [1986], ECLI:EU:C:1986:204, and C-270/97 *Sievers* [2000], ECLI:EU:C:2000:76), in which trade union officials represented the applicants in the main proceedings. See more generally: M Guerrero (European Network of Legal Experts in Gender Equality and Non-discrimination), *Strategic litigation in EU gender equality law* (Luxembourg, European Commission, 2020).

[34] G Garrett, RD Kelemen and H Schulz, 'The European Court of Justice, National Governments, and Legal Integration in the European Union' (1998) 52(1) *International Organization* 167; the *Barber* judgment, C-262/88 *Barber v Guardian Royal Exchange Assurance* [1990], referred to the *Bilka* judgment (n 33) in para 27.

[35] Case C-270/97 *Sievers* [2000], ECLI:EU:C:2000:76. See also G Fuchs, 'Strategische Prozessführung, Tarifverhandlungen und Antidiskriminierungsbehörden – verschiedene Wege zur Lohngleichheit?' (2010) 2 *Femina Politica*.

[36] Case C-55/18 *Federación de Servicios de Comisiones Obreras (CCOO) v Deutsche Bank* [2019], ECLI:EU:C:2019:402.

[37] Ibid, para 65.

European law. The respective trade union concluded: 'In other words, there is no going back, whoever governs.'[38]

Another example of (at least partly) successful litigation by a union is the *FNV v Van den Bosch Transporten* case.[39] An action seeking better protection of drivers in the international road sector as posted workers had been initiated by the Dutch trade union FNV Transport and Logistics before the domestic court and was successful.[40] On appeal, the Supreme Court asked several questions[41] of the CJEU, which acknowledged that Directive 96/71/EC must be interpreted as applying to the transnational provision of services in the road transport sector.[42]

In a more general way, strategic litigation was discussed in particular to combat austerity measures, mainly concerning Greece.[43] At least for a certain period, Greek trade unions used different avenues:[44] while GSEE favoured following ILO procedures, ADEDY preferred European paths, namely the EU Courts,[45] the ECtHR[46] and the ECSR,[47] although the latter was approached later also by GSEE.[48] Whereas the judicial procedures (CJEU and ECtHR) proved to be unsuccessful,[49] the quasi-judicial avenues had largely positive results. No real sustainable impact on the actual situation was achieved, however.[50]

The Italian trade union CGIL also tried to obtain a decision of non-application of Legislative Decree No 23 of 2015 (the so-called Jobs Act) on sanctions for unlawful collective dismissal, for discrimination between workers hired before 7 March 2015 (who enjoy strong protection) and those hired after that date, based on EU law. However, the CJEU did not forbid the use of collective dismissals

[38] 'El Tribunal de Justicia de la Unión Europea da la razón a CCOO', CCOO Press release, 14 May 2019, www.ccoo.es/noticia:382532-El_Tribunal_de_Justicia_de_la_Union_Europea_da_la_razon_a_CCOO_en_la_obligacion_de_implantar_un_sistema_que_permita_computar_la_jornada_laboral_diaria.

[39] Case C-815/18 *FNV v Van den Bosch Transporten* [2020], ECLI:EU:C:2020:976.

[40] ETF, 'FNV wins court case against Dutch haulier', 23 January 2015.

[41] Fair Transport Europe, 'Dutch Supreme Court hands down important rulings for road transport workers', 24 November 2018.

[42] However, see for a more critical comment: ML Markey, '*FNV v Van den Bosch*, or the thin line between the free movement of services and "social dumping" in the never-ending story of posted workers', 8 December 2020.

[43] (Several contributions in) N Bruun, K Lörcher and I Schömann (eds), *Economic and Financial Crisis and Collective Labour Law in Europe* (Oxford, Hart Publishing, 2014).

[44] In respect of restriction of freedom of association, they had started with a common approach (ILO CFA case 2820, *GSEE/ADEDY ea v Greece*, CFA 365th Report, paras 784 seq.

[45] Case T-215/11 [2012], ECLI:EU:T:2012:627 and T-215/11, *ADEDY ea/Council*, ECLI:EU:T:2012:627.

[46] *Koufaki und ADEDY/Greece* No 57665/12 ea (ECtHR, 7 May 2013).

[47] *ADEDY ea v Greece* Nos 65 and 66/2011 (ECSR, 23 May 2012).

[48] *Greek General Confederation of Labour (GSEE) v Greece* No 111/2014 (ECSR, 23 March 2017): violation of Art 4 (fair remuneration), Art 7 (protection of young persons) and Art 3 of the 1998 Additional Protocol (the right to take part in the determination and improvement of the working conditions and working environment).

[49] For a deeper analysis see A Koukiadaki, *Can the austerity measures be challenged in supranational Courts? The cases of Greece and Portugal*, study for the ETUC, Brussels (30 June 2014).

[50] ECSR, Findings 2020, published 24 March 2021: 3rd assessment of follow-up in the cases mentioned above in n 47 and (1st) assessment of follow-up in the case mentioned in n 48.

reformed by the Jobs Act.[51] Nevertheless in a multi-layer litigation approach, it turned out that the quasi-judicial avenues had more positive results.[52]

In attempting to improve the framework for information and consultation in France the complaining trade union CGT also lost its case before the CJEU mainly on the direct effect of the fundamental rights guarantee in Article 27 CFREU. However, this *AMS v CGT* judgment has been analysed as showing, on one hand, that the mobilisation of European law by trade union actors is being carried out progressively, and on the other hand, that recourse to EU law and justice has had the effect of reformulating the case defended by the trade union to become an issue of the CFREU itself.[53]

Cross-border disputes are of specific relevance, particularly in the transport sector. In a long-standing case on the applicable law, cabin crew members successfully prevented the airline company Ryanair from applying Irish law instead of more protective (Belgian) labour law[54] on the basis of a CJEU preliminary judgment.[55] The underlying strategy was connected with the ITF, ETF and the Belgian affiliate CNE/LBC transnational campaign to change Ryanair's business model in this respect.[56]

Directly at EU level, the rights of trade unions are at stake in relation to the EU social dialogue. Sectoral agreements to which ETUC affiliates are parties were not submitted by the Commission to the Council to be implemented by a decision for a Council Directive. Whereas the first ('hairdressers') case was not challenged,[57] the other ('central government administration') case was brought to the General Court and subsequently to the CJEU, which both ruled negatively (*EPSU* case).[58] The strategic aspect of this action has been discussed and its outcome is a blow against the EU social dialogue.

[51] Case C-652/19 *KO v Fallimento Consulmarketing SpA*, ECLI:EU:C:2021:208. CGIL and its affiliate Filcams CGIL (of which the applicant was a member) participated in the proceedings before the CJEU, as they had 'voluntarily entered an appearance in support of the forms of order sought by the applicant, in their capacity as trade union organisations' (para 22) at the domestic level. The request for a preliminary ruling referred to the CJEU by the Tribunal of Milan was decided by the CJEU in Case C-652/19 *Consulmarketing* ECLI:EU:C:2021:208.

[52] *CGIL v Italy* No 158/2017 (ECSR, 11 September 2019,), which ruled that the entire sanctions regime provided for by the Jobs Act (including that for unlawful collective dismissals) was contrary to Art 24 ESC.

[53] Case C-176/12 *Association de médiation sociale* [2014], ECLI:EU:C:2014:2, see J Louis, '"Qui perd gagne!" L'affaire "AMS c CGT": recours à la justice et passage à l'Europe d'un conflit syndical', (2017) 2(118) *Politix* 29–53.

[54] Cour du travail de Mons, 14 June 2019, 2013/AM/441 N. S.et crts / C Société de droit irlandais (application of local labour law to Ryanair employees).

[55] Case C-168/16 and C-169/16 *Nogueira ea* [2017], ECLI:EU:C:2017:688 (on the concepts of 'place in which the employee habitually carries out his work' and of 'home base').

[56] ETF, 'Landmark ruling in favour of Ryanair crew', 14 June 2019.

[57] For the arguments for challenging it see F Dorssemont, K Lörcher and M Schmitt, 'On the Duty to Implement European Framework Agreements: Lessons to be Learned from the Hairdressers Case' (2019) 48(4) *Industrial Law Journal* 571–603.

[58] For the CJEU see Case C-928/19 P *EPSU v Commission*, ECLI:EU:C:2021:656.

2.6.2. Non-union Activities

A nationwide campaign started by a TV event against the practice of resorting to low-paid temporary agency workers led, despite substantial difficulties, finally to a reference order by the German Federal Labour Court to the CJEU for a preliminary ruling.[59] It was strategically initiated and continues to be supported by a well-known labour law professor.[60] Significant difficulties arise from the fact that the low remuneration was included in collective agreements concluded by several trade unions affiliated to the German Confederation of Trade Unions (DGB) and the applicant was a member of one of the signatory trade unions (ver.di). Of the large number of workers concerned, only a few went to court. However, it is important to note that the signatory trade union provided legal assistance.

3. Strategic Enforcement beyond (or in Combination with) Litigation

Beyond litigation in the strict sense of the term there are many more fields, institutions, organisations, bodies and so on at EU level that have to be considered when aiming at defending or improving existing EU labour law. Within the framework of a strategic approach they can be combined with litigation.

There is a substantial number of means for (strategic) enforcement beyond (judicial) litigation in the strict sense of the term, many of which are discussed in the present volume. They range from administrative law, particularly by the European Labour Authority,[61] and criminal law[62] via soft law,[63] collective action and actors,[64] whistleblowing[65] to public procurement and EU economic and monetary policy.[66]

3.1. Petitions

Several institutions at EU level offer access to petitions. The obvious problem is that even if it is construed as a (fundamental) right based on a transparent procedure there is no legally binding outcome. Nevertheless, they can form part of an enforcement strategy. Positive results might lead to legal procedures or might be used as arguments in legal proceedings.

[59] BAG (German Federal Labour Court) Order 16 December 2020, 5 AZR 143/19 (A), on the remuneration of temporary agency workers.

[60] See for recent developments CJEU Case C-232/20 *Daimler* ECLI:EU:C:2022:196 and commentary by W Däubler, *EuGH zur Leiharbeit: Vorübergehend ist (fast) alles, was vorübergeht* [CJEU on temporary agency work: Temporary is (almost) everything that passes by].

[61] See Chapter 18 in this volume.

[62] See Chapters 4 and 5 in this volume.

[63] See Chapter 6 in this volume.

[64] See Chapters 16 and 17 in this volume.

[65] See Chapter 19 in this volume.

[66] See Chapters 20 and 21 in this volume.

The CFREU explicitly provides for the European Ombudsman (Article 43) who can be addressed to deal with cases of maladministration in the activities of the institutions, bodies, offices or agencies of the Union. EU citizens have the right to petition the European Parliament (Article 44). Besides those fundamental rights, the Commission has instituted the possibility to file petitions for non-application of EU law.[67] This opportunity has to be seen in the framework of possible infringement procedures.

3.2. EU Institutions and Bodies

As a general rule it is the Commission that, as guardian of the Treaties, is obliged to ensure application of EU law (Article 17(1) TEU), obviously including EU labour law.[68] For rare areas EU labour law provides for specific enforcement agencies. The most important is the newly created European Labour Authority (ELA).[69] Social partners at national level are entitled to bring to the attention of this body specific cases in the field of labour mobility with a view to triggering a cross-border labour inspection.[70] On the other hand, the Fundamental Rights Agency (FRA) might be the most appropriate organisation for enforcing fundamental (social) rights, but its mandate excludes 'individual' cases.[71] Nevertheless, it at least examines the CFREU's application in a thematic or structural way. Its results thus can contribute to a litigation strategy.

A new enforcement dimension has been opened up for trade matters. Recently, the Commission created the position of a Chief Trade Enforcement Officer (CTEO), who is supposed to take forward the implementation and enforcement of trade rules in the EU and with its trading partners. One of their tasks is to ensure that countries the EU has trade agreements with meet the relevant commitments, among others on workers' rights. NGOs (meaning also trade unions) can submit complaints about non-EU countries not meeting the commitments they have made in trade agreements, including on workers' rights.[72]

3.3. Beyond EU Institutions

There is a further dimension of enforcement that is not institutionalised, namely the media. Looking at strategic cases litigated before courts, it is becoming evident

[67] See: https://ec.europa.eu/info/about-european-commission/get-involved/petition-eu_en.

[68] See Chapter 2 in this volume.

[69] For more details see Chapter 18 in this volume.

[70] ELA (ed), Workflow guidance for Social partner organizations at national level to bring cases to the attention of ELA (October 2020).

[71] For National Human Rights Institutions, see MB Moraru, *Report on the Use of the EU Charter on Fundamental Rights by National Human Rights Bodies and Practical Guidelines on the Strategic Use of the EU Charter by National Human Rights Bodies*, July 2017 (Centre for Judicial Cooperation, CJC_2017).

[72] See: https://ec.europa.eu/trade/trade-policy-and-you/contacts/chief-trade-enforcement-officer/.

that they are increasingly forming an integral part of the litigation process in strategic terms. For EU labour law this might appear less obvious because the EU context is often not easily understood by the public. However, generally speaking, labour law is quite concrete and represents situations most people have experienced and thus can imagine or relate to. In any event, this approach can have important impact for better enforcement, including by 'naming and shaming' specific employers who do not properly enforce the relevant legislation.

For trade unions there is, besides the media, the possibility to combine litigation with their own collective/political activities[73] (possibly coupled with boycotts of companies against whom the litigation is directed). As a form of protest expression, they can help to create protest narratives about the need to change the situation in question, along the lines of 'losing your case, but winning your cause'.

4. Conclusions

This contribution has tried to highlight important elements for developing an effective enforcement strategy. While not being exclusive, they demonstrate an impressive variety. Nevertheless, it will be indispensable to examine them carefully and individually, including their interrelations, in order to successfully weigh advantages and disadvantages before coming to a conclusion in a specific case. In any event, decisions and further developments in strategic litigation will also have to take into account the dynamic and, at the same time, problematic developments in respect of the 'digitalisation' of law.[74]

Table 1 Possible Legal Avenues for Possible Actors

Levels of action	**Possible legal avenues for possible actors**		
	(Individual) workers	**Trade unions**	
		National level	**European/ international level**
	Judicial avenues		
	Main advantages: - Legally binding outcome Main disadvantages: procedures are potentially - very time-consuming (unless injunctions would be possible) - costly		

(continued)

[73] See Chapter 16 in this volume.

[74] See, for example, the debate on 'The Rule of Law versus the Rule of the Algorithm', https://verfassungsblog.de/category/debates/rule-of-algorithm/.

Table 1 ***(Continued)***

Levels of action	**Possible legal avenues for possible actors**		
	(Individual) workers	**Trade unions**	
		National level	**European/ international level**
	Judicial avenues		
	Legal standing	Possibly: – in their own name – on behalf of their member(s) – representing their member(s)	As a general rule: in its own name (but internally in cooperation with the affiliate(s) concerned)
National level	Court proceedings (possibly up to the constitutional and/or European level, see below)		[a]
European level			
EU	Preliminary references[b]		(Indirect support)
		CJEU cases on EU Social Dialogue Framework Agreements/Directives	ETUC[c] invited by the Commission (DG EMPL, Social Dialogue Unit) to submit opinions in such cases
CoE	Applications to the ECtHR[d]	Legal representation or support	Third-party interventions[e]
	Quasi-judicial avenues		
		Main <u>advantages</u>: – Procedures are usually quicker and less costly than judicial proceedings Main <u>disadvantages</u>: – Legally non-binding outcome	
National level	-	– (Parliamentary) Petition – National supervisory bodies: Ombudsman, data protection supervisor etc.	

(continued)

Table 1 *(Continued)*

Levels of action	**Possible legal avenues for possible actors**		
	(Individual) workers	**Trade unions**	
		National level	**European/ international level**
		Quasi-judicial avenues	
	European level		
EU	-	– EP Petition – Ombudsman – European Labour Authority (ELA)[f] – EU Chief Trade Enforcement Officer	– EP Petition – Ombudsman – European Labour Authority (ELA) – EU Chief Trade Enforcement Officer
CoE		(ESC) Collective complaints[g]	
	-	– Collective complaints (possibly jointly with ETUC)	– Collective complaints (possibly jointly with affiliates) – (ESC) third-party interventions (and possible participation/ inter-ventions in oral hearings)[h]
		(ESC) Reporting procedures[i]	
			– Written/oral interventions in/to the Governmental Committee/ECSR
		Steering Committee for Human Rights (CDDH)[j]	
			– Written/oral interventions in the (reporting) work of the CDDH (subgroups)
	International level		
UN	-	– Individual communications[k]	

(continued)

Table 1 *(Continued)*

Levels of action	Possible legal avenues for possible actors		
	(Individual) workers	Trade unions	
		National level	European/ international level
	Quasi-judicial avenues		
ILO	-	– Complaints[l] – Representations[m] – Complaints before the Committee on Freedom of Association (CFA)[n] – Coordination (with ITUC) of defence of EU/European cases before Committee on the Application of Standards (CAS)	

[a] (Very rarely) third-party interventions depending on the domestic order.
[b] Requires a domestic court decision (Art 267 TFEU, see in particular para (3)).
[c] Depending on the requirements foreseen in the Directive concerned.
[d] Requires inter alia exhaustion of domestic remedies (Art 35(1) ECHR).
[e] President (of Section) has to decide on granting leave for an intervention (Art 36(2) ECHR).
[f] In accordance with the ELA founding Regulation, national social partners (trade unions) can submit cases to the attention of the Authority. However, the first cases were reported by ETUFs and this did not meet any particular (procedural) objection, see for more details Chapter 18 in this volume.
[g] Depends on ratification of the 'Collective Complaints Procedure Protocol' (CCPP).
[h] According to Art 7(2) CCPP the ETUC has the right to submit observations. Participation in/ interventions at oral hearings are possible only if ETUC has submitted observations in the preceding written procedure.
[i] Depends on ratification of the ESC or RESC and à la carte ratification of the respective (RESC) articles. As for written/oral interventions on the so-called 'ECSR Findings' on the follow-up to the ECSR decisions on the merits of collective complaints, this depends on ratification of the CCPP.
[j] The Steering Committee for Human Rights (CDDH) conducts the intergovernmental work of the Council of Europe in the human rights field in the light, in particular, of the Council of Europe legal standards and the relevant jurisprudence of the European Court of Human Rights. It advises and provides its legal expertise to the Committee of Ministers on all questions within its field of competence. Since 2014, the ETUC has obtained permanent observer status in the CDDH and can thus participate, in principle, in all meetings of the CDDH and its subgroups with full speaking rights but no voting rights.
[k] Depends on ratification of the respective instruments, in particular the International Covenant on Economic Social and Cultural Rights (ICESCR) or the Convention on the Rights of Persons with Disabilities (CRPD), acceded to by the EU, as well as the relevant 'Optional Protocols' providing for the possibility of complaints named 'individual communications'.
[l] Only for delegates to the International Labour Conference (Arts 26 et seq ILO Constitution).
[m] Only in relation to ratified Conventions (Arts 24 and 25 ILO Constitution).
[n] Only in relation to Freedom of Association issues.

8

Enforcement of EU Labour Law in a Transnational Context

MIJKE HOUWERZIJL*

1. Introduction

The focus of this chapter is on issues of EU labour law enforcement concerning transnational employment situations[1] across the EU internal market.[2] In the years leading up to the global pandemic, several legislative initiatives were taken to establish 'clear, fair and enforceable rules',[3] to fight abuse and to foster fair cross-border movement for work. In the Covid-19 era, repeated outbreaks among mobile workers in low-wage sectors, such as the meat industry, have underlined the urgent need to combat the drivers of their precarious circumstances. As part of the European Pillar of Social Rights (EPSR) Action Plan launched in Spring 2021, the European Commission stated: 'The EU's social rulebook is only as good as its implementation ... Protecting and improving the rights and working conditions

* This contribution draws on a combination of earlier work, together with other authors – in particular: J Cremers and M Houwerzijl, *Subcontracting and social liability*, report commissioned by the ETUC, Brussels, April 2021; M Houwerzijl and LE Berntsen, 'Posting of workers: from a blurred notion associated with "cheap labour" to a tool for "fair labour mobility"?' in J Arnholtz and N Lillie (eds), *Posted Work in the European Union. The Political Economy of Free Movement* (Routledge, 2019); M Houwerzijl and H Verschueren, 'Free movement of (Posted) Workers and Applicable Labour and Social Security Law' in T Jaspers, F Pennings and S Peters, *European Labour Law* (Intersentia, 2019); Z Even, R Houweling, M Houwerzijl and A Zwanenburg, 'The Analysis of Private International Law in the EU with Regard to EU Cross-Border Road Transport: Competency and Applicable Law' in A Zwanenburg and B Bednarowicz (eds), *Cross-Border Employment and Social Rights in the EU Road Transport Sector* (Eleven International Publishing, 2019).

[1] For the purpose of this chapter, the term 'transnational employment situations' covers mobile (posted) workers and some situations concerning the mobility of companies (in the context of the freedom of establishment). Employee involvement at transnational level, as laid down in the European Works Councils Directive, is beyond the scope of this chapter. See in this respect ch 16 by Dorssemont.

[2] This chapter focuses on intra-EU employment situations and thus does not concern third-country nationals (TCN) in the EU. The bulk of EU law also applies in substance to Iceland, Liechtenstein and Norway, however, through the Agreement on the European Economic Area ('EEA Agreement').

[3] These words were used when launching the agreement on the European Labour Authority: see: https://ec.europa.eu/social/main.jsp?langId=en&catId=89&newsId=9301&furtherNews=yes.

[of mobile workers], while making labour mobility work seamlessly for businesses and administrations, is key to a well-functioning internal market'.[4]

The expression 'mobile workers' used by the European Commission – for example, in the EPSR Action Plan – is an umbrella term covering transnational workers in all forms of contractual situations[5] and includes both workers who move in the context of free movement of workers (FMOW) and posted workers in the context of free provision of services (FMOS). While the right to FMOW is only for EU citizens (and their family members), posted workers within the framework of FMOS can also be third-country nationals (TCN), legally residing and working in an EU member state. The specific legal status of mobile workers is often decisive for the context in which they have rights: EU nationals using the FMOW rights to move for employment reasons within the EU can base their claims on a different set of norms from posted workers or migrants from outside the EU.

Despite the differences with regard to their legal status, what all (newly arrived) mobile workers have in common is that they are alien to the laws of the Member State in which they (temporarily) work. Therefore, mobile workers (in particular, the low-waged) may be cheated (even) more easily out of their rights than their local co-workers. Effective protection against violation of mobile workers' rights should include information regarding the applicable law and the judicial system, made clear in accessible language. Because labour standards are not harmonised within the EU, it can make a major difference which law applies to their employment relationship and which court has jurisdiction and will apply its own national procedural rules.[6] These rules belong to the area of private international law[7] and are addressed in section 2.

As is well known, the status of posted workers is particularly challenging in this regard, as their employment (and social security and tax) situation is always linked to more than one legal system. This provides an (additional) obstacle to compliance and enforcement, because it is more difficult for employers, intermediaries, workers, trade unions and other worker representatives, as well as for inspectorates to identify, apply and/or monitor and control posted workers' rights. As shown in recent research, court practice varies greatly as well, even within EU

[4] See EPSR Action plan May 2021, ch 3.

[5] Such as full-time or part-time workers and frontier workers on standard contracts, seasonal workers, temporary agency workers, (bogus) self-employed, students/trainees with a side job, multiple job holders and so on.

[6] While Art 47 of the Charter imposes on Member States an obligation to ensure effective judicial protection of the rights conferred by EU law within the meaning of Art 51(1) of the Charter (CFREU), the principle of procedural autonomy still gives a crucial role to Member States' own monitoring and enforcement instruments. See eg M Kullmann, *Enforcement of Labour Law in Cross-Border Situations – A Legal Study of the EU's Influence on the Dutch, German, and Swedish Enforcement Systems* (Kluwer, 2015). See also Chapter 1 of this volume.

[7] Since the entry into force of the Treaty of Amsterdam, the European legislator has been provided with near to full competences in the field of private international law (Art 81(1) and (2)(c) TFEU). This has led to the 'Europeanisation of private international law'.

Member States.[8] Therefore, in section 3, attention shifts to information, monitoring and enforcement tools regarding the rights of this specific category of posted workers.[9]

In view of the persistent gap between (enforcement) rules on paper and rules in action, section 4 takes a 'contextual' perspective by sketching the emergence of cross-national subcontracting chains and letterbox companies. After these phenomena are explained and situated, (scarce) enforcement tools are identified whose purpose is to foster compliance with labour law within subcontracting processes. Section 5 ends the chapter with some concluding remarks and recommendations.

2. Guaranteeing the Rights of EU Mobile Workers in Private International Law

Where a court action is to be brought in an international dispute, three key issues arise in the context of private international law. The first question concerns which country's court shall have jurisdiction. It is only after the competence of the court has been determined that this court will decide the second question, namely, which law is applicable to the dispute. Another important third question pops up after the judgment and concerns its recognition and enforceability. This question has in principle been answered satisfactorily by the Brussels I bis Regulation[10] (hereinafter 'Brussels I bis') to the extent that it concerns recognition and execution on the territory of EU Member States. Article 39 of Brussels I bis provides that judgments given in a Member State do not need any declaration of enforceability to be enforced in any other Member State. In other words, a judgment given in Member State A can be executed without the need for special procedures by Member State B where the execution is being requested. This is beneficial for employees if they are the claiming party. Moreover, in all cases where the employee is the defendant, they are protected against recognition and enforcement of a decision concerning the employment contract, if this would conflict with the rules on jurisdiction pursuant to Article 45 of Brussels I bis.[11]

When determining which law applies (question 2) to contractual obligations in an employment relationship with a cross-border element, the Rome I Regulation

[8] See for a recent examination of posting-related case law in 11 European countries: Z Rasnača and M Bernaciak, *Posting of workers before national courts* (Brussels, ETUI, 2020).

[9] For more details concerning mobile workers in the context of FMOW and TCN migrant workers, see Chapter 12 of this volume.

[10] Regulation (EU) No 1215/2012 of 12 December 2012 on jurisdiction and the recognition and enforcement of judgments in civil and commercial matters, [2012] OJ L 351/1 (hereafter referred to as Brussels I bis).

[11] Moreover, the Regulation puts in place a system of practical safeguards, such as communicating the decision prior to any enforcement being undertaken (Art 43(1) Brussels I bis); the possibility to request a translation of the documents when these are communicated in a language that the persons against whom enforcement is sought does not understand (Art 43(2) Brussels I bis).

(hereinafter 'Rome I')[12] should be applied.[13] To improve consistency between the competent court and the applicable law there is a close link between Rome I and the related instrument in matters of conflicts of jurisdiction, Brussels I bis, which is also confirmed and further developed in Court of Justice of the European Union (CJEU or 'the Court') case law. Both question 1 and 2 will, in chronological order, be further elaborated below for situations of transnational employment within the EU.

2.1. Question 1: Which Court is Competent?

The formal scope of Brussels I bis requires that the dispute be connected to more than one country. Brussels I bis is applicable in international employment disputes if: (i) the defendant is domiciled in a Member State;[14] or (ii) if the parties have agreed that a court or the courts of a Member State are to have jurisdiction to settle disputes that have arisen or which may arise in connection with a particular legal relationship (hereafter referred to as 'choice of forum clause'). Importantly, Brussels I bis explicitly states that in relation to employment contracts, the weaker party (such as employees or consumers) should be protected by rules of jurisdiction more favourable to their interests than the general rules.[15]

2.1.1. Choice of Forum Clause

In line with the concept of weaker party protection, Brussels I bis leaves only limited room for party autonomy in departing from these protective rules so as to choose the court in employment disputes. Parties can conclude a choice of forum[16] only in two situations: (i) after the dispute has arisen, or (ii) if the agreement allows the employee to bring proceedings in courts other than the one that would otherwise be available for the employee under the rules of the Regulation. The clause

[12] Regulation (EC) No 593/2008 of 17 June 2008 on the law applicable to contractual obligations [2008] OJ L 177/6.

[13] Besides Rome I, the Rome II Regulation (864/2007) determines the law applicable to non-contractual obligations. Art 9 contains a conflict of law rule regarding collective actions, such as strikes. See F Dorssemont and A Van Hoek, 'Collective action in labour conflicts under the Rome II regulation' in E Ales and T Novitz (eds), *Collective Action and Fundamental Freedoms in Europe* (Intersentia, 2011). It is beyond the scope of this chapter, but see Chapter 15 of this volume.

[14] If an employee enters into a contract of employment with an employer who is not domiciled in a Member State but has a branch, agency or other establishment in one of the Member States, the employer shall, in disputes arising out of the operations of the branch, agency or establishment, be deemed to be domiciled in that Member State. See Art 20(2) Brussels I bis.

[15] Preamble (18) Brussels I bis. For an elaborate discussion, see U Grusic, 'Recognition and Enforcement of Judgments in Employment Matters in EU Private International Law' (2016) *Journal of Private International Law* 521–44.

[16] Usually, a choice of forum is made explicitly in a clause in the international employment agreement. Nevertheless, a tacit choice of forum is also possible.

must therefore widen the choice available to the employee of choosing between several courts with jurisdiction,[17] while the employer is prevented from imposing restrictions on the employee's rights under the Regulation (Article 23). In general, a court of a Member State before which a defendant enters an appearance, shall have jurisdiction ex Article 26(1) Brussels I bis, even though that court may not be competent according to the general rules of Brussels I bis. If the defendant is an employee, however, Article 26(2) Brussels I bis obligates the court to ensure, before assuming jurisdiction, that the defendant is informed of their right to contest the jurisdiction of that court and of the consequences of entering or not entering an appearance.

2.1.2. Claim Brought by the Employee against the Employer

The weaker party protection concept also impacts claims brought by employees against their employer. In such a situation, the employee has a choice to sue the employer at the latter's domicile[18] or at the place where the employee habitually carries out their work (or, if there is no such place, at the place where the business which engaged the employee is or was situated). Furthermore, according to Article 6(1) in connection with Article 21 (2), Brussels I bis applies when an employer is not domiciled in a Member State, and is sued by the employee: (i) in the courts of the place where or from where the employee habitually carries out their work, or in the courts of the last place where they did so; or (ii) if the employee does not or did not habitually carry out their work in any one country, in the courts of the place where the business which engaged the employee is or was situated.

2.1.3. Claim Brought by the Employer against the Employee

In case of a dispute, an employee domiciled in an EU Member State[19] can be sued by the employer only in the Member State where they are domiciled (pursuant to Article 22(1) Brussels I bis). Furthermore, the employer has the right to bring a counter-claim in the court in which, in accordance with Brussels I bis, the original claim is pending.

[17] The Court confirmed this in its judgment of 19 July 2012, C-154/11, *Mahamdia*, ECLI:EU:C:2012:491.

[18] Art 63 Brussels I bis provides that the employer (in case it is a company or other legal person) is domiciled at the place where it has its statutory seat, or central administration, or principal place of business. The company is thus domiciled in the EU even when only one of those criteria is fulfilled. Where an employer is not domiciled in a Member State but has a 'branch, agency or other establishment' in a Member State, the employer shall, in disputes arising out of the operations of that branch, agency or establishment, be deemed to be domiciled there (Art 20(2) and (8)). See, for example, the CJEU judgment in the *Mahamdia* case.

[19] In order to determine where the employee is domiciled, the court shall apply its internal law (Art 62(1) Brussels I bis).

2.1.4. The 'Habitual Place of Work'

The main connecting factor in Brussels I bis is the place where the employee habitually carries out their work. The habitual place of work is also the main connecting factor for Rome I, the regime for the applicable law. This means that the employee has access to court in the Member State where they habitually carry out their work and that that Member State's law will generally apply. As the concept is common to both the Rome I and the Brussels I Regulations, it has been interpreted and applied in parallel in the case law.

According to settled case law regarding an employee working in different countries, the national court should try to determine in which place the employee has established the effective centre of their working activities.[20] When the employee carries out a large part of their work in the country in which they have established their office, that country is deemed to be the country *in or from which* the work is habitually performed. However, if a worker is sent to different locations to perform one and the same activity (cooking on oil rigs on the Continental Shelf, for example), no such effective centre of working activities can be determined, nor can any qualitative criterion be used to determine the 'essential' part of the performance. In that case, the relevant criterion for establishing an employee's habitual place of work is the place where they spend most of their working time engaged on their employer's business.[21] In principle, the whole duration of the contract should be taken into account, unless there is a clear intention on the side of both parties to change the place of work, in which case only the most recent place of work will be relevant.[22]

The CJEU has given guidance most recently in a judgment concerning mobile workers in the air transport sector.[23] Former Ryanair cabin crew employees took the view that Belgian law applied to their employment agreements and summoned their former employer Ryanair before a Belgian court to pay various compensations with respect to Belgian law. The question was which country was the habitual place of work: Ireland or Belgium? The facts of the case can be summarised as follows. Ryanair is an airline with its head office in Ireland. According to the employment contract, drafted in English, the Irish courts have jurisdiction over possible disputes, and Irish law governs the work relationship between the employees and Ryanair.[24] The contract furthermore stipulated that the work was regarded as being carried out in Ireland, given that the duties were carried out on

[20] See CJEU 9 January 1997, Case C-383/95 *Rutten v Cross Medical*, ECLI:EU:C:1997:7, para 23.

[21] See CJEU 27 February 2002, Case C-37/00 *Weber*, ECLI:EU:C:2002:122, para 50.

[22] Ibid, paras 52–54.

[23] CJEU 14 September 2017, Case C-168/16 and C-169/16 *Ryanair*, ECLI:EU:C:2017:688. This concerned a 'strategic litigation' case. See Chapter 7 in this volume on that topic.

[24] To illustrate the relevance of what was at stake, one can point to an estimate that roughly 60 per cent of Ryanair cockpit and cabin crew at the time were based in jurisdictions with more favourable labour laws than those of Ireland. Analysts expected that Ryanair could face a €100 million increase in labour costs following the CJEU ruling. See: 'European Court ruling could cost Ryanair €100m and swell costs 5%', *The Irish Times*, 14 September 2017, www.irishtimes.com.

board aircraft registered in that country. However, that same contract nominated Charleroi Airport (Belgium) as 'home base'. The contract required the employees to live within an hour's journey of the home base that they were assigned to. The employees started their working days at Charleroi Airport and ended them there. Similarly, they sometimes had to stay there on standby in order to replace a potentially absent member of staff. The employees were subject to Irish law in the field of tax and social security.

As regards determining the concept of 'place where the employee habitually carries out their work' the Court referred to its settled case law, in which it repeatedly held that the concept must be interpreted broadly. When an employment contract is performed in the territory of several countries, and where there is no effective centre of professional activities, the 'place where the employee habitually carries out their work' covers the place where, or from which, the employee in fact performs the essential part of their duties vis-à-vis their employer. In the present case, that meant that the court must identify 'the place from which' the aircrew principally discharged their obligations towards their employer. To determine that place specifically, the national court must refer to a set of indicia. In the transport sector, it is necessary in particular to establish in which Member State is located: (i) the place from which the employee carries out their transport-related tasks, (ii) the place where they return after completing their tasks, receive instructions concerning their tasks and organise their work, and (iii) the place where their work tools are to be found (C-29/10 *Koelzsch*, and C-384/10 *Voogsgeerd*). In this case, the place where the aircraft on which the work is habitually performed is stationed must also be taken into account.

2.1.5. The Place of Business

In situations in which there is no habitual place of work, employees can sue their employer at the place where the business which engaged them is or was situated. This also applies if there are two places that are equally important.[25] For these exceptional (or so far even theoretical) situations, the Court's interpretation in the *Voogsgeerd* case is important. In this case, the CJEU interpreted Rome I, but this case is also relevant for Brussels I bis.[26]

2.1.6. A Specific Jurisdiction Clause for Posted Workers

Article 6 of the Posted Workers Directive (PWD)[27] stipulates that in order to enforce their rights to the terms and conditions of employment guaranteed in

[25] CJEU 15 December 2011, C-384/10 *Voogsgeerd/Navimer*, ECLI:EU:C:2011:842.

[26] Vice versa, answers to questions regarding jurisdiction are (most often) also relevant to determining the applicable law, as a result of the desired consistency between jurisdiction and applicable law.

[27] Directive 96/71/EC on the posting of workers in the framework of the provision of services.

this Directive,[28] posted workers must, alongside the possibilities of suing pursuant to Article 21 of Brussels I bis (such as in the Member State where they habitually perform their contracted employment), have the possibility to institute judicial proceedings in the host Member State.[29] Hence, all Member States have had to ensure that workers posted to their country and covered by the Directive can bring judicial proceedings for enforcement in the territory to which they have been posted. Because the jurisdiction rules under the PWD and Brussels I bis are concurrent, the rules on connected and related actions under Brussels I bis remain applicable. This provides the possibility to sue more than one employer before a court in the domicile of only one of them in situations of multiple postings in multiple countries.[30]

2.1.7. Access to Justice, both on Paper and in Reality?

All in all, from a 'law on paper' perspective, mobile (posted) workers' access to justice,[31] as established in Brussels I bis and Art 6 of the PWD, seems to be adequate. Workers' ability in fact to start legal proceedings depends on their knowing (how to determine) their rights and on support (for instance, legal aid systems) in exercising them. Precisely this gap between having a possibility on paper to bring a claim to court and exercising this right in practice is inherent in labour law, because of fears of retaliation or dismissal if one insists on one's rights, but also, say, a lack of awareness of rights. Not surprisingly, (low-waged) mobile workers encounter several extra difficulties when they consider pursuing a legal claim in another Member State.[32] In this regard, the practical relevance of the Legal Aid Directive (2003/8/EC) for cross-border workers needs examination (and, if need be, improvement). Extension of the scope of the Small Claims Regulation, which currently excludes outstanding wages claims, might also be helpful.[33]

[28] Issues governed by the law of the habitual country of work (such as conclusion and termination of the contract), however, do not fall within the jurisdiction of the host state.

[29] The *lex specialis* principle under Art 67 Brussels I bis facilitates this.

[30] See I Queirolo, CE Tuo et al, 'Article 67 Brussels I bis: overall critical analysis' in CE Tuo, L Carpaneto and S Dominelli (eds), *Brussels I bis Regulation and special rules: opportunities to enhance judicial cooperation* (Arane editrice, 2021) 84.

[31] In general on this topic, see Chapter 3 of this volume. On the empirical aspect of whether posted workers bring claims and which kind, see Z Rasnača and M Bernaciak, *Posting of workers before national courts* (Brussels, ETUI, 2020).

[32] As was made clear, for instance, by Advocate General Alber in a passing observation in his Conclusion on the (non-posted worker) case *Commission v Italy*, see C-279/00 *Commission v Italy*, points 34–36.

[33] Regulation (EU) 2015/2421 of 16 December 2015 amending Regulation (EC) No 861/2007 and Regulation (EC) No 1896/2006 creating a European order for payment procedure. Since its enactment (14 July 2017) the Regulation has applied to both contested and uncontested cross-border civil and commercial claims of a value not exceeding €5,000. In line with Brussels I bis, it also ensures that the judgments given within this procedure are enforceable without any intermediate procedure, in particular without the need for a declaration of enforceability in the Member State of enforcement (abolition of *exequatur*).

2.2. Question 2: Which Law Is Applicable?

Concerning applicable law, the uniform rules of Rome I apply to contractual obligations in any situation involving the laws of different countries (Article 1), that is, in situations in which not all the contractual elements are connected to the legal order of one and the same state. Consequently, Rome I does not apply to purely domestic situations with connecting factors with a single country. Furthermore, Article 2 states clearly that Rome I asks for universal application, meaning that Rome I is applicable not only among Member States of the European Union.[34] It also applies in case the law of a non-Member State is made applicable (for instance by choice of the parties) and the dispute is brought before a court in an EU Member State.

Article 3 of Rome I embodies the principle of party autonomy and therefore vests parties with a wide freedom of choice of contract law. But Article 8(1) Rome I limits the effect of a choice of law in employment contracts because such a choice by the parties cannot deprive employees of the protection afforded them by mandatory provisions of the law applicable in absence of this choice (the 'objectively applicable law'). Hence, employees will be protected by the law that offers better protection; if the employer and employee agree on better employment conditions than those put into the law applicable in the absence of choice, Article 8(1) Rome I prioritises the chosen law. By contrast, if the parties agree on worse employment conditions than those laid down in the objectively applicable law, the latter law prevails. This 'favourability principle' is meant to prevent employers from abusing their superior bargaining position.

2.2.1. Habitual Place of Work

Because the objectively applicable law acts as a 'floor', or a minimum standard of protection, it is always relevant to ascertain the latter law, which can be done following the rules in Article 8(2)–8(4) Rome I. Rome I provides two connecting factors in Article 8(2) and (3): the 'habitual place of work' and the 'place of business'. In the *Koelzsch* and *Voogsgeerd* cases already mentioned, the CJEU decided to go for a broad interpretation of the state of employment principle (*lex locis laboris*). The CJEU made clear that even in the case of a truck driver working in international transport (*Koelzsch*) or a sailor working on a seagoing vessel (*Voogsgeerd*), the national court should try to establish whether, based on the circumstances as a whole, a country can be identified where or from which the work is actually performed.[35] The main argument for this broad interpretation is that it complies

[34] Being an EU Regulation, Rome I in principle would be in force in the Member States of the European Union. However, since it has not opted in, Rome I is not in force in Denmark.

[35] See CJEU 15 March 2011, Case C-29/10 *Koelzsch*, ECLI:EU:C:2011:151, paras 47–49.

with the objective of Article 8 Rome I (which is to guarantee protection to the weaker party).

2.2.2. The 'Place of Business'

Article 8(3) Rome I contains an alternative reference rule in case a country where the work is habitually carried out cannot be identified. In that case the contract shall be governed by the law of the country where the place of business through which the employee was engaged is situated. The connecting factor serves to provide legal certainty in a case in which the primary connecting factor is not able to provide a clear link to any particular jurisdiction.[36] However, taking into account the very broad interpretation of the 'habitual place of work' in Article 8(2) Rome I, there seem to be hardly any situations that will be covered by Article 8(3) Rome I,[37] which refers to 'the place of business through which the employee was engaged'.[38] For (so far theoretical) situations in which Article 8(3) would apply, the term 'place of business' encompasses not only the subsidiaries and branches but also other units, such as the offices of an undertaking, even though they do not have legal personality. However, the undertaking is required to have a degree of permanence.[39]

2.2.3. Escape Clause

Under Article 8(4) Rome I, both pre-established connecting factors – habitual place of work and engaging place of business – may be set aside where it appears from the circumstances as a whole that the contract is more closely connected with another country, in which case the law of that other country shall apply. This clause has been interpreted by the Court in a case[40] with rather unusual factual circumstances, in particular that after 11 years of working in one Member State, the frontier worker in question was still affiliated to the social security system of her former habitual country of work.[41] The Court ruled that even where an employee carries out the work in performance of the contract habitually, for a

[36] See CJEU 15 December 2011, Case C-384/10 *Voogsgeerd/Navimer*, ECLI:EU:C:2011:842, para 47.

[37] Nevertheless, the provision may remain of or regain relevance for the emerging group of 'hyper-mobile' workers.

[38] The CJEU clarified this concept in the *Voogsgeerd* judgment. As the elements related to the performance of the contract are already taken into account in determining the habitual place of work, the assessment of the place of engagement has a more formal character and focuses on the place where the recruitment activities were situated. Accordingly, this connecting factor does not establish a relevant link to the performance of the employment contract but is fixed at the very beginning thereof.

[39] See CJEU 15 December 2011, Case C-384/10 *Voogsgeerd/Navimer*, ECLI:EU:C:2011:842, paras 54–55.

[40] See CJEU 12 September 2013, Case C-64/12 *Schlecker/Boedeker*, ECLI:EU:C:2013:551.

[41] Under the current (policy) rules of the Regulations for the coordination of social security systems this is possible only for a maximum of five years.

lengthy period and without interruption in the same country, the law applicable in that country may be disregarded, if it appears from the circumstances as a whole that the contract is more closely connected with another country. Among the significant factors suggestive of such a close and lengthy connection with a country are, in particular, the country in which the employee pays taxes on their income and where they are covered by a social security scheme and pension, sickness insurance and invalidity schemes. In addition, the national court must also take account of all the circumstances of the case, such as the parameters relating to salary determination and other working conditions.[42]

2.2.4. Overriding Mandatory Provisions

If we apply the Rome I rules to mobile workers covered by the FMOW, Article 8 Rome I will almost always point to the *lex loci laboris*, being the law of the country to which they moved in order to carry out their work in performance of the contract. In terms of outcome, this means that all mandatory laws and collective agreements in the Member State of habitual employment are applicable to their contracts. This implies that (only) in a system with relatively few mandatory and/or collectively agreed labour law standards, the equal treatment principle enshrined in Article 45 TFEU may suffer from the private international law rules. However, Article 9(2) Rome I allows courts to apply domestic 'overriding mandatory' provisions (law of the forum), regardless of the (objectively) applicable law. Many labour law rules have an overriding mandatory character, though the Member States traditionally draw the line differently between law or laws chosen by a forum court from among the relevant legal systems and overriding mandatory provisions.

Regarding the posting of workers within the framework of FMOS, it is important to note that, in essence, the PWD uses the same technique as Article 9 Rome I to achieve its aims. From the perspective of the host state, the PWD fills the 'gap'[43] that Article 8 Rome I would create for the territorial application of labour law. However, the interaction of private international law and the internal market-related PWD has created a highly complex legal system for posted-workers situations, exacerbating the 'usual' difficulties involved in guaranteeing the rights of mobile workers. This has (eventually) been acknowledged by the European legislator. Below, we take a closer look at the legal instruments concerning (the monitoring and fostering enforcement of) their position.

[42] The employer and employee were domiciled in Germany, remuneration was paid in German marks (prior to the introduction of the euro), the pension arrangements were made with a German pension provider, the employee had continued to reside in Germany, the employment contract referred to mandatory provisions of German law, and the employer reimbursed the employee's travel costs from Germany to the Netherlands.

[43] Because Art 8(2) Rome I stipulates that the country in which the work is habitually carried out shall not be deemed to have changed if a worker is temporarily employed (posted) in another country.

3. Strengthening the Protection of Posted Workers

3.1. Rights of Posted Workers

Currently, three Posted Workers Directives are in place: the original PWD, amended by the revised PWD,[44] and a Posted Workers Enforcement Directive (PWED; see section 3.2 below). The revised (2018) PWD amends the original PWD and complements the PWED, rather than replacing these Directives. As stated in its recital 5, the (1996) PWD is intended to reconcile the exercise of companies' fundamental freedom to provide cross-border services under Article 56 TFEU with the need to ensure a climate of fair competition and respect for workers' rights. The revised (2018) PWD resets the balance between said goals in favour of the latter (see eg recitals 4 and 10), in order 'to safeguard the freedom to provide, in both the short and the long term, services on a fair basis, in particular by preventing abuse of the rights guaranteed by the Treaties'. According to its recital 16: 'In a truly integrated and competitive internal market, undertakings compete on the basis of factors such as productivity, efficiency, and the education and skill level of the labour force, as well as the quality of their goods and services and the degree of innovation thereof'.[45]

Article 1(3) PWD defines three categories of posting: (1a) posted workers by service providers (subcontractors); (1b) intra-concern posted workers; and (1c) posted workers via intermediaries such as temporary work agencies (TWAs). In order to achieve its aims, the PWD coordinates Member States' legislation in a way that it provides a core of mandatory rules with which employers who post workers to the Member State in which the service is to be provided,[46] must comply in the host country. According to Article 3(1) PWD, Member States are to ensure

[44] Directive 2018/957/EU amending Directive 96/71/EC on the posting of workers in the framework of the provision of services.

[45] Moreover, the principle of equal treatment, equal pay and the prohibition of any discrimination on grounds of nationality in Union law is emphasised (recital 6) and recital 3 refers expressly to Article 3 TEU, establishing that the Union is to promote social justice and protection and Article 9 TFEU, stating that, in defining and implementing its policies and activities, the Union takes into account requirements linked to, for instance, the guarantee of adequate social protection.

[46] As explained in a practical guide on posting issued by the European Commission, workers who are sent temporarily to work in another Member State, *but do not provide services there* are not posted workers. European Commission, *Practical Guide on Posting* (Luxembourg, Publications Office of the European Union, 2019), 10 (answer to question 2.4). For example, this concerns workers on business trips (when no service is provided), attending conferences, meetings, fairs, following training and so on, but also workers sent (seconded) abroad for a longer period of time, such as foreign correspondents for a newspaper, performing tasks directly belonging to the core services of their employer in the home country). The implication of the distinction between workers posted and 'sent' abroad, seems to be that the latter are covered by the FMOW. If they are only (short-term) business travellers in the other Member State, private international law rules will still designate the law of the habitual country of work as applicable law. In the example of the journalist, the habitual country might however (partly) switch (depending on the specific circumstances of the case), because of private international law rules and in light of the equal treatment principle enshrined in Art 45 TFEU and operationalised in Art 7 of Regulation 492/2011.

that undertakings falling within the scope of the Directive guarantee to workers posted to their territory certain terms and conditions of employment laid down by mandatory law, including collective agreements that have been declared universally applicable. Hence, Article 3(1) PWD determines the nature of the labour standards that must be applied in the host state, but not the substance of these standards.

The revised PWD focuses on three main areas: the remuneration of posted workers, where it introduces the principle of equal pay for equal work, rules applying to long-term posting[47] and rules on temporary work agencies.[48] The minimum wage guarantee is replaced by a guarantee of equal remuneration, including all elements of remuneration that are mandatory in the host state (both in statutory law and in mandatory or generally binding collective agreements) and apply to both local and posted workers.[49] Moreover, Article 3(8) PWD is amended in a way that allows application of generally applicable agreements or agreements concluded by the most representative organisations not only in the absence of, but also 'in addition to' universally applicable ones.[50] Hence, there is still a ceiling of protection for posted workers, but at a higher level.

3.1.1. *Social Security Issues in Posted Workers Situations*

Undisputedly, the revised PWD has solved – at least on paper – many issues, such as wage differentiation between local and posted workers, which prevented the establishment of a level playing field for companies, and a lack of clarity regarding the temporary nature of postings as well as vis-à-vis rotational postings. However, the inconsistencies between the PWD and legal instruments concerning

[47] Once the duration of the posting exceeds 12 months (or 18 months) following a motivated notification from the employer, all of the mandatorily applicable terms and conditions of employment in the host state should be guaranteed to the posted worker, with the exception of procedures and conditions of conclusion and termination of the employment contract and the rules on supplementary occupational pension schemes, which will remain covered by the law of the habitual country of work, in accordance with Art 8(2) Rome I.

[48] The revised directive links the protection of posted agency workers to the 'equal treatment provision' of the Temporary Agency Work Directive 2008/104 (Art 5 TAWD), stipulating equal treatment of temporary agency workers in the user company. In addition to the provisions of Art 5 TAWD, Member States are entitled to require that posted temporary agency workers benefit from other terms and conditions that apply to temporary agency workers in the Member State where the work is carried out (see Art 1(2)(e) revised PWD, amending Art 3(9)). Moreover, Art 1(1)(c) of the revised Directive adds to the protection of temporary agency workers in specific situations.

[49] Arts 1(2)(a) of the revised Directive, amending Art 3(1) PWD. The explicit exclusion of supplementary occupational retirement pension schemes remains.

[50] Art 1(2)(d) of the revised Directive. This solves certain problems, such as in Germany after the *Rüffert* judgment (C-346/06). However, certain problems encountered in Sweden and Denmark after the *Laval* judgment (C-341/05) seem not to be solved, although it remains to be seen whether Art 1(b)(1a) of the revised Directive will make a difference in this respect. This clause stipulates that the Directive does not affect inter alia the right to take collective action, as well as the right to negotiate, to conclude and enforce collective agreements. Regarding the (possible) impact on the right to strike of this 'safeguard clause' see Chapter 16 of this volume.

the coordination of social security systems, Regulations (EC) Nos 883/2004 and 987/2008 on the Coordination of Social Security Systems, have not yet been resolved.

Posted workers remain insured under the social security schemes of the sending Member State, pursuant to Article 12 of Regulation 883/2004. In principle, during the first 24 months of posting, the worker remains affiliated to the social security system of the state where their employer is normally supposed to carry out its economic activities and where the worker and/or their employer continue to pay social contributions. This 'posting provision' is a derogation from the main rule in the Regulation, which is the state-of-employment principle (*lex loci laboris*). The application of the social security system of a state other than that where the actual activities are carried out, may provide the sending company with a competitive advantage over companies established in the host state, in particular when the former has to pay a lower level of social security contributions. Therefore, the CJEU explicitly regards the posting provision as an exception to the state-of-employment principle and holds that it can be applied only if a number of conditions are met.

Notably in practice, as reported in various studies, the sending state's social security legislation and/or policy rules or practice sometimes facilitate abuse of the posting rule, such as the requirement of having substantial activities in the state of establishment of the employer. The so-called 'A1 posting certificate' plays a key role in these strategies. The A1 certificate is a document issued by the competent body of the sending state, attesting that its legislation applies to the posted worker. As confirmed by the CJEU, as long as the A1 certificate is not withdrawn or declared invalid, the competent body of the host state must take into account that the legislation of another state should be applied to the workers concerned, meaning that it may not subject them to its own social security legislation. In recent years, the CJEU has nuanced 'home state control' of the A1 certificates, however the host state court is allowed to disregard certificates only in situations of intentional fraud and under strict conditions.[51] Other loopholes allowing for sham posting arrangements have also been addressed in recent judgments, such as in *Alpenrind*, regarding the so-called non-replacement condition for posting in the context of social security coordination. This judgment makes more difficult the recurrent use of posted workers to fill the same role, or undertake the same activity at the premises of the (same) host country entity.[52] Moreover, in *AFMB*, the Court pierced the corporate veil in order to make clear that purely artificial arrangements are not acceptable and that national courts should have regard to 'all relevant circumstances' in determining the 'true' employer within the meaning of Regulation 883/2004.[53] Finally, in its most recent *Team Power Europe*

[51] CJEU, C-359/16 *Altun* and CJEU, joined Cases C-370/17 and C-37/18, *Vueling*.

[52] CJEU 6 September 2018, Case C-527/16 *Alpenrind*, ECLI:EU:C:2018:669.

[53] CJEU Case C-610/18 *AFMB*, ECLI: EU: C:2020:565. See for an extensive discussion of this judgment in relation to a possible development towards a uniform EU employer concept M van Schadewijk,

judgment, the Court made clear that a temporary workers agency posting workers to another Member State can make use of the exception in Article 12 of Regulation 883/2004 only if it carries out a significant part of its activities assigning temporary agency workers in the territory of the Member State in which it is established.[54] Together, all these judgments may be considered to be important game-changers. Nevertheless, it remains difficult to effectively combat sham posting arrangements ex ante without the adoption of a pending reform package of the Coordination Regulations,[55] which is crucial to make sure that genuine posting is fostered not only in the field of labour law but also regarding posted workers' social security position.

3.2. Fostering the Actual Enjoyment of Rights by Posted Workers

To remedy the monitoring and enforcement lacunae regarding the labour law position of posted workers, a proposal for a Posted Workers Enforcement Directive (PWED) was launched in 2012 and – after initial fierce resistance from 'sending countries' – adopted on 15 May 2014.[56] Its title acknowledges that the PWD did not (at that moment) guarantee in practice any protection against abusive and exploitative practices. Notably, Article 4 PWED provides some 'ammunition' for checking whether workers are 'genuinely' posted. The provision lists elements that can be used by labour inspectorates and other stakeholders to check whether the employer of the posted worker is really established in the 'sending' country, instead of being a so-called letterbox company or empty shelf, established purely to enable posting of workers from a country with low wages, taxes and social security contributions.[57]

The PWED focuses on those elements of the PWD that were considered problematic by stakeholders and that pertain to enforcement of compliance, improvement of legal certainty and strengthening administrative cooperation. The PWED's overall objective is to ensure that posted workers actually enjoy the protection offered by the (revised) PWD, while also facilitating the free provision

'The notion of "employer": Towards a uniform European concept?' (2021) 12(3) *European Labour Law Journal* 363–86.

[54] CJEU 3 June 2021, C-784/19 *Team Power Europe*.

[55] Launched by COM (2016) 815 final. See for an elaborate discussion and plead of shared responsibility of host and sending state: N Rennuy, 'Posting of workers: Enforcement, compliance and reform' (2020) 22(2) *European Journal of Social Security* 212–34.

[56] COM (2012) 131. The proposal was adopted as Directive 2014/67/EU on the enforcement of Directive 96/71/EC concerning the posting of workers in the framework of the provision of services and amending Regulation (EU) No 1024/2012 on administrative cooperation through the Internal Market Information System ('the IMI Regulation') [2014] OJ L159/11.

[57] For an extensive legal analysis of labour, social security, company and tax law aspects of this phenomenon and how to combat it, see M Houwerzijl, E Traversa and F Henneaux, *A hunters game: How policy can change to spot and sink letterbox-type practices* (Brussels, ETUC, 2016).

of services. To achieve its aims, the PWED sets a common framework of measures and control mechanism. Its most important measures include:

- a non-exhaustive list of indicative factual elements to help competent authorities such as labour inspectorates to determine whether there is a genuine establishment of the posting company in the sending state (Article 4(2) of the Directive) and to assess whether a posted worker is only temporarily carrying out their work in a Member State other than the one in which they normally work (Article 4(3) of the Directive);[58]
- a stricter framework for improving access to information in host Member States, relevant for the posting of workers (Article 5) to enhance legal certainty for service providers;
- a framework for enhancing administrative cooperation between authorities and other stakeholders across countries (Articles 6 and 7);
- a (non-limitative) list of justified and proportionate administrative requirements and control measures that might be applied by the Member States (Article 9);
- an obligation upon Member States to ensure effective mechanisms for posted workers to lodge complaints and institute juridical/administrative proceedings (also through trade unions) against their employers also in the Member State where they are posted (Article 11);
- a subcontracting liability arrangement for wages (Article 12).[59] Member States can escape the liability arrangement through implementation of 'equivalent measures' in a direct subcontracting relationship. On the other hand, Member States are allowed to take more stringent liability measures, such as chain liability affecting all subcontractors in the chain.[60]

Clearly, the PWED facilitates and stimulates enforcement in some respects, but requires a real effort with budgetary implications and strong political will at the level of the host Member State. Ensuring that posted workers' rights are adequately protected requires comprehensive cooperation – such as joint visits to work sites of posted workers, enhanced information exchange – on the part of different national actors (depending on the national system, these may be inspectorates, other state bodies, social partners). Moreover, although posting of workers falls under both sending and receiving country regulations, enforcers of the rights of posted workers (for example, trade unions, labour inspectorates) do not have the competence to act beyond their own national jurisdictions. In order more effectively

[58] In line with Art 8(2) Rome I.

[59] In section 4 this measure is examined in the context of transnational subcontracting chains.

[60] The best-known and most far-reaching example of chain liability was established in Germany in 1995 for the construction sector and since then has been extended to several other sectors. See V Bogoeski, 'Chain liability as a mechanism for strengthening the rights of posted workers. The German chain liability model' (PROMO, 2016).

to monitor and enforce posted workers' rights, cross-border cooperation seems crucial. Although cross-border cooperation has increased during the past decade, especially in relation to posting, procedures are long and time-consuming and no proper sanctions are available. Some enhancement may be expected from the PWED where it links the inspectorates' information exchange to the so-called Internal Market Information (IMI) System. Moreover, in 2019 the Regulation to establish a European Labour Authority (ELA) was adopted. The ELA is meant to provide more comprehensive and easily accessible information and services, to stimulate cooperation because authorities, including joint inspections, across the legal areas of, for example, social security and labour law. 'It will serve the double mission of helping national authorities fight fraud and abuse and making labour mobility easier for EU citizens.'[61]

Stricter registration rules (such as notification systems, dissuasive penalties for not following the rules, making service recipients co-responsible for registration) for service providers posting their workers are allowed (but not obligatory) under the PWED and have been introduced in several Member States in order to enhance the quality of data collection on postings and to facilitate monitoring and enforcing the rights of posted workers. The Belgian LIMOSA scheme was one of the first and certainly the best-known and advanced notification system. At the same time, it is a contested notification system, from the perspective that it would limit the free provision of services too much. It has been the subject of several proceedings before the CJEU, with mixed outcomes.[62] More recently, the advantages of the advanced LIMOSA database have been highlighted by statistical research, making reliable estimates of the extent to which posting in the Belgian construction sector has resulted in displacement of local labour.[63]

In the revised PWD, some other surveillance and control measures are further developed. To foster legal certainty and law enforcement, Member States are obliged to publish 'without undue delay and in a transparent manner' information on the constituent elements of remuneration on their single official national website, next to the other information referred to in Article 5 PWED, as well as information on additional terms and conditions of employment applicable to postings exceeding 12 or, where applicable, 18 months. Each Member State should ensure that the information on the single official national website is accurate and updated on a regular basis. Failure to comply with this obligation shall be taken into account when determining the fines applicable for infringement of the national provisions adopted pursuant to the (revised) Directive, 'to the extent

[61] See Press Release: https://ec.europa.eu/social/main.jsp?langId=en&catId=89&newsId=9301&furtherNews=yes. For more details on the ELA see Chapter 17 in this volume.

[62] Belgium, for instance, had to reduce the amount of information they collected initially because, according to the Court of Justice, the scheme restricted, without good reason, the free movement of services. See ECJ 2010, Case C-515/08 *dos Santos Palhota ea;* ECJ 2012, C-577/10 *Commission v Belgium*; ECJ 2014, C-315/13 *De Clercq and others.*

[63] F De Wispelaere and J Pacolet, *De omvang en impact van intra-EU detachering op de Belgische economie. Met een specifieke focus op de bouwsector* (HIVA KU Leuven, 2017).

necessary to ensure the proportionality thereof'.[64] Moreover, the revised PWD complements the PWED by establishing an obligation for the host state to create a sanctions regime.[65]

3.2.1. *Posted Workers' Awareness of Rights*

Finally, regarding information and awareness-raising tools, the recent Directive on Transparent and Predictable Working Conditions[66] (TPWC Directive) is worth mentioning. This instrument must be implemented in the national law of the Member States before August 2022, and aims to ensure a transparent basic level of universal protection across existing and future contractual forms. With such a general and broad personal scope, the TPWC Directive promises to become a more effective instrument than separate legislative initiatives targeted at specific forms of employment, which may easily be superseded by the rapid pace of changes on the labour market. The idea is that all (mobile) workers, including those in short-term and casual employment relationships, will benefit from clarity about their working conditions and new minimum standards.[67] Article 6 of the TPWC Directive updates Article 4 on 'Expatriate workers' of the abolished Directive 91/533/EEC, to align with the relevant provisions of the PWD and the related PWED. Workers posted or sent abroad should receive additional information specific to their situation. In order to limit burdens on employers, the obligations set out in this Article apply only if the duration of the work period abroad is more than four consecutive weeks, unless Member States specifically provide otherwise. Information provided before the first departure may cover several grouped work assignments and may subsequently be modified in case of change.[68] Where they qualify as posted workers under the PWD, workers should also be notified of the single national website developed by the host Member State[69] where they will find the relevant information on the working conditions applying to their situation.

This, however, is easier said than done in transnational networks of companies, which put mobile 'posted' workers to work as cheap labour in high-wage Member States. As will be addressed in the next section, in the context of such cross-border subcontracting chains, mobile workers typically lack awareness of their genuine (and often volatile) legal status and employer. Moreover, they

[64] Art 1(2)(a) of the revised Directive.

[65] Finally, the revised PWD and Directive 2020/1057 have specific implications for the road transport sector, which are beyond the scope of this chapter. See F van Overbeeke, 'The Gordian knot is cut – CJEU rules that the Posting of Workers Directive is applicable to road transport', 10 December 2020, https://conflictoflaws.net/2020/the-gordian-knot-is-cut-cjeu-rules-that-the-posting-of-workers-directive-is-applicable-to-road-transport/.

[66] Directive (EU) 2019/1152 of 20 June 2019 on transparent and predictable working conditions in the European Union [2019] OJ L 186, replacing the 'Written Statement' Directive 91/533/EEC.

[67] COM 2017 797 final, 3.

[68] COM 2017 797 final, 13.

[69] Pursuant to Art 5(2) of the PWED.

are often[70] effectively excluded from the well-established fundamental right of collective representation.[71]

4. Challenges to Guaranteeing Decent Work in Transnational (Chains of) Companies

Sectoral collective bargaining by strong, representative trade unions is generally acknowledged to be the most effective instrument on national labour markets to lift *and enforce* pay levels above the minimum,[72] as well as to establish other good working conditions and more generally as a redistribution tool and a mechanism for 'workplace democracy'.[73] There is also historical proof for this broadly supported assumption. In the first four decades of post-war Europe, in all democratic countries the sectoral level became firmly rooted as the most important collective bargaining level. This system was supported by national legal or conventional regulative frameworks,[74] and by recognition in (post-war) international treaties such as ILO Conventions Nos 87 and 98, Articles 5, 6 and 19 of the European Social Charter[75] and the International Covenant on Economic, Social and Cultural Rights (ICESCR). As a default, both skilled and unskilled workers on standard full-time contracts were employed under the supervision and authority of one (large) liable and responsible employer, bound by a (generally applicable) sectoral collective agreement. All in all, this socio-economic model brought an unprecedented increase in the living standards and purchasing power of 'the working class'.

Since the 1980s however, many industries have gone through processes of outsourcing and externalisation of activities.[76] These processes were stimulated by privatisation, deregulation and Europeanisation of product and services markets in the context of the 'completion' of the EU internal market (1985–92), and since

[70] Despite the CJEU ruling in Case C-396/13 that trade unions cannot be prevented from representing in court posted workers who have become trade union members, in just the same way as they represent domestic workers.

[71] K Kall and N Lillie, *Protection of Posted Workers in the European Union: Findings and Policy Recommendations based on existing research* (PROMO briefing paper 2017) 5.

[72] Also by its fierce opponents, who often argue that the only purpose of collective bargaining laws is to cartelise the labour market so that workers can get higher wages, and that this is merely a result of interest group pressure. See, eg, RA Posner, 'Some Economics of Labor Law' (1984) 51 *University of Chicago Law Revue* 988.

[73] See G Davidov, 'Collective Bargaining Laws: Purpose and Scope' (2004) 20 *International Journal of Comparative Labour Law and Industrial Relations* 81–106.

[74] And by social security models, based on the so-called Ghent system, as in Nordic Europe and Belgium.

[75] See also the Council of Europe's *European Convention on the Legal Status of Migrant Workers*, European Treaty Series, No 93.

[76] For a global account of this development, see D Weil, *The Fissured Workplace. Why Work Became So Bad for So Many and What Can Be Done to Improve It* (Harvard University Press, 2014).

1994 by the Europeanisation of labour markets under the influence of association agreements and from 2004 onwards enlargements of the EU involving central and eastern European countries. Against this backdrop, first the rise of transnational subcontracting chains and letterbox companies is outlined (section 4.1) and then tools are identified that combat abuses and foster the (enforcement of) the rights of (mobile) workers in said context (section 4.2).

4.1. The Rise of Transnational Subcontracting Chains and Letterbox Companies

Demand for (cheap) labour in the 'old' Member States was matched with supply from 'new' Member States facilitated by legally permitted arrangements, partly based on EU law, such as fixed-term contracts and (posted) temporary agency work, posting of workers in (sub)contracting processes and self-employment. Hence, on top of the ongoing fragmentation of firms and labour within national labour markets, a layer of cross-border fragmentation of labour within the EU emerged. This led to well-known challenges to the territorial application of labour law and to posting of workers as a new business model based on 'regime competition'.[77]

Through cost-driven transnationalisation of subcontracting and outsourcing practices, often but not only in the context of European-wide public procurement,[78] production processes may take the form of a fragmented multiple network of economic activities (often) across several Member States.[79] In many sectors, outsourcing activities made companies replace direct employees with all kinds of flexible employment relations, such as posting as a business model based on 'regime competition'. Characterised as these processes are by unequal bargaining power, crucial social risks are transferred away from the main contractor to SMEs and/or individuals, such as (bogus) self-employed persons.[80] Such a cost-driven chain can ultimately reach the informal economy, especially when large settled companies transfer labour recruitment to labour-only subcontractors that drive costs down even further by using temporary work agencies, gangmasters and other intermediaries. The lower parts of the chain then tend to feature an irregular supply of cheap labour, resulting in low pay, poor working conditions, inadequate

[77] See eg S Evju (ed) *Regulating Transnational Labour in Europe: The quandaries of multilevel governance*, Skriftserie No 196 (Oslo, UiO, 2014).

[78] See Chapter 19 in this volume.

[79] Related to this subject but beyond the scope of this chapter is the upcoming proposal for an EU Directive on sustainable corporate governance, including a mandatory EU system of human rights due diligence for supply chains. See eg: www.etuc.org/en/time-act-human-rights-due-diligence-and-responsible-business-conduct.

[80] For recent investigations of abusive labour practices in (partly transnational) subcontracting chains, see S Borelli and G Frosecchi et al, *Securing workers' rights in subcontracting chains. Case studies* (Brussels, ETUC, 2021).

occupational health and safety, a lack of corporate responsibility and sometimes even 'modern slavery'.[81]

A crucial loophole, hampering enforceability of the regulatory framework, is linked to corporate mobility law. Some legal advisers specialise in setting up letter-box companies, which are legal entities with little or no activity in the country of registration. These companies have strategies for operating across legal areas, whereas inspectorates are often divided along the lines of legal areas ('silos'). A major difficulty in combating such exploitative bogus arrangements is that EU law in principle does not prohibit these companies.[82]

Notably, the CJEU has facilitated the establishment of letterbox companies through its case law in a number of judgments, starting with *Centros* and more recently confirmed in *Polbud*.[83] According to this case law, the 'host state' may not refuse to recognise the legal capacity of a company incorporated under the law of another Member State, even if that company does not pursue any economic activity in the latter state. Hence, such corporate forms may benefit in the same way as any 'genuine' company with real economic activities from the internal market principles that guarantee the freedom of establishment (Article 49 TFEU) and the freedom to provide services (Article 56 TFEU). These registered corporate forms are free to move around and enjoy market access elsewhere in Europe. This is facilitated by many websites that promote incorporation of businesses in, for example, Estonia, Romania and Slovakia.[84] Furthermore, the Supreme Court of Latvia has interpreted posted workers case law in a facilitative manner for letterbox practices.[85] This again underlines the importance of ensuring that, in cases of posted workers,[86] each service provider involved should perform a 'genuine activity' in the Member State where the posted worker habitually works (see Section 2 above on this) and therefore should be a genuine undertaking. Currently, Article 4(2) and Article 4(3) PWED (see section 3.2 above) are not formulated strongly enough to make companies comply with such preconditions for bona fide posting.

In sum, after some 15 years of measures and case law prioritising EU fundamental economic freedom, the need to combat 'regime shopping', fraudulent posting, the use of 'letterbox companies' and (too) complex cross-border subcontracting

[81] The European Agency on Fundamental Rights (FRA) has called for 'zero tolerance for severe forms of labour exploitation' in its report on *Severe Labour Exploitation: Workers Moving within or into the European Union, States' Obligations and Victims' Rights* (Brussels, 2015).

[82] K McGauran, *The impact of letterbox-type practices on labour rights and public revenue* (Brussels, ETUC, 2016).

[83] CJEU 25 October 2017, Case C-106/16 *Polbud*, ECLI:EU:C:2017:804.

[84] www.estoniancompanyregistration.com, www.companyincorporationestonia.com, www.romania-company.com, www.theromanianclub.com, www.slovenskespolocnosti.sk/en, http://zugimpex.com/slovakia-company.html.

[85] Z Rasnača, 'Identifying the (dis)placement of "new" Member State Social Interests in the Posting of Workers: The Case of Latvia' (2018) 14 *European Constitutional Law Review* 150ff.

[86] Many fraudulent situations involve posted (temporary agency) workers who have never actually been employed on the territory of the Member State of establishment of the employer (although this state is allegedly their habitual place of work).

chains was (finally) widely acknowledged from 2016 onwards, as evidenced by the revised PWD and the launch of the ELA (see section 3.2). These are not magic bullets, but only first steps in the right direction. To achieve 'fair labour mobility' and a 'level playing field' between domestic and cross-border companies in the internal market, the EU *acquis* still needs further strengthening.[87]

4.2. Tools to Guarantee (Posted) Workers' Rights in Subcontracting Chains Across the EU

Abuses of (EU) labour law in (transnational) subcontracting chains can be combatted by instruments that stipulate joint or shared employer responsibility. At European level, to date, this approach has been taken only in relation to health and safety instruments. If a worker employed by a subcontractor performs activities at a workplace of the main undertaking, responsibility for some aspects of occupational health and safety are shared.[88] In some other areas of EU law, co-responsibility between levels in the subcontracting chain has been created by provisions regarding transnational subcontracting liability.[89] A number of studies have provided an extensive overview of liability tools at both national and EU level, revealing loopholes as well as fraudulent practices.[90] The most recent update was in 2017 in a report commissioned by the European Parliament (hereafter: the

[87] Interesting in this respect is a passage in the so-called 'Nahles report' of February 2021 on improving social dialogue, which advises the EC to close existing regulatory loopholes that could adversely affect workers' involvement at company level and to 'assess whether to propose a revision of the European framework directive 2002/14/EC on workers' involvement and information and consultation rights so as to include common minimum standards for European and national companies, to prevent misuse in the form of letter box companies or chains of subcontractors'.

[88] The Framework Directive for safety and health at the workplace (89/391/EEC) prescribes that an 'employer shall take appropriate measures so that employers of workers from any outside undertakings and/or establishments engaged in work in his undertaking' receive adequate occupational safety and health information (Article 10). This was implemented in sector-specific Directives. The Directive on temporary agencies (91/383/EEC) adds that 'the user-undertaking is responsible, for the duration of the assignment, for the conditions governing performance of the work' (Article 8). The Directive on the implementation of minimum safety and health requirements at temporary or mobile construction sites (92/57/EEC) introduces mandatory coordination between the various parties in a chain, including self-employed persons on site (from the project preparation stage to the completion of work). See further on effective enforcement of occupational safety and health, Chapter 14 of this volume.

[89] The Employers Sanctions Directive 2009/52/EC provides – at least in theory – the most far-reaching subcontracting liability measures. The Directive is targeted solely against employers of illegally present third-country nationals. This Directive establishes full-chain liability, which implies in principle the strongest protection and highest preventive effect possible, because every link of the subcontracting chain is a possible debtor. However, the wording of Article 8(2) suggest that all links must have knowledge ('the main contractor and any intermediate subcontractor, where they knew that the employing subcontractor employed illegally staying third-country nationals').

[90] B Haidinger, *Liability and co-responsibility in subcontracting chains. Social standards at risk: making the case for labour citizenship in Europe* (LABCIT Project, 2016); Y Jorens, S Peters and M Houwerzijl, *Study on the protection of workers' rights in subcontracting processes in the European Union* (Project DG EMPL/B2-VC/2011/0015, 2012); M Houwerzijl and S Peters, *Liability in subcontracting processes in the European construction sector*, Comparative Report (Dublin, Eurofound, 2008).

2017 European Parliament study).[91] It provides an overview of liability provisions at EU level and a comprehensive picture of the legal systems in five EU Member States regarding liability in (transnational) subcontracting chains.[92]

Because posted workers are often employed in transnational subcontracting chains, the PWED includes in Article 12 a provision on cross-border joint and several liability for the payment of wages in subcontracting chains. This provision stipulates direct joint and several liability, extending liability to one link up the chain only, in respect of any outstanding net remuneration (according to the minimum rates of pay of the host state) and/or contributions due to common funds or institutions of social partners regulated by law or collective agreement (insofar as these are covered by Article 3(1) PWD). While Member States are required to introduce such subcontracting liability in the construction sector and cover at least unpaid net remuneration corresponding to the minimum rates of pay (pursuant to Article 12(1)), they may provide for it in any sector, also for more tiers than only towards the direct contractor and with broader scope than minimum rates of pay (Articles 12(2) and 12(4) PWED). Instead of such a system of subcontracting liability, Member States may take other appropriate enforcement measures (Article 12(6)).[93] All these measures have to be taken on a non-discriminatory and proportionate basis. A 'flanking' measure which might help in invoking the liability instrument in practice is laid down in Article 11 PWED. This provision enables trade unions and other third parties, such as associations, organisations and other legal entities having a legitimate interest in compliance with the PWD, to engage, on behalf or in support of the posted workers, and with their approval, in any judicial or administrative proceedings.

In their implementation, some Member States introduced new measures on joint and several liability, in particular in the context of public procurement and regarding temporary agency work. Nevertheless, considerable differences were observed in the European Parliament study of 2017 in terms of scope. While Germany, Italy[94] and the Netherlands have very far-reaching and elaborate systems of chain liability, sometimes even covering all wage components, Poland, the United Kingdom and – in part – Hungary are pursuing a policy strictly according to the minimum requirements of the PWED.[95]

In line with previous assessments, the authors of the European Parliament study in 2017 assessed the effectiveness of the PWED's chain liability measure as limited,

[91] A Heinen, A Müller and B Kessler, *Liability in Subcontracting Chains: National Rules and the Need for a European Framework* (Brussels, 2017), commissioned by the European Parliament.

[92] Germany, Italy, Hungary, the Netherlands, Poland.

[93] Only Denmark and Finland made use of that, according to the EC evaluation report (COM (2019) 426 final).

[94] Regarding Italy, the assessment showed very strict liability rules, but because foreign subcontractors and posting are less significant than in other Member States and Italy is 'traditionally facing issues with the enforcement of rules', there were doubts regarding the preventive impact in reality.

[95] The report *Transnational posting of workers within the EU. Guidelines for administrative cooperation and mutual assistance in the light of Directive 67/2014/EU*, ENACTING project (VS /2015/0013) (2016), also contains an examination of the subcontracting liability rules in Belgium, Germany, Italy and Romania.

because it is relatively easy to circumvent by inserting a letterbox company.[96] Moreover, the provision includes an escape clause (Article 12(5)), according to which a contractor who has undertaken due diligence obligations as defined by national law shall not be liable.[97] Specific requirements are not defined and are left, according to recital 37, to the discretion of the Member States.[98] This results in a wide margin of interpretation and therefore legal uncertainty.[99] Furthermore, liability is still restricted to the construction sector despite clear evidence that the practice of subcontracting has spread to other sectors, such as transportation, meat processing, agriculture and other labour-intensive sectors (albeit that Member States are free to expand the scope to these sectors). According to the 2019 evaluation by the European Commission,[100] the liability rules have not yet been frequently applied in practice as there are no relevant court cases. Nonetheless, 12 Member States[101] indicated that the introduction of these rules has increased the effective protection of workers' rights in subcontracting chains.[102]

With regard to the need to combat letterbox-type practices (see section 4.1 above), a so-called EU company law package adopted in spring 2019 is noteworthy.[103] In its proposal, the Commission introduced into company legislation a check by the competent authority of the Member State of departure against the risk of abuses in case of cross-border company mobility.[104] Unfortunately, in the compromise text of the adopted Directive 2019/2121 the anti-abuse check is a generally formulated obligation to stop abusive cross-border restructuring processes. The procedure for the anti-abuse check is to be defined in national law. Therefore, it will depend on how ambitiously the Directive is implemented at national level with regard to safeguards against letterbox companies.

5. Concluding Remarks

This chapter identified and examined legal tools and instruments to strengthen and guarantee the rights of mobile (posted) workers, including shared liability tools to overcome the most salient enforcement challenges related to employment

[96] However, because of the – at that time – recent implementation in mid-2016, there was no reliable data or practical experience with the flanking measures of Arts 4 and 11 of the PWED.

[97] 16 Member States introduced the option of a due diligence defence.

[98] Due diligence may include, among other things, measures taken by the contractor concerning documentation of compliance with administrative requirements and control measures in order to ensure effective monitoring of compliance with the applicable rules on the posting of workers.

[99] In contrast, para (2) of the first draft of Art 12 provided a prestructured due diligence proposing how reasonable due diligence could be performed and transposed to national legislation.

[100] COM (2019) 426 final.

[101] Belgium, Bulgaria, Croatia, Denmark, Germany, Finland, Italy, Lithuania, Luxembourg, Malta, the Netherlands and France.

[102] COM (2019) 426 final, 17–18.

[103] Press release 13 March 2019: 'Commission welcomes agreement on the cross-border mobility of companies'.

[104] COM (2018) 241.

in transnational (chains of) companies in the EU. Together, these tools contribute to a 'comprehensive approach to enforcement'. This approach was explained – almost 10 years ago – in the proposal for the PWED as follows:

> The comprehensive approach to enforcement includes awareness-raising (better information), state enforcement mechanisms (inspections and sanctions) and private law enforcement mechanisms (joint and several liability). All aspects are deemed important for a balanced approach. Weakening one of the aspects would imply strengthening other aspects of enforcement in order to achieve a similar result.[105]

Although the view of enforcement taken in this chapter has focused on the position of low-wage mobile (posted) workers vis-à-vis other mobile workers in the EU, the political discourse in the past decade justifies such a selective approach. In order to safeguard and maintain 'one of the most cherished freedoms of our EU',[106] it is important to reinforce intra-EU labour mobility as the human face of the Union, allowing *all* mobile workers to improve their living and working conditions and to improve their social advancement, while preventing (unfair) competition on social standards with non-moving workers in the Member States.

The steps recently taken and subject to a follow-up within the framework of the EPSR are going in the right direction and will hopefully be supported by the ongoing but bumpy process (in CJEU case law) of the 'constitutionalisation of the EU internal market'.[107] However, it is of key importance to insist that respect for and even promotion of effective enforcement of EU labour and social rights is safeguarded in other legal areas as well.[108] This calls for a consistent and genuine operationalisation of the so-called horizontal social clause in Article 9 TFEU, requiring that the EU legislator and policymakers take into account the objectives of social protection, social inclusion and high levels of (good quality) employment in all its policy initiatives, instead of limiting this to the scope of its social policy.[109]

[105] COM (2012) 131, 20.

[106] As the European Commission likes to emphasise: more than eight out of 10 Europeans support the free movement of citizens and the possibility to live, work, study and do business anywhere in the EU. See leaflet *Social priorities under the Juncker Commission*, 29 January 2019.

[107] If the potential impact of the CFREU as a 'counterweight to the neo-liberal orientation of the Treaties' were truly realised. See C Barnard, *European Employment Law* (OUP, 2012) 33. See for further exploration and a proposed approach to a constitutionally conditioned internal market: D Schieck, *EU Social and Labour Rights and EU Internal Market Law* (European Parliament, Policy Department A: Economic and Scientific Policy, 2015) 80–93.

[108] As became clear in the *Laval* quartet, freedom to exercise economic rights may considerably limit the granting or exercising of social rights. Moreover, until summer 2020, it was not compulsory for service providers to pay cross-border posted workers equally to national workers, on the grounds that this would infringe the freedom of services.

[109] In essence, the twofold strategy boils down to a consistent and coherent exercising of labour and social rights in line with internal market law and vice versa. If there is a conflict between those rights, mutual optimisation will have to be achieved. See D Schieck, n 109 at 89. See also R Ferrara, 'The horizontal social clause and the social and economic mainstreaming: a new approach for social integration?' (2013) *European Journal of Social Law* 295; P Vielle, 'How the Horizontal Social Clause can be made to Work: The Lessons of Gender Mainstreaming' in N Bruun, K Lörcher and I Schömann (eds), *The Lisbon Treaty and Social Europe* (Hart, 2012) 105.

9

The EU's Role in the Extra-territorial Enforcement of Labour Laws

SIMON DEAKIN AND BHUMIKA BILLA

1. Introduction

The issue of the EU's role in the extra-territorial enforcement of labour law arises in the juridically complex and politically contested question of the relationship of labour and social rights to international trade. For several years now, the EU has been using free trade agreements and association agreements to exercise regulatory influence in the social policy field (among others) beyond its own borders. In the case of association agreements, the EU is effectively imposing its own social *acquis* on potential future Member States in return for granting them certain trade privileges. This is a type of extra-territorial enforcement of EU labour law that follows a model first established for the central and eastern European states that became members of the EU in the 2000s. It can be understood as a process of alignment that anticipates eventual accession.

The insertion of labour clauses into free trade agreements with third countries is somewhat different. This process does not, as such, extend the EU's own social *acquis* to its trading partners. Rather, according to the template that has developed over time, the parties agree a number of things: a non-regression clause locking in their pre-existing level of labour protection; a reaffirmation of their intention to comply with ILO standards; and a commitment to improving standards of labour protection over time. On the face of it, then, it is not EU law that is being extended. The process can, however, be seen as a variant of the 'Brussels effect', in accordance with which European standards come to acquire global influence.[1] European labour laws are, on the whole, more protective than those in other regions.[2] While international labour law is not the exclusive property of any one country or region, European countries, and by extension the EU, have a particular interest in

[1] A Bradford, *The Brussels Effect: How the European Union Rules the World* (Oxford, OUP, 2020).

[2] Z Adams, P Bastani, L Bishop and S Deakin, 'The CBR-LRI Dataset: Methods, Properties and Potential of Leximetric Coding of Labour Laws' (2017) 33 *International Journal of Comparative Labour Law and Industrial Relations* 55.

ensuring that international labour standards are respected, nurtured and further developed over time. In seeking to enforce international labour standards through the mechanism of trade, the EU is both protecting the European social model, and diffusing it to the rest of the world.

The EU-UK Trade and Cooperation Agreement (EU-UK TCA)[3] includes a novel 'rebalancing mechanism' under which divergences in labour standards with a distortionary impact on investment and trade can be addressed by responses of varying degrees of severity, up to and including trade sanctions. The responses set out in the EU-UK TCA range from arbitration of a mostly advisory character to the unilateral imposition of tariffs.[4] Because until recently the United Kingdom was an EU Member State, the non-regression clause contained in the TCA effectively locks it in to the pre-existing EU social *acquis*, while the rebalancing clause envisages a degree of continuing alignment between UK labour law and EU standards. In this case, then, it is not inappropriate to talk of EU labour law having an extra-territorial effect.

Against the background of these developments, the aim of this chapter is to explore the EU's emerging role in enforcing labour laws beyond its borders and to explore the features of the area of law – which can be thought of as a hybrid of international trade law and international labour law – which has come into being over the past decade as this role has expanded. In section 2 we review justifications for linking trade and labour rights at the level of international agreements. In sections 3 and 4 we take a closer look at the relevant provisions of the EU's association agreements (AAs) and free trade agreements (FTAs). Section 3 examines the provisions of association agreements that in effect extend the EU's social *acquis* to potential accession states, and the enforcement mechanisms that accompany them. Section 4 analyses the labour clauses that have appeared in recent EU FTAs.

As we shall see, labour clauses in association agreements and FTAs come in a number of forms:

- *reaffirmation of commitments clauses*, under which state parties confirm their intention to abide by and implement ILO conventions and other international labour standards;
- *non-regression clauses*, under which the parties agree not to use the implementation of an FTA as the occasion to reverse or downgrade labour laws already in place;
- *best endeavour obligations*, committing the parties to upgrade their laws in future so as to achieve high levels of labour protection; and
- *enforcement mechanisms*, among the latter being the rebalancing mechanism included in the EU-UK TCA, which permits unilateral action to restrict

[3] Trade and Cooperation Agreement between the European Union, the European Atomic Energy Community, of the One Part, and the United Kingdom of Great Britain and Northern Ireland, of the Other Part, [2021] OJ L 149/10. (henceforth TCA).

[4] See below, sections 4 and 5.

market access in the event that divergences in the parties' labour laws emerge over time.

Section 5 then takes a closer look at the types of arguments that may justify a finding that a party is in breach of a trade-orientated labour clause. In some cases, a breach can occur without a specific need to show any impact on trade or investment. In others, a distorting impact on trade or investment may be presumed, if only as a default position that is open to being rebutted by evidence. In a further category, the impact on trade must be demonstrated by the party seeking to invoke the clause in its favour. As we shall see, issues of the burden of proof play a role in determining when a labour clause can be invoked as the basis for the imposition of tariffs or other restrictions on trade. Finally, section 6 offers some concluding remarks. We consider here the likely impact of trade-orientated labour clauses in extending the 'Brussels effect' and its implications for the EU's social policy more generally.

2. Exploring the Trade–Labour Nexus

The link between trade and labour rights goes back to the founding documents of the ILO. In 1919, the Preamble to Part XIII of the Treaty of Versailles, the origin of the ILO Constitution, asserted that 'the failure of any nation to adopt humane conditions of labour is an obstacle in the way of other nations which desire to improve the conditions in their own countries'.[5] However, with the advent of the General Agreement on Tariffs and Trade (GATT) from the 1940s and the World Trade Organization (WTO) from the 1990s, the link was broken: access to the global trading system was not to be made conditional on compliance with even the most basic ILO standards. The Singapore Declaration of 1996, while noting that the ILO 'is the competent body to set and deal with' what it referred to as 'internationally recognised core labour standards', claimed that these standards would best be promoted by 'economic growth and development fostered by increased trade and further trade liberalisation'.[6] Without quite saying that ILO conventions themselves could amount to an interference with trade, it noted that labour standards could be used for 'protectionist purposes',[7] and insisted on the need to preserve the 'comparative advantage' of 'low-wage developing countries'.[8]

Since the 1960s, however, the rules of the GATT, and subsequently those of the WTO, have allowed states to modify the basic non-discrimination or

[5] Part XIII of the Treaty of Peace with Germany (Treaty of Versailles) (adopted 28 June 1919, entered into force 10 January 1920) (1919) 225 CTS 188 (ILO Constitution), Preamble.

[6] Singapore Ministerial Declaration, WT/MIN(96)/DEC, 18 December 1996, para 4.

[7] On the distinction between 'protectionism' and 'protection', see B Billa, *Anti-Dumping in the Globalized World* (Alphen aan den Rijn, Wolters Kluwer, 2019), ch 3 ('Anti-Circumvention in the Free Trade Spectrum').

[8] Ibid.

'most favoured nation' rule by extending tariff exceptions or 'privileges' to selected trading partners. Over time, the practice has developed of countries in the global North extending trading access to middle- and low-income countries if they could demonstrate compliance with social and environmental standards. The EU's 'generalised system of preferences' (GSP) has generally taken a 'promotional' or dialogue-based approach to compliance, in contrast to the USA's more 'conditional' stance, which links compliance with labour standards to economic consequences at the level of the (re)imposition of tariffs and other restrictions on trade.[9] The recent US-Mexico-Canada Agreement (USMCA), in contrast to the North American Free Trade Agreement (NAFTA) that it replaces, contains provisions enabling the United States to restrict the flow of goods into its internal market in the event of non-compliance by producers based in Mexico with certain labour norms, including a minimum hourly wage in the vehicle production sector.[10] The USMCA also requires Mexico to strengthen its laws governing collective bargaining and trade union recognition.[11]

The EU's position is evolving. The policy non-paper released by the European Commission in 2015 entitled *Trade for all: towards a more responsible trade and investment policy*[12] set out the aim of 'an ambitious and innovative sustainable development chapter in all trade and investment agreements'.[13] It argued that sustainable development goals – including labour rights and environmental protection – should form a core component of the EU's trade partnerships. This 'trade for all' approach is reflected in the 'new-age FTAs' signed by the EU over the past decade or so, all of which include a 'trade and sustainable development' (TSD) chapter. Over time, the TSD provisions of the EU's FTAs have become both more extensive and subject to greater conditionality at the level of enforcement.[14]

[9] E Postnikov and I Bastiaens, 'Does Dialogue Work? The Effectiveness of Labor Standards in EU Preferential Trade Agreements' (2014) 21 *Journal of European Public Policy* 923–40.

[10] This is the effect of USMCA Chapter 4 ('Rules of Origin') Appendix ('Provisions Related to the Product-Specific Rules of Origin for Automotive Goods').

[11] USMCA, Chapter 23 ('Labor'), Annex 23A ('Worker Representation in Collective Bargaining in Mexico'). According to the US Department of Labor, the USMCA 'has the strongest and most far-reaching labor provisions of any trade agreement. The agreement contains a labor chapter that prioritizes labor obligations by including them in the core of the agreement and making them fully enforceable. This is a major change from NAFTA, which only contained a side agreement on labor, and it will dramatically benefit American workers and businesses. Complementing the USMCA's cutting-edge labor provisions, the agreement also contains a groundbreaking enforcement provision. The Rapid Response Labor Mechanism is the first of its kind and allows the United States to take enforcement actions against individual factories if they fail to comply with domestic freedom of association and collective bargaining laws. Similarly, the USMCA includes provisions aimed at directly improving wages and bringing jobs back to the American auto industry. The deal contains novel rules of origin that require 40–45% of auto content be made by workers earning at least $16 USD per hour in order to receive USMCA tariff relief.' US Department of Labor, Bureau of International Labor Affairs, 'Labor Rights and the US-Mexico-Canada Agreement (USMCA)', www.dol.gov./agencies/ilab/our-work-/trade/labor-rights-usmca.

[12] European Commission, *Trade for All: Towards a more trade and investment policy* (Brussels, 2015).

[13] Ibid at 24.

[14] M Gillis, 'Let's Play? An Examination of the "Level Playing Field" in EU Free Trade Agreements' (2021, forthcoming) 55(5) *Journal of World Trade*.

This approach is consistent with a so-called 'developmental' view of labour standards. This accepts that trade is in principle advantageous to both sides because of its potential to enhance specialisation, deepen the division of labour and permit the exploitation of respective comparative advantages.[15] To this basically pro-trade position, it adds the point that labour laws can generate mutual gains by disciplining capital to be more productive and achieve a higher level of equality and social cohesion.[16] Social rights promoting income and wealth equality, in addition to their inherent normative justification,[17] have a role in promoting sustainable growth through their positive impact on consumption and capacity utilisation.[18] Thus international labour standards occupy part of a 'decision space' in which countries at different levels of development can reconcile their otherwise divergent interests through a version of 'fair' trade: more developed nations can preserve high levels of social protection against erosion and continue to aim for their improvement, while those in the course of development can avoid entering a 'low-level' equilibrium in which they come to depend on informal work and economic insecurity as the basis of competitive advantage.[19]

In practice, this mutual-gains outcome is very far from guaranteed: as restraints on capital mobility have been increasingly removed over the past few decades, countries have inevitably 'come under pressure to compete to attract trade and investment by lowering their labour standards'.[20] States thereby find themselves in a 'grim trap':[21] even those that are first to 'defect' by undercutting others will eventually lose out once non-cooperation becomes the general strategy.[22] Under these

[15] On the importance of this general point for the operation of labour standards, see the report of the Ohlin Committee, 'Social Aspects of European Economic Cooperation' (1956) 74 *International Labour Review* 99.

[16] On the relationship between labour standards and economic progress, see C Craig, J Rubery, R Tarling and F Wilkinson, *Labour Market Structure, Industrial Organisation and Low Pay* (Cambridge, CUP, 1982); W Sengenberger, 'Labour Standards: An Institutional Framework for Restructuring and Development' in W Sengenberger and D Campbell (eds), *Creating Economic Opportunities: The Role of Labour Standards in Industrial Restructuring* (Geneva, International Institute for Labour Studies, 1994); W Streeck, 'Beneficial Constraints: On the Economic Limits of Rational Voluntarism' in J Rogers Hollingsworth and R Boyer (eds), *Contemporary Capitalism: The Embeddedness of Institutions* (Cambridge, CUP, 1997).

[17] 'The case for fundamental employment rights must rest, in the final analysis, on factors which lie beyond any purely economic calculus': S Deakin and F Wilkinson, 'Rights vs. Efficiency? The Economic Case for Transnational Labour Standards' (1994) 23 *Industrial Law Journal* 289, at 310.

[18] P Sarkar, 'Does Labor Regulation Reduce Total and Youth Employment?' (2020) 52 *Structural Change and Economic Dynamics* 374.

[19] See A Hyde, 'A Stag Hunt Account and Defense of Transnational Labour Standards – A Preliminary Look at the Problem' (2005) Cornell Law School research paper No 06-008; A Hyde, 'The ILO in the Stag Hunt for Global Labor Rights' (2009) 3 *Law and Ethics of Human Rights* 154. For a discussion of Hyde's use of the stag-hunt game, see G Davidov, 'Comment on Alan Hyde: The Perils of Economic Justifications for International Labor Standards' (2009) 3 *Law and Ethics of Human Rights* 180; M Menashe, 'The Race to the Bottom Revisited: International Labour Law, Global Trade and Evolutionary Game Theory' (2020) 40(53) *Oxford Journal of Legal Studies* 65–66.

[20] Menashe, n 19, at 54.

[21] E Ostrom, *Governing the Commons: The Evolution of Institutions for Collective Action* (Cambridge, CUP, 1990) 5.

[22] Menashe, n 19, at 60.

circumstances, international labour standards can play a role as 'correlating devices', penalising defection and thereby altering the pay-offs from undercutting.[23] For this to be a meaningful solution, however, a combination of sanctions, of varying degrees of severity, is required. On one hand, states need to have the option of retaliating against undercutting by closing off access to trade; on the other, mechanisms must be in place to publicise breaches of social rights.

The justifications offered for international labour standards (including trade-orientated labour clauses) can be revisited in light of this analysis. References to a *level playing field* (LPF) are long-standing both in legal texts and in the wider secondary literature concerning the labour–trade nexus. If anything, they are becoming more common, as the recent drafting of the EU-UK TCA indicates.[24] The idea that the ILO exists to 'equalise conditions of competition among the nations' so that trade can be liberalised 'without danger to standards of living'[25] is far from new.

It is doubtful, however, that legal mechanisms can be used to create a *parity of costs* in any real sense. There is an imprecise correlation, at best, between standards understood as 'normative or prescriptive' rules, on one hand, and standards as practice or 'actual terms of employment, quality of work and well-being of workers at a particular location and point in time', on the other.[26] Common adherence to a labour standard in the first sense does not imply convergence of standards in the second sense. Moreover, there will be many factors, in practice, that affect firms' costs, aside from labour laws. Thus if 'parity of costs' is the goal, standards described as aiming at a 'level playing field' are likely to lack coherence.[27]

A more coherent goal of transnational labour law rules is to establish a *floor of rights*. This sees norm-setting as a dynamic process, in which the goal of labour standards in the prescriptive or normative sense is to rule out a 'race to the bottom' or 'destructive competition' through undercutting, while encouraging states to experiment with new forms of labour regulation above the floor. This idea finds a concrete form in the 'minimum harmonisation' provisions that are found in most EU social policy directives.[28] The idea of a 'minimum' here does not necessarily imply that the common level of protection is low but, instead, that the directive is framed in such a way as to leave space to the Member State to adopt 'more favourable' measures. The same principle is observed in the case of ILO conventions.[29]

[23] On the idea of the correlating device in this context, see Menashe, n 19, at 63; S Deakin, 'Legal Evolution: Integrating Economic and Systemic Approaches' (2011) 7 *Review of Law and Economics* 659.

[24] See below, sections 4 and 5.

[25] K Polanyi, *The Great Transformation: The Political and Economic Origins of Our Time* (Boston MA, Beacon Press, 1957), at 27–28.

[26] Sengenberger, 'Labour Standards: An Institutional Framework for Restructuring and Development', n 16, at 3.

[27] See Deakin and Wilkinson, 'Rights vs Efficiency', n 27, at 303–304; Billa, *Anti-Dumping in the Globalized World*, n 7, ch 3.

[28] See the examples given by Deakin and Wilkinson, 'Rights vs Efficiency', n 27 at 305–306.

[29] According to Art 19.8 of the ILO Constitution, 'In no case shall the adoption of any Convention or Recommendation by the Conference, or the ratification of any Convention by any Member, be deemed to affect any law, award, custom or agreement which ensures more favourable conditions to the workers concerned than those provided for in the Convention or Recommendation'.

Non-regression clauses of the kind also contained in EU social policy directives, and which are normal in the LPF provisions of FTAs,[30] can be seen in the same light.

A third conception of labour standards goes further in stressing their *developmental* role as the legal justification for their inclusion in FTAs. This is to see labour standards as 'guarantors of economic development and participation':[31] the interaction of labour rights with trade openness alters the structure of the economy, moving it away from reliance on low pay and informal or precarious work. It follows that labour standards are an 'input into economic development of the kind needed to ensure that strategic factors do not lead either corporations or states to adopt a low-wage route to competitive survival'.[32] The idea of 'social policy as a productive factor' is one that finds expression from time to time in the justifications given for EU-level interventions in the area of labour law, for example in the Green Paper and White Paper on social policy of the early 1990s[33] and, more recently, the European Pillar of Social Rights.[34]

Although the most recent FTAs negotiated by the EU – most notably the EU-UK TCA – use the language of the 'level playing field' in terms that echo the idea of parity of costs, they are arguably consistent with both the 'floor of rights' and 'developmental' conceptions of labour standards, as set out above. Until the TCA the relevant chapters of FTAs were referred to as 'trade and sustainability' provisions, and despite the inclusion of the 'level playing field' terminology in the TCA, its Title XI retains references to sustainable development as the goal that this part of the agreement is seeking to achieve. Thus the overarching 'principles and aims' of Title XI are stated to be based on the recognition that 'trade and investment between the Union and the United Kingdom under the terms set out in this Agreement require conditions that ensure a level playing field for open and fair competition between the Parties and that ensure that trade and investment take place in a manner conducive to sustainable development'.[35] Sustainable development 'encompasses economic development, social development and environmental protection, all three being interdependent and mutually reinforcing';[36]

[30] See below, section 3.

[31] Deakin and Wilkinson, 'Rights vs Efficiency', n 27 at 307; S Deakin, 'The Lisbon Treaty, the Viking and Laval Judgments and the Financial Crisis: In Search of New Foundations for Europe's "Social Market Economy"' in N Bruun, K Lörcher and I Schömann (eds), *The Lisbon Treaty and Social Europe* (Oxford, Hart, 2012).

[32] Deakin and Wilkinson, 'Rights vs Efficiency', n 27 at 308.

[33] Respectively, Green Paper. European Social Policy Options for the Union COM (93) 551 final; White Paper, European Social Policy – A Way Forward for the Union (COM (94) 333).

[34] 'Modern social policy … should be conceived as a productive factor, which reduces inequality, maximises job creation and allows Europe's human capital to thrive. This conviction is confirmed by evidence on social and economic performance. The best performing Member States in economic terms have developed more ambitious and efficient social policies, not just as a result of economic development, but as a central part of their growth mode': COM(2016)127 Launching a Consultation on a European Pillar of Social Rights (Strasbourg, 8 March 2016), at para 2.1.

[35] TCA, Art 355(1).

[36] TCA, Art 355(2).

while the parties 'affirm their common understanding that their economic relationship can only deliver benefits in a mutually satisfactory way if the commitments relating to a level playing field for open and fair competition stand the test of time, by preventing distortions of trade or investment, and by contributing to sustainable development'.[37]

3. Labour Clauses in the EU's Association Agreements

Association agreements (AAs) are bilateral agreements between the EU and a non-EU country that provide for an association involving reciprocal rights and obligations.[38] They traditionally served as the basis for implementation of the accession process,[39] but the EU has gradually used them to create deeper long-term political relations and create 'privileged links' with neighbouring countries. The objective is to create a relationship that exceeds one that can be attained by the conclusion of a trade or commercial accord, and yet falls short of membership.[40] Third countries are granted certain forms of market access in return for demonstrating compliance with the EU *acquis*, including those applying in the field of social policy.

A case in point is the EU-Ukraine association agreement, which has been of strategic importance to both the parties and seems to have served as a template for agreements with Moldova and Georgia.[41] A key element of the agreement is the gradual approximation of Ukrainian legislation with EU norms and standards, which can be both supervised and enforced through the mechanisms provided in the agreement.[42] As opposed to the new-generation EU FTAs, which have mostly been seen as 'promotional',[43] association agreements can be considered closer to the US 'conditionality' model. The EU-Ukraine association agreement's preamble, for instance, states that the 'political association and economic integration of Ukraine will depend on progress in the implementation of the current agreement, as well as Ukraine's track record in ensuring respect for common values, and progress in achieving convergence with the EU in political, economic and legal areas'.[44]

[37] TCA, Art 355(4).

[38] Their legal basis is provided by Art 217 of the Lisbon Treaty, according to which 'the EU may conclude with one or more third countries or international organisations, agreements establishing an association involving reciprocal rights and obligations, common action and special procedures'.

[39] The very first association agreement was signed by Greece in 1961.

[40] W Feld, 'The Association Agreements of the European Communities: Comparative Analysis' (2009) 19 *International Organization* 223–49, at 227.

[41] G Van der Loo, P Van Elsuwege and R Petrov, 'The EU-Ukraine Association Agreement: Assessment of an Innovative Legal Instrument', EUI Working Papers, Law 2014/19, at 1.

[42] O Spiliopoulos, 'The EU-Ukraine Association Agreement as a Framework of Integration between the Two Parties' (2014) 9 *Procedia Economics and Finance* 256–63.

[43] See above, section 2.2.

[44] EU-Ukraine association agreement, Preamble.

The EU-Ukraine association agreement's TSD chapter reiterates the obligations of the parties to effectively implement the fundamental and priority ILO Conventions that they have ratified, and the ILO 1998 Declaration on Fundamental Rights and Principles at Work, and maintain the core labour standards, namely: (a) freedom of association and effective recognition of the right to collective bargaining; (b) elimination of all forms of forced or compulsory labour; (c) effective abolition of child labour; and (d) elimination of discrimination in respect of employment and occupation.[45] The chapter also contains a non-regression clause that prohibits the parties from 'weakening or reducing' existing standards of labour protection.[46]

The relatively novel implementation mechanism of the EU-Ukraine association agreement includes a multi-level institutional framework that includes annual summit meetings at the highest political level,[47] an association council with dedicated sub-committees to oversee legislative approximation,[48] a parliamentary association committee to assist and advise the association council[49] and a bilateral Civil Society Platform consisting of members of the European Economic and Social Committee and representatives of Ukraine's civil society.[50] The extent of market access to be granted to Ukraine will be determined on the basis of assessments made by these committees of the progress Ukraine has made in achieving the EU *acquis*. The market access conditionality is therefore very strong and leaves much power in the hands of the EU.[51] For disputes concerning the interpretation or implementation of the association agreement, the standard dispute settlement mechanism provides for the association council to issue binding decisions,[52] which can be followed by 'appropriate measures' by the complaining party within three months.[53]

For the TSD chapter, there is a specific procedure for consultations followed by arbitration.[54] In case of further non-compliance with the arbitration award, the mechanism incorporates the WTO model wherein the complaining party is entitled to suspend obligations, including increasing tariff rates, 'at a level equivalent to the nullification and impairment caused by the violation'.[55] For specific areas including customs and trade facilitation, competition, electronic commerce, it is required that the dispute be taken to the Court of Justice of the European Union (CJEU) instead of an arbitral panel to preserve the CJEU's exclusive jurisdiction to interpret the EU *acquis*.

[45] Ibid, Art 291.
[46] Ibid, Art 296.
[47] Ibid, Art 460.
[48] Ibid, Arts 464, 466.
[49] Ibid, Art 467.
[50] Ibid, Art 469.
[51] Van der Loo, Van Elsuwege and Petrov, 'The EU-Ukraine Association Agreement', n 41 at 13.
[52] EU-Ukraine association agreement, Art 477.
[53] Ibid, Art 478.
[54] Ibid, Arts 305, 306.
[55] Ibid, Art 315.

4. Labour Clauses in the EU's Free Trade Agreements

The labour clauses contained in the EU's new generation FTAs fall into broadly the same categories as those found in association agreements, namely reaffirmation of commitments clauses, non-regression clauses, and enforcement mechanisms.[56] They also contain best endeavour clauses, which are not such a regular feature of association agreements, which already contain a commitment to bring domestic laws into line with the EU *acquis*. The enforcement clauses of FTAs, unlike those of association agreements, emphasise dialogue rather than conditionality, and do not provide for a role for the CJEU. While best endeavour obligations in FTAs have broadly remained the same over time, the shift towards a fair trade approach, coupled with stricter enforcement, can be observed in the other three categories over each subsequent trade agreement.

4.1. Reaffirmation of Commitments

The EU's new generation FTAs emphasise the importance of compliance with general international labour standards. Article 13.4 of the EU-Korea Free Trade Agreement (EU-Korea FTA), which was signed on 15 October 2009 and entered into force on 13 December 2015, states that the parties 'recognise the value of international cooperation and agreements on employment and labour affairs' and 'commit to consulting and cooperating' on trade and employment issues of mutual interest.[57] The Canada-EU Trade Agreement (CETA), which was signed on 30 October 2016 and provisionally applied from 21 September 2017,[58] states in Article 23.3 that the parties 'shall ensure' that their labour laws provide protection for the 'fundamental principles and rights at work'.[59] The provision also explicitly mentions three kinds of labour law standards, namely those relating to health and safety at work, acceptable minimum standards for wage earners, and non-discrimination with respect to working conditions.[60] The EU-Singapore Free Trade Agreement (EU-Singapore FTA), which was signed on 19 October 2018 and came into effect on 21 November 2019,[61] strengthens reaffirmation of obligations by stating in Article 12.3 that the parties 'commit to respecting, promoting and effectively implementing the principles concerning the fundamental rights at work'.[62]

[56] The first three of these categories are those identified by Gillis, n 14 at 11.

[57] Free Trade Agreement between the European Union and its Member States, on the one part, and the Republic of Korea, on the other part, [2011] OJ L 127/6, Art 13.4.1.

[58] Comprehensive Economic and Trade Agreement between Canada, on the one part, and the European Union and its Member States, of the other part, [2017] OJ L 11/23.

[59] CETA, Art 23.3.1.

[60] Ibid, Art 23.3.2.

[61] Free Trade Agreement between the European Union and the Republic of Singapore, [2019] OJ L 294/3.

[62] Ibid, Art 12.3.1.

It further expands the scope of these commitments by explicitly defining the principles to include: '(a) the freedom of association and the effective recognition of the right to collective bargaining; (b) the elimination of all forms of forced or compulsory labour; (c) the effective abolition of child labour; and (d) the elimination of discrimination in respect of employment and occupation'.[63] The provision additionally states that the parties will make 'continued and sustained efforts towards ratifying and effectively implementing' the fundamental ILO conventions,[64] and that 'the violation of fundamental principles and rights at work cannot be invoked or otherwise used as a legitimate comparative advantage'.[65] Article 13.4 of the EU-Vietnam Free Trade Agreement (EU-Vietnam FTA),[66] which was signed on 30 June 2019 and is currently subject to ratification, sets out a similar reaffirmation clause, as part of which the parties 'recognise that the violation of fundamental principles and rights at work cannot be invoked or otherwise used as a legitimate comparative advantage and that labour standards should not be used for protectionist trade purposes'.[67]

The LPF Chapter of the EU-UK TCA is broadly equivalent to these reaffirmation provisions. It defines the scope of 'labour and social levels of protection' to include: '(a) fundamental rights at work; (b) occupational health and safety standards; (c) fair working conditions and employment standards; (d) information and consultation rights at company level; [and] (e) restructuring of undertakings'. Pensions and social security law are not included.[68] With regard to the EU, the meaning of the term 'labour and social levels of protection' is stated to refer to 'labour and social levels of protection that are applicable to and in, and are common to, all Member States'.[69]

4.2. Non-regression

Non-regression clauses restrain the parties from backtracking on pre-existing labour laws. Article 13.7 of the EU-Korea FTA and Article 23.4 of CETA prohibit parties from '[encouraging] trade or investment' by 'weakening or reducing' labour protection.[70] The EU-Korea FTA provides that neither party shall 'fail to effectively enforce its environmental and labour laws, through a sustained or recurring course of action or inaction, in a manner affecting trade or investment',[71] while CETA provides that a party 'shall not waive or otherwise derogate from'

[63] Ibid, Art 12.3.3.
[64] Ibid, Art 12.3.4.
[65] Ibid, Art 12.3.5.
[66] Free Trade Agreement between the European Union and the Socialist Republic of Viet Nam, [2020] OJ L 186/3.
[67] Ibid, Art 13.4.5.
[68] EU-UK TCA, Art 386(1).
[69] Ibid, Art 386(2).
[70] EU-Korea FTA, Art 13.7.2; CETA, Art 23.4.1.
[71] EU-Korea FTA, Art 13.7.1.

its labour standards to 'encourage trade or the establishment, acquisition, expansion or retention of an investment'.[72] The EU-Japan Economic Partnership Agreement (EU-Japan EPA)[73] provides that the parties 'shall not encourage trade or investment' by 'relaxing or lowering' labour protection levels,[74] while under the EU-Singapore FTA the parties recognise that 'it is inappropriate to encourage trade or investment by weakening or reducing the protections afforded by their domestic labour and environment law'.[75]

Title XI of the EU-UK TCA explicitly links the content of national labour law rules with their enforcement: under Article 387(2), 'A Party shall not weaken or reduce, in a manner affecting trade or investment between the Parties, its labour and social levels of protection below the levels in place at the end of the transition period, *including* by failing to effectively enforce its law and standards'.[76] This additional sub-clause reflects the diminishing role of the intention of the parties in determining what amounts to a breach of the clause; as long as the effect of a targeted or series of actions or inactions is a lowering of the standard of protection (regardless of its original policy objective), the clause would be violated.

4.3. Best Endeavours

Article 13.3 of the EU-Korea FTA, while recognising 'the right of each Party to establish its own levels of environmental and labour protection, and to adopt or modify accordingly its relevant laws and policies', also commits each party to 'seek to ensure that those laws and policies provide for and encourage high levels of environmental and labour protection, consistent with the internationally recognised standards or agreements'. Article 23.2 of CETA, Article 16.2 of the EU-Japan EPA, Article 12.12 of the EU-Singapore FTA, Article 13.2 of the EU-Vietnam FTA and Article 8.3 of Title XI of the EU-UK TCA are in broadly similar terms. Article 8.3, in addition to referring to the ILO Constitution, the ILO Declaration on Fundamental Principles and Rights at Work of 1998, the ILO Declaration on Social Justice for a Fair Globalisation and the ILO Decent Work Agenda, goes somewhat further than its predecessors in committing the parties to 'protect and promote social dialogue on labour matters among workers and employers, and their respective organisations, and with relevant government authorities',[77] and to 'work together on trade-related aspects of labour policies and measures, including

[72] CETA, Art 23.4.2.

[73] Agreement between the European Union and Japan for an Economic Partnership, [2018] OJ L 330/3. The agreement was signed on 17 July 2018 and came into force on 1 February 2019.

[74] Ibid, Art 16.2.2.

[75] EU-Singapore FTA, Art 12.1.3, which continues: 'At the same time, the Parties stress that environmental and labour standards should not be used for protectionist trade purposes.' The EU-Vietnam FTA contains a similar clause.

[76] EU-UK TCA, Art 387(2).

[77] Ibid, Art 399(7).

in multilateral fora, such as the ILO, as appropriate'.[78] The parties to the TCA also agree to take into account views provided by representatives of workers, employers, and civil society organisations when identifying areas of cooperation and when carrying out cooperative activities.[79]

4.4. Enforcement

Although all the FTAs entered into force by the EU since the 1990s have contained a labour element, the EU-Korea FTA was the first to introduce a specific mechanism for the enforcement of its labour clauses. The parties excluded the TSD chapter from the scope of the general state-to-state dispute resolution mechanism set out in the agreement, and created instead a TSD Committee to overlook implementation of the chapter. It also provided for domestic advisory groups with representation from stakeholders and civil society, tasked with advising the governments on implementation.[80] The envisaged enforcement mechanisms were essentially advisory: continuous dialogue between the parties, regular government consultations, annual civil society forums, and establishment of panels with the power to make resolutions, which the parties had to 'make their best efforts to accommodate'.[81] A similar approach was followed by the EU in its subsequent agreements with Canada, Japan, Singapore and Vietnam.

The enforcement mechanisms of TSD chapters in these FTAs have, unsurprisingly, been criticised for being 'toothless'.[82] Excluding the labour clauses from the general state-to-state dispute resolution framework meant that, at worst, a state party found to have violated the clauses might face a non-binding resolution or decision of an arbitral panel. Critics were not slow to draw a comparison with the US model of enforcement, and to point to empirical studies demonstrating the concrete impact of US agreements on state practice and outcomes in its trading partners. In particular, there is evidence of improvement in the trading partners' labour standards through an 'ex-ante due-diligence mechanism'; in other words, countries had strengthened their labour standards prior to signing the relevant FTA with the USA.[83] Despite some predictions that the EU FTAs might have similar impacts, both ex ante, given the scope for signalling in advance the need to demonstrate compliance with international labour standards as a condition of reaching agreement, and ex post, given the provision they make for social

[78] Ibid, Art 399(8).
[79] Ibid, Art 399(9).
[80] EU-Korea FTA, Arts 13.12–13.15.
[81] Ibid, Art 13.15.2.
[82] A Marx, B Lein and N Brando, 'The Protection of Labour Rights in EU Bilateral Trade Agreements: A Case-Study of the EU-Colombia Agreement', International Conference EU Trade Policy at the Crossroads: between Economic Liberalism and Democratic Challenges, Centre for International Development, Vienna (February 2016).
[83] M Kim, 'Ex Ante Due Diligence: Formation of PTAs and Protection of Labor Rights' (2012) 56 *International Studies Quarterly* 704–19.

and civil dialogue following their coming into force,[84] there is limited evidence of either trend to date.[85] A study of the implementation of EU-Peru-Colombia FTA reported a weakening of labour standards in the EU's trading partners following implementation of the agreement, as a result of a variety of domestic factors, including systematic failure to enforce labour laws in practice.[86]

The EU-UK TCA, on the other hand, includes a number of enforcement tools that mark a move away from the dialogue model. Article 388 obligates the parties to maintain an effective system of domestic enforcement, as in the case of other FTAs. Articles 409 and 410 lay down standard procedures for consultation and the establishment of panels, but what sets the TCA apart is the new 'rebalancing' provision in Article 411. While recognising 'the right of each party to determine its future policies and priorities with respect to labour and social protection', under Article 411(1) parties acknowledge that 'significant divergences in these areas can be capable of impacting trade or investment between the Parties in a manner that changes the circumstances that have formed the basis for the conclusion of this Agreement'. Article 411(2) goes on:

> If material impacts on trade or investment between the Parties are arising as a result of significant divergences between the Parties in the areas referred to in paragraph 1, either Party may take appropriate rebalancing measures to address the situation. Such measures shall be restricted with respect to their scope and duration to what is strictly necessary and proportionate in order to remedy the situation. Priority shall be given to such measures as will least disturb the functioning of this Agreement. A Party's assessment of these impacts shall be based on reliable evidence and not merely on conjecture or remote possibility.

The wording here is comparable to the Chapeau of GATT Article XX which limits its application by providing for measures that would otherwise violate GATT 'to be restricted with respect to their scope and duration to what is strictly necessary and proportionate in order to remedy the situation'.

Rebalancing measures under the TCA may include the imposition of tariffs and other restrictions on trade. By contrast, in the event of an alleged breach of the 'reaffirmation' and 'best endeavour' clauses of the TCA, the remedies available to an aggrieved party are confined to dialogue and the convening of a panel that may issue a non-binding ruling.[87] The TCA's non-regression clause, likewise, can lead to a panel ruling, although in this case the winning party is entitled to request compensation or, in certain circumstances, to suspend part of the Treaty, again opening up the possibility of retaliatory tariffs.[88]

[84] E Postnikov and I Bastiaens, 'Does Dialogue Work? The Effectiveness of Labor Standards in EU Preferential Trade Agreements' (2014) 21 *Journal of European Public Policy* 923–40.

[85] J Harrison et al, 'Labour Standards Provisions in EU Free Trade Agreements: Reflections on the European Commission's Reform Agenda' (2018) 18(4) *World Trade Review* 635–57.

[86] J Orbie and L Van den Putte, *Labour Rights in Peru and the EU Trade Agreement: Compliance with the Commitments under the Sustainable Development Chapter*, OFSE Working Paper (2016).

[87] See EU-UK TCA Art 409(9), (19).

[88] This is the effect of Art 402(3) read with Art 402(19), Art 749 (temporary remedies) and Art 750 (review of any measure taken to comply after the adoption of temporary remedies).

The possibility of tariff-based sanctions being employed to enforce the labour clause provisions of the TSD chapter of an EU FTA is a novelty. The shift can be attributed to a number of factors. The TCA is unusual in managing divergence rather than convergence.[89] It can also be seen as a response to criticisms of the earlier dialogue-based approach.

5. A Closer Look at 'Divergences' with 'Material Impacts on Trade and Investment'

The operation of the rebalancing provisions of the TCA will turn on whether there is a '*significant* divergence' of labour laws giving rise to a '*material* impact' on trade and investment (emphasis added). These qualifying words might be supposed to set a high threshold for the party relying on them. Under the Vienna Convention on the Law of Treaties (VCLT), which is relevant to the interpretation of the TCA, a breach of a Treaty is 'material' if it violates 'a provision essential to the accomplishment of the object or purpose of the treaty'.[90] The concept of a material 'impact' is, it might be thought, not exactly coterminous with the idea of a material 'breach' in the VCLT, but materiality in the context of the TCA can plausibly be read as referring to an impact of a substantial and continuing nature. The requirement that rebalancing measures should be 'strictly necessary and proportionate' can be taken to imply, in accordance with their normal meaning in customary international law, that the measures must be both essential and the least restrictive available.

There is limited guidance from the experience of other FTAs on how Article 9 might be interpreted. In 2017 an arbitral panel convened under the terms of the Dominican Republic-Central America-United States Free Trade Agreement (CAFTA-DR) rejected the US government's claim that Guatemala was in breach of the agreement for (among other things) allowing victimisation of union activists, on the basis that the United States had failed to show a relevant effect on trade. Under Article 16 of CAFTA-DR, 'A Party shall not fail to effectively enforce its labor laws, through a sustained or recurring course of action or inaction, in a manner affecting trade between the Parties'.[91] The breaches alleged by the United States in the Guatemala dispute included: failure to organise regular inspections of factories; not acting on labour inspectors' reports of employers' violations; failing to enforce court orders for the reinstatement and compensation of union officials who had been subject to unfair dismissals; and failure to investigate and prosecute homicides of union officials. The panel found that a number of these breaches had indeed occurred, but it concluded that sufficient evidence of a resulting impact

[89] E White and L Van Den Hende, 'The View from Brussels: EU-UK Trade and Cooperation Agreement Level Playing Field Provisions and their Enforcement', Legal Briefing, Herbert Smith Freehills (31 December 2020).

[90] VCLT, Art 60.

[91] Dominican Republic–Central America–United States Free Trade Agreement, August 5, 2004, 119 Stat 462, 43 ILM 514, Art 16.2.

on trade or investment had not been demonstrated, as a result of which it ruled against the US claim.[92]

The analysis in the Guatemala-US dispute turned on the question of whether Guatemala's failure to enforce its labour laws had conferred an economic advantage on specific employers. After a review of the evidence submitted by the United States, the panel found that a competitive advantage had not been demonstrated, largely because it could not be shown that enforcement failures had led to a 'sustained and recurring impact' on employers' costs, as required by Article 16. The panel's ruling 'creates a significant barrier for labor advocates looking to use the labor provisions in CAFTA-DR to enforce labor laws in countries with poor labor rights protections'.[93]

Of more significance for interpretation of the TCA is the ruling issued on 20 January 2021 by the panel of experts convened to consider a dispute between the EU and Korea concerning alleged breaches by the latter of Article 13 of the EU-Korea FTA.[94] The EU argued that Korea was in breach of the 'reaffirmation clause' in Article 13.4.3, under which the Parties 'commit to respecting, promoting and realising, in their laws and practices', the terms of the ILO Declaration of Fundamental Principles and Rights at Work of 1998, including 'freedom of association and the right to collective bargaining'. The alleged breaches took the form of what the EU claimed were deficiencies in certain provisions of the Korean Trade Union Act, namely those addressing the definition of 'workers' qualifying for protection, which excluded certain self-employed persons in a position of economic dependence, dismissed persons and unemployed persons from the scope of freedom of association; the definition of a 'trade union'; the conditions governing election as a trade union official; and the procedures for certifying a trade union.[95]

Article 13.4 makes no reference to the need to show an interference with trade or competition, and the panel rejected an argument that such a reference should be read into the Article by having regard to the overall scope of the TSD Chapter, as set out in Article 13.2. It also rejected as irrelevant Korea's claim that, in light of the ruling of the panel in the CAFTA case, a failure to enforce or comply labour laws should not, without more ado, be seen as 'necessarily and automatically [resulting] in trade diversions or distortions or [affecting] trade flows'.[96] The panel in the EU-Korea case noted that the CAFTA case was concerned with enforcement rather than with the scope of legislative protections.[97]

[92] *In re Guatemala – Issues Relating to the Obligations (US v Guatemala)*, Final Report, CAFTA-DR Arb. Panel (June 14, 2017).

[93] P Paiement, 'Leveraging Trade Agreements for Labor Law Enforcement: Drawing Lessons from the US-Guatemala CAFTA Dispute' (2018) 40 *Georgetown Journal of International Law* 649, 692.

[94] Panel of Experts Proceeding Constituted under Article 13.15 of the EU-Korea Free Trade Agreement, Report of the Panel of Experts, 20 January 2021.

[95] Ibid, at [101].

[96] Ibid, at [58].

[97] Ibid, at [90], [92].

The panel made some broader observations on the way in which the EU-Korea agreement conceptualised the relationship between trade and labour rights. Noting that the 'contextual setting' in which labour rights appeared in the EU-Korea FTA was one of 'sustainable development', the panel clarified that in 'finding that complaints about measures based on Article 13.4.3 are not limited to trade-related aspects of labour' it did not mean to conclude 'that the EU's Panel Request refers to matters which have no connection to trade'.[98] In this regard it was relevant to note that:

> the Parties have drafted the Agreement in such a way as to create a strong connection between the promotion and attainment of fundamental labour principles and rights and trade. The various international declarations and statements referred to in the EU-Korea FTA, discussed above, have been referenced by the Parties to show that decent work is at the heart of their aspirations for trade and sustainable development, with the 'floor' of labour rights an integral component of the system they commit to maintaining and developing. In the Panel's view, national measures implementing such rights are therefore inherently related to trade as it is conceived in the EU-Korea FTA.[99]

This is a strong endorsement of the 'developmental' conception of labour standards,[100] which, elsewhere in its ruling, the panel distinguishes from the idea that labour standards are designed to induce uniform conditions of competition:

> The ILO has explained the modern relationship between trade and labour standards in the following terms: 'the aim is not for the ILO to achieve uniformity in the level of social protection' because 'differences in conditions and levels of protection are linked to a certain extent to differences in levels of development.' Rather, there should be 'universal recognition of certain basic rights … respect of certain common rules of the game …' including those fundamental rights and principles included in Article 13.4.3. This is akin to the idea of the core labour standards as the 'floor' underpinning the concept of Decent Work. The fundamental principles and rights in the 1998 Declaration and the core labour standards are seen as enabling rights, a pre-condition to the attainment of some of the aspirational goals enumerated in the multilateral declarations and statements referred to by the Parties. Once the rules of the game are set, domestic labour law may then be set in accordance with local economic and social conditions, norms and cultures. The EU's Panel Request is, speaking broadly, directed at the former (the rules of the game as they are given effect in domestic law), not the latter (the domestic labour law regime and practices as a whole).[101]

The panel went on to rule in favour of the EU on the substance of its complaint.

Given the placing of the labour clauses of the TCA in a Title that envisages a 'level playing field for open and fair competition and *sustainable development*' (emphasis added), it would be plausible to suggest that they should be broadly interpreted in a way that is consistent with the 'developmental' understanding of

[98] Ibid, at [94].
[99] Ibid, at [95].
[100] On which, see section 2, above.
[101] Ibid, at [82] (citations omitted).

labour standards set out in the panel's ruling in the EU-Korea dispute. So viewed, the issue of whether a post-Brexit 'divergence' in labour laws between the United Kingdom and the EU has a 'material impact on trade and investment' should not be reduced, as it was in the US-Guatemala case, to whether it gives rise to a cost advantage for particular enterprises or sectors. The issue should be addressed more holistically: is a given divergence of such a nature as to undermine the role of labour standards in promoting competition that is both 'fair' and 'open', and development that is 'sustainable'?

It can very well be argued that deregulatory labour law reforms that seek to make firms competitive by cutting their regulatory and compliance costs will create competition that is far from 'fair' and development that is not 'sustainable'. Restricting protections for workers may enable some firms to increase their profits and to undercut others, but these are likely to be short-run effects.[102] In the medium to long term, labour law rights tend, other things being equal, to promote productivity (understood as the relationship between labour inputs and outputs), and to provide a firmer foundation for the competitive position of both firms and nations. If 'fair' competition means anything in this context, it should mean competition based on improved productivity, and not on costs alone. This would be to offer an understanding that is consistent with the idea of social policy as a resource or input into the process of production, which, as we have seen, has a certain traction within the EU's internal social policy.[103]

Would it then be necessary for a party seeking to rely on the rebalancing clause to present evidence in the form of an econometric study or forecast predicting negative social and economic effects of a certain labour law reform? Studies of this kind are sometimes carried out in the context of competition or antitrust law, but to require them in the context we are considering would be to erect a high and arguably artificial barrier to any complaint. Article 411(2) of the TCA refers to 'reliable evidence', which could include statistical studies and forecasts but would not be confined to them.

Nor does it follow that a simple assertion of impact – a 'conjecture or remote possibility', as Article 411(2) puts it – would suffice. There are a number of intermediate possibilities. One is that a divergence of a significant kind would create a presumption of an adverse developmental impact, which the party implementing it would have to rebut or justify.[104] Another possible approach is to require

[102] Menashe, n 19 at 60.

[103] See above, section 2. In addition to the references to social policy as a productive factor in the texts accompanying the European Pillar of Social Rights, reference may also be made to the distinction between competing on grounds of productivity, on one hand, and competing on the basis of (nominal) wage costs on the other, the recent judgments of the Court of Justice rejecting challenges to the revisions to the Posting Directive (Directive (EU) 2018/957, amending Directive 96/71/EC). See Case C-206/18 *Hungary v EU Parliament*, Judgment, at [106].

[104] It may also be noted that the burden of showing that the invocation of unilateral rebalancing measures was not warranted lies on the party wishing to see them discontinued, that is, the party whose labour laws are in issue. See Editorial Comment, 'The Trade and Cooperation Agreement with the UK: A Hard Brexit in Sheep's Clothing', *EU Law Live*, 2 February 2021, noting that 'the burden of proof will

the party defending a divergence to justify its position if it adopted a regulatory change with the explicit intention of gaining a cost advantage. This is by no means an implausible position, as the UK government has frequently invoked the idea of labour laws as a 'burden on business' to justify deregulatory changes to them.[105]

None of this is to suggest that invoking the rebalancing clause of the TCA would be straightforward. The TCA, as an international treaty, creates no directly effective rights for workers and trade unions. The decision to trigger it would lie with the UK government and, representing the Union, the European Commission. However, the existence of the clause will provide opportunities for political action and the exercise of voice by relevant stakeholders. The Parliament may have a role, as would the social partners. While the decision to act ultimately lies in the political realm, the Commission will not be immune to pressure coming from the Parliament and social partners.[106]

For these various reasons, it would seem premature to write off the labour clauses of the TCA. They may well play a role in maintaining the alignment of UK labour law with the EU social *acquis* and, more generally, with the international labour standards which the TCA requires the parties to observe and implement.

6. Conclusion

The growing role of the EU in the extra-territorial enforcement of labour laws is a striking feature of developments over the past decade at the intersection of international trade law and international labour law. It is part of the wider 'Brussels effect' according to which EU standards become a template for companies and countries beyond Europe. This can occur both *de jure*, as a result of the direct extension of laws, and *de facto*, through the adoption of EU standards as an increasingly accepted global norm for the organisation of commerce and trade.[107]

become decisive in future disputes between the EU and the UK. In this context is remarkable to observe the careful drafting of the procedures … Given that the text of these measures was probably carefully drafted by their alleged main user, the European Commission … this distribution of the burden of proof and the possibilities of certain pathways towards unilateral remedial measures hints at a pre-paved path that the EU intend to make use in order to implement its high-level policy goal to ensure a fair level playing-field between the EU and the UK' (https://eulawlive.com/editorial-comment-the-trade-and-cooperation-agreement-with-the-uk-a-hard-brexit-in-sheeps-clothing, retrieved 21 April 2021).

[105] For examples, see Z Adams, C Barnard, S Deakin and S Fraser Butlin, *Deakin and Morris' Labour Law* 7th edn (Oxford, Hart, 2021) [1.22]–[1.25].

[106] As Paiement notes in his analysis of the US-Guatemala dispute, 'the inclusion of labor provisions in FTAs offers opportunities for labor unions and labor rights advocates to take part in disputing alleged violations of labor rights. While the FTAs are formal agreements among national governments, this case demonstrates how a transnational coalition of labor unions can initiate disputes. Notably, the Dispute began with an action by the coalition of United States and Guatemalan labor unions and workers' organizations', which in due course triggered a response from the US government: 'Leveraging Trade Agreements for Labor Law Enforcement', at 691.

[107] Bradford, *The Brussels Effect*, n 1, ch 1.

The EU's social *acquis* is directly extended to potential accession states through its association agreements, a process that can be enforced through trade-based sanctions if the country in question fails to demonstrate sufficient compliance with labour and other laws. In its free trade agreements, the EU assumes a role of diffusing not just its own social *acquis* but, more generally, core international labour standards as defined by the ILO, and given effect through reaffirmation and best endeavour clauses. The EU can also find itself policing other countries' labour laws through the operation of non-regression clauses. In its FTAs the EU has been gradually moving from reliance on dialogue and advisory panel rulings to forward its external labour law agenda, to the use of unilateral trade sanctions as the preferred mode of enforcement.

This development may turn out to have profound implications for Brexit. The UK's departure from the EU can be seen as a major challenge to the Brussels effect in both its *de jure* and *de facto* senses: a large economy is removed from the EU's direct sphere of influence and its laws cease to have the effects previously accorded to them.[108] The LPF clauses of the EU-UK TCA, however, may well end up aligning much of domestic British labour with the EU social *acquis*. It is not just the existing laws that will be locked in as a result of the operation of the principle of non-regression; the novel rebalancing mechanism contained in the TCA envisages some degree of future alignment. How that will actually turn out cannot be straightforwardly predicted.

At the same time, the evolution of the trade–labour nexus poses many questions. As the recent EU-Korea dispute shows, the EU is prepared to use FTAs to enforce core ILO standards on freedom of association. Yet its own compliance with these standards is far from clear. The right of association is one of the matters expressly excluded from the scope of the EU's power to legislate in the social policy field,[109] and the status of the right to strike and the right to collective bargaining as in EU law is, to say the least, uncertain.[110] If the EU is failing to implement internally standards which it seeks to impose externally, it will inevitably lay itself open to the charge of using the labour clauses of FTAs to pursue a 'protectionist' agenda.

As the EU assumes a role in the enforcement of core international labour standards beyond its borders, its failure to address internal shortcomings, in the form of gaps and enforcement deficits in its own social policy, will be thrown into stark relief. Thus one consequence of recent developments may be to revive the case for a European labour code in place of the patchwork approach to EU social policy which has prevailed until now.

[108] Ibid, at [69].

[109] TFEU Art 153(5).

[110] F Dorssemont and M Rocca, 'Article 28 –Right of Collective Bargaining and Action' in F Dorssemont, K Lörcher, S Clauwaert and M Schmitt (eds), *The Charter of Fundamental Rights of the European Union and the Employment Relation* (Oxford, Hart, 2019).

PART II

Enforcement in Specific Areas of EU Labour Law

10

Enforcing Non-discrimination

CSILLA KOLLONAY-LEHOCZKY

1. Introduction: Historical Background and Scope of the Chapter

The evolution of the European Union's non-discrimination has followed the general Community line of developing from an economic community, guaranteeing economic freedoms and free competition under the Rome Treaty, to a supranational constitutional system with enforceable fundamental rights under the Amsterdam and Lisbon Treaties.

The right to non-discrimination under European law is part and parcel of this progress. In the Rome Treaty of 1957 (Treaty establishing the European Economic Community – EEC) the prohibition of discrimination between workers was present as a guarantee of the right to free movement, prohibiting discrimination based on nationality.[1] Similarly, Article 119, guaranteeing equal remuneration and prohibiting discrimination based on sex with regard to remuneration for equal work, was inserted into the Rome Treaty with the intention of guaranteeing equal competition between Member States. Human rights (gender equality) considerations did not play a role. However, the 'human rights nature' of this provision revealed itself in its enforcement[2] and became a fertile seed for the development of EU anti-discrimination law.

The interpretation of the – at that time progressive – European Court of Justice, which developed fundamental rights in its case law, based on 'fundamental values' and 'common constitutional traditions' of the Member States,[3] constituted the

[1] Art 48(2) EEC prohibited discrimination based on nationality as regards employment, remuneration and other working conditions.

[2] As a result of remarkable advocacy work by the Belgian lawyer Éliane Vogel-Polsky in the *Defrenne* cases, in particular in Case 43/75 *Gabrielle Defrenne v Société anonyme belge de navigation aérienne Sabena (No 2)* [1976], dragging the Court of Justice heavily into the interpretation of the non-discrimination provision and promoting its enforcement.

[3] See: A Lyon-Caen and S Simitis, 'Community Labour Law: A Critical Introduction to its History' in P Davies, A Lyon-Caen, S Sciarra and S Simitis (eds), *European Community Labour Law: Principles and Perspectives*, Liber Amicorum Lord Wedderburn of Charlton (Oxford, Clarendon Press, 1996) 13–14.

prohibition of discrimination as one of those values of the Community (EC). From 1999, the year the Amsterdam Treaty entered into force, Article 13 TEC – according to which the EC may take appropriate action to combat discrimination based on sex, racial or ethnic origin, religion or belief, disability, age or sexual orientation – meant that dynamic progress permeated the law of the European Union and promoted social and human rights, including enforceable equality in matters other than equal pay and sex equality. Directive 2000/43/EC implementing the principle of equal treatment between persons irrespective of racial or ethnic origin ('Anti-racism Directive'), Directive 2000/78/EC establishing a general framework for equal treatment in employment and occupation ('Equality Framework Directive') and the progress of the case law led to the thorough revision of the norms of gender equality and the adoption of Directive 2006/54/EC on the implementation of the principle of equal opportunities and equal treatment of men and women in matters of employment and occupation (recast) ('Gender Recast Directive').

Compliance with the Directives still requires that Member States – besides abolishing regulations and public provisions contrary to the principle of equal treatment – declare contracts, agreements, internal rules violating these provisions null and void unless amended.[4] Some Member States have such or similar specific provisions in their legislation (Belgium, Spain, Ireland), but invalidity is not automatic, it requires specific litigation. Most countries have found it enough for compliance to rely on constitutional or general labour law provisions.[5]

The history of EU non-discrimination law is intertwined with the issue of direct applicability of EU norms. The direct applicability – including in horizontal relations – of equal pay norms in the Treaties[6] has been clarified early and confirmed in multiple cases, recently in the *Tesco* case.[7]

The direct effect of secondary legislation (Directives) could result in individual enforcement of non-discrimination rights within the liability of the state for failing to comply with obligations under the Directives.[8] Successful litigation in national courts was possible, except between private parties, blocked by the principle that a Directive could not of itself have horizontal effect.[9]

This changed with the adoption of the Charter of Fundamental Rights of the European Union (CFREU) as part of the Lisbon Treaty. All grounds covered by Article 19 TFEU (grounding the three non-discrimination Directives) are enumerated in its Article 21(1) CFREU. This changed the approach of the CJEU,

[4] Anti-Racism Art 14(b), Framework: Art 16(b), Recast 23(b).

[5] European Commission, DG for Justice and Consumers, *A Comparative Analysis 2020* ('Comparative Analysis 2020') 119.

[6] EEC Treaty Art 119, Art 157 TFEU.

[7] C-624/19 *K and Others v Tesco Stores Ltd* [June, 2021], para 21.

[8] E Ellis and P Watson, *EU Anti-Discrimination Law* (OUP, 2012) 306 – reference to the *von Colson* and *Dekker* cases.

[9] Ibid at 302.

explicitly stating, for the first time in the *Egenberger* judgment, that Article 21(1) CFREU 'is sufficient in itself … to confer on individuals a right which they may rely on as such'.[10] The milestone decision has been followed and confirmed in the *IR v JQ* case of a religious but divorced and re-married employee of a Catholic charity organisation[11] and in the *CRESCO* decision on the differentiation by a private agency between employees in respect of days off for religious holidays,[12]

This chapter covers the issues of enforcement of these three Directives on the concretisation of the fundamental human right of non-discrimination, where '[a]t the heart of discrimination lies prejudice and bias pertaining to the protected ground' of less favourable treatment in employment.[13] This prohibition of discrimination, as a human rights principle, will be examined as distinct from a 'market-type' prohibition of discrimination aiming at free movement and free competition, between otherwise equal competitors, which can easily be removed by applying the same rule to everyone (falling under Article 20 CFREU). The human rights concept of equal treatment (enshrined in Article 21 CFREU) concerns equal treatment between the 'standard' and 'non-standard', the 'mainstream' and the 'other', when 'otherness' is associated with a presumed lower value, a label of inferiority imposed on the group. A further differentiating element is the extent to which the 'suspect' attribute is part of the person's personal identity, which cannot be changed without serious damage to their dignity and human personality.

Enforcement of EU regulations related to non-discrimination outside employment or outside the scope of human rights indicated above are not covered by this chapter.[14]

The chapter first presents the concept of discrimination and protected attributes: the two factors determining the ways of enforcing the right to non-discrimination. This will be followed by consideration of the procedural and substantive issues of the available legal and non-legal forms of enforcement.

2. The Concept of Discrimination

The human right of all persons to equal treatment and non-discrimination is a universal right recognised by international instruments and constitutional

[10] See N Bruun, 'Articles 20 and 21 – Equality and Non-discrimination', ch 19 in F Dorssemont, K Lörcher, S Clauwaert and M Schmidt (eds), *The CFREU and the Employment Relation* (Bloomsbury, 2019) 390 – referring to Case C-414/2016 *Egenberger v Evangelisches Werk für Diakonie und Entwicklung eV*, para 78.

[11] Case C-68/17 *IR v JQ* (11 September 2018), para 69.

[12] Case C-193/17 *Cresco Investigation v Markus Achatzi* (22 January 2019), para 76.

[13] L Farkas and O O'Farrell, *Reversing the burden of proof: Practical dilemmas at the European and national level*, European Network of Legal Experts in the Non-discrimination Field (2015), available at www.equalitylaw.eu/downloads/1076-burden-of-proof-en, 88.

[14] The Directives on fixed-term and part-time employment are the subject of a separate chapter (Chapter 13) in this volume.

provisions of national laws. Although formulated as a 'fundamental right', its effective enforcement requires a broad variety of special means over and above the general toolbox for enforcing labour rights.

Enforcement of the right to non-discrimination is determined by two factors: (i) the definition and concept of discrimination, and (ii) the protected attributes, in respect of which different treatment is prohibited.

2.1. Direct Discrimination

Discrimination occurs when a person is treated less favourably than others in a comparable situation, when this differentiation is based on one of the grounds (sex, racial or ethnic origin, religion or belief, disability, age or sexual orientation) protected in the relevant Directives.[15]

The term 'treatment' covers all rules (including collective agreements) and employers' actions related to terms and conditions of employment: access to employment and dismissal, wages and other forms of remuneration, determination of working conditions such as working time, designation of workplace, health and safety conditions, rules of workplace conduct.

These conditions are taken broadly when it comes to finding instances of discrimination. For example, while the issue of social security pensions is beyond the scope of the Gender Recast and the Equality Framework Directives, pension rules are found discriminatory by the extended interpretation of 'dismissal' or 'pay', in other words as employment, not pension matters. The term 'dismissal' is taken in a broad sense; the dismissal of a woman solely because she has reached pensionable age (lower for women) constitutes sex discriminatory dismissal, and has been established case law since the 1984 *Marshall* case.[16] In the *Palacios de la Villa* case on automatic retirement at a certain age in a collective agreement the Court treated it as purely an age discrimination issue, apart from retirement rules in Recital 14 as an exemption from the Directive.[17] The landmark decision in the *Barber* case[18] drew occupational pensions within the ambit of pay, under the prohibition of pay discrimination.

'Less favourable treatment' is based on comparison, and raises the issue of a comparator. This puts the question of access to information about the comparator(s) or the acceptability of a hypothetical comparator at the heart of the issue of enforcement. The Directives add two further types of conduct to 'less

[15] Art 2(2) in both the Anti-Racism Directive and the Equality Framework Directive, Art 2(1)(a) Gender Recast Directive.

[16] Case 152/84 *MH Marshall v Southampton and South-West Hampshire Area Health Authority*, para 38.

[17] Case C-411/05 *Palacios de la Villa v Cortefiel Servicios SA* [2007], paras 44–45.

[18] Case C- 262/88 *Barber v Guardian Royal Exchange Assurance Group* [1990].

favourable treatment' and direct discrimination, namely 'instruction to discriminate' and 'harassment'.[19] They rightly extend the concept.

2.1.1. Instruction to Discriminate and Harassment – Who Is Liable?

'Instruction to discriminate' is not explained in the Directives; nor is it interpreted in the case law. It depends mainly on the rules and practice in national laws. Implicitly, the term can be found in the reference in the Opinion of AG Sharpston in the *Bougnaoui* case[20] on religious discrimination to a decision of the Dutch Institute of Human Rights. This held that a rule or instruction expressly prohibiting the wearing of a religious sign falls to be considered as direct discrimination. An interpretation that allows action against an employer not only in the case of an explicit, formal instruction but also in case of tolerance (let alone tacit approval) of discrimination would be a prerequisite for effective enforcement.[21]

Harassment and sexual harassment are also forms of 'less favourable treatment', constituting direct discrimination and the clear definition of such conduct is identical in the Directives: unwanted conduct related to the protected attribute, with the purpose or effect of violating the dignity of a person and of creating an intimidating, hostile, degrading, humiliating or offensive environment.[22]

Harassment, but also an instruction to discriminate raises the question of when discriminatory conduct is attributable to and protection enforceable against the 'employer'. The meaning of 'instruction', whether both the instructor and the discriminator or only one of them is liable,[23] whether harassment by a co-worker or external actor (service provider on the sites of the employer) belongs to the concept and is enforceable against the employer – these are just examples of the multitude of questions surrounding the provisions. It should be made clear that, in the context of an employment relationship, irrespective of the concrete person of the harasser or the instructor or perpetrator – the employer, as the party exercising control over the workplace as a whole and over those present there, is responsible for what happens on the premises and shall be held liable to the employee whose rights have been infringed. The employer may then hold the offending employee liable under the employment relationship. Requiring the victim to bring action against a private person or agent of a service partner of the employer would seriously obstruct effective enforcement.

[19] Race Directive and Framework Directive, Art 2(4) in both, Recast Directive: Art 2(2)(b).

[20] C-188/15 *Asma Bougnaoui and Association de défense des droits de l'homme (ADDH) v Micropole SA* (14 March 2017).

[21] See, for more, I Asscher-Vonk, 'Instruction to discriminate' (2012) 1 *European Gender Equality Law Review* (EGELR).

[22] Anti-Racism and Equality Framework Directives: both Art 2(3), Recast Directive, Art 2(1)(c), (d) and (2).

[23] For divergent national rules see *Comparative Analysis 2020*, n 5 above at 48.

The only CJEU judgment on harassment as a form of discrimination was the *Coleman* case[24] regarding the harassment of a woman who was her disabled son's primary carer. Here, however, the question was not the person of the harasser, rather that of the victim. The Court extended the prohibition of direct discrimination beyond people who are themselves disabled to those who are associated with a disabled child.[25]

It might be indicative of the slow development of European gender culture that no sexual harassment case has reached the CJEU so far, unless in appeal cases from the General Court (or its predecessors) in EU staff matters. National court cases are also infrequent. Hopes emerged in the wake of the 'Me-Too' movement that public attention and growing awareness would increase litigation and decrease occurrences in the future.

2.1.2. Discriminatory Public Statement – Discrimination or Just Presumption?

Employers generally avoid making open statements on their discriminatory views, even if they act in a discriminatory way, just to avoid producing evidence against themselves. In three cases – the *Firma Feryn*,[26] *Asociația Accept*[27] and *NH*[28] cases – the CJEU had to assess the inclusion of such speeches in the concept of discrimination, especially the enforceability of non-discrimination in the absence of specific victims and the role of civil organisations in enforcement. While the Court has clearly shown progress through the sequence of the three cases, and has been hailed for a number of landmark elements, some final steps are missing to ensure complete protection.

The *Firma Feryn* case was launched by the Belgian equality body against an employer (one of the firm's directors) who had publicly declared that they 'did not wish to recruit "immigrants"'. The CJEU recognised that the words of the director established a presumption of directly discriminatory recruitment practice, independently of the lack of any identifiable complainant.[29] On the other hand, the judgment was criticised[30] for concluding that the prima facie case can be rebutted by indicating that the actual recruitment practice of the undertaking does not correspond to such statements.

[24] C-303/06 *S Coleman v Attridge Law and Steve Law* [2008] ECR I-5603.

[25] *Coleman*, para 56.

[26] C-54/07 *Centrum voor gelijkheid van kansen en voor racismebestrijding v Firma Feryn NV*, 10 July 2008.

[27] C-81/12 *Asociația Accept v Consiliul Național pentru Combaterea Discriminării*, 25 April 2013.

[28] C-507/17 *NH v Associazione Avvocatura per i Diritti LGBTI – Rete Lenford*, April 2020.

[29] *Firma Feryn*, paras 31, 32.

[30] K Henrard, 'The Effective Protection against Discrimination and the Burden of Proof Evaluating the CJEU's Guidance Through the Lens of Race' in U Belavusau and K Henrard (eds), *EU Anti-Discrimination Law Beyond Gender* (Oxford, Hart Publishing, 2019) 104.

In the *Asociaţia Accept* case, a person known to the public as a leading figure at a football club made discriminatory statements about the recruitment of homosexuals. The Court found that the presumption of discriminatory recruitment policy was established despite the fact that the person had no legal competence in recruiting. However, regarding the shift of the burden of proof onto the football club, the CJEU did not find it necessary to require proof of opposite practice because it would be 'impossible to adduce without interfering with the right to privacy'.[31]

In both cases the dissuasive force of such public speech was the reason for both praise and criticism of the judgment. Recognising its power to create a prima facie case without the presence of a concrete victim, and in *Asociaţia Accept* even extending it to statements by a person without legal power in recruitment, is a step forward. At the same time the CJEU failed to recognise the strong and de facto dissuasive effect as a self-standing instance of discrimination regardless of corresponding practice.[32]

In the third case, *NH*, a senior lawyer at an Italian law firm made homophobic statements in a radio programme, to the effect that he would never hire a gay person to work for the law firm. An Italian association of lawyers engaged in protecting the rights of LGBTI people initiated a legal procedure against him, among other things for non-material damages and to have the court decision made public. The CJEU found that, even if no recruitment process was opened, the case covered the concept of 'conditions for access to employment' (thereby implicitly accepting that the statement constituted discrimination).[33] Furthermore, the Court confirmed the standing of the association to bring legal proceedings for enforcing non-discrimination rights and claim damages within its scope of activity recognised under national legislation, irrespective of its non-profit or for-profit nature.[34]

Despite the progress made by extending the possible material and personal scope of enforcement, the judgment has been criticised for focusing on actual access to employment, passing over the negative impact of such a homophobic statement by a responsible member of the firm on the current staff and their working conditions, potentially generating a homophobic climate that might also constitute harassment.[35]

Discriminatory statements like the one in the *NH* case fit both harassment and the instruction to discriminate, thereby justifying enforcement action against direct discrimination.

[31] *Asociaţia Accept*, Operative part 1, 2.

[32] K Henrard, n 30 at 106, 115.

[33] *NH*, para 43.

[34] *NH*, para 65.

[35] A Tryfonidou, Case C-507/18 *NH v Associazione Avvocatura per i diritti LGBTI – Rete Lenford*: Homophobic speech and EU anti-discrimination law. Case Report (2020) 27(4) *Maastricht Journal of European and Comparative Law* 518, 519.

2.2. Indirect Discrimination

A broader scope of conduct is outlawed by the concept of indirect discrimination, developed by the CJEU in its early judgment concerning adverse treatment of part-timers[36] and included in the non-discrimination Directives as an explicit prohibition.[37] When a measure, formally treating everyone equally, brings about disadvantages for a protected group, regardless of their differences, it amounts to indirect discrimination and in such cases an individual enforcement procedure can be launched.

The explicit prohibition of indirect discrimination – transposed into law by all Member States using similar phrasing – has special significance for sex equality with regard to the disparity between child rearing and other private responsibilities of women and men and its impact to workplace performance. In such cases the courts' interpretation is quite clear: differentiation on the basis of a worker's leave of absence for family reasons is considered indirectly discriminatory.[38]

The protection of persons with disabilities seems to have been increased, too, by the interpretation of indirect discrimination. One example is protection against dismissal due to absence. While dismissal solely on account of sickness does not fall within the scope of protection under the Equality Framework Directive,[39] dismissal of a worker due to intermittent absences (sanctioned as a form of combatting absenteeism, a legitimate goal of employers) linked to disability was considered by the CJEU to be a form of indirect discrimination.[40] The lack of reasonable accommodation (defined as direct discrimination by Article 5 of the Equality Framework Directive), might also be a reason to suppose indirect discrimination.[41]

On the other hand, the applicable rules justifying indirect discrimination in the case of religious discrimination invite efforts to portray instances of unfavourable treatment rather as indirect than direct discrimination. Past cases of religious discrimination reflect such efforts, primarily the case of Ms Bougnaoui,[42] dismissed because certain customers objected to her wearing an Islamic headscarf: clearly, direct discrimination and the cautious attitude of the Court might encourage further weakening of effective enforcement in terms of the false or exaggerated 'neutrality' of clearly discriminatory provisions. The emerging case law can also

[36] C-170/84 *Bilka-Kaufhaus GmbH v Weber von Hartz* (1986).

[37] Art 2, Anti-Racism Directive, Recast: Art 2(1)(b), Framework: Art 2 (2) (b), Self-Employed Art 3(b), 4(1).

[38] In addition to European case law, the EGELR 2010-2 issue provides ample examples of national legislative changes and court decisions that contribute to the effective elimination of indirect gender discrimination with regard to parental roles.

[39] C-13/05 *Chacón Navas*, para 52.

[40] C-270/16 *Carlos Enrique Ruiz Conejero v Ferroser Servicios Auxiliares SA, Ministerio Fiscal*, 18 January 2018, paras 39, 57.

[41] C-397/18 *DW v Nobel* Plastiques *Ibérica SA*, para 75.

[42] See n 20.

confirm views in the academic literature on the hierarchy of prohibited grounds. This issue will be touched upon in the next section.

2.3. Prohibited Grounds

The second factor determining the ways and possibilities of enforcement of non-discrimination are the protected grounds: these are attributes that may not be legitimate grounds of differentiation between workers, apart from narrowly defined exceptions. In other words, any measure to the disadvantage of persons belonging to the protected group is automatically suspected of discrimination. Under EU non-discrimination law such prohibited or suspect grounds are: sex, race or ethnic origin, religion or belief, disability, age and sexual orientation. The available protection against unfavourable treatment depends on the interpretation of the supposed ground of different treatment and of the permitted derogations linked to the given ground.

None of the non-discrimination Directives contain a definition of the protected attributes. The Court has developed its interpretation of the scope of certain grounds but not all. Thus, the CJEU extended the concept of 'sex' to encompass pregnancy (pregnancy discrimination)[43] and to discrimination arising from gender reassignment[44] (now this extension is included in Recital (3) of the Gender Recast Directive).

Definitional issues have emerged in the context of disability, and the Court has made progressive efforts to broaden the scope and enforceability of protection. Thus, besides the abovementioned *Conejero* case, in which sickness attributable to disability was deemed not to be a just reason for dismissal, the CJEU extended the concept and protection of disability to obesity in the *Kaltoft* case, in which an obese childminder who had been working for approximately 15 years was dismissed after several visits and inquiries regarding his weight-loss. The Court interpreted the Equality Framework Directive as meaning that a worker's obesity constitutes a disability.[45]

2.3.1. Hierarchy of Grounds – Its Impact on Enforcement; Multiple Grounds

There is a dispute in the academic literature about whether there is a hierarchy of prohibited grounds of discrimination. Hierarchy has relevance for enforcement in that it affects the strength and preconditions of derogations and exceptions.

[43] C-177/88 *Elisabeth Dekker v VJV-Centrum Plus* [November, 1990], para 12.

[44] C-13/94 *P v S and Cornwall County Council*, EU:C:1996:170, [1996] ECR I-2143, para 20.

[45] C-354/13 *Fag og Arbejde (FOA), acting on behalf of Karsten Kaltoft, v Kommunernes Landsforening (KL), acting on behalf of the Municipality of Billund*, para 64.

Theoretically, the nexus of personal identity, the dignity of the person can be indicated as a factor. Without going into the debate on hierarchy of grounds, the interpretation and case law of the various enforcement bodies seem to reinforce hierarchical differences.

There are hardly any direct exceptions regarding race other than positive action, and no such case has yet reached the Court. Exceptions from sex discrimination require the highest level of justification, under strict interpretation, and there has clearly been progress in enforceability as gender stereotypes have tended to wither away. In 1983 the Court dismissed the Commission's claim of a violation of equal treatment in the UK regulation excluding male applicants from training to become a midwife.[46] The UK reaction was to abolish the exception. Public safety might be a reason in a situation of frequent assassinations (not generally) to restrict policing duties to men equipped with firearms,[47] while the risks pertaining to hiring women as prison guards in an exclusively male prison are not accepted as derogating from the prohibition of sex discrimination.[48]

At the other end of the scale, religious and age discrimination show clear examples of occupying a lower place in the hierarchy by their permitted specific exceptions. They explicitly allow, in Articles 4(2) and 6, further flexibility on the part of the national legislator. Enforcement of the prohibition of age discrimination – the recent offspring of European non-discrimination, and consolidated by the Court's carefully crafted interpretation of both young-age and old-age discrimination[49] – is weakened by the almost boundless interpretation of subordination to labour market considerations already in the Equality Framework Directive (Article 6(1)). The confirmation of automatic dismissal in the *Rosenbladt* case[50] uses the vague and not really verified statement on 'better distribution of work between generations',[51] which returns in other cases as well. Another standard and unverified argument weakens the enforcement of non-discrimination on the ground of young age, too: lowering job security with the alleged aim of promoting access to the labour market. More clearly, the aim is to impose cost-saving flexible solutions for employers. This was first assessed in the *Bordonaro* case, when under new regulations the labour contract was converted into an on-call contract for an indefinite period and after some months the worker in question was notified that his contract had ended on his 25th birthday under the new law. Despite the strong concerns of AG Bobek, the CJEU concluded that,

[46] C-165/82 *Commission of the European Communities v UK.*

[47] Case C-222/84 *Marguerite Johnston v Chief Constable of the Royal Ulster Constabulary*, para 40.

[48] C-14/83 *Sabine von Colson and Elisabeth Kamann v Land Nordrhein-Westfalen* (10 April 1984).

[49] See the first, landmark cases outlawing old age and young age discrimination: Case C-144/04 *Werner Mangold v Rüdiger Helm* (22 November 2005) as a principle, and, on the ground of the Equality Framework Directive: Case C-411/05 *Palacios de la Villa v Cortefiel Servicios SA* (2007) for old age discrimination, and C-555/07 *Kücükdeveci v Swedex GmbH* (2010) for young age discrimination.

[50] C-45/09 *Gisela Rosenbladt v Oellerking Gebäudereinigungsges. mbH* (2 February 2009), paras 53, 77, 80.

[51] Ibid, para 62.

as serving a legitimate aim of labour market policy, the means are appropriate and necessary and therefore not precluded by Directive 2000/78/EC.[52]

The prohibition of religious discrimination seems to fall victim to business interests and low justification requirements. In the name of a 'policy of neutrality' the Court accepted – attracting huge criticism – the ban on wearing a headscarf in the *Achbita*[53] and *Bougnaoui* judgments,[54] qualifying (questionably) indirect discrimination and thereby lowering the level of permitted exceptions. Recently in the joined cases of *IX v WABE eV* (child care centres) and *MH Müller Handels GmbH v MJ* (drugstore chain)[55] the Court found that internal rules prohibiting wearing a religious symbol or veil in the workplace do not constitute direct discrimination on the grounds of religion or belief, provided that the rule is applied in a general and undifferentiated way and might be justified, if preconditions were fulfilled, as indirect discrimination.[56] 'Undifferentiated' points at the core of discrimination here: the prohibition is not 'neutral', but seriously differentiates to the disadvantage of those whose religion strictly requires wearing or displaying certain things.

'Preserving prejudice in the name of profit'[57] is a suitable description of these cases exposing workers to tough decisions regarding their job and dignity. This might indicate disappointing developments with regard to effective enforcement of non-discrimination and confirm a hierarchy of protected grounds.

These headscarf cases call attention to a gap in EU non-discrimination law: the lack of an adequate response to discrimination on multiple grounds either in legal provisions[58] or in jurisprudence. In both cases the victim of discrimination was not only a member of a religious minority, but also a woman and also belonging to a racial minority – in this instance deprived of their job in the name of religious neutrality. The issue of multiple (or intersectional) discrimination was not raised.

Multiple discrimination on the grounds of sex, ethnic origin and age was expressly referred to by *Galina Meister*,[59] although because, according to the CJEU, she had no right to information about the reasons for the rejection, the discriminatory grounds could not be examined.

Z[60] was born without a uterus and had her biological child through a surrogate pregnancy. Her request for maternity leave was refused on the ground that she

[52] C-143/16 *Abercrombie & Fitch Italia Srl v Bordonaro* (July 2017), para 47.

[53] Case C-157/15 *Samira Achbita, Centrum voor gelijkheid van kansen en voor racismebestrijding v G4S Secure Solutions NV* (3 April 2015).

[54] See n 20.

[55] Cases C-804/18 *IX v WABE eV* and C-341/19 *MH Müller Handels GmbH v MJ.*

[56] Ibid, para 55.

[57] Comment by M van den Brink: https://verfassungsblog.de/preserving-prejudice-in-the-name-of-profit/.

[58] Enshrined only in recitals 14 and 3 of the Anti-Racism and the Equality Framework Directives.

[59] C-415/10 *Galina Meister v Speech Design Carrier Systems GmbH*, January 2012.

[60] C-363/12 *Z v A Government department and the Board of Management of a community school.*

was not pregnant; she claimed discrimination on the ground of sex and disability. The claim failed; the CJEU found no breach either of the Gender Recast Directive, or of the provisions of the Equality Framework Directive prohibiting disability discrimination.

The *Parris* case[61] – the combined effect of sexual orientation and age – presented the Court with an important opportunity to rule on multiple discrimination. The same-sex partner of Mr Parris was declared ineligible for a survivor's pension because eligibility was limited to surviving civil partners who had entered their civil partnership prior to their 60th birthday. Mr Parris was over 60 when they established their civil partnership. However, same-sex marriage was recognised in Ireland only after his 60th birthday. The Irish court referring the case to the CJEU put three questions: (i) whether the prescription of the 60th birthday limiting entitlement of same-sex partner to survivor's benefit constitutes discrimination on the ground of sexual orientation, in circumstances in which they were not permitted by national law to enter a civil partnership prior to the partner's 60th birthday? (ii) Does the same limitation, under the same conditions, constitute discrimination on grounds of age? And (iii), clearly addressing the issue of multiple discrimination, if the answer to both previous questions is negative, would it constitute discrimination if the limitations on entitlements arose from the combined effect of age and sexual orientation?

AG Kokott, finding discrimination on both alleged grounds separately, did not consider the question relevant in the case, but nevertheless emphasised that splitting and exclusively assessing one or the other ground in isolation would be inconsistent with the principle of non-discrimination.[62] In contrast to her Opinion, the Court found no discrimination on the ground of either age or sexual orientation, and concluded that the combined effect of the two cannot create discrimination.

2.3.2. Extension of Grounds: Victimisation and Discrimination by Association

Effective enforcement of the principle of equality requires adequate judicial protection against victimisation. Because of the weaker position and vulnerability, the fear of adverse consequences in response to a complaint may deter victims from initiating an enforcement procedure. For this reason, the Equality Directives require that Member States prohibit victimisation,[63] that is, introduce measures in their national legal systems that protect people from dismissal or any adverse treatment in response to a complaint or to proceedings aimed at enforcing compliance with the principle of equal treatment.

[61] C-443/15 *David L Parris v Trinity College Dublin and Others.*
[62] Opinion, §§153, 155.
[63] Art 9 Anti-Racism Directive, Art 11 Equality Framework Directive, Art 24 Gender Recast Directive.

Victimisation is prohibited as a self-standing form of offence: the adverse treatment is not based directly on the prohibited ground, but instead on the act of stepping up against discrimination. The wording of the Directives left it unclear who shall be protected by this prohibition: only the complainant or are others, acting in support of her, also protected? Only the Gender Recast Directive makes reference to third persons: 'employees' representatives provided for by national laws and/or practices'.

Similarly, the meaning of 'adverse treatment' as victimisation remained unclear, in national laws limited to dismissal. In *Coote*[64] the Court clearly dissented from the view that only the threat of dismissal 'may effectively deter a worker from making use of the right to judicial protection', and considered the refusal to provide references and thereby obstruct the dismissed employee's attempts to find new employment as a deterrent reaction to legal proceedings.

The first victimisation judgment under the Recast Directive may give an impetus to a clearer and more extended interpretation of protection. In the *Hakelbracht* case[65] the job applicant was found suitable for the job by the interviewer but was nevertheless rejected because of her pregnancy. The interviewer warned the employer of the prohibited discrimination. Hakelbracht submitted her complaint, and the interviewer was dismissed, being blamed for this outcome. The Court declared that Belgian law, in restricting the protection to employees who appeared formally as a witness in the case and excluding employees who informally supported the discriminated person, was not in conformity with Article 24 of the Directive. Hopefully this clarification will guide and broaden future interpretation, not limiting personal scope by any formal condition, but instead extending it to any worker involved in the claim.

Another extension of the concept is 'discrimination by association', when the ground of unfavourable treatment is not the protected attribute of the worker but rather the victim's association with a person belonging to the protected group. The *Coleman* case – pioneering also in establishing harassment[66] – extended the concept to 'discrimination by association', the harassment of the worker due to her disabled child, extending the protected grounds, as well as the concept of 'direct discrimination'.

3. Litigation and the Burden of Proof[67]

For the enforcement of non-discrimination, the Equality Directives stipulate the Member States' obligation to establish judicial and/or administrative procedures

[64] C-185/97 *Coote v Granada Hospitality Ltd* [1998] paras 27–28.
[65] C-404/18 *Jamina Hakelbracht and Others v WTG Retail BVBA*, 20 June 2019.
[66] See n 24 above.
[67] For a general description, see Chapter 3 in this volume.

available for those who consider themselves wronged by a failure to apply the principle of equal treatment to them.[68]

The primary mode of enforcement is civil litigation or equivalent procedure before a court, tribunal or other body. Administrative and criminal procedures[69] are also available, rather of a complementary nature, exceptionally as a substitute for a civil enforcement procedure.

3.1. Access to Court

Guaranteed access to justice (courts or other independent judicial bodies), and to real and efficient remedies for victims of employment discrimination are of primary importance for ensuring effective enforcement of EU equality law. Its importance has been increased by the double vulnerability of the victims: the weaker party is in a legally dependent position, in addition to belonging to a socially disadvantaged group. These factors enhance the likelihood of being deterred from standing up for their rights. Therefore, the Directives lay down multiple forms of protection and support for enforcement.

First of all, Member States are obliged to ensure the availability of judicial procedures for all persons who consider themselves wronged by a failure to apply the principle of equal treatment to them. Access to the judicial process must be guaranteed even after the employment relationship in which the discrimination allegedly occurred has ended.[70]

In the *Johnston* case[71] the CJEU deemed that the principle of effective judicial control does not allow the exclusion of review by the courts even in cases in which public safety would dictate keeping the case closed from external view. It concluded that the right of access to court excludes treating as conclusive evidence a certificate issued by a national authority, derogating from the principle of equal treatment between men and women for the purpose of protecting public safety.[72]

3.2. Burden of Proof

3.2.1. Establishing a Prima Facie Case for Shifting the Burden of Proof

Standard rules of evidence – whoever alleges something has the burden of proving it – would make it impossible to challenge discrimination. CJEU jurisprudence

[68] Art 7(1) Anti-Racism Directive, Art 9(1) Equality Framework Directive, Art 17 (1) of the Recast Directive. Identical text in Art 9(1) Self-Employed Directive.

[69] See Chapters 4 and 5 in this volume.

[70] Art 17(1) Recast Directive, Art 7 Anti-Racism Directive, Art 9 Framework Directive.

[71] See n 47.

[72] Para 21.

pointed out in case law on pay discrimination from the late 1980s – first in the two landmark judgments *Danfoss*[73] (dispute over gender-discriminatory pay supplements) and *Enderby*[74] (dispute over different pay rates for jobs of equal value) – that without shifting the burden of proof workers would be unable to enforce their right to equal pay. This approach to the burden of proof was later codified into EU law.

All Member States now have the obligation to adopt rules ensuring

> that, when persons who consider themselves wronged because the principle of equal treatment has not been applied to them establish, before a court or other competent authority, facts from which it may be presumed that there has been direct or indirect discrimination, it shall be for the respondent to prove that there has been no breach of the principle of equal treatment.[75]

Criminal procedures are excluded from this rule.

Even if 'shift' was the term used by the CJEU in the *Enderby* judgment (para 18), the Directives rather divided it between the two parties. The complainant has the burden of establishing the presumption that there was discrimination, and when this is established, the burden shifts to the defendant to show that the difference in treatment is not discriminatory.

The initial burden rests with the complainant to establish 'prima facie discrimination': facts from which it may be presumed that there has been direct or indirect discrimination. The wording of the Directives contains uncertainties. According to the dominant interpretation this means two things: providing sufficient evidence of the disadvantage suffered by the victim, and showing the likelihood of a causal relationship between the disadvantage and the protected attribute.

Apart from the difficulties involved in showing the disadvantage (discussed in the next section) the second requirement can create insurmountable obstacles, undermining the rule on the burden of proof itself and effective enforcement overall. Even if it decreases the onus on the complainant, not to prove, but 'only' to establish 'likelihood' it needs the presentation of facts that are, in the majority of cases, not available to the litigant (for example, documents or witness statements). The power of this provision in the Directives consequently depends on the concrete national rules and the attitude of the court or other adjudicating body, as well as on the access of interest representatives or other civil organisations to the procedure.

In some countries the regulation putting the burden on the complainant is coupled with judicial interpretation that is more supportive of claimants. Such couplings are reported from France, where, despite the petitioner's obligation

[73] C-109/88 *Handels og Kontorfunktionarernes Forbund i Danmark v Dansk Arbejdsgiverforening (acting on behalf of Danfoss)*, para 13.

[74] C-127/92 *Enderby v Frenchay Health Authority and Secretary of State of Health*, para 18.

[75] Art 8(2) Anti-Racism Directive, Art 10(1) Framework Directive, Art 19(1) Recast Directive. The second paragraph in each provision permits the introduction of rules more favourable to plaintiffs.

to establish the presumption of discrimination, the *Conseil d'Etat* held that the judge has the duty 'to actively ensure that the respondent provides evidence' that its decision had objective grounds and was devoid of discriminatory objectives.[76] The Court of Cassation, too, recently revised its former interpretation that the petitioner had to bear the burden of verifying arbitrariness of differential treatment of persons in comparable situations arising from collective agreements.[77]

An opposite example might be raised concerning Hungary, the exemplary rule of the 2003 Equal Treatment Act.[78] It requires merely that the aggrieved party establish the likelihood of the disadvantage and that they possess (or are assumed to possess by the perpetrator) a protected characteristic. This is enough to shift the burden to the defendant who has to prove that either there was no disadvantage or the unfavourable treatment was not related to the characteristic, or that it was a situation exempted from the prohibition.

3.2.2. Access to Information; Transparency

Establishing a presumption of differential treatment requires the submission of information on the treatment of others. Lack of access to such information is one of the main obstacles facing victims of discrimination in their efforts to take action and it can render the rule on the burden of proof impracticable.[79] To tackle this deterrent effect at least partially, a robust approach on the part of adjudicating bodies would be necessary, either to enable access to the relevant documents – perhaps already in the pre-litigation phase – or to draw the proper conclusions on the presumption of discrimination.

The CJEU has had to adjudicate such a situation in two cases. In the *Kelly* case[80] a rejected applicant to an MA course in social sciences (social worker) submitted a complaint that he had been rejected because of discrimination on grounds of sex. He claimed that he was better qualified than the least-qualified female candidate who had been admitted and demanded disclosure of applications. The CJEU held that the EU anti-discrimination rules did not entitle applicants to access information about the qualifications of other applicants for the purpose of establishing a prima facie case of discrimination and also that such disclosure would be against EU rules on confidentiality of personal data.[81]

A similar rejection came from the Court in the *Galina Meister* case.[82] Meister, a Russian national, born in 1961, had applied to a job advertisement in Germany,

[76] *Comparative Analysis 2020*, n 5 at 92, quoting France, Conseil d'Etat, No 298348, 30 October 2009.
[77] Ibid, referring to: Court of Cassation, Social Chamber, decision of 3 April 2019, Case No 17-11970.
[78] Act CXXV of 2003 on Equal Treatment and the Promotion of Equal Opportunities, Art 19(1).
[79] Henrard, n 30 at 95.
[80] C-104/10 *Patrick Kelly v National University of Ireland (University College, Dublin)*, July 2011.
[81] See n 80, *Kelly*, paras 38, 48 and 53.
[82] See n 59.

being in possession of a Russian degree recognised as equivalent in Germany to the degree required for the advertised job. Her application was rejected in October 2006, but the same company soon advertised the same job again. She made another attempt to apply, but was not even invited to an interview. She believed that she was the victim of discrimination on the grounds of sex, age and ethnic origin. In this case, too, the CJEU expressed, with reference to *Kelly*, that the Directives must be interpreted as not entitling her – even if she could plausibly claim that she met the job requirements – to gain access to information on the process.[83]

At the same time, the Court expressed its awareness that the refusal of disclosure may conceal information suggesting discrimination, and acknowledged that it may call into question the efficacy of the burden of proof provision and the achievement of the Directives' objectives. Nevertheless, it left it to the national courts to ascertain whether that was the case.[84]

3.2.3. Specific Role of Access to Information and Transparency in Eliminating Pay Gaps

The right to equal pay for the same work or work of equal value for female and male workers is contained in Article 119 EEC Treaty, with a purely economic intention. Already the early interpretation of the CJEU established it as part of the foundations of the Community, including its direct vertical and horizontal enforceability.[85] With Europe's turn from a free market economic area to a constitutional community based on human rights and values, the equal pay rule became the expression of one of the fundamental principles of European labour law, included in Article 157 TFEU, specified in Article 4 Gender Recast Directive, and surrounded by multiple guarantees and provisions to facilitate enforcement.

Notwithstanding multiple protections the pay gap has not decreased accordingly: it still stands at 14 per cent, 55 years after the *Defrenne (2)* case. The persistence of gender stereotypes, and women's unequal status and role in society are unequivocally the root cause, but legal enforcement mechanisms have an important, albeit limited function.

The small number of cases brought to court compared with the high level of pay discrimination point to a serious gap in the enforcement mechanisms: the lack of access to information coupled with the so-called 'individual rights strategy'; in other words, individual employees have to initiate action to claim their right to equal pay.

In order to establish a prima facie case, complainants have to establish that comparable male workers are receiving higher pay and also that the complainant's work is identical or 'of equal value'. Confidentiality, personal data protection,

[83] See n 59, *Meister*, para 46.
[84] See n 80, *Kelly*, paras 39, 54; n 59, *Meister* paras 40, 47.
[85] *Defrenne* No 2. See n 2 above, para 39.

occasionally even reference to business interests are invoked most frequently as reasons for refusing access to the (potential) complainant. In the absence of a comparator, even the first element – the disadvantage suffered – cannot be established, never mind the fact that information on which workers are doing equal work or work of equal value is frequently not available.[86]

The vicious circle here is evident from the statement of the Court in the *Brunnhofer* case (an equal pay dispute with reference to *Danfoss*[87]): where a pay system lacks transparency it is for the employer to prove that the system is not discriminatory, if (!) a female worker establishes, in relation to a relatively large number of employees, that women's average pay is less than that of men.[88] In the absence of access to information on wages, this seemingly beneficial approach cannot help effective enforcement.

Because of an overall lack of transparency of pay systems in most Member States, in March 2014 the Commission adopted a Recommendation[89] on transparency with the aim of guiding and assisting Member States in combating pay discrimination and tackling the persistent gender pay gap. The core measures include: (i) the right of employees to obtain information on pay levels by gender for those doing the same work or work of equal value; (ii) a duty of employers to report on their average remuneration by category or position, broken down by gender; (iii) pay audits that include job evaluation and classification, as well as pay differentials on grounds of gender; (iv) discussion of equal pay at the appropriate collective bargaining level.

Analysis of the Recommendation's implementation shows a desperately low level of acceptance. The most important step – granting the individual the right to demand information on pay levels – has been introduced by only three countries (Finland, Ireland and Norway). Of the 31 countries surveyed (the then 28 Member States and Iceland, Liechtenstein and Norway) transparency measures have been developed in only ten, making more detailed information on these instruments available.[90]

On 4 March 2021 the Commission published its proposal on a Directive to strengthen application of the principle of equal pay through pay transparency and enforcement mechanisms[91] that would make these obligations mandatory.

[86] Case C-400/93 *Royal Copenhagen* [May 1995], para 24.

[87] See n 73.

[88] Case C-381/99 *Susanna Brunnhofer v Bank der österreichischen Postsparkasse AG*, 26 June 2001, para 54.

[89] Commission Recommendation of 7 March 2014 on strengthening the principle of equal pay between men and women through transparency, C(2014) 1405 final, 8.3.2014, 112–16.

[90] J Hofman, M Nightingale, M Bruckmayer, P Sanjurjo, *Equal Pay for Equal Work: Binding Pay-transparency Measures*. Study commissioned by the EMPL committee. Directorate-General for Internal Policies, February 2020, 24.

[91] Commission Proposal for a Directive of the European Parliament and of the Council to strengthen the application of the principle of equal pay for equal work or work of equal value between men and women through pay transparency and enforcement mechanisms. Brussels, 4.3.2021 COM(2021) 93 final.

It did so in a more elaborate form than the Recommendation, taking certain experiences into consideration. Pay gap audits at both public and private employers that might remedy the problem of the individual litigation model are not included, and more emphasis is needed on the peer-review system, mainly for larger companies. Considering the contradictory opinions on the advantages and disadvantages of binding transparency measures,[92] the extent to which the Directive will promote transparency and non-discrimination in setting pay is to be seen.

3.3. Obstacles and Assistance

Despite guaranteed access to courts and other procedures in all Member States, the level of non-discrimination litigation in the EU remains low overall. The most common reasons (beyond the transparency problem of pay litigation) include low awareness of possibilities and the weak position of the victims, but other reasons are specific to the type or ground of discrimination.

3.3.1. Legal, Financial, Social Obstacles

Some reasons derive simply from the characteristics of legal regulation and legal procedures that entail increased difficulties for victims of discrimination with particular regard to their status compared with other labour law litigants. The complexity of legal regulations, the need for (or even the mandatory presence of) a legal representative, the limited deadlines, and the uncertainties regarding the outcome are all deterrent factors for them. The expense of the procedure, the level of court fees, the low level of available compensation, the risk of losing the case, which might indeed be followed by additional costs (paying the court fees and other expenses of the defendant) or the overall lack of trust in the legal system may pose further barriers.

The legal and financial barriers may be coupled with social, mental and psychological reasons, fear of revealing private matters in public (such as religion, LGBTQI identity), specific barriers in the case of disabled persons or concerns about undermining their own position at the workplace, may all contribute to the deterrent factors.

These obstacles can be decreased or removed by well-considered legal revisions, by legal and financial aid for victims, and not least by the measures, institutions and procedures included among state duties in the Directives regarding relevant bodies, other procedures beyond litigation, dissemination of information and dialogue (to be reviewed below).

[92] Hofman et al, n 90 at 26–27.

3.3.2. Assistance and Support to Cope with Obstacles; the Role of Trade Unions

The importance of removing obstacles to effective enforcement is reflected in the inclusion of identical text in each of the Anti-discrimination Directives prescribing the duty of the Member States to

> ensure that associations, organisations or other legal entities which have … legitimate interest in ensuring that the provisions of this Directive are complied with, may engage, either on behalf or in support of the complainant, with his/her approval, in any judicial and/or administrative procedure provided for the enforcement of obligations under this Directive.[93]

Such organisations might include trade unions or civil organisations engaging in the abovementioned forms of support. Together with interest groups and organisations, equality bodies in several countries may also engage in legal proceedings on behalf of victims of discrimination (see section 5.1 below).

Financial assistance is one aspect of legal support. Under the last non-numbered paragraph of Article 47 CFREU national law must promote effective access to justice by making legal aid available to those who lack sufficient resources.[94] Besides providing free legal assistance, and contributing to or reducing procedural expenses there is also a wide range of variations among Member States. The different criteria enshrined in national laws concerning organisations and assistance provided would be worth surveying; not only national regulations but also their correlation with the frequency of enforcement procedures.

It would be interesting to look at the dual role of the trade unions and its development. On one hand, they participate in rule-setting together with employers – in collective agreements and other norms governing conduct at work – which might sometimes give rise to disputes for being discriminatory.[95] On the other hand, similarly to NGOs they provide protection, support and – most importantly – legal assistance and legal representation to their members or any workers treated in a discriminatory way by their employers. Their exact legal standing depends on national legislation. In some countries a distinction is drawn between trade unions representing members (or workers), and NGOs representing other victims. Trade unions in a number of cases have contributed to developing non-discrimination jurisprudence.[96]

[93] Art 17(2) Recast Directive, Art 8(3) Anti-Racism, Employment and Services Directives.

[94] See Chapter 3 of this volume, n 67.

[95] See eg Case C-132/2011 *Tyrolean Airways*, concerning disputed collective agreement seniority rules regarding pay categories.

[96] Eg joint Cases C-335/11 and C-337/11 *HK Danmark*, on disability discrimination, Case C-/14 *Mr Rasmussen*, on age discrimination. For further examples see chapter 2 by Koukiadaki.

The diverse landscape of national circumstances certainly shows overall progress in regulatory-participatory activity aimed at promoting the prohibition of discrimination (together with changing attitudes of employers towards discrimination), in addition to continued legal activities to enforce non-discrimination effectively.

4. Sanctions: Compensation, Administrative and Criminal Penalties

4.1. Substantive Remedy[97]

In addition to procedural rights through judicial process (access to court, shift of the burden of proof, prohibition of victimisation), EU rules guarantee substantive remedy and reparation. This shall include not only the restoration of rights but also compensation that is effective, proportionate and dissuasive in order to achieve the objective of the Directives.

The right to effective, proportionate and dissuasive compensation is a result of the development of the case law on the ground of the earlier gender equality Directives, which did not yet include such a right. In the early case of discriminatory rejection of women's applications for the job of prison guard in a male prison, the Court laid down that while the Sex Equality Directive leaves the Member States free to choose between different solutions for achieving the objective, if the approach taken is to award compensation it must be adequate and deterrent.[98]

Under the Anti-Racism and the Equality Framework Directives, compensation is included as a possible sanction,[99] but there is a separate and specific compensation provision only in the Gender Recast Directive. Its Article 18 requires compensation or reparation that is not 'only' real and effective, dissuasive and proportionate to the damage suffered but also 'may not be restricted by the fixing of a prior upper limit' (except when the employer can prove that there was no damage beyond the refusal of the job application).

Such a specific provision on the amount of compensation is missing from the Race and Equality Framework Directives adopted earlier, hopefully 'merely as a consequence of a slip of the drafter's pen'.[100] No case law is yet available on

[97] For more see Chapter 2 of this volume.
[98] See *von Colson and Kamann*, n 48, para 28.
[99] Art 15 Anti-Racism Directive, Art 17 Framework Directive.
[100] E Ellis and P Watson, n 8 at 311.

interpretation of the 'prior upper limit' in cases other than those on sex discrimination.

The interpretation given by the Court in its *Camacho* judgment[101] may bring some clarification, distinguishing between Article 18 (on damages) and Article 25 (penalties) of the Gender Recast Directive. The plaintiff – a victim of sex discriminatory dismissal – claimed significantly higher damages than suffered, and the referring court was uncertain whether 'dissuasive' compensation may mean an amount going beyond the total amount of losses and damages suffered by the victim. The CJEU decision makes clear that the genuine deterrent effect required by Article 18 did not involve awarding punitive damages that go beyond full compensation for the loss and damage actually sustained.

4.2. Penalties

There seems to be a difference between 'damages' (under Article 18) and 'penalties' under Article 25 Gender Recast Directive, which may include compensation for damages. The Court adds that if Member States opt for 'penalties' under Article 25, in that case the Directive allows, but does not require, 'providing for the payment of punitive damages'. The Court refers to the provision permitting 'more favourable' rules for the victims, confirming the opportunity to adopt punitive damages.[102] The same provisions in the Anti-Racism and the Equality Framework Directives[103] may promote effective enforcement also by way of additional (punitive) damages. However, rendering such punitive measures enforceable would require a clear and express provision of national law setting the criteria for determining the extent of the penalty, provided that the principles of equivalence and effectiveness are respected. In the concrete case of *Arjona Camacho*, as punitive damages do not exist in Spanish law, effective compensation could not go beyond an amount covering the total loss and damage sustained.[104] Because achieving the award of damages may take a considerable time, pre-fixed upper limits cannot exclude the award of interest as a result of the passage of time.[105]

CJEU case law has consistently stated that within the framework of civil liability there cannot be exemptions with reference to a lack of fault on the employer's side; any breach of the prohibition of discrimination must be sufficient to make the employer liable. This was established in the *Dekker* judgment, which also established for the first time that a refusal of employment due to pregnancy constitutes

[101] Case C-407/14 *María Auxiliadora Arjona Camacho v Securitas Seguridad España, SA* [December 2015].

[102] *Camacho*, see n 101 above, paras 40, 41.

[103] Art 6(1) Anti-Racism Directive; Art 8(1) Framework Equality Directive.

[104] *Camacho, n 101*, Operative part.

[105] Case C-271/91 *Marshall* 2, para 32.

direct sex discrimination.[106] The similar conclusion in the *Draehempaehl* case has made the Directive directly enforceable, precluding the provisions of German law, which made reparation of damage resulting from discrimination subject to the requirement of fault.[107]

While the requirement of dissuasiveness is in principle attached to administrative and criminal sanctions, the fact of the matter is that in most countries prescribing such sanctions, the level of the sanctions, in the laws and/or in practice, is not very high, not fully corresponding to the requirements of effectiveness and dissuasiveness.[108] Labour inspectorates may initiate administrative procedures, while criminal sanctions are applied reluctantly and infrequently, rather in gender discrimination cases or in case of discrimination against the disabled. The Italian government's preference for decriminalisation and substitution of criminal sanctions by administrative monetary sanctions (of higher amounts) may increase effective enforcement.[109]

In contrast to such easing, in Romania there was a tightening of sanctions in the wake of the CJEU judgment in *Asociaţia ACCEPT*.[110] The Romanian National Council on Combatting Discrimination (NCCD), empowered to adopt sanctions, changed its former practice of issuing recommendations and warnings rather than fines and started to issue fines more frequently, also increasing their amount.[111]

5. Other Institutions and Procedures

Institutions and procedures outside the court system, such as equality bodies, pre-litigation procedures and strategic litigation, which got going in the 2000s with the development of anti-discrimination regulation, have already contributed to greater awareness and improvements in the enforcement of non-discrimination.

5.1. Equality Bodies

Equality bodies play an essential role in the promotion of equal treatment, in different ways. Both the Anti-Racism Directive (Article 13) and the Gender Recast Directive (Article 20) require that Member States establish equality bodies or

[106] *Dekker*, n 43, para 22.
[107] Case C-180/95 *Draehmpaehl v Urania Immobilienservice OHG* [April, 1997], para 22.
[108] DG Justice and Consumers, *A Comparative Analysis of Gender Equality Law in Europe* (2020), 156–58; *Comparative Analysis 2020* 94–96.
[109] *Comparative Analysis 2020*, 156.
[110] See n 27 above, section 2.1.
[111] *Comparative Analysis 2020*, 95.

agencies for the promotion of equal treatment of persons regardless of race, ethnic origin or sex. The Equality Framework Directive does not have such a provision, however, the 2018 Commission Recommendation on standards for equality bodies[112] expressly suggests that Member States consider designating an equality body to cover the grounds protected by Directive 2000/78/EC.

In fact, the grounds covered by the mandates of such bodies include, from the beginning, the grounds protected by the Equality Framework Directive in most Member States and are even broader than those covered by the three Directives, extending most frequently to political views/activity, trade union views/activity, civil status, social status and property (wealth).[113] Member States have a wide degree of discretion with regard to the nature, organisation and mandates of the specialised bodies; consequently, there is wide range of variations in terms of their organisational framework, structures, mandates and competences.

These bodies may form part of existing agencies with responsibility at national level for the defence of human rights or the safeguarding of individual rights, or might be bodies specialising in non-discrimination.

The Directives enumerate their functions in an open manner that makes it possible to allocate more tasks or powers. At a minimum they must be authorised with the competence to provide independent assistance to victims in pursuing their complaints about discrimination.[114] This function is fulfilled in each Member State and can take different forms. Frequently, assistance entails the initiation of legal procedures either representing the victim or in their own name. Such actions may conclude in strategic litigation, as in the milestone *Feryn* case initiated by the Belgian equality body, Unia.[115]

They also have to conduct independent surveys and make independent reports. They may issue recommendations and, even if not required by the Directives, they can fulfil quasi-judicial functions and adopt binding decisions, also imposing fines. Considering the easier – less costly, less formal – access to these bodies victims feel more comfortable turning to them, despite the fact that not all of them have quasi-judicial functions and clearly only a minority are empowered to adopt binding decisions.

The Belgian model specified only equality affairs and distinguished between protected grounds (Unia for all grounds except sex, and the Institute for the Equality of Women and Men). It appears to be an efficient model, while multi-mandate models may experience challenges regarding effectiveness, staffing and financing.[116]

[112] Commission Recommendation of 22.6.2018 on Standards for Equality Bodies, C(2018)3850 final, Brussels, 2018, https://ec.europa.eu/info/sites/info/files/2_en_act_part1_v4.pdf.

[113] *Comparative Analysis 2020*, Survey on equality bodies, 101–107.

[114] Art 20(2) Recast Equality Directive, Art 13(2) Anti-Racism Directive, the first indent in both provisions.

[115] *Firma Feryn NV*, n 26.

[116] The Croatian People's Ombudsman is noted for steps taken to safeguard the effectiveness of its broad mandate, which might be a good example of merged mandates. EELR 2021/01, 8.

The element of independence of functioning is emphasised in the Directives. The 2018 Recommendation[117] aims at improving and increasing the independence and effectiveness of equality bodies, as well as extending the subject matters within their mandate. Moreover, in the proposal for the new 'Transparency Directive' equality bodies are designated to play a crucial role in enforcing non-discrimination.[118] Significant cuts in funding for equality bodies in several countries imposed ostensibly in response to the economic crisis (for instance, in Greece, Ireland, Hungary, Latvia and the United Kingdom)[119] inevitably have an impact on their operations. The 2018 Recommendation emphasises the importance of sufficient budgeting for both the independence and effectiveness of equality bodies.[120] Besides the formally laid down tasks of these bodies fulfil a significant role in the enforcement of concrete cases within the framework of, or beyond assistance to victims of discrimination, as well as in the various forms of soft means promoting equal treatment (reviewed below).

5.2. Pre-litigation Procedures

Each of the Equality Directives makes possible recourse to other – non-judicial – procedures, complementary to and preceding but not substituting access to courts.[121] Two kinds of such procedures can be distinguished, although not separated clearly in the Directives: mediation and conciliation between the victim and the employer in order to achieve peaceful settlement of the dispute; and second, administrative intervention by external institutions, such as labour inspectorates, ombudsmen, human rights institutions or the equality body.

The regulation of both kinds of procedures might be laid down with a general character for all private legal disputes or all kinds of labour disputes, or procedures (organs) might be established specifically for discrimination cases. In the latter category, equality bodies may have a significant role when empowered with quasi-judicial functions, depending on national regulations.

Mediation or conciliation proceedings may be available either as a mandatory part of court proceedings, or the procedures may be brought to such organs by the decision of the victim, independently of court procedures. Such peaceful settlements are preferred because of their speed, lower cost and because they avoid an unpleasant impact on future workplace relations. At the same time, the various forms of amicable settlement between unequal parties may harbour dangers, because the stronger party (the defendant employer) is likely to have the upper hand. For this reason, the availability of judicial review remains of crucial importance.

[117] See n 91 above.
[118] See n 93, Art 25.
[119] *Comparative Analysis 2020*, 113.
[120] Commission Recommendation (2018) on Equality Bodies, Recital 20, Section 1.2.
[121] Art 17 Recast Directive, Art 7 Anti-Racism Directive, Art 9 Framework Directive.

5.3. Collective Redress and Strategic Litigation[122]

5.3.1. Group Action and Actio Popularis

Broadened legal standing for civil and industrial parties and modes of collective redress are considered a useful form of protection against discrimination by the Commission and by organisations concerned with equal treatment. The relevant two forms are class or group action (litigation on behalf of an undefined group – 'class' – of victims or identified victims with multiple claims) and *actio popularis* (started in the public interest or on their own behalf).

None of these procedures are regulated in the Directives, but they are known in several Member States. Group action is more of an option in various forms representing multiple victims than class action in its classic form.

Actio popularis is a highly effective tool for fighting discrimination in various situations, but its public nature might seem to contradict the provisions that make judicial procedures available 'to all persons who consider themselves wronged' by a violation of equal treatment. The Opinion of AG Maduro in the *Firma Feryn* case[123] recognised that such actions 'in the nature of an *actio popularis*' are not precluded by the Directives. Rather, such provisions are permitted, as more favourable than the minimum protection of the principle of equal treatment, subject to assessment by the national court.

5.3.2. Strategic Litigation

Strategic litigation means the selection of cases taken to court with the goal of achieving changes, serving the public interest or the collective interest of workers and trade unions, going beyond the significance of the particular case. Strategic litigation has had, in the field of non-discrimination, a considerable impact on the interpretation and jurisprudence of the relevant EU law by the Court from the earliest period, improving the level of enforcement.[124]

Such 'impact cases' can be brought to the Court by the advocacy of individual litigators or by collective or public bodies (civil organisations, equality bodies). The *Defrenne* series championed by Eliane Vogel-Polsky is to be mentioned first, leading to the CJEU's recognition of the right to non-discrimination on the ground of sex as a fundamental right that takes precedence over national laws.[125] As a special example the more recent *Egenberger* case[126] might be mentioned, initiated by a leading non-discrimination activist in her own case on the interpretation of the

[122] For a general description see Chapter 7 of this volume.
[123] See n 26, Opinion, paras 12–13.
[124] M Guerrero, 'Strategic litigation in EU gender equality law' (European Commission, DG for Justice and Consumers, 2020) 10.
[125] See n 2 above.
[126] See n 10 above.

Article 4(2) Equality Framework Directive, an exception from the prohibition of religious discrimination permitted to religious employers.[127]

More frequent and typical are instances in which civil (human rights) organisations or equality bodies submit cases that can 'essentially revolutionise future development of anti-discrimination law in Europe'.[128] The *Firma Feryn* case was litigated by the Belgian Unia, 'a strong and genuinely independent equality body'[129] established under Article 13 of the Anti-Racism Directive. An interesting contrast is the *Asociaţia ACCEPT* case launched not by, but against Romania's national equality body by an LGBT organisation. Both cases managed to reach the Court and obtain an affirmative interpretation on the rights of the disadvantaged groups (African workers and homosexuals) in the absence of a specific plaintiff.

A more recent case demonstrates the advancement of effective protection resulting from strategic litigation by the other Belgian equality body, the Institute for Equality of Women and Men, in the *Hakelbracht* case, successfully expanding the personal scope of the protection against victimisation.[130]

6. Soft Instruments: Information and Dialogue[131]

6.1. Dissemination of Information

Member States are obliged to ensure that the provisions and measures adopted to transpose the non-discrimination Directives, together with relevant provisions already in force, are brought to the attention of the persons concerned by all available means.[132] According to the relevant reviews, these provisions are the least implemented in the Member States, at least formally, from among all of the Directives' articles, even though phrased as a duty.[133] Similarly, activities aimed at disseminating information about the anti-discrimination legal framework are rarely organised by the Member States. Despite a few positive examples (for example, publications, media information campaigns, seminars in Finland, Germany, Malta and Sweden, or a website run by the Slovak Ministry of Labour) dissemination of information is 'not a high priority at national level' in the EU, and in the majority of countries there is serious concern about public perception and

[127] M Möschel, 'Litigating anti-discrimination cases in Germany: what role for collective actors?' (2017) 2 *Anti-Discrimination Law Review* 80.

[128] U Belavusau and K Henrard, 'A Bird's Eye View on EU Anti-Discrimination Law: The Impact of the 2000 Equality Directives' (2019) 20 *German Law Journal* 629.

[129] Ibid.

[130] See n 65 above.

[131] For a more general overview see Chapter 6 of this volume.

[132] Art 10 Anti-Racism Directive, Art 12 Framework Directive, Art 25 Recast Directive.

[133] *Comparative Analysis 2020*, n 5 at 114.

awareness, as individuals are often not informed of their non-discrimination rights and of protection mechanisms.[134] Evidently, reducing the information gap, and raising awareness about rights and available means of redress is one way of removing hindrances afflicting effective enforcement and lowering the high rate of latency of employment discrimination. The workplace, as suggested in Article 30 Gender Recast Directive, can be an appropriate site for the dissemination of information.

6.2. Social and Civil Dialogue

Each of the Directives stipulates the Member States' obligation to 'take adequate measures to promote social dialogue between the two sides of industry with a view to fostering equal treatment'. A similar obligation is laid down to encourage dialogue with appropriate non-governmental organisations that have a legitimate interest in promoting equal treatment and in the fight against discrimination on the grounds protected under those Directives.[135]

Dialogue between social partners, coupled with dialogue with civil organisations have become established tools for implementing European social policy and fundamental rights within the framework of the Lisbon Strategy and the open method of coordination, significantly strengthened and broadened in the provisions of the EPSR.[136] These channels are a natural completion of the toolbox of prohibitions, legal procedures and other non-legal policy measures for achieving equality in the workplace and in society more generally.

Social partners, within the framework of their powers and practices of concluding agreements and adopting codes of conduct or similar internal regulations, are best positioned to regulate and monitor workplace practices in the area of equal treatment. This applies in particular to their negotiations within the scope of collective bargaining.

On the other hand, the partners' bargaining autonomy has repeatedly led directly or indirectly to discriminatory wage agreements, as seen in both the case law and the literature of EU labour law. It was in the *Enderby* case that the Court first pointed out that separate bargaining processes for two professional groups, with no discrimination within those groups, can easily circumvent the principle of equal pay.[137] The importance to be accorded to the fact that the discrimination arises in a collective bargaining context returned in several cases[138]

[134] Ibid, 114–15.

[135] Art 11–12 Anti-Racism Directive, Art 13–14 Framework Directive, Art 21–22 Recast Equality Directive.

[136] For a general description see Chapter 20 of this volume.

[137] *Enderby*, n 74, para 22.

[138] C-400/93 *Royal Copenhagen* [1995] (basis of a lot of later reference), and C-447/09 *Prigge and Others v Lufthansa*.

The formal implementation of the provisions on social and civil dialogue for the promotion of equal treatment in employment remained scarce. In the area of disability there seem to be more examples of structured dialogue compared with other grounds of discrimination. These may take the form of joint councils with representatives of NGOs and government bodies, or representative organisations commenting on legislative actions or reviewing developments.[139] Specific structures of such dialogue play a role in promoting equality of the Roma in various areas of social and economic life, less so in relation to employment.

In closing this overview of soft instruments, it might be mentioned once again that equality bodies are important tools for disseminating information as well as promoting social dialogue in many Member States, although this task is not expressly listed among their mandates in the Directives.

7. Conclusions

Non-discrimination has developed from a formal competition rule into a fundamental right of European law today. Primary and secondary legislation prohibiting discrimination on a broad range of grounds grants direct enforceability, not only in front of the state, but also between private parties. Violation of the rules, breaching the prohibition on discrimination is surrounded by guarantees, both procedural and material. Sanctions on violations and compensation for damages are prescribed in a complex way.

Member States have transposed the EU norms into national legislation, sometimes verbatim. Nonetheless, as this chapter shows, the developed legal framework has shortcomings at the level of practical implementation and enforcement. The difficulties are in part caused by interpretational problems at national courts and the CJEU, by a lack of effort to translate legal norms into practice, and by some gaps in implementation. The reasons for enforcement deficiencies vary along with the grounds of discrimination.

Perhaps the greatest deficiency is the persistence of the gender pay gap across Europe, and relatedly the low number of claims. The main obstacle to submitting such claims is a lack of access to information. The 2021 Commission proposal for a Directive to strengthen pay equality by promoting transparency and enforcement[140] might bring some improvement, if adopted. The lack of information and its restrictive treatment by the CJEU can prevent successful enforcement beyond wage claims, too.[141]

[139] *Comparative Analysis 2020*, n 5 at 115.
[140] n 93.
[141] See *Kelly* (n 82) and *Meister* (n 59).

The uncertainties in the rules on reversal of the burden of proof (requiring a prima facie case of discrimination), coupled with the information problems, also contribute to the low degree of enforcement.

Encouraging developments in the interpretation of racial discrimination and sexual orientation have been accompanied by mixed developments in relation to religious belief, such as the interpretation of permitted exceptions, facilitating exemptions by the CJEU blurring the boundaries between direct and indirect discrimination.

The increasing role of equality bodies has promoted enforcement, primarily by their function, in tandem with civil organisations and trade unions, of assisting victims in accessing justice. Equality bodies also carry out institutional activities, providing governments with advice and recommendations, awareness-raising and promoting good practices in numerous ways.

An overall assessment of the history and present state of enforcement of non-discrimination underlines the importance of legal and non-legal measures to further narrow the gap between non-discrimination in the law books and in practice.

11

Enforcing EU Information and Consultation Rights

SILVIA RAINONE

1. Introduction

This chapter discusses the enforcement of EU workers' right to information and consultation. At the outset, it is important to stress that information and consultation rights operate on two different levels and can therefore be approached from two different perspectives. On the first level, information and consultation rights are substantive rights that help workers to overcome their weaker bargaining position by giving them a voice within the company. Perceived in this guise, information and consultation rights may be asserted in pursuit of the ideals of industrial and workplace democracy.[1] On a second level, information and consultation rights can be regarded as instrumental to the enforcement of other labour rights.[2] From this point of view, they can be understood as enabling rights, because workers' representatives and trade union delegates are not only holders of information and consultation prerogatives, but also actors who, through the functions assigned by information and consultation legislation, promote the effective enforcement of workers' rights.

This premise is necessary to clarify that this chapter deals with information and consultation rights only as substantive rights, and that their function as a means of monitoring and promoting the enforcement of other workers' rights is discussed by Dorssemont in Chapter 17.

With this clarification, I can proceed by observing that, over the years, EU policymaking has developed a fairly composite set of rules on information and consultation rights. However, the adoption of information and consultation legislation is only the first step; without proper enforcement, workers remain

[1] I Schoemann, 'Information and consultation in the workplace: a long and difficult path towards democracy in the company' (2010) *Europe et Société* 29–43.

[2] E Ribarova, 'Information and consultation arrangements: results from a transnational study' (2011) 17(2) *Transfer: European Review of Labour and Research* 229–37; D Walters, 'The Role of Worker Representation and Consultation in Managing Health and Safety in the Construction Industry', ILO WP 270 (2010).

unprotected. To better illustrate how non-compliance with information and consultation rights may impact working conditions, it is helpful to provide two salient examples that underline the importance of establishing adequate enforcement mechanisms.

The first example is the inadequate enforcement of the EU information and consultation framework in relation to the introduction of technology into the work environment. EU rules should apply in relation to all substantial changes in work organisation, production processes and working methods.[3] The deployment of data processing tools, AI, and people-analytics in the workplace undoubtedly results in circumstances that require the launch of information and consultation processes with workers' representatives. Despite this, a survey conducted by ETUC between 2017 and 2018 revealed that, in relation to the introduction of technology into the workplace technological innovations, the EU legal framework on information and consultation rights is often disregarded.[4] Only 14 per cent of respondents said they were aware of collective agreements regulating the matter, and it was reported that only 65.2 per cent of the companies analysed have established information and consultation processes that address the impact of digitalisation on company organisation and working conditions.

A second example of the relevance of an adequate information and consultation rights enforcement was provided by the Covid-19 crisis. The pandemic forced a rethinking of work organisation and resulted in a wave of company closures, corporate restructuring, profound changes in working arrangements (eg teleworking) and compliance with health protocols. This has led to all sorts of company protocols and company reorganisations whose enactment would have, at least theoretically, required the application of EU information and consultation law. Even in this case, however, the regulatory tools offered by EU law have been applied insufficiently.[5] So much so that in a joint declaration in June 2020, ETUC and some of the main European trade union federations declared that 'company practices show very limited or no involvement of workers and union representatives in the decision-making process of strategies, if any', and called on European and national institutions to ensure greater enforcement of EU information and consultation rights.[6]

[3] R Beaujolin-Bellet and G Schmidt, *Les Restructurations d'entreprises* (La Découverte, Collection Repères, 2012) 7–28.

[4] E Voss and H Riede, 'Digitalization and Workers' participation: What Trade Unions, Company Level Workers and Online Platform Workers in Europe Think', Report to the ETUC, September 2018.

[5] A Hoffmann, R Jagodziński, C Degryse, S Lafuente Hernandez, S De Spiegelaere and S Vitols, 'Democracy at work in a pandemic' in *Benchmarking Europe 2020 – Covid-19 and the World of Work: The Impact of a Pandemic* (ETUI, 2021); J Kirton-Darling and I Barthès, 'Anticipating the Covid-19 restructuring tsunami' (2020) *Social Europe* (3 September). According to the data collected by European Monitoring Centre on Change, from 1 January 2019 to 1 March 2020, 691 cases of restructuring were reported in the EU, with a total of 325,719 job losses. Then, from 1 March 2020 to 16 April 2021 a total of 1,029 instances of restructuring took place, with a total of 613,868 job losses – almost double.

[6] Joint Statement of the European Trade Union Confederation (ETUC) and the European Trade Union Federations IndustriALL Europe, UNI Europa, EFFAT, EPSU, ETF, EFBWW on 'Worker involvement in managing the Covid-19 crisis', Brussels, 24 June 2020.

These examples are valuable reminders of the importance of adequate enforcement of information and consultation rights. It should also be mentioned that, in consideration of the strong procedural component of such rights, effective enforcement can be guaranteed only by suspending the violation and restoring the situation prior to it; remedies of a compensatory nature have only a deterrent value and do not guarantee compliance with the violated norms.

In addressing the issue of enforcement of EU information and consultation rights, this chapter adopts two complementary approaches. First, in section 2 the inadequacy of the enforcement mechanisms that are in place at EU level is discussed. Section 3 then illustrates how the scarcity of enforcement mechanisms available at the EU level is further aggravated by important limitations on the enforceability of the rules providing for information and consultation rights. Finally, Section 4 provides concluding reflections on potential avenues to improve and render more effective the institutional response to non-compliance with information and consultation rights.

2. Enforcement of EU Information and Consultation Rights: Not an EU Concern?

This section provides a two-level analysis of the enforcement mechanisms that, in the context of EU law, are made available in the area of information and consultation rights. At first, the focus is on the text of the relevant EU Directives, in relation to the provisions that address the effective application of the information and consultation procedures laid down therein. The second level of analysis concerns the assessment of the contribution of the case law of the Court of Justice (hereinafter CJEU or the Court) to the enforcement of EU information and consultation rights. The EU judiciary has, at least potentially, the capacity to increase the normative effectiveness of legislation and to provide further avenues for stronger enforcement of rights.

All in all, it appears that, in relation to information and consultation rights, the issue of enforcement is dealt with only marginally, both in the legislative and in the jurisprudential context, with the partial exception of the EWC Directive.

2.1. Enforcement Aspects in the Information and Consultation Directives

Employees' right to information and consultation has been part of the European legislative debate since the 1970s, as its regulatory development coincided with the emergence of one of the first bodies of EEC labour law.[7]

[7] CA Holle, 'Workers' Participation and EC Legislation, in Workers' Participation: Influence on Management Decision-Making by Labour in the Private Sector' (1992) 23 *Bulletin* 19–35.

As Laulom correctly observed, the legislative development of information and consultation rights at the European level can be seen as a reaction by the European legislator to periods of intensified corporate restructuring.[8]

A first set of legislative measures concerning information and consultation rights was in fact adopted following an intensification of what may be called 'crisis or defensive reorganisations', generally caused by plant or business closures. The number of these closures had increased following the first phase of single-market integration and the oil crisis that erupted in 1975.[9] Directive 75/129/EC (now Directive 98/59/EC) on collective redundancies and Directive 77/187/EC (now Directive 2001/23/EC) on transfer of undertakings were thus adopted to mitigate the social impact of restructuring on the workers concerned. Both Directives established information and consultation practices, which were part of a set of broader guarantees for workers in the case of the Directive on transfers and were the central topic of the Directive on collective redundancies. However, only mild norms on enforcement were introduced.

Article 6 of Directive 98/59/EC and Article 9 of Directive 2001/23/EC merely stipulate that Member States are obliged to ensure the existence of administrative and/or judicial procedures to which workers' representatives and employees can have recourse in the event of violation of their rights. The European legislator therefore preferred to devolve the issue of enforcement entirely to its national counterparts, avoiding the establishment of ad hoc procedures and remedies and specifying minimum levels of adequacy of responses to infringements.

Then, in the mid-1990s and early 2000s, the European framework on information and consultation rights was enriched with Directive 94/45/EC (now Directive 2008/39/EC) on the European Works Council (hereinafter EWC) and Directive 2002/14/EC establishing a general framework on information and consultation rights.[10] Furthermore, the right to information and consultation was also included among the fundamental principles of the European Union, enshrined in Article 27 of the EU Charter of Fundamental Rights (hereinafter CFR).[11]

As in the past, this second legislative moment did not result in more effective remedies for information and consultation rights. Both Directives essentially limited themselves to indicating that Member States have a duty to ensure that administrative and/or judicial procedures are in place to deal with non-compliance.

[8] S Laulom, 'Le Droit Européen des restructurations' (2012) *Le Droit Ouvrier* (Juin), 767.

[9] European Commission, Green Paper on Employee Participation and Company Structure in the European Countries, COM(75)887.

[10] R Blanpain, 'Involvement of Employees in the European Union: European Works Councils, The European Company Statute and Information and Consultation Rights' (2002) *Bulletin of Comparative Labour Relations* 42.

[11] B Veneziani, 'Article 27 – Worker's Right to Information and Consultation within the Undertaking' in F Dorssemont, K Lörcher, S Clauwaert and M Schmitt (eds), *The Charter of Fundamental Rights of the European Union and the Employment Relation* (Hart, 2019) 429–65.

Directive 2002/14/EC, while having a rather broad scope that would have provided the ideal context for more robust enforcement provisions, contains only a general reference to the fact that sanctions must be effective, dissuasive and proportionate.[12]

As regards the EWC Directive, it is interesting to note that the absence of references to enforcement in the original version was partially corrected with the adoption of the Recast Directive in 2008, probably in an effort to curb the ineffective practical implementation of the original Directive.[13] Directive 2009/38/EC eventually introduced a rule aimed at supporting employee representatives who wish to obtain redress in the event of non-compliance with the Directive.[14] Article 10 now provides that 'the members of the European Works Council shall have the means necessary to apply the rights arising from this Directive, in order to represent collectively the interests of the employees of the Community-scale undertaking or Community-scale group of undertakings'. This represents a step forward, but still not much to cling to.

The existence, on one hand, of a fairly rich legal framework for information and consultation rights and, on the other hand, the almost total lack of consideration of their enforcement is quite a contradiction. One possible reading is that the laxity that pervades the issue of enforcement of information and consultation rights has been influenced by a perception, fostered by EU policymaking, that information and consultation practices are valuable managerial tools rather than fundamental workers' prerogatives.[15] This approach emerges quite clearly from the EWC Directive and the General Framework Directive which, unlike the two pieces of legislation adopted in the 1970s, are no longer focused on specific corporate restructuring events, but have integrated information and consultation rights practices into ordinary company management.[16]

This, in turn, can be seen as a reflection of the general political pressure in favour of labour market flexibility and the promotion of firms' ability to adapt their production and organisation to external competition. Corporate restructuring was no longer synonymous with 'crisis', but rather with 'structural emergency', leading to the normalisation of reorganisation and corporate strategies aimed at higher productivity and competitiveness.[17]

[12] Recital 28 and Article 5(2) Directive 2002/14/EC.

[13] S De Spiegelaere, 'Too Little, Too Late? Evaluating the European Works Councils Recast Directive', Report 18 (ETUI, 2016).

[14] R Jagodziński and P Lorber, 'Enforcement Frameworks and Employees' Rights of Access to Enforcement Procedures' in R Jagodziński (ed), *Variations on a Theme? The Implementation of the EWC Recast Directive* (ETUI, 2015).

[15] See Recital 9 Directive 2002/14/EC. Also, the fallback provisions of Directive 2009/38/EC indicate that the EWC shall have the right to meet with the central management once a year.

[16] I Schömann, 'The Current State of Information and Consultation Rights in the European Union' in S Vitols and J Heuschmid (eds), *European Company Law and the Sustainable Company: A Stakeholder Approach* (Brussels, ETUI, 2013).

[17] R Beaujolin-Bellet and G Schmidt, above n 3 at 7–28.

2.2. Enforcement through the EU Judiciary

In this section it is argued that, despite producing a rather rich jurisprudence, the EU judiciary has not emerged as a particularly effective channel for enforcing information and consultation rights.

2.2.1. Directive on Transfers of Undertakings

Starting with Directive 2001/23/EC on transfers of undertakings, an analysis of the case law shows that the judicial avenue has not, at least to date, proved to be a useful tool in strengthening the enforcement of information and consultation rights established therein.[18] Of a total of 75 judgments handed down by the Court of Justice, only two have dealt with the rules on information and consultation, and one of these (the *UGT* case) did not even concern information and consultation practices, but rather the preservation of trade union delegates' role following a transfer of undertaking.[19]

The only judgment that is relevant from an enforcement perspective is the *Commission v UK* case, which concerned also Directive 75/129/EC (now 98/59/EC on collective redundancies).[20] The case stemmed from a claim by the Commission that the United Kingdom had failed to implement those Directives by making the appointment of workers' representatives dependent on the employer's willingness to accept a trade union delegation in the company. The UK government, on the other hand, argued that the obligation set out in the Directives could apply only to the extent allowed by the existing national system of industrial relations. It goes without saying that this solution would represent an obstacle to the enforcement of the information and consultation rights set out in the Directives. The Court of Justice eventually ruled that the United Kingdom had to adapt its domestic legislative framework. In particular, it established that the Member States must ensure that employees have the possibility to elect employees' representatives in all circumstances covered by the Directives, and that the employer should be obliged to pay a penalty in case of non-compliance.[21]

2.2.2. Directive on Collective Redundancies

Turning now to Directive 98/59/EC on collective redundancies, it is worth considering that, unlike Directive 2001/23/EC, this instrument focuses entirely on the information and consultation rights of employees. This implies that all the

[18] S Rainone, 'Labour Rights in the Making of the EU and in the CJEU Case Law: A Case Study on the Transfer of Undertakings Directive' (2018) 9(3) *European Labour Law Journal* 299–325.

[19] Case C-151/09 *UGT-FSP*, 29 July 2010, ECLI:EU:C:2010:452.

[20] Case C-382/92 *Commission v United Kingdom of Great Britain and Northern Ireland*, 8 June 1994, ECLI:EU:C:1994:233.

[21] Ibid, para 55.

judgments that the CJEU has adopted on this Directive deal with some aspects related to information and consultation practices. Not all judgments, however, have addressed the actual exercise of these rights. Bearing in mind that each judicial proceeding can deal with more than one legal issue and that 29 rulings have been issued to date, 12 relate to the personal scope of application, 10 to the quantitative threshold of dismissed workforce and to the concept of establishment, 14 to the concept of 'dismissal' or 'redundancy' and just 11 to actual information and consultation practices with workers' representatives.[22]

Despite a fairly rich jurisprudence, the issue of enforcement has been addressed only indirectly and, moreover, most often in judgments that have had the effect of making the enforcement of the Directive more difficult. For example, the Court has interpreted the personal scope of application in a narrow manner, thus restricting the perimeter of the subjects who can activate enforcement mechanisms and against whom these mechanisms can be directed. In the *Akavan* case, the CJEU established that, from the managerial side, the information and consultation Directives bind only the direct employer of the dismissed workers, even when the actual corporate entity in charge of decisions with redundancy implications is a different one for instance the controlling parent company.[23] This entails that the workers' representatives can only engage with a managerial level that often is not in a position to influence the course of the business restructuring operations or to obtain adequate information in good time. Then, in the *Mono Car* decision, the Court asserted that the collective nature of the rights to information and consultation legitimised a restriction of the persons entitled to bring legal action to enforce them.[24] In particular, the Court accepted that the rights laid down in the Directive can be claimed only by workers' representatives and not by the individual workers affected by the redundancies.

The CJEU has also contributed to indirectly limiting the enforceability of Directive 98/59/EC through a rather extensive reading of the employer's margin of discretion. As will be further explained in the next section, a flexible interpretation of managerial obligations is allowed by the vagueness of the text of the Directive. For instance, Article 2 stipulates that employers must begin consultation with the workers' representatives in good time whenever they *contemplate* collective redundancies. The notion of 'contemplating' redundancies seems to have been understood by the Court in a manner quite favourable to the employer. On several occasions, the CJEU has in fact stressed that the employer must be free to decide when to draw up plans for redundancies.[25] In the *Dansk Metalarbejderforbund*

[22] S Rainone, 'Workers' Involvement in Collective Redundancies in EU Law – What for? A Case Study' (2019) *Bulletin of Comparative Labour Relations*.

[23] Case C-44/08 *Akavan and Others*, 10 September 2009, ECLI:EU:C:2009:533, paras 57 and 69.

[24] Case C-12/08 *Mono Car Styling SA v Dervis Odemis and Others*, 16 July 2009, ECLI:EU:C:2009:466, paras 38–40 and 44.

[25] Case C-284/83 *Dansk Metalarbejderforbund*, 12 February 1985, ECLI:EU:C:1985:61, para 15; Case C-12/08 *Akavan*, para 39; Case C-323/08 *Ovidio Rodriguez Mayor and Others*, 10 December 2009, ECLI:EU:C:2009:770, paras 40, 42; Case C-201/15 *AGET Iraklis*, 21 December 2016, ECLI:EU:C:2016:972, para 31.

case, for instance, the Court ruled that the presence of a situation of clear corporate crisis – such as that triggered by a declaration of insolvency – does not necessarily imply that the employer is obliged to 'contemplate' redundancies, and thus to inform and consult the workers.[26]

More recently, this broad understanding of the discretion of employers in deciding whether and when to draw up dismissal plans has been restricted by the *Socha* and *Ciupa* decisions.[27] In those cases, the Court ruled that the employer is under an obligation to initiate the consultation process if it decides to make unilateral changes to the employment contract, and that this obligation materialises from the moment the changes are communicated to the employees. The Court found that, in these situations, the employer must in fact contemplate that there is a strong possibility that many workers might decide to terminate their employment contract.[28] Therefore, with these rulings, the Court accepted that the obligation to consult the workers' representatives can arise before the employer actually decides to terminate the contract and, in specifying that, increased the legal certainty around the concept of 'contemplating' redundancies. This arguably represents a first positive judicial development for the enforceability of the Directive.

2.2.3. Directive on EWCs

As regards the EWC Directive, the Court has so far issued only four judgments, all concerning to Directive 94/45/EC (the predecessor of the Recast Directive 2009/38/EC). It is interesting to note that, despite the scarcity of pronouncements, for this Directive the judicial avenue before the Court of Justice has proved to be a rather effective method of enforcement.

In the *Bofrost* case, for example, the CJEU upheld the claim of the trade union representatives and gave a broad interpretation of the type of information that, during the negotiations that will then lead to the setting up of the EWC, the workers' delegation is entitled to acquire from the management of a company that is part of the corporate group.[29] Another interesting case concerns the EWC of the company Kühne & Nagel. The proceeding related to the refusal of the company performing the role of central management to disclose to the workers' representatives the information relevant for the establishment of a EWC, with the justification that this information had not been provided by the subsidiary companies. This is often the case when the actual controlling company is located outside the EU and, pursuant to Article 4(2), had to designate another deputee central management in the

[26] Case C-284/83 *Dansk Metalarbejderforbund.*

[27] Case C-149/16 *Halina Socha and Others*, 21 September 2017, ECLI:EU:C:2017:708; Case C-429/16 *Malgorzata Ciupa and Others*, 21 September 2017, ECLI:EU:C:2017:711.

[28] Case C-149/16 *Socha*, para 32; Case C-429/16 *Ciupa*, paras 35 and 29.

[29] Case C-62/99 *Betriebsrat der Bofrost*, 29 March 2001, ECLI:EU:C:2001:188.

EU territory.[30] In addressing the matter, the CJEU supported the position of the workers' delegation and ruled that this refusal was contrary to Article 4 of Directive 94/45/EC. In particular, the CJEU found that the company fulfilling the conditions of 'central management' has the responsibility to supply its subsidiary companies with information requested by employees in the context of the setting up an EWC. In order to make that possible, the subsidiary companies are also under an obligation to provide the central management with the relevant information that will enable workers' representatives to conduct their negotiations.[31]

Finally, the Court further reinforced its jurisprudence in favour of workers' representatives in the *ADS Anker* case. In this ruling the CJEU established that the Member States are obliged to require that undertakings established on their territory, and constituting the central management of a Community-scale group of undertakings, supply the other undertakings of the same group with the information requested by employees' representatives when that is essential for opening negotiations for setting up an EWC.[32]

2.2.4. Directive 2002/14/EC

Finally, there is Directive 2002/14/EC establishing a general framework on information and consultation rights. The Court of Justice has ruled only eight times on this legal instrument. Five of these rulings were initiated by the European Commission in the context of enforcement actions and in all those cases the Court condemned the Member State (Spain, Luxembourg, Belgium, Greece and Italy) for having failed to implement the Directive in the prescribed time. Certainly, these proceedings were positive for the enforceability of the Directive in the concerned Member States. However, this judicial contribution might have been offset by the *AMS* case, in which the CJEU did not recognise horizontal direct effect to the Directive's provisions, while this would have been crucial for strengthening the enforcement of information and consultation rights.[33]

The *AMS* case originated from a preliminary reference of the French Court of Cassation, which asked whether the EU fundamental right to information and consultation laid down in Article 27 CFR could have direct horizontal effect, meaning that it could be claimed to settle a dispute between individuals, so as

[30] Case C-440/00 *Kühne & Nagel AG*, 13 January 2004, ECLI:EU:C:2004:16.

[31] Ibid, para 64.

[32] Case C-349/01 *ADS Anker GmbH*, 15 July 2004, ECLI:EU:C:2004:440, para 62.

[33] Case C-176/12 *AMS v CGT and Others*, 15 January 2014, ECLI:EU:C:2014:2; for literature: V Papa, 'The Dark Side of Fundamental Rights Adjudications? The Court, the Charter and the Asymmetric interpretation of fundamental rights in the AMS case and Beyond' (2015) 6(3) *European Labour Law Journal* 190–214; N Lazzerini, '(Some of) the Fundamental Rights Granted by the Charter May Be a Source of Obligations for Private Parties: AMS' (2014) 51 *Common Market Law Reports* 907; F Dorssemont, 'The Right to Information and Consultation in Article 27 CFR of the EU' (2014) 21(4) *MJECL* 704–22.

to remedy the inadequate national implementation of Directive 2002/14/EC. In fact, French legislation had not correctly implemented the Directive in that it had improperly excluded certain categories of workers from the calculation of the quantitative threshold of workers employed in the establishment and the undertaking. This threshold is decisive for defining the scope of application of information and consultation rights. With this reference for a preliminary ruling, the CJEU was therefore given the opportunity to provide information and consultation rights more effective enforceability, as the attribution of horizontal direct effect would have allowed workers' representatives to invoke Article 27 CFR in litigation against employers when the information and consultation rights Directives were not properly applied. However, and different from previous cases on the principle of non-discrimination on the ground of age,[34] the Court decided not to take this important step. At first, the Court rightly found that there had been a violation of EU law and held that the right of workers to information and consultation is among the fundamental principles of the EU legal system. Then, however, the Court ruled that, unlike what had been determined in relation to other fundamental principles of EU law, Article 27 CFR could not find direct application in the case brought to the Court's attention, and could therefore not be invoked by the workers' representatives against the employer.

More precisely, the Court held that the quantitative threshold determining the scope of application of Directive 2002/14/EC (which was the provision violated by French law) could not be considered an expression of the general principle of EU law established in Article 27 CFR.[35] This conclusion is somewhat perplexing. It is difficult to be persuaded that the legislative criteria on which the application of a Directive whose objective is to establish a general framework on information and consultation rights depends do not constitute an expression of those rights. The reasoning of the Court is thus unconvincing, and seems to conceal a certain reluctance to encroach upon national legislation, even at the cost of weakening the enforceability of the EU right to information and consultation.[36]

What emerges from the case law analysis is that the EU judiciary has not proven to be a particularly effective tool from the perspective of enforcing information and consultation rights. It is true that, in some cases, the Court has been able to remedy shortcomings in the application of the legislation. However, it is only with respect to the EWC Directive that the balance is actually positive. For the information and consultation rights enshrined in the other legislative instruments, the CJEU cannot be said to have helped to give the EU rules more 'teeth'.

[34] Case C-144/04 *Mangold v Ruediger Helm*, 22 November 2005, ECLI:EU:C:2005:420; case C-555/07 *Seda Kucukdeveci*, 19 January 2010, ECLI:EU:C:2010:21.

[35] *AMS*, paras 47–49.

[36] See Dorssemont, n 33.

3. Additional Intrinsic Barriers to the Enforcement of Information and Consultation Rights

From the preceding section it has emerged that, although information and consultation rights are relatively well established in EU law in substantive terms, the enforcement dimension is not as well developed. Evident shortcomings are to be found in the legislation, where references to remedies and sanctions in case of non-compliance consist mostly of a generic mandate to Member States to ensure access to judicial and/or administrative redress. As a result, there is a lack of ad hoc instruments that take into account the specificity of information and consultation rights, as they also have a strong procedural component. The minimalist legal text is not remedied by EU case law which, as has been described, does not offer particularly effective solutions for the enforcement of the Directives.

Now, in this third section, I would like to draw attention to two other aspects that further aggravate the absence of EU mechanisms dedicated to the enforcement of information and consultation rights. First, in section 3.1, the high level of regulatory vagueness that afflicts the Directives and makes it difficult to attribute a precise and coherent meaning to the rules dedicated to information and consultation practices. Normative indeterminacy thus contributes negatively, albeit indirectly, to enforceability. Section 3.2 will instead focus on the fact that, at least so far, there is a lack of institutional ownership by EU institutional actors with respect to the enforcement of information and consultation rights. Most importantly, this attitude especially characterises the approach of the European Commission, which is the institution responsible for stimulating new regulatory input. There is therefore a risk that this disregard for the effective application of information and consultation practices will be an obstacle to overcoming the current shortcomings in favour of the status quo.

3.1. Normative Indeterminacy

The information and consultation rules established in the Directives discussed in section 2 are characterised by a substantial degree of regulatory vagueness. This is relevant from the point of view of enforcement because rules with an imprecise normative spirit and uncertain scope are arguably characterised by a lower degree of enforceability than well defined legal norms.[37] The reason is that

[37] H Avila, *Certainty in Law* (Springer, 2016) 21ff, 59.

if the preceptive meaning of a norm is unclear or refers to concepts that are not purely legal, then it becomes quite complex to determine whether that norm has actually been violated. In turn, this uncertainty as to the very existence of the violation is reflected in a reduced incentive (or even a practical impossibility) to remedy it.

An example that occurs in the EU information and consultation Directives is the requirement that management and workers' representatives should conduct consultations *with a view to reaching an agreement*.[38] In fact, nothing in the legislation offers normative criteria to effectively qualify the existence of a genuine intent to reach an agreement, and this leads to great difficulty in enforcing this provision.

Another example relates to the fact that, according to the information and consultation Directives, information and consultation should be guaranteed *in good time*.[39] Here too, the concept is not further defined in the legislative framework and is thus emptied of its enforceability.

It is worth noting that the CJEU attempted to remedy the insubstantiality of both these notions by ruling, in the *Junk* case, that the employer's obligations to inform and consult arise prior to the decision to terminate the employment contract. Moreover, the Court held that 'consultation' implies an obligation to negotiate. However, this still offers no concrete elements to sharpen the enforceability of the workers' rights, since it is not clear how the formative moment of the decision to dismiss should be determined.[40]

The remainder of this section shows that normative indeterminacy affects also several other aspects of the EU information and consultation rights.

3.1.1. *Material Scope of Application*

With regard to the material scope of application of the EU provisions on information and consultation, legal uncertainty affects, first of all, the circumstances giving rise to the workers' rights. Considering Directive 2001/23/EC on the transfer of undertakings, the event that gives employees the right to information and consultation is the transfer of a business or part of a business to another employer.[41] This alone would be sufficient to confer statutory vagueness, because the concept of 'transfer to another employer' has been the object of a profusion of case law and

[38] Art 4(4)e Directive 2002/14/EC; Art 2(1) Directive 98/59/EC; Art 7(2) Directive 2001/23/EC; Art 6(1) Directive 2009/38/EC.

[39] Recital 46 Directive 2009/38/EC; Art 2 Directive 98/59/EC; Art 7 Directive 2001/23/EC.

[40] Case C-188/03 *Junk*, 27 January 2005, ECLI:EU:C:2005:59, paras 37–40, 43.

[41] Among many, RM Beltzer, 'The Transfer of Undertakings and the Importance of Taking Over Personnel – A Vicious Circle' (2007) 23(1) *International Journal of Comparative Labour Law and Industrial Relations* 139–55; J McMullen, 'Leaving a Legacy: Recent Jurisprudence of the European Court on Transfer of Undertakings' (2021) 50(1) *Industrial Law Journal* 130–57.

has given rise to many interpretative doubts. Then, Article 6 on the rights of workers' representatives provides that

> if the undertaking, business or part of the undertaking or business preserves its autonomy, the status and functioning of the representatives or of the representation of the employees affected by the transfer shall be preserved on the same terms and subject to the same conditions as existed before the date of the transfer.

The maintenance of the employees' representative structure therefore depends on preserving the autonomy of the part of the business that has been transferred. However, the norm does not offer any indication of how to define the notion of autonomy. The Court of Justice intervened in the *UGT* case in relation to this interpretative concern and gave the concept of 'autonomy' a meaning coinciding with the right to self-government of the transferred business entity.[42] The Court also ruled that the existence of this requirement must be assessed after the existence of a transfer of an economic entity has been established.[43] However, it is doubtful that this interpretative clarification succeeded in putting an end to the legal uncertainty. Suffice to say that in other cases, both before and after *UGT*, the Court has created further confusion by ruling that the autonomy of the transferred entity is a condition that must be met in order for the Directive to apply, thus making it a criterion for the existence of the transfer and not only for the application of Article 6.[44]

Another example in which the wording of the legislation does not allow for a clearer appreciation of the events that give rise to information and consultation rights can be found in the EWC Directive. In particular, this Directive establishes that management is obliged to inform and consult the EWC in the case of transactions and decisions with a *transnational impact*.[45] But how can it be determined, especially in situations in which the business is one of global scale, whether a management decision is transnational in nature? An important advance was made with the introduction in the recast EWC Directive of a definition of 'transnationality' that, in addition to the scope of the potential effects of the decision, also considers the level of management that took that decision.[46] However, this may not have sufficiently alleviated the interpretative difficulties. It is indeed significant to note that the vagueness of the notion of 'transnationality' has in several instances negatively affected judicial enforcement in domestic contexts.

[42] Case C-151/09 *UGT-FSP*, para 37.

[43] Ibid, para 44.

[44] For instance, in Case C-127/96 *Hernandez Vidal*, 10 December 1998, ECLI:EU:C:1998:594, the Court introduced autonomy as one of the requirements for the transfer operation to be within the scope of the Directive and then, in Case C-458/12 *Amatori v Telecom Italia*, 6 March 2014, ECLI:EU:C:2014:124 the Court mixed up the notion of autonomy with that of 'independence'.

[45] Art 1(4) Directive 2009/38/EC.

[46] Recital 16 Directive 2009/38/EC.

In the dispute before the German Labour Court of Lorrach against the Australian packaging company Amcor, the workers representatives in the EWC had alleged that the management did not comply with the obligations attached to the information and consultation rights because it adopted too narrow an interpretation of the concept of the 'transnational competence' of the EWC.[47] Eventually, the judicial avenue proved inconclusive and the parties decided to resolve the matter by negotiating an addendum to their existing EWC agreement with a more precise definition of the transnationality requirement.

A similar dispute had also arisen in France before the Nanterre Tribunal, concerning the Veolia Transdev company.[48] Here the delegates in the EWC applied for an injunction against the decision of the company management to demand a repayment of a loan to SNCM, a company belonging to the same group, which led the latter into bankruptcy. The request for an injunction was motivated by the fact that, in taking this crucial decision, the management had not complied with its obligation to inform and consult the EWC. The Tribunal, however, rejected the claim, stating that the management's decision did not have, in its view, transnational scope because it only affected the employees of SNCM, who make up 2.5 per cent of the group workforce.

The *Veolia* case is not an isolated one in French jurisprudence, and follows on from a 2006 judgment of the Cour d'Appel de Versailles, in a proceeding that the EWC brought against British Airways.[49] This case concerned the company's decision to outsource British Airways customer services at the Charles de Gaulle airport. According to the Court, the management was correct in considering this decision as devoid of transnational character because it concerned just one airport. In the decision, the Court even ordered the EWC to pay the costs of the proceedings.

Another notable regulatory ambiguity related to the material scope of application of the information and consultation rights concerns the concept of 'establishment' as interpreted by the CJEU in relation to Directive 98/59/EC on collective redundancies. Article 1 of the Directive anchors the employer's obligation to inform and consult the workforce with a minimum quantitative threshold based on the number of redundancies. This threshold is calculated on account of the number of workers assigned to a certain establishment.[50] It follows that, depending on how one interprets the concept of 'establishment', the scope of application of the Directive will differ. So far, in the *Rockfon* case, the CJEU has clarified that 'establishment' must be understood to be the unit to which the workers made

[47] 5 BV 8/14.

[48] Ordonnance of 26.11.2014, RG 14/02861.

[49] Decision of 14.06.2006, RG 06/03337.

[50] Art 1 Directive 98/59/EC establishes the following thresholds: 10 workers made redundant in an establishment employing more than 20 and less than 100 workers; at least 10 per cent of the workers in establishments normally employing between 100 and 300 workers; at least 30 workers in establishments normally employing 300 workers or more or, in alternative, at least 20 in a period of 90 days.

redundant are assigned to carry out their duties.[51] It is worth noting that this reading gives a fairly wide margin of manoeuvre to the employer, which has the possibility of circumventing the Directive by creating sub-units and distributing the redundancies among them, thus not reaching the thresholds established in the Directive and escaping its application. The issue of the possible circumvention of information and consultation obligations on the part of the employer was brought to the CJEU's attention by the Industrial Tribunal of Belfast, in the *Lyttle* case. In its request for a preliminary ruling, the Northern Ireland judge indicated the opportunity to adopt a purposive interpretation of the notion of establishment and to opt for the interpretation that would cover the largest possible number of redundancy-related dismissals.[52] The Court of Justice, however, rejected this option and confirmed the *Rockfon* doctrine. This reasoning, and the consequent volatility (and non-enforceability) that it entails for information and consultation rights, was then reiterated by the CJEU in subsequent rulings.[53]

3.1.2. Personal Scope of Application

Still with regard to Directive 98/59/EC, but this time in relation to the personal scope of application, the enforceability of information and consultation rights may also be hindered by another definitional problem, concerning the figure of the employer who is bound to observe information and consultation obligations and practices. As already mentioned in section 2.2, Directive 98/59/EC provides that it is the 'direct' employer of the workers affected by the dismissals – namely the person in charge of the establishment where the redundancies are effected – who has to fulfil the information and consultation obligations. The problem with this rule is that this person is not necessarily located at the managerial and corporate level at which the decision to proceed with the redundancies is taken.[54] Indeed, the 'direct' employer may not have adequate information and elements available to conduct the consultation. This is a clear limitation of the enforceability of information and consultation rights: even if information and consultation rights practices take place formally, the rights cannot be fully and effectively exercised.

As already mentioned, this issue was addressed by the Court of Justice in the *Akavan* case. There the dispute related to a situation where the decision to proceed with collective redundancies had been taken centrally by the parent company when it was not yet clear which subsidiary would be affected and, therefore, which 'direct employer' would be bound by the information and consultation obligations. In the *Akavan* judgment, the Court indirectly acknowledged the impossibility of implementing the information and consultation procedures effectively, but, at the same

[51] Case C-449/93 *Rockfon A/S*, 7 December 1995, ECLI:EU:C:1995:420, para 32.

[52] Case C-182/13 *Lyttle*, 13 May 2015, ECLI:EU:C:2015:317, para 24.

[53] Case C-80/14 *USDAW*, 30 April 2015, ECLI:EU:C:2015:291; Case C-392/13 *Canas v Nexea Gestion Documental*, 13 May 2015, ECLI:EU:C:2015:318.

[54] Art 2(4) Directive 98/59/EC.

time, did not take steps to remedy the paradoxical effect of the norm. Indeed, the CJEU ruled that 'whether the obligation has arisen from the employer to start consultations on the collective redundancies contemplated does not depend on whether the employer is already able to supply to the workers' representatives all the information required by Article 2(3)b of Directive 98/59/EC'.[55] And yet, Article 2(3)(b) is a crucial provision for the concrete fulfilment of the employer's obligations with regard to the information and consultation of employees, because it stipulates that the employer shall notify the employees' representatives in writing of: (i) the reasons for the projected redundancies; (ii) the number of categories of workers to be made redundant; (iii) the number and categories of workers normally employed: (iv) the period over which the projected redundancies are to be effected; (v) the criteria proposed for the selection of the workers to be made redundant insofar as national legislation and/or practice confers that power on the employer; and (vi) the method for calculating any redundancy payments other than those arising out of national legislation and/or practice. It is clear that if the employer can claim to have conducted information and consultation practices even without disposing of this information, then the Directive is emptied of its normative force, making its enforcement merely formal.

3.1.3. Wide Discretion for Management and Negotiating Parties

Finally, it is important to note that the EU legislator has preferred to leave to the discretion of management and employee representatives the definition of some crucial aspects for the effective enforcement of information and consultation practices.

Directive 2009/38/EC leaves ample room for manoeuvre for the representatives of management and of the workforce who sit in the 'special negotiating body', and who are responsible to adopt the agreement that will govern the operation of the EWC. Often these agreements suffer from a lack of clarity and precision in their clauses, and thus fall into a hardly enforceable regulatory limbo.[56] Only if the 'special negotiating body' cannot reach an agreement does the Directive provide for fallback provisions.[57] Yet even these fallback provisions fail to define essential aspects for the proper functioning of the EWC and thus do not provide for precise and actually enforceable prerogatives. For instance, the fallback provisions do not specify how to convene the first EWC, or how to cover travel and language interpreting costs. This can be a major obstacle for workers' representatives on the EWC, especially if they are spread across several countries.[58]

[55] Case C-44/08 *Akavan*, para 55.

[56] F Dorssemont, 'Directive 94/45: A General Analysis, in European Workers Councils – A Legal Analysis of the EWC: Towards a Revision of Directive (EC) No 94/45?' (1999) *Intersentia*, edited by M Rigaux and F Dorssemont.

[57] Annex 1 Directive 2009/38/EC.

[58] S De Spiegelaere, 'Too Little, Too Late? Evaluating the European Works Council Recast Directive', ETUI Report (2016) 42ff.

Another example of legal vagueness as a result of the legislator's choice to give room for manoeuvre to the very people to whom the Directive is addressed is found in the area of confidentiality.[59] Article 6 of Directive 2002/14/EC and Article 8 of Directive 2009/38/EC allow employers to leave information they consider confidential outside the obligation to inform and consult employees' representatives. However, there is a lack of objective criteria in the legislation for employee representatives to use as a basis for challenging possible abuses by managers, who may be tempted to adopt an inappropriately broad definition of confidentiality.[60]

These obstacles to enforceability of information and consultation rights connected with the notion of 'confidentiality' seem to be confirmed by the analysis of the legal proceedings at national level concerning Directive 2009/38/EC. The EWC database coordinated by the European Trade Union Institute shows that, out of a total of 105 cases reported, only two deal with a possible abuse by the employer of the confidentiality exception.[61] This may indicate practical difficulties for workers' representatives to challenge the actual confidential nature of the information that is withheld by management. Similarly scarce are judicial proceedings where workers' representatives have brought claims concerning those prerogatives that are essential to the effective exercise of information and consultation rights and the proper functioning of the EWC. These are, for instance, access to language assistance, time off work to fulfil the functions of workers' representatives, and coverage of travel expenses.[62]

Ultimately, the lack of clear procedures and definitions in the Directives regarding the effective exercise of information and consultation rights is beneficial to the employer. Lack of legal certainty is a deterrent for employees' representatives, who may reasonably prefer not to attempt to enforce their prerogatives through the judicial route, given the procedural costs and the uncertain outcome.

3.2. Lack of Institutional Ownership

In this section it is contended that the marginalisation of enforcement in the EU legislative and judicial context could also be an expression of a lack of institutional ownership by EU policymakers and especially by the European Commission. Indeed, the Commission holds the exclusive right of legislative initiative in the EU and is therefore the institution from which proposals to strengthen the enforcement

[59] S Laulom and F Dorssemont, 'Fundamental Principles of EWC Directive 2009/38/EC in R Jagodziński (ed), *Variation on a Theme? The Implementation of the EWC Recast Directive* (Brussels, ETUI, 2015).

[60] L Meylemans and S De Spiegelaere, 'EWC Confidential', ETUI Working Paper 2020.02.

[61] *Verizon EWC*, London central arbitration committee, Case Number EWC/22/2019; *Exxon Mobile*, Arbeidseechtbank Antwerpen, KG 08/9/C.

[62] *Mayr-Melnhof Cartonboard*, Arbeitsgericht Oldenburg, 3 BV 9/19; *Kuehne & Nagel*, AZ:5 TaBV 5/15 Urteil Lag Rheinland Pfalz, where the EWC representatives attempted, but failed, to claim the right for EWC members to have time off their working hours in order to complete their duties as workers' representatives.

of information and consultation rights would eventually emanate.[63] Moreover, it is within the Commission that periodical assessments of the effectiveness of existing EU law are undertaken, usually under the name of a 'refit exercise' or 'fitness check'.[64] When problematic issues emerge, the Commission generally follows up with policy initiatives to address the shortcoming. If the Commission would be interested in strengthening the impact of EU information and consultation rights, this would emerge from these evaluation exercises.

Despite its responsibilities in promoting the effectiveness of EU law, the Commission to date has not sufficiently addressed the shortcomings in the enforcement of the EU legal framework on information and consultation of workers. This could be a manifestation of the preference, already indicated in section 2, for a decentralised model of enforcement, left to the responsibility of national institutional actors or even to the non-institutional actors to whom the information and consultation legislation is addressed. As previously mentioned, the non-prescriptive approach to enforcement may be linked to business-oriented approach to information and consultation practices. These appear to be regarded by the Commission more as part of a toolkit for sound and efficient corporate restructuring than as crucial prerogatives for safeguarding workers' dignity and rights.[65]

The lack of any sense of urgency on the part of the European Commission with respect to improving the enforcement of information and consultation rights became clear from the fitness check initiative launched in 2011 to assess the effectiveness of information and consultation rules in the Directives on transfers of undertakings and collective redundancies, and as set out in the general framework Directive 2002/14/EC (basically, only the EWC Directive 2008/39/EC was excluded).[66] The Commission's assessment was conducted on the basis of a report that had been commissioned to external experts (the consultancy firm Deloitte), who had described substantial problems with enforcement arrangements and the adequacy of sanctions: 'Slow, complex and otherwise inadequate enforcement procedures and insufficiently dissuasive sanctions are reported in a third of the countries covered, notably but not exclusively in many "new" Member States'.[67]

Despite this negative assessment of the enforcement of information and consultation rules, the report eventually concluded that the Directives were still effective and recommended the Commission to address the enforcement issues merely by non-legislative means. More precisely, it suggested initiatives to raise awareness of information and consultation rights among workers, and to promote action at national level to speed up and simplify procedures and ensure appropriate

[63] Art 17 TEU.

[64] For an in-depth analysis of the Refit exercise and its role within the Commission's Smart Regulation Strategy, see COM(2010)543 final and COM(2014)268 final.

[65] DG Employment, Toolkits for Restructuring Based on the Innovative Actions of European Social Fund Article 6 Projects; Communication from the Commission, EU Quality Framework for Anticipation of Change and Restructuring, COM(2013)882 final.

[66] This fitness check initiative was carried out as part of the 2010 Commission work programme – Commission work programme, COM(2010)135 final, p 10.

[67] P Wauters, JJ Lennon, L Kapff and J Morley, 'Final Synthesis Report, Operation and Effects of Information and Consultation Directives in the EU/EEA Countries – Fitness check' (2012) 17.

sanctions. Based on this report, the Commission's assessment was that the EU information and consultation rules were 'fit for purpose'.[68]

This positive evaluation is surprising, to say the least, since not only the Deloitte report but also the Commission's fitness check communication highlighted major enforcement problems:

> There is evidence to suggest that there are some shortcomings with respect to the effectiveness of the information and consultation Directives … It seems that there are also shortcomings relating to the enforcement of the national transposing legislation, which mainly falls within the competence of the national authorities. There is also evidence in several countries of insufficient awareness of rights and obligations relating to information and consultation rights at company level.[69]

Or again:

> Overall, few complaints are made to national authorities, in particular labour inspectorates. There are also few judicial cases and court decisions. In case of non-compliance, low-level sanctions are occasionally imposed. The situation varies from one Member State to another. It also varies across the three Directives; for instance, there are extremely few information and consultation-related complaints or court decisions regarding Directive 2001/23/EC.[70]

Following what was suggested by Deloitte's experts about prioritising non-legislative responses to enforcement problems, the Commission committed to raising awareness among workers. However, not even this rather bland endeavour found expression in any concrete action by the Commission in the years to come.

Then, in 2015, the Commission launched a consultation with the EU social partners on a possible 'recast' (ie simplification through consolidation in a single text) of the existing EU information and consultation rules. However, it is worth noting that, while describing possible actions, there was no mention of addressing enforcement issues.[71] Eventually, the initiative did not find support from the social partners and the idea of a recast Directive was taken off the table. The ETUC saw the Commission's proposal as an attempt to simplify the three Directives in order to make them less burdensome for companies, with a risk of a regression of workers' rights.[72] Since then, the Commission has taken no further action on these Directives, despite the fact that the poor compliance with the information and consultation practices was also reported by other institutional actors.[73]

[68] Refit communication of 2 October 2013, COM(2013)685 final.

[69] Commission Staff Working Document 'Fitness check' on EU law in the area of Information and Consultation of Workers, SWD(2013)293 final, p 3.

[70] Ibid, 22.

[71] Commission Consultation Document, First Phase Consultation of Social Partners under Article 154 TFEU on a Consolidation of the EU Directives on information and consultation of workers, C(2015)2303.

[72] ETUC position, 18 June 2015.

[73] See for example, 2012/2061 INL, European Parliament resolution of 15 January 2013 with recommendations to the Commission on information and consultation of workers, anticipation and management of restructuring.

As for the EWC Directive, in 2018 this measure was also the subject of a Refit exercise, which revealed serious enforcement problems:

> Labour law experts from 10 Member States indicated enforcement issues and specifically the lack of dissuasive sanctions as an obstacle to the effectiveness of the Recast EWC Directive … Employees' representatives stressed that differences in the levels and scope of sanctions set at national level were an obstacle to effective redress and an insufficient incentive for the respect of EWC rights. They argue for a revision of the Recast Directive to introduce an obligation to nullify company decisions where information and consultation procedures have been breached.[74]

Here too, despite the clear need to take action to strengthen enforcement mechanisms, the Commission remained essentially inactive; the only initiative that was taken was very modest, consisting of a proposal to adopt an EWC handbook for workers' representatives and to invest in raising awareness of information and consultation rights.[75]

All in all, EU policymaking has neglected the enforcement aspect of EU information and consultation rights. Importantly, this laxity towards enforcement persists despite the Von der Leyen Commission's increased emphasis on strengthening the social dimension of EU policies. For instance, the Action Plan that the Commission adopted in March 2021 to implement the European Pillar of Social Rights stresses the importance of promoting information and consultation rights, but does not include any concrete initiatives in this regard.[76]

4. Concluding Reflections and Possible Ways Forward

The analysis carried out in the previous sections shows that, when observed from the EU perspective, the situation of enforcement of information and consultation rights is rather bleak. It is at the national level, however, that the implications of this inadequacy become apparent.

As highlighted in the context of the fitness checks conducted by the Commission, the lack of an effective EU approach to enforcement translates into the strong variability of sanctions and remedies provided by national legal systems.[77]

[74] Commission Staff Working Document – Evaluation Accompanying the Report on the implementation by Member States of Directive 2009/38/EC, SWD(2018)187 final, 35.

[75] Commission Report on the implementation by Member States of Directive 2009/38/EC, COM(2018)292 final, 9.

[76] Commission Communication on The European Pillar of Social Rights Action Plan, COM(2021)102 final.

[77] According to R Jagodziński and P Lorber, 'Enforcement Frameworks and Employees' Rights of Access to Enforcement Procedures in R Jagodziński (ed), *Variations on a Theme? The Implementation of the EWC Recast Directive* (Brussels, ETUI, 2015) 129–31, in case of non-compliance with information and consultation rights, in only half of the Member States (Bulgaria, Hungary, Ireland, Denmark, Estonia, Finland, France, Germany, Belgium, Bulgaria, Cyprus, Italy, Spain and the Netherlands) can workers' representatives demand the immediate suspension of the infringement by means of an injunction.

For instance, in some countries, such as the Netherlands, workers' representatives have at their disposal cheap and fast procedures to stop management from violating information and consultation rights.[78] In other countries, instead, the absence of legal standing of workers' representative bodies and the costs of acting before the judiciary constitute a deterrent. This results in a low reliance on judicial means of enforcement.

While a comprehensive analysis of the data on enforcement of the four information and consultation Directives is lacking, the EWC Database coordinated by the European Trade Union Institute collects useful data on the enforcement of the EWC Directive.[79] Despite the fact that this Directive contains enforcement provisions that are more developed than those in the other information and consultation Directives, the database shows that the use of judicial enforcement is extremely diverse across the Member States. A total of 1,652 EWC bodies have been established to date, but only around 105 court proceedings have been reported, including the different degrees of judgment in the same dispute. The number of proceedings per Member State is also not proportionate to the number of EWC bodies established. In Germany alone over 360 EWC bodies have been created, and the reported disputes number 23, while in France, with fewer than 200 EWCs, there have been 46 court proceedings.[80] As has become apparent from the previous sections, often workers' representatives lose their claim before the Court.

The national variability and the overall weak enforcement of the information and consultation Directives constitute sufficient ground to call for a fundamental change in the EU approach. In light of what has been presented in this chapter, this change should touch on several aspects.

The first aspect relates to a shift of narrative within EU policymaking (and in the approach of the EU Commission) concerning the rationale of information and consultation practices. The Commission should return to emphasising the emancipatory dimension of information and consultation rights. This would re-equilibrate the current predominant focus on their functionality with respect to the agile management of the company in situations of business restructuring. A more worker-oriented narrative would then arguably lead to greater cogency of the enforcement issue, because, as has emerged across this chapter, enforcement failures are ultimately suffered by the workers and not by the management.

Second, it is crucial to intervene with a legislative review that introduces specific enforcement mechanisms for information and consultation rights. Because of their highly procedural nature, violations of information and consultation prerogatives cannot be remedied by the generic solutions existing in the context of labour law,

[78] ATJM Jacobs, 'The Netherlands' in F Hendrickx (ed), *International Encyclopaedia for Labour Law and Industrial Relations* (2020) 337–40.

[79] www.ewcdb.eu. It should be noted that the database depends on information provided by national experts, therefore it cannot guarantee full accuracy.

[80] Distribution of the court proceedings on EWC across Member States: Germany 23; France 46; UK 17; Italy 3; Austria 2; Spain 3; Belgium 5; Luxembourg 1; Sweden 2; the Netherlands 1; Slovakia 2.

which are suited to enforcing rights with more tangible and substantive reverberations (such as wage issues, or challenges to unfair dismissals). Instead, a system should be put in place to ensure prompt intervention by a third and impartial decision-making authority with the power to impose immediate suspension of managerial decisions taken in breach of information and consultation rights and to accompany such suspension with effectively deterrent sanctions. Moreover, workers' representatives should be able to bring a claim before this authority incurring no or only moderate costs and with the guarantee that the raising of such claims will not affect the employment position of the workers concerned.

Thirdly, it is important for the EU legislator to intervene in the text of the Directives in order to remedy the regulatory indeterminacy which, as discussed in section 3.1, is detrimental to the enforceability of the rules.

Both of these legislative interventions should be carried out in consultation with the social partners and involving workers' representatives in the identification of better regulatory solutions.

Finally, it may also be of interest to workers' representatives to reconsider obtaining from the Court of Justice a declaration of direct horizontal effect of Article 27 CFR, which was denied in the *AMS* case. Indeed, in the recent *Egenberger* case, the Court recognised the direct applicability of an EU fundamental right in the employment field (the right not to be discriminated against because of religious beliefs).[81] There, for the first time in years the Court revived the doctrine of horizontal direct effect in relation to EU fundamental rights, which translates into the possibility for an individual to claim the enforcement of an EU fundamental right before the judiciary. The *Egenberger* case is thus an important precedent through which workers' representatives could argue for a reversal of the *AMS* jurisprudence.[82]

In conclusion, current institutional unresponsiveness and regulatory failures in enforcement weigh heavily on workers' effective enjoyment of information and consultation rights. This is a crucial issue that should be urgently addressed, especially considering that, in today's increasingly unstable economy, corporate restructuring phenomena have become largely normalised. And the EU rule-makers' emphasis on the digital and green transitions will only accentuate this trend. It is therefore necessary that EU institutional actors mobilise and take responsibility for improving the implementation and enforceability of these EU rules. At the same time, it is to be hoped that trade union delegates and workers' representatives will continue to insist and stand up for the enactment of information and consultation rights, including through the national and EU judiciary.[83]

[81] Case C-414/16 *Vera Egenberger*, 17 April 2018, ECLI:EU:C:2018:257.

[82] E Franziou, 'Mangold recast? The CJEU's flirtation with Drittwirking in Egenberger' in *European Law Blog*, 24.4.2018.

[83] P Olsson, 'Possible Shielding Effects of Article 27 on Workers' Rights to Information and Consultation in the EU Charter of Fundamental Rights' (2016) 32(2) *International Journal of Comparative Labour Law and Industrial Relations* 251–73.

12

Enforcing Migrant and Mobile Workers' Rights

ZANE RASNAČA

1. Introduction

The profiles of migrant workers in the EU are very diverse. Some move as intra-EU migrant workers, planning to stay in the host country for a long time. Others use intra-EU labour mobility for a short time only (such as seasonal workers). Yet others are 'mobile' workers, working in multiple countries in quick succession, sometimes based on the freedom to provide services rather than the free movement of workers.[1] Furthermore, workers from outside the EU – so-called 'third-country nationals' – are a separate category because they are subject to stringent immigration rules in addition to their labour rights. Sometimes they can also benefit from the rules of free movement (for example, as family members) but this is not always the case. Finally, some workers may be undocumented migrants.

Because of this remarkable diversity, it is hard to gauge how many migrant workers there are in the EU. Regarding third-country nationals, in 2020 – according to the European Commission – 8.7 million non-EU citizens were employed in the EU.[2] Intra-EU mobility reveals higher numbers, although it is difficult to assess exactly. In 2019, 13 million people of working age moved to another Member State, among whom the employment rate was 78 per cent.[3] These (intra-EU) migrant workers most often work in manufacturing, wholesale and retail and are overrepresented in accommodation and food services, construction and administrative and support services.[4] On top of this, there are also undocumented or irregular migrants; some of them work (undocumented) and they usually do not appear in the official workforce statistics. Overall, while not excessive, these numbers are

[1] For enforcement issues related to the posting of workers please see Chapter 8 in this volume.

[2] European Commission, 'Overall figures of immigrants in European society', https://ec.europa.eu/info/strategy/priorities-2019-2024/promoting-our-european-way-life/statistics-migration-europe_en.

[3] European Commission, Annual Report on Intra-EU Labour Mobility 2020, European Union, 2021, https://ec.europa.eu/social/BlobServlet?docId=23293&langId=en, 14.

[4] Ibid.

stable and illustrate that labour mobility is a structural and essential feature of the European labour market.

With the creation of the European Labour Authority (ELA),[5] and given that the exploitation of migrant workers has been all over the European media during the Covid-19 pandemic,[6] enforcement of their rights is high on the EU agenda. The rights of migrant workers, however, including those migrating inside the EU and from third countries, often fail to be realised or enforced in practice.[7] In part, it is because it is indeed very difficult to ensure adequate enforcement of migrant workers' rights, more difficult than in the case of local workers. In part, migrant workers themselves are reluctant to enforce their rights, fearing retribution from their employer or (worse) even expulsion from the EU. In part, however, the free movement of workers, albeit protected as one of the cornerstones of the EU integration project,[8] has simply become a somewhat controversial topic, condemned as the reason for Brexit,[9] blamed for Euroscepticism,[10] and associated with social dumping[11] and brain drains[12] at the same time.

In this chapter I look at the enforcement of migrant workers' rights from the perspective of the 'justice gap'.[13] In relation to mobile and migrant workers, one can speak about a justice gap (or enforcement gap) in several ways. First, in terms of formal equality and the idea that migrant workers should be able to access justice on the same basis as local workers. As we will see, this approach has largely been adopted by the EU.

Exactly because migrant workers are not usually in a situation comparable to local workers, however (because of their lack of language knowledge, support network, union membership, resources, lack of permanent resident status and

[5] See Chapter 17 in this volume.

[6] Eg M Apuzzo and S Gebrekidan, 'Trapped at sea by Covid-19 lockdowns, crew members plead for help', *The New York Times*, 25 March 2020; https://nyti.ms/2AiAQJk; R Bejan, 'Covid-19 and disposable migrant workers', Verfassungsblog, 16 April 2020; https://verfassungsblog.de/covid-19-and-disposable-migrant-workers. See also Z Rasnača, *Essential but unprotected: highly mobile workers in the EU during the Covid-19 pandemic*, ETUI Policy Brief No 9/2020.

[7] See eg N Lillie and L Berntsen, 'Hyper-mobile migrant workers and Dutch trade union representation strategies at the Eemshaven construction site' (2014) *Economic and Industrial Democracy* 1–17.

[8] Free movement of workers is protected in both the founding Treaties (Art 3(2) TEU and Arts 4(2)(a), 20, 26 and 45–48 TFEU) and as a fundamental right in Arts 15(2) and 45.

[9] Euractiv, Refugee crisis and EU migration policy to blame for Brexit, 29 June 2016; www.euractiv.com/section/uk-europe/news/refugee-crisis-and-eu-migration-policy-to-blame-for-brexit-says-hungarys-orban.

[10] S Vasilopoulou and L Talving, 'Opportunity or threat? Public attitudes towards EU freedom of movement' (2019) 26(6) *Journal of European Public Policy* 805–23.

[11] European Parliament, Report on social dumping in the European Union, 2015/2255(INI), 2016.

[12] C Bruzelius, 'Why the EU must debate and address the challenges arising from emigration', LSE Blog, 2019; https://blogs.lse.ac.uk/europpblog/2019/06/24/why-the-eu-must-debate-and-address-the-challenges-arising-from-emigration/.

[13] S Marsden, 'Migrant workers, rights, and the rule of law: Responding to the justice gap' (2019) 42(1) *Dalhousie Law Journal*.

so on), one also must look at them separately. The distance between such workers' rights 'on paper' and 'in practice' is especially wide.

Even this perspective does not reveal the whole picture, however: it might be that migrants in fact have fewer rights 'on paper', in which case they will be disadvantaged in comparison to local workers. Taking this on board, one could also look at the enforcement of migrant workers' rights in terms of substantive equality by examining whether the existing enforcement framework is capable of remedying the structural injustice faced by these workers. In this context, Mantouvalou has argued that migrant workers are put in a position of special structural vulnerability and systematically subjected to exploitation. One can certainly make a similar point concerning the enforcement of migrant workers' rights; the very existence of migration regimes puts workers in a vulnerable position and this vulnerability naturally extends also to enforcement of their rights.[14] Even though this raises some sensitive issues because it implies that migrant workers should have extra rights and should be better protected enforcement-wise than local workers, as I argue below, this is probably the only approach that would yield actual improvement in their situation.

This chapter unfolds as follows. In the first section, I explore the idea of a 'justice gap' and its application to the enforcement of migrant workers' rights in their diversity. In the second section, I look at what the EU has already done to bridge this gap and review the existing enforcement infrastructure for migrant workers, as well as the elements that make the enforcement of their rights different. In the third section, I try to identify some elements that are important if an enforcement structure is ever to fit the needs of migrant workers and develop some elements and criteria that should be considered when constructing it. Finally, I conclude.

Because the enforcement of migrant workers' rights is a very broad topic, I will concentrate primarily on the enforcement of mobile and short-term migrant workers' rights, namely, those who move for work and do not yet remain in the 'host' Member State for more than five years and those who travel for work a lot (change countries of work often) or carry out their work '*en route*' (mobile workers). I will not look at posted workers because enforcement of their rights,[15] disputes over jurisdiction and other specific issues related to the cross-border enforcement of EU labour law are discussed elsewhere in the book.[16] Finally, I look primarily at the enforcement opportunities for migrant and mobile workers in the EU rather than review how these workers enforce EU law in practice. That would require an empirical inquiry.

[14] V Mantouvalou, 'Legal Construction of Structures of Exploitation' in H Collins, G Lester and V Mantouvalou (eds), *Philosophical Foundations of Labour Law* (OUP, 2018).
[15] See Chapter 8 of this volume.
[16] Ibid.

2. A 'Justice Gap'

Data shows that migrant workers suffer from violations more commonly than other workers.[17] Holgate, Massey and others have highlighted the role of ethnicity and nationality in shaping divisions of labour and the (in)ability of workers to draw upon social networks and legal systems to enforce their rights.[18] Thus, migrant workers face problems with enforcement of their rights and asserting justice can be especially difficult. This results in a sort of 'justice gap', which could be understood in at least three ways regarding enforcement.

2.1. 'Comparative' Justice Gap

First, we can speak of a 'justice gap' between migrant workers and local workers in a comparative perspective. There are certainly gaps between migrant workers and local workers concerning substantive rights. Grimshaw et al[19] have showed that vulnerable workers face employment protection gaps and gaps in social protection and integration, for example, gaps in entitlement, and contributions.[20] Such workers (at least initially) often are not eligible for social assistance, and they also usually have to pay social contributions for a certain time before being able to draw benefits.[21]

While the gaps can be obvious concerning substantive rights, they are less so when it comes to enforcement mechanisms. The basic idea underlying the EU project is that the national level enforcement mechanisms are also available for enforcing EU law at the national level. Hence there is normally no distinction between migrant workers and native workforce in their formal access to enforcement mechanisms. Migrant workers are free to use them just as local workers (formal equality).

This has not always been so, at least when it comes to enforcement via representation mechanisms, such as workers' participation or trade unions. Multiple cases have been brought before the CJEU over the years in this regard. In all of them the CJEU has ruled in favour of workers. First, in 1991 the CJEU ruled that Article 8(1) of Regulation No 1612/68 precludes national legislation that refuses migrant workers the right to vote in elections held by an occupational guild to which they are compulsorily affiliated.[22] The same position was confirmed and

[17] G Davidov, 'Compliance with and Enforcement of Labour Laws: An Overview and Some Timely Challenges' (2021) 3 *Soziales Recht* 111–27 at 112.

[18] J Holgate, 'Organising migrant workers: a case study of working conditions and unionization at a sandwich factory in London' (2005) 19(3) *Employment and Society* 463; D Massey, *Spatial Divisions of Labour* (London, Macmillan, 1995).

[19] D Grimshaw et al (eds), 'Reducing Precarious Work. Protective gaps and the roles of social dialogue in Europe', November 2016.

[20] Ibid, 3.

[21] For example, six months until eligibility to paid maternity leave in Belgium.

[22] Judgment in Case C-213/90 *ASTI v Chambre des employés privés*.

extended to both passive and active election rights in *Commission v Luxembourg* in 1994.[23] Finally, in *Commission v Austria* the CJEU clarified that this protection extends also to third-country nationals, ruling that the principle of non-discrimination on grounds of nationality requires that all migrant workers – including third-country nationals – enjoy equal conditions and are allowed to participate in the representation and defence of workers' interests through such bodies as works councils and workers' chambers.[24]

Unfortunately, however, the formal equality approach is not particularly conducive to the effective enforcement of migrant workers' rights. It completely ignores the specific problems migrant workers face in accessing existing enforcement mechanisms that have been designed with local workers in mind.

2.2. 'Law-in-action' Justice Gap

Another way of conceptualising the justice gap is to consider it as the gap between someone's rights and (the possibility of) their enforcement: the difference between rights de jure and de facto. Migrant workers are less likely to attempt to enforce their rights and might be even less likely than local workers to achieve justice if they attempt enforcement.[25] Sarah Marsden has argued that there is a justice gap not only between eg migrant workers and citizen workers, but also between the promise of law and its actual functioning in the case of these workers.[26]

Enforcement barriers that migrant workers experience are typically reported to be much more pronounced and their possibilities of accessing justice severely limited.[27] Research carried out in the United Kingdom before Brexit by Barnard et al concerning enforcement of rights by EU8[28] workers showed that not only are migrant workers much less likely to enforce their rights or even to complain, but, according to authors, UK-born workers were more likely to report specific work-related problems and twice as likely to take some form of action than non-UK-born respondents.[29] Workers might not have adequate knowledge of the enforcement mechanisms available to them; it might be extremely difficult for them to obtain legal advice in a language they understand; they might lack support networks or have no free resources and savings to spend on enforcement.

[23] Judgment in Case C-118/92 *Commission v Luxembourg*.

[24] Judgment in Case C-465/01 *Commission v Austria*, see especially paras 30, 33, 40, 48–49, 56 and operative part.

[25] See in this regard, especially C Barnard, 'The Rule of Law and Access to the Courts for EU Migrants' (2020) 58)(6) *Journal of Common Market Studies* 1621–34 and Barnard et al, n 25 above.

[26] Marsden, n 12 at 159.

[27] Picum, 'A Worker is a Worker: How to Ensure that Undocumented Migrant Workers Can Access Justice' (2020), https://picum.org/wp-content/uploads/2020/03/A-Worker-is-a-Worker-full-doc.pdf.

[28] Latvia, Lithuania, Poland, Czechia, Slovenia, Slovakia, Hungary and Estonia.

[29] C Barnard et al, 'Beyond Employment Tribunals: Enforcement of Employment Rights by EU-8 Migrant workers' (2018) 47(2) *Industrial Law Journal* 231.

Additional dependency on their employer (eg for accommodation or even residence rights) creates further barriers for them to achieve justice. Simply put, they have much to lose and little to gain in asserting their rights. Thus, they tend to seek justice only in extremely dire situations.

Another significant issue faced by migrant workers is the absence of 'social solidarity'[30] and meaningful access to trade union representation in the host state, beyond the formal equality they largely enjoy.[31] For example, construction workers perceive the whole of Europe as their labour market, and their interactions with particular work contexts and national union organisations are inevitably temporary and limited, yet can last for years in case of large construction projects.[32] Tonia Novitz and Rutvica Andrijasevic investigated a situation in which Serbian workers worked in Slovakia in extremely exploitative conditions. The local trade union organised a strike against a violation of the collective agreement when the 342 Serbian agency workers outnumbered the 300 Slovak workers.[33] The trade union representatives or labour inspectorate in this case did not assist these workers, but supported actions that heightened their vulnerability.[34] This is unfortunate but understandable because trade unions represent the interests of their members and in such situations are often caught between a rock and a hard place. Unions want to enforce their collective agreements to prevent a downward spiral in wages and conditions which would affect their native membership as well. They are therefore confronted with the dilemma of representing migrants who are not members, are unlikely to become members, and are willing to take little or no action on their own behalf.[35]

To an extent, such justice gaps exist for all workers. Some, if not the majority, might be tempted to ignore certain breaches of their rights, for example, minor issues with overtime pay or other such matters; other breaches, such as discriminatory practices, might remain unknown even to the workers affected because such injustices are often structurally entrenched and visible only within the framework of certain data and at a certain level of aggregation. According to Barnard et al, the enforcement of working time rights is a particularly good example of a right that is sometimes thought to conflict with personal ambitions: migrant workers might want to work hours that considerably exceed the maximum working week prescribed by working time rules because that enables them to earn more and to get back to their country of origin more quickly after earning the desired amount

[30] B Refslund and I Wagner, 'Cutting to the Bone: Workers' Solidarity in the Danish-German Slaughterhouse Industry' in V Doellgast et al (eds), *Reconstructing Solidarity: Labour Unions, Precarious Work, And the Politics of Institutional Change in Europe* (OUP, 2018) 67–83.

[31] T Novitz and R Andrijasevic, 'Reform of the Posting of Workers Regime – An Assessment of the Practical Impact on Unfree Labour Relations' (2020) 58(5) *Journal of Common Market Studies* 1325–41, at 1326.

[32] Berntsen and Lillie, n 6 at 176.

[33] T Novitz and R Andrijasevic, n 31 at 1328.

[34] Ibid, 1332.

[35] Berntsen and Lillie, n 6 at 172.

of money.[36] Indeed, taking a dispute to the courts might be seen as a waste of time by some migrant workers, and in the face of dispute they might prefer moving to another job.[37] At the same time, these rights should still be enforced. Working time rules not only protect workers' health but also customers from mistakes that may occur due to tiredness. Also, employers should not unduly benefit simply because a worker does not see enforcement as a viable option for achieving justice.

Only in extremely rare situations are migrant workers duly informed about local law and the rights to which they are entitled under the equality established in EU law. This informational asymmetry, together with other factors already prima facie creates an unfavourable situation for enforcement, at least enforcement of the kind that needs to be triggered by the migrant worker, even before we take into account structural inequality.

2.3. 'Structural' Justice Gap

Finally, one should look at the idea of a 'justice gap' from a perspective of a substantive equality approach. This allows us to better grasp the overall picture of the obstacles migrant workers face in enforcing their rights.

Substantive equality is a contested concept, whose scope ranges from the idea of equal opportunities to equal outcomes and other approaches. Fredman takes a four-dimensional approach to this concept, proposing that to achieve substantive equality one must redress disadvantage, address stigma and stereotyping, enhance voice and participation, and accommodate difference and achieve structural change.[38] This approach has in a way been 'translated' for the migration context by Grimshaw et al. For them, migrant workers face gaps in employment protection, social protection and integration, representation, and enforcement. The latter result from mechanism gaps (gaps in access, process, sanctions, protection), awareness gaps (knowledge, transparency), power gaps (fear of losing job, fear of exclusion from unemployment support, lack of access to employer) and coverage gaps (unregistered workplaces, informal and undocumented employment).[39] This approach goes beyond formal and comparative justice gap approaches and identifies structural disadvantages and discrimination migrant workers face aiding in achieving substantive equality in a broad sense and can be seen as complementary to the approach taken by Mantouvalou, who argues that migrant workers face

[36] C Barnard, A Ludlow and S Fraser Butlin, 'Beyond Employment Tribunals: Enforcement of Employment Rights by EU-8 Migrant workers' (2018) 47(2) *Industrial Law Journal* 239. C Barnard et al, n 25 at 239.

[37] C Barnard, A Ludlow and S Fraser Butlin, n 36 at 239.

[38] S Fredman, 'Substantive equality revisited' (2016) 14(3) ICON 712–38.

[39] Grimshaw et al, n 17 at 3.

special structural injustice, as also social structures and law itself play a role in creating a vulnerability to exploitation.[40]

There is also another dimension to these gaps. Namely, not all migrant workers suffer significant breaches of their rights and face difficulties accessing justice on an equal basis. A migrant worker who knows the local language, or can more easily become a member of the local trade union, may have better access to resources and support systems and will probably experience a smaller justice gap than a fixed-term employee, working as a seasonal worker in a low-paid sector, not a trade union member and without any local support system. For example, it has been reported that in the Netherlands and Germany, repeat offenders in this regard are employers in agriculture, meat processing and construction, all of which are heavily reliant on migrant workers.[41] Seasonal workers have also been distinguished as especially vulnerable and unlikely to enforce their rights.[42] Temporary employment can often create vulnerability; however, it can also be fictitious, as the employer hires (and re-hires) workers on short-term contracts to avoid becoming subject to more stringent obligations.

Intersectionality also can play a significant role in expanding or narrowing the width of the justice gap. The combination between the status of a worker, especially a worker working in 'atypical' circumstances – for example, at the employer's home (domestic workers, individual care workers) – together with gender-based and racial discrimination[43] can also significantly reduce the incentives and opportunities for enforcement. Migrant workers will always by default suffer from intersectionality because of their status as workers and as migrants, which reinforces vulnerability. This, coupled with other factors, such as gender, race, nationality or religion – among others – may contribute to expanding the justice gap they face in terms of enforcement.

To make sure that justice is achievable and that access to justice[44] (broadly conceived) is ensured, one needs to aim to close the justice gaps in all their dimensions. While probably all migrant workers suffer to some extent from the third type of 'justice gap' because of their structural disadvantages on the labour market; and many, if not the majority certainly also suffer from the 'law-in-action' gap;

[40] Mantouvalou, n 14 above.

[41] T de Lange, S Mantu and P Minderhoud, 'Into the unknown: Covid-19 and the global mobility of migrant workers' (2020) *American Journal of International Law* AJIL Unbound, published online by CUP, 334.

[42] MH Zoeteweij-Turhan, 'The Seasonal Workers Directive: "but some are more equal than others"' (2017) 8(1) *European Labour Law Journal*.

[43] See eg G Alberti, J Holgate and M Tapia, 'Organising migrants as workers or as migrant workers? Intersectionality, trade unions and precarious world' (2013) 24 *The International Journal of Human Resource Management* 22.

[44] This concept, laid down in Art 47 CFREU, means that the victim of a rights violation is entitled to an effective remedy and a fair trial. Access to justice must not be theoretical or illusory, but practical and effective. The concept covers all forms of legal redress provided by criminal, civil and administrative justice services (Fundamental Rights Agency, 'Protecting migrant workers from exploitation in the EU: workers' perspectives', 2019, 9). See also Chapter 4 in this volume.

some especially vulnerable groups face a comparative justice gap. While for some (groups of) migrant workers the traditional enforcement routes might largely suffice, for others more intervention and aid are necessary to make the enforcement structure effective and functional for them. Third-country-national workers are especially vulnerable. As soon as they lose their job, they are at risk of losing their right to stay and work in the host country. The whole discussion on unfree labour[45] typically deals with workers who are very unlikely to have adequate access to redress.

Finally, even if migrant workers manage to get through the enforcement process, the enforcement of judgments is another issue. Usually, there are no special mechanisms in the Member States to ensure that migrant workers receive any compensation awarded to them by the courts. Often, they have already left the country (because they lost their job or their residence permit expired in the case of third-country nationals) and do not receive compensation. For example, in the Republic of Ireland, based on cases between 2006 and 2015, it was established that while more than 1.1 million euros had been awarded to migrant workers for breaches of employment law, only one-third of this sum had actually been paid out.[46] In the Netherlands, in order to get migrant labour rights enforced, Dutch trade unions are increasingly turning to judicial enforcement, because other options – such as social dialogue with management and industrial action – are only rarely effective in improving migrant conditions. However, according to Berntsen, because judicial proceedings usually extend beyond the duration of a worker's stay in the country, these procedures have a limited effect on changing the conditions of the workers involved.[47]

3. The EU's Current Approach to Enforcing Migrant and Mobile Workers' Rights

This section will look at how far and in what ways the EU legislator has filled in the justice gap faced by migrant workers. While enforcement-related provisions in the EU social and labour law *acquis* are rather rare, migrant workers are a bit of an exception. Historically, some enforcement-oriented provisions could be found in EU secondary law regulating labour migration because the free movement of workers is one of the fundamental objectives of the European integration project

[45] J Fudge and K Strauss, *Temporary Work, Agencies and Unfree Labour. Insecurity in the New World of Work* (Routledge, 2014).

[46] The Migrant Rights Centre Ireland, *All Work and Low Pay: The Experience of Migrants Working in Ireland* (Dublin, 2015).

[47] L Berntsen, 'Precarious Posted Worlds: Posted Migrant workers in the Dutch construction and meat processing industries' (2015) 31(4) *The International Journal of Comparative Labour Law and Industrial Relations* 371–90, at 384.

and it has been recognised that these workers should be able to enforce their rights.[48] In more recent years, enforcement of some migrating workers' rights, fuelled by concerns over protection of these workers, as well as fears of social dumping, has been high on the EU agenda. In fact, initiatives, such as the ELA, show that enforcement of migrating workers' rights is being prioritised. In this sense there is some recognition that the justice gap indeed exists and there have been attempts to (partly) close it.

At the same time, the approach taken by the EU can be characterised as sporadic. Certain types of enforcement are prioritised over others, and it seems that the overall approach is (1) not to do much at all to empower migrant workers who are EU citizens, (2) to grant and emphasise enforcement powers of the host countries when it comes to mobile workers, and (3) to balance the objectives of preventing undocumented migration somewhat unequally with the interests of protecting migrant workers from third countries. It is questionable whether this helps in closing the justice gap because the individual and collective interests of migrant and mobile workers in asserting and benefiting from their own rights remain in the background. The enforcement efforts differ significantly, depending also on the 'type' of worker. In other words, there is a comparatively more developed *acquis* concerning the enforcement of the rights of third-country-national workers, followed by increased attention to mobile workers but especially posted workers.[49] Not much attention is being paid to enforcing 'standard' intra-EU migrant workers' rights.

3.1. General Directives – Applying to All Workers

Typically, the EU's approach to the enforcement of migrant workers' rights is to have rules that apply only to certain types of workers; namely, different kinds of migrant and mobile workers receive different treatment when it comes to enforcement of their rights. Some general enforcement elements can be found in the general EU labour law Directives adopted under the Social Policy title (title X) that have the potential to aid migrant workers in enforcing their rights.

The right to information is very significant for successful enforcement. Migration Directives do not seem to contain a lot of rules for strengthening access to information for either workers or their representatives. However, the Transparent and Predictable Working Conditions Directive[50] contains not only general rules on providing information to workers (Article 4), but also in Article 7 sets out an additional duty of information for employers concerning workers sent

[48] For example, judgment in Case 36/74 *Walrave and Koch*, para 18.
[49] See Chapter 8 in this volume.
[50] Directive (EU) 2019/1152.

to work in another Member State or to a third country.[51] This obligation to provide information could be very useful; unfortunately, there is no requirement to provide this information in a language the worker understands and it can also be provided simply 'in the form of reference to applicable laws', which is a serious limitation (Articles 4(3) and 7). Also, the limit that the information can be provided up to seven days after the start of work could create additional difficulties for migrant workers (Article 5(1)). Because workers are reluctant to seek redress, the same Directive also aims to introduce enforcement provisions that ensure a favourable presumption where information about the employment relationship is not provided. Alternatively, there may be a procedure under which the employer may be required to provide the missing information and may be subject to a penalty if they do not (for example, Article 15).

While some enforcement-related provisions useful for migrant workers can also be found in the Temporary Agency Work Directive, especially in Article 10,[52] overall, the general EU social and policy law Directives do not contain further rules that would aim specifically to facilitate enforcement of migrant workers' rights.

However, it seems that also third-country national workers in some situations can rely on the Directives adopted under the Social Policy title. The CJEU ruled in *Tümer* that, in the context of the Insolvency Directive,[53] Article 153 TFEU (ex-136 EC) is not limited to Union nationals but can also include third-country nationals, and Member States cannot define the term 'employee' in a way that would undermine the social objective of this Directive.[54]

3.2. Enforcement of Intra-EU Migrant Workers' Rights

Overall, the EU Member States grant other EU nationals more rights than non-EU nationals.[55] Free intra-EU movement of EU workers is one of the fundamental freedoms, and the underlying objective is not only to protect them but also to facilitate such movement.

The whole idea of free movement of workers is centred around the prohibition of discrimination on grounds of nationality (Article 45(1) TFEU) between workers of the Member States in respect of employment, remuneration and other work

[51] This includes countries of work, anticipated duration, currency for payment of remuneration, any benefits, information whether there has been repatriation. Moreover, a posted worker also has to receive information on remuneration he is entitled to, any allowances specific to posting and reimbursement of travel, board and lodging, and a link to a single website with information (Art 7(1) and (2)).

[52] Member States should provide for administrative or judicial procedures to safeguard temporary agency workers' rights and should provide for effective, dissuasive and proportionate penalties for breaches of the obligations laid down in this Directive (Art 10(1)).

[53] Directive 80/987/EEC which has in the meantime been replaced by Directive 2008/94/EC.

[54] Judgment in Case C-311/13 *Tümer*, para 32, 42.

[55] W van Ginneken, 'Social protection for migrant workers: national and international policy challenges' (2013) 15(2) *European Journal of Social Security* 213.

and employment conditions. However, strikingly, TFEU Part 3, Title IV, Chapter 1 on workers does not mention enforcement of their rights as one of the aspects in which equality must be guaranteed. Instead, reference to the EU's potential role in developing an enforcement structure for workers (but not migrant workers specifically) can be found in Article 153(1) TFEU (see (e) and (f) in particular)[56] and broader EU competences to act in enforcement matters (but not specifically for migrant workers or within the area of social policy law and labour law) is embedded in judicial cooperation in civil matters, which allows the EU to develop judicial cooperation in civil matters having cross-border implications (including approximation) (Article 81(1) TFEU) including on conflict of laws and jurisdiction and effective access to justice (Article 81(2)(c) and (e)).

Regulation No 492/2011 on freedom of movement for workers[57] (Article 7(1)) demands equal treatment with national workers in relation to any conditions and work, including reinstatement or re-employment; however, it does not specifically regulate access to justice.[58] Instead, Directive 2014/54/EU on facilitating exercise of rights conferred on workers in the context of free movement for workers is the key instrument dealing with enforcement of migrant workers' rights. Unfortunately, it applies only to EU citizens (Article 1), which is a serious limitation because it means that non-EU citizens cannot rely on it independently of how long they have already worked in EU territory. One could try to apply reasoning similar to *Tümer* (mentioned above) to expand its scope, but this has not been done yet and would seem to go explicitly against the text of the Directive.

Generally, Directive 2014/54/EU requires that Member States ensure that after administrative recourse and, where appropriate, conciliation procedures, judicial procedures are available to all EU workers who have suffered from restrictions on their right to free movement or consider themselves wronged by a failure to apply the principle of equal treatment (Article 3(1)). Notably, this is a rather general right to enforcement and in practice means that, for the most part, migrant workers simply have recourse to the same enforcement mechanisms as local workers.[59] Therefore enforcement will take place largely via formal equality in terms of available enforcement mechanisms. But, as we saw in the previous section, it is not sufficient to reduce either the 'law-in-action' or 'structural' justice gap faced by migrant workers.

Two more safeguards have been introduced. First, entities having a legitimate interest in ensuring that this Directive is complied with can engage in any judicial or administrative procedure either on behalf or in support of migrant workers

[56] See Chapters 16 and 11 in this volume.

[57] See also former Regulation 1612/68.

[58] At the same time, it might be used to enforce some enforcement-related rights (see judgment in Case C-317/14 *Commission v Belgium*).

[59] See national implementation measures: https://eur-lex.europa.eu/legal-content/EN/NIM/?uri=CELEX:32014L0054.

(Article 3(2)). This, together with Article 8 of Regulation (EU) No 492/2011 that requires equal treatment regarding the membership of the trade unions for migrant workers who are EU citizens, might help in facilitating organising to enforce one's rights. However, such an enforcement route might again be difficult for vulnerable migrant workers who, lacking the information and language access needed to join a trade union, are afraid that their employer will retaliate if they join or have joined or simply are not yet eligible for legal advice from the union because of the shortness of their membership. The relative unimportance of this Directive for enforcement is also indirectly revealed by the lack of cases brought before the CJEU concerning its interpretation. It has been mentioned in only two judgments[60] without any cases being brought based on it.

Second, Member States must designate a body responsible for the promotion, analysis, monitoring and support of equal treatment of Union workers and members of their family (Article 4(1)). In cases where such bodies offer aid in legal proceedings, such assistance has to be free of charge to persons who lack sufficient resources (Article 4(2)). Under this Article some Member States have designated their labour inspectorates while others their national equality bodies as responsible;[61] though Germany, for example, has specifically established a dedicated Office for the Equal Treatment of EU Workers. This office, however, does not offer legal aid, only information and access to their media library.[62] Research on the work of these national-level bodies suggests that they face significant obstacles in the form of insufficient mandate and resources[63] and there are no clear trends yet in the evolution of the cases they investigate.[64] While this is a beginning, it is not very promising.

In large part the EU has adopted a formal equality approach. This is clearly not enough. First, to assess equality a local worker comparator might be needed, but in many sectors and positions held by migrant workers it might not be available. Where the same rights are available, they will usually not suffice because of further disadvantages faced by migrant workers (language barriers, no knowledge of local legal system, no resources, among other things). The problem is not only empirical or practical; it is a problem of law, at least if one sees the law's ultimate role as offering justice. There are very few provisions that attempt to close the law-in-action and structural justice gaps. While for long-term privileged migrant workers only small adjustments might be enough (such as additional information and facilitation of organising), for others, much more intervention would be necessary.

[60] Judgment in joined Cases C-401/15 and C-403/15 *Depesme and Kerrou* and judgment in Case C-802/18 *Caisse pour l'avenir des enfants*.

[61] European Commission, 'Bodies promoting equal treatment and supporting workers in the European Union and their family members'; https://ec.europa.eu/social/main.jsp?langId=en&catId=1277.

[62] See: www.eu-gleichbehandlungsstelle.de/eugs-en/service.

[63] EQUINET, Freedom of Movement in the EU: Equality Bodies Tackling Discrimination of Union Workers, Discussion paper, 2021, 10–12.

[64] See n 63 at 18.

One such recent attempt, however, has been the establishment of the European Labour Authority (ELA).[65] The ELA's activities have limited scope, and are focussed mainly on posting of workers,[66] social security[67] and freedom of movement for workers (intra-EU),[68] as well as free movement in road transport.[69] It has some own powers but functions mainly as a support system for (administrative) enforcement mechanisms at the national level.

The most interesting of the ELA's functions is probably its role in organising joint inspections. At the request of one or more Member States, the ELA must coordinate and support concerted or joint inspections in the areas within its competence. It can also, on its own initiative, suggest a concerted or joint inspection to Member States. Interestingly, social partner organisations at national level may bring cases to the attention of the Authority (Article 8(1) of ELA Regulation[70]). The ELA Guidelines indicate that social partner cases can be submitted on the grounds of 'serious complaints, reoccurring cross-border issues or risk assessment outcomes'.[71] However, Member States remain the ultimate holders of power when it comes to inspections, and they need to agree for the inspection to be carried out in their territory. At the same time, in line with Article 41(2)(c) CFREU we could at least expect a motivated answer if the ELA decides to reject a case signalled by the social partners. Furthermore, if the ELA becomes aware of suspected irregularities in the application of EU law, it can report to the concerned Member State and the European Commission (Article 9(10) of ELA Regulation). In such cases inspections can potentially result in administrative enforcement at the national level or infringement procedures at the Union level.

It seems that at least for the areas covered by the ELA Regulation the EU legislator has gone a little further than formal equality because a special procedure has been created at the EU level, with problems faced by many migrant workers in mind. At the same time, the central approach to the enforcement of intra-EU workers' rights still largely remains the same, which does little to address two out of three of the justice gaps identified above.

[65] Regulation (EU) 2019/1149. Please see also Chapter 17 in this volume.

[66] Directive 96/71/EC, Directive 2014/67/EU.

[67] Regulation (EC) No 883/2004 and Regulation (EC) No 987/2009 and Regulation (EU) No 1231/2010.

[68] Directive 2014/54/EU, Regulation (EU) No 492/2011, Regulation (EU) 2016/589.

[69] Regulation (EC) No 561/2006; Directive 2006/22/EC; Regulation (EC) No 1071/2009.

[70] Regulation (EU) 2019/1149.

[71] ELA Guidelines for concerted and joint inspections: www.ela.europa.eu/sites/default/files/2021-02/Item01_Guidelines-for-concerted-and-joint-inspections.pdf. In line with Art 41(2)(c) CFREU we might expect that in case of a refusal to pursue such a case, the ELA will offer motivation and hence there is some hope of the development of a sort of 'case law' in this context.

3.3. Enforcement of Third-country National Migrant Workers'[72] Rights

In contrast to free movement of workers, the underlying objectives of EU policies differ when it comes to labour-oriented migration by third-country nationals. The objectives of 'efficient management of migration flows' and 'combatting of illegal immigration and trafficking in human beings' stand alongside fair treatment of third-country nationals residing legally in the Member States.[73] EU secondary law regulating rights of third-country national workers is to a large extent emblematic of this – different – rationale. Special rules on enforcement are included in most of the Directives dealing with third-country national workers. However, there is a clear emphasis on administrative and coercive enforcement that leads to the punishment of employers who employ workers illegally and aim at making sure that third-country-national workers leave the country when losing employment (their reason for staying in the EU territory).

For example, the Seasonal Work Directive[74] includes a passage that states that sanctions must be effective, proportionate and dissuasive, like most EU secondary law regulating labour law matters. However, it is probably the only example where this aspect is developed further: sanctions are supposed to include liability of the employer to pay compensation to seasonal workers and enforcement mechanisms enabling seasonal workers to obtain compensation are supposed to be in place, even if they are no longer on the territory of the Member State in question (Recital 36).

The Seasonal Work Directive also contains some provisions aimed at prevention of breaches (so that recourse to means of enforcement is not necessary). First, it allows the Member States to reject authorisations of seasonal work where the employer has committed infringements of social security, taxation or labour law within the last 12 months or where the relevant third-country national has not complied with the obligations arising from a previous decision on admission as a seasonal worker (Article 8(4)). Second, Member States must withdraw authorisation where documents have been fraudulent or falsified, the holder is staying in the country for purposes other than seasonal work, and where the employer has been sanctioned for undeclared work or undocumented employment (Article 9(1) and (2)). Third, the Member States must require (concrete) evidence that accommodation for workers will be adequate (Article 20(1)). This, much more preventive, approach is rare when it comes to the enforcement of migrant workers' rights and could not be found in any measures regulating free movement of workers analysed

[72] There is also a privileged category among third-country-national workers: those who come from EEA countries or accession countries. However, enforcement rules often remain the same for such workers, except if special procedures are introduced bilaterally. This chapter will look only at third-country national workers in general, without examining in detail these special regimes.

[73] Recital 2 of the Seasonal Work Directive.

[74] Directive 2014/36/EU.

above. It is more akin to rules typically included in the occupational health and safety *acquis*.[75] It illustrates the rationale of also regulating immigration flows and minimising undocumented employment. The Seasonal Work Directive also extends the liability for breaches beyond the direct employer: the main contractor and any intermediate subcontractor may be liable where no due diligence was done and be subjected to sanctions, liable for any compensation due to seasonal workers and liable to pay any back payments (Article 17(3)).

Finally, the Directive also contains some specific rules when it comes to access to justice. The equal treatment principle is applied to the right to strike and to take industrial action, together with freedom of association and affiliation or membership of organisations representing workers, as well as to back payments (Article 23(1)). At the same time, it may still be difficult for these workers to enjoy the benefit of organising in the host country because of many barriers (such as language, short-term stay, remote location of their work and often also living arrangements) and a lack of more specific framework for facilitating organisation or at least representation of their rights. In addition, administrative enforcement is meant to play a significant role when it comes to seasonal workers, and according to Article 24(1) Member States must prevent possible abuses and sanction infringements. That must include monitoring, assessment and inspections; importantly, access to workplaces should be ensured not only to inspection services but also to organisations representing workers' interests, and with the agreement of workers. There must also be access to accommodation.

Member states have to ensure 'effective mechanisms' for submitting complaints against employers directly, through third parties or competent authorities, such as labour inspectorates (Article 25(1)). With the authorisation of the worker, third parties can engage in administrative or civil proceedings on behalf of seasonal workers. Protection from adverse treatment and measures against dismissal because of complaint must be ensured, based on the principle of equality with national workers. This latter aspect might be problematic because seasonal workers will typically be in much more dependent situations in their relationship with the employer than local workers. Furthermore, their right to legally remain in the country may be tied to their employment contract. Thus, equal protection from victimisation might not suffice.

Despite the comparatively rich set of enforcement-related provisions, no cases have been brought before the CJEU that concern interpretation of the Seasonal Work Directive. In general, while there is abundant research on the dire conditions of seasonal workers, there is not that much discussion on the enforcement of their rights, besides claims that it is insufficient. A recent study commissioned by the European Commission reveals that, among other challenges, seasonal workers severely lack access to information concerning their employment situation

[75] Please see Chapter 14 in this volume.

and related rights, as well as information on how to claim these rights.[76] Even though organisations representing seasonal workers have a right to access workplaces, their work is still hampered by language barriers and workers' fear of losing their jobs. Moreover, in many countries – for example, Italy – many third-country nationals perform undeclared work and often reside undocumented. This vulnerability further creates a vacuum in the enforcement of their rights because they not only fear losing their job but also being deported.[77]

At the same time, while there are several initiatives to address the gaps in access to information faced by seasonal workers,[78] and the first joint ELA inspection between France and Bulgaria was organised specifically to tackle recurring serious violations of the labour and social rights of seasonal workers in agriculture,[79] there is little to no information on any cases brought on behalf of seasonal workers to enforce their rights. There also seems to be little strategic litigation in this field.[80] While at the national level there are some examples of reforms that allow more unity in the enforcement of seasonal workers' rights, few instances lead to actual enforcement. For example, in Belgium a range of actors – including labour inspectorates, trade unions and organisations defending the interests of migrant workers – claim to protect seasonal workers.[81] The main trade union representing seasonal workers is the FGTB.[82] However, no information is targeted at seasonal workers on their website and there is no information on enforcement of their rights. Only in 2018 did the national authorities agree to cooperate on sharing information about seasonal workers beyond an ad hoc basis.[83] To this day there are no specific procedures in Belgium to ensure that seasonal workers and their employers are informed about their rights and duties, and no special procedures for monitoring, inspections or complaints.[84] Hence seasonal workers seem to experience a significant law-in-action and also a structural-justice gap despite an EU *acquis* providing enforcement-oriented rights.

A second Directive that contains enforcement-related provisions for third-country national workers is the Employers Sanctions Directive.[85] It prohibits employment of undocumented third-country nationals and is illustrative of the

[76] European Commission, 'Intra-EU mobility of seasonal workers: Trends and challenges', 2021, 48.

[77] Ibid, n 76 at 49.

[78] For example, a phone helpline in Romania, a guide informing Spanish seasonal workers in France of their rights (ibid, p 50), leaflets and activities organised by the ELA in their campaign 'Rights for All Seasons'; www.ela.europa.eu/en/campaigns/rights-for-all-seasons

[79] ELA, 'European Labour Authority organised first joint inspection', 2021, www.ela.europa.eu/en/news/european-labour-authority-organised-first-joint-inspection.

[80] See Farmworker Justice and their advocacy programme in the United States for comparison.

[81] European Migration Network Belgium, 'Attracting and protecting the rights of seasonal workers in Belgium', January 2021, https://emnbelgium.be/publication/attracting-and-protecting-rights-seasonal-workers-emn, 20.

[82] Ibid, n 81 at 21.

[83] See n 81 at 21.

[84] Ibid, n 81 at 22.

[85] Directive 2009/52/EC.

underlying objectives of regulating and preventing illegal immigration. It lays down minimum common standards on sanctions to be applied in the Member States against employers who infringe prohibition (Article 1). To offer compensation to workers, the Directive requires that employers pay any outstanding remuneration, an amount equal to any taxes and social security contributions that the employer would have paid if the third-country national had been employed legally, and any costs arising from sending back payments to the country to which the third-country national has returned or been returned (Article 6(1)). To foster access to justice, liability beyond the direct employer – albeit though only one level in the subcontracting chain – is also introduced (Article 8(1)). Member States must introduce various enforcement elements in their national systems:

(1) criminal penalties for the breaches of this Directive (Articles 9 and 10 and 12);
(2) effective mechanisms through which third-country nationals may lodge complaints directly or through third parties (including unions) (Article 13(1));
(3) effective and adequate inspections that are based primarily on a risk assessment to be drawn up by the competent authorities (Article 14(1)); and
(4) with a view to increasing the effectiveness of inspections, Member States must regularly identify the sectors of activity in which the employment of undocumented third-country nationals is concentrated (Article 14(2)).

Both the Seasonal Work Directive and the Employers Sanctions Directive introduce rules on enforcement. However, they apply only to very specific kinds of workers (seasonal workers and workers in undocumented employment). They also do not seem to be able to meaningfully bridge the justice gap illustrated by inter alia no cases having been brought before the CJEU concerning their interpretation. To a large extent these Directives rely on individual workers to fight for their own rights despite their organisational capacity being very weak. Even though Member States have to ensure a certain level of administrative enforcement, it might not be enough to deliver justice for workers because by the time the investigation has finished most of them will probably have already lost their jobs and right of residence along with it. While victimisation is prohibited,[86] that does not mean that, for example, third-country national seasonal workers will retain their right to stay in the country. In most Member States, they lose their residence rights automatically if they lose their job.[87]

Vulnerable workers require a structural and far-reaching approach to the enforcement of their rights. However, until they are able to rely on adequate protection in either EU or national law, detached from their immigration status,

[86] See Art 25(3) of the Seasonal Work Directive.

[87] W Zwysen et al, 'Labour market and social developments crisis further entrenches inequality', *ETUI Benchmarking* 2021, 69–70.

their situation will probably remain dire. Even though *Tümer* offers some hope that third-country nationals might also be able to rely on general safeguards established in EU law, even when finding themselves in an irregular situation,[88] the judgment dealt with one particular Directive and the CJEU has not yet expanded that approach beyond the specific case.

3.4. Enforcement of Mobile Migrant Workers' Rights

EU law does contain several sector-specific or worker type-specific EU secondary law measures that include enforcement-oriented rules for mobile workers. The main examples are rules on work in the transport sector (mainly road transport and concerning seafarers), on one hand, and rules on the enforcement of posted workers' rights, on the other. While enforcement of the latter's rights is analysed elsewhere in this volume,[89] I will here briefly mention enforcement rules for transport workers.

One of the very few labour law Directives that focuses solely on enforcement is the Directive on Enforcement of Seafarers' Hours of Work.[90] It regulates administrative enforcement (via inspections) and, importantly, both EU workers and third-country-national workers can benefit from it (indirectly) because it applies to any ships finding themselves in EU territory. There is an obligation to have on-board complaint procedures and some other rules on enforcement,[91] and if the conditions on board are hazardous to workers, Member States must ensure that the ship does not leave port until deficiencies are rectified or the seafarers have rested.[92]

Also, Directive (2002/15/EC) on working time in road transport requires that Member States create a system of penalties for breaches[93] and that precise rules be laid out on what enforcement authorities should be able to check when it comes to tachographs.[94] The checks concerning road transport are regulated in quite a detailed way compared with other measures dealing with EU labour and social policy law. For example, it is stated that roadside checks should 'each year [cover] a large and representative cross-section of mobile workers, drivers, undertakings and vehicles'[95] and 'each Member State shall organise checks in such a way that at least 3 per cent of days worked by drivers of vehicles [are covered]'.[96] Furthermore,

[88] See judgment in Case C-311/13 *Tümer*.
[89] See Chapter 8 in this volume.
[90] Directive 1999/95/EC.
[91] Directive 2009/13/EC, see especially Regulation 4.2 and Regulation 5.1.5. This Directive is based in a procedural way on an agreement between social partners and in a substantive way on the ILO Maritime Labour Convention.
[92] Directive 1999/95/EC (Art 5(1) and (2)).
[93] Penalties have to be 'effective, proportional and dissuasive' (Directive 2002/15/EC).
[94] Regulation (EC) No 561/2006 (Recitals 4, 14 and 15).
[95] Directive 2006/22/EC as amended by Amended in 2020 by Directive 2020/1057 (Art 2).
[96] Ibid.

concerted checks by Member States have to be organised both roadside and at the premises of undertakings at least six times per year.[97] Finally, there is a special procedure for exchanging information on enforcement cases between the Member States.[98] Hence, transport is one area in which the EU has introduced enforcement-related provisions but they do seem to be aimed mainly at administrative enforcement and ensuring that the Member State through which the transportation takes place can carry out effective inspections rather than at enforcing workers' rights per se.

When taken together with the enforcement of posted workers' rights and such developments as the adoption of the Enforcement Directive,[99] the revision of the Posted Workers Directive,[100] the establishment of the ELA and the adoption of posting rules for road transport,[101] one could argue that there has been an overall tendency in the past decade at least to adopt more and more detailed and empowering rules for enforcing mobile workers' rights. This approach of focusing on the few instead of the many cannot be fully explained, however, because many other groups of migrant workers are in equally bad or even worse situations in terms of enforcement of their rights (eg workers in care services or domestic workers). Besides, while working conditions and social security fraud concerning mobile workers has been high on the EU agenda, what is still missing is any empowerment of these workers and any attempts to organise them across borders to assert their rights, as well as any attempts to ensure that justice (at least in the form of compensation) reaches them. Thus, overall, the focus has not truly been on protecting workers' rights. One could argue that these legislative developments are rather illustrative of a struggle between various systems of labour law and of the difficulties involved in applying the territoriality principle in the multi-level reality of the internal market.

In terms of reducing the justice gaps, the focus has been largely on equality and on closing gaps in administrative enforcement mechanisms, especially in terms of inspections. While that is a start, it is not enough to meaningfully address the justice gaps experienced by migrant workers. EU rights and enforcement frameworks tend to frame workers and employers as isolated individuals.[102] Workers become eligible for individual remedies based on any harm they have suffered individually, and the employer is considered to be a wrongdoer and, implicitly, an outlier who does not conform. Most of the mechanisms discussed in this section rely on workers to initiate complaints or at least to participate actively in enforcement of their rights, while not guaranteeing that they will benefit from any administrative enforcement of their rights. This approach does not leave much space for examining or challenging the structurally embedded disadvantages faced

[97] Ibid.
[98] Ibid, Art 8.
[99] Directive 2014/67/EU.
[100] See consolidated text of Directive 96/71/EC.
[101] See Directive (EU) 2020/1057.
[102] See Marsden, n 12 at 161.

by migrant workers and does not allow examination of the conditions under which unfree labour becomes structurally embedded, nor the role of states in fostering conditions in which the most severe forms of exploitation can thrive.[103] Hence the law-in-action and structural-justice gaps remain largely unaddressed.

A second problem – which might in fact be a direct consequence of the adoption of the formal equality model by the EU legislator – has to do with the social rights of migrants in a more direct sense. Despite formal equality with local workers in this regard, they are cut off from meaningful representation of their interests, not only in collective bargaining and workplace-level representation, but also in the enforcement of legal rights[104] and participation in the workplace and political life.[105] Labour law is an area in which workers' collective voice is necessary to ensure that justice is achieved. To date, however, migrant workers have not really benefited from their formally equal but substantively unequal right to representation of their interests.

4. Quo vadis? An Enforcement Structure Fit for Migrant Workers' Needs

There are several enforcement gaps affecting migrant workers in the EU. They need to be identified and remedied if 'justice gaps' are to be narrowed in any way. While this is by no means an exhaustive list, the ways in which the enforcement of migrant and mobile workers' rights might be strengthened include the following:

(i) strengthening migrant workers' collective voice;
(ii) improving their access to resources;
(iii) strengthening liability beyond direct employers;
(iv) untangling enforcement of labour law from workers' residence status; and
(v) addressing structural disadvantages, including the precarious circumstances in which migrant workers are embedded.

All these elements could also be seen alongside Grimshaw et al's typology of enforcement gaps (in terms of enforcement mechanisms, awareness, power and coverage). They generally respond to one or more 'needs' identified in their research.[106] They are also offered here as possible pathways towards reducing the law-in-action and structural-justice gaps identified in section 1.

[103] See Marsden, n 12 at 161.

[104] JE Dølvik and J Visser, 'Free Movement, equal treatment and workers' rights: can the European Union solve its trilemma of fundamental principles?' (2009) 40(6) *Industrial Relations Journal*.

[105] I Greer, Z Ciupijus and N Lillie, 'The European Migrant Workers Union and the barriers to transnational industrial citizenship' (2013) 19(1) *European Journal of Industrial Relations* 5–20, at 9. This reality might also be a direct result of the adoption of a formal equality approach, which does not take into account migrant workers' structural disadvantages and special experiences of vulnerability.

[106] See the Conclusion for details.

4.1. Strengthening Migrant and Mobile Workers' Collective Voice

Industrial relations systems in the EU tend to be somewhat isolated from one another. Workers' representation is still largely national in its level of activity[107] and developed with the needs of local workers in mind. Giving migrant workers a voice necessarily requires a cross-border and transnational approach, which is very difficult for organisations such as trade unions to achieve. A migrant worker who is an EU national enjoys equality of treatment regarding trade union membership.[108] There is no further facilitation of collective organising for EU workers and migrant workers specifically, however. For now, as Greer and others have put it, 'while workers in the EU have new civil rights to live and work in different countries, in accessing these rights they [often] give up the rights of industrial democracy'.[109]

Despite this there are some hopeful examples of organising a unified bargaining agenda across borders.[110] Furthermore, attempts to organise beyond borders, albeit only partially successful, have taken place in Europe before.[111] Collective voice does not only mean workers' representation by trade unions, especially when it comes to enforcement. There are other mechanisms that could be used to strengthen collective enforcement of migrant workers' rights. Introduction of pan-European collective redress opportunities at either the EU or the national level might also be a step in the right direction. The EU recently adopted a Directive on Representative Action in Consumer Protection. Similar mechanisms should be in place also for migrant workers. Probably, to provide incentives for litigation, any such mechanism should also involve some class action elements modelled on the US system, which also allows pecuniary damages and goes beyond mere compensation for harm suffered, as well as including contingency fees. Even largely worker-friendly enforcement mechanisms do not reach some workers (eg seasonal workers). For such especially vulnerable workers justice mechanisms should be easier to access and also provide more effective incentives. All in all, in some situations in which the 'justice gap' is particularly wide, private and public enforcement, as it currently stands, might not reach or at least not provide sufficient protection. Collective redress mechanisms might be able to complement the enforcement system and bring (some) justice to some groups of these workers or at least contribute to reducing employer breaches in future.[112] To be effective in vulnerable situations, however, collective redress must be effective and provide plenty of incentives for workers to pursue it. It is by no means the only option in

[107] S Lafuente Hernandez and Z Rasnača, 'Can workers' rights ever catch up? The Erzberger case and EU cross-border reality' (2019) 48(1) *Industrial Law Journal* 98–116.

[108] Art 8 Regulation (EU) No 492/2011.

[109] Greer, Ciupijus, and Lillie, see n 100 at 17.

[110] Ibid, n 100 at 9.

[111] Ibid, n 100 at 17. The example of the European Migrant Workers Union, created by the German union IG BAU.

[112] Z Rasnača, 'Collective redress in labour and social law disputes: An (attractive) option for the EU?' (2021) 12 (4) *European Labour Law Journal* 415–435.

the enforcement toolbox to address and fill the justice gap. But it seems a suitable instrument for situations in which the rights of certain groups of workers are not being adequately respected and they have little chance of achieving justice individually. This is not to say that collective redress would not be a useful instrument for defending any workers' rights, merely that such a mechanism might be more pertinent than others simply for filling the gaps in the enforcement system for migrant workers.

4.2. Improving Access to Resources

A not so cardinal, but necessary step is to strengthen migrant workers' resources and to ensure that they receive assistance and opportunities to enforce their rights. Even an obligation to make it possible to submit claims in multiple languages and to make information available to them in other languages than that of the host country would go a long way towards facilitating enforcement. While the CJEU on a few occasions has held that enforcement proceedings should be accessible in a language known by the worker[113] and has ruled that very rigid language rules can at times breach free movement rules,[114] this line should be pursued even further. Legal aid and assistance, as well as improved mechanisms for delivering compensation to migrant workers even when they have already left the territory of the relevant Member State or EU territory in general, might enhance enforcement. The difficulty of enforcing judgments is often reported by researchers.[115]

Further necessities include solutions for inspecting workplaces that are in private homes or outside; increased resources for translation; explanations of the rules in force; and protection of workers' right of residence beyond the specific employment contract.

4.3. Strengthening Liability Beyond Direct Employers

Another specific feature of the European labour market is the widespread use of subcontracting, especially in public procurement.[116] Liability for most work-related aspects still lies largely with the direct employer, however, even though profits are largely shared between contractor and subcontractors, often with a larger share going to the general contractors. There have been some attempts to change this situation (one-step liability is provided by the Posting Enforcement Directive, and subcontracting liability in the Seasonal Work Directive, and to

[113] Judgment in Case C-137/84 *Ministere public v Mutsch*.

[114] Judgment in Case C-317/14 *Commission v Belgium*.

[115] C Murphy, DM Doyle and M Murphy, 'Still Waiting for justice: Migrant workers' perspectives on labour exploitation in Ireland' (2020) 49(3) *Industrial Law Journal* 347.

[116] See also Chapter 19 in this volume.

some extent also in the Illegal Work Directive). These options should be explored further, and a more radical change might yield more benefits. The direct liability of the general contractor for some employment aspects, beyond health and safety, including remuneration, working time, holiday pay and other similar aspects – with the possibility for the contractor to recover sums from subcontractors – might go a long way towards avoiding situations in which employers cannot be found, and workers remain uncompensated. It would also put the liability where most of the profit lies (namely, with the main contractors).

Mainstreaming of social conditionality in the other areas of EU law might help, too. Jo Hunt has argued that space for social conditionalities should be made in the Common Agricultural Policy, making subsidies conditional on respect for employment rights for all workers.[117] The key mechanism by which this could be achieved is the system of direct subsidies for farmers, with payments tied to compliance with a range of statutory requirements. At the very least, a basic floor of employment rights should be provided for all workers among the statutory requirements.[118]

4.4. Untangling Enforcement of Labour Law from Workers' Residence Status

Migrant workers from third countries tend to be in a rather difficult situation because their work permit tends to be linked to their residence permit. There is thus a strong possibility that they will be deported if they lose their job. This, together with other aspects that increase their dependency on their employer, makes them much less likely to assert their rights. This is often tantamount to unfree labour – a workforce caught within the supply chain that they have entered voluntarily, but find difficult to exit as they are tied into a contract with a particular employer, under a menace of penalty and/or non-payment of wages. They may also be subject to illicit pay deductions, vulnerable to deportation, risk homelessness because of tied accommodation, be isolated by geography and language, and have little access to meaningful legal protection.[119] Giving a decent grace period and not restricting residence permits to a single employment contract would at least partly free them from this burden and empower them to assert their rights. Any migrant workers who are not permanent residents are still vulnerable, however, especially in terms to their limited access to some rights and also because they may lose rights as soon as they lose employment. This does not mean, of course, that in some instances temporary migration might be better accepted by the indigenous

[117] J Hunt, 'Making the CAP fit: Responding to the exploitation of migrant agricultural workers in the EU' (2014) 30(2) *International Journal of Comparative Labour Law* 131–52, at 131.

[118] Ibid, at 132.

[119] Novitz and Andrijasevic, n 27 at 1334.

population, and take better account of migrants' interests and the well-being of their country of origin.[120] Nevertheless, temporary migration should not be facilitated by making workers more vulnerable.

This is an especially difficult dilemma for the administrative enforcement of migrant workers' rights. This often prevents them from being 'on the same side' as labour inspectors. They fear losing employment and not gaining anything, even compensation, in return. There is some empirical research showing that this is indeed the case.[121] Hence one should put remedying individual workers' suffering as the main priority in administrative enforcement. Otherwise, there is a tendency to see administrative enforcement and especially non-payment of social contributions in the host country as a financial loss for the state rather than a loss of benefits and rights for the worker. This is a rather dangerous approach.[122] In fact, one should make sure that, regardless of the shortness of their period of service, workers can always benefit, at least proportionally, from the social protection benefits due to them. It is important to make sure that the most vulnerable actors in this process – the workers – do not become mere casualties in the enforcement process.

4.5. Addressing Structural Disadvantages

Finally, there are structural disadvantages to being a migrant worker that are very hard to address. This is especially so because of the economic and social differences between Member States, between regions, between groups of workers and even individual workers. Often the terms under which migrant workers are ready to work are already exploitative. But reality often turns out to be even worse. Some employers even try to exacerbate workers' vulnerability by eg moving them illegally and not paying health and social security contributions.[123] As long as the underlying structures remain unchallenged, the justice gap between the promise of rights and sanctions and their limitation will not be closed by the accretion of more individual rights, better access to existing rights, or more sanctions. The persistence of justice gaps for migrant workers signals a need to challenge this naturalisation of labour unfreedom and the specific legal and institutional forms it takes.[124] The answer lies, to some extent, in addressing the state directly and examining how we understand the EU's functions. States should not only offer access to the same rights, but special conditions and structures should be created that consider and are responsive to the vulnerability of migrant workers.

[120] Van Ginneken, n 54 at 210.

[121] See European Commission, n 75 above.

[122] See eg the discussion on enforcement of social security and A1 forms, and especially N Rennuy, 'Posting of Workers: Enforcement, Compliance, and Reform' (2020) 22 *European Journal of Social Security* 212–34.

[123] Novitz and Andrijasevic, n 27 at 1328.

[124] Marsden, n 12 at 174.

5. Conclusion

In this chapter, I have tried to reveal the main structural deficiencies in the enforcement regime for migrant workers in the EU. Currently, the EU largely takes a formal equality approach to enforcing migrant workers' rights. That is, they have to rely on the existing enforcement structures designed with native (or local) workers in mind. In this situation, migrant workers are formally equal in terms of enforcement, but still face significant justice gaps.

In systemic terms, one could imagine approaching these gaps in a way similar to the categorisation offered by Grimshaw et al, by addressing gaps in mechanisms, awareness, power and coverage.[125]

I have sketched some ideas on how to address key deficiencies in all four of these contexts. First, migrant workers need special mechanisms, created with their needs in mind, which would help to close the justice gap they face. Collective redress, improved access to administrative enforcement and better protection of workers' interests in this process, together with more efficient enforcement of judgments and compensatory mechanisms, could be the way forward.

Second, access to information (awareness) should be further improved, especially by introducing a multilingual approach to enforcement in sectors in which migrant workers have a permanent structural presence, as well as by improving their access to knowledge-based aid and resources.

Third, the organisation of migrant workers' voice is clearly the weak point. There have been no legislative initiatives in this area from the EU so far. In fact, organising workers cuts across the categories developed by Grimshaw et al and needs to be addressed if any of the problems we have dealt with are to be address properly. The imbalance between employers and migrant workers needs to be tackled, at least in terms of dedicated measures to empower migrant workers to organise (ideally, at a transnational level), to improve the enforcement of their rights in a meaningful way.

Furthermore, and especially relevant to reducing the justice gap for third-country-national workers, loss of residency should not be automatic after the (abrupt) end of an employment relationship. The interdependency between the employment relationship and the right to legal residence in the country needs to be untangled. The justice gaps in terms of enforcement are especially wide for workers in unregistered workplaces, whose employment is informal and undocumented. One could start to address these things via organisation, strong protection against exploitation and a strong presumption of an employment relationship.

[125] Grimshaw et al, n 17 at 3.

13

Enforcing the Rights of Non-standard Workers

BARBARA KRESAL

1. Introduction

Non-standard employment is a very broad issue,[1] which goes beyond the scope of this chapter. In order to remain within the thematic borders of the book – the effective enforcement of EU labour law – this chapter focuses on the EU legal framework for non-standard forms of employment and analyses it from an enforcement perspective.

Because this analysis cannot be entirely separated from a broader perspective on non-standard and precarious work, a short schematic overview of types and characteristics of non-standard employment is sketched out in this introductory section. In section 2, the existing EU legal framework for non-standard employment is analysed and in section 3, the initiatives for further EU legal regulation

[1] There is a huge literature on this topic. To mention only a few items: ILO, *Non-standard employment around the world* (Geneva, 2016); Eurofound, *New forms of employment* (Dublin, 2015); A Broughton et al, *Precarious Employment in Europe* (Strasbourg, European Parliament, 2016); J Buelens and J Pearson (eds), *Standard Work: An Anachronism?* (Cambridge, Intersentia, 2013); W Eichhorst and V Tobsch, *Risk of Precariousness: Results from European Working Conditions Survey 2010 and 2015* (Strasbourg, European Parliament, 2017); J Kenner, I Florczak and M Otto (eds), *Precarious Work – The Challenge for Labour Law in Europe* (Cheltenham, Edward Elgar, 2019) 114–32; D McCann and J Fudge, 'Unacceptable forms of work: A multidimensional model' (2017) 2 *International Labour Review* 147–84; A Blackham, M Kullmann and A Zbyszewska (eds), *Theorising Labour Law in a Changing World – Towards Inclusive Labour Law* (Oxford, Hart, 2019); K Kresal Šoltes, 'Vpliv prekarizacije dela na kolektivne pravice delavcev' in K Kresal Šoltes et al (eds), *Prekarno delo* (Ljubljana, PF and EF, 2020) 29–44; D Senčur Peček, 'Social protection of workers in non-standard forms of employment in Slovenia' (2018) 39(4) *Zbornik Pravnog fakulteta SR* 1561–99; G Schmid and J Wagner, *Managing social risks of non-standard employment in Europe* (Geneva, ILO, 2017); I Mandl, *New forms of employment: 2020 update* (Dublin, Eurofound, 2020); P Schoukens and A Barrio, 'The changing concept of work: When does typical work become atypical?' (2017) 8(4) *European Labour Law Journal* 306–32; E Ales, O Deinert and J Kenner (eds), *Core and Contingent Work in the European Union – A Comparative Analysis* (Oxford, Hart, 2017); A Koukiadaki and I Katsaroumpas, *Temporary contracts, precarious employment, employees' fundamental rights and EU employment law* (Strasbourg, European Parliament, 2017) and many others.

in this area are presented, namely, those concerning platform work and the self-employed. In section 4, the main findings and some concluding thoughts in relation to the effective enforcement of non-standard workers' rights are gathered.

In case of non-standard employment, legal forms within which work is performed for another are non-standard and not workers themselves. Workers are not and cannot be 'non-standard'. Nevertheless, the term 'non-standard workers' has become widely used in the literature and can be found in various formal documents. We thus use it in this chapter as well. I would like to emphasise, however, that workers in non-standard forms of employment are not 'non-standard workers', despite the term used. They are just workers, ordinary people like everyone else and with the same human rights. Workers in non-standard forms of employment have the same right to decent working and living conditions as all others.

An abundance of research and studies show, however, that such workers often experience less favourable working conditions than workers in standard employment, and face various obstacles in realising their labour rights.[2] The problem can also be analysed from the perspective of 'gaps that may reproduce and/or reinforce a process of precarisation [*sic*] of work … inter-linked and mutually constitutive "protective gaps" categorised as employment protection, representation and enforcement gaps'.[3]

Non-standard forms of employment deviate from standard employment in one or more characteristics,[4] and include, in particular, fixed-term work, temporary agency work, part-time work and home/telework. In a broader sense, non-standard employment comprises also self-employment, with an emphasis on bogus and also dependent self-employment, as well as various forms of contract work under civil law contracts, where the work is performed on the legal basis that is outside the scope of labour law. In the broadest sense, undeclared work, informal work or work performed outside legally regulated forms can also be placed in this framework.[5] Recently, most attention in this area has focused on platform work and (bogus) self-employment (see section 3 below).

As the ILO study notes, non-standard forms of employment have become 'a contemporary feature of labour markets around the world', for some, working in non-standard employment is a choice and has positive outcomes, but for most

[2] See n 1 above.

[3] A Koukiadaki and I Katsaroumpas, n 1 at 13–14; see also D Grimshaw, M Johnson, A Keizer and J Rubery, *Reducing Precarious Work: Protective Gaps and the Role of Social Dialogue in the UK* (University of Manchester, EWERC, 2016), https://documents.manchester.ac.uk/display.aspx?DocID=48990.

[4] Standard employment is understood as employment based on a contract of employment for an indefinite period, with full working-time, where the work is performed directly for the employer with whom an employee has concluded a contract of employment and on the employer's premises.

[5] B Kresal, 'Vpliv prekarizacije dela na individualne pravice delavcev' in K Kresal Šoltes et al (eds), *Prekarno delo* (Ljubljana, PF and EF, 2020) 16. The ILO study identified five different types: temporary employment, part-time work, multi-party employment relationships, disguised employment and dependent self-employment (ILO (no 1), xxi, 2). For a similar typology see also M Frosch, *The Challenges of Analysing Non-Standard Employment* (Geneva, ILO, 2017). See also OECD, *Policy Responses to New Forms of Work* (Paris, OECD, 2019).

workers it is associated with insecurity.[6] Not all workers in non-standard employment are precarious and not all precarious workers are in non-standard forms of employment. Precariousness can also be found within standard employment. Non-standard forms of employment, however, although not precarious per se, attract higher risks of precariousness, especially if they concern non-voluntary engagement because a worker could not find a 'regular' job. Workers in non-standard employment in general experience less favourable working and living conditions, have fewer opportunities for training and promotion, are less likely to receive additional benefits and bonuses, have lower remuneration on average, and find it more difficult to reconcile their professional and family responsibilities. They are also less likely to be unionised. They are more often unemployed and are exposed to a higher risk of poverty (the problem of the working poor) than regular workers. Precariousness spills over to other areas of life (it is more difficult for them to get a bank loan, to obtain adequate housing, their children more often have fewer opportunities in school or out-of-school activities and so on). There is a higher share of people from various vulnerable, disadvantaged groups among non-standard workers. Therefore, they are all the more exposed to discriminatory practices and exploitation. Non-standard workers often do not dare to claim their rights because they are in a precarious, insecure position; but on top of that, the fact that they do not claim their rights makes them even more vulnerable and their situation even more precarious.[7] This is a simplified and generalised overview; there are various non-standard forms of employment and the characteristics and the risks of precariousness differ accordingly. This must also be taken into account when discussing the enforcement of non-standard workers' rights.

From the legal point of view, the following distinction is important. First, there are legal forms (special contracts of employment) that fall within the scope of labour law, but the rules governing a particular form of non-standard employment (fixed-term, part-time and so on) deviate from those applicable to a standard employment relationship. In addition, discussions on non-standard employment also address – recently, even predominantly – 'non-standard' forms outside the scope of labour law, such as self-employment.[8]

The problem arises when these persons perform work in the same or similar manner as persons in an employment relationship and, taking into account the characteristics of the relationship in which they work (primacy of the facts), they should be recognised and treated as workers. They need labour law protection, but are denied the status of worker and, consequently, labour rights. A similar situation occurs if a worker is employed under a fixed-term contract or as a temporary agency worker, but should be employed as a regular worker under a standard

[6] ILO, n 1 at xxi, 1. The majority of workers in the EU still work within standard employment relationships, however, non-standard employment is increasing in Europe (Mandl, n 1 at 53).

[7] Kresal, n 5 at 17; see also n 1 above.

[8] Some legal systems recognise also a 'third', intermediate status (dependent self-employed, employee-like and so on).

contract of employment. From the legal point of view, the main problem in these situations is misclassification and abuse of non-standard employment, which must be addressed adequately also from the enforcement perspective (how to prevent abuses and how to remedy misclassification).

Even if there is no abuse and/or misclassification, non-standard workers often find themselves in a more precarious situation than workers in standard employment and face various obstacles in realising and enforcing their rights, which must also be addressed accordingly.

These can be legal obstacles. For example, non-standard workers are not entitled to the same rights as workers in standard employment, a different legal regime applies to them. In addition, there are practical/factual obstacles, which make it more difficult for non-standard workers to realise their (formally recognised) labour rights in practice. When analysing whether non-standard workers are entitled to a certain right, a constitutional and human rights perspective on the rights of non-standard workers must be taken into account. Often, legal and practical/factual obstacles overlap and are interrelated.

Recognition of the same level of rights and the principle of equal treatment for non-standard workers is a first step, whereby only limited and well-substantiated exceptions to this principle should be allowed, inherently linked to essential characteristics of a particular non-standard form of employment and subject to the proportionality test. As a second, simultaneous step, ensuring effective enforcement mechanisms through which their rights, if not respected voluntarily, can be realised in practice is also necessary and equally important. Special characteristics of non-standard forms of employment should be taken into account, because a 'standard' set of existing enforcement mechanisms does not always suffice.

2. EU Legal Framework: Focusing on Substantive Rights rather than Enforcement of Rights

At the EU level, only certain types of non-standard employment have been regulated so far. This section analyses Directive 91/383 on safety and health of fixed-term and temporary workers, the Fixed-term Work Directive (1999/70), the Part-time Work Directive (97/81) and the Temporary Agency Work Directive (2008/104). Although not dealing specifically with non-standard work, the Transparent and Predictable Working Conditions Directive (2019/1152) is also very important here.

Currently, there are two important initiatives at the EU level, namely on platform work and on the self-employed. These are presented in section 3.

From the perspective of effective enforcement of non-standard workers' rights, not only Directives that deal specifically with non-standard forms of employment are relevant, but also other EU labour law Directives (some more than others). EU equal treatment and non-discrimination Directives are particularly important, because the research and data show that among non-standard workers, there are higher shares from various vulnerable, disadvantaged groups (women, older, younger, migrant workers and so on).[9] Many EU labour law Directives explicitly stipulate that they also apply to non-standard workers.

In general, all EU labour law is relevant to non-standard workers, except if they are explicitly excluded from the personal scope of a particular EU labour law Directive, or if the issue regulated there is not relevant for a particular non-standard worker. That means also that enforcement of labour rights regulated at the EU level must be guaranteed to non-standard workers in an equally effective manner as for all other workers. As a starting point, the same enforcement mechanisms must be at the disposal of non-standard workers. Non-standard forms of employment have certain specific characteristics, however, and non-standard workers may face additional obstacles with respect to the enforcement of their rights, as already mentioned. Therefore, it seems reasonable, if not necessary, that these special characteristics and additional obstacles be addressed and taken into account, not only with respect to substantive rights but also as regards procedural and enforcement aspects of the labour law protection of non-standard workers.

2.1. First Steps in the Early 1990s: Directive 91/383/EEC

Directive 91/383 of 1991[10] addresses only a very specific and narrow, yet fundamental aspect of labour law protection, namely safety and health at work for fixed-term and temporary workers. The Preamble acknowledges that these workers are more exposed to risks than other workers and that their specific situation 'calls for special additional rules'. As can be seen from the Preamble and all provisions of the Directive, the focus was on substantive rights (the principle of equal treatment; some additional rules as regards information, training and medical surveillance), whereas the problem of enforcement of rights of these non-standard workers was not tackled specifically.

It is sometimes difficult to distinguish strictly between substantive rights and the enforcement aspects; better information and training, as well as stricter medical surveillance can also function as 'enabling rights',[11] which can improve the situation of these workers in general and increase the possibility that they become aware of their rights and actually decide to seek their enforcement in practice. The Directive also contains some provisions on the responsibility of the user undertaking, which could also indirectly improve possibilities for better enforcement of rights (in the area of safety and health at work) for these non-standard workers.

[9] J Fudge and R Owens (eds), *Precarious Work, Women, and The New Economy* (Oxford, Hart, 2006).

[10] Council Directive 91/383/EEC of 25 June 1991 supplementing the measures to encourage improvements in the safety and health at work of workers with a fixed-duration employment relationship or a temporary employment relationship, [1991] OJ L 206/19–21.

[11] On 'enabling rights' see Chapter 12 of this volume. See also Chapter 14 dealing specifically with health and safety at work.

It seems that it was perceived at the time of adoption of Directive 91/383 that the main problem was uncertainty as regards (equal) rights of fixed-term and temporary workers and that clear provisions recognising equal rights for those workers, at least as regards safety and health at work, and some additional provisions with respect to information, training, medical surveillance and responsibilities of the user undertaking would suffice and solve the problems.

2.2. Late 1990s: Fixed-term and Part-time Work Directives

The next legislative steps followed at the end of the 1990s: the Part-time Work Directive (97/81/EC)[12] from 1997 and the Fixed-term Work Directive (1999/70/EC)[13] from 1999. The Temporary Agency Work Directive (2008/104) was a more delicate issue and was adopted a decade later.[14] These three Directives are the core of EU legal rules on non-standard forms of employment.

As regards enforcement, the approach taken in these two Directives is similar to that in Directive 91/383: they are focused primarily on substantive rights and no special attention is paid to enforcement problems. This gap has been filled, at least to a certain extent, by CJEU case law, which is presented later in this section.

No special provisions can be found in Directive 1999/70 which would address obstacles for effective enforcement of fixed-term workers' rights. Nevertheless, its adoption is an important step forward. It has a broader material scope and covers all aspects of fixed-term contracts. It introduces many important rules at the EU level to the benefit of fixed-term workers, in particular, the principle of non-discrimination/equal treatment[15] and a framework to prevent abuse arising from the use of successive fixed-term employment contracts or relationships. The whole Directive can therefore indirectly also improve the possibilities for better enforcement of the rights of fixed-term workers.

Clause 5 on measures against abuses of successive fixed-term employment contracts is of particular importance in this respect. However, a broad margin of appreciation is left to the Member States. It is left to the Member States to decide, after consultations with social partners, which of the measures indicated in the Directive, one or more, are introduced into the national legal system. It is also

[12] Council Directive 97/81/EC of 15 December 1997 concerning the Framework Agreement on part-time work concluded by UNICE, CEEP and the ETUC, [1998] OJ L 14/9–14.

[13] Council Directive 1999/70/EC of 28 June 1999 concerning the framework agreement on fixed-term work concluded by ETUC, UNICE and CEEP, [1999] OJ L 175/43–48.

[14] EU rules on temporary agency work were announced in the Preamble of the Framework agreement on fixed-term work in Directive 1999/70 (which excluded from its personal scope of application the temporary agency workers). However, the social partners were unable to conclude such a Framework agreement and the Directive was then adopted only in 2008.

[15] 'In respect of employment conditions, fixed-term workers shall not be treated in a less favourable manner than comparable permanent workers solely because they have a fixed-term contract or relation unless different treatment is justified on objective grounds.' (Clause 4.)

left to the Member States to decide whether and how it is defined under what conditions fixed-term employment contracts are regarded as 'successive' and when they are deemed to be contracts for indefinite periods. It is not necessary for the Member State to introduce the possibility of transformation/conversion into an open-ended contract of employment as a sanction for abuses of successive fixed-term contracts. It is for the Member States to decide, after consultations with social partners, whether or not such sanction is introduced, 'where appropriate'. Such vagueness and broad margin of appreciation certainly weakens the potential of the EU legal framework for measures against abuses of (successive) fixed-term contracts.

In this respect, the CJEU emphasised, for example, in *MV and Others*,[16] that where abuse of successive fixed-term employment contracts has occurred, the national courts must, to the fullest extent possible, 'interpret and apply the relevant provisions of national law in such a way that it is possible duly to penalise the abuse and to nullify the consequences of the breach of EU law', and that if the conversion of fixed-term employment contracts into contracts of indefinite duration is not possible, because that would amount to an interpretation *contra legem*, 'the court should ascertain whether there are other effective measures for that purpose', whereby such measures must be 'sufficiently effective and act as sufficient deterrent'.[17]

In *Santoro*,[18] which also concerns successive fixed-term contracts in the public sector, this time in Italy, the CJEU decided that Directive 1999/70 does not preclude national legislation 'which, on the one hand, does not punish the misuse of successive fixed-term contracts by a public sector employer through the payment of compensation to the worker concerned for the lack of conversion of the fixed-term employment relationship into an employment relationship of indefinite duration', but, on the other hand, provides for other effective measures, 'provided that such legislation is accompanied by an effective and dissuasive penalty mechanism, a matter which is for the referring court to verify'. In its reasoning, the CJEU explained that the fact that in the private sector the transformation, conversion of a fixed-term contract into an employment contract for an indefinite period is foreseen to penalise the misuse of fixed-term contracts – which is 'the most extensive protection that may be granted to a worker' – cannot, in itself, result in a reduction of the effectiveness of the national measures applicable to workers in the public sector.[19] The CJEU again pointed out that it is for the national court to verify whether penalties for the misuse of fixed-term contracts, are effective and dissuasive.[20]

[16] CJEU, Case C-760/18 *MV and Others*, judgment of 11 February 2021.
[17] Ibid, paras 69, 70.
[18] CJEU, Case C-494/16 *Santoro*, judgment of 7 March 2018.
[19] Ibid, paras 51–52.
[20] Ibid, para 53.

Despite certain limits, the provision of Clause 5 is important from the broader perspective of enforcement of workers' rights. If such measures are effective in preventing abusive fixed-term contracts, that means that standard, open-ended employment becomes more attractive also for employers and that, consequently, access to standard employment becomes easier for workers. If employers are prevented from (ab)using successive fixed-term contracts, they will have to offer the workers they need standard employment. More workers will be able to obtain a standard contract of employment for an indefinite period, either ex post (in case conversion is possible as a sanction), but also ex ante if the (ab)use of fixed-term contracts is limited by effective prevention. And because a regular job with adequate protection against unjustified dismissal means, as a rule, also a better position as regards the enforcement of all other rights, such measures directed against abusive fixed-term employment can actually improve the enforcement of workers' rights in general. Of course, this is only on condition that the enforcement of rights in general is adequately regulated and implemented. There are problems with the enforcement of workers' rights in general, not just for non-standard workers, but – as a rule – workers with a standard, open-ended contract are nevertheless in a better position as regards enforcement of their rights.

Prevention of abuses is only one aspect of the enforcement problem in the case of fixed-term work. These measures address situations in which workers formally employed under fixed-term contracts should in fact be employed under a standard contract of employment for an indefinite period of time. But what about workers with a fixed-term contract concluded in accordance with the law and in respect of whom there has been no abuse in relation to the conclusion of a non-standard contract of employment? These workers can also have problems with the enforcement of their rights. They are often denied certain rights that standard workers enjoy. For example, their remuneration may be lower than that of regular workers. They may not enjoy equal access to training or promotion. And other rights of fixed-term workers may be less favourable than those of a comparable permanent worker.

In *Universitatea 'Lucian Blaga' Sibiu and Others*,[21] the Court of Justice of the European Union (CJEU) dealt with lower remuneration for fixed-term workers. The CJEU emphasised that the Fixed-term Work Directive and the principle of equal treatment preclude the application of such national legislation and that budgetary considerations as such cannot justify different treatment to the detriment of fixed-term workers. In a similar case, *Daniel Ustariz Aróstegui*, the CJEU decided that Directive 1999/70 precludes a national legal provision that restricts entitlement to particular additional remuneration to teachers employed for an indefinite duration as established public officials, to the exclusion of, in particular, teachers employed under fixed-term contracts governed by public law.[22] The CJEU decided

[21] CJEU, Case C-644/19 *Universitatea 'Lucian Blaga' Sibiu and Others*, judgment of 8 October 2020.
[22] CJEU, Case C-72/18 *Daniel Ustariz Aróstegui*, judgment of 20 June 2019.

twice in *de Diego Porras* as regards compensation on the expiry of fixed-term contracts (this compensation was compared to compensation paid to dismissed workers employed for an indefinite period).[23] Sometimes non-standard workers, when enforcing their rights, rely on another EU labour law Directive, for example, on the Working Time Directive,[24] or one of the equal treatment Directives.[25] Fixed-term workers in question triggered national judicial procedures and the issues came before the CJEU through preliminary ruling proceedings.

The Fixed-term Work Directive is clear about 'what' is at issue, namely the same rights as comparable permanent workers unless different treatment is justified on objective grounds,[26] but mute about 'how'. The measures against abuses, albeit adequate and effective, do not address this problem.

The only provision relevant from the procedural and enforcement perspective is a standard provision that 'the prevention and settlement of disputes and grievances arising from the application of this agreement shall be dealt with in accordance with national law, collective agreements and practice' (Clause 8, para 5). The issue of enforcement of the rights of fixed-term workers is left entirely to national legal systems and national rules governing enforcement mechanisms (judicial, administrative and so on).

It is therefore important that the CJEU has developed certain minimum requirements as regards effective enforcement (the principle of effective judicial protection).[27] With regard to the Fixed-term Work Directive, these principles were applied in *Impact*.[28] The case concerned fixed-term workers who claimed employment conditions equal to those of comparable permanent workers and some of them (with more than three years of continuous service) also claimed conversion

[23] CJEU, Case C-596/14 *de Diego Porras*, judgment of 14 September 2016; CJEU, Case C-619/17 *de Diego Porras*, judgment of 21 November 2018.

[24] The CJEU confirmed that the Working Time Directive 2003/88 applies to fixed-term contracts in C-428/09 *Union syndicale Solidaires Isère*; and similarly in relation to the previous Directive 93/104 in C-173/99 *BECTU*. The famous *BECTU* case concerned around 30,000 workers, members of the Broadcasting, Entertainment, Cinematographic and Theatre Union employed as sound recordists, cameramen, special effects technicians, hairdressers, make-up artists and similar who were engaged on short-term contracts, frequently for less than 13 weeks with the same employer, so that many of them did not satisfy the condition laid down in domestic law for entitlement to paid annual leave. The CJEU decided that the EU Working Time Directive does not allow such a domestic regulation and emphasised that such workers 'often find themselves in a more precarious situation' (para 63). The case *Zentralbetriebsrat der Landeskrankenhäuser Tirols* (C-486/08) concerns enforcement of the right to annual leave by part-time workers and fixed-term workers.

[25] See, for example the CJEU judgments in C-144/04 *Mangold*, C-109/00 *TeleDanmark*, and C-438/99 *Melgar*. In the famous CJEU case *Mangold*, for example, while a person could not successfully rely on provisions of the Fixed-term Work Directive, by referring to Directive 2000/78/EC, the worker successfully enforced his rights and protection against discriminatory fixed-term employment.

[26] As regards the interpretation of 'objective grounds justifying different treatment' see, for example, CJEU Case *de Diego Porras*, n 23, paras 67–68, and CJEU Joined Cases C-30/18 and C-44/18 Cobra Servicios Auxiliares SA v José David Sánchez Iglesias and Others, judgment of 11 April 2019, paras 46–54.

[27] J Malmberg et al (eds), 'Effective enforcement of EC labour law' (2004) 10(2) *European Labour Law Journal* 219–29.

[28] CJEU, Case C-268/06 *Impact*, judgment of 15 April 2008.

of fixed-term contracts into contracts of indefinite duration. The CJEU stressed that it would be contrary to the principle of effectiveness if a specific regulation of jurisdiction for the claims concerning fixed-term contracts regulated by Directive 1999/70, depending on whether they concern the period before the legislation transposing this Directive entered into force or the period after that date, 'would result in procedural disadvantages for those individuals, in terms, inter alia, of cost, duration and the rules of representation, such as to render excessively difficult the exercise of rights deriving from that directive'.[29]

The CJEU noted in its reasoning that Directive 1999/70 does not define the detailed procedural rules governing judicial actions for safeguarding their application.[30] In explaining the principles of equivalence and effectiveness in relation to the rights of non-standard workers stemming from Directive 1999/70 the CJEU referred extensively to its well-established case law in this respect, namely *Rewe-Zentralfinanz and Rewe-Zentral*,[31] *Comet*,[32] and *Unibet*.[33]

The CJEU emphasised that 'it is important to note that the principle of effective judicial protection is a general principle of Community law' and that Member States are responsible for ensuring that those rights are effectively protected in each case, and that 'the detailed procedural rules governing actions for safeguarding an individual's rights under Community law must be no less favourable than those governing similar domestic actions (principle of equivalence) and must not render practically impossible or excessively difficult the exercise of rights conferred by Community law (principle of effectiveness)' and that 'a failure to comply with those requirements at Community level is … liable to undermine the principle of effective judicial protection'.[34] The CJEU also emphasised that it is for the domestic courts 'to interpret the domestic jurisdictional rules in such a way that, wherever possible, they contribute to the attainment of the objective of ensuring effective judicial protection of an individual's rights under Community law'.[35]

From the perspective of effective enforcement of EU rules on non-standard forms of employment the case *MV and Others*,[36] already mentioned, is also very important. The Greek Constitution was amended after the entry into force of Directive 1999/70 and before the time limit for its transposition and imposed an absolute prohibition on the conversion of fixed-term employment contracts into contracts of indefinite duration in the public sector. In the reasoning of its decision, the CJEU emphasised that 'all the authorities of the Member States are

[29] Ibid, paras 51, 53, 55.
[30] Ibid, para 39.
[31] CJEU, Case C-33/76, in particular para 5.
[32] CJEU, Case C-45/76, in particular paras 13–16.
[33] CJEU, Case C-432/05, in particular paras 37–39, 43.
[34] CJEU, *Impact*, paras 43, 45, 46, 48.
[35] Ibid, para 54.
[36] CJEU, Case C-760/18 *MV and Others*, judgment of 11 February 2021.

subject to the obligation to ensure that the provisions of EU law take full effect, and that applies also when those authorities amend their Constitution'; in such a situation, the referring national court must check 'whether the provisions of earlier national legislation, which remain in force, and which permit the conversion of a succession of fixed-term contracts to one employment contract of indefinite duration, may, where appropriate, be applied for the purposes of that interpretation in conformity with EU law, even though national constitutional provisions impose an absolute prohibition, in the public sector, on such conversion'.[37]

Directive 97/81 on part-time work follows the same pattern as Directive 1999/70 as far as the enforcement issue is concerned. The Directive is clear about 'what' – equal treatment, equal rights on a pro-rata basis with certain exceptions, whereby here, the rights of part-time workers are compared with a comparable full-time worker – but mute about 'how' compliance with this rule is to be achieved. Exactly the same provision on prevention and settlement of disputes as in the Fixed-term Work Directive can be found in the Part-time Work Directive (Clause 6). Worth mentioning is the rule on the provision of information to workers' representative bodies, which also appears, in nearly the same wording, in both Directives.[38] Information is the first step towards effective enforcement and compliance. And by giving relevant information to workers' representatives, a kind of supervision can be established and problems detected with respect to obstacles and deficiencies in the enforcement of rights. Workers' representatives can play an important role in the enforcement (in its broadest meaning) of non-standard workers' rights. Various enforcement mechanisms are possible[39] and the role of workers' representatives should not be overlooked. However, the above-mentioned provision is very limited and quite vague.

All in all, it seems that in the late 1990s, when Directives 1999/70 and 97/81 were adopted, it was still perceived, as in the early 1990s, that the main problems with regard to non-standard workers were: (i) adequate regulation of their substantive rights, in particular the principle of equal treatment, with certain exceptions, (ii) the prevention of abuses (in case of fixed-term), and (iii) the promotion of non-standard forms of employment (in particular, part-time work, especially as a work–life balance measure); whereas non-compliance with the rules regulating the rights of non-standard workers – the problems with enforcement of their rights, and specific obstacles they might face in realising their rights in practice – have not yet been perceived as issues worth addressing and regulating at the EU level.

[37] Ibid, paras 71–75.

[38] Directive 1999/70, Clause 7.3 and Directive 97/81, Clause 5.3(e).

[39] For an overview of different enforcement mechanisms see the chapters in Part I of this book, in particular, on the notion of effective enforcement by A Jacobs, on access to justice by K Lörcher, on sanctions and remedies by A Koukiadaki, on administrative law and criminal law enforcement by J Unterschütz, on soft law mechanisms by C Kollonay-Lehoczky and on strategic enforcement by I Schömann et al.

2.3. A Decade Later: The Temporary Agency Work Directive

An important step forward in strengthening the enforcement perspective of the protection of non-standard workers was Directive 2008/104 on temporary agency work (TAW) from 2008.[40]

Here, too, one of the cornerstones is the principle of equal treatment.[41] But a lot of room is left for autonomous regulation and there are many possibilities for derogations and exceptions from the equal treatment rule. The aim of the Temporary Agency Work Directive is not just to improve working and employment conditions in temporary agency work, but also to identify and remove possible obstacles preventing undertakings from using it. From the perspective of effective enforcement of workers' rights, the provisions on prevention of abuses[42] are particularly important, in the same way as for fixed-term contracts.

In addition, there are other relevant provisions in this Directive, namely on (non-)compliance, administrative and judicial procedures for enforcement of rights, and penalties, which are more detailed and demanding than the vague provisions on prevention and settlement of disputes and grievances that can be found in the Directives on fixed-term and part-time work.

The focus at the EU level is no longer only on the substantive rights of particular non-standard workers, but also – at least to a certain extent – on the question of how these rights can effectively be enforced in practice in cases of non-compliance with these rules. This could be ascribed partly to specific characteristics of temporary agency work, but also to better understanding of enforcement problems and the need to pay special attention to enforcement. This is reflected in the Preamble (Recital 21) and further regulated in Article 10, titled 'Penalties'. Member States shall 'provide for appropriate measures in the event of non-compliance with this Directive by temporary-work agencies or user undertakings' and 'ensure that adequate administrative or judicial procedures are available to enable the obligations deriving from this Directive to be enforced'. They must 'lay down rules on penalties applicable in the event of infringements of national provisions implementing this Directive' and 'take all necessary measures to ensure that they are applied'. For the first time in relation to non-standard work, the explicit requirement is included in the Directive that the penalties provided for must be 'effective, proportionate and dissuasive', the standard developed by CJEU case law. Article 10 is clear that Member States 'shall ensure that workers and/or their representatives have adequate means of enforcing the obligations under this Directive'.

[40] Directive 2008/104/EC of the European Parliament and of the Council of 19 November 2008 on temporary agency work, [2008] OJ L 327/9–14.

[41] Preamble, Recital 14 and Art 5 *et subseq*. The basic working and employment conditions of temporary agency workers shall be, for the duration of their assignment at a user undertaking, at least those that would apply if they had been recruited directly by that undertaking to occupy the same job.

[42] Preamble, Recital 18, and Art 4 and Art 5, para 5.

When it comes to improving the possibilities for effective enforcement of rights the following is also relevant. First, a clear provision to ensure the protection of temporary agency workers by recognising temporary work agencies as employers. It is a *sine qua non* condition for the effective enforcement of rights that it is clear not just who the holder of a right is and what its contents are, but also who is responsible on the other side for fulfilling an obligation. The practical problem with 'triangular relationships' was quite often the uncertainty who the employer was. Second, and equally important, are the rules imposing certain obligations on the user undertaking.

Last but not least, the Temporary Agency Work Directive contains a special provision on information of workers' representatives: the user undertaking must provide suitable information on the use of temporary agency workers to bodies representing workers. Workers' representatives could and should have an important role in informing, raising awareness, supervising compliance with the rules and enabling more effective enforcement of temporary agency workers' rights in practice.

Important CJEU case law has also been developed in relation to the Temporary Agency Work Directive. To mention only one example, case *JH*[43] concerned successive assignments of a temporary agency worker to the same user undertaking and the question was raised whether a permanent employment relationship was concealed behind successive temporary agency contracts and whether these were designed to circumvent the objectives of Directive 2008/104, in particular 'the temporary nature of temporary agency work'.[44] The CJEU emphasised that

> if successive assignments of the same temporary agency worker to the same user undertaking result in a period of service with that undertaking that is longer than what can reasonably be regarded as 'temporary', that could be indicative of misuse of successive assignments …
>
> … successive assignments of the same temporary agency worker to the same user undertaking circumvent the very essence of the provisions of Directive 2008/104 and amount to misuse of that form of employment relationship, since they upset the balance struck by that directive between flexibility for employers and security for workers by undermining the latter.[45]

2.4. Recent Trends: Directive on Transparent and Predictable Working Conditions

Although not specifically dealing with non-standard forms of employment, Directive 2019/1152[46] of 2019 opens up new dimensions of the discussion on how

[43] CJEU, Case C-681/18 *KG*, judgment of 14 October 2020.
[44] Ibid, para 67.
[45] Ibid, paras 69, 70.
[46] Directive (EU) 2019/1152 of the European Parliament and of the Council of 20 June 2019 on transparent and predictable working conditions in the European Union, [2019] OJ L 186/105–21.

the effective enforcement of rights of workers in non-standard forms of employment can be better achieved. Adopted a decade after the Temporary Agency Work Directive, Directive 2019/1152 reflects a fresh approach to the problem of effective enforcement of workers' rights.

It can be understood as a response to practical developments. Especially since the 2008 financial crisis, various non-standard forms of employment have become even more common than before (much research shows that regular jobs lost because of the crisis were subsequently replaced with lower-quality, non-standard jobs).[47] This trend has constantly intensified, also more recently. Fixed-term and temporary work, zero-hours contracts, on-demand contracts etc. Self-employment (much of it bogus) is more and more widespread. More and more people are engaging in platform work, characterised by the persistent denial of workers' rights.

The most evident feature of these 'new'[48] forms of employment is the lack of adequate labour law protection for many workers and weak enforcement of their rights in practice. Precarious work and the need to address this problem have become an important part of the academic debate, but also of the dialogue between social partners. Finally, it is also now an item on the political agenda at both the national and EU levels. Demands have strengthened that a certain basic floor of rights must be recognised for all workers and that more effective enforcement of their rights should be ensured. Furthermore, better protection of all workers, including non-standard workers, must be ensured by clear requirements as regards transparency and predictability of employment patterns and working conditions, and this needs to be regulated at the EU level.

Directive 2019/1152, which replaces (transposition August 2022) the Written Statement Directive (91/533/EEC) of 1991, applies to all workers. It is particularly important for non-standard workers. This special focus on non-standard employment and reaffirmation that standard employment should still be the core of the system of employment relations in the EU is reflected in the Preamble. Already in Recital 1, for example, the Preamble explicitly refers to 'every worker', and states in Recital 2 that 'regardless of the type and duration of the employment relationship, workers have the right to fair and equal treatment', that 'the transition towards open-ended forms of employment is to be fostered', and that 'employment relationships that lead to precarious working conditions are to be prevented, including by prohibiting abuse of atypical contracts'. Furthermore, Recital 36 states that '[w]here employers have the possibility to offer full-time or open-ended employment contracts to workers in non-standard forms of employment, a transition to more secure forms of employment should be promoted'.

Further on, it is noted that 'labour markets have undergone far-reaching changes … leading to the creation of new forms of employment' and that

[47] D Vaughan-Whitehead (ed), *Work Inequalities in the Crisis – Evidence from Europe* (Geneva, ILO, 2012); J Hurley, D Storrie and J-M Jungblut, *Shifts in the job structure in Europe during the Great Recession* (Dublin, Eurofound, 2011).

[48] As addressed by this Directive, although it is questionable what is really 'new' about these forms.

'[s]ome new forms of employment vary significantly from traditional employment relationships with regard to predictability, creating uncertainty with regard to the applicable rights' and that 'gaps in protection have emerged for new forms of employment' (Recital 5).

Directive 2019/1152 recognises, to a certain extent, that misrepresentation and misclassification of (self-)employment status and denial of the status of 'worker' is at the core of the problem. Recital 8 of the Preamble refers to CJEU case law as regards the criteria for determining the status of a worker and explicitly states that '[p]rovided that they fulfil those criteria, domestic workers, on-demand workers, intermittent workers, voucher based-workers, platform workers, trainees and apprentices could fall within the scope of this Directive' and, further on, explicitly exposes the problem of bogus self-employment and confirms the principle of 'primacy of facts' from the ILO Recommendation No 198 on the employment relationship, and explicitly states that 'such persons should fall within the scope of this Directive'. Recital 8 is clear that 'the determination of the existence of an employment relationship should be guided by the facts relating to the actual performance of the work and not by the parties' description of the relationship'. Unfortunately, corresponding rules cannot be found in the binding provisions of the Directive.

From the perspective of ensuring better access to justice and effective enforcement of workers' rights, the questions 'who is the employer?' and 'who is responsible for fulfilling employers' obligations?' are very important.[49] In practice, a real legal and/or factual obstacle that non-standard workers often face is that they cannot identify their employer against whom they could enforce their rights. Clear rules in this respect are thus crucial for effective enforcement of workers' rights. But this issue is left entirely in the hands of Member States.

As already mentioned, the problems of misclassification and, in particular, of what enforcement mechanisms and procedures, as well as supportive measures should be in place for challenging misclassification are not regulated by the binding provisions of the Directive.

A rebuttable presumption of an employment relationship of a particular quality has also been included in the Directive. This can be a very useful legal instrument that supports more effective enforcement of workers' rights in practice. Together with measures to prevent abuses of non-standard forms of employment – in particular, those with highly unpredictable working patterns – a rebuttable presumption is already mentioned in the Preamble, Recital 35, and regulated in Article 11.

The most important part of Directive 2019/1152 as regards the enforcement aspect are horizontal provisions enshrined in Articles 15 to 19 (Chapter IV), already announced in the Preamble, Recitals 39 to 45.

The Directive requires of Member States that they introduce provisions on favourable presumptions where information about the employment relationship

[49] Recital 13 and Art 1.5.

is not provided; for example, a presumption that the worker has an open-ended employment relationship, that there is no probationary period or that the worker has a full-time position, where the relevant information is missing (Article 15, see also Recital 39). Not just the worker concerned, but also 'a third party such as a worker's representative or other competent authority or body' could initiate an adequate enforcement procedure (Recital 39).

Access to effective and impartial dispute resolution, such as a civil or labour court, and a right to redress, which may include adequate compensation, is part of this Directive (Article 16, see also Recital 40), whereby workers should continue to enjoy such protection even after the end of their employment relationship.

An important precondition for effective enforcement of rights is adequate judicial and administrative protection against any adverse treatment and protection against dismissal, which is regulated in Articles 17 and 18 (and announced in Recital 42). For non-standard workers the wording used in combination with the protection against dismissal 'or its equivalent' in Article 18 ('or equivalent detriment, such as an on-demand worker no longer being assigned work' in Recital 43) is of a particular importance, with the burden of proof on the employer.

Last but not least, there is a standard requirement that penalties for infringements must be 'effective, proportionate and dissuasive' (Article 19, Recital 45).

As can be seen from the above analysis, Directive 2019/1152, which applies to non-standard forms of employment in general, with certain very limited exceptions, and in addition addresses some specific issues relevant specifically to particular types of non-standard forms of employment, pays special attention not just to substantive rights, but also – to a much greater extent than previous Directives on non-standard employment – to the enforcement of rights.

The importance of this Directive for better enforcement of rights of non-standard workers is threefold:

(i) it guarantees that all workers be informed by their employer (in written form or, under prescribed conditions, in electronic form) of the essential aspects of the employment relationship; information and awareness of existing rights raise the probability that they will be respected, implemented and, if necessary, enforced in practice;
(ii) some additional minimum rights for all workers, including non-standard workers, have been introduced, whereby particular attention has been paid to various non-standard forms of employment and specific guarantees for them have been introduced (for example, various favourable presumptions), which can also function as 'enabling rights' for non-standard workers and their ability to enforce their workers' rights;
(iii) it includes much stronger horizontal provisions on enforcement, remedies and sanctions, on procedural aspects of protection of workers' rights in general, with some sensitivity also to specific challenges related to non-standard forms of employment.

It remains to be seen whether this Directive, when transposed into the national legal systems (deadline August 2022) and implemented in practice, will actually add any strength to the existing EU legal rules aimed at improving the situation of non-standard workers and prevent misuse of non-standard forms of employment, and whether it will strengthen non-standard workers' ability to enforce their rights in practice.[50]

3. New Initiatives at the EU Level: Platform Work and Self-employed Workers

Platform work is an open issue and highly debated topic, also in the EU. There have already been various initiatives to regulate this issue at the EU level suggesting that a new Directive on platform work is needed.[51] The Commission announced a legislative initiative on improving the working conditions of platform workers by the end of 2021,[52] which identifies the following as the key challenges in platform work: the employment status of platform workers is unclear and many are misclassified as 'self-employed'; automated decision-making by algorithms which can be discriminatory, non-transparent; limited access of platform workers to collective representation and collective bargaining; the cross-border nature of platform work.

A separate initiative at the EU level that concerns non-standard workers addresses the relationship between EU competition law and collective bargaining for the self-employed.[53] It is of particular importance for platform work as well. Both issues overlap considerably. According to the Commission, the purpose of this (second) initiative is 'to ensure that EU competition law does not stand in the way of collective agreements that aim to improve the working conditions of self-employed in a weak position'.[54] This issue has already been discussed and

[50] See the special chapter on enforcement in a recently published report: European Commission, *Transposition of Directive (EU) 2019/1152 on transparent and predictable working conditions in the European Union*, expert group report (Luxembourg, Publications Office of the European Union, 2021) 64–75.

[51] See, for example, M Risak, *Fair working conditions for platform workers – Possible regulatory approaches at the EU level* (Berlin, Friedrich Ebert Stiftung/International Policy Analysis, 2018); M Risak and C Berger, 'Platform Work' (2021) 3 *Policy Brief* 1–4; L Chaibi, 'A proposal to legislate for the rights of platform workers' (2020) *Social Europe* 16.11.2020, https://socialeurope.eu/a-proposal-to-legislate-for-the-rights-of-platform-workers. The text of the proposal: https://left.eu/content/uploads/2020/11/English.pdf.

[52] The Commission Work Programme 2021: A Union of vitality in a world of fragility (COM(2020) 690 final, Brussels, 19.10.2020). In February 2021, the Commission launched the first-stage consultation and in June 2021, it launched the second-stage consultation of European social partners on this issue (European Commission, Consultation document, C (2021) 4230 final, Brussels, 15.6.2021, https://ec.europa.eu/commission/presscorner/detail/en/IP_21_2944).

[53] See: https://ec.europa.eu/info/law/better-regulation/have-your-say/initiatives/12483-Collective-bargaining-agreements-for-self-employed-scope-of-application-EU-competition-rules_en.

[54] Ibid.

analysed extensively in the labour law literature, so we only mention it here due to lack of space.[55]

It is questionable whether a partial approach to regulating platform work is the best way to address this problem. On one hand, it is only part of a more general issue of self-employed workers, bogus self-employment and misclassification. At the same time, it raises other questions (such as algorithmic decision-making) that are also relevant for other workers, not just for platform workers. On the other hand, it is not just collective bargaining that is problematic in relation to self-employed workers.

As a starting point, it is important to stress that platform workers are not and should not be dealt with as a new category of workers as such, and that platform work should not be perceived and treated as a completely new non-standard form of employment.

Platform work is just a consequence of new patterns in work organisation, enabled by the use of modern technology. Of course it raises certain issues that have to be regulated, but labour law rules can and should apply to it.[56] It is actually more a problem of enforcing existing rights, in combination with misclassification and abuse of 'non-labour law' legal forms for performing work. As the ETUC has emphasised, a European initiative should focus on the protection of all non-standard workers and workers in platform companies, including the self-employed, but it 'should not be a pretext to wrongly categorise all platform workers as self-employed or to create a third category of workers'; what is relevant is that these workers 'have no real possibility of claiming their rights, otherwise they will not be called back the next day'.[57] The enforcement of their rights is often much more difficult for them than for workers with a standard contract of employment.

There have already been many attempts to enforce the rights for platform workers, some successful, some not.[58] 'As platform work spreads around the world,

[55] See, for example, B Waas and C Hießl, *Collective Bargaining for Self-Employed Workers* (Alphen aan den Rijn, Kluwer, 2021); S Rainone and N Countouris, *Collective bargaining and self-employed workers* (Brussels, ETUI, 2021); M Doherty and V Franca, 'Solving the "Gig-saw"? Collective rights and platform work' (2020) 49(3) *Industrial Law Journal* 352–76; and many others.

[56] Of course, platform work is very diverse and heterogeneous, which needs to be taken into account, but there is no room to go into detail here.

[57] ETUC (2020), ETUC Resolution on the protection of the rights of non-standard workers and workers in platform companies (including the self-employed), Brussels, 28.10.2020, www.etuc.org/en/document/etuc-resolution-protection-rights-non-standard-workers-and-workers-platform-companies#_ftn2. See also ETUC (2021), ETUC reply to the Second stage consultation, Brussels, 9.9.2021, www.etuc.org/en/document/etuc-reply-second-phase-consultation-social-partners-under-article-154-tfeu-possible.

[58] For an overview of disputes before courts and developing case-law in this respect see: V De Stefano et al, *Platform work and the employment relationship* (Geneva, ILO, 2021) 30–40; C Hießl, 'Case Law on the Classification of Platform Workers: Cross-European Comparative Analysis and Tentative Conclusions' (2 May 2021), *Comparative Labour Law & Policy Journal* (forthcoming), https://papers.ssrn.com/sol3/papers.cfm?abstract_id=3839603; De Groen et al, *Employment and working conditions of selected types of platform work* (Dublin, Eurofound, 2018) 45–46.

so has litigation brought by workers against platforms', note De Stefano et al.[59] Most of the cases brought before courts so far concern misclassification, the issue of bogus self-employment of platform workers and the question of whether the platform workers concerned are employees or self-employed. This is of course logical, because most platforms deny their platform workers the status of worker/employee. The existence of an employment relationship is, as a rule, the basis for access to labour rights.

Most of these cases were brought before courts by platform workers and the trade unions that represented them, but also administrative bodies, such as labour inspectorates or social security administration play an important role. Not all cases concerning platform work are labour law cases. There are also disputes before courts dealing with platform work which concerned, for example, fiscal issues or transport rules, in which the employment status of platform workers appeared as a preliminary or 'side' issue.[60] Trade unions are becoming more and more engaged, and other types of organising or assisting platform workers have developed, such as cooperatives or umbrella companies.[61] Alternative dispute resolution bodies have emerged alongside (labour) courts, which deal with disputes in platform work, such as the 'Ombuds Office' in Germany overseeing enforcement of the 'Crowdsourcing Code of Conduct' adopted by platforms.[62] According to the Leeds Index of Platform Labour Protest, '[m]ainstream unions play a vital role in defending platform workers' interests, especially in western Europe, while in the global South, protests are much more likely to be led by grassroots unions' and '[m]ainstream unions rely more frequently on legal challenges, while unofficial unions rely more frequently on strike actions'.[63] The Eurofound study on platform work also showed that trade unions in many countries 'endeavour to organise platform workers and provide a collective voice for them' and that one of their important activities in this respect is also to 'support court cases'.[64]

[59] V De Stefano et al, n 58 at 4. From the Consultation document of the European Commission (op cit, 8): 'To date, more than 100 court decisions and 15 administrative decisions dealing with the employment status of people working through platforms have been identified in nine Member States. Most of these cases concern ride-hailing or food-delivery platforms, but some also cover other forms of on-location platform work. Court rulings have gone in different directions, but most judges have decided in favour of reclassifying nominally independent contractors as workers and platforms as employers.'

[60] For a comparative overview see also C Hießl, n 48 above. For an example of trade union action in this area with a rich overview of trade union activities in enforcing rights of platform workers and various awareness-raising activities, see H Johnston et al, *Working on digital labour platforms A trade union guide for trainers on crowd-, app- and platform-based work* (Brussels, ETUI, 2020).

[61] See, for example, B Palli, *Regulation of platform work in France: From voluntary charters to sector-wide collective agreements?* (Brussels, European Commission, 2020) 5; De Groen et al, n 58 at 53–58; J Drahokoupil and A Piasna, *Work in the platform economy: Deliveroo riders in Belgium and the SMart arrangement* (Brussels, ETUI, 2019).

[62] Available at: http://faircrowd.work/2017/11/08/ombudsstelle-fuer-crowdworking-plattformen-vereinbart/; see also O Deinert and C Freudenberg, *Platform work in Germany: How to improve working conditions and social protection?* (Brussels, European Commission, 2020).

[63] S Joyce et al, *A global struggle: worker protest in the platform economy* (Brussels, ETUI, 2020) 1.

[64] De Groen et al, n 58 at 58.

CJEU case law has also addressed certain legal aspects of this issue. The first case, *Uber France*, did not deal directly with labour law issues.[65] The most recent relevant case *Yodel*[66] attracted much attention and also criticism.[67] Labour law theory is more or less clear that employment status should be recognised to platform workers under the same general principles as to any other workers (of course, applied accordingly, by taking into account specific characteristics of this new type of work organisation).[68] This should be based on the principle of 'primacy of facts', and where there are elements of an employment relationship, they should be considered to be workers just like any others. The sole fact that the work is organised through the digital platform should not be a decisive factor denying employee status and labour rights to platform workers.

The aim of this section is not to provide an overall and in-depth analysis of platform work in general (the issue is no longer new and has already been dealt with extensively in the labour law literature),[69] but to focus on platform work from the perspective of EU labour law and its enforcement. It remains to be seen whether the EU initiative on platform workers will be successful and actually improve platform workers' situation in practice, strengthening their ability to enforce their labour rights in practice.

Looking at the consultation documents, it seems that, although the EU initiative on platform work focuses mainly on various aspects of substantive rights, it nevertheless does not entirely overlook the enforcement aspects. Among four key challenges in platform work identified by the Commission, the enforcement aspect is not mentioned explicitly.[70] But various ideas on possible measures aimed

[65] CJEU, Case C-320/16 *Uber France*.

[66] CJEU, Case C-692/19 *Yodel*.

[67] See, for example, A Aloisi, '"Time Is Running Out" The Yodel Order and Its Implications for Platform Work in the EU' (2020) 13 *Italian Labour Law e-Journal* 2, https://doi.org/10.6092/issn.1561-8048/11777; J Adams-Prassl, A Aloisi, N Countouris, V De Stefano, *EU Court of Justice's decision on employment status does not leave platforms off the hook*, http://regulatingforglobalization.com/2020/04/29/eu-court-of-justices-decision-on-employment-status-does-not-leave-platforms-off-the-hook/.

[68] A purposive approach is strongly advocated here. See, in particular, A Aloisi, n 67, J Adams-Prassl et al, n 67; on the purposive approach more generally see also G Davidov, *A purposive approach to labour law* (Oxford, OUP, 2016).

[69] For more on platform work, see, for example, V De Stefano and A Aloisi, *European legal framework for 'digital labour platforms'* (Luxembourg, EU, 2018); V De Stefano et al, *Platform work and the employment relationship* (Geneva, ILO, 2021); J Prassl, *Humans as a Service: The Promise and Perils of Work in the Gig Economy* (Oxford, OUP, 2018); M Kullmann, 'Platform Work, Algorithmic Decision-Making, and EU Gender Equality Law' (2018) 34(1) *International Journal of Comparative Labour Law and Industrial Relations* 1–21; J Unterschütz, 'Collective Bargaining for Platform Workers: a Hope for new Developments?' (2020) *Hungarian Labour Law E-Journal* 2, www.ias.jak.ppke.hu/letolt/2020_2_a/06_Unterschutz_hllj_uj_2020_2.pdf; J Prassl and M Risak, 'Uber, TaskRabbit, and Co: Platforms as Employers? Rethinking the Legal Analysis of Crowdwork' (2016) 37(3) *Comparative Labor Law & Policy Journal* 619–649; SP Choudary, *The Architecture of digital labour platforms: Policy recommendations on platform design for worker well-being* (Geneva, ILO, 2018); ILO, *Job Quality in the Platform Economy* (Geneva, 2018); MC Urzi Brancati et al, *New evidence on platform workers in Europe*, (Luxembourg, Publications Office of the European Union, 2020).

[70] European Commission, Staff Working Document (SWD(2021) 143 final) accompanying Consultation document, C (2021) 4230 final, Brussels, 15.6.2021, https://ec.europa.eu/commission/presscorner/detail/en/IP_21_2944.

at improving enforcement of platform workers' rights can be found in consultation documents. They include a rebuttable presumption of employment status with a shift in the burden of proof; the possibility of establishing a presumption of an employment relationship in the country where the worker operates; the possibility of an administrative procedure to examine the employment status of people working through platforms, which could 'spare them the cost and risk involved in legal proceedings and thus lower the burden of reclassification action'; and certification of work-related contracts, carried out at the request of either party, by labour authorities or by independent bodies as another out-of-court option.[71] In relation to algorithmic management rights, appropriate channels for redress are suggested, such as setting up internal procedures or mediation structures within companies to look into complaints.[72] It is also worth mentioning the proposals from the Eurofound study. One is that platforms should be required to provide effective dispute-resolution mechanisms to ensure fair treatment of workers.[73]

The Commission emphasised in its consultation document that

> Enforcement of rules and collective action are key, given the imbalance of power between platforms and people working through them. This is particularly true for workers who often face obstacles or risks to claim their rights in the absence of any support from trade unions or other organisations. It is also true for certain self-employed who are sometimes in a weak position to defend their rights and interests. The initiative could introduce measures to ensure compliance with the new material and procedural rights and obligations in platform work that the initiative will establish ... They could cover access to effective and impartial dispute resolution, procedures on behalf of or in support of workers (eg by trade unions), the right to compensation, protection against adverse treatment or consequences for claiming rights, access to evidence, and penalties. Another avenue to be considered is the promotion at national level of ombudspersons responsible for resolving disputes between platforms and people working through platforms ... Finally, clarity on rules and a broader data basis can contribute to better enforcement and compliance.[74]

With regard to a broader data basis as a necessary precondition for effective enforcement of rights, it is worth noting that in the digital era there is constant and substantial gathering of data, also on the most important employment-related issues. This can also be used for supervision of compliance and enforcement purposes. It also means that access to 'virtual employer's premises' – that is, the platform – is crucial also for trade unions. As Doherty has pointed out,

> one implication of the growth of digital work, and a key means by which gig workers can be monitored and controlled by platforms, is that vast quantities of data (information) are collected, stored and accessed instantaneously. It is relatively easy, therefore,

[71] Ibid, n 70 at 81–82; European Commission, Consultation document, at 22.
[72] Ibid.
[73] De Groen, n 58 at 63.
[74] European Commission, SWD, n 70 at 84–85; European Commission, Consultation document, n 70 at 25.

> for regulators and other actors to seek access to information on working time, remuneration rates and so on … If knowledge is power, those concerned with enforcement of basic labour standards have potentially more access to power than ever before … Trade unions have long fought, and in many jurisdictions continue to fight, to gain access to physical workspaces in order to police employment standards. Now, the fight must move to digital space; 'virtual access' to platforms, and the data that there reside, similarly, is key in order to police employment standards for 'gig work'.[75]

4. Conclusion

More and more people are working in various non-standard forms of employment, which are often precarious. The situation of such workers is usually more insecure and less favourable than that of workers in standard employment. Although not precarious per se, non-standard forms of employment entail higher risk of precariousness and consequently higher risk that the rights of such workers will not be effectively enforced in practice.

Precariousness is often the reason for, but even more the consequence of non-application of existing labour law rules. The problem is lack of effective enforcement of labour rights rather than their non-existence, especially if fundamental labour rights and legally binding international treaties on human rights at both global and European level are taken into account. Precarious workers often do not dare to claim their rights because they are in such an insecure, precarious position. Failure to respect their (existing) rights and their non-enforcement puts these workers in an even more precarious situation. Another important reason for non-enforcement of rights is that non-standard workers are often not unionised. And it is difficult to step out of this vicious circle. In the case of non-standard employment, effective enforcement of rights in practice (access to courts, supervision by labour inspectorates, collective enforcement and so on) is especially problematic.

Full realisation of labour rights in practice, also for non-standard workers, is crucial for the improvement of their working and, consequently, living conditions, but it also is necessary to stave off pressure to lower the general level of labour law protection also for standard employment relationships.

It is not enough to regulate the rights of workers in non-standard forms of employment. Special attention should also be paid to establishing adequate enforcement mechanisms to ensure compliance with the existing rules on non-standard work in practice. Specific characteristics of non-standard forms of employment should be taken into account when regulating the substantive rights of non-standard workers, as well as when designing mechanisms for their enforcement. However, there are a variety of non-standard forms of employment with

[75] M Doherty, 'Trade unions and the Gig Economy' in F Hendrickx and V De Stefano (eds), *Game Changers in Labour Law – Shaping the Future of Work* (Alphen aan den Rijn, Kluwer, 2018) 108–109.

different characteristics, and the risks of precariousness and vulnerability differ accordingly. This also affects enforcement of rights.

Analysis of EU labour law Directives on non-standard employment and other relevant Directives shows that the enforcement aspect has long been neglected. The EU legal rules regulating non-standard forms of employment were initially, and to some extent still are focused predominantly on substantive rights rather than on practical enforcement of rights of non-standard workers. More and more attention has been paid to the enforcement aspect, however, and more recent EU Directives include more provisions aimed at improving non-standard workers' ability to actually enforce their rights.

We have also seen that EU labour law addresses this problem mainly from the perspective of preventing abuses of non-standard forms of employment. The main problem is, to be sure, that many non-standard workers should in fact be employed under a (standard) contract of employment and that misrepresentation/misclassification – in other words bogus self-employment and similar – pose a major challenge to labour law today. Effective enforcement of EU labour law in general and in relation to non-standard employment is not possible without effective enforcement mechanisms to ensure recognition of a status of a worker/employee and recognition of an existence of a (standard) contract of employment in accordance with the principle of the primacy of facts. This can also be seen in the case of platform work.

Persons who find themselves in non-standard employment such as self-employment as a result of an abuse of this legal form should first and foremost have adequate enforcement mechanisms at their disposal which would ensure that they are able to obtain a contract of employment and be recognised as a worker/employee. Or if they are, for example, employed under a fixed-term contract or as a temporary agency worker, but should actually be employed under a standard contract of employment, they should be able to obtain such a contract and be recognised as a 'regular', 'standard' worker. These enforcement mechanisms should not rely solely or predominantly on the individual worker concerned.

The need for effective enforcement of EU labour law in the area of non-standard employment, however, goes beyond measures that would effectively prevent abuses of non-standard forms of employment, including those formally outside the scope of labour law, such as bogus self-employment and similar. Non-standard workers in general, also in cases where non-standard forms of employment have not been abused/misused, face many problems with asserting their labour rights in practice. The main principle of EU labour law concerning non-standard workers is the principle of equal treatment. This means that non-standard workers should, in principle – with certain exceptions – have the same rights as comparable 'standard' workers. That means the same level of remuneration, and equal access to training, promotion, additional facilities and bonuses, not to mention equal opportunities to exercise their collective labour rights and so on. In practice, however, non-standard workers often experience less favourable treatment with regard to working conditions and enforcing their rights is often difficult in practice. Sometimes non-standard workers are not aware of their rights and even if they are, often do not dare to enforce them.

In addition to enforcement mechanisms or, even better, as an integral part of the legal framework on enforcement of rights in the area of labour law, including with regard to non-standard workers, adequate legal protection of workers is needed against unjustified dismissal and equivalent measures resulting in job loss. Such protection amounts to much more than protection of individual workers against the loss of a particular job. It functions as protection against insecure, precarious and thus unacceptable employment patterns and it is also a *sine qua non* condition for the effective realisation of all other workers' rights.[76] If workers do not enjoy adequate protection against dismissal and equivalent measures resulting in job loss, they might be afraid to assert their rights. And this is equally true for standard, as well as non-standard workers. Therefore, non-standard workers should also enjoy some kind of protection against unjustified loss of employment (non-renewal of a fixed-term contract, not receiving new assignments, deactivated/disconnected from the platform and similar).

Adequate enforcement mechanisms must be available to ensure that workers' rights are respected, realised and, if necessary, enforced. It is equally necessary that all workers, in standard and in non-standard employment, should be adequately protected against unjustified loss of their job, so that they dare to realise and, if necessary, enforce their rights in practice.

Taking into account their vulnerable, precarious situation, it is self-evident that enforcement of the rights of non-standard workers cannot rely solely on the individual initiative of (non-standard) workers. In addition to judicial enforcement, *ex-officio* supervision and administrative law enforcement is necessary. Labour inspectorates and other public bodies should play an important role in the whole structure of enforcement mechanisms. The role of collective actors cannot be overestimated, but is often overlooked. Collective action and collective redress mechanisms may overcome many obstacles that individual non-standard workers face as regards effective enforcement of their rights. Additional supportive measures that take into account specific characteristics of particular types of non-standard employment and make it easier for non-standard workers to enforce their rights should be put in place as well.

[76] B Kresal, 'Protection against dismissal in contemporary labour law' in F Hendrickx and V De Stefano, *Game Changers in Labour Law* (Alphen aan den Rijn, Kluwer, 2018) 165–75. In the same sense, for example, Malmberg, 'Protection against dismissal is of key importance in enabling individual employees to enforce their rights' in J Malmberg (ed), *Effective enforcement of EC labour law* (Stockholm, 2004), https://ilo-ilera.org/wp-content/uploads/2020/04/track_5_malmberg.pdf, 9; see also J Malmberg et al (eds), *Effective enforcement of EC labour law* (Alphen aan den Rijn, Kluwer, 2003).

14

Towards Effective Enforcement of Occupational Health and Safety Law in the European Union

AUDE CEFALIELLO

1. Introduction

The adoption of the so-called 'Framework Directive' (Directive 89/391/EEC) marked the beginning of the 1990s, the decade in which most of the EU occupational safety and health (OSH) Directives were adopted.[1] This Directive has been the basis for more than 30 Directives covering a variety of risks (eg biological agents, working conditions and working equipment). The decade 'ended' with the adoption of the Charter of Fundamental Rights of the European Union, and in particular Article 31 on fair and just working conditions, which provides that 'every worker has the right to working conditions which respect his or her health, safety and dignity'. Previous research emphasised the strong relationship between these two instruments; Directive 89/391/EEC 'has made the fundamental right to occupational health and safety operational and will serve as the basis for' Article 31 CFREU.[2]

To complete the EU occupational safety and health legal framework and depending on what their Member States have ratified, workers can also rely on various legally binding international agreements. All the Member States have ratified the International Covenant on Economic, Social and Cultural Rights recognising the right of everyone to just and favourable working conditions, including safe and healthy working conditions (Article 7(b) OSH Convention, 1981, No 155). The

[1] *See:* L Vogel, 'The machinery of occupational safety and health policy in the European Union. History, institutions, actors' (Brussels, ETUI, 2015); K Liu and W Liu, 'The Development of EU Law in the Field of Occupational Health and Safety: A New Way of Thinking' (2015) 40(3–4) *Management and Labour Studies* 207–38.

[2] K Lörcher, 'Article 31 – Fair and Just Working Conditions' in F Dorssemont, K Lörcher, S Clauwaert and M Schmitt (eds), *The Charter of Fundamental Rights of the European Union and the Employment Relation* (London, Bloomsbury Publishing, 2019) 538.

ILO's Promotional Framework for Occupational Safety and Health Convention, 2006 (No 187) has also been ratified by many Member States. Finally, Article 3 of the (Revised) European Social Charter, providing that all workers have the right to just conditions of work, has also been ratified by most Member States.[3]

Therefore, there is a full and complementary set of legally binding international and European provisions that provides a set of workers' rights and protection in occupational safety and health, at least in theory.[4] Being legally binding does not necessarily mean that these provisions have a direct effect, however; to be effective, these principles must be implemented and enforced at the national level, relying therefore on domestic mechanisms. Despite national differences, the first part of this book stressed some commonality in the ways European labour law is enforced.[5] Member States share three main forms of enforcement: (i) industrial relations enforcement, (ii) administrative enforcement and (iii) judicial enforcement.

To contrast a similar analysis of occupational safety and health at the European level, one might highlight that there is no such thing as a 'European Labour Inspectorate'. Similarly, there is no European health and safety committee. Finally, there is no European Labour Court. Nevertheless, there are some mechanisms that allow an investigation of these three forms of OSH enforcement at the EU Level. Indeed, all the Member States have labour inspectorates or some other authority in charge of monitoring compliance and enforcing occupational safety and health. Similarly, following implementation of Directive 89/391/EEC, all Member States have provisions to appoint or elect health and safety representatives.[6] Finally, even if the CJEU might not specialise in labour law, some decisions have significantly improved and clarified the way EU occupational safety and health is applied at the national level.[7] Therefore, it would be appropriate to follow a similar typology to examine the different forms of OSH enforcement in the EU.

Enforcement is one aspect, but how do we guarantee effective enforcement? What does effective enforcement mean for occupational safety and health? One interpretation of effective enforcement would be the guarantee, or fulfilment, of the purpose of occupational safety and health: prevention. The aim of occupational safety and health, both internationally[8] and at the European level, is to introduce measures to encourage improvements of workers' health and safety.[9]

[3] *See:* K Lörcher, 'Article 3 – The Right to Safe and Healthy Working Conditions' in N Bruun, K Lörcher, I Schömann and S Clauwaert (eds), *The European Social Charter and the Employment Relation* (London, Bloomsbury Publishing, 2019) 181–98.

[4] Lörcher, n 2 at 535.

[5] Chapter 3 by Lörcher, 'Access to justice', and Chapter 4 by Unterschütz, 'Enforcing EU labour law by using administrative law means'. See also: previous research such as J Malmberg, 'Effective enforcement of EC labour law: a comparative analysis of community law requirements' (2004) 10(2) *European Journal of Industrial Relations* 2219–29.

[6] ILO Convention No 187 also refers to 'workers and their representatives', Art 4(2)(d).

[7] A Cefaliello, 'Towards an improvement of the legal framework governing occupational health and safety in the European Union' (doctoral dissertation, University of Glasgow, 2020), 150–52.

[8] Art 4(2) ILO Convention C-155.

[9] Art 1(1) Framework Directive 89/391/EEC.

To achieve this preventive goal, the Framework Directive provides general principles of prevention.[10] The basic general principle of prevention is the evaluation of risks; it constitutes the basis for development of a coherent overall prevention policy in cooperation with workers and/or workers' health and safety representatives. Thus, the 'DNA' of occupational safety and health concerns avoiding occupational illnesses and accidents before they occur.

Thus, this chapter aims to explore the three dimensions of enforcement of EU occupational safety and health law, solely through the prevention prism. In other words, how would it be possible to effectively enforce the preventive function of EU occupational safety and health principles? The main argument developed in this chapter is the existence of a possible hierarchy of regulatory options in terms of the effective enforcement of the prevention function of occupational safety and health in the EU. To support this idea the analysis proceeds in three steps. First, by examining the ability of workers' health and safety representatives to monitor the enforcement of the OSH principle of prevention, exercising their right to consultation (Article 11(1) Directive 89/391/EEC), and their right to appeal to labour authorities (Article 11(6), Directive 89/391/EEC). Their capacity to hold the employer accountable for adopting an adequate OSH prevention plan makes workers' health and safety representatives the primary actors for enforcing OSH prevention principles. The effectiveness of this approach, however, relies on the presence of health and safety representatives, but also on the capacity of the labour inspectorate to react. Thus, in section 3 we provide an overview of the main structural challenges that labour inspectorates face in effectively enforcing OSH principles in the EU. Unfortunately, the lack of support at the EU level has resulted in the general development of risk-based approach because of understaffed and under resourced labour inspectorate services. Additionally, labour inspectorates face significant changes because of the evolution of the labour market. As a result, labour inspectorates often enforce the OSH legal framework only after an accident has occurred, despite the prevention principle. Therefore, the fourth and last section stresses that the capacity for workers and their representatives to go before a court to enforce OSH prevention principles appears to be the fundamental safeguard of effective enforcement. Recent CJEU cases have addressed the question of risk assessment and the burden of proof, which provides a procedural tool for workers towards effective prevention. Additionally, at the national level, some recent jurisprudence illustrates the potential role of the court in re-assessing the importance of involving health and safety representatives in the development of OSH prevention plans. Another case resulted in broadening the OSH protective framework to workers (and not only employees); this extension might be an alternative way to effectively enforce (or here apply) OSH principles to more people.

[10] Art 1(2) Directive 89/391/EEC.

2. Health and Safety Representatives on the Front Line to Guarantee Effective Enforcement of Occupational Safety and Health in the EU

Effective prevention involves the concept of communication and cooperation with the workers or their representatives. Indeed, according to Article 20 ILO C-155: 'Co-operation between management and workers and/or their representatives within the undertaking shall be an essential element of organisational and other measures taken in pursuance of' the Convention. Similarly, Article 11(1) Directive 89/391/EEC stresses that employers have a duty to consult workers and/or their representatives and allow them to take part in discussions on all questions related to safety and health at work. Workers' representatives are not only passively consulted; they can also make proposals, which turn them – in theory – into prevention actors. Therefore, this section examines the provisions at the disposal of workers' health and safety representatives and whether they provide effective means to enforce OSH prevention measures.

2.1. Presence of Workers' Health and Safety Representatives as a Prerequisite of Effective Enforcement of OSH Prevention

The Framework Directive defines workers' health and safety representatives as 'any person elected, chosen or designated in accordance with national laws and/or practices to represent workers where problems arise relating to the safety and health protection of workers at work'.[11]

Even though most countries already had a form of workers' representation on health and safety, the implementation of Directive 89/391/EEC has incentivised national initiatives.[12]

The presence of workers' health and safety representatives is essential because they have an active role in guaranteeing the enforcement of OSH legislation.[13] Indeed, the safest workplaces are those that have active and well-recognised collective representation.[14] Their role is of the utmost importance in a context of weaker administrative enforcement. As underlined by Tombs and Whyte:

> The retreat of proactive inspection and enforcement clearly brings the regulatory significance of the day-to-day regulatory functions of workers themselves, the monitoring

[11] Art 3(c) Directive 89/391/EEC.

[12] L Vogel and D Walters, 'An Afterword on European Union Policy and Practice' in D Walters and T Nichols (eds), *Workplace Health and Safety* (London, Palgrave Macmillan, 2009) 100.

[13] Malmberg, n 5 at 224.

[14] See P James and D Walters, 'Worker representation in health and safety: options for regulatory reform' (2002) 33(2) *Industrial Relations Journal* 141–56.

> role of worker organizations and the safety management role of systems of workplace safety committees into sharp focus.[15]

Therefore, effective enforcement of OSH principles by occupational safety and health representatives will be achieved through their influence on managerial decisions and the enforcement of employer's duties in that regard.[16] Their scope for monitoring employers' responsibilities would cover the general employers' obligation to prevent risks in all aspects of work and to adapt the workplace accordingly (Article 6), competent support (Article 7) and through systematic risk assessment (Article 9).[17] Workers' representatives perform their enforcement role when they are consulted and informed,[18] but also in their capacity to issue alerts and to appeal to the responsible authorities.[19] In some Member States, workers' representatives have a right to draw on the expertise of outside consultants and experts and to order that dangerous work cease.[20] Thus, Directive 89/391/EEC not only regulates employers' duties, but also explicitly deals with the industrial relations process as a means of enforcement.

2.2. Right to Appeal to National Authorities: Between Myth and Reality at the National Level

One of the main means of enforcement for workers' representatives in occupational safety and health might be the possibility to appeal to the responsible authorities, as provided for in Article 11(6) Directive 89/391/EEC:

> Workers and/or their representatives are entitled to appeal, in accordance with national law and/or practice, to the authority responsible for safety and health protection at work if they consider that the measures taken and the means employed by the employer are inadequate for the purposes of ensuring safety and health at work.
>
> Workers' representatives must be given the opportunity to submit their observations during inspection visits by the competent authority.

But is this right a guarantee of effective enforcement? Is it actually enforced at the national level?

[15] S Tombs and D Whyte, 'The myths and realities of deterrence in workplace safety regulation' (2013) 53(5) *British Journal of Criminology* 758.

[16] D Walters, R Johnstone and K Frick, 'Introduction: Inspecting health and safety management and the consequences of restructuring in the modern world of work' in D Walters, R Johnstone, K Frick, M Quinlan, G Baril-Gingras and A Thébaud-Mony (eds), *Regulating Workplace Risks: A Comparative Study of Inspection Regimes in Times of Change* (Cheltenham, Edward Elgar, 2011) 3–20.

[17] Vogel and Walters, n 12 at 96.

[18] Vogel and Walters, n 12 at 98.

[19] Art 11(6) Directive 89/391/EEC.

[20] P James, 'Worker Representation and Health and Safety: Reflections on the Past, Present and Future' in D Walters and T Nichols (eds), *Workplace Health and Safety* (London, Palgrave Macmillan, 2009) 205.

This right can take different forms at the national level, which sometimes are not equally effective. Article 11(6) has been implemented almost word for word in Sweden by the Work Environment Act.[21] Some studies show, however, that even if workers' representatives should in theory benefit from these rights, there are severe problems with application.[22] As underlined by Trägårdh, the implementation of this right is linked to the presence of health and safety representatives, which is not the case in every workplace because of the applicable minimum threshold. This author also shares additional concerns for the near future, because cuts at the Swedish Work Environment Authority have led to a substantial reduction in inspections (20–25 per cent) and staff. Therefore, workers' representatives do not have the opportunity to report to labour inspectorates, but even if they do, the latter do not have the capacity to respond.

In other countries, such as the United Kingdom, the provisions of Article 11(6) are implemented via general provisions on whistleblowing. The main idea is that employees can report any wrongdoing (illegal behaviour/malpractice) by their employer, and that such employees should be protected. In that context, employees reporting such behaviour should be regarded as 'dedicated individuals who provide a valuable safety net when other forms of regulation fail'.[23] The applicable provision is section 43B(1) Employment Rights Act 1996 defining a case of 'qualifying disclosure' as one in which a worker reasonably believes that the employer's wrongdoing constitutes a danger to the health and safety of any individual (ie not necessarily a worker). The main problem with that interpretation of Article 11(6) is that it does not encourage employees to report wrongdoing, because it places the burden and the risk on the individual, which is unreasonable.

Based on these two examples, it seems that one of the main obstacles to effective enforcement by health and safety representatives is that, under Directive 89/391/EEC, they can appeal only to the 'authority responsible for safety and health protection at work', which has been understood to mean the labour inspectorates. Therefore, the effectiveness of occupational safety and health 'industrial relations' enforcement is interlinked with the strength and effectiveness of the administrative enforcement provided by labour inspectorates.

[21] Ch 6, para 6(a) Swedish Work Environment Act.

[22] B Trägårdh, 'The role of health and safety representatives in Sweden–The implementation of EEC Directive 89/391' (2008) 1 *Studies of Organization and Society* 9–10, University of Gothenburg, Department of Business Administration.

[23] D Lewis and S Trygstad, 'Protecting whistleblowers in Norway and the UK: a case of mix and match?' (2009) 51(6) *International Journal of Law and Management* 375 (fn 34).

3. Essential Structural Support to Guarantee Effective Enforcement of Occupational Safety and Health Prevention: Administrative Enforcement/Labour Inspectorates

The role of labour inspectorates is recognised in most countries as being essential to ensure the effectiveness of legal measures designed to protect workers.[24] There is a recognition that labour law enforcement cannot rely entirely on self-enforcement. The regulatory philosophy of 'regulated self-regulation' means that employers in collaboration with their workforces are identified as the primary mechanisms for maintaining and improving standards of workplace health and safety.[25] Law enforcement requires external surveillance and sanctions, either by the courts or by the labour inspectorates.[26]

As underlined previously by Unterschütz (in this volume), even if Member States' administrative decisions follow the principle of procedural autonomy, this principle is limited by the obligation to ensure full effectiveness of EU law.[27] Therefore, the national labour inspectorates should be under an obligation to ensure the full effectiveness of the EU OSH Directive, in particular the preventive dimension embodied by the Framework Directive.

This section will examine the means accessible to labour inspectorates to effectively enforce the preventive dimension of occupational safety and health principles in the EU.

3.1. Dissonance between the EU Institutions on the role of Labour Inspectorates in the Enforcement of Occupational Health and Safety

Even though there is a European principle of the effectiveness of EU Law, supranational enforcement powers are highly limited on the ground, and according to Article 4 TFEU, social policy (and so occupational safety and health) is a shared competence.[28] Therefore, in accordance with the principles of proportionality and subsidiarity, the EU will take action only when the objectives of an action cannot

[24] Walters, Johnstone and Frick, n 16 at 5.

[25] James, n 20 at 207.

[26] Chapters 3 and 4 in this volume.

[27] Chapter 4 in this volume.

[28] M Hartlapp, 'Enforcing social Europe through labour inspectorates: changes in capacity and cooperation across Europe' (2014) 37(4) *West European Politics* 805.

be sufficiently achieved by the Member States, but can be better achieved at Union level, 'by reason of the scale and effect of the proposed action'. Thus, as of now, Member States remain mainly responsible for enforcement of occupational safety and health principles.[29]

As guardian of the treaties, however, the Commission has the role of guaranteeing implementation of EU Directives at the national level, which is necessary to guarantee effectiveness later on. Also, even if the EU does not have extensive competence for the enforcement of OSH prevention, it still has to monitor it at the EU level. Indeed, one might say that distortions in the enforcement of OSH principles can be a factor in social dumping and therefore interfere with the European labour market.

At the EU level, the importance given to enforcement and compliance has evolved over time. In the 1990s, enforcement was seen as the corollary of implementation; therefore, proper implementation of Directives was a way to guarantee the effectiveness of minimum standards set by Directives at the national level. With the arrival of the Barroso Commission in 2004, the position towards the adoption of new Directives was that they should be the last resort, and that priority should be given to existing legislation. What differed from previous Commissions, however, is that implementation was guaranteed through compliance, not enforcement. In the Community strategy on health and safety at work (2007–12), adopted during Barroso's time, the aim is to guarantee proper implementation of EU legislation and to 'encourage changes in the behaviour of workers and encourage their employers to adopt health-focused approaches', without mention of enforcement.[30] Overall, in 2004, the preoccupation was with the costs of preventive regulation and the desire to 'simplify' or replace it with 'soft' law and voluntary measures (this was the main theme of the Dutch presidency's health and safety conference in Amsterdam in 2004).[31] This approach was also in line with the development of the Open Method of Coordination: the Commission encouraged and supported national labour inspectorates to play an advisory role on occupational safety and health and to support employers. Even in the recent EU Strategic Framework on Health and Safety at Work (2014–20), the Commission stressed that 'it is crucial that labour inspectors are seen as facilitating compliance with legislation rather than obstacles to business activity'.[32]

[29] An exception can be made for the mandate of the European Labour Authority (ELA) on cross-border work when this Authority might intervene in the future to enforce OSH principles. The case of the ELA will be discussed further below.

[30] European Commission, COM(2007) 62 final, Communication from the Commission to the European Parliament, the Council, the European Economic and Social Committee and the Committee of the Regions. Improving quality and productivity at work: Community strategy, 2007–2012 on health and safety at work.

[31] Vogel and Walters, n 12 at 98.

[32] European Commission, COM(2014) 332 Final, Communication from the Commission to the European Parliament, the Council, the European Economic and Social Committee and the Committee of the Regions on an EU Strategic Framework on Health and Safety at Work 2014–2020, 8.

This decreasing importance attached to enforcement and sanctions to guarantee proper implementation of OSH legal frameworks echoed a broader political shift within the EU. All over Europe, more 'business friendly' environments have been fostered, in which there is political enthusiasm for deregulation to remove perceived 'burdens on business'.[33] In that context, self-regulation and self-enforcement are perceived as enough to guarantee health and safety at work. Therefore, labour inspectorates are supposed to intervene only when this system fails (reactive inspection) or when severe occupational risks are extremely likely to occur (a risk-based approach). Thus, over the same period, there has been a parallel reduction in the resources available to regulatory inspection in most countries.[34] With the adoption of REFIT,[35] it seemed that the Commission endorsed this shift from the national level and the vision that effective OSH enforcement was a burden on competition – which needed to be lightened or removed.[36] The problem is that 'the general deterrence effect depends on employers anticipating that they are likely to receive an inspection and are likely to be punished in the event of non-compliance. The higher the expectation of detection and punishment the greater the general deterrent effect will be.'[37] By recommending lowering the number of preventive inspections, the Commission might weaken effective enforcement at the national level.

In that respect the position of the European Commission contrasts with that defended by the ILO (and the principles provided in the ILO Conventions), stressing the importance of the power of labour inspectorates (covering also OSH).[38] The ILO also underlined that labour inspectorates shall have the status, the material means and the financial resources necessary to perform their duties effectively.[39] The ILO has expressed strong concerns about the current situation, in which labour inspection services in many countries are not able to carry out their roles and functions.[40]

Similarly, the lack of emphasis on enforcement by the Commission ill matches the official statements and the Advisory Committee (ACSH), which has a mandate on OHS. Indeed, the ACSH stressed that facilitating Member State enforcement of OSH legislation is a priority of current of EU OSH policy and should remain high on the agenda of any future EU OSH framework initiative (ACSH opinion, June 2019).

[33] Walters, Johnstone and Frick, n 16 at 11–12.

[34] Hartlapp, n 28 at 815.

[35] The European Commission's regulatory fitness and performance programme (REFIT) aims to ensure that EU laws deliver on their objectives at a minimum cost for the benefit of citizens and businesses. See further details: https://ec.europa.eu/info/law/law-making-process/evaluating-and-improving-existing-laws/refit-making-eu-law-simpler-less-costly-and-future-proof_en.

[36] See: www.socialeurope.eu/one-in-one-out-is-a-danger-to-workers-health-and-safety.

[37] Tombs and Whyte, n 15 at 755.

[38] ILO Labour Inspection Convention, 1947 (No 81).

[39] ILO Labour Administration Convention, 1978 (No 150).

[40] *See* G Casale and A Sivananthiran, *The fundamentals of labour administration* (International Labour Organization, 2010).

The European institution that contrasts most with the European Commission is the European Parliament (EP). Indeed, in 2014, the European Parliament emphasised the essential role played by labour inspectorates in ensuring health and safety at the workplace, and therefore

> advocates stiffer penalties for companies that fail to meet their obligation in relation to employees' basic rights, and considers that such penalties must have a sufficiently deterrent and dissuasive effect to ensure that employers shall by no means profit from circumventing the existing rules on employment and health protection; calls Member States to consider in their sanction-setting systems to make the level of fine proportionate to the damage as well as to ensure that it is above the profit gained from the circumvention.[41]

The European Parliament also calls on Member States to increase and to provide sufficient resources to labour inspectorates in order to have the capacity to carry out inspections with regard to online platforms to impose sanctions where rules have been breached.[42] With this resolution, the European Parliament highlighted that, if sufficiently funded, labour inspectorates could have a decisive role in effectively enforcing OSH principles (by increasing preventive inspections, including regarding 'new' forms of work).

The current discord at the EU level has raised multiple obstacles to guaranteeing effective enforcement of the EU OSH framework (and so preventive principles). One of the main problems is that it relies entirely on national systems. While obliged to ensure the application of EU law in general (Article 17(1) 2nd sentence TEU), the Commission is not equipped in practice to control effectively the way in which labour law, and so OSH, is enforced at the national level (with perhaps the exclusion of cross-border workers).

Some authors have explored the possibility of creating a Transnational Labour Inspectorate (TLI) dealing with transnational private instruments of multinational enterprises (MNEs) into the ILO, in addition to national labour inspections.[43] At the EU level, some hopes have been placed on the new European Labour Authority (ELA).[44] The purpose of ELA is to address the challenges of cross-border tensions between national authorities and market disruptions. One study examining the Commission impact assessment[45] and the mandate given to ELA and its potential

[41] European Parliament resolution of 14 January 2014 on effective labour inspections as a strategy to improve working conditions in Europe (2013/2112(INI)) Art 34.

[42] S Garben, *Protecting workers in the online platform economy: an overview of regulatory and policy developments in the EU* (EU-OSHA, 2017) 84.

[43] See AGM Alhambra, B Ter Haar and A Kun, 'Harnessing Public Institutions for Labour Law Enforcement: Embedding a Transnational Labour Inspectorate within the ILO' (2020) 17(2) *International Organizations Law Review* 233–60.

[44] See S Fernandes, 'What is our ambition for the European Labour Authority?', *Notre Europe*; J Cremers, 'The European Labour Authority and Enhanced Enforcement' (Policy Department for Economic, Scientific and Quality of Life Policies, European Parliament, Brussels, 2018) 148–61.

[45] Commission impact assessment – Accompanying the document, Proposal for a Regulation of the European Parliament and of the Council establishing a European Labour Authority – COM (2018) 131 final – SWD(2018) 69 final.

impact in OSH concluded that it will have a limited impact at the domestic level.[46] The impact will be limited because it is restricted to cross-border situations, and the fact that ELA does not have its own inspectors and relies on national labour inspectorates. The current structure and functioning of the ELA do not resolve the problem of the lack of national resources.

As we will see, the national labour inspectorate and national authorities in charge of occupational safety and health are facing a strong challenge, and preventive inspections are declining. The second problem is that the emphasis on compliance without mentioning enforcement seems to suggest that the idea still prevails (by way of an endorsement) that enforcing occupational safety and health legislation and the principle of prevention are first and foremost a burden for companies. Not having effective enforcement of the OSH principle, however, risks workplace accidents and occupational diseases. That is certainly a burden in terms of workplace organisation, but also for society as a whole. That is without even mentioning the 'burden' and 'weight' on the social security system, and on national welfare systems if workers find themselves unable to work anymore. Additionally, the lack of equivalent power to enforce OSH preventive principles at the national level represents a significant obstacle to OSH effective enforcement in the EU.

3.2. Labour Inspectorates at the National Level: United in Diversity and Adversity

Despite the minimum standard laid down by ILO Convention No 81, which has been ratified by all Member States, previous literature has underlined that enforcement systems differ from one Member State to another, with dual and central systems of enforcement.[47] Indeed, depending on the national tradition, labour inspectorates or authorities can have a specific or a general mandate (either labour law in general, or exclusively OSH). Other studies have reported that, in some countries, the role of labour inspectorates has developed more towards support and guidance, and in other countries rather towards a punitive approach.[48]

Additionally, there are differences among Member States regarding the legal nature of sanctions, the amounts of fines, and combination with soft enforcement. These differences can lead not only to inconsistency but also to the ineffectiveness of EU OSH standards at the national level.[49] From a more theoretical perspective, it has been observed that if sanctions are applied too strictly, there is no incentive

[46] Cefaliello, n 7 at 210–23.

[47] See Hartlapp, n 28 at 809. See also Walters, Johnstone and Frick, at n 16.

[48] D Walters, E Wadsworth, P Hasle, B Refslund, M Ramioul and AB Antonsson, *Safety and health in micro and small enterprises in the EU: the view from the workplace* (EU-OSHA, 2018) 8.

[49] Cefaliello, n 7 at 178–83.

for employers to apply OSH standards. Indeed, if there is absolutely no understanding and flexibility from labour inspectorates, employers may well refrain from implementing OSH standards and 'take the risk' of being sanctioned if there is an inspection (which might be rare in some sectors because of the risk-based approach), rather than trying and being sanctioned anyway. A more flexible way to control the application of OSH would lead to better self-compliance and cooperation only if it is complemented strictly by legally binding rules that act as a threat. Therefore, to guarantee effective enforcement (even through advice and support), labour inspectorates should have appropriate deterrent powers.

In addition to these 'structural' differences, other aspects should be taken into consideration to assess whether national labour inspectorates actually contribute to effective enforcement of OSH principles. The first element is the threshold (or ratio) of one labour inspectorate for every 10,000 workers to assess whether there is an adequate number of labour inspectorates at the national level. This number was adopted when the majority of employment relationships were standard (ie full-time, usually workers centralised in a single workplace). The evolution of the labour market might even turn this ratio into an inappropriate threshold (or make it 'fictional').

Secondly, even if some workplaces remain centralised and have to deal mainly with physical risks, the labour market and the nature of work as it has evolved (and associated risks, too) complicate the role of labour inspectorates in the enforcement of OSH. Labour inspectorates have to conduct more inspections in the case of temporary work(places), but also because of the fragmentation of workplaces (more small and medium companies, but also the development of remote work).[50] The use of subcontracting makes it difficult for them to define who is responsible for the general principle of prevention. Additionally, the numerous cases of bogus self-employed (especially in the gig economy) complicates the situation and labour inspectorates find themselves in a situation in which they have to examine more general aspects than occupational safety and health strictly speaking (eg employment status or minimum wages).[51]

Similarly, there is a change of regulation from a prescriptive approach with technical standards to a process-based approach focused on improving the management of health and safety.[52] It requires more time to assess management organisation and interactions with workers. This modern setting puts labour inspectorates in situations in which they have to assess the nature and extent of legal responsibilities and recommend suitable preventive strategies.[53] This is the concept of 'risk management', within the framework of which the entire

[50] Garben, n 41 at 19. Opinion on future EU OSH Enforcement Priorities contributing to a renewed EU OSH Strategy. A submission from the Senior Labour Inspectors' Committee (SLIC).

[51] EU OSH, *Foresight on new and emerging occupational safety and health risks associated with digitalization by 2025* (EU-PSH, 2018) 14.

[52] Walters, Johnstone and Frick, n 16 at 6.

[53] Walters, Johnstone and Frick, n 16 at 11.

environment must be examined. 'Risk management' is in line with the broader conception and scope of occupational safety and health as covering all working conditions. All of this requires more time, and so more resources – and necessitates measures in strict contrast to risk-based inspection.

Thus, the third complicating factor is the overall turn toward risk-based inspection in Member State. As EU-OSHA describes it:

> The spread of the risk-based approach means that most modern labour inspectorates have embraced the idea of pulling back resources from low-risk objects and concentrating more resources for enforcement on objects with the highest risks.[54]

This approach impacts negatively on the likelihood of a visit from the labour inspectorate, depending on risk prioritisation in the inspection strategy.[55] Priority is often given to higher-risk sectors – with more physical and 'traditional' risks – to the detriment of 'lower risk sectors'. This approach and way of prioritising do not take into account the modification of the nature of risk in these 'low risk sectors', but risks still exist, under a different form.

For example, musculoskeletal disorders and psychosocial risks (PSR) are the issue reported most frequently by European workplaces.[56] Paradoxically, these risks are more likely to be under-reported. Indeed, according to ESNER, fewer than 50 per cent of companies have a plan to assess stress or harassment.[57] Even if the risks of stress and harassment are not covered by individual Directives, they are covered by Directive 89/391/EEC and have been the object of European framework agreements signed by the social partners.[58] Therefore, they should be assessed and explicitly integrated in an appropriate prevention plan. These risks are often observed in the low risk sectors, and will not be the object of preventive inspections. One could argue that there is a direct link between the lack of inspections and the absence of preventive plans to assess psychosocial risks. This illustrates a clear failure of labour inspectorates to prevent modern risks; especially considering that these workplaces would benefit from preventive inspections.

According to ESENER-3, between 2014 and 2019, the proportion of workplaces reporting a visit by the labour inspectorate in the previous three years fell in almost all countries.[59] One might hypothesise that this decline is one effect of the shift in prioritisation of inspections. The structural repercussion might be

[54] See Ø Dahl and A Starren, *The future role of big data and machine learning for health and safety inspection efficiency* (Bilbao, Spain, EU-OSHA, 2019).

[55] EU-OSHA, *Safety and health in micro and small enterprises in the EU: the view from the workplace* (EU-OSHA, 2018) 8.

[56] European Agency for Health and Safety at Work (EU-OSHA), *Third European Survey of Enterprises on New and Emergent Risks, 2019* (European Union, Bilbao, Spain, 2020) 7.

[57] Ibid 11.

[58] Framework agreement on harassment and violence at work (2007); Framework agreement on stress at work (2004).

[59] European Agency for Health and Safety at Work (EU-OSHA), *Third European Survey of Enterprises on New and Emergent Risks, 2019* (European Union, Bilbao, Spain, 2020) 18.

an externalisation or shift of responsibility for effective prevention to individual workers, thereby negating the organisational and collective aspect of effective prevention. Therefore, the answer to the question 'does the labour inspectorate effectively enforce the preventive dimension of the Occupational Health and Safety Principles/Framework in the European Union?' would be that, under the current circumstances, it is particularly complicated for labour inspectorates to effectively enforce the preventive dimension of OSH principles.

Accordingly, it seems that administrative enforcement cannot provide the required structural support for health and safety representatives to strengthen them in their role of actors tasked with effective enforcement of OSH prevention. Thus, the only way for workers and their representatives to effectively enforce their rights and compliance with OSH principles is through judicial enforcement.

4. Judicial Enforcement as a Fundamental Safety Net Guaranteeing Effective Enforcement of OSH Prevention

It is important to underline that even if Directive 89/391/EEC provides a common ground for OSH workers' rights, their enforcement will vary depending on the specificities of national systems. There are two factors to take into consideration when examining the possibilities of effective OSH judicial enforcement. The first, impacting how occupational safety and health is enforced judicially is the (legal) capacity for trade unions and workers' health and safety representatives to lodge actions. The second element is that, often, cases raised are individual cases that are legally permissible only when there is a breach (and sometimes a fault) by the employer of their duty of care to protect workers' OSH. Therefore, the majority of the cases brought before courts and tribunals in relation to OSH are of a compensatory (reparative) nature, and not centred around prevention.

With the aim of this chapter/book in mind, however, we examine only cases with the direct potential of improving enforcement of the general principle of prevention, either by discussing principles of prevention (eg risk assessment) or by workers' representatives enforcing their rights leading to better prevention (national level).

4.1. Conjunction of Obligation to Assess OSH Risks and Reversal of the Burden of Proof: A Winning Combination towards Improving Effective Enforcement of OSH in the EU? CJEU Case Studies

The enforcement of the OSH principles laid down by Directive 89/391/EEC at the EU level is characterised by a form of duality. On one hand, a common set of principles is supposed to be applied (and so enforced) equivalently through all the Member States, which is also the key to providing equivalent protection to all workers. On the other hand, the Framework Directive can be qualified as reflexive law: it provides general principles and goals. Even if some OSH Directives are more specific in terms of exposure (eg Carcinogens and Mutagens Directive (EU) 2019/130), none provide specific rules of procedure or sanctions. The aim is to guarantee that these principles are applied at the national level: it would then depend on the national procedure and sanctions. Nevertheless, as shown in the first part of this book, the CJEU has developed some requirements that limit the autonomy of Member States in providing specific rules of procedure and sanctions according to which substantive provisions are to be enforced.[60] Under these circumstances, one fundamental task might be to determine the extent to which the CJEU can contribute to the effective enforcement of OSH in the EU. How can we ensure equality in occupational safety and health provisions if there is no way to control how they are enforced or applied Europe-wide?

A number of different legal actions are available before the CJEU: infringement proceedings, preliminary rulings and annulment proceedings. Various authors have shown an overall trend towards decentralisation from infringement proceedings towards preliminary rulings.[61] One study explicitly draws a connection between the decline in infringement proceedings and the restrained policy activism of the second Barroso Commission.[62] This tendency has been confirmed regarding OSH cases, with more than 60 per cent of the decisions lodged before the CJEU being preliminary rulings.[63] Based on this assessment, one might suggest that the Commission is lacking in its role as guardian of the Treaties.[64] The section focuses only on available ways for workers and workers' representatives to effectively enforce OSH principles, thus, only preliminary rulings will be examined in what follows.

Article 267(2) TFEU provides definitions and conditions in relation to preliminary rulings. According to this article, the CJEU has jurisdiction to give preliminary rulings concerning the interpretation of the Treaties and the validity and interpretation of acts by institutions, bodies, offices, or agencies of the Union – including Directives. Preliminary rulings have a central place in the Community legal order,[65] and contribute to Europe's legal integration by allowing national courts to enforce EU law over national law.[66]

[60] Chapter 3 in this volume; see J Malmberg, n 7 at 219–29.

[61] A Hofmann, 'Is the Commission levelling the playing field? Rights enforcement in the European Union' (2018) 40(6) *Journal of European Integration* 737–51.

[62] H Kassim, S Connolly, R Dehousse, O Rozenberg and S Bendjaballah, 'Managing the house: The presidency, agenda control and policy activism in the European Commission' (2017) 24(5) *Journal of European Public Policy* 666.

[63] See Cefaliello, n 6 at 138–54. The study examined a total of 161 CJEU decisions related to OSH Directives. There were 65 infringement proceedings and 96 preliminary rulings.

[64] Cefaliello, n 7 at 143.

[65] MA Dauses, 'Practical considerations regarding the preliminary ruling procedure under Article 177 of the EEC Treaty' (1986) *Fordham Int'l LJ* 10, 539.

[66] CJ Carrubba and L Murrah, 'Legal integration and use of the preliminary ruling process in the European Union' (2005) 59(2) *International Organization* 399.

Previous studies show that the use of preliminary rulings and requests might be a suitable way to ensure the correct application of EU OHS standards in cases in which the claim is based on individual workers' rights, as opposed to employers' obligations.[67] A close examination of the topics of the argument affirms that, in order to be feasible and successful, such claims have to be based on rights granted to workers individually, which is rare in OSH, given the reflexive nature of the provisions embodied in the Directives. Consequently, most claims relate to the Working Time Directive and the Directive on the Protection of Pregnant Workers (often combined with the Directive on Equal Treatment). One hypothesis explaining this tendency is that these claims often lead, if successful, to monetary compensation. Even if such jurisprudence improves workers' OSH rights by clarifying some aspects – such as what can be considered working time, or the definition of a pregnant or breastfeeding worker – these cases do not deal with how prevention is organised at the workplace.

The CJEU rulings *Otero Ramos* (C-513/15) and *Castro* (C-41/17) differ from the general pattern by shedding some light on the preventive aspect of OSH. Indeed, even if, in both cases, initial claims partly follow the general pattern by involving workers breastfeeding (falling under the scope of Directive 92/85/EEC), the discussions and questions raised relate directly to the employers' obligation to assess and prevent risks.

Before *Otero Ramos* and *Castro*, CJEU rulings revolved around the question of definition (Article 2), maternity leave (Article 8), and the prohibition of dismissal (Article 10) or other discriminatory behaviours (eg refusing to hire a woman because of her pregnancy). For the first time, these two cases raise questions about risk assessment (Article 4) and actions following such assessment (Article 5). According to the later article, the employer shall take the necessary measures to ensure that, by temporarily adjusting the working conditions and/or working hours of the worker concerned (within the meaning of Article 2), the exposure of that worker to such risks is avoided. If such adjustment is not possible, the employer shall take the necessary measures to move the worker concerned to another job. As a last resort, if the worker cannot perform any work, she shall be granted leave in accordance with national legislation for the whole period necessary to protect her safety or health. This covers the effect on breastfeeding.

In both cases, workers were breastfeeding and argued that their working conditions had negative impact on it. They both argued that their employer did not correctly assess the risks, and the only way for them to be safe was to be granted paid leave. The question raised before the CJEU involved determining which party had to meet the burden of proof. In principle, the claimant must provide proof of a breach. The only exception is in case of discrimination, as provided by Article 19(1) of Directive 2006/54/EC. In case of direct or indirect discrimination,

[67] Cefaliello, n 7 at 148–55.

persons or workers who consider themselves wronged must establish, before a court or other competent authority, a fact from which it may be presumed that there has been discrimination; it shall be for the respondent to prove that there has been no breach of the principle of equal treatment. It has been consistent jurisprudence that less favourable treatment of women because of pregnancy is direct discrimination.[68] According to the CJEU, the fact that employers did not carry out an adequate risk assessment resulted in less favourable treatment against women breastfeeding, which constitutes direct discrimination on the basis of sex.

For the first time, the CJEU confirmed that Article 19 of Directive 2006/54/EC applies to the assessment of any risks to the safety or health of breastfeeding of workers for all activities liable to involve a specific risk of exposure (Article 4.1),[69] particularly when the working conditions include night work (Article 7),[70] even when the worker is only partially working at night.

The reversal of burden of proof is a major improvement in effective OSH enforcement, because usually workers have to prove that the risks have not been assessed and that there was a risk. Similarly, usually workers must prove not only a breach but also damage (physical or psychological) and a causal link. Here the Advocate General justified the shift of the burden of proof on the grounds that: 'it is the employer that has the general overview of working conditions and requirements for these employees and that is best placed to evaluate what measures are suitable for dealing with any risks that are identified.'[71]

Therefore, it reinforces the procedural guarantee for workers and effective enforcement. Indeed, it is sufficient for the worker to provide prima facie evidence of risks to her safety and health and/or her child for the employer to have to assume the burden of providing otherwise.[72] 'It is then for the respondent to prove that the risk assessment did actually include such a specific assessment.'[73] The reversal of the burden of proof is essential in guaranteeing the effective enforcement of equal treatment, and the prevention of OSH risks.[74]

Beyond providing procedural clarifications, the Court also reflects on what risks should be assessed and how. In both cases, the workers' working conditions included complex shifts or partial night shifts. Risks related to night shifts are well-known, as highlighted by Commission Guidelines emphasising that the risk assessment should cover 'mental and physical fatigue and other types of physical and mental stress connected with the work done by workers within the meaning

[68] Eg Case C-32/93 *Webb*, Case C-177/88 *Dekker*.

[69] Case C-531/15 *Elda Otero Ramos v Servicio Galego de Saude and Instituto Nacional de la Seguridad Social.*

[70] Case C-41/17 *Isabel Gonzalez Castro v Mutua Umivale and Others.*

[71] Opinion pt 82, Case C-41/17 *Castro;* similar point made in Opinion pt 66, Case C-531/15 *Otero Ramos.*

[72] See I Marin Alonso, 'Preventive Protection of Breastfeeding and Sex Discrimination in European and National Judicial Practice: Reversal of the Burden of Proof in Cases of Incorrect Assessment of Occupational Risks (2019) 11 *Cuadernos Derecho Transnacional* 459–77.

[73] Summary of the judgment, Case C-41/17 *Castro.*

[74] Opinion pt 12, Case C-41/17 *Castro.*

of Article 2 of Directive 89/391/EEC'.[75] The Advocate General insists that the employer is the party required to conduct the risk assessment, which is consistent with Directive 89/391/EEC placing a duty on employers to take preventive action to ensure workers' safety and health for all aspects related to work.[76] And the risk assessment of Directive 92/85/EEC must take into account the preventive aspects of Directive 89/391/EEC.[77] According to the Court, risk assessment is a

> systemic examination of all aspects of work which comprises at least three phases:
>
> 1) identification of hazards (physical, chemical and biological agents; industrial processes; movements and postures; mental and physical fatigue; other physical and mental burden),
> 2) identification of worker categories which are exposed to one or several of those risks,
> 3) qualitative and quantitative risk assessment to assess whether or not the hazard identified entails a risk situation for workers.[78]

Therefore, these rulings from the CJEU contribute to the effective enforcement of the OSH principle of prevention by providing references on what risks should be assessed, how the employer should assess them, and providing workers with the 'procedural advantage' of the reversal of the burden of proof.

Even though the personal scope of these decisions is limited and Directive 92/85/EEC provides direct protection only to pregnant women, women who recently gave birth or are breastfeeding; there are still substantial references to the general provisions of Directive 89/391/EEC. Future research might want to investigate a way to expand the reasoning or the application of these decisions to all workers (eg the three phases of risk assessment). Indeed, the Advocate General in *Castro* highlighted the fact that risk assessment is a dynamic process and should be re-evaluated every time an individual worker's circumstances change.[79] One might hope that similar reasoning could be applied to working conditions in general, and that employers should be under an obligation to evaluate risk every time working conditions change.

4.2. Trade Unions as Key Actors in Litigation to Improve Occupational Safety and Health Prevention – Cases of France and the United Kingdom

At the national level, trade unions – through the appointment or election of health and safety representatives – are central actors in developing global prevention

[75] European Commission, DG for Employment, Social Affairs and Equal Opportunities (2010) *Study to support an Impact Assessment on further action at European level regarding Directive 2003/88/EC and the evolution of working time organisation*. Annex 1 Study on health and safety aspects of working time.

[76] Opinion pt 62, Case C-41/17 *Castro*.

[77] Opinion pt 44, Case C-531/15 *Otero Ramos*.

[78] Case C-531/15 *Otero Ramos*, pt 47–48.

[79] Opinion pt 44, Case C-531/15 *Otero Ramos*.

plans at the workplace. As already underlined, one essential way of enforcing the OSH principle effectively is through industrial enforcement. Trade unions have the capacity to contribute to effective enforcement of OSH prevention before the courts in two ways: (i) demanding the effective enforcement of their right to be consulted (within the meaning of Article 11 Directive 89/391/EEC), (ii) using litigation strategically to extend the protective scope of EU OSH Directives to atypical workers. Both have been illustrated by successful litigation in France and the United Kingdom. It is particularly interesting to compare them because these two countries have different legal traditions (ie civil law and common law), while still implementing the EU OSH Directives.[80] Additionally, the two situations examined in this section are complementary: in France, trade unions are enforcing rights that have been granted (Amazon's workers are employees, for example), while in the United Kingdom trade unions are using litigation to 'conquer new territory' by ensuring the prevention of risks for atypical workers (ie so-called 'limb (b) workers', who are not employees *stricto sensu* but who satisfy the legal criteria defining workers). The key element is that in all cases there has been reference to the purpose of Directive 89/391/EEC and none had a compensatory goal, but rather a preventive one.

4.2.1. France: Trade Unions and Workers' Representatives

The Covid-19 pandemic has massively disturbed societies at all levels, requiring major curtailments of individual freedoms and exceptional public health measures. Paradoxically, while the pandemic has been presented publicly as an invisible risk that could be anywhere (especially because of the risk of asymptomatic people spreading the virus), it seemed at first that workplaces had escaped the emergency. At the beginning of the pandemic, there was a narrative that Covid-19 was a public health issue, not an OSH one: it was enough to apply the public health recommendations and there would be no need to change workplace organisation. A ruling from the French Court of Appeal and a referee order issued in April and May 2020 – in the middle of the first wave – combined to alter this logic, highlighting that Covid-19 was indeed an OSH matter. This change was due to trade unions seizing the opportunity to stress the centrality of OSH in work organisation. The unions played a crucial role in elaborating a prevention plan in the workplace.

The first turning point was the decision of the Court of Appeal of Versailles on 24 April 2020 on working conditions at Amazon.[81] At that time, too, the French government adopted the first strict lockdown and closed all non-essential shops. Meanwhile, Amazon was considered to be providing 'essential services' and no

[80] Note that the case covered here was ruled on before 31 December 2020, so before the coming into force of the Brexit Withdrawal Agreement. At the moment of the ruling, EU OSH Directives were still fully applicable and part of the national legal system.

[81] Versailles, 14e ch, 24 avril 2020, no. 20/01993, SAS Amazon France Logistique c. Union syndicale solidaire.

limitations or restrictions were imposed. Therefore, and no doubt triggered by the fact that no one could leave their homes (except 'essential workers'), there was a huge increase in the volume of orders from Amazon. Amazon hired new workers to meet demand, but did not have time to train them properly. This combination of factors led to an increase in the density of workers in warehouses and an increase in the rhythm of work. Amazon's management sought to prevent Covid-19 infections by providing hand gel and masks and by recommending that workers maintain social distancing.

There were two main problems with this situation. First, the preventive measures were neither adequate nor adapted to what workers were experiencing, putting them at risk. Second, health and safety representatives were not consulted by the employer regarding changes in working conditions that might impact OSH, even though this is required by French and European law. Therefore, the trade unions launched an action to halt operations at Amazon until they had been consulted and appropriate measures – including a change in work organisation – could be adopted to provide adequate protection to all workers in the warehouse.

The Court of Appeal confirmed the decision of the *juge des référés du tribunal judiciaire de Nanterre*, requiring Amazon to restrict its activities to food products and medication, judging that the degree of workers' exposure to Covid-19 was too substantial. According to the Court, the employer's assessment of Covid-19 risk was insufficient and the protective measures inappropriate. It was the first time that the activity of an undertaking had been stopped as precautionary measure. It sent a strong signal that workers' health and safety were more important than a company's economic interest. The Court conditioned the restart of Amazon's activities on the carrying out by workers' representatives of an assessment of the risks due to Covid-19 in all its establishments, in light of Article L.4121-1 of the Labour Code (echoing Article 11 Directive 89/391/EEC). With this decision, the Court stressed that the workers' representatives should not have been informed a posteriori but should have been consulted a priori regarding the evaluation of the risk and the planning of preventive measures. With this, the Court recognised the fundamental role of health and safety representatives in the effective enforcement of the general principle of prevention. The Court also said that the nature of the risk (Covid-19) justified a re-organisation of work (and not only an adaptation, with the introduction of sanitary measures). In that respect, the Court observed that Amazon had not evaluated psychosocial risks (PSR) – particularly high in this context – and that the way the company proceeded was not 'enough considering the challenges posed by a pandemic'.

Here, the role of workers' representatives (with a mandate in OSH) is at the heart of the decision, but also the scope of what risk assessment should have covered (including psychosocial risks). Although this ruling was made in extraordinary times, it effectively enforces the rights of workers' representatives and contributes to better risk prevention at a time when workers are at their most vulnerable.

Similarly, in the *Renault* decision, the judge ruled that restarting operations during a pandemic is an important undertaking and likely to affect workers' health and safety. Workers' representatives should therefore be consulted (and not only informed).[82] The consultation should be some time in advance, so the workers' representatives have the necessary time to read the relevant documents and to assess the situation. Here once again, the main question was whether to include workers' representatives in the process of risk assessment and what the appropriate measures (collective and individual) would be to prevent the risk of contracting Covid-19. The tribunal also emphasised that before re-opening the factory, each worker should be trained (to apply the measures) before restarting work.

In both rulings before the French Court and Tribunal, the judges ruled in favour of the workers. This also illustrates that judicial enforcement can actively be used for prevention to fulfil the principal aims of OSH regulation, ie ongoing prevention of workers' infection, not only the provision of a remedy when there is a breach. Therefore, there might also be some space for the trade unions and workers' representatives to adopt a more strategic use of judicial enforcement to ensure the application of their rights at the workplace.

4.2.2. United Kingdom: Trade Unions as Actors of Regulatory Change

The pandemic has also been an important factor in emphasising the existing gaps in the legislative scope of OSH. The jurisprudence mentioned previously demonstrates that judicial enforcement can be an effective way to enforce OSH principles for employees. However, labour market deregulation, the casualisation of work and the fragmentation of employment status have been going on for several decades now.[83] Existing research has already examined the impact and consequences of these changes on the OSH protection afforded to workers, depending on employment status.[84] The most striking – and seen most often in the media – face of this has been on-demand gig-workers. To ensure clarity, 'on-demand gig-workers' in this sense are workers who utilise smartphones and mobile applications in performing their work locally.[85] These workers have been called 'essential workers',

[82] *Trib Jud Havre*, réf, RG 20/00143.

[83] See S Deakin, 'Addressing labour market segmentation: The role of labour law' (Cambridge, University of Cambridge, Centre for Business Research, 2013); V De Stefano, 'A tale of oversimplification and deregulation: the mainstream approach to labour market segmentation and recent responses to the crisis in European countries' (2014) 43(3) *Industrial Law Journal* 253–85; P Schoukens and A Barrio, 'The changing concept of work: When does typical work become atypical?' (2017) 8(4) *European Labour Law Journal* 306–32.

[84] See R Johnstone, M Quinlan and D Walters, 'Statutory occupational health and safety workplace arrangements for the modern labour market' (2005) 47(1) *Journal of Industrial Relations* 93–116; M Quinlan, C Mayhew and P Bohle, 'The global expansion of precarious employment, work disorganization, and consequences for occupational health: a review of recent research' (2001) 31(2) *International Journal of Health Services* 335–414.

[85] D Howcroft, T Dundon and C Inversi, 'Fragmented Demands: Platform and Gig-Working in the UK' in Sullivan et al (eds), *Zero Hours and On-call Work in Anglo-Saxon Countries* (Singapore, Springer, 2019) 216.

for whom working from home was not an option, and whose services are necessary to society. These categories of workers were on the front line and exposed to Covid-19. In contrast to regular employees, who could rely on the OSH protective framework (and go to court to demand its effective enforcement if necessary), gig workers, because they count as self-employed, could not benefit from the protective dimension of OSH principles and their legal framework.

In the United Kingdom over recent years there has been a judicial battle around the status of on-demand gig workers, such as Uber drivers. In February 2021, the Supreme Court ruled that Uber drivers should be recognised as limb (b) workers and not as self-employed.[86] However, even as limb (b) workers there was a risk that they would not benefit from the same level of protection as employees. This question of equivalent levels of OSH protection provided in the United Kingdom in relation to EU law has been raised by the Independent Workers Union of Great Britain (IWGB).

The IWGB brought an application for judicial review in the High Court (HC) seeking a declaration that the United Kingdom had failed to implement in national law two EU-OSH Directives: Framework Directive 89/391/EEC and the Directive on Personal Protective equipment (PPE).

In November 2020, IWGB won a judicial review claim against the UK government (*IWGB v SSWP and Others*), effectively establishing that the UK government had failed to implement Articles 8(4) and 8(5) of Directive 89/391/EEC and Article 3 of Directive 89/656/EC (on personal protective equipment). The direct effect of this ruling has been to ensure that limb (b) workers have access to PPE and can withdraw from work in case of serious and immediate danger without fearing any less favourable treatment. What was interesting was the concepts discussed in the course of reaching this judgment.

One key discussion revolved around the personal scope of Directive 89/391/EEC and the meaning of 'worker' (Article 3(a) Directive 89/391/EEC). The main argument of the defendant (ie the UK government) was that Directive 89/391/EEC is supposed to be implemented according to national legal tradition, and thus there was a certain degree of flexibility in defining who could be considered a 'worker' within the meaning of the Directive. Therefore, the UK government defended a restrictive national approach limiting the scope of implementation of Directive 89/391/EEC to employees and not workers. On the other side, the claimant (ie the IWGB) argued for a broad understanding of the definition of 'worker' by claiming that a purposive approach must be applied to the interpretation of the OSH Directives.[87] In their legal argument, the IWGB referred to previous CJEU jurisprudence in which a broad interpretation was applied to the concepts of 'working environment', 'safety' and 'health' to clarify the scope of Article 118a (now 153

[86] *Uber BV v Aslam* [2021] UKSC 5 ('Uber (SC)').

[87] *R (on the application of the IWGB) v Secretary of State for Work and Pensions and others*, pt 54.

TFEU),[88] but also to a case in which a broad interpretation of the scope of Article 2 of the Framework Directive was applied.[89]

In the Court ruling, Judge Chamberlain J referred to the 13th recital of the Framework Directive to justify a single meaning of 'worker' common to all Member States to avoid 'different levels of safety and health protection' as between Member States and 'competition at the expense of safety and health'. According to him, 'the *objectives* of the Framework Directive suggest a scope fixed by reference to a single EU-wide meaning'.[90] He also referred to Article 31 of the Charter as an interpretive aid to determine the purpose, and so the scope of the Framework Directive. The judgment reads as follow:

> The broad reading is also supported by Article 31 of the Charter. I accept that the Charter is no more than an interpretive aid … But the fact that the drafters, drawing on the Framework Directive, chose to confer the right to 'working conditions which respect his or her health, safety and dignity' on 'every worker', without seeking to confine the application of that term, seems to me to support as broad an interpretation as possible of the term when used in the Framework Directive.[91]

This judgment improves effective enforcement of OSH in two ways. First, the direct effect on effective enforcement is to guarantee the right of (limb (b)) workers to have access to PPE and to have the right to withdraw from dangerous and imminent danger. These rights have been particularly relevant in a time of pandemic when PPE might be the only way to ensure adequate protection, and leaving the workplace is sometimes the only choice left to workers to preserve their OSH when the employer is not respecting their obligations. The second effect is indirect, or more theoretical. Nevertheless, the rationale and reference to the Framework Directive to justify the extension of scope to atypical workers can lead to the application of the general principle of prevention to 'more' workers, which improves the effective enforcement of OSH to situations in which the framework did not apply previously. Even though it is a UK domestic ruling, one can hypothesise that similar reasoning and reference to OSH Directives and the Charter might lead to similar developments in other Member States.

5. Conclusion

The three main forms of enforcement complement each other in a 'hierarchical' way to guarantee effective enforcement of the EU OSH preventive principles. Industrial relations enforcement via workers' health and safety representatives

[88] Case C-84/94 *United Kingdom v Council* [1997] ICR 443 at [15].

[89] Cases C-397/01 to 403/01 *Pfeiffer v Deutsches Rotes Kreuz, Kreisverband Waldshut eV* [2005] ECR 1307 at [52].

[90] *R (on the application of the IWGB) v Secretary of State for Work and Pensions and others*, pt 82(i).

[91] Ibid, pt 82(n).

is the 'immediate'/direct way to enforce OSH at the workplace. Workers' health and safety representatives report the reality of shop-floor risks and integrate it into a prevention plan, when they are consulted. This aspect guarantees adequate prevention. However, it is their complementary role to monitor employers' decisions impacting OSH, combined with their possibility of appealing to the labour inspectorate when there is a breach of the principle of prevention, that has the potential to turn them into effective enforcers. Two crucial factors are required to realise this potential: (i) the presence of health and safety representatives and (ii) a responsive labour inspectorate. Thus, administrative enforcement represented by national labour inspectorates can be seen as a supportive form of enforcement, and even as the primary way of enforcement in situations where there are no health and safety representatives. Unfortunately, a common shift within the EU towards risk-based inspections, coupled with significant cuts in labour inspectorate resources has resulted in under-staffed national labour inspectorates that cannot always adequately address health and safety representatives' complaints. Even though, historically, labour inspectorates have been – and should be – essential to enforce OSH preventive principles effectively, it is unlikely that they are fulfilling their preventive role under the current circumstances. Hence, judicial enforcement through litigation appears to be a fundamental safeguard to effective enforcement of OSH principles. Cases before both the CJEU and national courts have demonstrated the potential roles of judicial bodies in enforcing the preventive dimension of OSH principles. The CJEU provided clarification on the circumstances leading to the reversal of the burden of proof and the obligation to assess risks, which is an important procedural improvement towards effective enforcement of OSH principles. Additionally, national judicial bodies have effectively enforced the right of health and safety representatives to be consulted during the employer's elaboration of the prevention plan, leading to better prevention and protection of workers' health. Judicial enforcement has also proven to broaden the protective scope of the OSH legislative framework, hence extending the application of OSH prevention principles to workers who did not benefit from them previously. Thus, the only way to guarantee effective enforcement of OSH prevention principles by workers and their representatives, at a time when labour inspectorates are reduced to reactive inspections, is to grant access to courts to workers and their representatives whenever employers do not respect their obligations, even in the absence of damages.

PART III

Mechanisms and Specific Actors for Enforcing EU Labour Law

15

Enforcing EU Law via Collective Action

GIOVANNI ORLANDINI

1. Introduction

It is of course superfluous to point out that national regulations on the right to strike differ considerably in the Member States of the European Union (EU). Each national law on strike action is conditioned by the characteristics of national industrial relations systems, to the point that it is even difficult to trace the various regulations to common regulatory 'models'.

An attempt was masterfully ventured by Bill Wedderburn, in an essay that has become (with good reason) a classic of European labour law.[1] This British scholar, wondering about the possibility of identifying a common European standard, found one of the main elements of divergence between national systems in the distinction between disputes over rights and disputes over interests, unknown in many of them. The question is connected with the more general one of the purposes that can be pursued with strike action and the function attributed to industrial conflict in the legal system.

Therefore, the issue of the enforcement of EU law 'via' collective action needs, first of all, to be addressed on a comparative level, in order to highlight how this path is precluded in many Member States. This is, however, an approach that obviously cannot be dealt with in a thorough and systematic manner here. Only a few hints will therefore be devoted to issues of national law in the initial part of this chapter (section 2).

If, from a comparative perspective, the analysis moves to the level of the EU legal order, any reasoning – both *de jure condito* and *de jure condendo* – on the legal foundation of the right to take collective action to enforce EU law seems to find an insurmountable limit in Article 153.5 TFEU which, as known, excludes the competence of the EU legislator to intervene in the matter. Considering this limit, the issue under consideration should be approached only according to a 'negative

[1] W Wedderburn, 'The Right to Strike: Is There a European Standard?' in W Wedderburn, *Employment Rights in Britain and Europe: Selected Papers in Labour Law* (Lawrence & Wishart, 1991) 276 ff.

approach': that is, it is only possible to ask whether EU law limits or allows the use of the strike as an enforcement tool, when this is legitimate in a Member State. And as is well known, the huge debate following the *Viking* and *Laval* cases developed on the basis of this approach.

In the following pages we will try to overcome this approach and to propose a possible 'positive approach' to the topic at stake: it is a question of analysing whether, and in what way, on the contrary, in EU law there are legal instruments for protecting collective action that may ensure its exercise even in the event that (for the aforementioned limits regarding conflicts over rights) national law does not recognise it as an enforcement tool. The issue of enforcing EU law via collective action is then intertwined and overlaps with the broader one of enforcing the right to strike via EU law.

To deal with this issue, it is first of all necessary to ask whether Article 28 of the EU Charter of Fundamental Rights (CFREU) incorporates a notion of the right to strike that is broader – in relation to its purposes – than that present in the national legal systems inspired by the so-called 'organic' model of the regulation of industrial conflict. If an 'evolutionary and progressive' notion of the right to strike can be based on EU primary law (section 3), the question is how and to what extent can such a norm be invoked in disputes related to the implementation of EU law, as provided for by Article 51.1 CFREU.

A first answer to this question can be found in the context of the single market. Indeed Article 28 could be used to 'subvert' the *Laval* doctrine, expanding the scope for collective action when exercised to enforce the employment rights of posted workers: section 4 is dedicated to this perspective, in which the legal reasoning is conducted taking into account both the possible effects of the clauses safeguarding the right to strike included in the recent EU legislation on posting of workers (both the 2014 Enforcement Directive and the 2018 Directive amending the Posted Workers Directive) and the evolution of CJEU case law (namely, the 'twin' judgments *Hungary v European Parliament* and *Poland v European Parliament*).

The adoption of the aforementioned 'positive approach' suggests looking for legal tools in the EU legal order to protect the right to strike, beyond the scope of the single market. Therefore, the second part of the chapter is focused on asking whether it would be possible to use EU law to oppose acts of the employer sanctioning workers who go on strike to claim their rights (that is, to contest retaliatory behaviour). This question is tackled by means of references to both anti-discrimination law (section 5) and provisions on protection against victimisation widespread in many labour law Directives (section 6).

Finally, the question of a possible legal basis for transnational collective action is treated. This kind of action raises issues of private international law, that is, whether disputes regarding the selection of competent jurisdiction and of applicable law derive from its exercise. It is therefore worth asking whether and in what way private international rules (provided both in Rome I and Rome II Regulations, and also in the Posted Workers Directive) can serve to protect the workers involved in a transnational action, allowing selection of the legislation of the Member State more favourable to the exercise of the right to strike (section 7).

2. Conflicts Over Interests and Conflicts Over Rights

The distinction between disputes over interests and disputes over rights is associated with a traditionally 'participatory' model of industrial relations with a high rate of 'institutionalisation', characterised by the presence of strong centralised trade unions (as in German-speaking and Scandinavian countries), whereas this distinction tends to lose importance the more pluralist and conflictual an industrial relations system is (as in the systems of Mediterranean countries).[2] In the latter, strike action is considered to be a worker's individual right, while in the former it is a collective right, and as such considered a trade union prerogative. In these systems – which can be defined 'organic' models of strike regulation[3] – strikes are functionally connected with collective bargaining, and the signing of a collective agreement generally entails a peace obligation. Moreover, the legitimacy of political strikes is usually excluded, because the aim of collective action in this case is not the signing of a collective agreement, and the employer is not the counterpart of the unions calling for the strike. Conversely, in 'individualist' systems, no implicit peace obligation follows from the signing of a collective agreement, and strike action can legitimately be also aimed at demands of a 'political' nature.

The Italian and the German systems, respectively, can be taken as ideal types of the two models. In Germany, the labour courts have derived the right to strike from the Constitutional provision recognising freedom of association;[4] and from the Constitution, national courts have deduced the principle of *extrema ratio*. It is therefore undisputed that, if a dispute arises over the recognition of a 'right', it is up to the competent courts to decide; just as it is common ground that the conflict is legitimate only if its purpose is the conclusion of a collective agreement. This, however, does not mean that there are no margins of uncertainty regarding the legitimacy of a strike proclaimed during the validity of a collective agreement, because this depends on whether or not the claim is strictly attributable to the matters governed by such a collective agreement. It should not be ignored that in Germany (as in other 'organic' systems, such as in Scandinavia) the peace obligation emanating from the collective agreement is, as a starting point, relative, not absolute.[5]

Lacking a definition of 'strike' in Article 40 of the Italian Constitution – which affirms it as a fundamental right – national courts have recognised that it is up to workers and trade unions to identify the aim to be pursued, and no 'aprioristic'

[2] On the historical roots of the different 'models' of industrial relations systems in Europe see, for all, C Crouch, *Industrial Relations and European State Traditions* (Oxford University Press, 1993) esp ch 1.

[3] Wedderburn, n 1 above at 297.

[4] B Waas, 'The Right to Strike: Germany' in B Waas (ed), *The Right to Strike: A Comparative View* (Kluwer Law Int, 2016) 236 ff.

[5] In Swedish, Danish and Finnish labour law, also during the period when a collective agreement is in force trade unions can use collective action to force the employer to pay outstanding wages due indisputably to the employees. Also sympathy action is regarded not to be related to their own collective agreement and therefore as falling outside the peace obligation (on Sweden, see Malberg and Johansson in Waas, n 4 at 525 ff).

limitation can be imposed regarding the purposes of the strike.[6] As the right to strike is qualified as an individual worker's right,[7] not only does the signing or conclusion of a collective agreement not entail an implicit peace obligation, but also peace clauses provided for by a collective agreement bind only the signatory trade unions and not the workers.

A comparison between the Italian and German systems allows one to highlight the profound divergence existing within the EU regarding the aims that can be pursued with strike action. It should therefore be concluded that the question of collective action as a possible tool for enforcing EU law can be addressed and resolved only on the basis of the law of individual Member States.

It is obviously not possible to carry out such a comparative analysis here. It is enough therefore to suggest some issues that may arise in systems in which the distinction between conflicts over interests and conflicts over rights is relevant; indeed, such issues do not arise in the systems that admit the strike to enforce rights deriving from national legislation or collective agreements in force.

The distinction between conflicts over rights and conflicts over interests can become problematic if it refers to rights recognised by EU sources, instead of by national sources of law. This can make assessment of the legitimacy of strike action in the Member States that recognise this distinction problematic. The issue can in fact be declined in different terms, depending on the type of sources on the basis of which (hypothetically) the enforcement is claimed through collective action. Surely a dispute concerning the interpretation or application of a national law transposing an EU source should be considered a dispute over rights. But the distinction between disputes over interests and over rights vanishes if applied to strikes aimed at claiming rights recognised in a directive not correctly transposed (or not transposed at all) by national legislation. Or again, we can hypothesise a strike aimed at demanding interests that find their legitimacy in EU law rules that do not have direct effect, and which therefore do not confer rights in the proper sense on the workers of a given Member State (as is the case with reference to most of the 'social' provisions of the CFREU).[8] In other words, collective action can be configured as a (potentially) legitimate tool for enforcing EU law even in countries that deny their legitimacy when it concerns a dispute over rights, in cases where such rights are recognised in provisions of EU law without direct effect in national law (and therefore cannot be considered rights in the strict sense in the national legal order).

With reference to the 'conventional' sources of EU law, the (unsolved) problem of the effectiveness of transnational collective agreements comes into play,

[6] See the seminal judgment of the Corte di Cassazione n 711/80.

[7] See Giugni, *Diritto sindacale* (Cacucci, 2014) 257 ff on the right to strike as an individual right to be executed collectively.

[8] Case C-176/12 *Association de médiation sociale v Union locale des syndicats CGT* [2014], para 36, concerning Art 27 CFREU.

or of sectoral collective agreements not implemented by an act of the EU pursuant to Article 155.2 TFEU.[9] A strike to ensure their implementation in national legal systems should not (in principle) involve a dispute over rights, nor should any peace obligations be inferred from the agreement; on the contrary, collective action becomes (in the absence of legal constraints that oblige companies or national social partners to implement it) an essential tool for its implementation in national law.

3. For an Evolutionary and Progressive Interpretation of Article 28 CFREU

The double reference to the 'interests' of workers contained in Article 28 CFREU indicates that its drafting was influenced by the German model of strike regulation.[10] The sources of international law, however, that concur with Article 28 to define the content of the right of collective action in the EU legal system (namely, Article 6.4 ESC rev and ILO Convention No 87) do not provide clear and consistent indications regarding its teleological limits. Precisely the absence of a defined framework of principles in this regard leaves possible 'progressive' readings of the norm of the Charter open, that is, aimed at expanding the spaces of practicability of collective action. Moreover, the right to strike is by its nature a right with variable content and exposed to evolutionary interpretations, that is, conditioned by changes affecting the legal systems and systems of industrial relations in which it exists.

Such an evolutionary interpretation is testified to by both the jurisprudence of international bodies (namely, ECSR and CFA) and the case law of the ECtHR.[11] If it is true that all international sources seem to incorporate principles present in the organic model, it is equally true that the competent international bodies have progressively adopted an approach aimed at expanding the margins of practicability of industrial conflict beyond the borders in which such a model limits it. In particular, this has occurred by excluding the possibility of attributing a mere

[9] On the right to strike in relation to sectoral social dialogue process see also: T Novitz, 'The EU and the Right to Strike' (2016) 27(1) *King's Law Journal* 50–51.

[10] On Art 28 CFREU see: comments by C Barnard, in S Peers, T Harvey, J Kenner, A Ward (eds), *The EU Charter of Fundamental Rights: a Commentary* (Hart, 2014) and F Dorssemont and M Rocca, 'Article 28 – Right of collective bargaining and action' in F Dorssemont, K Lörcher, S Clauwaert, M Schmitt (eds), *The Charter of Fundamental Rights of the EU and the Employment Relation* (Hart, 2019).

[11] The reference is to the approach inaugurated in the *Demir and Baykara v Turkey* judgment (Application No 34503/97, 12.11.2018) based on an intertextual canon of interpretation that makes Art 11 ECHR permeable to the most progressive interpretations of the various sources of international labour law (on the recent judgments of the ECtHR on the right to strike, following *Demir and Baykara*, see Vogt et al, *The Right to Strike in International Law* (Hart, 2020) 87ff.

instrumental function to collective action with regard to the signing of a collective agreement.[12] Once the right to strike has been released from the mere 'contractual' function, any social and economic interest of workers should be included among the purposes pursued with it,[13] just as exercise of the right should be released from the peace obligation resulting from the stipulation of the collective agreement.[14]

This does not allow the conclusion that international law definitely guarantees the possibility of acting collectively also to assert rights. But neither does it make it possible to exclude that Article 28 could be interpreted and applied in such a way as to protect workers who act for these purposes.

This conclusion is corroborated by the peculiar legal context in which Article 28 is placed. The open and polysemic character of this provision is in fact imposed precisely by its particular (and problematic) field of application, which is quite different from that of the other sources of international law. Indeed, Article 28 is not aimed at setting minimum standards compliance with which by a Member State is to be monitored; but its function is to ensure that both the Member States and the EU respect its content when they apply EU law in their respective fields of competence (Article 51.1 CFREU).

This brings us to the question of the effects that the adoption of a certain notion of the right to strike can produce in the EU legal system (and, consequently, in national legal systems). If the perspective from which one starts is that of *effet utile*, the norm must be given a meaning that ensures it some effect.

As even the *Viking* and *Laval* judgments show, any collective action (whatever its purposes or form) must be considered in principle legitimate if it is so for national law; indeed, only 'external' limits are imposed by EU law, deriving from respect for other rights or freedoms protected by it (namely, the fundamental economic freedoms). It remains to be seen whether Article 28 can be invoked to raise national standards. Starting from the perspective of the *effet utile*, it should be assumed that Article 28 can (hypothetically) serve to strengthen and broaden the space for exercising collective action, compared with what is provided for in some Member States, or to prevent limitations not compatible with it. The question that needs to be answered is whether and when Article 28 can be applied in this sense, taking into account the limits that Article 51.1 CFREU laid down regarding the scope of application of the provisions of the Charter.[15]

[12] The concept of collective bargaining is understood by the experts of Strasbourg in a broad sense (conclusions XIX-2010, Germany); an even broader notion of the right to strike, in relation to its purposes, can be derived from ILO Convention No 87 as interpreted by the CFA; see T Novitz, *International and European Protection of the Right to Strike* (Oxford University Press, 2003) 290 ff.

[13] F Dorssemont, 'The Right to Take Collective Action in the Council of Europe: A Tale of One City, Two Instruments and Two Bodies' (2016) 27(1) *King's Law Journal* 80.

[14] In this sense, see: R Quintana and DMC Barreto, 'Collective Bargaining and Right to Strike: New Challenges' in J López (ed), *Collective Bargaining and Collective Actions* (Hart, 2019) 71.

[15] A Koukiadaki, 'Application (Article 51) and Limitations (Article 52(1))' in Dorssemont et al, above n 10, especially 109 ff.

The issue of enforcement of EU law through collective action is thus intertwined and overlaps with the broader one of enforcement through EU law of the right to strike. In fact, it is a question of understanding whether Article 28 is judicially cognisable to guarantee the right to strike even beyond the limits configured in individual Member States, so that such a right can be exercised to assert the application of and compliance with EU law.

To raise, if not to answer this question, or at least to suggest some interpretative path that makes a positive answer plausible, it is worth addressing it first of all in the context of EU law in which the issue of strike action has been more widely debated to date, namely that of the single market for services.

4. Subverting the *Laval* Doctrine: The Scenarios Opened Up by the Legislative and Case Law Counter-movement

It is not a stretch to assert that the *Laval* case concerns a dispute regarding the use of collective action as an instrument for enforcing EU law. In fact, by censuring a strike by Swedish workers, the ECJ denied that it could be used to impose compliance with the protections due to posted workers on the basis of Directive 96/71. Industrial action, the Court affirmed, cannot replace national law transposing the Posted Workers Directive to determine the remuneration due to workers posted to the territory of a Member State; nor can the weapon of industrial conflict be used to obtain application of collective agreements that have no general effect. The uncertainty that would ensue is not compatible with the principles on which the services market is based, which the Court deduces from Article 56 TFEU.[16]

The Swedish legislator has managed to preserve the use of collective action as an enforcement tool in the specific context of transnational posting, while respecting the dicta of the CJEU. The current legislation provides that social partners can define the minimum standard to be paid for posted workers and that the Swedish authorities must provide information on these standards to foreign service providers. If the conditions of a foreign service provider fall below these standards, trade unions are allowed to take collective action to enforce the Swedish minimum standards for posted workers. And the law explicitly states that collective action is not unlawful as long as the trade union demands do not exceed the minimum under the Posted Workers Directive.[17]

The question of the protection of the right to strike within the single market, however, certainly cannot be considered resolved by the *Laval* judgment, although it is thanks to the judgment that the issue has acquired centrality in the EU legal system.

[16] Case C-341/05 *Laval* [2007] ECR I-11767, para 110.

[17] The current rules are the result of the Social Democratic government repealing the so-called *Lex Laval* in June 2017.

As controversial and questionable as the *Laval* judgment may be considered, it must be acknowledged that it has one undoubted merit: that of having 'revitalised' the debate around industrial conflict, at an historical moment in which its decline has been highlighted or even its disappearance announced by many. The alarm caused by the potential effects of the 'generalised' application of the *Laval* doctrine in the Member States has fuelled a huge debate at both academic and institutional level around the right to strike,[18] reinforcing awareness that the defence of the European social model cannot ignore the effective protection of this right. It can be said that the *Laval* case provoked a sort of Polanyian 'counter-movement',[19] aimed at damming the effects of the judgment, first on the level of the academic debate, then on the level of EU legislation and of the case law of the CJEU.

This counter-movement, on a legislative level, has obviously found its limit in Article 153.5, which prevents the EU from adopting acts with a 'direct' impact on regulation of the right to strike. With the Monti II Regulation proposal, the Commission tried to intervene in the matter, moving within the narrow limits of competence recognised by the Treaty, in the wake of what it had already done with free movement of goods.[20] But, as known, the proposal was blocked by the activation of the so-called 'yellow card procedure'. The proposal found an insurmountable obstacle in the diffidence (widespread in the Member States and among the social partners) towards an act which, instead of damming the effects of the *Laval* doctrine, risked making them even more binding.[21] Because Monti II regulation has not seen the light, it is not possible to assess whether this fear was founded. Therefore, the question remains whether (contrary to what was feared), through the proposed special mechanism for mediation of industrial conflicts coordinated by the Commission, the exercise of collective action could have found unprecedented spaces for legitimation at the level of the EU legal system, even wider than those recognised in national legal systems.

It is a fact that, after the failure of the Monti II regulation, the legislative 'counter-movement' has firmly followed an approach based on clauses safeguarding the right to strike as guaranteed at national level (so-called 'Monti clauses').[22] First, pending the *Viking* and *Laval* cases, the Directive on the single market was intended to neutralise the effects of the (imminent) judgments of the Court by providing

[18] A critical synthesis in C Barnard, 'The calm after the storm: Time to reflect on EU (labour) law scholarship after the decisions in Viking and Laval' in A Bogg, C Costello and ACL Davies (eds), *Research Handbook on EU Labour* (Cheltenham, Edward Elgar, 2015) 337 ff.

[19] The reference is to the classic book by K Polanyi, *The Great Transformation. The Political and Economic Origin of Our Time* (Beacon Press, 2001).

[20] European Commission, COM(2012)130 def.

[21] M Rocca, 'The Proposal for a (So-Called) 'Monti II' Regulation on the Exercise of the Right to Take Collective Action within the Context of the Freedom of Establishment and the Freedom to Provide Services: Changing without Reversing, Regulating without Affecting' (2012) 3(1) *European Labour Law Journal* 19 ff.

[22] The term 'Monti clause' is due to the 'Monti' Regulation No 2679/98 regarding free movement of goods, which first provided for it (Art 2).

that this 'Directive does not affect the right … to take industrial action in accordance with national law and practices which respect Community law' (Article 1, para 7, Directive 2006/123); similar 'safeguard clauses' have been inserted in subsequent directives on posted workers.[23] It can therefore be said that there is no area of the single market for services in which the right to take collective action is not protected by EU legislation. This does not necessarily guarantee the legitimacy of any collective action falling within the scope of this legislation. The illegitimacy of a strike could in fact derive from two reasons. The first relates to the (in fact) purely 'immune' value of the provisions at stake: if they were intended only to avoid interference of EU law in national systems, the right to strike is guaranteed if and within the limits in which such systems recognise it. That is, the safeguard clause would be compatible with any limit to the right to strike provided for by national law, even if in contrast with the standards fixed by Article 28 CFREU. The second reason concerns the persistent applicability of the *Laval* doctrine which, as it is based on Article 56 TFEU, should not be superseded by European legislation.

This second issue was addressed by the CJEU in the 'twin' judgments *Hungary v European Parliament* and *Poland v European Parliament*,[24] with which the appeal of the two states for the annulment of Directive 96/71 was rejected. Among the points of the Directive challenged by the applicants there was also the supposed contrast between the 'safeguard clause' provided for by Article 1, paragraph 1, letter b), Directive 2018/957 and what the CJEU affirmed in the *Laval* judgment on the basis of Article 56 TFEU. According to the CJEU, the question is unfounded because such a clause does not 'in any way' remove the right of collective action from the application of EU law:

> On the contrary, since that provision refers to fundamental rights as recognised at Union level, it means that the exercise by workers of their rights of collective action, in the context of a posting of workers subject to the provisions of the amended Directive 96/71, must be assessed in the light of EU law, as it has been interpreted by the Court.[25]

The Court therefore excludes that the 'safeguard clauses' have a properly 'immune' efficacy, or that thanks to them the judgment of balancing between the right to collective action and economic freedom is excluded 'a priori'. This conclusion can lead to an interpretation of these clauses that deprives them of any legal effect. As such, it would be an interpretation that is incompatible with the abovementioned principle of the *effet utile* which, on the contrary, requires recognising some legal effect to Article 1, paragraph 1, letter b), Directive 2018/957. The words (indeed ambiguous) of the CJEU can then be read not as a mere confirmation of the *Laval* doctrine, but rather as an opening to its possible overcoming.

[23] Art 1, para 2, Directive 2014/67 and Art 1, para 1, letter b), Directive, 2018/957 which introduces the new Art 1, para -1 bis in Directive 96/71.

[24] Case C-620/18 *Hungary v European Parliament and Council of EU* [2020]; Case C-626/18 *Poland v European Parliament and Council of EU* [2020].

[25] Case C-620/18, para 168.

This conclusion is suggested by the assertion that the evaluation – 'in the light of EU law' – of the right to collective action must be made by referring to the fundamental rights recognized at the level of the Union. In fact, one can grasp the implicit reference to a different balance between economic freedoms and the right to collective action, which places the latter (at least) on the same level as market freedoms, in the wake of the well-known theory of 'double balancing' by several parties proposed in legal literature[26] and endorsed by Advocate General Trstenjiack in her opinion on the *Commission v Germany* case.[27]

What is most interesting to ask here, however, is whether there is another scenario which would lead not so much to a simple 'correction' of the *Laval* doctrine, but rather to its 'subversion'. In other words, it is a question of reflecting on the possibility of basing the workers' right to take collective action on the 'safeguard clause', even if this is considered to be unlawful under national law. That is, one might ask whether it is possible to establish a 'balance' between economic freedom and the right to strike at the level of the EU legal system that prevents Member States from limiting the latter in a way that is not compatible with the standards deducible from Article 28 CFREU. Doing this in order to attribute a 'positive' legal effect to this provision is excluded if the question of the protection of the right to strike is expressed in exclusively 'immunity' terms (ie defence of national law from the 'infiltration' of EU law).

This perspective is at least conceivable by going back to what the CJEU affirms in the 'twin' judgments mentioned above. The fact that the Court does make reference to the fundamental rights recognized at the level of the Union implicitly suggests reading Article 28 as a rule that establishes 'distinct and autonomous' standards for the protection of collective action with respect to national laws; and therefore, hypothetically, even higher. This sentence must then be read in light of what the Court affirms in the same judgments to justify the legal basis of Directive 2018/957.

In tackling the questions related to the legal basis, the Court in fact resolves a crucial theoretical problem regarding the principles of the single market, a problem raised by Paul Davies in the aftermath of the adoption of Directive 96/71,[28] but which until now has been unanswered: how can a directive be based on the Treaty provisions on freedom to provide services (Articles 53 and 62 TFEU) if it clearly does not serve to protect such freedom but rather to limit its exercise? According to the Court, the answer lies in the fact that:

> in relation to the free movement of goods, persons, services and capital the measures adopted by the EU legislature … not only have the objective of facilitating the exercise of one of those freedoms, but also seek to ensure, when necessary, the protection of

[26] First, C Barnard, 'A Proportionate Response to Proportionality in the Field of Collective Action' (2012) 37(2) *European Law Review* 117ff.

[27] Opinion of AG Trestenjak, 14.4.2010. C-271/08.

[28] P Davies, 'Single Market or Protection of National Labour Systems?' (1997) 34(3) *Common Market Law Revue* 571ff.

> other fundamental interests recognised by the Union which may be affected by that freedom.[29]

In particular with regard to the possibility of changing the balance between economic freedom and workers' rights in favour of the latter, as happened through Directive 2018/957:

> the EU legislature cannot be denied the possibility of adapting that act to any change in circumstances or advances in knowledge, having regard to its task of safeguarding the general interests recognised by the FEU Treaty and of taking into account the overarching objectives of the European Union laid down in Article 9 of that Treaty, including the requirements pertaining to the promotion of a high level of employment and the guarantee of adequate social protection. (para 41)

The Court therefore uses the so-called horizontal social clause of Article 9 TFEU to (re)interpret the Treaty rules that protect economic freedoms. In the opinion of the Court, Article 9 TFEU justifies an EU intervention whose purpose is not simply to protect the freedom to provide services, but rather to ensure the freedom to provide services 'on a fair basis'.[30] The social aim of the protection of workers is thus assumed as co-essential with the market freedoms on which the single market is based, and not as a mere 'external' limit that may be invoked by the Member States in defence of public interests protected by their national systems: for this reason, the provisions of the Treaty that recognise economic freedoms can also act as a legal basis for interventions by the European legislator aimed, in fact, at limiting them.

The systematic consequences of these statements are potentially very significant, because the consolidated relationship between market rules (guaranteed by EU sources) and social and labour rights (guaranteed at national level) is reversed; a relationship which is at the origin of the process of downgrading labour standards induced by the integration of the single market. In the twin judgments the Court seems to affirm that workers' rights are no longer to be considered only in terms of 'exceptions', which the Member States can invoke just in order to derogate from the principles promoting fundamental economic freedoms.

It is therefore possible to argue that through the 'safeguard clauses' the European legislator not only intended to preserve national laws protecting the right to strike, but also to ensure that (also in this area) the freedom to provide services must be guaranteed 'on a fair basis', that is, in a way which respects the fundamental right of collective action recognised 'at Union level' (ie by Article 28 CFREU). If this perspective is adopted, Article 28 would become judicially cognisable to the benefit of workers and trade unions sanctioned under national law for strikes aimed at claiming the rights provided for by Directive 96/71, both in the case of strikes '*à*

[29] Case C-620/18, para 105.
[30] Case C-626/18, paras 56 and 90.

la Laval' (ie carried out by the workers of the host state), and in the case of strikes carried out by posted workers in violation of the limits established by their own national law.[31] The latter hypothesis is very likely, given the limits to exercising the right to strike often provided for in the laws of the Member States 'exporting' posted workers within the EU (first and foremost, central and eastern European Member States[32]).

The fact that the safeguard clause is also included in the Enforcement Directive (Article 1, paragraph 2, Directive 2014/67) helps to strengthen the proposed perspective. This provision should be considered invokable by workers if they act to claim compliance with the conditions of employment provided for by Directive 96/71; otherwise, such provision would be deprived of any legal meaning. Indeed, because the Enforcement Directive concerns enforcement measures rather than the employment conditions of posted workers, Article 1, paragraph 2 should be applicable if workers take collective action as a means of enforcement, complementary to those prescribed and regulated by the same Directive. This is regardless of whether such collective action is provided for by Member State law.

By adopting the proposed approach, not only would Article 28 become a norm producing some legal effect in the EU and Member State legal orders, but the single market would be preserved from imbalances and inequalities produced by the excessive heterogeneity of national law on strikes. Nor would the reserve of state competence pursuant to Article 153.5 TFEU be violated because the safeguard clause thus interpreted would affect national legislations only 'indirectly' and only to the extent strictly necessary to ensure the exercise of economic freedom 'on a fair basis'.

The same reasoning should suggest using Article 28 as a basis for the protection of collective actions different from strikes, such as boycotting or blockades of movement of goods. Such actions should be included within the notion of 'collective action' laid down by the norm and they can be taken in order to enforce EU law provisions fixing social and environmental standards, possibly regarding products from third countries.[33] An internal market built 'on a fair basis' would imply that such actions not only justify restriction of free movement of goods (as already recognised by the ECJ in *Schmidberger*, albeit conditioned by the proportionality test[34]), but are also protected on the basis of Article 28, even if the law of a Member State does not legitimate them.

[31] On private international law issues related to this kind of strike, see section 7 below.

[32] D Petraylaité and C Woolfson, '"Missing in Action": the Right to Strike in the New Member States – an Absent EU Competence' (2006) 22(4) *International Journal of Comparative Labour Law and Industrial Relations* 439–468.

[33] See, for instance, Regulation (EU) No 978/2012 on generalised tariff preferences; finally, European Parliament Resolution of 10.3.2021 with recommendations to the Commission on corporate due diligence and corporate accountability (2020/2019(INL)), concerning a possible directive on the matter.

[34] C-112/00 *Schmidberger* [2003] ECR I-5659.

5. Enforcing the Right to Strike through Anti-discrimination Law

The *Laval* doctrine suggests also other lines of argument in the EU legal order to protect the right to strike, beyond the narrow scope of the single market for services. The European Court of Justice has in fact proved that Article 153.5 TFEU does not preclude EU law from affecting the right to strike. In fact, the general principle always applies according to which

> in the areas in which the Community does not have competence, the Member States remain, in principle, free to lay down the conditions for the existence and exercise of the rights at issue, they must nevertheless exercise that competence consistently with Community law.[35]

The same principle led the Court to justify the application of the principle of equal treatment on 'remuneration', despite the fact that this matter also falls within the areas reserved for Member States by Article 153.5 TFEU.[36]

Starting from this premise, the question arises whether it is possible to use anti-discrimination law to protect workers against the conduct of the employer, in case sanctions are applied by reason of their participation in a strike. In other words, it is a question of reflecting on whether the right to non-discrimination guaranteed by EU law also includes discrimination due to exercise of the right to strike. The answer to this question presupposes that 'trade union belief' can be included among the beliefs referred to in Directive 2000/78, as well as in Article 19 TFEU and Article 21 CFREU.

Indeed, as some scholars suggest, it is possible to adopt an extensive reading of the concept of 'belief' such as to also include 'trade union' ones, based on a systematic reading of EU sources, conducted in the light of other sources of international law.[37] In fact, 'belief' is indicated in EU law as a distinct ground for discrimination from 'religious'; which means that the prohibition of discrimination also should apply to the employee's opinions that are not of a religious nature, such as those of a political or, indeed, trade union nature.[38]

Nevertheless, the CJEU has expressed a different opinion on the matter in its *Wabe and Müller* judgment, excluding political or other opinion from the scope of application of Directive 2000/78.[39] As a consequence, trade union discrimination

[35] See n 16, para 87.

[36] Case C-268/06 *Impact* [2008] ECR I-2483, concerning fixed-term workers.

[37] S Borelli, 'Esiste un principio di non discriminazione per ragioni sindacali nel diritto dell'Unione Europea?' in S Borelli, A Guazzarotti and S Lorenzon (eds), *I diritti dei lavoratori nelle Carte europee dei diritti fondamentali* (Jovene, 2012) 63 ff, also in light of ECtHR, *Danilenkov v Russia* (Application No 67336/01, 30.7.2009).

[38] About the difficulties of reconciling the proposed interpretation with the term 'belief', as translated in the legislation of some Member States (Germany first), see Chapter 16 in this volume.

[39] Case C-804/18 & C-341/19 *Wabe and Müller* [2021], para 47, where the Court states that 'for the purposes of the application of Directive 2000/78, the terms "religion" and "belief" must be analysed as

should be 'covered' only by Article 21 CFREU, which explicitly refers to 'political or any other opinion'. Moreover, as Filip Dorssemont highlights in his chapter in this volume, the need to combat discrimination related to trade union activities on the basis of EU law also derives from the fundamental principle of equality before the law enshrined in Article 20 CFREU.

Despite the opinion of the CJEU, the qualification of trade union discrimination in terms of 'personal belief' is now accepted by many courts in various Member States. A different interpretation of the EU source between the CJEU and (at least some) national Courts follows: an anomalous scenario, but admitted by Directive 2000/78, as this latter does not preclude MSs to extend the protections against discriminations provided by it beyond its proper scope of application.

The Belgian Constitutional Court has intervened to declare federal and 'regional' legislation implementing Directive 2000/78 contrary to the Constitution precisely because it does not include trade union discrimination among the reasons for prohibited discrimination.[40] In France, Loi No 2008-496 implementing EU law includes trade union discrimination within its scope of application. Similarly, the Italian Court of Cassation recently recognised that Directive 2000/78 also protects against trade union discrimination, because

> union affiliation represents the profession of an ideology of a different nature from religious belief, characterised by specific reasons for belonging to an organism socially and politically qualified to represent opinions, ideas, beliefs requiring protection as the object of possible prohibited discriminatory acts.[41]

The rationale that unites the case law of the various Member States should also serve to guide future decisions on the matter by the European Court of Justice, based on both Article 20 and Article 21 CFREU. It is a question of recognising a key principle: the same protections guaranteed to those who suffer discrimination for their religious beliefs should, in a secular and democratic State, be applied to those who suffer discrimination for their non-religious beliefs.

The inclusion of trade union discrimination within the scope of EU anti-discrimination law has significant consequences precisely regarding the enforcement tools that can be used to ensure effective protection of the right to strike. In particular, the provisions of Directive 2000/78 relating with remedies and enforcement are relevant: Article 9 (defence of rights), Article 10 (burden of proof) and Article 11 (victimisation), as well as, obviously, Article 17 which requires states to impose 'effective, proportionate and dissuasive' sanctions on employers who are guilty of discrimination.

two facets of the same single ground of discrimination. As is apparent from Article 21 of the Charter, the ground of discrimination based on religion or belief is to be distinguished from the ground based on "political or any other opinion" and therefore covers both religious beliefs and philosophical or spiritual beliefs'.

[40] Constitutional Court, 16.6.2009, No 123/2009.

[41] Court of Cassation, 2.1.2020, No 1.

The Italian Labour Courts offers some significant examples of the concrete application of these provisions to contrasting employers' behaviour restricting the right to strike. The Court of Bergamo, for example, based on national legislation transposing Directive 2000/78,[42] ordered Ryanair to compensate the applicant union (Filt-Cgil) for the discriminatory nature of the rules contained in the Cabin Crew Agreement for Crew Operations.[43] This latter document (incorporated in employment contracts) in fact contained a clause under which participation in a strike entailed termination of the employment relationship. In condemning the air company, the national court relied on the '*Feryn* doctrine', according to which the existence of discrimination under Directive 2000/78 does not necessarily require the existence of a victim;[44] the court action by the trade union, on the other hand, was possible thanks to the provisions of domestic law that incorporate Article 9.2 Directive 2000/78.

Still on the basis of the national legislation transposing Directive 2000/78, the Court of Bologna recently ruled against the Deliveroo food delivery platform for the discriminatory nature of an algorithm it uses to manage its staff.[45] The rules on the burden of proof (provided for by Article 10 of Directive 2000/78) allowed the applicant union (pursuant to Article 9.2) to obtain from the judge recognition that the algorithm, although it was apparently based on neutral criteria, disadvantaged workers who participate in a strike: the refusal to answer customer calls during the period of the strike damaged the reputation ranking of the worker, on which the possibility of being called in the future depends. Hence the indirectly discriminatory nature (pursuant to Article 2.2 letter b) of the company's conduct. Also in this case, in compliance with the *Feryn* doctrine, the purely 'potential' nature of the discrimination and the absence of a victim did not exclude the condemnation of the employer.[46]

6. Searching for a 'Link' with EU Law: Right to Strike and Protection against Victimisation

Although there are comforting signals from national legal systems about the possibility of using the rules of the EU anti-discrimination law to guarantee more effective protection of the right to strike, this prospect nevertheless seems to reach an insurmountable limit in the reserving of state competence in the matter provided for by Article 153.5 TFEU. Access to anti-discrimination protection is in

[42] Legislative Decree No 216/03.
[43] Tribunale of Bergamo, 30.3.2018, No 1586.
[44] Case C-54/07 *Feryn* [2008] ECR I-5187.
[45] Tribunale of Bologna, Ordinanza 31.12.2020.
[46] The decision is important also because protection against discrimination is applied to platform workers regardless of the nature of their contracts of employment.

any case conditioned by the legitimacy of strike action, according to national law. The illegality of a strike puts workers in a condition of contractual liability, which prevents 'upstream' any evaluation on the discriminatory nature of the employer's conduct. Nor does this obstacle seem to be overcome simply by virtue of using Article 28 CFREU, which could be considered invokable in a case concerning the interpretation of Directive 2000/78. To argue the opposite would mean admitting that the last word on the legitimacy of a strike (whether or not this is legitimate under national law) always rests with the European Court of Justice, called on to apply Article 28 to assess the discriminatory character of an employer's conduct sanctioning strikers. This is a scenario that is clearly incompatible with Article 153.5 because it would open the way to a redefinition by the CJEU of national laws regarding strike action across the board, that is, well beyond what happened in virtue of the *Laval* doctrine.

And yet, the conclusion that the principle of non-discrimination finds its insurmountable limit in national rules regulating strike action cannot satisfy us, given that, if so, there could be no infringement of EU law even on the extreme hypothesis of a Member State that introduced a total ban on strikes, radically denying the right enshrined in Article 28 CFREU. It is therefore appropriate to try to put forward possible arguments that may give some substance to the right to strike, as recognised by Article 28, allowing the use of this provision in order to partially expand the scope of industrial conflict beyond the limits provided by the relevant national law. What is most interesting here is that the objective is to recognise conflict as an enforcement tool for EU law, even when this is not provided for by the applicable national legislation.

A legal argument for reaching such an objective can be based on the strict link with EU law which exists if collective action is taken to enforce an EU law provision. In other words, the link with EU law – which is needed to make Article 28 applicable pursuant to Article 51.1 CFREU – should be identified in the strict relationship between collective action and a clear infringement by the employer of a national labour law provision implementing EU law. This conclusion can be further strengthened by the rules that protect workers from victimisation, present in many directives; first of all, as seen in the previous paragraph, those concerning discrimination. According to these provisions, states must ensure workers protection in the event that they suffer dismissal or other unfavourable treatment 'as a reaction to a complaint within the undertaking or to any legal proceedings aimed at enforcing compliance' with EU law protecting workers' rights.

In the *Hakelbracht* judgment the CJEU seems to adopt a broad reading of the scope of the protection against victimisation.[47] The case involved the dismissal of a worker who had intervened in support of a candidate for a job interview, who was not hired because she was pregnant. The Court rejected the employer's demand to limit the application of Article 24 Directive 2006/54 (concerning victimisation)

[47] Case C-404/18 *Hakelbracht* [2019].

only to cases of complaint made in the context of a formal procedure, and specified that

> Article 24 of Directive 2006/54 should be interpreted in the sense that employees covered by that article, other than the person who has been discriminated against on grounds of sex, must be protected to the extent that such employees are likely to be disadvantaged by their employer because of the support they have provided, formally or informally, to the person who has been discriminated against. (Para 35.)

The reference even to 'informal' support provided to a worker who has been the victim of discrimination deserves particular attention. Indeed, such reference makes it possible to exclude that, for EU law, the only channel for proceeding against the infringement of a right is a 'formal' proceeding before the competent authorities.

Read in this perspective, the provisions on victimisation can be understood as a reflection of a general principle of EU law, which, as such, also inspires other pieces of legislation aimed at guaranteeing spaces for 'direct' action by workers, both to denounce illegitimate behaviour on the part of an employer (as in the case of the Directive on whistle-blowers) and to protect fundamental rights (as in the case of the rules on the *droit d'alert*, in the health and safety Directive[48]). These rules are intended to protect direct action exercised by a 'single' worker. However, it is legitimate at least to question the reasonableness of a differentiated treatment between claims promoted by 'individual' workers and claims promoted collectively by a plurality of workers. The legitimacy of the former should in fact entail the admissibility of the latter as well. If this is true, the aforementioned provisions can be considered the expression of a general principle that can be invoked in the event of collective actions, hypothetically also implemented in the form of a 'strike'.

Collective action can take many forms. First, collective action can be taken if an employer omits to adopt the protective and prevention measures laid down in Article 6 of Directive 1989/391 (and the relevant provisions of the subsequent occupational safety and health directives); a fortiori, when failure to comply with obligations regarding safety at work causes 'serious and imminent danger' pursuant to Article 8.5.[49] Protection against victimisation could also be invoked in case of an action called both to enforce the right of workers' representatives to be consulted pursuant to Article 11.1, Directive 89/391, and because an employer ignored requests and proposals submitted by them pursuant to Article 11.3.

More generally, every action taken to induce an employer to respect the right to information and consultation based on a labour law directive (such as the Directive on Transfer of Undertakings), can be considered a way to assert a right recognised

[48] Art 8.4, Directive 89/391.

[49] During the Covid-19 crisis, in several Member States strikes have been called to demand protection against the risk of infection in the workplace. In Italy the authority regulating strikes in public services has intervened, prohibiting such strikes; Orlandini, 'Diritto di sciopero e tutela della salute durante lo stato d'emergenza epidemiologica' in Bonardi et al (eds), *Covid 19 e diritti dei lavoratori* (Ediesse, 2020) 103ff.

by EU law. In case of a transfer of undertaking, collective action could also be taken in order to ask the transferee to respect the same conditions of employment applied by the transferor, pursuant to Article 3 of Directive 2001/23. Similarly, strikes can be used for the effective application of a 'social clause' in the context of public procurement (see Niklas Bruun in this volume). Indeed, trade unions can use collective action to prevail upon contractors or subcontractors to respect the labour standards laid down by law or by collective agreement, if this obligation is provided as a condition for the performance of the contract. In this case, the legitimacy of the action should derive also from Article 18, Directive 2014/24 which states that Member States must 'take appropriate measures to ensure that in the performance of public contracts economic operators comply with applicable obligations in the fields of environmental, social and labour law established by Union law, national law, collective agreements'.

These are just some relevant cases in which a national court could protect workers against victimisation by an employer by means of direct application of Article 28, even if the collective action would not (hypothetically) be 'covered' by national law regarding industrial conflict. In this latter case, a preliminary question before the CJEU could also be raised by the national judge. In other words, it is plausible to hypothesise a preliminary question in the context of a dispute regarding the dismissal of a worker who took part in a strike called to assert a right provided for by EU law. As the reference for a preliminary ruling would be made precisely in the event that national law did not consider such collective action legitimate, the CJEU should assess whether the need to protect workers against victimisation precludes framing such actions as illegal. Such an assessment should be made in light of Article 28 CFREU which, in this case, would be applicable pursuant to Article 51.1, because the dispute is related to the 'implementation of EU law'.

A positive response to this hypothetical preliminary question seems plausible, precisely because Article 28 would affect national legal systems in a limited way, justified by the relationship between collective action and its aims, namely to counteract an infringement of EU law. Because protection would be indirectly guaranteed to workers on strike by virtue of the application of provisions not 'directly' concerning the right to strike, the limits set by Article 153.5 TFEU on the EU's power to regulate the matter of strikes would be safeguarded.

7. Protecting and Enforcing the Right to Transnational Collective Action Through Private International Law

Reflecting on the possible basis of a right of collective action in EU law also means providing legal tools to make this right practicable at a transnational level. The 'immune' logic that inspired the European legislator's approach to the issue of strikes (from the adoption of Article 153.5 TFEU up to the present time) renders this problem insoluble, because, on the basis of it, workers in the Member States can at most require that EU law should not prejudice the rules on industrial conflict configured by national law. The perspective we have been describing goes in the opposite direction. But it is a theoretical perspective, which is not reflected in current EU law.

As things stand, the problem of the legitimacy of collective action remains exclusively in the purview of national law, even when this is exercised at transnational level. This is confirmed in the Explanations related to the Charter, where it is specified that 'the question of whether [collective actions] may be carried out in parallel in several Member States … come[s] under national laws and practices'. This is clearly a non-committal attitude because the problem is not solvable by individual Member States, each of which provides its own rules (substantive or procedural) on industrial conflict, which cannot be coordinated with those of the others.

Transnational collective action, precisely because it is regulated by the law of each Member State, can, however, raise issues of private international law, when its exercise gives rise to disputes related to the selection of competent jurisdiction and applicable law.[50] It is therefore worth asking, at the end of this chapter, if and in what way the private international rules of EU law can serve to protect workers involved in transnational action, allowing selection of the Member State jurisdiction most favourable to the exercise of the right to strike.

Article 9 of Rome II Regulation (EC) No 864/2007 on the law applicable to non-contractual obligations is the only conflict-of-law rule expressly dedicated to industrial action.[51] This provision has its origin in the *Tor Caledonia* case,[52] with which the European Court of Justice was called on to resolve a problem of jurisdiction (that is, the selection of the competent court) arising in the context of a dispute between a Danish shipping company and a Swedish trade union. The latter had called a strike and organised boycott actions to induce the former to apply better working conditions to its crew (consisting mainly of Polish sailors). The Court selected the competent forum on the basis of the criterion of *locus damni* – that is, the place where the damage was produced (in this case Denmark, the ship's country of nationality) – applying the rule provided for by Article 5.3 of the (then current) Brussels Convention (current EU Regulation Brussels I bis no 1215/12).

The *Tor Caledonia* rule highlighted the inadequacy of the current regulatory framework, given that the *locus damni* criterion corresponds primarily to the interests of the injured party (ie the employer). Hence the intervention of the European legislator, which established special conflict-of-law rules to be complied with in the

[50] This happens in the case of transnational secondary action, but not if a transnational action, called at supranational level (possibly by a European federation), is simply taken by national trade unions in different Member States.

[51] See F Dorssemont and A van Hoek, 'Collective action in Labour Conflict under the Rome II Regulation' in E Ales and T Novitz (eds), *Collective Action and Fundamental Freedoms in Europe* (Intersentia, 2011) 213ff.

[52] Case C-18/02 *Danmarks Rederiforening c LO* [2004] ECR I-01417.

event of non-contractual damages produced by collective actions. Article 9 of the Rome II Regulation therefore provides that a worker, an employer or a representative organisation must assume liability for damages caused by industrial action, according to the law of the country 'where the action is to be, or has been, taken'. The different criterion of the locus actus is waived only if 'the person claimed to be liable and the person sustaining damage both have their habitual residence in the same country at the time when the damage occurs' (pursuant to Article 4.2).[53]

The criteria laid down in Article 9 are, however, applicable only if the employer seeks damages for non-contractual liability towards the union organising the industrial action or, possibly, the workers who take part in it, but they are not relevant in disputes concerning contractual and disciplinary liability for strike. In this case, the choice of applicable law is left to application of the criteria laid down in Article 8 of Regulation (EC) Rome I No 593/2008; first of all, the *lex loci laboris* criterion, which involves regulating transnational collective action on the basis of the legislation of the home states of all the workers who join it.

In this composite framework of conflict-of-law rules, however, possible ways are open for workers of one State to use the strike legislation of other Member States if it is more favourable to them.

German legal doctrine has highlighted how, thanks to private international law rules, solidarity actions prohibited by a given national law can become legitimate.[54] An example is the case of a solidarity strike organised by German trade unions in support of a political strike by workers from another Member State. If the 'primary' action is legitimate under national law, the secondary action also becomes legitimate under German law, although a strike for non-contractual purposes in Germany is not permitted. More generally, the law applicable to a primary action can serve to legitimise secondary action in a different state. This (to return to the specific subject of this chapter) would therefore legitimise the secondary action even if the primary action were aimed at demanding the application of EU law.

Private international law can make it possible to strengthen the protection of strikers in the event of transnational action also thanks to Article 9 of the Rome I Regulation concerning overriding mandatory provisions. The rules that protect the right to strike in a Member State can in fact be included within 'provisions the respect for which is regarded as crucial by a country for safeguarding its public interests, such as its political, social or economic organisation', pursuant to Article 9. This conclusion is reinforced by the inclusion of the right to strike within the fundamental rights enshrined by the EU. The judge will therefore be able to protect workers on the basis of the *lex fori* regardless of the law applicable to their

[53] A similar provision has not been inserted in the Brussels I bis Regulation; as a consequence, jurisdiction is still selected on the basis of the *Tor Caledonia* rule.

[54] The reference to German doctrine is in F Dorssemont, 'Collective Action Against Austerity Measures' in N Bruun, K Lörcher and I Schömann (eds), *The Economic and Financial Crisis and Collective Labour Law in Europe* (Hart, 2016) 168.

employment relationship. This, again, can legitimise a strike carried out by posted workers, if it is legitimate under the law of the host State but illegitimate for that of the country of origin; indeed, the overriding mandatory provisions coincide with the 'public policy provisions' of the host state that Article 3.10 of Directive 96/71 allows to be applied to posted workers. On the other hand, the (possibly) more favourable legislation of the host state may be applied on the basis of Directive 96/71 also to contest the discriminatory nature of a dismissal (or other disciplinary sanction) imposed on strikers, because 'provisions on non-discrimination' fall within the matters listed in Article 3.1.

Finally, the conflict-of-law rules provided for by the Rome I and Rome II Regulations certainly serve to counteract law-shopping by companies, especially within the international transport sector. This of course does not guarantee the legitimacy of the transnational action but it does prevent it from (possibly) being limited by the legislation chosen by the employer. The union actions taken in 2018 by Ryanair crew are an example of virtuous cooperation between national unions, favoured by the support of the ETF and the ITF. At the same time, however, this winning trade union strategy indicates the difficulties facing the workers of various Member States in coordinating transnational strikes taking into account their respective national rules.[55]

8. Conclusions

The examples of the use of private international law to legitimise transnational collective action mentioned in the last paragraph should not tempt us to underestimate the problem of the absence of a legal basis in the EU legal system. The complex problems to which the application of private international law gives rise rather confirm that only the definition of common standards between Member States would make it possible to establish legal certainty for this kind of trade union action. If reform of Article 153.5 TFEU which made it possible to bring strike action within the competence of the EU is unrealistic (and not even wanted by many national trade unions), this provision should not prevent intervention by the European institution aimed at legitimising trans- and supranational actions, involving trade unions and workers from different Member States for common aims. The same logic that guided the European Commission in adopting the proposal for a directive on an adequate minimum wage could be followed,[56] leaving it to the Member States to choose how to guarantee the exercise of the right to cross-national industrial action, consistent with the law and internal practices of their legal systems.

[55] S De Spiegelaere, 'Transnational union action at Ryanair' (2020) 26(2) *Transfer* 229ff, where the role of social media (Facebook and WhatsApp) in coordinating action is underlined.

[56] European Commission, COM(2020)682 def.

An act of EU law providing that Member States must make such collective actions practicable (while at the same time preserving them from the constraints of the single market), would not unduly alter the features of national industrial relations systems, but would lay down only that those features cannot preclude the development of a supranational system of industrial relations, which is a prerequisite (necessary but never achieved) of a less unbalanced relationship between the economic and social dimensions of the EU.

Similarly, neither Article 153.5 TFEU nor the general principles of subsidiarity and proportionality should preclude the possibility of extending the protection provided by EU law to workers who fall victim to retaliation in the case of strike action, especially if the collective action is aimed at demanding and enforcing their rights under EU law. It would be a matter of incorporating in EU law the broad interpretation that has been suggested above, concerning both the principle of non-discrimination enshrined in Article 21 CFREU (amending Directive 2000/78) and the scope of protection against victimisation provided for by EU law (amending the relevant Directives). Also in this case, there is no doubt that only intervention by the European legislator could guarantee a certain basis for the exercise of collective action as an instrument for enforcing EU law.

Indeed, the scenarios outlined in this chapter, although plausible, presuppose an interpretation of current EU law inspired by the desire to confer substance on the right to strike at the level of the EU legal order, forcing (even if only indirectly) the limit established by Article 153.5 TFEU to protect national sovereignty in this matter. Perhaps it is optimistic to expect the European Court of Justice to accept such a perspective. On the other hand, it is even more optimistic to trust in a clarifying intervention by the European legislator in the sense proposed. The history of European integration has shown, however, that (as Gramsci teaches) the optimism of the will sometimes prevails over the pessimism of reason.

16

Collective Actors Enforcing EU Labour Law

FILIP DORSSEMONT

1. Collective Actors and Enforcement

This contribution deals with the issue of collective actors representing workers' interests as actors of enforcement of EU labour law. This complicated relationship presupposes that the notion of enforcement is elucidated *in liminis*.

This question needs to be examined against the background of the European Union's limited competences for regulating on the issue of representation and collective defence of workers' interests and the EU's obligation to take account of the diversity of national industrial relations systems.

The chapter's focus is a proper understanding of whether and how EU law can institute and/or empower such collective actors with regard to *implemented EU labour law* and how they can play a role in enforcing EU labour law. It examines the role of collective actors at both Member State and EU level as actors of enforcement of EU labour law. It seeks to reconstruct the legal tools empowering collective actors to implement enforcement.

Last but not least, it raises the issue of the protection of these collective actors – in particular if they are employees – against retaliation from the employer's side.

1.1. Enforcement Versus Implementation

For the purpose of this chapter enforcement is construed as any action that contributes to the effective application or observance of *implemented* and pre-existing (EU) labour law standards. The Oxford English Reference Dictionary defines 'to enforce' as 'to compel observance of a law'.

In this chapter, I will not deal with the issue of implementation itself. Implementation is an issue of standard-setting, not of the enforcement of standards. Hence, the setting of standards by means of collective agreements will *not* be treated as an issue of enforcement. This approach deviates from the approach adopted by Van Peijpe in a seminal book on the enforcement of EU labour law.[1] On one hand, implementation of EU labour law by means of collective agreements might need to be complemented by measures ensuring enforcement. On the other hand, EU labour law can be an obstacle to the enforcement of collective agreements at the level of the Member States.

The conclusion of collective agreements can raise issues of implementation in two ways affecting EU labour law. First, Article 153(3) TFEU authorises Member States to 'entrust management and labour, at their joint request', with the implementation of Directives in the field of social policy. In such a scenario, an EU Directive will be implemented at national level primarily by means of a collective agreement. A clear indication that implementation needs to be distinguished from enforcement stems from the fact that Article 153(3) states that, in such a situation of implementational bargaining, a Member State still needs 'to guarantee the results imposed by that directive'. In my view, the notion of 'guarantee' is intertwined with enforcement. In rare cases, EU Directives have even allowed Member States to empower management and labour to derogate from EU labour standards.[2] Without calling for such *in pejus* bargaining, there may be good reasons to assume that autonomous implementation of EU labour standards by means of collective agreements might work more effectively in real life than a heteronomous implementation driven by state actors. Thus, in Belgian law the social partners were able to implement EU Directives more speedily than the legislature and this modus operandi is more consistent with horizontal subsidiarity.

Secondly, Article 155(2) TFEU, reversing the dynamics, states that collective agreements concluded by social partners at EU level *shall* be implemented either in accordance with the procedures and practices specific to management and labour and the Member States, or in matters within the scope of the Social Policy Title at the joint request of the signatory parties by a Council decision on a proposal from the Commission. In such a scenario an intervention by social partners at national level or an intervention of the Commission and the Council will be necessary to implement a collective agreement concluded at EU level.

Collective agreements can be subject to enforcement of EU labour law, insofar as they are not in conformity with it. The landmark *Defrenne I* judgment has prefigured the extent to which enforcement of EU labour law can indeed be detrimental to an abusive exercise of collective autonomy.[3]

A number of Directives in the field of equal treatment provide that provisions of (national) collective agreements that are unjustifiably discriminatory need to be

[1] For a different approach dealing with negotiations as a means of enforcing rules derived from EU labour law, see T Van Peijpe, 'Industrial relations processes' in J Malmberg (ed), *Effective enforcement of EC Labour Law* (The Hague, Kluwer Law International, 2003) 77–108.

[2] Art 17 EU Directive 2003/88 and Art 5 EU Directive 2002/14.

[3] Case 43-75 *Defrenne* [1976] ECR 455. See also Joined Cases C-297/10 and C-298/10 *Sabine Hennigs v Eisenbahn-Bundesamt and Land Berlin (C-298/10) v Alexander Mai* [2011] and Case C-312/17 *Surjit Singh Bedi* [2018].

declared null and void.[4] The Temporary Agency Directive adopted another stance, stating that collective agreements are subject to a review procedure by the state concerned.[5] This provision does not allow private individuals to ask for the annulment of provisions of these agreements, on the ground that they would unduly restrict recourse to temporary agency workers.[6]

1.2. Collective Actors and EU Law

The TFEU sets a number of constitutional thresholds for interference by the EU legislator in industrial relations, especially where workers' representation is concerned. Thus, Article 152 TFEU states that in recognising and promoting the role of social partners *at its level*, the EU needs to take into account the diversity of national systems. In my view, it is hazardous to state that the Union should not take into account the diversity of national systems, while adopting legislation affecting the role of social partners at Member State level. Thus, EU Directives adopted in the field of representation and the collective defence of the interests of workers and employers, including codetermination, can be adopted only with unanimity.[7]

In practice, this unanimity requirement needs to be and has been mitigated. Prior to the adoption of the Maastricht and Lisbon Treaties, some Directives had been adopted with unanimity on the distinct basis of Article 115 TFEU. Thus, the Collective Redundancy Directive 98/59 and the Transfer of Undertakings Directive 2001/23 were adopted in 1975 and 1977, respectively. An analysis of these Directives demonstrates that they have had an impact on the issue of workers' representation. Both Directives prescribe an obligation incumbent on an employer to inform and consult workers' representatives in scenarios of collective redundancy or transfer of undertaking. Although the notion of a workers' representative is defined by means of a *renvoi* to the law of the Member States, the CJEU, in two judgments following an infringement procedure, has made it abundantly clear that a Member State should provide sufficient guarantees that the existence of workers' representation is not dependent solely on arbitrary recognition by an employer.[8] Hence, both Directives generated a positive *spillover* effect in the area of workers' representation. The Acquired Rights Directive also provides some safeguards for the continuity of existing institutions of workers' representation after

[4] See: Art 16 (b) Directive 2000/78 (general framework for equal treatment in employment and occupation); Art 14 (b) Directive 2000/43 (equal treatment between persons irrespective of racial or ethnic origin); Art 23 (b) Directive 2006/54 (equal opportunities and equal treatment of men and women in matters of employment and occupation).

[5] Art 4 (2) EU Directive 2008/104/EC.

[6] Case C-533/13 *AKT* [2015].

[7] Art 153(2) TFEU.

[8] Case C-382/93 *Commission v UK* [1994].

the transfer of an undertaking, provided that the undertaking, business or part of an undertaking or business preserves its autonomy.[9]

This case law related to Directives adopted prior to the entry into force of the Maastricht and Amsterdam Treaties makes it abundantly clear that information and consultation are intertwined with the issue of representation. This link came even more to the fore when the EU legislator acquired competences to adopt Directives on the basis of a qualified majority to improve the right to information and consultation because of the Agreement on Social Policy (Maastricht) and the modification of the Social Policy Title (Amsterdam). The provision that Directives dealing with representation should be adopted on the basis of unanimity did not at all prevent the aforementioned spillover in practice, now on the basis of a qualified majority.

In fact, the first EU Directive adopted on the basis of Article 2(2) of the Agreement on Social Policy, namely EWC Directive 94/45, introduced two bodies of workers' representation unprecedented in national statutory law, as well as EU law. These are the so-called ad hoc Special Negotiating Body (SNB), which is endowed with bargaining power, and the European Works Council (EWC).[10] Furthermore, this Directive also shaped some corollary rights to information and consultation that tend to strengthen the activities of workers' representatives.

Article 6 of the EWC Directive provides a right to protection and guarantees for employees' representatives under national legislation and/or practice in force in their country of employment, including the payment of wages during their work as EWC members. The subsequently adopted Recast EWC Directive has fleshed out these guarantees in more minute detail. It explicitly recognises a right of EWC members to 'represent collectively the interests of the employees of the Community-scale undertaking or Community-scale group of undertakings'. To some extent this new provision generalises a pre-existing and still existing right of EWC members to have access to judicial or administrative procedures in order to challenge the use made by central management of the provisions allowing them not to convey information or to demand confidentiality.[11]

Insofar as this protection entails protection against dismissal a clear-cut example is given of how issues that should be formally regulated on the basis of unanimity (dismissal protection)[12] tend to be regulated on the basis of a qualified majority, insofar as they are encapsulated in a broader issue for which a qualified majority seems sufficient.

The EWC Recast Directive has also corroborated some corollary rights previously mentioned in the so-called subsidiary requirements of the EWC Directive,

[9] Art 6 Directive 2001/23. See Case C-151/09 *Ayuntamento de la Linea della Concepcion* [2010].

[10] See on the question of whether this was compatible with the fact that representation requires unanimity: J Kenner, *EU Employment Law: From Rome to Amsterdam and Beyond* (Oxford, Hart Publishing, 2003) 241.

[11] See in this respect: Art 11 Recast EWC Directive 2009/38.

[12] Art 153(1) (d) TFEU.

integrating them into the body of the Recast Directive. Thus, EWC members need to inform the representatives of the employees of the establishments or undertakings of a Community-scale group of undertakings, or, in the absence of representatives, the workforce as a whole, of the content and outcome of an information and consultation procedure carried out in accordance with this Directive. Although the Directive has phrased this provision as entailing an obligation, it is important to note that the central management needs to facilitate these operations, including the financial costs it might entail. Last but not least, the members of the SNB and the EWC have a right to be provided with training without loss of wages. Unfortunately, an important corollary right – the right to be assisted at the expense of the employer by expert(s) – has not yet been integrated into the body of the Recast Directive.

The subsequent Framework Directive on Information and Consultation (2002/14) also stressed, in a less elaborated way, the existence of a corollary right to enjoy adequate protection and guarantees to representatives enabling them to perform properly the duties that have been assigned to them. Last but not least, the adoption of this Directive confirms the idea that information and consultation and representation go hand in hand, because in a joint Declaration of the European Parliament, the Council and the Commission on employee representation, the aforementioned ECJ judgments were recalled (Cases C-382/92 *Safeguarding of employees rights in the event of transfers of undertakings* and C-383/92 *Collective redundancies*).

Directives adopted in order to ensure equal treatment of men and women can be adopted on the basis of a qualified majority, contrary to other Directives combatting discrimination on a number of other grounds, which require unanimity. It is important to consider that the EU legislator did not refrain from using a qualified majority basis in order to ensure that associations, organisations or other legal entities which have, in accordance with the criteria laid down by their national law, a legitimate interest in ensuring that the provisions of the Equal Treatment Directive are complied with, may engage, either on behalf or in support of the complainants, with his or her approval, in any judicial and/or administrative procedure provided for the enforcement of obligations under Directive 2006/54.

The implementation of this provision has in fact empowered trade unions defending the rights of employees who have fallen victim to sex discrimination.[13] Other Directives combating discrimination have followed this good legislative practice, but they do not make a difference, insofar as the adoption of these Directives also requires unanimity.[14]

Looking more closely at this *acquis* in the field of representation, adopted under these provisions, a number of characteristics can be discerned. As a general rule,

[13] Directive 2002/73/EC of the European Parliament and of the Council of 23 September 2002 amending Council Directive 76/207/EEC.

[14] Directives 2000/78 and 2000/43.

the EU legislature seems to privilege a system of indirect representation of workers through their representatives, instead of opting for a system of direct involvement, in other words, the exercise of the prerogatives by the workers themselves.

This approach is exemplified by Recital 16 of EU Directive 2002/14, which states:

> (16) This Directive is without prejudice to those systems which provide for the direct involvement of employees, as long as they are always free to exercise the right to be informed and consulted through their representatives.

The only exception to the rule is the Framework Directive on Health and Safety, which consistently seems to suggest there is an arbitrary choice to be made between the exercise of involvement through workers or representatives.

In sum, direct involvement is a second best or subsidiary solution, applicable in rare instances in which no system of representation exists, for a reason independent of the will of the employees.[15]

Another feature is the fact that the EU legislature recognises that the Member States should define how workers' representatives in their country are designated. There is no 'autonomous' concept of workers' representatives. Thus, Framework Directive 2002/14 provides that the notion 'employees' representatives' means the employees' representatives provided for by national laws and/or practices. Hence, the European legislature has refrained from interfering with the autonomy of Member States or of management and labour at national level to define that notion. The only exception to the rule might be the capacity of the SNB to define the composition of workers' representatives with a seat in the conventional EWC. Because the SNB is composed of workers' representatives from Member States, however, and the Member States shall determine the method to be used for the election or appointment of the SNB's members in their territories, it is likely that the SNB will indeed respect national law and practices. As indicated above, the CJEU has indicated that this *renvoi* precludes that a system of workers' representation be completely dependent upon the will of the employer.

[15] Eg Art 7(6) Directive 2001/23:

> '6. Member States shall provide that, where there are no representatives of the employees in an undertaking or business through no fault of their own, the employees concerned must be informed in advance of:
>
> - the date or proposed date of the transfer,
> - the reason for the transfer,
> - the legal, economic and social implications of the transfer for the employees,
> - any measures envisaged in relation to the employees.'

Art 10 Directive 2009/38:

> '3. Members of special negotiating bodies, members of European Works Councils and employees' representatives exercising their functions under the procedure referred to in Art 6(3) shall, in the exercise of their functions, enjoy protection and guarantees similar to those provided for employees' representatives by the national legislation and/or practice in force in their country of employment.'

The most important obstacle to the adoption of EU legislation dealing with representation and collective defence of interests is the enumeration of excluded matters, listed in Article 153(5). Paragraph 5 states that the 'provisions of this Article shall not apply to pay, the right of association, the right to strike or the right to impose lock-outs'.

In view of the competences concerned, the right of association, the right to strike or the right to impose lock-outs are of immediate interest to the issue of representation and collective defence. In fact, although Article 153(5) TFEU is a rule of exclusion relevant for all the competences listed in Article 153, Article 153(1)(f) TFEU is the only competence referring to exclusion explicitly.

In sum, one might ask which issues of representation could be argued to fall outside the exception. As a general rule, a clear-cut exception needs to be interpreted narrowly. It is hardly questionable that codetermination (*co-gestion*, *Mitbestimmung*, *medezeggenschap*, *co-gestione*) falls outside the exception: if it did not, it would not have been mentioned explicitly in Article 153(1)(f) TFEU. The only problem is that the notion of codetermination is to some extent ambiguous and that the different language versions are not very convergent. Codetermination can be interpreted in a strict sense, as a kind of organic participation at board level of workers' representatives or people who owe their seat to the support of workers. To some extent the use of the words *cogestion* and *cogestione* confirms such an interpretation. Such a form of codetermination comes close to participation within the meaning of Directive 2001/86. In my view, codetermination could also be related to the veto rights of workers' representatives outside corporate governance structures. Thus, in Germany and the Netherlands some employers' decisions are subject to approval by works councils. This means of collective defence goes beyond information and consultation rights, because the latter do not affect the managerial prerogative. The use of a more generic expression such as *Mitbestimmung*, codetermination and even *medezeggenschap* are not limited to issues of board-level representation.

In my view, the notion of right of association needs to be construed narrowly, as referring to the right to form and join trade unions or employers' associations, with the exclusion of the collective dimension of this freedom. Inevitably, this raises the issue of whether, for this reason, there is an EU competence to tackle the issue of discrimination against workers on the basis of trade union membership. In my view, a categorical exclusion of such a competence could be seen as problematic for a number of reasons, both legal and political.

The European Union has prohibited trade unions from discriminating against workers on the basis of sex, religious convictions or belief, age, handicap, sexual orientation and nationality. These provisions might be related to issues of trade union membership[16] and to (legitimate) restrictions of collective autonomy. Article 153(5) TFEU has never been seen as an obstacle to such clear-cut

[16] See Directives 2006/54, 2000/43 and 2000/78.

restrictions on freedom of association and the corresponding internal and collective autonomy. Why therefore should it be seen as an obstacle to prohibiting discrimination on the basis of trade union membership? Can the EU only adopt rules that restrict freedom of association, rather than rules that promote it? By analogy, the mere fact that pay is included in the list of excluded matters has not prevented the Court or the legislature from using Article 153 to combat unequal treatment of men and women as with regard to pay. Should the fact that freedom of association is mentioned prevent the European Union from combating discrimination based on trade union membership? In practice, it cannot be denied that the EU has a competence to protect workers where their employment contract is terminated. Insofar as this protection deals with a need to protect people against unjustified dismissal, it is intertwined with Article 30 CFREU, an instrument that the EU institutions are obliged not just to respect, but to promote. In this respect, it is important that the protection of workers against discriminatory dismissals based upon trade union membership is explicitly mentioned in Article 5 of the ILO's Termination of Employment Convention No 158, which states in Article 5:

> The following, inter alia, shall not constitute valid reasons for termination:
>
> (a) union membership or participation in union activities outside working hours or, with the consent of the employer, within working hours;

The right of association in my view does not need to be interpreted in a generic way, despite the choice of vocabulary. The context of this reference within the Social Policy Title suggests an interpretation of the meaning of the right for workers and employers to organise (*liberté syndicale* or *Koalitionsfreiheit*). Furthermore, the mere fact that the TFEU mentions the right to strike and the right of association suggests that the 'right of association' only refers to the right of an individual to form and join trade unions or employers' associations as opposed to the collective rights held by the association or its members taken collectively.

2. Tools for Enforcement at Grassroots Level

There are various ways in which collective actors representing workers can facilitate effective enforcement of EU labour law standards. Some of these enforcement tools are provided solely by national labour law, others are imposed on Member States by provisions of EU Directives.

Thus, there is the role attributed to workers' representatives in a number of Member States to monitor employers' compliance with (EU) labour law at grassroots level. An essential tool for exercising such monitoring is information, in the sense of data on past managerial decisions, which will help workers' representatives to trace management compliance. Hence, the question arises whether EU Directives in the field of information and consultation, as well as participation can be used to exercise such a control.

A number of EU Directives have empowered collective actors to have access to justice in defence of individual or collective workers' rights.

Another question is whether recourse to collective action to exert pressure against an employer unwilling to abide by the law is allowed under EU law.[17]

2.1. Monitoring or Control of Compliance

2.1.1. At Member State Level

'Control' here refers to the traditional notions of *contrôle ouvrier* or *droit de regard* in relation to enterprise management. 'Control' does not refer to 'directing' the enterprise but to monitoring the management of the enterprise. Such control on the part of collective actors representing workers' interests has a retrospective character. It seeks to assess whether a management has effectively observed labour law standards. Empowering collective actors at enterprise level to exercise such control is an example of enforcement through monitoring at grassroots level.

Thus, Belgian Intersectoral Agreement No 5 institutes a trade union delegation at enterprise level. Its competences include monitoring observance in the enterprise of social legislation, collective agreements, 'shop rules' and individual employment contracts (*l'application dans l'entreprise de la législation sociale, des conventions collectives de travail, du règlement de travail et des contrats individuels de louage de travail*). In a similar vein, the Belgian Works Council, a mixed body, has competence under Article 15 d) of the *Loi portant Organisation de l'Entreprise* to control the strict observation of industrial and social legislation adopted in view of workers' protection (*de veiller à la stricte application de la législation industrielle et sociale protectrice des travailleurs*). Dutch works councils have a specific competence on the basis of Article 28 Works Councils Act to promote the observation of provisions on working conditions applicable to the enterprise, as well as rules in the field of health and safety, working time and rest time with regard to people active in the enterprise (*De ondernemingsraad bevordert zoveel als in zijn vermogen ligt de naleving van de voor de onderneming geldende voorschriften op het gebied van de arbeidsvoorwaarden, alsmede van de voorschriften op het gebied van de arbeidsomstandigheden en arbeids- en rusttijden van de in de onderneming werkzame personen)*.

French works councils have a specific instrument for monitoring compliance with social legislation, the so-called *droit d'alerte* (right to warn).[18] Although

[17] In this respect see also Chapter 15 in this volume.
[18] Art L2312-59:

> 'Si un membre de la délégation du personnel au comité social et économique constate, notamment par l'intermédiaire d'un travailleur, qu'il existe une atteinte aux droits des personnes, à leur santé physique et mentale ou aux libertés individuelles dans l'entreprise qui ne serait pas justifiée par la nature de la tâche à accomplir, ni proportionnée au but recherché, il en saisit immédiatement

Dutch Works Councils do not enjoy a similar right, Dutch trade unions have a right of enquiry against company management on the basis of Article 2(344–359) of the Dutch Civil Code.

In the same vein, German Works Councils, on the basis of sections 80[19] and 89[20] of the Works Constitution Act (*Betriebsverfassungsgesetz*),[21] have the right to monitor compliance with the relevant laws and the application of rules related to a number of issues, such as health and safety and environmental protection, respectively.

2.1.2. At EU Level

Under EU labour law no similar prerogatives have been bestowed on workers' representatives. The question arises solely whether the information given to workers' representatives provides them with an opportunity to monitor compliance with labour law. Not all Directives dealing with worker involvement are relevant in this regard; in particular, those concerning information and consultation with regard to envisaged managerial decisions (*cf* transfer of undertaking and, especially, collective redundancies) are less relevant to the issue. These instruments do not enable monitoring of the legality of managerial decisions.

EWC Directive 1994/45 was a pioneering instrument insofar as it instituted a recurring kind of generic information and consultation not related to specific circumstances in which workers' representatives were allowed to assess the past performance of central management. This model of recurring information was

l'employeur. Cette atteinte peut notamment résulter de faits de harcèlement sexuel ou moral ou de toute mesure discriminatoire en matière d'embauche, de rémunération, de formation, de reclassement, d'affectation, de classification, de qualification, de promotion professionnelle, de mutation, de renouvellement de contrat, de sanction ou de licenciement.

L'employeur procède sans délai à une enquête avec le membre de la délégation du personnel du comité et prend les dispositions nécessaires pour remédier à cette situation.

En cas de carence de l'employeur ou de divergence sur la réalité de cette atteinte, et à défaut de solution trouvée avec l'employeur, le salarié, ou le membre de la délégation du personnel au comité social et économique si le salarié intéressé averti par écrit ne s'y oppose pas, saisit le bureau de jugement du conseil de prud'hommes qui statue selon la procédure accélérée au fond.

Le juge peut ordonner toutes mesures propres à faire cesser cette atteinte et assortir sa décision d'une astreinte qui sera liquidée au profit du Trésor.'

[19] '(1) The works council shall have the following general duties:

1. to see that effect is given to Acts, ordinances, safety regulations, collective agreements and works agreements for the benefit of the employees; …'

[20] Section 89 on health and safety as well as environmental protection at work:

'(1) The works council shall endeavour to ensure that the provisions on safety and health at work and accident prevention, as well as environmental protection are observed in the establishment. It shall support the competent occupational safety and health authorities, the statutory accident insurance institutions and other relevant bodies in their efforts to eliminate safety and health hazards by offering suggestions, advice and information.'

[21] See: www.gesetze-im-internet.de/englisch_betrvg/englisch_betrvg.html.

copied in Framework Directive 2002/14 (Information and consultation). The data that may be the object of the information and consultation procedure under both Directives are in my view so generic that they will not enable an EWC or a local body of workers' representatives to monitor management compliance. They rather make it possible to reconstruct a company's economic and financial situation retrospectively and prospectively and to assess the social impact and prospects of that financial and economic situation. The focus is on employment, not on the legality of the conditions of employment.

The most effective way to control or monitor management is participation, as defined in Article 2 e) of the SE Directive 2001/88, namely the

> influence of the body representative of the employees and/or the employees' representatives in the affairs of a company by way of:
>
> - the right to elect or appoint some of the members of the company's supervisory or administrative organ, or
> - the right to recommend and/or oppose the appointment of some or all of the members of the company's supervisory or administrative organ.

This would enable employees to monitor the observance of EU labour law indirectly. This situation is restricted to companies that opt to establish a *Societas Europae* (SE as a holding company or a subsidiary or by means of transformation). Furthermore, the SE Directive does not guarantee that all SEs will be endowed with participation rights.

2.2. Access to Justice and to Administrative Procedures

The question arises of the extent to which collective actors have been granted access to justice and to administrative procedures on the basis of EU law to defend proper institutional interests, collective interests or even the individual interests of particular individuals. After providing an inventory of the provisions empowering collective actors to obtain such access to justice, the conditionality of such access will be examined.

The following provisions of EU Directives confer a right on collective actors to obtain access to justice. Article 11(3) Directive 2014/67 (on the enforcement of Directive 96/71/EC concerning the posting of workers):

- Article 7(2) Directive 2000/43 (equal treatment between persons irrespective of racial or ethnic origin);
- Article 9(2) Directive 2000/78 (general framework for equal treatment in employment and occupation);
- Article 17(2) Directive 2006/54 (equal opportunities and equal treatment of men and women in matters of employment and occupation);
- Article 9(2) Directive 2010/41 (equal treatment between men and women engaged in an activity in a self-employed capacity).

All these provisions are formulated in an almost identical manner. Although the notion of 'trade union' is seldom used,[22] trade unions can be considered to have access to justice because they qualify as 'associations, organisations or other legal entities which have, in accordance with the criteria laid down by their national law, a legitimate interest in ensuring that the provisions of this Directive are complied with'. The Directives indicate that these entities may engage 'either on behalf or in support of the complainant' and that they should act 'with his or her approval'. In order for such a provision to work effectively, it needs to be implemented properly. The *renvoi* to the notion 'in accordance with the criteria laid down by their national law' might be used as an argument for leeway granted to Member States. This leeway is reduced to the benefit of equality bodies, which need to be instituted on the basis of Directives 2000/43 and 2006/54 and 2010/54, although these provisions do not insist on access to justice as a minimum competence of these bodies.

In all these situations, workers' organisations can act either as agents of the victim of a violation of EU labour law or in their own right as litigants. Both scenarios presuppose that the victim acts. Furthermore, the EU Directives make the admissibility of this claim conditional on an agreement with the victim of the violation of EU labour law. This approach is based on two assumptions that are not necessarily well founded. First, it presupposes that an instance of unlawful conduct was detrimental to an identifiable person. Second, it presupposes that such a person is willing to instigate proceedings against the perpetrator of the breach of EU labour law, who may be his or her current employer. The question arises of how realistic such a scenario is. In a number of Directives this risk is mitigated by a provision containing a kind of 'victimisation clause' protecting employees against dismissal or other adverse treatment in case they file a complaint within the undertaking or any legal proceeding aimed at enforcing compliance. Directive 2014/67 lacks such a provision, however, as does Directive 2010/41, which is not relevant to genuine employees.

The formula used in the Belgian law implementing Directive 2000/78, 2000/43 and 2006/54 differs from that used in the Directives in two respects. It allows for a claim 'in the organisation's own name'. Furthermore, the consent of the victim is required only if a victim can be identified.

In the *Feryn* case, an employer had made a public statement about his inability, allegedly because of pressure from his clients, to recruit employees with a migrant background. Ruling on a preliminary reference, the CJEU decided that this constituted direct discrimination. In what seems an obiter dictum indirectly related to this question, the Court also gave its blessing to the less rigorous formulation of the consent conditionality in Belgian law in relation to enforcement procedures. It stated that:

> 26. The question of what constitutes direct discrimination within the meaning of Directive 2000/43 must be distinguished from that of the legal procedures provided

[22] One exception is Art 11 (3) Directive 2014/67 (on the enforcement of Directive 96/71/EC concerning the posting of workers).

> for in Article 7 of that directive for a finding of failure to comply with the principle of equal treatment and the imposition of sanctions in that regard. Those legal procedures must, in accordance with the provisions of that article, be available to persons who consider that they have suffered discrimination. However, the requirements of Article 7 of Directive 2000/43 are, as stated in Article 6 thereof, only minimum requirements and the Directive does not preclude Member States from introducing or maintaining provisions which are more favourable to the protection of the principle of equal treatment.
>
> 27. Consequently, Article 7 of Directive 2000/43 does not preclude Member States from laying down, in their national legislation, the right for associations with a legitimate interest in ensuring compliance with that directive, or for the body or bodies designated pursuant to Article 13 thereof, to bring legal or administrative proceedings to enforce the obligations resulting therefrom without acting in the name of a specific complainant or in the absence of an identifiable complainant. It is, however, solely for the national court to assess whether national legislation allows such a possibility.[23]

In my view, this approach is only to be welcomed. If no employee can be identified, it is essential that organisations can step in. Otherwise, practices could be deemed directly discriminatory and prohibited, but such a prohibition could not be enforced at all in view of the lack of an employee with an interest and of an organisation empowered to step in. In my view, the leeway that the CJEU still leaves to Member States is problematic. It gives rise to a situation in which no enforcement of a prohibition of direct discrimination is possible at all.

Recast EWC Directive 2009/38 contains a provision that could be interpreted as having such a judicial scope. Thus, Article 10(1) provides that the 'members of the European Works Council shall have the means required to apply the rights arising from this Directive, to represent collectively the interests of the employees of the Community-scale undertaking or Community-scale group of undertakings'. This provision ensures that access to justice is not limited to the European Works Council. This is extremely helpful for two reasons. First, in a number of situations, European Works Councils are mixed bodies composed of representatives of central management and of workers. This might constitute a major obstacle to a decision of the European Works Council to go to court. Furthermore, in a number of countries, EWCs do not have corporate personality, which might be an essential condition for the admissibility of a case.[24]

On the other hand, there is the issue of trade unions' difficulty in accessing the European Court of Justice, given that they are seldom considered to be individually and directly concerned. This is in stark contrast to the recognition of access to justice as an essential means to defend workers' interests within the meaning of Article 11 ECHR (*cf Adefdromil v France*, §60).

[23] Case C-54/07, *Firma Feryn NV*.

[24] On this issue, see F Dorssemont, 'The European Works Council Directive and the domestic Courts. A critical analysis of the legal issues at stake' in F Dorssemont and T Blanke (eds), *The Recast of the European Works Council Directive* (Antwerp, Intersentia, 2010) 233–35.

These thresholds are at odds with the obligation of all institutions, including the ECJ, to promote the role of social partners at its level (Article 152 TFEU) and to promote and ensure the right to access to justice (Article 47 CFREU).

2.3. Collective Action

Recourse to collective action as a means to enforce the law needs to be distinguished from the exercise of collective action as a means to settle disputes about collective interests. In a number of legal systems this means of enforcement is at odds with the idea that a strike needs to be seen as an *ultimum remedium*. If a legal avenue is open to enforce a right, such an avenue needs to be followed. This simplistic and reactionary scheme is fallacious. It erroneously suggests that judicial enforcement would produce results identical to, and as fast and as efficient as collective action. First, legal procedures are slow; second, they might result in sanctions deemed insufficient as compared, for example, to reinstatement. The use of *ultimum remedium* has been severely criticised by the ECSR,[25] but *in casu* this case law might not even be operational. Collective actions in order to enforce rights would probably fall outside the scope of Article 6(4) ESC because they might not qualify as collective action in case of conflict of interests.[26]

The more important and decent issue, in my view, concerns how the right to collective action can be enforced. This right can be effective only insofar as workers are sufficiently protected against management retaliation, hence against act of anti-union discrimination. Furthermore, labour law should also outlaw practices that allow an employer to replace striking workers. Adding a recital in order to *allow* Member States to continue to prohibit the use of agency workers in order to replace workers on strike (*cf* Recital 20 in Directive 2008/104 EC) is not sufficient. This recital, which tends to mitigate an obligation on Member States to justify prohibitions or restrictions affecting recourse to agency work within the framework of a review procedure entailing obligations for Member States in relation to the Commission, does not create any obligation to preclude recourse of agency workers to replace workers on strike. The new provision Article 1a of the revised Posted Workers Directive stipulates that 'this Directive shall not in any way affect the exercise of fundamental rights as recognised in the Member States and at Union level, including the right or freedom to strike or to take other action covered by the specific industrial relations systems in Member State'. This provision, which is more binding than a recital, does not clearly and precisely prohibit the use of posted workers to replace striking workers in an enterprise situated in a host state,

[25] See F Dorssemont, 'Article 6. The right to bargain collectively' in N Bruun, K Lörcher, I Schömann and S Clauwaert (eds), *The European Social Charter and the Employment Relation* (Oxford, Hart Publishing, 2017) 276–77.

[26] Ibid, 272.

but has been used as a catalyst to introduce such a prohibition in the German legislation on posted workers (§11 para 5 Arbeitnehmerüberlassungsgesetz [Temporary Employment Act]).

This issue affects a major loophole in EU anti-union discrimination law. The European Union has prohibited trade unions discriminating against workers on the basis of sex, religious convictions or belief, age, handicap, sexual orientation and nationality. These provisions might relate to issues of trade union membership[27] and to (legitimate) restrictions on collective autonomy. Article 153(5) TFEU has never been seen as an obstacle to such clear-cut restrictions on freedom of association and the corresponding internal and collective autonomy. Why, then, should it be seen as an obstacle to prohibit discrimination on the basis of trade union membership? Can the EU only adopt rules that restrict freedom of association, rather than rules that promote it? By analogy, the mere fact that pay is used in the list of excluded matters should not prevent the legislature from using Article 153 to combat unequal treatment of men and women with regard to pay, even though other grounds had to be used in the past. Should the fact that freedom of association is mentioned thus preclude the EU's competence to combat discrimination based upon trade union membership? In practice, it cannot be denied that the EU has a competence in the area of workers' protection where their employment contract is terminated. Insofar as this protection deals with a need to protect people against unjustified dismissal, it is in fact intertwined with Article 30 CFREU, an instrument which the EU institutions are obliged not just to respect, but to promote. In this respect, it is important that the protection of workers against discriminatory dismissal based upon trade union membership is explicitly mentioned in Article 5 of the ILO's Termination of Employment Convention No 158, which states in Article 5:

> The following, inter alia, shall not constitute valid reasons for termination:
>
> (a) union membership or participation in union activities outside working hours or, with the consent of the employer, within working hours.

More importantly, the Appendix attached to the revised European Social Charter disqualifies this very same ground in identical wording as a valid reason to terminate employment.[28]

The price of non-intervention is high. At present, EU law rightly prohibits unions from discrimination and enforces this prohibition through effective sanctions, such as the nullity of provisions of collective agreements. But it turns a blind eye to victims of anti-union discrimination. Thus, EU non-discrimination law is contaminated by the virus it is combating. It has created unequal treatment of

[27] See Directives 2006/54, 2000/43 and 2000/78.

[28] See on Art 24 ESC revised: M Schmitt, 'Article 24 The right to protection in cases of termination of employment' in N Bruun, K Lörcher, I Schömann and S Clauwaert (eds), *The European Social Charter and the Employment Relation* (Oxford, Hart Publishing, 2017) 412–38.

victims of discrimination. This modus operandi is problematic because it is incompatible with the general principle of equality before the law, contained in Article 20 CFREU. In fact, the Belgian Constitutional Court has been confronted on two occasions with a demand to declare the implementation of EU Directive 2000/78 at odds with the principle of equality. In 2004 it considered that the sole reference to religion or belief violated that principle by not protecting victims of discrimination based upon political convictions.[29] In 2009 the Belgian Constitutional Court ruled that the Belgian legislation which had in the meantime included political convictions, violated the principle of equality by not combatting discrimination based upon trade union convictions.[30] A major element in the Court's reasoning was the Belgian legislator's wish to combat all kinds of discrimination intertwined with fundamental rights. As a result of this case law, the Belgian legislation does enforce all freedoms of the mind: freedom of association, freedom of religion and freedom of expression. It has not been possible to question the nexus between non-discrimination and the effective enforcement of the right to organise since the landmark judgment *Danilenkov v Russia*.[31] In sum, the issue here is not just Article 20 CFREU, but also Article 12 CFREU.

A creative way of overcoming this hurdle *de jure condito* is to interpret the prohibition of discrimination based upon religion or belief so broadly as to include convictions related to trade union affiliation. In my view, this is a hazardous undertaking. However, the principle of equality might serve as a catalyst for the kind of audacity that the CJEU imposes on domestic judges as well. The notions used in various language versions of Directive 2000/78, as well in the Article of the TFEU that constitutes the legal basis of this Directive. The fact that the word 'or' is used between 'religion' and 'belief' suggests, in my view, that the convictions concerned relate not just to any kind of philosophical, let alone political conviction, but to convictions of a more metaphysical nature. The use of the German word *Weltanschauung* seems to make this abundantly clear. In an obiter dictum of *IX v Wabe eV and MH Müller Handels GmbH v MJ*, the ECJ stated that 'as it is apparent from Article 21 of the Charter, the ground of discrimination based on religion or belief is to be distinguished from the ground based on "political or any other opinion"'.[32]

The contribution of Giovanni Orlandini, however, demonstrates that Italian judges have interpreted the notion of 'belief' in implementing EU Directive 2000/78 within the context of the generic legislation combatting discrimination in a broad manner.[33] The added value of this interpretation is important because the more specific protection in the *Statuto dei lavoratori* is applicable solely to workers

[29] Cour Constitutionnelle, No 157/2004.
[30] Cour Constitutionnelle, No 64/2009.
[31] *Danilenkov v Russia* ECHR 2004 67336/01.
[32] Cases C-804/18 and C-341/19 *IX v Wabe eV and MH Müller Handels GmbH v MJ*, § 47.
[33] See Chapter 15 in this volume.

in a contractual employment relationship based on subordination. Furthermore, the remedies in the statutory instrument implementing Directive 2000/78 are more diverse and stronger.

3. Quis Custodem Custodiet?

Last but not least, it is important to assess the extent to which EU law gives some kind of dismissal protection, *casu quo* protection against discrimination to the benefit of workers' representatives. Insofar as these representatives function as actors of enforcement of European labour law, such dismissal protection is vital in order to ensure enforcement of EU labour law at grassroots level.

In this respect, it is worth recalling the following from the ILO's Workers' Representatives Recommendation, 1971 (No 143):

> 5. Workers' representatives in the undertaking should enjoy effective protection against any act prejudicial to them, including dismissal, based on their status or activities as a workers' representative or on union membership or participation in union activities, in so far as they act in conformity with existing laws or collective agreements or other jointly agreed arrangements.
>
> 6. (1) Where there are not sufficient relevant protective measures applicable to workers in general, specific measures should be taken to ensure effective protection of workers' representatives.
>
> (2) These might include such measures as the following:
>
> (a) detailed and precise definition of the reasons justifying termination of employment of workers' representatives:
> (b) a requirement of consultation with, an advisory opinion from, or agreement of an independent body, public or private, or a joint body, before the dismissal of a workers' representative becomes final;
> (c) a special recourse procedure open to workers' representatives who consider that their employment has been unjustifiably terminated, or that they have been subjected to an unfavourable change in their conditions of employment or to unfair treatment;
> (d) in respect of the unjustified termination of employment of workers' representatives, provision for an effective remedy which, unless this is contrary to basic principles of the law of the country concerned, should include the reinstatement of such representatives in their job, with payment of unpaid wages and with maintenance of their acquired rights;
> (e) provision for laying upon the employer, in the case of any alleged discriminatory dismissal or unfavourable change in the conditions of employment of a workers' representative, the burden of proving that such action was justified;
> (f) recognition of a priority to be given to workers' representatives with regard to their retention in employment in case of reduction of the workforce.

Although effective enforcement of both the Collective Redundancy Directive and the Transfer of Undertakings Directive necessitates the institution of workers' representatives, neither of these Directives explicitly provides protection for the workers' representatives concerned. The very first Directive to institute a principle of protection was the original EWC Directive 94/45. Article 10 of the EWC Directive stated under the heading 'protection of employees' representatives':

> Members of special negotiating bodies, members of European Works Councils and employees' representatives exercising their functions under the procedure referred to in Article 6 (3) shall, in the exercise of their functions, enjoy the same protection and guarantees provided for employees' representatives by the national legislation and/or practice in force in their country of employment
>
> This shall apply in particular to attendance at meetings of special negotiating bodies or European Works Councils or any other meetings within the framework of the agreement referred to in Article 6 (3), and the payment of wages for members who are on the staff of the Community-scale undertaking or the Community-scale group of undertakings for the period of absence necessary for the performance of their duties.

The issue of attendance at meetings and payment of wages is erroneously categorised under 'protection', whereas it clearly concerns facilitation of activities. The aforementioned ILO Recommendation No 143 clearly distinguishes both issues in a way that is more satisfactory from a conceptual point of view.

Three major loopholes characterise this system of protection in the context of European Works Councils. First, it presupposes the existence of a system of protection for employees' representatives by national legislation and/or practice in force in the country of their employment. At the time of the adoption of the EWC Directive, EU law did not require Member States to institute such a system. Second, there is no victimisation clause for the sake of workers or their representatives who request the establishment of an EWC, which would compel central management to enter into negotiations. Third, the question arises whether this principle of protection also applies to EWC structures functioning prior to the entry into force of EU Directive 94/45. On a strict reading of the grandfather clause in Article 13 EWC Directive, the obligations arising from this Directive shall *not* apply to structures that predated its adoption. The Recast Directive does not seem to have altered this loophole.

Directive 2002/14 is important because it introduced the principle of protection of workers' representatives at the level of the undertaking. Thus Article 7 states that:

> Member States shall ensure that employees' representatives, when carrying out their functions, enjoy adequate protection and guarantees to enable them to perform properly the duties which have been assigned to them.

The provision does not explain what 'adequate protection' entails, but some inspiration can be drawn from the generic principle enshrined in the subsequent provision of Article 8 which states that adequate sanctions in the case of infringement of the Directive must be effective, proportionate and dissuasive.

In *Ingeniørforeningen i Danmark*[34] the CJEU had to deal with the legal niceties of the Danish industrial relations system. The case concerned a workers' representative affiliated to another union than the one that signed a Cooperation Agreement aimed at implementing Directive 2002/14. Whereas this Agreement provided dismissal protection for representatives equivalent to an extra six weeks' notice in order to sanction the unfair character of the dismissal, under Danish law workers' representatives who fell victim to unfair dismissal would be entitled to the same protection as that granted to union representatives in the same professional groups or equivalent, and moreover dismissal could take place only if there were compelling grounds for it. Although the Court did not reject as such the existence of a variety of dismissal regimes, it elucidated the essence of the adequate protection provided under Article 7 Directive 2002/14. Thus, the Court made it abundantly clear that the 'dismissal of an employees' representative on grounds of his status or the functions which he performs in his capacity as a representative is incompatible with the protection required by Article 7'. Hence, it ruled that

> an employee's representative who has been the subject of a dismissal decision must therefore be in a position to ascertain, in the context of the appropriate administrative or judicial proceedings, whether that decision was taken on grounds of his status or performance of his functions as a representative and adequate sanctions must be applicable should it transpire that there is a connection between that representative's status or functions and the measure dismissing him.[35]

The Court did not – and did not have to – indicate, however, how this prohibition of unfair dismissal due to the representative's status or function had to be sanctioned, in other words, by compensatory measures or by reinstatement.

Council Directive 89/391/EEC of 12 June 1989 on the introduction of measures to encourage improvements in the safety and health of workers at work provides a role for both individual workers as experts in the field of health and safety and for workers' representatives in developing and monitoring a policy to improve the protection of health and safety. Unfortunately, Directive 89/391 provides protection only for these specific workers, stating that 'designated workers may not be placed at any disadvantage because of their activities related to the protection and prevention of occupational risks'. For workers' representatives, the issue of facilities (adequate time off work without loss of pay and necessary means) is addressed, but the Directive is mute on the issue of their dismissal protection.

It is worth comparing the protection of workers' representatives under EU law, with the protection provided by EU law to whistleblowers, who are not as such endowed with a representative mandate. The mere fact that Directive 2019/1937 is not applicable to breaches of EU labour law does not make the comparison pointless. The Whistleblowers Directive could serve as a source of inspiration regarding

[34] Case C-499/08 *Ingeniørforeningen i Danmark* [2010].
[35] §59.

what might constitute 'protection'. The Whistleblowers Directive refers to the notion of retaliation, which is exemplified by a non-exhaustive enumeration.

Article 19 mentions the following examples of retaliation:

(a) suspension, lay-off, dismissal or equivalent measures;
(b) demotion or withholding of promotion;
(c) transfer of duties, change of location of place of work, reduction in wages, change in working hours;
(d) withholding of training;
(e) a negative performance assessment or employment reference;
(f) imposition or administering of any disciplinary measure, reprimand or other penalty, including a financial penalty;
(g) coercion, intimidation, harassment or ostracism;
(h) discrimination, disadvantageous or unfair treatment;
(i) failure to convert a temporary employment contract into a permanent one, where the worker had legitimate expectations that he or she would be offered permanent employment;
(j) failure to renew, or early termination of, a temporary employment contract;
(k) harm, including to the person's reputation, particularly in social media, or financial loss, including loss of business and loss of income;
(l) blacklisting on the basis of a sector or industry-wide informal or formal agreement, which may entail that the person will not, in the future, find employment in the sector or industry;
(m) early termination or cancellation of a contract for goods or services;
(n) cancellation of a licence or permit;
(o) psychiatric or medical referrals.

Furthermore, a subsequent provision, Article 21 clearly deals with the issue of enforcement of this prohibition by requiring that Member States provide the necessary measures to protect workers against retaliation. It provides a non-exhaustive list of measures, ranging from immunity from liability to interim relief and full compensation.

4. Conclusion

A distinction should be made between enforcement and implementation of EU labour law. Whereas the first concept is related to any action that contributes to the effective application or observance of labour law standards, the second refers to the setting of those standards. In the case of collective agreements implementing EU Directives in the field of social policy, Member States entrusting management and labour with the implementation of such Directives, according to Article 153(3) TFEU, still need to 'guarantee the results imposed by that Directive'. This obligation includes the adoption of measures ensuring the enforcement of these collective agreements.

Although Article 153(1)(f) seems to provide unanimity for EU Directives as regards representation and collective defence of the interests of workers (and employers), the Council has adopted Directives derived from other provisions – often on the basis of a qualified majority – that were favourable for workers' representatives. They have introduced and institutionalised a collective actor at transnational level, rarely present in a spontaneous order (European Works Councils and the Special Negotiating Body) and have necessitated, empowered and protected workers' representatives at national level.

These collective actors are able to function as actors of enforcement of EU labour law mainly because three important tools are available to them: (i) monitoring the legal exercise of the managerial prerogative, (ii) access to justice, and (iii) recourse to collective action. The competence of workers' representatives stems mainly from provisions of Member State labour law and has not yet been the object of any harmonisation. As far as collective actors' access to justice is concerned, it is laid down in a variety of EU Directives, including Article 7(2) Directive 2000/43 (equal treatment between persons irrespective of racial or ethnic origin), Article 9(2) Directive 2000/78 (general framework for equal treatment in employment and occupation), Article 17(2) Directive 2006/54 (equal opportunities and equal treatment of men and women in matters of employment and occupation) and Article 9(2) Directive 2010/41 (equal treatment between men and women engaged in an activity in a self-employed capacity). These provisions offer considerable leeway, entrusting trade unions with access to justice. They also provide an option between judicial and administrative enforcement. Furthermore, they do not guarantee that these entities can act without the consent of the victim or in the absence of an identifiable victim. However, the minimal character of these provisions should not prevent Member States from empowering trade unions and works councils over and above them. The analysis of the tool of collective action demonstrates that the recourse to collective action as a means of enforcing EU labour law is hampered by too narrow an interpretation of the notion of 'conflict of interests' and by the fact that EU secondary instruments do not provide sufficient guarantees against the replacement of striking workers by agency or posted workers. EU law against discrimination is itself discriminatory, turning a blind eye to victims of discrimination against trade unions, while trade unions are rightly prohibited from discriminating on the grounds of religion or belief. This is remedied only partially by EU provisions on information and consultation, which provide protection that, in the words of the late Brian Bercusson (used to describe the development of EU labour law), are 'spasmodic, episodic and unsystematic'.[36]

[36] See B Bercusson, 'The conceptualisation of European Labour Law' (1995) *Industrial Law Journal* 3–18.

17

The European Labour Authority: Missing Link in the Cross-Border Enforcement of EU Labour Law

PIET VAN NUFFEL[1]

1. Introduction

The European Labour Authority ('ELA') is one of the youngest agencies of the European Union (EU). Set up in 2019, it was one of the flagship initiatives of the Juncker Commission, aimed at reinforcing the EU's social image by ensuring fair labour mobility in the EU. In line with the traditional set-up of EU labour law, in which enforcement is left primarily to the competent authorities of the Member States,[2] the ELA is aimed at facilitating the effective enforcement of EU labour law by reinforcing the tools for cooperation available to national administrations. Its focus on operational support for administrative enforcement distinguishes the ELA from existing EU agencies in the area of labour law, such as the European Agency for Safety and Health at Work (EU-OSHA), the European Centre for the Development of Vocational Training (CEDEFOP) and the European Foundation for the Improvement of Living and Working Conditions (EUROFOUND), which have essentially been tasked with collecting and exchanging information and disseminating expertise in the field of social and labour policy.[3] Whereas the knowledge provided by these agencies undoubtedly contributes to improved enforcement of EU labour law, the objectives set for the European Labour Authority were, from the outset, of a different nature, concentrated on operational support in a field of action limited to cross-border labour mobility.

It was then Commission President Jean-Claude Juncker who announced the establishment of the European Labour Authority in his speech on the State of the

[1] Legal Service, European Commission; Professor of European Law, KU Leuven. As a member of the Cabinet of Commissioner Marianne Thyssen the author has been involved with the preparation and negotiation of the Commission's proposal establishing the ELA. All views in this chapter are personal.

[2] See Chapter 1 in this volume.

[3] See Chapter 4 in this volume.

Union of 13 September 2017,[4] following which Commissioner Marianne Thyssen, in March 2018, submitted a legislative proposal[5] that the European Parliament and the Council (the 'co-legislators') adopted one year later.[6] On 16 October 2019, the ELA's Management Board met for the first time in Brussels, following a formal opening ceremony. Since then, the ELA has recruited staff, adopted its first work programmes and appointed an Executive Director.[7] At cruising speed, it will have 144 employees and an annual budget of 50 million euros.[8] The ELA will thus have more resources at its disposal than the existing agencies in the social area,[9] although it will not attain the size of other operational EU agencies, such as Europol or Frontex.[10] In 2021, the ELA is still functioning with only 60 per cent of its envisaged total staff and budget, but will gradually expand its operational capacity.[11] Also this year, the agency is set to exchange temporary premises in Brussels for offices in Bratislava. This contribution attempts to explain the choice made by the EU legislature for an agency that does not itself act as enforcer of European labour law but rather reinforces the operational capacities of national enforcement authorities by facilitating their cooperation. Before analysing the specific tools that ELA makes available for the enforcement of EU social law, it is therefore necessary to situate the agency in the political context in which it was created.

2. Establishing the ELA as an Instrument for Fair Labour Mobility

The background for the creation of the ELA is the increased cross-border labour mobility in the EU. In the past decade, the number of citizens working or residing in a Member State other than that of their nationality has doubled.[12] Whereas

[4] See: https://ec.europa.eu/commission/presscorner/detail/en/SPEECH_17_3165.

[5] Commission proposal of 13 March 2018 for a Regulation of the European Parliament and of the Council establishing a European Labour Authority, COM (2018) 131 final (hereinafter the 'Commission proposal').

[6] Regulation (EU) 2019/1149 of the European Parliament and of the Council of 20 June 2019 establishing a European Labour Authority, [2019] OJ L 186/21 (hereinafter the 'ELA Regulation').

[7] See the ELA website: www.ela.europa.eu. On 22 October, the Management Board appointed Cosmin Boiangiu as Executive Director.

[8] Explanatory memorandum to the Commission proposal, 10.

[9] According to the information available on their websites, the 2021 budget available for EU-OSHA is around €16 million (for 65 temporary and contractual staff), for CEDEFOP around €18 million (for 123 temporary and contractual staff) and for EUROFOUND around €21 million (for 112 temporary and contractual staff).

[10] See the overview in Annex VIII (The composition of the budget of EU agencies and other bodies – 2018) to the European Court of Auditors' 2020 Special Report 'Future of EU agencies – Potential for more flexibility and cooperation' (mentioning of 2018 budgets of €288.7 million for FRONTEX and €135.7 million for Europol – compared with €38.4 million for Eurojust and €23 million for the EU Fundamental Rights Agency).

[11] See the work programme for 2021, available on the ELA website, at 38 (envisaging almost 100 staff members by end 2021 of which 45 seconded national experts).

[12] Impact assessment accompanying the Proposal for a Regulation of the European Parliament and of the Council establishing a European Labour Authority (SWD(2018)68 final, 7) (referring to 17 million citizens in 2017 as compared with 9 million in 2006).

overall the number of mobile citizens still represents no more than 4 per cent of the EU workforce,[13] in several Member States this labour mobility is having a significant impact. Since the accession of new Member States in 2004 and 2007, there has been a remarkable increase in the employment, often for short periods, of workers from central and eastern European Member States in western European Member States with higher wage levels.[14]

In that context the Juncker Commission launched its programme for promoting fair labour mobility. While most attention was paid to the proposal to review the 1996 Posted Workers Directive[15] in order to lay down the principle of equal pay for equal work at the same place,[16] the Commission also proposed to revise the regulations on coordination of national social security systems.[17] It also proposed revision of the legislation on road transport in order to improve the position of lorry drivers and lay down specific rules on the application of the Posted Workers Directive in that extremely mobile sector.[18] Meanwhile, practical difficulties in the application of the rules on posting of workers showed that fair labour mobility must be ensured not merely by improving the substantive rules, but also by facilitating and strengthening their enforcement.[19] Also, the European Parliament had been insisting on increased cooperation between the Member States, with better exchange of information between national labour inspections.[20] In 2014, the European Parliament and the Council agreed on a directive on the enforcement of the rules on posting of workers[21] and in 2016 on a decision establishing a European Platform to tackle undeclared work.[22] The Juncker Commission also presented the improved enforcement of EU labour law as implementing the

[13] Ibid.

[14] See P Van Nuffel and S Afanasjeva, 'Enhancing the Protection of Workers in the Cross-border Provision of Services' (2018) *European Papers* 1401–27.

[15] Directive 96/71/EC of the European Parliament and of the Council of 16 December 1996 concerning the posting of workers in the framework of the provision of services, [1997] OJ L 18/1.

[16] See J-C Juncker, 'A New Start for Europe: My Agenda for Jobs, Growth, Fairness and Democratic Change- Political Guidelines for the next European Commission – Opening Statement in the European Parliament Plenary Session', Strasbourg, 15 July 2014, 7.

[17] Commission proposal of 13 December 2016 for a Regulation of the European Parliament and of the Council amending Regulation (EC) No 883/2004 on the coordination of social security systems and Regulation (EC) No 987/2009 laying down the procedure for implementing Regulation (EC) No 883/2004, COM(2016)815 final.

[18] Commission proposals of 31 May 2017, COM (2017) 278 final, COM (2017) 277 final, and COM (2017) 281.

[19] See also H Verschueren, 'De Europese Arbeidsautoriteit: een nieuw orgaan aan het Europese firmament' (2020) *SEW – Tijdschrift voor Europees en economisch recht* 21, at 23.

[20] See the resolutions of 14 January 2014 on effective labour inspections as a strategy to improve working conditions in Europe (2013/2112(INI)) and of 14 September 2016 on social dumping in the European Union (2015/2255(INI)).

[21] Directive 2014/67/EU of the European Parliament and of the Council of 15 May 2014 on the enforcement of Directive 96/71/EC concerning the posting of workers in the framework of the provision of services, [2014] OJ 2014 L159/11.

[22] Decision (EU) 2016/344 of the European Parliament and of the Council of 9 March 2016 on establishing a European Platform to enhance cooperation in tackling undeclared work, [2016] OJ L 65/12.

European Pillar of Social Rights, in particular its principles supporting fair working conditions, fair and well-functioning labour markets and welfare systems.[23] The establishment of a European Labour Authority came as the final piece of the Commission's programme to achieve fair labour mobility.

As expected, the Commission's programme on fair labour mobility triggered a difficult discussion in both the European Parliament and in the Council. In certain western European Member States, such as France and Belgium, the growing phenomenon of posted workers has led to stricter control measures in order to combat what is perceived as 'social dumping' on their labour markets.[24] Therefore, the revision of the Posted Workers Directive to introduce the mandatory application of rules on remuneration for posted workers was particularly controversial in central and eastern Europe. It has been by pointing out that providing for equal conditions of remuneration for posted workers is essential for ensuring fair play in the Single Market, and that the revised Directive seeks to preserve the cross-border movement of services against national protectionism, rather than to restrict that movement of services,[25] that the Commission, in 2018, eventually managed to find sufficient support for the review of that Directive, both in central and eastern Europe and in western Europe.[26] That proved more difficult for the proposed revision of the coordination of social security rules, which, like the reform of the rules on road transport could not be completed before the May 2019 elections to the European Parliament.[27]

[23] Eg principles 4 (active support to employment), 5 (secure and adaptable employment), 6 (wages) of the European Pillar of Social Rights. See also the Explanatory Memorandum of the Commission proposal, at 10.

[24] The European Parliament defined the concept of social dumping in its Resolution of 14 September 2016 on social dumping in the European Union (A8-0255/2016) as 'cover[ing] a wide range of intentionally abusive practices and the circumvention of existing European and national legislation (including laws and universally applicable collective agreements), which enable the development of unfair competition by unlawfully minimising labour and operation costs and lead[ing] to violations of workers' rights and exploitation of workers'. The Court of Justice has recognised the protection of workers of the host State against possible social dumping as an overriding reason of public interest capable of justifying a restriction of one of the Treaty economic freedoms, see, eg Case C-60/03 *Wolff & Müller* EU:C:2004:610, paras 35 and 36; Case C-315/13 *De Clercq and Others* EU:C:2014:2408, para 65. Still, the notion of social dumping is controversial, as it is influenced by considerations concerning the legitimacy of such protection. See eg the opinion of Advocate General Szpunar in Case C-16/18 *Dobersberger* EU:C:2019:638, paras 29–32 ('To put it bluntly, what is "social dumping" for some is, quite simply, "employment" for others.').

[25] See also the confirmation of the internal market legal basis by the Court of Justice when rejecting the actions for annulment against the revised Posted Workers Directive: Case C-620/18 *Hungary v European Parliament and Council* EU:C:2020:1001 paras 49–64 and Case C-626/18 *Poland v European Parliament and Council* EU:C:2020:1000, paras 54–69.

[26] Leading to the adoption of Directive (EU) 2018/957 of the European Parliament and of the Council of 28 June 2018 amending Directive 96/71/EC concerning the posting of workers in the framework of the provision of services, [2018] OJ L 173/16. At the time of final approval in the Council on 21 June 2018, only Poland and Hungary voted against, with Croatia, Latvia, Lithuania and the United Kingdom abstaining.

[27] At the time of writing, the negotiators of the European Parliament and the Council could not agree on the revision of the social security coordination regulations. On road transport, the co-legislators achieved a political agreement in December 2019, formally adopted as Directive (EU) 2020/1057 of the European Parliament and of the Council of 15 July 2020 laying down specific rules with respect

It is therefore noteworthy that the EU co-legislators were able to reach agreement rather swiftly on the Commission's proposal on the ELA. In line with the approach taken on the revision of the Posted Workers Directive, the Commission opted not to conceive the ELA as an enforcement tool aimed at combating breaches of social legislation by foreign undertakings. The Commission realised that its proposal would find support only if it was not perceived as solely serving the interests of Member States with a large share of incoming (posted) workers. The ELA therefore equally had to respond to obstacles to the correct application of EU labour and social security law as also encountered in sending Member States. Moreover, whereas the establishment of an agency facilitating the enforcement of social legislation was certainly likely to be received positively by trade unions, the Commission considered that its adoption would also need to obtain support from employers' associations, whose needs also needed to be accommodated. From the outset, the Commission therefore presented the ELA as a body with primary responsibility for informing and supporting undertakings and workers of their rights and obligations in cross-border situations, with the ELA thus 'supporting' rather than 'restricting' the provision of cross-border services and labour mobility.[28] Accordingly, the Commission proposed to make the ELA also responsible for facilitating the cross-border matching of job vacancies, including the coordination of the existing European network of employment services (EURES).[29] The transfer of the EURES Coordination Office from the Commission's services should provide the ELA with useful expertise on labour mobility, including information on shortages in the labour market and mismatching of skills.[30] Furthermore, as regards the enforcement of EU legislation, the Commission proposed to make the ELA responsible not only for the rules on posting of workers, but also the regulations on free movement of workers and coordination of social security systems, which ensure social protection and protection against discrimination for all mobile workers, wherever they are active in the EU.[31] To further increase the ELA's added value, the Commission also sought to simplify the institutional landscape by integrating existing structures and networks involved with labour mobility as

to Directive 96/71/EC and Directive 2014/67/EU for posting drivers in the road transport sector and amending Directive 2006/22/EC as regards enforcement requirements and Regulation (EU) No 1024/2012, [2020] OJ L 249/49.

[28] On the importance of this 'positive mission', see S Fernandes, *What is our ambition for the European Labour Authority?*, Policy Paper No 2019 (Jacques Delors Institute, 8 March 2018), 3.

[29] Commission Proposal, Art 7. See Regulation (EU) 2016/589 of the European Parliament and of the Council of 13 April 2016 on a European network of employment services (EURES), workers' access to mobility services and the further integration of labour markets, [2016] OJ L 107/1.

[30] See also R Pedersini, 'How to design the European Labour Authority to ensure greater efficiency social and dumping' (2019, Brussels, European Economic and Social Committee), 11.

[31] Commission proposal, Recital 7. The Commission proposed to base the ELA not only on Arts 46 (free movement of workers) and 48 (coordination of social security systems) TFEU, but also on Arts 53(1) and 62 (free movement of services) and 91 (international transport) TFEU. Based on the accessory nature of the activities regarding posted workers and international transport, the co-legislators agreed to base the ELA Regulation solely on Arts 46 and 48 TFEU.

much as possible into the ELA.[32] That included the European Coordination Office of EURES and the European Platform against undeclared work, but also various expert committees on free movement and social security coordination.[33]

As expected, the proposal received immediate support from Member States such as France and Belgium, which had also been those insisting on the revision of the rules on posting of workers. Several other Member States changed their initial criticism of the establishment of a new EU agency into support after evaluating the Commission's proposal. That was also true for many central and eastern European Member States, some of which also soon demonstrated their interest in hosting such a new agency.[34] When issuing its proposal, the Commission immediately set up an advisory group in which it invited representatives of the Member States and the social partners to exchange experiences and information on the tasks to which the ELA could pay attention once set up.[35] Without interfering with the legislative procedure dealing with the Commission's proposal, the advisory group allowed national experts to brainstorm with employers' associations and trade unions on the practical needs underpinning certain envisaged tasks, in particular the coordination of cross-border inspections. In the Council's working parties, meanwhile, a majority of delegations rather quickly reached agreement on the set of tasks they wished to allocate to the ELA, with some amendments to the Commission's proposal, such as a refusal to transfer the expert committees on social security coordination and the emphasis on the supportive role that the agency had to perform vis-à-vis national authorities and their competences in social matters. In the negotiation mandate that the Council approved on 6 December 2018 (the Council 'general approach') this transpired also in the request to have the term 'authority' changed to 'agency'.[36] On 11 December 2018, the European Parliament agreed on its negotiating mandate by validating, with a very large majority, the report adopted within the Committee on Employment and Social Affairs, produced by Dutch MEP Jeroen Lenaers.[37] Curiously, this report took on board both concerns from trade unions, such as the request to have social partners directly represented in the Management Board of the ELA, but also some concerns expressed mainly by employers' associations, such as the proposed slimming down of the ELA's tasks.[38]

[32] See the explanatory memorandum to the Commission Proposal, 9–10.

[33] The Commission succeeded in this ambition, except as regards social security coordination; see n 137 and accompanying text.

[34] Candidates for hosting the ELA were Sofia (Bulgaria), Nicosia (Cyprus), Riga (Latvia) and Bratislava (Slovakia).

[35] Commission Decision (EU) 2018/402 of 13 March 2018 establishing the European Advisory Group for the European Labour Authority, [2018] OJ L 72/20.

[36] Council of the European Union, Document 15392/18, 10 December 2018 (see: http://data.consilium.europa.eu/doc/document/ST-15392-2018-INIT/en/pdf). In the Council, only Hungary and Sweden did not support the general approach.

[37] European Parliament, document A8-0391/2018, 26 November 2018 (the 'Lenaers Report', see: https://www.europarl.europa.eu/doceo/document/A-8-2018-0391_EN.html).

[38] See, for example, the critical position of the German employers' organisation BDA considering tasks such as taking over the EURES Coordination Office as an unnecessary duplication of structures: European Labour Authority offers no added value, improve coordination between existing EU

Because time was pressing at the end of the European Parliament's mandate, the Parliament convened on the same 11 December 2018 the first of seven trialogue meetings with the Council and the Commission. A comparison of the Council's general approach and the 'Lenaers Report' indicated that the co-legislators largely agreed with the set of tasks proposed by the Commission. The main difference was that the Parliament wanted the ELA to concentrate on enforcement activities and not to deal with employment services.[39] Both institutions preferred the ELA not to have the power of mediation in matters of social security coordination and opposed the Commission's proposal to have the ELA contribute to resolving cross-border labour market disruptions.[40] On the last point, the co-legislators effectively amended the Commission's proposal; on the other points, the text as finally agreed in the trialogues – as explained further below – did not substantially depart from the set of tasks proposed by the Commission. The politically most sensitive differences between the co-legislators' positions concerned the question of whether the social partners should be represented in the Management Board, the method for determining the agency's seat and its final name ('agency' or 'authority'). Thanks to constructive negotiations skilfully organised by the Romanian Presidency of the Council and the EP rapporteur, with the Commissioner acting as honest broker, a compromise was found on 14 February 2019 according to which the Management Board includes four social partner representatives without voting rights,[41] the founding Regulation does not determine the seat[42] and the term 'authority' has been maintained. That compromise was approved by a broad majority of Member States on 20 February 2019[43] and by an equally large majority within the

structures – BDA position on the European Commission's proposal for a regulation establishing the European Labour Authority, June 2018. On the trade unions' views on the ELA's management structure, see the position of the European Trade Union Confederation (ETUC) in ETUC Position on the European Labour Authority – Ensuring fairness for workers in the single market, 13–14 December 2017, www.etuc.org/sites/default/files/document/files/etuc_position_on_a_european_labour_authority_-_ensuring_fairness_for_workers_in_the_single_market.pdf.

[39] Thus, the European Parliament's rapporteur initially asked to entirely remove for the ELA the task of promoting access to services in the field of cross-border labour mobility, which, in the Commission's proposal, was generally formulated to also include, eg, targeted mobility schemes. Eventually, the Parliament could agree to a less general formulation, limiting the relevant services to the coordination of the EURES Network of Employment Services. See ELA, Regulation, Art 6.

[40] For further details, see the analysis below.

[41] On the ELA's management structure and the discussion on the representation of social partners, see further P Van Nuffel, 'De Europese Arbeidsautoriteit: een nieuw agentschap voor arbeidsmobiliteit in de interne markt' in H Verschueren (ed), *Detachering – Nieuwe ontwikkelingen in het Europees recht vanuit Belgisch en Nederlands perspectief* (Die Keure, 2019) 229, at 252–54.

[42] On the margins of the Council meeting on 13 June 2019, the Member States organised a vote resulting in the selection of Bratislava. That outcome has been formalised in Decision (EU) 2019/1199 taken by common accord between the Representatives of the Governments of the Member States of 13 June 2019 on the location of the seat of the European Labour Authority, [2019] OJ L 189/68. The European Parliament disagrees that the power to determine an agency's seat is left to the Member States and has therefore brought an action for annulment against that decision (C-743/19, pending). See Van Nuffel, n 41 at 254–56.

[43] Within the Council's Committee of Permanent Representatives (Coreper) only Hungary, Austria and Sweden indicated to vote against, with the Czech Republic and Poland indicating their abstention.

Parliament on 16 April 2019.[44] On that basis, the Regulation establishing the ELA was formally adopted on 20 June 2019 and entered into force on 31 July 2019.

3. What EU Legislation is to be Enforced by the ELA and for Whom?

As set out above, the European Parliament and the Council largely preserved the diversified tasks that the Commission proposed to allocate to the ELA as regards provision of information, enforcement of social law, tackling of undeclared work and mediation. These tasks are aimed at facilitating the application and enforcement of existing EU legislation and do not create new rights or obligations for workers or employers.[45] Before discussing these tasks, it is necessary to specify the areas in which and for which persons the ELA will be active.

Article 1(2) of the ELA Regulation defines the domain in which the ELA is to assist the effective application and enforcement of EU rules as 'Union law related to labour mobility across the Union and the coordination of social security systems within the Union'. In this domain, the ELA 'shall act within the scope of the Union acts listed in paragraph 4, including all directives, regulations, and decisions based on those acts, and of any further legally binding Union act which confers tasks to the Authority'.[46]

The EU acts listed in Article 1(4) comprise the regulations on coordination of social security,[47] legislation implementing the free movement of workers,[48] the EURES regulation,[49] the rules on posting of workers[50] and social legislation concerning road transport.[51] The Commission had referred in its proposal to all those situations concerning 'cross-border labour mobility', a term that some in the

[44] Approved with 472 votes in favour, 142 against and 39 abstentions.

[45] ELA Regulation, Recital 14.

[46] ELA Regulation, Art 1(2).

[47] Regulation (EC) No 883/2004 of the European Parliament and of the Council of 29 April 2004 on the coordination of social security systems, [2004] OJ L 166/1; Regulation (EC) No 987/2009 of the European Parliament and of the Council of 16 September 2009 laying down the procedure for implementing Regulation (EC) No 883/2004, [2009] OJ L 284/1.

[48] Regulation (EU) No 492/2011 of the European Parliament and of the Council of 5 April 2011 on freedom of movement for workers within the Union, [2011] OJ L 141/1; Directive 2014/54/EU of the European Parliament and of the Council of 16 April 2014 on measures facilitating the exercise of rights conferred on workers in the context of freedom of movement for workers, [2014] OJ L 128/8.

[49] See n 29.

[50] See nn 15 and 21.

[51] Regulation (EC) No 561/2006 of the European Parliament and of the Council of 15 March 2006 on the harmonisation of certain social legislation relating to road transport, [2006] OJ L 102/1; Directive 2006/22/EC of the European Parliament and of the Council of 15 March 2006 on minimum conditions for the implementation of Council Regulations (EEC) No 3820/85 and (EEC) No 3821/85 concerning social legislation relating to road transport activities, [2006] OJ L 102/35; Regulation (EC) No 1071/2009 of the European Parliament and of the Council of 21 October 2009 establishing common rules concerning the conditions to be complied with to pursue the occupation of road transport operator, [2009] OJ L 300/51.

European Parliament feared could be easily misunderstood as limited to frontier workers,[52] for which they insisted on using the term 'labour mobility across the European Union'. Either way, it should be clear that only cross-border situations are concerned here. It is indeed in those situations that it is less easy for workers and employers to find adequate information on their rights and obligations and for national authorities to apply the relevant legislation without cooperation from other Member States. That is true not only for the enforcement of labour law provisions on workers posted from other Member States, but also for the application of social security rules to persons who have acquired, or are likely to acquire, rights in other Member States.

Admittedly, also in other areas of social law, information on rights and obligations and effective enforcement may pose problems to Member States, for which cooperation at EU level could be useful. Still, the added value of an agency such as the ELA exists above all in areas where it is precisely the cross-border dimension that creates obstacles to information about and enforcement of rights and obligations under EU law. That is why a large part of EU labour law remains outside the ELA's scope of action, for example the rules on occupational safety and health, working time and non-discrimination. Also, the rules on the information and consultation of workers, in particular the European Works Councils, which may raise issues of application across Member States, have not been brought within the ELA's remit.[53] The action of the ELA remains indeed focused on those situations in which workers or their employers make use of their free movement rights. Extending the scope of the ELA's activities to 'domestic' labour law issues would also have impacted on the legal basis for the ELA Regulation, which relies on the Treaty provisions on free movement[54] and not on the social policy provisions of Article 153 TFEU. Various stakeholders had from the outset made clear that they would only be able to accept a European labour authority if endowed with a focused set of tasks with clear added value,[55] thereby excluding any agency with a general competence as regards enforcement of EU social law. Nevertheless, the co-legislators accepted the Commission's proposal to enable the ELA to report to national and EU authorities on any suspected irregularities in areas of Union law of which it might become aware in the course of its activities. This may include breaches of working conditions, health and safety rules or labour exploitation.[56]

[52] Despite Recital 8 to the ELA Regulation clearly 'including the freedom of movement for workers, the posting of workers and highly mobile services'.

[53] It should be noted that trade unions also saw a role for the ELA in that area; see the position of the European Trade Union Confederation (ETUC) mentioned in n 38.

[54] See n 31.

[55] Eg the amendment proposed in the Lenaers Report to Recital 5, which eventually resulted in Recital 6 of the ELA Regulation. Thus, the added value of the ELA was also questioned by Business Europe, the European organisation of national employers' federations, in its position paper of 7 May 2018: www.businesseurope.eu/sites/buseur/files/media/position_papers/social/2018-05-07_european_labour_authority.pdf, and by German employers' organisations (see n 38).

[56] ELA Regulation, Art 9(9) and Recital 8. Meanwhile, the ELA has developed a template and workflow guidance on reporting suspected irregularities (see the ELA website).

Apart from the abovementioned terminological issue, the European Parliament and the Council largely agreed on the focus on cross-border labour mobility proposed by the Commission. What needed to be discussed in the trialogues was the Council's request to delimit the ELA's scope of activities by means of a closed list of applicable EU legislation. The Parliament had no problems with the content of that list, which includes the legislative acts mentioned above, but preferred giving the ELA the power also to enforce other EU legislation, for example social provisions included in sector-specific legislation. In order to ensure legal certainty, the co-legislators eventually accepted the definition of the scope of activities laid down in Article 1(2), which refers to the closed list of EU legislation contained in Article 1(4), yet not without stipulating that this list should be extended whenever new EU legislation is adopted in the field of labour mobility across the Union.[57] Although the co-legislators thus precisely defined the ELA's field of action, they equally intend all new EU legislation containing rights or obligations related to cross-labour mobility to be added to the list in Article 1(4). Somewhat ambiguously, the co-legislators also indicated that 'within the scope of this Regulation' the ELA may also deal with cross-border aspects of specific EU legislation in certain sectors, such as international transport.[58]

It is important to note that, contrary to the narrow impression that the term 'Labour Authority' may have on some people, the agency's scope of activities is not limited to workers and employment relationships. It rather covers the whole of the 'labour market' with the applicable EU legislation indeed also extending to self-employed persons and jobseekers and, as far as social security coordination is concerned, even non-economically active EU citizens who as family members or in another capacity are insured in a Member State and find themselves in a cross-border situation. On that basis the ELA may also need to deal with third-country nationals legally resident in the Union, either as posted workers, intra-corporate transferees or long-term residents or as family members of workers or self-employed persons.[59]

Territorially, the ELA's scope of action coincides with that of the relevant EU legislation, which applies not only to the EU Member States but also to certain third countries, such as the non-EU member countries of the European Economic Area (Iceland, Liechtenstein and Norway) and Switzerland.

4. ELA's Tasks Aimed at Facilitating and Enhancing Enforcement of EU Labour Law

The ELA Regulation grants the agency a diversified set of tasks, allowing it to intervene at several stages in which labour mobility may need support from public

[57] ELA Regulation, Recital 9.

[58] Ibid, Recital 12 (adding that the ELA's scope of activities should be periodically evaluated and, where appropriate, reviewed).

[59] ELA Regulation, Recital 13.

authorities. In four respects the ELA is to contribute to ensuring fair labour mobility across the Union and assist in the coordination of social security systems: (1) facilitating access to information on rights and obligations and access to relevant services in relation to labour mobility; (2) enhancing cooperation in the enforcement of EU law; (3) mediating and facilitating a solution in case of cross-border disputes between Member States; and (4) supporting cooperation between Member States in tackling undeclared work.[60] Compared with the tasks set out in the Commission's proposal, the EU legislator only added that of tackling undeclared work, clarifying that the ELA is taking over the mission granted to the European Platform specifically set up to that end in 2016. Although 'enforcement' of EU law is specifically highlighted in the second task, it is actually served by all four tasks, which require the ELA to cooperate with – and ultimately support – the competent national authorities in order to assist mobile workers, their employers and public authorities in the application of the relevant EU legislation.

4.1. Support in the Provision of Information to Workers and Employers

Also as regards enforcement of EU labour law, it is thus relevant to refer to the task granted to the ELA in order to facilitate access to information on rights and obligations regarding labour mobility.[61] As follows from the Regulation, this task does not mean that workers and employers will henceforth be able to contact the ELA with any question on the legislation applicable in other Member States. Rather, it is the ELA's task to assist the Member States with the fulfilment of requirements imposed by existing EU legislation as regards information to be provided to workers, employers or their organisations, in particular by helping them improve the availability, quality and accessibility of that information.[62] Some information is more linked to employment services, such as information on cross-border vacancies that must be accessible on the EURES portal.[63] Other information requirements, however, directly facilitate the application of legislation, such as information that Member States must provide on the rights of migrant workers pursuant to the Enforcement Directive on the free movement of workers[64] or on working conditions applicable to posted workers pursuant to the Enforcement Directive on posting of workers.[65] Thus, the ELA has started to review information provided through the Member States' websites concerning posting of workers on aspects such as remuneration, long-term posting, sanctions, and declaration

[60] ELA Regulation, Art 2.
[61] ELA Regulation, Art 2(a).
[62] Ibid, Art 5.
[63] See Art 22 of Regulation No 2016/589 (see n 29 above).
[64] See Art 6 of Directive 2014/54 (see n 48 above).
[65] See Art 5 of Directive 2014/67 (see n 21 above).

requirements, and to develop recommendations as to the presentation of a Member State's collective agreements on those websites.[66] At the request of the European Parliament, the ELA will have to contribute to the provision of information also through a website that, as a single portal, provides access to information sources in the Member States and at EU level in all official languages.[67] Meanwhile, the ELA has set up a Working Group on Information, which started mapping information gaps and reviewing the information currently provided by Member States, as well as an Information Support Service and a Translation Facility.[68]

4.2. Cooperation between Member States in the Enforcement of EU Legislation

As indicated above, it is the concern about effective enforcement of EU labour law in cross-border situations that directly instigated the establishment of the ELA.[69] Although the Member States' authorities are required under Article 4(3) TFEU to respect their duty of sincere cooperation, the implementation thereof frequently faces serious practical problems. In that context, reference is often made to the difficulties encountered by host Member States in case of posting of workers to obtain timely and accurate information on sending undertakings from the Member States in which those undertakings are established.[70] More generally, however, the ELA is bound to play a key role in the exchange of information and in coordinated enforcement activities building on the experiences and best practices that some Member States have already been developing bilaterally.[71] Before discussing these matters, it should be noted that the ELA will also assist the operational work of enforcement authorities through risk assessment and analyses and will support Member States with capacity-building through exchanges of staff and experiences and training and awareness-raising programmes.[72]

In order to strengthen cooperation between Member States in enforcement matters, the ELA will primarily provide operational support in the exchange of

[66] See, eg, the Summary of deliberations of the Fifth meeting of the European Labour Authority Working Group on Information, 2 March 2021 (published on ELA's website).

[67] ELA Regulation, Art 5(a).

[68] See the 2021 work programme, 13.

[69] Eg, President Juncker's speech on the State of the Union of September 2017 (see n 4): 'We should make sure that all EU rules on labour mobility are enforced in a fair, simple and effective way by a new European inspection and enforcement body. It is absurd to have a Banking Authority to police banking standards, but no common Labour Authority for ensuring fairness in our single market. We will create such an Authority.' See also the Commission's Impact Assessment accompanying the Proposal for a Regulation of the European Parliament and the Council establishing a European Labour Authority (n 12 above), 11–16.

[70] See J Cremers, *Towards a European Labour Authority – Mandate, Main Tasks and Open Questions* (Brussels, Friedrich-Ebert-Stiftung, 2018) 4–5; N Rennuy, 'Posting of workers: Enforcement, compliance and reform', (2020) *European Journal of Social Security* 212–34.

[71] Pedersini, n 30 above at 15.

[72] Ibid, Arts 10 and 11.

information and the organisation of joint and coordinated inspections.[73] From certain angles, the Commission's proposal has been criticised and the ELA has been depicted as toothless.[74] For example, trade unions suggested that the ELA should supervise the extent to which national authorities respond to requests for information from other Member States and should be empowered to take non-cooperating Member States to the European Court of Justice.[75] The Commission, however, took the view that granting such police powers to the ELA was not necessarily the best way of leading national inspectorates to better cooperation[76] and that such powers would be difficult to reconcile with the responsibility for defining enforcement structures that, especially in matters of social policy, is largely left to the Member States. It also referred to the specific role exercised in some Member States (in particular the Nordic countries) by social partners, not only in the implementation of social law, but also in supervising its enforcement.[77] Furthermore, there was also the political fact that central and eastern European Member States generally were not eager to create a European enforcement body for legislation which they often perceive – particularly as regards posted workers – as intended to restrict competition by central and eastern European undertakings, despite its possible beneficial effects for the workers concerned.

4.2.1. Exchange of Information between National Authorities

As regards information exchange, the ELA is supposed to facilitate cooperation between the competent national authorities and to contribute to an accelerated exchange of information and effective fulfilment of cooperation obligations laid down in the applicable EU legislation.[78] To that end, the ELA must help national authorities in identifying the relevant contact points in other Member States.[79] It must facilitate contacts between national authorities by providing logistical and technical support, such as translation and interpreting services.[80] The ELA will also promote the use of electronic exchange mechanisms and databases between the Member States.[81] In order to encourage the authorities to respond effectively

[73] ELA Regulation, Arts 7 to 9.

[74] See, for example, the explanatory statement to the Lenaers Report: 'Second, the Authority must have the means to make an actual difference in practice. It should not become a toothless tiger; the voluntary nature of Member States' authorities' participation – as proposed by the Commission – is not enough to achieve this.'

[75] See, for example, the position of the Austrian employers' association, *Bundesarbeitskammer, AK Position Paper – May 2018 – Proposal* on establishing a European Labour Authority: www.akeuropa.eu/sites/default/files/main_report_en_502.pdf.

[76] See also R Pedersini, n 30 above at 24.

[77] As confirmed also in Art 1(6) and Recital 19 of the ELA Regulation.

[78] Ibid, Art 7(1).

[79] Ibid, Art 7(1)(a).

[80] Ibid, Art 7(1)(b).

[81] Ibid, Art 7(3) and (4). The ELA does not have the means to develop its own mechanisms for electronic exchange and databases, but may suggest improvements to existing mechanisms: ibid.

and timely to another Member State's request for information, the ELA shall keep and exchange the status of such requests.[82] Where a Member State so requests, the ELA will also facilitate and support the cross-border enforcement of penalties and fines.[83]

In order to make national authorities cooperate effectively, the ELA has been modelled on the structure used by Europol[84] and Eurojust,[85] with Member States seconding liaison officers to the agency.[86] The national liaison officers should ensure that a request for information from their own Member State is instantly transmitted to the liaison officer of the requested Member State, who can then forward it directly to the proper authorities within that Member State.[87] Each Member State is to give its liaison officer the right to internally request and receive all relevant information.[88] It may be hoped that through their day-to-day cooperation within a single agency, these national experts will develop shared views on enforcement needs and also be able within their respective Member States to demonstrate the utility of the ELA's cooperation channels for the effective and uniform application of the relevant EU legislation.

Because the Commission conceived the ELA as an instrument at the service of national authorities, it has not proposed any system of sanctions against Member States that would not, or not sufficiently, cooperate with the ELA. That does not mean that the ELA Regulation requires the ELA to simply abide by such a situation. As stated above, the ELA will keep a record of the progress of requests for information that it has received, together with responses and failures to respond. Furthermore, the ELA is to report twice a year to the Commission about unresolved requests.[89] As guardian of the Treaties, the Commission may then investigate whether there has been an infringement of cooperation requirements imposed by EU legislation and, if necessary, start infringement proceedings against a Member

[82] Ibid, Art 7(1)(b).

[83] Ibid, Art 7(1)(d). Although the Council had initially requested so during the legislative process, that competence has eventually not been limited to those penalties and fines for which Arts 13 to 19 of the Enforcement Directive on the posting of workers lays down a system of cross-border enforcement.

[84] Contacts between Europol and Member States' competent authorities are ensured by national units, which each designate at least one liaison officer to be attached to Europol. See Arts 7 and 8 of Regulation (EU) 2016/794 of the European Parliament and of the Council of 11 May 2016 on the European Union Agency for Law Enforcement Cooperation (Europol), [2016] OJ L 135/53. Liaison officers are to assist in the exchange of information between Europol and their Member States: ibid, Art 8(3).

[85] Eurojust consists of national members seconded by each Member State in accordance with its legal system, who has his or her regular place of work at the seat of Eurojust. See Art 7 of Regulation (EU) 2018/1727 of the European Parliament and of the Council of 14 November 2018 on the European Union Agency for Criminal Justice Cooperation (Eurojust), [2018] OJ L 295/138. The operational information exchange between Eurojust and Member States takes place through the national members: ibid, Art 7(8).

[86] See ELA Regulation, Art 32 and Recital 17.

[87] Ibid, Art 32(2).

[88] Ibid, Art 32(3).

[89] ELA Regulation, Art 7(1)(e).

State.[90] Moreover, the ELA may itself consider initiating the mediation procedure between the Member States concerned set out in the ELA Regulation.[91]

4.2.2. *Joint and Concerted Inspections*

The enforcement instrument of the ELA that has received most attention during the legislative process, is the possibility to organise joint or concerted inspections.[92] The ELA has immediately focused on this task, setting up a Working Group on Inspections and supporting pilot inspections, the first being a concerted inspection on 21 September 2020 investigating construction companies in Belgium, Lithuania and Portugal, after months of preparation and unexpected setbacks caused by the COVID-19 pandemic.[93] Also as regards inspections, the Commission has opted to confer on the ELA supportive powers aimed at reinforcing and backing rather than controlling the national inspection services. In dealing with the Commission proposal, the co-legislators further ensured, at the instigation of the European Parliament, that the ELA would be more than an instrument in the hands of the Member States.

This can already be seen in the initiative for joint or concerted inspections. The ELA will set up those inspections not only at the request of one or more Member States, through their national liaison officers, but may itself suggest that Member States carry out a joint or concerted inspection.[94] Also the social partners may bring cases to the attention of the ELA.[95] The guidelines developed by the ELA explain that a national social partner organisation should first signal the relevant national authorities on their intention to bring a case to the attention of ELA, based on information obtained, for example, on irregular working conditions, subcontractors or fraud schemes.[96] If the national authorities agree on the need for a cross-border inspection, their national liaison officer will send the official request for support to ELA and other concerned Member States, following which the ELA should assess as soon as possible, but not later than in 14 days, whether it will participate in the proposed inspection.[97] If the national authorities do not agree with the suggestion of the social partner organisation, or do not take action, the social partner organisation may itself bring the case to the attention of the ELA for its assessment within 14 days. On the basis of this assessment, for which the

[90] See Arts 258 to 260 TFEU.

[91] ELA Regulation, Art 7(1)(e). See the discussion below of the ELA's mediation task.

[92] The difference being that 'joint inspections' are carried out in a certain Member State with the participation of the national authorities of one or more other Member States (and possibly of the ELA), whereas 'concerted inspections' are carried out simultaneously in several Member States by the respective national authorities (possibly with the ELA): ibid, Art 8(2).

[93] See the press release issued by the ELA on that date, available on the ELA website.

[94] ELA Regulation, Art 8(1), first subpara.

[95] Ibid, third subpara.

[96] Guidelines for concerted and joint inspections, available on the ELA website, point 4.2.

[97] Ibid, point 4.3, read together with points 2.3 and 2.4.

ELA will involve the national liaison officers of the concerned Member States, the ELA Executive Director will identify the measures appropriate for addressing the case and notify all parties involved.[98]

Still, joint or concerted inspections cannot take place against the will of the Member States and always require the agreement of all Member States concerned, as notified via the national liaison officers.[99] As regards Member States unwilling to participate in an inspection, the European Parliament had wished to enable the ELA to make recommendations as to how a problem should be dealt with and to require Member States to organise their own inspections and disclose the results thereof.[100] Neither the Council nor the Commission wanted to go so far, but eventually agreed a text that does not give the Member States absolute freedom to refuse to take part in a joint or concerted inspection.

First of all, the Regulation interprets the general principle of sincere cooperation as meaning that Member States must endeavour to participate in concerted or joint inspections when invited to do so.[101] Second, a Member State which does not wish to take part in such an inspection must inform the ELA and the other Member States without undue delay, not only of its reasons for doing so but also of the measures it plans to take to resolve the problem.[102] The ELA may suggest that a Member State that has not participated in a joint or concerted inspection must carry out its own inspection.[103] Even though such a Member State is thus not legally required to take part in an inspection coordinated by the ELA, it must inform the ELA and other Member States of alternative measures taken to resolve the problem and of the outcomes of those measures, once known.[104] Moreover, as members of the ELA Management Board, the Member States may develop additional obligations. The ELA is indeed required to adopt the modalities to ensure appropriate follow-up in cases where Member States decide not to take part in an inspection proposed by other Member States or by the ELA.[105] It should further be noted that Member States wishing to organise inspections among them are not obliged to set them up within the framework of the ELA. As regards those Member States that already carry out joint inspections on the basis of bilateral agreements or administrative cooperation arrangements, the ELA Regulation makes clear that it does not affect those existing systems.[106]

In line with its instrumental vision on the ELA, the Commission, in its proposal, had left it entirely to the Member States concerned and the ELA to agree on the

[98] Ibid, points 4.4 to 4.6. Besides concerted ad joint inspections, possible measures could also relate to information campaigns, capacity building and risk analysis.

[99] ELA Regulation, second subpara.

[100] See the amendments proposed in the Lenaers Report as regards Art 9(2a) and (3).

[101] ELA Regulation, Art 8(3).

[102] Ibid, Art 8(4).

[103] Ibid.

[104] Ibid.

[105] Ibid, Art 8(4).

[106] Ibid, Art 1(6).

conditions for carrying out joint or concerted inspections, whereby ELA staff members could not take part in an inspection without agreement of the Member State in which the inspection takes place.[107] Although the co-legislators confirmed that approach, they nevertheless inserted some guarantees intended to ensure the effectiveness of inspections. The principle has been maintained that inspections must be carried out in accordance with the law or practice of the Member States in which the inspections take place, and this has been extended to the follow-up to such inspections.[108] Nevertheless, the Regulation requires that it 'be possible' to use the information collected during concerted or joint inspections as evidence in legal proceedings in the Member States concerned.[109] A Member State cannot therefore deny such information any evidential value on the sole ground that it was obtained during a concerted or joint inspection. The Regulation does not require a Member State to grant participating inspectors from another Member State the same powers as its own inspectors, but requires that they be given an 'appropriate role and status', implying that a Member State may not altogether exclude those inspectors or deprive them of any function.[110] Staff of the ELA must be able to attend the inspection as observers, to provide logistical support or to actually participate in an inspection if the Member State where the inspection takes place so allows.[111] In any event and whenever requested by a Member State, the ELA as a body will provide conceptual, logistical and technical support for those inspections, including translation and interpreting services and, where appropriate, legal expertise.[112] In December 2020, the ELA issued the abovementioned guidelines for concerted and joint inspections, including templates for case descriptions and reporting, and a model agreement to be used by the Member States wishing to set up such inspections.[113]

Finally, the ELA Regulation requires Member States taking part in joint or concerted inspections to report to the ELA. Within six months they are to report on the outcome and the operational running of the inspection.[114] The ELA is to report twice a year to both its Management Board and Stakeholder Group.[115] Whenever the ELA suspects, in the course of inspections or other activities, irregularities in the application of EU law, it may notify the Member State concerned and the Commission of these irregularities.[116]

[107] Commission proposal, Art 10(1) and (4).
[108] ELA Regulation, Art 9(2).
[109] Ibid, Art 9(7).
[110] Ibid, Art 9(3).
[111] Ibid, Art 9(5).
[112] Ibid, Art 9(4).
[113] Guidelines for concerted and joint inspections, available on the ELA website.
[114] ELA Regulation, Art 9(6).
[115] Ibid, Art 9(8).
[116] Ibid, Art 9(9). This also goes for suspected infringements of EU law in areas outside the ELA's field of action: see n 56 and accompanying text.

4.3. Tackling Undeclared Work

As stated above, the ELA will take over the tasks of the European Platform for tackling undeclared work, set up in 2016.[117] Within that forum, national labour inspections and other law enforcement services regularly meet with the social partners and experts from the Commission and EU agencies in order to exchange information and best practices, to develop relevant expertise and, more generally, to promote cross-border cooperation in tackling undeclared work. Although that Platform does not merely discuss undeclared work in cross-border situations, it is particularly for those situations that cooperation between the Member States is useful. The expertise built up within the Platform should therefore be immediately relevant to the ELA.[118] Tackling undeclared work remains broadly defined as preventing, deterring and combating undeclared work, as well as promoting the declaration thereof.[119] It concerns undeclared work, but also falsely declared work, such as bogus self-employment.[120] The co-legislators could agree on the integration of the Platform only on condition that it continue to exist in its present composition as a permanent working group created within the ELA.[121]

4.4. Mediation between Member States

Finally, the ELA has been tasked with mediation between Member States in cross-border disputes within its scope of application. It is also a power that is not binding on the Member States. The ELA will propose its mediation services when a dispute cannot be resolved in direct contacts ('dialogue') between the Member States concerned.[122] Mediation may be initiated only with the agreement of all the relevant Member States. It will be initiated either at the request of one or more of the Member States concerned, or at the initiative of the ELA, but also in the latter case, mediation may be initiated only with the agreement of all Member States concerned.[123] Moreover, mediation will only lead to a non-binding opinion seeking to reconcile the positions of the Member States concerned.

One of the issues to be clarified in the legislative negotiations was how the mediating power of the ELA would coexist with the mediation between Member

[117] See Decision 2016/344 (n 22 above), to be repealed by Art 48 of the ELA Regulation on the date when the ELA becomes fully autonomous, which is still to be determined.

[118] Pedersini, n 30 above at 13–14.

[119] ELA Regulation, Recital 22.

[120] Ibid, Art 12(1)(a).

[121] Ibid, Art 16(2). In the legislative negotiations, this was a request from the European Parliament, also to retain the specific representation of the social partners within the Platform. Compare Art 12(3) and (4) of the ELA Regulation with Art 2 of Decision 2016/344.

[122] ELA Regulation, Art 13(2).

[123] Ibid.

States as organised by the Administrative Commission for the coordination of social security systems within its area of activity.[124] The Administrative Commission has established a conciliation procedure, under which disagreements in determining the applicable national legislation which cannot be resolved in dialogue, may be submitted to a Conciliation Board. There, experts from Member States not involved in the dispute come up with a legal opinion that is then to be confirmed by the Administrative Commission.[125] In the impact assessment accompanying the proposal for the ELA, the Commission had indicated that practical problems regarding cross-border labour mobility very often relate to disagreements between Member States regarding the application of social security rules.[126] Still, only a very small number of those disputes are settled by the Conciliation Board of the Administrative Commission, which works with volunteers and without any substantive support.[127] For that reason, it was clear to the Commission that the ELA should provide mediation not only on labour law issues falling within its remit, but also on social security issues, given also the fact that concrete cases often concern aspects of both labour law and social security that cannot always be separated. However, both the Council and the European Parliament were not eager to give the ELA such a broad mediation task, insisting that the Administrative Commission fully retain its powers.[128] In the course of the trialogues, the Commission managed to persuade the negotiators of the European Parliament and the Council to confer on the ELA a mediation power covering also social security matters, but the co-legislators maintained their position that the mediation powers of the Administrative Commission had to be preserved.

Unlike the Commission proposal, which merely indicated that a Mediation Board within the ELA would perform mediation in areas covered by the Regulation, the ELA Regulation now sketches out the main features of the mediation procedure before the ELA, which is to be further developed in rules of procedure,

[124] See Decision A1 of the Administrative Commission for the coordination of social security systems of 12 June 2009 concerning the establishment of a dialogue and conciliation procedure concerning the validity of documents, the determination of the applicable legislation and the provision of benefits under Regulation (EC) No 883/2004 of the European Parliament and of the Council, [2010] OJ C 106/1.

[125] Administrative Commission on Social Security for Migrant Workers, Mandate for the 5th Conciliation Board, Note of the Secretariat of 9 June 2017.

[126] Impact Assessment accompanying the Proposal for a Regulation of the European Parliament and the Council establishing a European Labour Authority (n 12 above), 14 (indicating that 60 per cent of the questions received by the SOLVIT network concern social security issues, whose number has doubled between 2012 and 2015 up to 1,100 a year).

[127] See S Fernandes, n 28 above at 6 (referring to the lack of resources of the Administrative Commission, whose Conciliation Board has only taken one decision in the past three years); H Verschueren, n 19 above at 29 (stressing the lack of effectiveness of the conciliation procedure before the Administrative Commission).

[128] Council general approach (n 36), Art 13; Lenaers Report, amendments to Art 13(1) to (6). The Parliament nevertheless proposed a conciliation procedure with some constraints for the Member States, such as requiring them to give reasons if they do not participate and inviting the Conciliation Board to give an opinion within six months.

which the ELA Management Board envisages adopting in 2021.[129] In a first phase, mediation is conducted between the Member States that are party to a dispute and a mediator.[130] Where this does not lead to a solution, the dispute may, in a second phase, be brought before the Conciliation Board of the ELA. Similar to the Conciliation Board of the Administrative Commission, the ELA Conciliation Board is composed only of experts from Member States other than those party to the dispute.[131] At each stage, experts from the ELA may be involved in an advisory capacity.[132] At both stages, the mediation remains voluntary in the sense that its initiation requires the agreement of all the Member States concerned and that it eventually leads to a non-binding opinion. That does not mean that the process remains entirely noncommittal. At the request of the European Parliament, the ELA Regulation contains the obligation for Member States that refuse to take part in mediation to give reasons for such a refusal.[133] In addition, as the Commission had proposed, the Member States concerned are required to report within three months on the measures they have taken to follow up on the opinion or the reasons why they have not taken measures.[134]

As indicated, disputes may be submitted for mediation in all areas covered by the Regulation, which includes issues of social security coordination (typically, the determination of applicable national legislation in situations with cross-border aspects). Where a dispute is related, fully or in part, to matters of social security, however, the ELA must inform the Administrative Commission for the coordination of social security systems. The issue of social security coordination may be referred to the Administrative Commission, at the request of the Member State concerned or at the request of the Administrative Commission, but, in the latter case only with the agreement of the relevant Member States.[135] In order to ensure good cooperation and coordination, the ELA and the Administrative Commission still need to establish a cooperation agreement.[136] The co-legislator also preferred not to encroach on the powers of the Administrative Commission in other respects. Thus, the technical committees on social security coordination, which the Commission wished to incorporate into the ELA in order to bring together relevant expertise, continue to exist in their current form.[137]

[129] See Art 12(6) of the ELA Regulation, which leaves it to the Management Board, eg, to fix applicable deadlines and the possibility for the Conciliation Board to sit in panels, and the 2021 work programme, at 30.

[130] Ibid, Art 12(3).

[131] Ibid, Art 12(4) and (5).

[132] This also applies to experts from the Member States and the Commission: ibid, Art 12(3) and (5).

[133] Ibid, Art 12(7).

[134] Ibid, Art 12(12).

[135] Ibid, Art 12(11). Furthermore, mediation is to take into account 'all relevant decisions' of the Administrative Commission: ibid, para 10.

[136] Ibid, Art 12(11). This is scheduled for 2021, according to the 2021 work programme, at 31.

[137] Besides the Conciliation Committee, this concerns the Technical Commission and the Audit Board of the Administrative Commission for the coordination of social security systems. See the amendments proposed in the Commission proposal to Arts 72 to 74 of Regulation No 883/2004, which have not been taken over in the ELA Regulation.

The ELA Regulation provides only for mediation with respect to disputes between Member States. The Commission had proposed making the ELA also responsible for facilitating cooperation between stakeholders in the event of cross-border labour market disruptions, such as large-scale restructuring events or major projects impacting employment in border regions.[138] This proposal was inspired by the task force set up by the Commission in September 2016 on the occasion of the closure of the Caterpillar plant in Gosselies (Belgium), in which the Commission sat together with the competent Walloon authorities and the social partners to ascertain how EU funds could be mobilised to support the jobless workers.[139] Making the ELA responsible for such activities, which have little to do with facilitating enforcement in cross-border situations, was promoted by European trade unions,[140] but strongly criticised by employers' organisations.[141] The proposal found some support in the Council,[142] but not in the European Parliament,[143] which saw little added value. Eventually, the co-legislators agreed not to incorporate such an activity in the ELA's set of tasks.

5. Conclusion

With the establishment of the European Labour Authority, the EU legislator has not created a European body to control the enforcement activity of national authorities, but an instrument to reinforce the operational capacity of national enforcement authorities and other instances involved with cross-border labour mobility. Although the ELA Regulation clearly encourages Member States to cooperate in many respects, it provides them with opportunities rather than requirements. Still, given the practical need for cooperation in cross-border situations, national enforcement authorities may be expected to have a real interest in turning to the ELA for assistance, instigated or not by their national liaison officers.

The supportive nature of the ELA goes together with a diversified set of tasks, which should enable it to facilitate not only the enforcement of EU legislation in cross-border situations, but also the provision of information to workers and employers making use of free movement rights. It has been suggested above that

[138] See Commission Proposal, Art 1(c), as further developed in Art 14.

[139] See press release from the European Commission of 23 March 2018, 'Commission proposes €4.6 million from Globalisation Adjustment Fund for former Caterpillar workers in Belgium', https://ec.europa.eu/commission/presscorner/detail/en/IP_18_2182.

[140] See the position of the European Trade Union Confederation of 13–14 December 2017 (n 38 above), 5.

[141] See the position of the European organisation of national employers' federations (n 55 above) and of the German employers' organisation BDA of June 2018 (n 38 above).

[142] See the Council general approach, amendment to Art 14.

[143] See Lenaers Report, amendment to Art 14 (proposed deletion of the article).

this is also the reason why sufficient support could be found for the establishment of this new EU agency both among the Member States and within the European Parliament.

Insofar as the ELA builds upon existing structures, it has been able to be operational right from the start. That goes, for example, for the coordination of EURES and the fight against undeclared work, which have been the core activities of the ELA in its first two years, with further deployment of activities also being restrained by Covid-19 restrictions.[144] The highest expectations concern the new operational activities that the ELA will develop in the area of information exchange, coordination of inspections, risk assessment and capacity-building, where the agency will have to develop its own expertise. It must be noted that in all of these activities, the ELA will be part of a network of national authorities, which it will coordinate and support. In that context, the key role played by the ELA will be to bring together experts and expertise from the Member States and other EU bodies and stakeholders, including the social partners. The success of the ELA will depend from the outset on the extent to which national authorities and stakeholders will be mobilised to pool their expertise and make use of and reinforce the services offered by the ELA.[145]

As regards the enforcement of EU social law, some have argued in favour of granting the ELA more far-reaching powers, such as monitoring of national authorities through binding decisions sanctioned by penalties, which would push authorities and employers even harder to comply with requirements as to the provision of information and respect for substantive law. It has been explained above why such coercive powers were out of question when establishing the ELA. Nevertheless, it cannot be ruled out that, after a few years' experience, the EU political institutions might wish to confer more extensive competences on the ELA, in particular if it were to transpire that not all national authorities invest in cooperation at EU level to the same extent. It is now primarily for the national authorities to implement the changes to the legislative framework that the Juncker Commission has pushed through as regards cross-border labour mobility and to make full use of the potential for cooperation that the ELA offers.

[144] Most of the operational expenditure also goes to EURES coordination (see the draft budget for 2021).

[145] See also Pedersini, n 30 at 16; Verschueren, n 19 at 32.

18

The Alert (Whistleblowing) in Light of the Enforcement of European Labour Law

ELLIOT COBBAUT

1. Introduction

The issue of labour law enforcement is crucial today. It appears, however, that institutionalised enforcement mechanisms are not always able to perform this task. This situation has led to an increase in studies on ways of improving legal enforcement. To this end, one important element is access to information on (potential) breaches in order to stop and sanction them, but also information on potential risks in order to meet prevention obligations. One means of making such information available is to encourage disclosures by people with privileged access to intelligence on breaches or risks because of their activities inside or around the entity concerned.

In recent years, a number of cases have been brought to light by people who sacrificed their own interests to promote the common interest.[1] Such (groups of) people tend not to be formally charged with any supervisory function, but acted because responsible authorities did not do so. They are called 'whistleblowers' or, in French, *lanceurs d'alerte*. According to sociological studies,[2] such cases are part of a global phenomenon, and a wide diversity of 'alerts' has developed in modern societies. They can be generally defined as disclosures by natural or legal persons that bring to light situations they believe are illegal, immoral, against the public interest or risky, and that have not been identified or properly dealt with. By making this information available, alerts can constitute an effective tool for better enforcement, especially of labour law. On one hand, they can reveal actual or imminent breaches of law in general, including labour law or human rights.

[1] Examples include the Snowden case, the Panama Papers, Wikileaks, the mediator case or Luxleaks; F Kain, 'Whistleblowing and labour law: the Whistleblower Directive – development, content and obstacles' (2020) 2(13) *Italian Labour Law e-Journal* 132.

[2] See F Chateauraynaud and D Torny, *Les sombres précurseurs: une sociologie pragmatique de l'alerte et du risque* (Paris, EHESS, 1999).

On the other, they can contribute to better prevention of risks, which is crucial in the very important area of labour law, occupational safety and health, where the preventive approach is fundamental.

In order for alerts to play this role, however, they need to be legally regulated to ensure the transmission of information, protect reporting persons and avoid abusive alerts. A large number of laws have been adopted at EU and Member State level to regulate alerts. Nevertheless, none of those laws recognise all existing forms of alert. Usually, they were adopted in response to particular events and only cover specific fields of law, constituting an addition of laws without coherence. Today, in some fields of EU law, legal provisions on alerts are well developed and protective, as in financial law. In others, including labour law, only a few legal instruments exist, sometimes with a poor framework and protection, and only cover some (very) specific fields.[3] This situation reduces the effectivity of alerts for better enforcement, including in labour law, and has led to the adoption of Directive 2019/1397, dedicated to the issue of enforcement, which aims to establish a general legal framework for alert practices.

This chapter will consider how the alert and alert law can contribute to better enforcement of EU law, especially labour law. To this end, it analyses different conceptions of alerts in order to assess how they can contribute to better EU law enforcement. It underlines the particular interest of alerts for better enforcement of EU labour law because of the importance of the duty of prevention in the field of the occupational safety and health protection. Then, it analyses the need for a solid legal framework as essential to enabling alerts to achieve their potential for better law enforcement. It studies the merits and limits of existing EU alert laws, with particular emphasis on EU labour law instruments, and highlights the general insufficiency of EU alert law, especially in labour law. Finally, it analyses how far Directive 2019/1397 can address the insufficiency of those alert laws as regards improving EU labour law enforcement. Although it appears that alerts can be a very efficient mechanism to improve labour law enforcement, existing EU alert provisions do not allow it to achieve its full potential, in particular EU labour law, despite the adoption of the new Directive. This analysis therefore calls for the adoption of a more comprehensive and ambitious EU alert law instrument or, at least, extensive implementation of the Directive in Member State law, to address its inadequacies.

2. The Regulation of Alert Practices as a Means of Improving the Enforcement of EU Law

This section underlines how the alert, if properly regulated, can contribute to better enforcement of EU law, especially EU labour law. Indeed, access to information on

[3] See Directives 1976/207/EEC, 89/391/EEC, 2009/13/CE, 2009/16/EC, 2009/65/CE, 2013/36/EU, 2013/54/EU, 2014/65/CE, 2015/849, 2015/2392 and Article 12 of the EU Staff Regulation.

breaches of the law and potential risks is a key element in improving labour law enforcement.

2.1. EU Law Enforcement and Access to Information

The progressive construction of EU law is in vain if legal provisions have no effect. Today, EU law enforcement is flawed. One of the main causes of this weakness lies in the difficulty of identifying potential breaches of the law and risks in a context in which practical situations and regulation are increasingly complex and technical. The issue is to identify breaches, stop them and better fulfil legal obligations, sometimes formulated in general or unclear terms, for example, the general duty of prevention in respect of occupational safety and health imposed on employers by Directive 1989/391.

Law enforcement therefore requires access to comprehensive knowledge on the activities of relevant entities to verify compliance with legal provisions. Obtaining such information, however, is difficult both for the authorities charged with supervising law enforcement with limited means and for the entity's management itself. It is indeed increasingly complex today because of the evolution of the economic context and of company structures, as well as scientific and technical development, which modify companies' organisation and activities. A growing number of companies are organised in networks, including several legal entities articulated at the transnational level and working not only with workers but (sub)contractors, independent workers and suppliers. In addition, from the use of new technologies new complex issues arise (such as the treatment of personal data, new risks to occupational safety and health and public health or the environment).

Therefore, employers and authorities need tools to improve access to information. One means of obtaining better information is to be 'alerted' by people involved in activities of the relevant entity, who have privileged access. Hence the importance of 'alert practices'.

2.2. The Rise of Alert Practices

Alerts may take various forms and concern various objects. They can contribute to better enforcement of the law, especially in certain areas that serve an important purpose of prevention, such as labour law.

Over the past few decades, a number of people have become famous for revealing questionable circumstances related to the activities of an entity in which they were involved, which were not identified or properly dealt with.

The interest of the information revealed and the risks taken by those who brought it to light caught the attention of the public and of researchers. The sociological works of F Chateauraynaud and D Torny show that these famous alert cases were only the best-known among an increasing number of alerts since the 1980s and underline the diversity of practices qualified as 'alerts'. The object of such alerts may be to report a breach of the law, at-risk situations or public interest information. Their authors may be any entity stakeholder who has privileged access to information (worker, (sub)contractor, manager, or a person living near the entity). They can reveal their information either inside or outside of the entity concerned, for instance to a competent authority or publicly. They can therefore be any natural or legal person who draws attention to an illegal, risky or public interest situation in order to stop it, to prevent risk or to submit information to public debate. The diversity of practices has resulted in the coexistence of a large number of alert definitions in official texts and in doctrine.[4]

Despite the diversity of these practices, two types or conceptions of alert can be identified. The first, called 'whistleblowing', comes from English-speaking countries. A whistleblower is a person, often a worker, who transmits to an authority (eg their employer or an external authority) information related to breaches of the legal or regulatory framework in order to stop them.[5] It is a means of remedying the limited resources of the authorities charged with identifying illegal conduct. It can therefore improve the enforcement of the law in general, whatever the field, including labour law.

The second, called a *lancement d'alerte* or 'early warning', is a term from the pragmatic sociology of risk. It is defined as reporting by a (group of) person(s) who observes a situation that they believe could constitute a risk and which has not been (properly) taken notice of by the institutions charged with managing it. Their reporting draws attention to this situation and therefore increases the likelihood of damage prevention.[6] Such behaviour is part, on the preventive side, of a potential collective and continuous due diligence process that is becoming increasingly necessary in a so-called 'risk society' such as ours.[7] The aim must be to open up the scope of risk management systems to the diversity of 'early warnings' and to develop mechanisms for handling alerts that can determine the reality of risks and the measures that need to be adopted. In the important field of labour law that is occupational safety and health, early warnings can contribute to better fulfilment of the employer's duty of prevention under Directive 1989/391 and therefore enable them to avoid liability. Early warnings are thus crucial in areas in which the stakes are high when it comes to anticipating risk. Early warnings also contribute to better enforcement in other fields of law where the emphasis is on anticipation,

[4] D Lewis, AJ Brown and R Moberly, 'Whistleblowing, its importance and the state of the research', in *International Handbook on Whistleblowing Research* (Cheltenham, Edward Elgar, 2014) 4; P Latimer and AJ Brown, 'Whistleblower Laws: International Best Practice' (2008) 31 *University of New South Wales Law Journal* 768.

[5] F Chateauraynaud, 'Lanceur d'alerte' in *Dictionnaire critique et interdisciplinaire de la participation* (Paris, GIS, Démocratie et Participation, 2013).

[6] Chateauraynaud and Torny, above n 2; F Chateauraynaud, *Alertes et lanceurs d'alerte* (Paris, Que sais-je, 2020) 13.

[7] See U Beck, *Risk Society. Towards a New Modernity* (London, Sage, 1992); O Godard, *Le principe de précaution dans la conduite des affaires humaines* (Paris, Ed. Maison des sciences de l'homme, 1997).

such as data protection. For these reasons, in labour law in particular, whistleblowing and early warnings must be developed in order to prevent damage, and if this is not possible to impose sanctions and put things right.

Alerts thus constitute an internal and external supervisory mechanism for illegal and risk situations, complementing traditional and institutionalised control by expert authorities. Alerts encompass various forms of enforcement (treated in the first part of this book), according to circumstances. It is a direct enforcement tool when it concerns a breach of the law and more indirect when it reveals a risk and makes it possible for actors to perform a duty of prevention. It assists private enforcement mechanisms when information is revealed inside the entity or public mechanisms when it is revealed outside. If the information is revealed to a competent authority, it can contribute to administrative enforcement. It may also contribute to enforcement by the social partners if they take charge of the alert inside the relevant entity. In this last example, this enforcement mechanism becomes less individual and more collective.

2.3. Need for Regulation

Alerts can contribute to better enforcement of the law, especially labour law, only if they are properly regulated. People who observe a breach or risk do not always issue a warning or alert, because they may be too afraid to report it or they tried to report it but were discouraged or not listened to.[8] It is also crucial to prevent reports that might be made that are knowingly false or with no reasonable grounds, to damage the person or entity concerned. Legal provisions must protect the reputation, honour or secrets of physical and legal persons. Regulation is needed to take advantage of the potential of alerts and to avoid abuses. The relevant legal provisions have to encourage alerts or warnings and to enable whistleblowers and early warnings to fully achieve their potential to foster better enforcement of the law, in particular labour law.

To this end, legal instruments have to provide solid, clear and comprehensive protection against the diverse forms of deterrents or reprisals applied to reporting persons.[9] This protection is even more important in instances of whistleblowing where violations have occurred and the person or entity concerned has an interest in keeping it hidden.[10] In addition, the legal framework for alerts has had to establish broadly available alert channels to ensure the transmission of information to

[8] That was so for example in the recent *Lubrizol* case. A French chemicals company suffered a fire after safety processes failed. It appeared that some workers had observed some problems before the accident but did not issue a warning.

[9] RG Vaughn, *The Successes and Failures of Whistleblower Laws* (Cheltenham, Edward Elgar Publishing, 2012) 55.

[10] That was typically so in the *Dieselgate* or *Luxleaks* cases, where the entity concerned had an interest in hiding the information reported.

the right receiver and mechanisms for dealing with it.[11] Finally, the legal framework for alerts has to discourage reports that are knowingly false or lack reasonable grounds.[12]

3. Classification of Legal Instruments Pertaining to Alerts

If an alert can contribute to better enforcement of EU labour law, we must analyse how far EU law can regulate it and whether existing EU legal instruments related to alerts allow them to achieve their potential. The legal framework for alerts varies according to the area of law. Some areas are not covered by any alert provisions, while others are covered by strong legal instruments. Most existing instruments regulate whistleblowing, while only a few regulate early warnings. In its current state, the EU legal regime for alerts is still inadequate, especially in labour law, and there is a need for more comprehensive and harmonised instruments to enable alerts to contribute to better enforcement of EU labour law.

Facing the need to improve the law on alerts, legal frameworks have been adopted progressively at the EU and national levels. However, none of them encompass alerts in all their diversity. They have been adopted sporadically, in response to crisis situations triggered by alerts, in order to cope with specific circumstances in a given sector. They have their own scope of application, conditions, channels and protection. Existing alert laws vary according to the particular field of law. In some areas, such as financial law, there are a number of solid protections. In others, such as labour law, there is less protection. The level of protection can be evaluated in light of different characteristics of legal instruments, such as material and personal scope of application, availability and effectiveness of alert channels, or the support and protective measures they offer to reporting persons. These differences may reduce the potential contribution of alerts to better enforcement of labour law.

In addition, it must be observed that alert provisions, even if they are not in labour law instruments, are closely linked to labour law logic: in most cases they are provisions that protect workers when they report and which are inspired by antidiscrimination laws, forbidding less favourable treatment for persons who have reported what they have seen. They are labour law instruments that contribute to better enforcement of the law.

[11] See K Kenny, *Whistleblowing: Towards a New Theory* (Cambridge MA, Harvard University Press, 2019); JP Near and MP Miceli, 'Effective Whistle-Blowing' (1995) 20 *Academy of Management Review* 679.

[12] Kain, n 1 at 132.

3.1. The Whistleblower Laws

Most existing laws on alerts adopt the whistleblowing approach and only regulate reporting of breaches of the law. They are especially developed in financial, accounting or anti-corruption laws.

The first whistleblowing laws can be found in the United Kingdom, indeed having existed since the fourteenth century. In the eighteenth century, there was an important development in the United States. More recently, one of the most important US instruments is the Sarbanes-Oxley Act of 2002, which implements a whistleblowing system concerning accounting and applies both to US and foreign companies listed on the New York Stock Exchange. The transborder scope of this law and the efficiency of the whistleblowing mechanisms in general have influenced European countries, which have progressively adopted their own legal whistleblowing instruments.[13]

Most EU whistleblowing provisions have been introduced in financial laws and establish quite similar regimes.[14] They cover reports of actual or potential breaches of the law in the field concerned, by the workers of the relevant entity. Some of them require that the reporting person be in good faith. They impose the establishment of effective, specific, independent and autonomous whistleblowing mechanisms, including procedures for the reception of reports and follow-up. They must include reporting channels inside the entity and in relation to the competent authority. They must protect both the reporting person and the person or entity affected, including confidentiality regarding their identity. The reporting person must be protected against retaliation, discrimination or other types of unfair treatment in connection with their reporting and cannot be held liable for a breach of an obligation due to their report. Some of these regimes organise the provision of information to reporting persons on the remedies and procedures available to them and provide them with effective assistance.

Directive 2016/943 on the protection of trade secrets can also be considered to regulate whistleblowing. Under Article 5, the measures provided for in the Directive must not be applied where there would be a breach of confidentiality in pursuit of 'revealing misconduct, wrongdoing or illegal activity'. Reporting is permissible only if it is in pursuit of protecting the 'general public interest'. This is an unprecedented notion that, depending on its interpretation, may strongly restrict the scope of reporting.

Some whistleblowing provisions also exist in the EU Staff Regulation (SR). Under Articles 22a, b and c any official who, in their work, becomes aware of possible *illegal activity* detrimental to the interests of the EU, or of serious failure

[13] See W Dorsey, 'An overview of whistleblower protection claims at the United States Department of Labor' (2006) 26 *Journal of the National Association of Administrative Law Judges* 43–122; F Chaltiel Terral, *Les lanceurs d'alerte* (Paris, Dalloz, 2018) 41.

[14] See Directives 2009/65/CE, 2013/36/EU, 2014/65/CE, 2015/849 and 2015/2392.

to comply with the obligations of EU officials, must inform their immediate superior or other authorities, such as their Director General or the OLAF. If they have previously disclosed this information to the OLAF or their own superior, they can inform the presidents of various EU bodies or the European Ombudsman. Here the provisions are focused on illegal situations without limitation to specific fields. The reporting person shall not suffer any prejudicial effects on the part of the relevant institution as a result of their report. In order to make this provision effective, each institution must establish a procedure for confidentially handling complaints made by officials concerning how they were treated as a consequence of fulfilling their obligations.

Very few EU laws regulate the reporting of breaches of labour law and only in specific fields. As a result, EU law can contribute only to a very limited extent to better enforcement of EU labour law.

Under Directive 1976/207/EEC concerning the equal treatment of men and women and the subsequent Directives adopted to reform it, the Member States must adopt necessary measures to 'protect individuals from any adverse treatment or adverse consequence as a reaction to a complaint or to proceedings aimed at enforcing compliance with the principle of equal treatment'. These provisions cover only equal treatment and are less developed and detailed than the alert provisions of financial laws. They address only protection of the reporting person. Although the provision is not entirely clear, it appears from implementation of these texts by the Member States that their personal scope covers both the victims and the witnesses of illegal conduct.

In the EU public sector, Article 12(2) SR provides that an official who gives evidence on harassment shall not suffer any prejudicial effects on the part of the institution, provided they acted in good faith. This provision is short but the alert process under Articles 22 a, b and c are pertinent because harassment is a breach of official duties.

In all these regimes, the key point is the protection of the reporting person. Such protection is also necessary to prevent abuses. To this end, some legal regimes require that the reporting person report 'honestly', 'in good faith' or with reasonable grounds. Another important regulated issue is the establishment of channels to transmit the information inside the entity or to the competent authority. The material scope of these legal instruments varies: some cover the breach of any legal provisions (eg Article 22a, b and c SR), while others are focused on a precise instrument. The process and method for dealing with the reported information are almost unregulated, as if reporting in itself was sufficient to ensure resolution of the problem.

The whistleblowing provisions cover only a very narrow scope of EU labour law and are still fairly general and underdeveloped, leaving a broad margin for the establishment of alert mechanisms, with no precise guarantees for whistleblowers. As such, they do not enable much scope for exploiting the potential of alerts for better enforcement of labour law. For this reason, it is necessary to extend to areas that are not yet covered and improve existing instruments.

3.2. The Early Warning Laws

Other legal instruments regulate early warning, mainly in relation to protection of (occupational) safety and health, and the environment. Usually, they have restricted material scope, covering either a specific sector or the prevention of a specific risk.

Some provisions in Directive 2013/30 on the safety of offshore oil and gas operations regulate early warning. Under Article 22, to ensure that relevant safety concerns are not overlooked or ignored, the Member States must ensure that the competent authority establishes mechanisms for confidential reporting on safety and environmental protection from any source and for investigation of such reports, while maintaining the anonymity of the individual concerned. It also requires provision of information to employees and contractors connected with the operations in question and their employees.

In the field of civil aviation, Regulation 376/2014 requires that the relevant entities, Member States and the European Aviation Safety Agency establish a mandatory and a voluntary reporting system covering the reporting of 'any safety-related event which endangers or which, if not corrected or addressed, could endanger an aircraft, its occupants or any other person'. Its provisions cover a broad range of categories of workers engaged in aerial transport. They can report inside the entity, to the state or to the European Aviation Safety Agency, and their identity must be kept confidential and reprisals are forbidden.

Some provisions also exist in labour law. In some respects, such as their material scope of application, they are interesting, but there are also weaknesses, especially concerning the establishment of channels for reporting and the protection granted. There is a need for improvements to allow early warnings to contribute to better enforcement of labour law by means of better risk prevention.

The instrument with the broadest scope is Directive 89/391/EEC[15] concerning occupational safety and health in the public and private sectors. Under its Articles 5 and 6, the employer has to ensure workers' safety and health. They must assess the risks and decide on the protective measures to be taken. The workers have to contribute to risk prevention and take care of their own safety and health and that of others. To this end, under Article 13, they must immediately inform the employer of any work situation they consider, on reasonable grounds, to represent a serious and immediate danger to safety and health and of any shortcomings in the protection arrangements.[16] Furthermore, in handling and reacting to reports,

[15] See on this issue Chapter 14 in this volume.

[16] Those provisions regulating early warning have been implemented in Member State law. In some Member States, such as Belgium, there is no case law concerning their application; in others, such as France, there is important case law. The French law for instance considers that a worker can have reasonable grounds for considering what represents a serious and immediate danger to safety and health if they work in a substandard, poorly lit unheated place, subject to gas emissions (CA Versailles, 12 November 1996, n° 852, *SA Asystel Maintenance c/ Michel*) or they are required to work on a defective scaffold (Cass Fr, ch soc, 2 June 2004).

workers and their representatives are entitled, under Articles 11 and 13, to take part in discussion of all questions related to occupational safety and health, to exchange with the employer information concerning potential risks, to ask them to take appropriate measures and, if they consider that the measures taken and the means employed are inadequate to ensure safety and health at work, to appeal to the responsible authority. The workers and their representatives cannot be placed at any disadvantage because of their action and must be protected against any harmful and unjustified consequences.

In a more specific area, Directive 2009/16/EC on port state control, which organises the protection of safety on ships, on-board living and working conditions and the prevention of pollution, regulates reports submitted by any person or organisation to the competent authority with a legitimate interest. The competent authority must assess the report and take the necessary action. The identity of the reporting person must remain confidential. A similar system is imposed concerning safety and health among maritime labour, under Directives 2013/54/EU and 2009/13/EC.

In comparison with the whistleblowing laws, in order to ensure that all elements that might contribute to risks are captured, the scope of the objects than can be reported under these legal instruments is far broader (any information that could help to reveal a risk). Another feature is the attention paid to handling reports. In this sense, Directive 89/391 integrates these alert practices inside the entity's risk management system, making its management more collective. The issue of the reporting person's protection is also present but has lower priority than the whistleblowing provisions. While some instruments cover 'any person', most cover only reports by workers.

These provisions, in adopting the early warning conception of alerts, even if they do not cover the reporting of 'breaches of the law', also contribute to better enforcement of EU law. Reports of risks contribute to better prevention of damages and then to better enforcement of the employer's obligation of prevention. Enforcement here is more preventive than curative, to avoid problematic situations that could lead to breaches of the law and damages that invoke the employer's liability.[17] Nevertheless, the existing provisions also appear less clear and detailed concerning the availability of reporting channels and the measures of protection and support that should be granted to people making reports in comparison with the whistleblowing provisions analysed in financial law. Some early warning provisions exist in labour law, but they have to be improved in order to contribute better to the enforcement of EU labour law.

It is crucial to distinguish early warnings and whistleblowing because they require different legal provisions (mainly broader scope of the potential objects of reporting and organisation of the follow-up). Merging them may lead to a lowering of protection for reporting persons. This was the case with the adoption in

[17] See on this issue Chapter 15 in this volume.

France of the 'Sapin II' Law (2016) which aims to extend and harmonise the legal framework pertaining to alerts. It appears that the Sapin II Law adopted only the whistleblowing approach, while neglecting early warnings. In this process of 'improvement' something has been abandoned, and while the reporting of breaches of the law is now better protected, protection is weaker for people reporting situations of risk.

3.3. Case Law of the European Courts and the Public Interest

Facing an increase in alerts and the patchy legal treatment of alerts in some areas, such as labour law, the competent authorities of the EU and the Council of Europe regarded alert cases to be covered by the fundamental right to freedom of expression guaranteed by Article 10 ECHR and Article 11 CFREU.

Analysis of ECtHR case law cannot be avoided because of the link between the ECHR and the CFREU. Under Article 52 CFREU, if a right guaranteed by the CFREU corresponds to a right guaranteed by the ECHR, its meaning and scope shall be the same as the one laid down by the ECHR.[18] This provision shall not prevent EU law from providing more extensive protection. Protection of the freedom of expression under Article 11 CFREU has to be at least the same as that of the ECHR. In addition, analysis of ECHR case law is necessary because all EU Member States are bound to respect the ECHR anyway while, under Article 51 CFREU, they are bound by the CFREU when they are implementing EU law.

Article 11 CFREU and Article 10 ECHR provide for a similar definition of this right to freedom of expression, which covers freedom of opinion and to receive and communicate information or ideas without interference by public authorities and without consideration of borders. Workers benefit from the right to freedom of expression within the framework of their work,[19] and alerts constitute a particular exercise of this right. This right is not absolute, however; it can be subject to restrictions. If a person reports an abuse, thereby exercising their right to freedom of expression, and falls victim to reprisals – for instance, if they are dismissed by their employer – the reprisal must be regarded as constituting a restriction on the reporting person's freedom of expression. Such restrictions are valid only on condition that they respect the conditions provided by Articles 10(2) ECHR and 52(1) CFREU limiting this fundamental right. They must be prescribed by law,

[18] See K Lörcher, 'Chapter 7 – Interpretation and Minimum Level of Protection' in F Dorssemont, K Lörcher, S Clauwaert and M Schmitt (eds), *The Charter of Fundamental Rights of the European Union and the Employment Relation* (Bloomsbury-Hart Publishing, 2019).

[19] Case C-100/88 *Oyowe and Traore v Commission* [1989], General Court (2nd Ch), pt 16; Case C-274/99 *Connolly v Commission* [2001], pt 43; Case T-585/16 *Carina Skareby v EEAS* (2nd Ch) [2017], pt 77; ECtHR, Gr Ch, *Guja v Moldova*, pt 70; *Heinisch v Germany*, 21 July 2011, 28274/08, pt 63-70; *Kudeshkina v Russia*, 26 February 2009, 29492/05, pt 86; *Vogt v Germany*, 26 September 1995, 17851/91, pt 53; *Wille v Liechtenstein*, 28 October 1999, 28396/95, pt 41.

pursue a legitimate aim and respect the principle of proportionality.[20] Both the first and second conditions are often easily fulfilled. Workers have a 'duty of loyalty, confidentiality and secrecy in respect of their employer'[21] provided by law, as long as the employer is considered to be pursuing a legitimate interest. The analysis of proportionality is more complex and requires a balance between existing rights and interests.[22] To this end, since its decision in *Guja v Moldova* of 2008[23] and on several occasions since then,[24] the ECtHR has established a list of six criteria to which the EU authorities refer.[25] To determine whether the right to freedom of expression of the reporting person has been breached, the Court analyses whether the reporting person had alternative channels to disclose their information before making it public,[26] whether the reported information is in the public interest, the authenticity of information, the harm to the employer caused by disclosure, whether the reporting person acted in good faith and the proportionality of the penalty imposed.[27]

Under its Articles 1 and 5, the Trade Secrets Directive recognised this case law in providing that it shall not affect 'the exercise of the right to freedom of expression and information' and in excluding from its protective regime the acquisition, use or disclosure of trade secrets carried out for the purpose of 'exercising the right to freedom of expression and information'.

This case law is a regulation of the disclosure of public interest information. This notion can cover both reports of serious risks or breaches of law. For this reason, it could be considered a kind of whistleblowing and early warning regulation that may contribute to better enforcement of labour law. Nevertheless, because public interest information is information regarding situations that could

[20] A Koukiadaki, 'Chapter 6 – Application (Article 51) and Limitations (Article 52(1))' in F Dorssemont, K Lörcher, S Clauwaert and M Schmitt (eds), *The Charter of Fundamental Rights of the European Union and the Employment Relation* (Bloomsbury-Hart Publishing, 2019).

[21] Case C-274/99 *Connolly v Commission* [2001], General Court, pt 44; 13 December 2012, Case T-199/11 *Strack v Commission*, pt 138; Case T-585/16, *Carina Skareby v EEAS* [2017], pt 79; ECHR, Gr Ch, *Palomo Sanchez and others v Spain*, 12 September 2011, 28955/06, 28957/06, 28959/06 and 28964/06, pt 76.

[22] Case C-274/99 *Connolly v Commission* [2001], General Court, pt 48.

[23] ECHR, Gr Ch., 2 February 2008, *Guja v Moldova*, 14277/04.

[24] ECHR, 21 October 2011, *Heinisch v Germany*, 28274/08, pt 64–70; Case C-40238/028 *Bucur and Toma v Romania* [2013], pt 93.

[25] Civil Service Tribunal, 5 December 2012, F-88/09 and F-48/10, *Z v CJEU*, pt 247; Court of First Instance, 28 October 2004, *Meister v OHMI*, T-76/03, pt 159.

[26] See W Vandekerckhove, 'European Whistleblower Protection: Tiers or Tears?' in D Lewis (ed), *A Global Approach to Public Interest Disclosure* (Cheltenham, Edward Elgar, 2010).

[27] Concerning this case law see: J Bowers et al (eds), *Whistleblowing: Law and Practice* (Oxford, Oxford University Press, 2007); V Junod, 'La liberté d'expression du whistleblower. Cour européenne des droits de l'homme (Grande Chambre), *Guja c Moldova*, 12 février 2008' (2009) 77 *Rev trim dh* 227–60. In its decision in *Gawlik v Liechtenstein*, the ECtHR reaffirmed these criteria and adopted a particularly strict interpretation of the requirement to verify the authenticity of the reported information. Such an interpretation reduces the scope of protection of the reporting person (ECtHR, 16 February 2021, *Gawlik v Lichtenstein*, 23922/19, pt 74–78).

constitute a threat or damage to the general interest, this notion excludes a number of disclosures of risk or breaches of the law. It must be underlined that if the reported information is not 'of public interest', freedom of expression can be invoked but the condition of proportionality will not be met given the six criteria of the *Guja* case.[28]

Despite the developments of both EU legal instruments pertaining to alerts and ECtHR protective case law, various cases, including *Dieselgate*, the *Panama Papers* and *Luxleaks*, have shown the inadequacy of the EU legal framework. The last may be the most obvious example: in 2014 two former workers of a consulting firm and a journalist revealed the existence of a massive system of aggressive 'tax optimisation' organised by their employer and the Luxembourg tax authorities. They were prosecuted before the Luxembourg courts. The case gave rise to several decisions of these courts which applied the protective case law developed by the ECtHR.[29] This case highlighted the insufficiency of the legal framework on alerts, both at the EU and the Member State level, in Luxembourg, to protect reporting persons, despite the uncontested interest in the information revealed.[30] Workers can only invoke their right to freedom of expression and ECtHR protective case law. This case also showed how complex this case law can be to interpret and apply.[31] There was therefore legal uncertainty that did not encourage potential reporting. EU law did not regulate alerts in a way that could contribute to better law enforcement. For this reason, an increasing number of demands have been expressed in favour of the adoption of a Directive regulating alert practices at the EU level by the Council of Europe,[32] the EU Parliament and Council,[33] various civil society organisations[34] and trade unions.[35]

[28] See for instance workers' right of criticism, ECtHR GC, 12 September 2011, *Palomo Sanchez v Spain*, 28955/06.

[29] Tribunal d'arrondissement du Grand-Duché de Luxembourg (12th Ch), 29 June 2016; Cour d'appel du Grand-Duché de Luxembourg (10th Ch), 15 March 2017, n 117/17; Cour de cassation du Grand-Duché de Luxembourg, 11 January 2018, n 01/18 and 3912/16; Cour d'appel du Grand-Duché du Luxembourg (5th Ch), 15 May 2018.

[30] A Luxembourg law of 13 February 2011 only protected workers reporting facts of corruption, trafficking of influence or illegal interest-taking. The reporting person cannot benefit from this instrument in this case.

[31] On these decisions see A Vandendriessche, 'Legal Developments in the Protection of Whistleblowers in the European Union' (2018) 4 *EDPL* 483–91.

[32] PACE Resolution 1729(2010); Committee of the Ministers of the Council of Europe (CMCE), Recommendation CM/Rec(2014)7 of 30 April 2014.

[33] The EU Parliament adopted several Resolutions along these lines: Resolutions (2013/2107 (INI)), (2015/2066 (INI)) (TAXE 1) (2015/2010(INL)), (2016/2055 (INI)) and (2016/2055 (INI)). In 2016, the Greens/EFA parliamentary group proposed an EU Directive to establish minimum levels of protection for whistleblowers. The Council of the European Union, in its conclusions on tax transparency of 11 October 2016, also invited the Commission to consider the possibility of future EU action.

[34] D Schmidt, 'Les secrets d'affaires et les étouffeurs d'alerte' (2016) *Rec Dalloz* 1425.

[35] V Abazi, 'The European Union Whistleblower Directive: A "Game Changer" for Whistleblowing Protection?' (2020) 49(4) *Industrial Law Journal* 640; S Gerdemann and N Colneric, 'The EU Whistleblower Directive and its Transposition: Part I' (2020) *European Labour Law Journal* 2.

4. The Promised Directive 2019/1937: Including Labour Law as a Tool, Excluding Labour Law from Its Scope

The general inadequacy of the EU legal framework pertaining to alerts was recognised and led to the adoption of a new Directive. While this text constitutes a step forward for EU alert law, it does not improve alert regulation with regard to labour law and therefore it does not contribute to better enforcement of EU labour law. Even if the extension of its scope to labour law could improve enforcement, it would not be sufficient because the Directive does not encompass early warnings, which is a crucial element of alerts, especially in labour law.

The Commission published a Directive proposal on 23 April 2018, which was accompanied by an intensive policy debate on the existence of legal grounds, the material scope of the future regime and the hierarchy of alert channels. Finally, Directive 2019/1937 on the protection of persons who report breaches of Union law was adopted in November 2019.[36] Its provisions were strongly influenced by the Council of Europe and the protective case law of the ECtHR.

Under Article 1, the Directive aims to contribute to better enforcement of EU law in specific areas by laying down common minimum standards of protection for the persons reporting breaches of Union law. This Directive is dedicated to the enforcement issue, which establishes an alert regime beyond the boundaries of the different areas of EU law, in contrast to existing EU alert law, in which each law includes provisions for better enforcement of its obligations.

This Directive is intended to improve existing law. Under its Article 25, its implementation 'shall under no circumstances constitute grounds for a reduction in the level of protection already afforded', but the Member States 'may introduce or retain provisions more favourable to the rights of the reporting persons'.

A careful analysis of this Directive is necessary to appreciate where it can be situated in relation to the diversity of existing EU alert laws and if it addresses their inadequacies, thereby promoting better enforcement of labour law.

4.1. Scope of the Directive

At first sight, the scope of the Directive appears quite broad. Nevertheless, a deeper analysis reveals it to be narrower.

Under Articles 2 and 5, the Directive covers the reporting of 'information, including reasonable suspicions, about actual or potential breaches [of EU law]

[36] The Member States are not at the same stage in implementation. According to the level of protection already granted to reporting persons, the implementation process is more or less important. In some countries, demands have already arisen for an extension of the material scope of application of the Directive (including from the 'Protecteur des droits' in France and from some political parties in Belgium).

which occurred or are very likely to occur'. These 'breaches' are acts or omissions that either are unlawful or defeat the object or the purpose of the rules. It clearly adopts the whistleblowing conception of alerts, focused on conduct not conforming to legal provisions. This is in line with Article 1 and Recital 6, and following that, only treats the notions of 'public interest issues' and 'risks' to underline that they can be consequences of insufficient enforcement of the legal provisions.[37] For this reason, the Directive is a 'global' legal framework pertaining to alerts, but a whistleblowing regulation, less inclusive than some Member State laws, such as the English or Irish Public Interest Disclosure Acts or even the French Sapin II Law. It does not cover 'risk to the public interest' or 'at risk' situations, as encouraged by the Council of Europe.[38] As a result, it missed an opportunity to address the need for improvement of the early warning provisions in labour law, and its interest in better enforcement of labour law.

While the Directive seems to establish a harmonised alert regime which is no longer limited to a particular legal instrument or field of law, it appears it only covers the breach of EU legal instruments listed in the Annex. It includes a broad range of areas, such as public procurement, financial services, product safety, protection of the environment, consumer protection and the protection of personal data, but also the breaches affecting EU financial interests or relating to the Single Market. In fields in which alert laws already exist, they will continue to apply. In a way, the fact that the Directive covers those matters enables it to govern some very specific fields of EU labour law. Indeed, some breaches of public procurement law, competition law or even data protection law may contain labour law dimensions. This could make it possible to cover, and then to encourage, the reporting of breaches of labour law and therefore to better enforcement of labour law. Nevertheless, this sole element is far from sufficient to truly improve the enforcement of EU labour law.

Under Article 3, specific areas are excluded from its scope, such as national security, legal and professional privilege in the medical domain or the secrecy of judicial deliberation.

A far less understandable omission from inclusion in the scope are EU labour law instruments as such, while, as underlined, the existing labour law alert provisions are sporadic, sometimes underdeveloped, and broad areas of labour law are still not covered by any alert provisions. Therefore, the Directive also missed the opportunity to address the need for improvement of the whistleblowing regulation in labour law, and its interest as regards better enforcement of labour law. No credible explanation of this choice can be found in the Directive. Under Recital 21, the Directive is supposed to be without prejudice to the protection granted to workers when reporting breaches of Union employment law, in particular in the area

[37] D Lewis, 'The EU Directive on the protection of whistleblowers: a missed opportunity to establish international best practices?' (2020) 9(1) *E-Journal of International and Comparative Labour Studies* 3.

[38] PACE, Resolution 1729(2010) and 2300(2019); CMCE, Recommendation CM/Rec(2014)7.

of occupational safety and health, where Article 11 of Directive 89/391 already requires Member States to protect workers who are reporting persons. It suggests that sufficient protection already exists in EU labour law. Under Article 3, the Directive will not affect the rules on, and the protection related to, the exercise by workers of their rights to consult their representatives or trade unions, as well as on the autonomy of the social partners and their right to enter into collective agreements. It adds that 'this is without prejudice to the level of protection granted by the Directive'. Therefore, it seems that the Directive does not affect labour law rules beyond the sole protection it grants to a worker when they make a report covered by its provisions. Despite this exclusion, the Directive nevertheless seems to recognise a specific place for labour law. Under Article 27, the Commission shall by December 2025, submit a report assessing the need for additional measures, including potential extension of the scope of the Directive to further areas 'in particular the improvement of the working environment to protect workers' health and safety and working conditions'. This provision is difficult to reconcile with the justification that EU labour law already contains sufficient alert law provisions. It appears that one reason influencing the decision to exclude labour law from the scope is the fact that it would have imposed, under Article 154 TFEU, consultation of the social partners and prevented adoption of the Directive during the mandate of the Commission. Therefore, it must be underlined that the Directive does not recognise and address the insufficiency of the legal framework pertaining to alerts in EU labour law.

The legality of this exclusion is questionable on the basis of the fundamental principle of equality in law under Article 20 CFREU. According this principle, people shall be guaranteed equal rights and freedoms irrespective of social conditions or circumstances. As it has been held there is inequal treatment concerning whether different categories of workers are covered in the same way by social laws, here it could be held as contrary to this principle to treat differently persons who report breaches of the law according the fields of the law concerned.

The weaknesses in scope can be addressed by the Member States, which are, under Article 6(2), free to 'extend protection under national law as regards areas or acts not covered'. This situation remains questionable because it leaves broad freedom to the Member States to determine the scope of the regulation and opens the door to great diversity among Member States, which is not in line with the aim of a more harmonised and understandable EU regulation. Furthermore, it could be considered that Member States have to extend the scope of this Directive under Article 51 CFREU, which requires that the Member States respect CFREU provisions when they apply EU law. Because this Directive concerns freedom of expression, in its implementation the States are bound by the Charter, including the right to freedom of expression in all its aspects. That means, in accordance with Article 11 CFREU as interpreted by the European authorities in alert cases, which covers the reporting of public interest issues without limiting these issues to breaches of some specific Union acts.

If the scope of implementation of the Directive were extended to cover more fields of law, including labour law, where existing provisions regulate early warnings, it should be ensured that it does not lead to the establishment of a single regime that regulates only whistleblowing and neglects early warnings.

As for its personal scope of application, the Directive takes account of the latest good practices in alert laws.[39] Under Article 4, it covers any reporting person, working in the public or the private sector, who acquires information about violations in a worker-related context, including a work-based relationship that has since ended or is yet to begin. According to the non-exhaustive list in Article 4, the reporting person can be a worker, a self-employed person, a shareholder, an administrative employee, a member of a management or supervisory body of an undertaking, including non-executive members, a volunteer or a paid or unpaid trainee, as well as a person working under the supervision and direction of (sub) contractors and suppliers. This broad personal scope guarantees better law enforcement because all the persons listed are likely to have a detailed understanding of how the organisation operates and able to detect breaches of the law. The Directive takes into account the fact that workers are no longer the only actors at the heart of the activities of modern firms, which are increasingly organised in networks.[40] It is far broader than the scope of existing EU alert law, especially labour law. The extension of this scope to alerts under labour law could help to improve it and therefore the enforcement of labour law overall. For this reason, the exclusion of labour law from the scope of the Directive appears even more disappointing. It appears that, to be even more effective, scope should be extended to people outside an organisation, such as people living nearby, but also to legal persons, such as associations or NGOs, which could act as filter of an alert if they were contacted by individuals and transmit the report to the proper authorities, which they would be better able to identify because of their expertise.

4.2. Channels and Reporting Conditions

Concerning the transmission of reports, the Directive establishes three channels for reporting persons.

(1) The first channel is internal reporting, meaning the communication of information within the entity concerned. Under Article 8(1), Member States must ensure that legal entities in the private (with 50 or more workers) and the public sector establish channels and procedures for reporting and follow-up, following consultation and in agreement with the social partners, where provided by national law. They shall enable an entity's workers to report and

[39] Abazi, n 35 at 641; Gerdemann and Colneric, n 35 at 7.

[40] N Nohria and C Garcia-Pont, 'Global strategic linkages and industry structure' (1991) 12 *Strategic Management Journal* 105–24.

may enable other persons covered by the relevant personal scope to report. The text details the requirements this channel must respect. Among others, under Article 9, it must ensure the confidentiality of the identity of both the reporting person and any third party mentioned and the follow-up must be diligent and be carried out by an impartial person or department.[41]

(2) Another channel is external reporting to the competent authority. Under Article 11, the competent authorities for receiving and following up reports are designated by the Member State and must be provided with adequate resources. Articles 11 and 12 also detail the requirements this channel must comply with. They must, notably, be independent and autonomous to receive and handle information. Protection of the confidentiality of the identity of the reporting person and any third person mentioned is also provided for. Under Articles 7, 9 and 13, concerning both internal and external reporting, the provision of information to potential reporting persons must be organised by the entities and the authorities concerned.

(3) Finally, reporting persons can make the report public. This is the first EU alert law that regulates public disclosure. All existing EU instruments only organise internal reporting and reporting to a competent authority. This improvement could be explained by the influence of ECtHR case law and the *Luxleaks* case, which highlighted the possibility that even the competent authority may be unable to deal with a particular situation.

In order to report, the reporting person must respect certain conditions, depending on the channel they use.

Under Article 6(1), the reporting person must have reasonable grounds to *believe* (they have the right to make a mistake in this respect) that the information they report is true at the time of reporting and that such information falls within the scope of the Directive. The major issue here is to interpret the notion of 'reasonable grounds'. Too strict an interpretation often excludes the reporting person from the scope of the law and discourages reporting; too broad an interpretation, on the other hand, potentially leads to abusive reporting. There is an important role for the relevant authorities here.[42] Under Article 10, the reporting person can freely choose to report internally or externally, and can decide who is the most appropriate receiver. This choice is innovative because most alert laws require that initially reporting must take place internally, where possible. The freedom to choose in this respect provides an important incentive to report.[43]

[41] This protection is not automatic as the interplay with other legislation, such as the protection of personal data, which is being debated in Germany and was recently the subject of a decision of the German Labour Court (Regional Labour Court Baden-Württemberg, judgment of 20 December 2018, 17 Sa 11/18). See Abazi, n 35 at 645.

[42] This was an important issue in the *Luxleaks* case where the practices of the employer were difficult to assess for anyone lacking expertise in taxation. In the ECtHR decision *Gawlik v Lichtenstein* this condition, which corresponds to a criterion of *Guja* case law, is interpreted particularly restrictively (ECtHR, 16 February 2021, *Gawlik v Lichtenstein*, 23922/19, pt 74–78). See Lewis, n 37 at 7.

[43] The French Sapin II Law, the English and Irish Public Disclosure Act or the case law of the ECtHR require reporting to the employer, then to the regulator and only then public disclosure.

Additional conditions are required for public disclosure, depending on the circumstances. Under Article 15, public disclosure is permitted if the person reported internally and/or directly externally, but no appropriate action was taken in response. It is also permitted if the person has reasonable grounds to believe either that the violation may constitute 'an imminent or manifest danger to the public interest'[44] or that there is a risk of retaliation or a low prospect of the violation being addressed effectively, given the particular circumstances of the case.

The Directive regulates in detail the establishment of procedures and channels and their requirements, which brings more certainty and encourages reporting. Its provisions are far more detailed than the existing EU legal provisions on alerts, especially in labour law, in which most provisions are quite short and general, leaving the Member States substantial scope for organising reporting. This runs the risk of giving rise to legal uncertainty. This is an additional reason for underlining the importance of inserting EU labour law within the scope of the Directive, in order to improve the status of alerts in labour law and its enforcement.

By contrast, one weakness of the Directive is that it does not sufficiently detail what procedure should be established for the follow-up of reports. This is potentially an extremely complex matter. The process of reporting follow-up is less developed than in some existing labour law instruments, as such Directive 89/391, which organises workers' involvement in the handling of reports.

4.3. Protection and Support

The protection offered by the Directive is far more comprehensive and detailed than in any existing EU legal instrument, especially in labour law, where most provisions simply state that the reporting person shall not suffer any detriment as a consequence of their reporting and do not provide specific support. This is another respect that underlines the importance of extending the scope of the Directive to include EU labour law instruments in order to encourage alerts and improve the enforcement of labour law.

Article 19 prohibits any form of (threats or attempts at) retaliation against reporting persons, meaning any act or omission that (may) cause(s) them unjustified harm. It lays down a long and non-exhaustive list of forms of retaliation. It also requires the adoption of measures to protect reporting persons. In addition, it provides for immunity from liability for the reporting person for obtaining and reporting the relevant information: they shall not be considered to have breached any restriction on disclosure and shall not incur liability, provided that they had reasonable grounds to believe that reporting was necessary to reveal a violation and that the acquisition of the relevant information did not constitute a criminal offence in its own right. The

[44] The notions of public interest and risk are used only on the assumption that they are consequences of a breach of the law.

Directive also meets a crucial need in organising the interplay between different legal regimes that might come into conflict in the case of reporting.

The Directive provides that, in court proceedings related to harm suffered by a reporting person, if they can establish that the harm occurred after they reported a violation, the harm will be presumed to have occurred in retaliation for the report and the perpetrators of the harmful measure will have to prove that it was based on justified grounds. Under Article 21(8), the reporting person who suffered retaliation must have access to remedial measures. In addition, the Directive provides for penalties for persons who (attempt to) hinder reporting, or who retaliate, bring vexatious proceedings against, or breach the duty of maintaining the confidentiality of the identity of reporting persons.

Besides protection, Article 20 of the Directive requires that the reporting person shall have access to support measures, including independent, accessible and free information and advice on procedures, available remedies and protection. It also requires the provision of effective assistance before any relevant authority to protect them against retaliation. The Member States must grant legal aid in criminal and cross-border civil proceedings and legal aid in further proceedings, as well as legal counsel or other legal assistance. But the Directive also leaves the Member States free to implement other measures, even some crucial ones, such as financial assistance.

Among the most interesting provisions of the Directive, Article 4(4) provides protection to natural persons who assist a reporting person in the reporting process, third persons who are connected with the reporting person and could suffer retaliation, and legal entities that the reporting person owns, works for or is otherwise connected with. This protection can therefore be awarded to trade union and workers' representatives who help the reporting person. This protection avoids indirect retaliation targeting people linked to the reporting person and recognises the necessarily collective dimension of alerts.

Because the natural or legal person to whom the breach is attributed also needs protection, under Article 22, the Member States shall ensure that they fully enjoy the right to an effective remedy, a fair trial, the presumption of innocence and the rights of defence. Their identity must be protected as long as investigations are ongoing. The rules concerning the protection of the reporting person's identity also apply to the person who is the object of reporting. Under Article 23 penalties must be applicable against reporting persons who knowingly report false information and measures must be available to affected persons to compensate them for damages arising from such reporting.

5. Conclusion

Provided they are properly regulated, alerts can constitute an effective tool for better enforcement of the law. This is especially true in relation to labour law, in relation to which whistleblowing can help to bring to light and stop violations, and early warnings can contribute to better prevention of risks and better fulfilment of preventive obligations. This is crucial in the vital area of occupational safety and health.

Despite the importance of such alerts, only few legal instruments regulate them in labour law. A number of areas of EU labour law are not covered by any alert laws and the existing texts are sometimes weak and could be improved in some respects, such as the development of alert channels and protections granted to reporting persons. This current situation reduces the effectiveness of alerts as a tool for better enforcement of EU labour law.

The adoption of Directive 2019/1937, which aims to improve and harmonise the alert rules in EU law, could have addressed these shortcomings. The Directive, however, only regulates whistleblowing and does not cover reporting of violations of EU labour law. Workers are mobilised for better enforcement of the law and better protection of the interests of a large number of actors, except in the case of the enforcement of labour law and the interests of workers themselves. This is very disappointing because the Directive could have covered EU labour law. In addition, its broad personal scope, its developed and detailed reporting channels and its comprehensive protection and support measures could have improved the existing alert provisions existing in EU labour law. The Directive missed the opportunity to address this insufficiency and improve the enforcement of EU labour law by means of alerts.

This observation may be mitigated by the fact that Member States remain free to extend the scope of application of the Directive also to labour law instruments, but there is no obligation on this point. As a result of this margin left to the Member States, great differences remain between Member State legislation, reducing the understandability and effectiveness of global alert regulation at the EU level. For these reasons labour law instruments should be integrated in the scope of the regulation in the implementation of the Directive. Furthermore, in extending the regime, attention should be paid to the approach adopted by existing labour law instruments, in particular by Directive 89/391, which regulates early warnings. The implementation of the Directive in this area should articulate both approaches without removing early warning.

If early warning, despite its importance, remains the poor relation of EU alert law, there may be some hope with the potential adoption of a Directive imposing a duty of diligence on private entities. The European Commission has taken some preliminary steps, including a study that confirmed the need for EU-wide legislation requiring companies to identify, account for and mitigate negative human rights and environmental impacts in their supply chains. The Commissioner for Justice announced in April 2020 that the Commission will introduce an initiative in 2021. In March, the European Parliament adopted Resolution 2020/2129 calling for a compulsory EU duty of diligence and including a proposal for a Directive inspired by the French law imposing a duty of vigilance. This proposal requires the establishment of an alert mechanism covering whistleblowing and early warnings, also in labour law. This Directive could represent an opportunity to develop the legal instruments regulating whistleblowing and early warnings in order to ensure a more coherent legal framework for alerts.

19

Enforcing Labour Law via Public Procurement

NIKLAS BRUUN

1. Introduction

The European Union has established a comprehensive and detailed legal regime for handling large-scale publicly funded projects. The legal regime is focused primarily on the tendering and awarding of public contracts, but indirectly it also has important implications for the content of these contracts.

Work performed by workers or employees might often take place within the framework of these contracts and as part of fulfilling them. Usually this work is governed by labour law in the country where the work is carried out. In such situations the fact that the work performed forms part of a publicly procured project usually does not have any significant impact on the terms and conditions of employees performing the work.

The fact that work is performed within the framework of a contract between a public authority and a private contractor might, however, bring in some additional important legal sources that might become relevant. These include the following:

- *Legislation on public procurement* that has stipulations with labour law relevance or effect. This legislation can have its basis either in EU Directives[1] or national regulations, which might be in place for instance in order to fulfil state obligations, not only included in public procurement legislation but also emanating from ILO Convention No 94 on labour clauses in public contracts.[2]
- The *contractual arrangement between the public authority and the contractor* can contain undertakings from the latter to meet certain labour law

[1] The relevant EU legislation can be found in the EU's 2014 legislative package, which has three elements or instruments: Directive 2014/23/EU on the award of concession contracts, [2014] OJ L 94/1; Directive 2014/24/EU on public procurement, [2014] OJ L94/65; and Directive 2014/25/EU on utilities, [2014] OJ L 94/243.

[2] See K Krüger, R Nielsen and N Bruun, *European Public Contracts in a Labour Law Perspective* (Copenhagen, DJØF Publishing, 1998), ch 7, 207–47.

obligations. The enforcement of such obligations can be ensured specifically through contractual solutions binding on the contractor and relevant in relation to their employees, and may also be extended to subcontractors.

- The fact that the European Union (EU) has created an open public procurement market for all its Member States and the EEA states has enhanced the relevance of *rules on cross-border working and posting of workers in the context of public procurement*.[3] When we discuss the enforcement of workers' rights in the context of public procurement we must pay close attention to the regulation of terms and conditions for posted workers in the EU.
- Recently, attention has been paid in EU law to the protection of persons who report breaches of EU law (so-called 'whistleblowers').[4] Such reporting has explicitly been allowed in cases of breaches of EU legislation on public procurement in order to strengthen the enforcement of this field of law within the EU.

This chapter is structured as follows. First, we will scrutinise the specific public procurement rules that are of relevance for social and labour law considerations. We will focus especially on Directive 2014/24/EU, which contains the general, classic public procurement regime. We will avoid entering into a detailed discussion on similar provisions in the other Directives on public procurement and their enforcement. Secondly, we will discuss different types of contractual arrangements and their enforcement, and thirdly enforcement of posted workers' rights in the context of public procurement.

2. Labour Law Obligations under Directive 2014/24/EU

2.1. Article 18(2)

Article 18(1) proclaims the traditional well-established basic principles of public procurement within the EU: 'Contracting authorities shall treat economic operators equally and without discrimination and shall act in a transparent and proportionate manner.' The new Article 18(2) proclaims principles that have until now not been formulated as part of the basic principles of EU procurement law:

> Member States shall take appropriate measures to ensure that in the performance of public contracts economic operators comply with applicable obligations in the fields of environmental, social and labour law established by Union law, national law, collective agreements or by the international environmental, social and labour law provisions listed in Annex X.

[3] Directive (EU) 2018/957 of the European Parliament and of the Council of 28 June 2018 amending Directive 96/71/EC concerning the posting of workers in the framework of the provision of services.

[4] Directive (EU) 2019/1937. See further section 5 in this chapter.

The international social conventions identified in Annex X reflect the ILO's eight core labour standards: ILO Conventions No 87 (Freedom of Association and the Protection of the Right to Organise), No 98 (the Right to Organise and Collective Bargaining), No 29 (Forced Labour), No 105 (the Abolition of Forced Labour), No 138 (Minimum Age), No 111 (Discrimination (Employment and Occupation)), No 100 (Equal Remuneration); and No 182 (Worst Forms of Child Labour).[5] At present there also is a debate on including safe and health provisions in the ILO's framework of fundamental principles and rights. Working environment is also regulated under EU law, however.

The 'labour law' clause in Article 18(2) is an important innovation. It is drafted in mandatory terms ('Member States shall take appropriate measures') and is generally framed ('social and labour law established by Union law,[6] national law, collective agreements'). The reference to collective agreements is general: there is no condition that the collective agreement must be universally applicable. It explicitly refers to Union law, which covers all EU labour law Directives, including EU law on non-discrimination.

Article 18(2) explicitly addresses the Member States, which must make sure that contracting authorities take the appropriate measures. From Recital 37, however, we can see that this para also is addressed directly to the contracting authorities. The Recital states:

> With a view to an appropriate integration of environmental, social and labour requirements into public procurement procedures it is of particular importance *that Member States and contracting authorities* take relevant measures to ensure compliance with obligations in the fields of environmental, social and labour law that apply at the place where the works are executed or the services provided and result from laws, regulations, decrees and decisions, at both national and Union level, as well as from collective agreements, provided that such rules, and their application, comply with Union law. [Emphasis added.]

Article 18(2) applies 'in the performance of public contracts'. Recital 40, however, indicates that 'performance' here covers the different stages of the procurement process because it prescribes that account should be taken of social (and environmental) provisions throughout the procurement process:

> Control of the observance of the environmental, social and labour law provisions should be performed at the relevant stages of the procurement procedure, when applying the

[5] In the context of the Follow-up to the resolution on the ILO Centenary Declaration for the Future of Work it has been proposed to also include safe and healthy working conditions in the ILO's framework of fundamental principles and rights at work. This would mean that also ILO Occupational Safety and Health Convention No 155 (1981) and its Protocol, as well as Conventions Nos 187 and 161 would be classified as core labour standards in the ILO system. See: www.ilo.org/gb/GBSessions/GB341/ins/WCMS_769712/lang--en/index.htm.

[6] Union law here refers not only to the Labour Law Directives adopted within the European Union, but also to European non-discrimination law and the EU OSH (occupational safety and health) legal regime consisting of Framework Directive 89/391/EEC of 12 June 1989 on the introduction of measures to encourage improvements in the safety and health of workers at work. This Framework Directive

general principles governing the choice of participants and the award of contracts, when applying the exclusion criteria and when applying the provisions concerning abnormally low tenders.

The interpretation of the new Article 18(2) has varied in different Member States. In some states the mandatory character of Article 18(2) has been taken seriously and transposed into national law; in other Member States the fact that the state has broad discretion when deciding on which measures are deemed to be 'appropriate' has led to the conclusion that Article 18(2) is primarily a declarative or 'programmatic' provision.[7]

The CJEU seems to agree with the first group of Member States that take the mandatory character of Article 18(2) seriously. In Case C-395/18 (30.1.2020) the Court noted (pp 38–39):

> In this respect, it should be noted that Article 18 of Directive 2014/24, entitled 'Principles of procurement', is the first article of Chapter II of that Directive devoted to 'general rules' on public procurement procedures. Accordingly, by providing in paragraph 2 of that article that economic operators must comply, in the performance of the contract, with obligations relating to environmental, social and labour law, the Union legislature sought to establish that requirement as a principle, like the other principles referred to in paragraph 1 of that article, namely the principles of equal treatment, non-discrimination, transparency, proportionality and prohibiting the exclusion of a contract from the scope of Directive 2014/24 or artificially narrowing competition. *It follows that such a requirement constitutes, in the general scheme of that Directive, a cardinal value with which the Member States must ensure compliance pursuant to the wording of Article 18(2) of that Directive.*
>
> In those circumstances, the need to ensure appropriate compliance with the obligations referred to in Article 18(2) of Directive 2014/24 must enable Member States, when determining the implementing conditions of the ground for exclusion referred to in Article 57(4)(a) of that Directive, to consider that the party responsible for the failure to fulfil obligations may be not only the economic operator who submitted the tender, but also the subcontractors which the latter intends to use. The contracting authority may legitimately claim to award the contract only to economic operators who, at the stage of the contract award procedure, demonstrate their capacity to ensure in an appropriate manner, during the performance of the contract, that those obligations are fulfilled, where appropriate by having recourse to subcontractors who themselves comply with those obligations. [Emphasis added.]

When specific additional (in relation to Article 18(2)) labour law obligations are included in a public procurement contract the economic operator has an obligation to apply them to its employees or to make sure that these obligations are applied in relations between its subcontractors and their employees.

is accompanied by further Directives focusing on specific aspects of safety and health at work. Together they form the fundamentals of European OSH legislation.

[7] For instance, the United Kingdom decided not to implement Art 18(2) as such. See further C Barnard, 'To Boldly Go: Social Clauses in Public Procurement' (2017) 46(2) *Industrial Law Journal* 208–44.

The fact that Article 18(2) contains an obligation for the Member States has an important implication for the relevance of Article 31(1) CFREU in this context. Under Article 51 CFREU Member States need to comply with the Charter when implementing EU law. Article 31(1) prescribes that workers have the right to fair and just working conditions and the Member States are bound to guarantee this within the context of public procurement because they are here 'implementing' EU law.[8]

When there are law-based obligations in place within the country where the work is performed, they apply normally. The public procurement contract might, however, introduce further possibilities to enforce the labour law obligations by traditional contractual economic means, such as contractual fines or damages, as will be explored further below. Such contractual sanctions might prescribe that the contractor will have to pay a fixed sum of for instance 10,000 euros if the employees working for a subcontractor do not receive stipulated minimum wages.

2.2. Further Implications of Article 18(2)

Article 56(1) of Directive 2014/24/EU obliges contracting authorities to check the tender's and bidders' compliance with all requirements and selection criteria. Under Article 56(1) contracting authorities may decide not to award a contract to the tenderer submitting the most economically advantageous tender where they have established that the tender does not comply with the applicable obligations referred to in Article 18(2).

Under Article 57(4 a) contracting authorities may exclude or may be required by Member States to exclude from participation in a procurement procedure any economic operator in relation to which the contracting authority can demonstrate by any appropriate means a violation of applicable obligations referred to in Article 18(2).

The language used in Articles 56(1) and 57(4a) is slightly contradictory. On one hand, it is stated that contracting authorities *may be* required to exclude economic operators not complying with Article 18(2); on the other hand, the Member States must ensure compliance with Article 18(2). It therefore seems clear that a Member State which does not introduce an obligation in national law to exclude a tenderer, when it is established that it does not comply with the obligations in Article 18(2), has not fulfilled its implementation obligations under EU law. In practice, however, it might be difficult ex ante to clearly establish that there are violations of the obligations referred to in Article 18(2).

[8] See R Zimmer, 'Living wages in international and European law' (2019) 25(3) *Transfer* 285–99. See also on the interpretation of Art 31(1) CFREU, K Lörcher in F Dorssemont, K Lörcher, S Clauwaert and M Schmitt, *The Charter of Fundamental Rights of the European Union and the Employment Relation* (London, Bloomsbury, 2019).

Under Article 69(3) the contracting authority shall assess the information provided by consulting the tenderer. During such a consultation the tenderer might ask the workers' representative, for example a shop steward, to testify that the working conditions in the tendering entity meet all the requirements. The public authority might during the process encourage the tenderer to involve workers' representatives, but it is up to the tenderer to decide how compliance with Article 18(2) can be proven.

Contracting authorities shall reject a tender where they have established that the financial sum given is abnormally low because it does not comply with applicable obligations referred to in Article 18(2). At this stage the rejection of the tender can only be done by the contracting authority; the decision not to reject a tender can however be challenged by a competitor tendering for the same project.

The conditions for performance of contracts are regulated in Article 70. Contracting authorities may lay down special conditions related to the performance of a contract, provided that they are linked to its subject matter and are indicated in the call for competition or in the procurement documents. Those conditions may include economic, innovation-related, environmental, social or employment-related considerations.

In the preamble (p 91) it is stated that contract performance conditions might also be intended to favour the implementation of measures for the promotion of equality of women and men at work, the increased participation of women in the labour market, the reconciliation of work and private life, the protection of the environment or animal welfare, and to comply in substance with fundamental ILO Conventions, and to recruit more disadvantaged persons than are required under national legislation.

Article 71 regulates subcontracting. Here it is stated that observance of the obligations referred to in Article 18(2) by subcontractors is ensured through appropriate action by the competent national authorities acting within the scope of their responsibility and remit.[9]

Article 71(2) states that in the procurement documents, the contracting authority may ask, or may be required by a Member State to ask, the tenderer to indicate in its tender any share of the contract it may intend to subcontract to third parties and any proposed subcontractors.

2.3. The EU and ILO Convention No 94

The development of the regulation of public procurement within the European Union has its origin in the EU rules on competition and state aid. The competition

[9] In practice, the sanctioning of subcontractors seems to be rather rare. It has been reported that in France, which has been a pioneer in introducing joint and several liability of local clients and general contractors by extending it to pay obligations, there has been little application in practice so far. See B Palli, 'Posting of workers in French courts' in Z Rasnača and M Bernaciak (eds), *Posting of Workers before National Courts* (Brussels, ETUI, 2020) 81 and 102.

rules restrict concerted practices between bidders, and restrictions on state aid regulate how state resources can be channelled to certain undertakings in order to help them to compete for public contracts.

As part of the single market programme in the late 1980s the Directives on public procurement were prepared and adopted.[10] Later, these Directives were revised and replaced by new ones, first in 2006 and then in 2014, when the Directives which are now in force were adopted.

In the late 1980s little attention was paid to the fact that several EU Member States were bound to ILO Convention No 94 when the first Directives on public procurement were adopted. As early as 1949 the International Labour Organization had adopted, during a period when post-war rebuilding within the framework of public contracts was common, a Convention regarding labour clauses in public contracts.[11]

The primary rule in Convention No 94 (Article 2) concerning labour clauses in public contracts states that contracts to which the Convention applies shall include clauses ensuring to the workers concerned wages (including allowances), hours of work and other conditions of labour that are not less favourable than those established for work of the same character in the trade or industry concerned in the district where the work is carried out. These conditions could be established by collective agreement or other recognised machinery of negotiation, by arbitration award or by national laws or regulations (Article 2.1). If labour conditions are not regulated in such a manner, the labour clauses must ensure conditions that are not less favourable than those established by collective agreement or other recognised machinery of negotiation, by arbitration, or by national laws or regulations, for work of the same character in the trade or industry concerned in the nearest appropriate district; or the general level observed in the trade or industry in which the contractor is engaged by employers whose general circumstances are similar (Article 2.2).

The aim of Convention No 94 is primarily to make sure that already established national working conditions in a district are safeguarded and not undermined. It is not, however, the purpose of the Convention to set up substantive minimum standards for conditions of work carried out under a public contract.[12]

Adequate sanctions shall be applied, by the withholding of contracts or otherwise, for failure to observe and apply the provisions of labour clauses in public

[10] See 86/665/EEC, OJ 1989 L 395/33 on the coordination of the laws, regulations and administrative provisions related to the application of review procedures for the award of public supply and public works contracts and Directives 93/36/EEC, [1993] OJ L 199/1 and 93/37/EEC.

[11] Convention No 94, which was adopted in 1949, and entered into force on 20 September 1952, has been ratified by a considerable number of Member States: Austria (1951), Belgium (1952), Denmark (1955), Finland (1951), France (1951), the Netherlands (1952), Italy (1952), Spain (1971). Among the 'new' Member States, at least Bulgaria (1955) and Cyprus (1960) have ratified the Convention. Also Norway, a Member State of the EES agreement, ratified the Convention in 1996.

[12] See K Krüger, R Nielsen and N Bruun, *European Public Contracts in a Labour Law Perspective* (Copenhagen, DJØF Publishing, 1998) 207.

contracts (Article 5.1). Appropriate measures shall be taken, by the withholding of payments under the contract or otherwise, for the purpose of enabling the workers concerned to obtain the wages to which they are entitled (Article 5.2). The Convention No 94 gives hereby rather general guidelines for the enforcement of the Convention which indicates that it is up for the Member States to develop and adopt the adequate sanctions.

2.4. Different Models for Implementation

The approach to the implementation of Article 18(2) has shown significant variations in different Member States.

In some Member States it has been left to the public authorities to choose how they require any social or labour-related stipulations to be included in their public contracts. In other countries, the legislator has put in some guidance or obligations for the public authorities in this regard. Finland and Sweden can here serve as examples of Member States where the legislator has introduced some obligations.

2.4.1. Finland

Section 98 in the Finnish Act on public procurement (29.12.2016/1397) stipulates that the contracting authority can put in place requirements related to the performance of the contract, provided that they are linked to the subject matter of the contract. Such requirements must be included in the call for tenders or in the documentation provided.

Section 98 is clearly influenced by ILO, No 94 which Finland has ratified. The public contract between a central public authority and the contracting party that has won the tender must contain a clause according to which the work that is to be performed in Finland in accordance with the contract must be performed under conditions which fulfil the minimum requirements which under Finnish law and provisions in collective agreements should apply in similar work.

Section 98 goes beyond ILO Convention No 94 by prescribing that all public contracts within the construction sector must contain commitments to follow the standards set by Finnish law and collective agreements.

2.4.2. Sweden

Under the new Swedish Act on Public Procurement 17:1 the public authority as a party to the public contract may stipulate special environmental, social, labour law or other conditions on the performance of a public contract.[13]

[13] Swedish Act 2016:1145 Lag om offentlig upphandling.

These conditions must be linked to the subject matter of the contract as defined in Act 16(2) and they must be mentioned in the tender documentation.

In Act 17(2) it is stated that the public authority must require that the contractor respects minimum conditions on wages, annual holidays and working time specified in the contract when work is performed for the fulfilment of the contract. This obligation applies only if there is a need for such minimum standards.

This obligation also applies to the subcontractor to the party in the public contract, which participates directly in fulfilling the contractual obligations.

The level of wages, working time and annual holidays shall follow the lowest standards contained in a central collective agreement which is applicable in the whole of Sweden in the sector concerned. They must, however, always meet the requirements laid down by law.[14]

When a purchasing public authority has to stipulate the minimum standards regarding wages, working time and annual holiday it should give the relevant central labour market organisations that are parties to the agreement an opportunity to express their views on the issue, unless there is no need for it.

If there are no preconditions for setting the level in accordance with Act 17(2), the public authority has no obligation to stipulate any specific standards. However, ordinary national labour law obligations apply.

2.4.3. Spain[15]

The main innovation of Act 9/2017 of 8 November on public sector contracts regarding social (and environmental) clauses is the reinforcing of the importance of social and environmental considerations in public contracts. Contracting bodies may establish these considerations as qualitative award criteria for evaluating the best price/quality ratio or as special performance conditions, provided that these are linked to the object of the contract, are not discriminatory, are compatible with EU law, and are established in the procurement documents or in the contract notice. The change in the context of special performance conditions under the 2014 Directive is that the Act obliges the contracting body to establish in the procurement document at least one special environmental, social or labour condition from among those set out in Article 202.

Breach of the special performance conditions can give rise to penalties. The Act also establishes sanctions for non-payment of salaries to workers assigned to the performance of the contract or breach of the conditions.

[14] See the preparatory works: Upphandling och villkor enligt kollektivavtal. SOU 2015:78.

[15] See the information on the home page of Uria Menendez: www.uria.com/documentos/circulares/955/documento/7259/UMBriefing.pdf. This new legislation has been used by the Catalan government to introduce a socially responsible framework agreement for cleaning services. See further the European Commission publication: Making Socially Responsible Public Procurement Work: 71 Good Practice Cases #WeBuySocialEU (May 2020), https//ec.europa.eu/DocsRoom – European Commission (europa.eu).

Another novelty under the Act is that trade union organisations are given standing to file special procurement appeals when decisions subject to appeal offer grounds to deduce that there will be a breach of social or labour obligations with respect to the workers participating in the process of executing the contract. There is also express recognition of standing for sectoral business organisations representing the collective interests affected by the challenged act.

2.4.4. Conclusion

It is not possible here to further explore the various national models for enforcing labour law obligations in the context of public procurement, but the broad variations in this respect indicates that the European Commission here has an important task to ensure the application of EU law (TEU Article 17.1).

3. Enforcement of Labour Law Obligations

3.1. Starting Points

When there are law-based obligations in the country where the work is performed, these obligations apply normally similarly to all work performed as indicated above. The public procurement contract might, however, introduce further possibilities or avenues for enforcing labour law obligations. Contractual remedies will apply in relations between the public authority and the contractor (annulment, cancellation of the contract as the extreme measure). Default fines might be a functioning remedy that can be imposed. The question is, however, how the contractual stipulations on 'additional' labour obligations can be controlled and surveillance organised.

One common form of 'additional' labour law obligations might emanate from collective agreements at different levels. Public procurement contracts can be used in order to lay down minimum standards based on stipulations in collective agreements, for instance at sectoral level. This can be done by including obligations for the economic contractor to apply at least conditions regulated in the collective agreements applicable in the sector when fulfilling the contract. Such an obligation might be included also in situations where the contractor is not bound by the collective agreement, for instance because the contractor is not a member in the employer federation has signed the agreement.

In these cases enforcement might cause challenges because the trade unions that are part in the collective agreement and can normally control its enforcement (from which the minimum standards emanate) do not have any automatic role in monitoring the contract. There might even be problems for trade union representatives related to GDPR regulations in relation to obtaining data on employees and paid wages.[16] On the other hand it is not out of the question that clauses on surveillance and enforcement can be included in the contract and that the trade unions are given some monitoring competences because of explicit provisions in the public procurement contract. Competences can be conferred on trade unions also through special legislation, as the Spanish example shows.

3.2. Transfer of Undertakings – Situations

In practice, the Transfer of Undertakings Directive (TUD)[17] has played an important role in the context of public procurement.

Public procurement procedures are used when public authorities outsource public functions or engage in competitive tendering. It has long been clear that the Transfer of Undertakings Directive may also be applicable when the change of contractors is the result of a public procurement procedure.[18] The precondition has been that there must be a transfer of an economic entity which retain its identity after the transfer. The relevance of regarding a situation as a transfer has been that the new contractor is bound to the terms and conditions of employment applicable in the old employer or transferor.

In practice, the Transfer of Undertakings Directive has been important, among other things, in the context of public passenger transport tendering, for instance for certain bus routes. Over a long period the extent to which the Transfer of Undertakings Directive applies has been slightly open because the CJEU has referred to an overall assessment. This has included the extent to which the new contractor has taken over staff from the old one. In the recent *Grafe and Pohle* case the CJEU reconsidered its view, however, and here it found that the situation could be regarded as a transfer of undertaking, although neither tangible assets nor staff were transferred to the new contractor after a tender competition.[19]

In order to make it clear that employment terms and conditions must be applied also by the new contractor the public authority should clarify in the tendering call that the situation in this respect will be regarded as a transfer of undertaking. Such a condition can reduce legal uncertainty and also create a base for transferred staff to enforce such claims.

[16] See Regulation (EU) 2016/679 of 27 April 2016 on the protection of natural persons with regard to the processing of personal data and on the free movement of such data.

[17] Council Directive 2001/23/EC of 12 March 2001 on the approximation of the law of the Member States relating to the safeguarding of employees' rights in the event of transfers of undertakings, businesses or parts of undertakings or businesses.

[18] See, for instance, the CJEU Case C-172/99 *Liikenne*, ECLI:EU:C:2001:59.

[19] See CJEU Case C-298/18 and further J McMullen, 'Leaving a Legacy: Recent Jurisprudence of the European Court on Transfer of Undertakings' (2021) 50(1) *Industrial Law Journal*.

4. Practical Experience from Enforcement

The detailed EU regulation of public procurement is basically silent on the issue of enforcement. The CJEU has stated, however, that the requirements that a public authority lays down must permit the accuracy of the information contained in the tenders to be effectively verified; for instance, the award criterion must be formulated sufficiently clearly so that it can satisfy the requirements of equal treatment and transparency of procedures for public contracts.[20]

In other words, the CJEU has stated that it must be possible to follow up and control different clauses and conditions in public contracts, but neither the legislation nor the Court's practice tell us anything about how follow-up and enforcement should take place when the contract has been signed and is in the stage of implementation. This starting point emphasised by the Court must, however, be taken into account when different national rules are applied and interpreted.

At the first stage of the enforcement of social and labour clauses in public contracts the public authority requires continuous and detailed information on the follow up of these clauses, for instance on what wages have been paid to employees, what working time schemes have been followed and so on. Such requirements must be included in the contract and mentioned already in the call for tender, in which the substantial requirements on working conditions must also be mentioned. This form of reporting is usually called self-reporting. The self-reporting is then supplemented with possibilities for inspections that the public authority or its agents can conduct.

The second stage in the enforcement process consists of any sanctions or consequences that can be imposed when labour clauses are not respected. These sanctions again must be part of the contractual framework. Usually the contractual sanctions must be preceded by a chance for the contractor to correct their practice and fulfil the contractual obligations. If, however, the contractor continues to breach labour clauses there might be specific economic sanctions in the form of contractual penalty clauses tailored with damages stipulated for these situations. The sanctions can also be extended to apply to situations in which a subcontractor is in breach of the contract and its labour clauses.

It is important to note that sanctions, as a starting point, should be proportional. In many situations it is therefore not enough to rely on general contractual remedies and sanctions where labour clauses are not respected. It may turn out that the whole contract, which might cover many elements and as a whole amount to millions of euros, might have to be revoked in a situation in which some labour law obligations are not respected. In such a situation it might be more efficient to stipulate fines, which can be repeatedly invoked and increased in situations of non-fulfilment of labour law obligations.

[20] See CJEU Case C-448/01 *EVN and Wienstrom*, EU:C:2003:651.

In Sweden, the trade unions in the city of Malmö developed a 'White Job' campaign (*Vita jobb*), within the framework of which the public authorities were offered enforcement consultants with a trade union background to monitor labour clauses in public contracts. These consultants were hired by the public authorities to help them with follow-up and monitoring of labour clauses in public contracts. Some employer organisations questioned this practice, but as long as the consultants stuck to their mandate and acted as impartial experts, this practice was found to be legitimate.

Follow-up for labour clauses is often fairly complicated and costly. In cases in which the contractor/employer is not bound by a collective agreement, the trade union within the contractor company has no mandate to obtain information and to control whether the labour clauses stipulated in the public contract are being respected. Information on wages, which shop stewards in companies bound by collective agreements are entitled to receive, might be regarded as sensitive personal information which the contractor will refuse to share with the trade union. Here again a contractual solution regarding follow-up and control is necessary.

5. Whistleblowing as an Enforcement Mechanism

Article 2.1 of Directive 2019/1937[21] states that the Directive lays down common minimum standards for the protection of persons reporting the following breaches of Union law: (a) 'breaches falling within the scope of the Union acts set out in the Annex that concern the following areas'. 'Public procurement' is listed as an example of such an area. It seems clear therefore that breaches related to Article 18(2) or other labour law obligations emanating from the public procurement Directives or contracts based on these Directives can also be a legitimate reason for whistleblowing. We recall that there are two basic material requirements for justified whistleblowing under the Directive: 'Reporting persons shall qualify for protection under this Directive provided that they had reasonable grounds to believe that the information on breaches reported was true at the time of reporting and that such information fell within the scope of this Directive' (Article 6.1 a).[22]

As mentioned in Recital 6 of the Directive, whistleblower protection is necessary to enhance the enforcement of EU law on public procurement. It is necessary, not only to prevent and detect procurement-related fraud and corruption in the context of the implementation of the EU budget, but also to tackle inadequate enforcement of rules on public procurement by national contracting authorities and contracting entities in relation to the execution of works, the supply of products or the provision of services. Breaches of such rules create distortions of

[21] Directive (EU) 2019/1937 of the European Parliament and of the Council of 23 October 2019 on the protection of persons who report breaches of Union law [2019] OJ L 305/17–56.

[22] See further Chapter 18 in this volume.

competition and create an uneven playing field for all businesses across the EU, thus affecting the proper functioning of the internal market.

The reference to public procurement rules in the Whistleblowing Directive is an important and significant exception to the Directive's restrictive approach to reporting breaches of labour law obligations.

The prohibition of retaliation in Article 19 of the Directive also protects whistleblowers in the context of public procurement against suspension, lay-off, dismissal or equivalent measures as consequences of whistleblowing and also against other forms of retaliation.

6. Enforcement of Labour Clauses in Public Contracts with an International Dimension

In what follows we will discuss the relationship between the Posted Workers Directive, EU public procurement law and ILO Convention No 94. In section 6.1 we will present the typical situations where posting of workers under EU law will become relevant in the context of public procurement. In section 6.2 we will discuss whether there is a tension between the requirements of Convention No 94 and the Posted Workers Directive, and in section 6.3 we will discuss the additional enforcement tools that can be used when posting of workers take place within the context of public procurement.

6.1. The EU Dimension

The legal regime pertaining to public procurement within the European Union has been adopted in order to make it easier for contractors to compete and bid on public contracts in other Member States than the one in which they are registered or have their seat.

Although the level of genuine cross-border contracts is lower than the European Commission might have expected, a considerable number of such contracts are entered into each year.

Contractors commonly want to use their own workforce to perform such contracts. In such situations the contractor might post its workers to the Member State where the contract is to be performed.

In such a situation the employment contract between the contractor and the employee is often subject to the regulations of the country of origin of the employment relationship. When setting the employment conditions for posted workers the Posted Workers Directive (PWD) will come into play. Furthermore, States that have ratified ILO Convention No 94 will have to respect their international obligations under this instrument. This means that in this area the scope of application of, on one hand, the Posted Workers Directive and, on the other, public procurement instruments (including Convention No 94) overlap. Both instruments have the same aim, establishing an obligation for the employer to guarantee a minimum standard of defined labour conditions in the particular context in which the work is performed.

Two main scenarios are likely when it comes to the posting of workers when a contractor wins a contract:

(i) Contractor C enters into a contract in Member State A to be performed in A, although C is based in Member State B. C sends out posted workers from B to A to perform the work.
(ii) Contractor C based in Member State A enters into a contract in Member State A with a public authority in A. The work is to be performed in State B by subcontractors to C. The workers in this case are not posted. Interpretation of Case C-549/13 *Bundesdruckerei* tells us that in this case national law in B applies, plus basic ILO standards.

6.2. The Posted Workers Directive

The *Rüffert* case[23] was a preliminary ruling requested by a German court. The *Land* of Lower Saxony's law on awarding public contracts contained provisions on awarding public contracts above a minimum value of €10,000. The preamble to the law stated:

> The Law counteracts distortions of competition which arise in the field of construction and local public transport services resulting from the use of cheap labour and alleviates burdens on social security schemes. It provides, to that end, that public contracting authorities may award contracts for building works and local public transport services only to undertakings which pay the wage laid down in the collective agreements at the place where the service is provided.

Paragraph 3(1) of the Land Public Procurement Act (*Landesvergabegesetz*), headed 'Declaration that the collective agreement will be complied with', states:

> Contracts for building services shall be awarded only to undertakings which, when lodging a tender, undertake in writing to pay their employees, when performing those services, at least the remuneration prescribed by the collective agreement at the place where those services are performed and at the time prescribed by the collective agreement. For the purposes of the first sentence, the term 'services' means services provided by the principal contractor and by subcontractors. The first sentence shall also apply to the award of transport services in local public transport.

The *Rüffert* case concerned a company, Objekt und Bauregie, that had been awarded a public contract. The company employed as a subcontractor another

[23] C-346/06 *Dirk Rüffert v Land Niedersachsen*, EU C:2008:189, 37.

company, established in Poland. In summer 2004 this firm came under suspicion of employing workers on the building site at a wage below that provided for in the 'Buildings and public works' collective agreement. Following investigations, the *Land* of Lower Saxony terminated the contract with Objekt und Bauregie, on the grounds that the company had failed to fulfil its contractual obligation to comply with the collective agreement. A penalty notice was issued against the person primarily responsible at the subcontractor undertaking established in Poland, accusing him of paying 53 workers engaged on the building site only 46.57 per cent of the minimum wage.

The issue went at first instance to the regional court in Hannover and then to the higher regional court, which referred the following question to the European Court of Justice (ECJ):

> Does it amount to an unjustified restriction on the freedom to provide services under the EC Treaty if a public contracting authority is required by statute to award contracts for building services only to undertakings which, when lodging a tender, undertake in writing to pay their employees, when performing those services, at least the remuneration prescribed by the collective agreement in force at the place where those services are performed?

The ECJ read the Posted Workers Directive[24] in light of Article 49 EC. The ECJ held that German federal legislation did not satisfy the conditions regarding minimum wages in the host country, which are binding on a service provider as regards payment of posted workers. According to the Court, the legislation did not declare collective agreements generally applicable, and applied only to a part of the sector (public contracts). Nor did the legislation satisfy the criteria laid down in Article 3(8) of the Directive. The ECJ gave a very restrictive interpretation of Article 3(7) of the Directive, which states that paragraphs 1 to 6 shall not prevent application of terms and conditions of employment that are more favourable to workers. In sum, the Court came to the conclusion that a Member State is not entitled to impose such legislation on contractors. The Posted Workers Directive, interpreted in light of Article 49 EC, did preclude a Member State from adopting legislation such as that in force in Lower Saxony.

The ECJ judgment was in many ways problematic from a legal point of view already when it was adopted.[25] Here we do not present a general critique of the controversial conclusions in the *Rüffert* case, but discuss only a few aspects related to ILO Convention No 94.

The *Land* legislation in Lower Saxony complied precisely with the obligation foreseen in ILO Convention No 94 on those states that have ratified it. Article 2 of the Convention states that '[c]ontracts to which this Convention applies shall

[24] Directive 96/71/EC concerning the posting of workers in the framework of the provision of services, [1996] OJ L18/1.

[25] See N Bruun, A Jacobs and M Schmidt, 'ILO Convention No 94 in the aftermath of the *Rüffert* case' (2010) 16(4) *Transfer* 473–88.

include clauses ensuring to the workers concerned wages (including allowances), hours of work and other conditions of labour which are not less favourable than those established for work of the same character in the trade or industry concerned where the work is carried on – (a) by collective agreement'.

Germany has not ratified Convention No 94 and this may be the formal reason why neither the AG in his opinion nor the ECJ in its judgment in Case C-346/08 (*Rüffert*) mentioned it. The tension between ILO Convention No 94 and the Posted Workers Directive was clear, however. The requirement presented in *Rüffert* according to which labour clauses can be demanded only in the same way as minimum (core) posting conditions of work under the Posted Workers Directive is contrary to ILO Convention No 94, as we explained thoroughly in an article published in 2010.[26]

This tension has never really been dealt with openly by the EU authorities; it has rather been denied or overlooked.[27] It is clear, however, that post-*Rüffert* ECJ case law, as well as new legislation regarding both posting and public procurement have made it possible to eliminate the conflict between ILO Convention No 94 and the Posted Workers Directive by way of interpretation. EU law can nowadays be interpreted in full conformity with the Convention.[28]

Furthermore, the new Directives on Public Procurement, as well as of Directive 2014/67/EU on the Enforcement of the Posted Workers Directive and the revision of the Posted Workers Directive 2018/957/EU have helped to eliminate the tension mentioned above.[29] Cases C- 115/14 *RegioPost* and C-549/13 *Bundesdruckerei* are also significant in this respect. In the *RegioPost* judgment the ECJ made clear that wage stipulations in a public contract do not normally restrict the free movement of services, and in any case such restriction is justified by the purpose of protecting workers. Furthermore, the ECJ has ruled, contrary to its position in *Rüffert*, that public contracts can contain elements that are not required for private contracts; in other words, a comparison between public contracts and private contracts is not relevant in this context. *Bundesdruckerei* introduced a restriction regarding

[26] See Bruun, Jacobs and Schmitt, n 25 above.

[27] The EU has asked the Member States to ratify ILO Convention No 94 as an 'up-to-date' Convention. See also the ILO report 'Labour clauses in public contracts', which was drafted by the Committee of Experts (ILO) and discussed at the International Labour Conference's 97th Session in 2008. The Committee noted 'the absence of specific binding national legal provisions concerning labour conditions in the execution of public contracts and the lack of effective enforcement measures' (para 313). The Committee did emphasise, however, that the purpose and object of Convention No 94 had remained intrinsically sound (para 314).

[28] This view is also shared by G Frosecchi and F Orlandini in their Working Paper 'An internationally oriented interpretation of EU law on public procurement: strengthening labour clauses through ILO Convention No 94', WP CSDLE Massimo D'Antona (ISSN 1594-817 X), http://csdle.lex.unict.it.

[29] The relationship between the developments in EU public procurement law and the Posted Workers Directive is also discussed by M Rocca, 'Stepping Stones over Troubled Waters, Recent Legal Evolutions and the Reform of the Posting of Workers Directive' in J Arnholtz and N Lille (eds), *Posted Work in the European Union. The Political Economy of Free Movement* (Routledge, 2020) 176–77.

application of the principle that the public authority can require the contractor to follow the core minimum labour standards under the Posted Workers Directive. When the work is performed outside the Member State in which the contractor is based, the minimum standards of the place of work are applicable.

6.3. Enforcement of the Posted Workers Directive and its New Elements in the Context of Public Procurement

The Enforcement Directive codifies and clarifies that certain enforcement mechanisms are not only deemed not to be restrictions on the free movement of services, but are also mandatory for Member States. Here we can look at them only briefly, as well as the debates that have taken place in the context of the implementation of this Directive. The relevant point, however, is that all these requirements concerning enforcement also apply when postings take place in order to fulfil a contract for a public authority under the legal regime of public procurement.

Before discussing the various instruments regulated in the Enforcement Directive, we shall examine the special role of the European Labour Authority (ELA)[30] with regard to the cross-border movement of workers in the context of public procurement and posting. One of the ELA's most important tasks is to facilitate and enhance cooperation between Member States in the enforcement of related law across the EU, including facilitating concerted and joint inspections. It remains to be seen how the ELA can contribute to the enforcing of labour standards in the context of public procurement; here we note only that also social partner organisations have a potential role in this context, because it is explicitly stated that they may bring cases to the attention of the authority (Art 8.1). It is possible that the ELA can contribute to most of the mechanisms listed in the Enforcement Directive.

6.3.1. Identification of a Genuine Posting and Prevention of Abuse and Circumvention

For the purpose of implementing, applying and enforcing the Posted Workers Directive, the competent authorities shall make an overall assessment of all factual elements that are deemed necessary to determine whether a situation is a genuine posting. The same elements may also be considered in order to determine whether a person falls within the applicable definition of a 'worker' in accordance with Article 2(2) Posted Workers Directive. Member States should be guided, among other things, by the facts related to the performance of work, subordination and

[30] Regulation (EU) 2019/1149 of the European Parliament and of the Council of 20 June 2019 establishing a European Labour Authority. See also Chapter 17 in this volume.

remuneration of the worker, notwithstanding how the relationship is characterised in any arrangement, whether contractual or not, that may have been agreed between the parties.

6.3.2. *Improved Access to Information*

Member States shall take the appropriate measures to ensure that the information on the terms and conditions of employment referred to in Article 3 Posted Workers Directive, which are to be applied and complied with by service providers, is made generally available free of charge in a clear, transparent manner.

In order to bring about further improvements with respect to access to information, Member States shall also indicate clearly, in a detailed and user-friendly manner and in an accessible format on a single official national website, and by other suitable means, which terms and conditions of employment and/or which parts of their national and/or regional law are to be applied to workers posted to their territory.

6.3.3. *Mutual Assistance – General Principles*

Member States shall work in close cooperation and provide each other with mutual assistance without undue delay in order to facilitate the implementation, application and enforcement in practice of the Posted Workers Directive and the Enforcement Directive.

6.3.4. *Administrative Requirements and Control Measures*

Member States may impose justified and proportionate administrative requirements and control measures necessary to ensure effective monitoring of compliance with the obligations set out in the Posted Workers Directive and the Enforcement Directive. Such requirements include various notification obligations, starting from an obligation to inform national authorities (for example, the health and safety authority) about the posting of a worker to the territory of a Member State. Furthermore, the posting undertaking can be requested to comply with specified documentation requirements. Another example is the requirement that the posting undertaking shall have a representative in the host country whom the posted worker and others can contact at all times during posting. According to Finnish law, staff representatives are also entitled to obtain information regarding the employment conditions and employment contract of posted workers.[31]

[31] See Finnish Act on Posting of Workers (447/2016 as amended 743/2020), Sec 12.

6.3.5. *Inspections*

Member States shall ensure that appropriate and effective checks and monitoring mechanisms provided in accordance with national law and practice are put in place and that the authorities designated under national law carry out effective and adequate inspections on their territory in order to control and monitor compliance with the provisions and rules laid down in the Posted Workers Directive, taking into account the relevant provisions of the Enforcement Directive, and thus guarantee their proper application and enforcement.

6.3.6. *Defence of Rights – Facilitation of Complaints – Back-payments*

For the enforcement of the obligations under the Posted Workers Directive, in particular Article 6 thereof, and this Directive, Member States shall ensure that there are effective mechanisms to enable posted workers to lodge complaints against their employers directly, as well as the right to institute judicial or administrative proceedings, also in the Member State in whose territory the workers are or were posted, where such workers consider they have sustained losses or damages as a result of a failure to apply the applicable rules, even after the relationship in which the failure is alleged to have occurred has ended.

6.3.7. *Subcontracting Liability*

In order to tackle fraud and abuse, Member States may, after consulting the relevant social partners in accordance with national law and/or practice, take additional measures on a non-discriminatory and proportionate basis in order to ensure that in subcontracting chains, the contractor of which the employer (service provider) covered by Article 1(3) Posted Workers Directive is a direct subcontractor can, in addition to or in place of the employer, be held liable by the posted worker with respect to any outstanding net remuneration covered by Article 3 Posted Workers Directive.

In addition, in accordance with Article 22 Enforcement Directive, Member States shall lay down rules on penalties applicable in the event of infringements of national provisions adopted pursuant to the Enforcement Directive and shall take all necessary measures to ensure that they are implemented and complied with. The penalties provided for shall be effective, proportionate and dissuasive.

7. Conclusions

There has been a gradual transformation regarding the enforcement of labour law via public procurement. For a long time the discussion focused on what labour clauses could be used in the context of public procurement and how they should be designed and included in the tendering documentation in order to fulfil the basic requirements of EU public procurement law.

The new Directives, which were adopted in 2014, clarify that Member States have an obligation to include labour law requirements and labour clauses in the national framework for public procurement. Therefore the new debate is focused on how we can ensure effective enforcement of these clauses. Here we still see an urgent need for practical development. In particular, contractual solutions in different countries should be adapted to the different features of national labour relations systems and include reporting obligations, follow-up procedures – which involve relevant stakeholders – and sanctions that are proportionate and efficient.

20

The European Pillar of Social Rights: Transforming Promises into Reality

OLIVIER DE SCHUTTER

1. Introduction

The European Pillar of Social Rights (EPSR), initially announced on 9 September 2015 by the President of the Commission in his State of the Union address,[1] was formally presented by the Commission in a communication of 8 March 2016.[2] It was endorsed by the European Parliament, the Council and the Commission on 17 November 2017, at the Social Summit for Fair Jobs and Growth held in Gothenburg, and approved the following month by the European Council. On 13 March 2018, in response to the request of the European Council, a communication from the Commission described how implementation of the EPSR would be monitored.[3] This monitoring includes a regular assessment of the employment and social performances of the EU Member States on the basis of a so-called 'Social Scoreboard', comprising 35 social, educational and employment indicators, broken down by age, gender and education. These are grouped into three dimensions corresponding to the broad areas covered by the EPSR (equal opportunities and access to the labour market; dynamic labour markets and fair working conditions; and public support, social protection and inclusion). The Social Scoreboard

[1] See also European Commission, *Commission Work Programme 2016*, COM(2015) 610 final of 27.10.2015 (in which, under the heading 'A deeper and fairer Economic and Monetary Union', the Commission announces its intention to contribute to the development of a 'European pillar of social rights', both by 'modernising and addressing gaps in existing social policy legislation' and by 'identifying social benchmarks, notably as concerns the flexicurity concept, built on best practices in the Member States with a view to upwards convergence, in particular in the euro area, as regards the functioning of the labour market, skills and social protection', 9).

[2] Communication from the Commission to the European Parliament, the Council, the European Economic and Social Committee and the Committee of the Regions, *Launching a consultation on a European Pillar of Social Rights*, COM(2016) 127 final, 8 March 2016.

[3] Communication from the Commission to the European Parliament, the Council, the European Economic and Social Committee and the Committee of the Regions, Monitoring the implementation of the European Pillar of Social Rights, COM(2018) 130 final of 13.3.2018.

is supposed to influence, in particular, the annual Joint Employment Report and the Country Reports presented as part of the European Semester, which seeks to promote macroeconomic convergence in the EU.[4] Finally, the EPSR was complemented by an Action Plan for its implementation, endorsed in March 2021 at the Porto Social Summit.[5] The Action Plan lists a number of initiatives the Commission proposes to take, or actions it recommends to other EU institutions or to the Member States, in order to make further progress. Three headline targets are stipulated: to increase the employment rate of the adult population in the EU to 78 per cent by 2030 (as compared with 73.1 per cent in 2019); to ensure that 60 per cent of adults participate in training every year (up from 37 per cent in 2016); and to reduce the number of people at risk of poverty or social exclusion (AROPE) by 15 million by 2030 (down from around 91 million AROPE in 2019).

The professed ambition of the Commission in presenting this proposal was to encourage a move towards a 'deeper and fairer economic and monetary union',[6] and to complement macroeconomic convergence with greater convergence in the three broad areas it covers, encompassing in total 20 principles formulated as rights. This chapter examines the extent to which the European Pillar of Social Rights and its Action Plan help to realise social rights in the European Union.[7] In order to answer this question, it is necessary, first, to recall the framework for the protection of fundamental social rights in the European Union's legal order. Section 2 of this contribution offers such a diagnosis. It identifies four major deficits in this regard, the most significant of which is that the new social and economic governance established in the EU following the public debt crisis of 2009–12 did not take into account until recently the impacts of fiscal and budgetary measures on social rights: it is to this deficit, indeed, that the adoption of the EPSR sought to respond. Section 3 of this study recalls the background of the initiative; it describes the contribution of the EPSR to the protection of social rights in the economic and social governance of the EU; and it identifies certain limitations. Section 4 offers a brief conclusion.

2. Protection of Fundamental Rights: Social Rights in the European Union Legal Order

The Court of Justice of the European Union (CJEU) has incorporated fundamental rights in its case law since the early 1970s, in response to concerns expressed

[4] See Proposal for a Council Decision on guidelines for the employment policies of the Member States, COM(2017) 677 final of 22.11.2017.

[5] COM(2021)102 final, 4.3.2021.

[6] Ibid, para 2.1.

[7] This chapter therefore is complementary to the companion Chapter 21 by Mélanie Schmitt and Marco Rocca in this volume. Whereas that chapter relates the EPSR to the legislative *acquis* of the EU, assessing the overlaps and potential competition between the two, I focus here on the EPSR as a tool to stimulate further legislative action, and on its role in strengthening the position of social rights in the socioeconomic governance of the EU.

by domestic constitutional courts that the supremacy of European law might otherwise undermine the protection of fundamental rights under national constitutions.[8] That case law was later endorsed by the other institutions, and it was gradually incorporated in the European treaties. This process culminated in the proclamation of the Charter of Fundamental Rights (CFREU) at the Nice Summit of December 2000,[9] and in the inclusion of the Charter as part of the constitutional *acquis* of the European Union in the Treaty of Lisbon.[10] In the area of social rights, however, a number of deficits remain. Three are well known and can be recalled briefly. The fourth deficit is most relevant to the adoption of the European Pillar of Social Rights, and deserves more emphasis.

2.1. Gaps in the Protection of Social Rights in the EU Constitutional Order

First, the CFREU has provided the main reference point for the protection of fundamental rights in the EU's legal order since it was proclaimed in 2000. While certainly a major improvement in comparison to the earlier situation, the Charter however essentially presents the *acquis* of fundamental rights in the European Union. As such, it is selective and remains provisional. In particular, a number of social rights (guaranteed either by the European Social Charter (ESC)[11] or by UN human rights treaties[12]) have been omitted from the Charter of Fundamental Rights, despite the references to the ESC in other parts of EU constitutional law.[13] The drafters of the Charter were instructed not to include social rights that were considered to be merely 'programmatic', that is, setting political objectives rather

[8] Case 4/73 J Nold, Kohlen- und Baustoffgroßhandlung v Commission of the European Communities, para 13 (emphasis added).

[9] [2000] OJ C 364/1.

[10] Art 6(1) of the Treaty on the European Union provides that: 'The Union recognises the rights, freedoms and principles set out in the Charter of Fundamental Rights of the European Union of 7 December 2000, as adapted at Strasbourg, on 12 December 2007, which shall have the same legal value as the Treaties.' For an extensive assessment of the contribution of the CFREU to the employment relationship, see F Dorssemont, K Lörcher, S Clauwaert and M Schmitt (eds), *The Charter of Fundamental Rights of the European Union and the Employment Relation* (Oxford, Hart, 2019).

[11] The original instrument was signed by 13 Member States of the Council of Europe in Turin on 18 October 1961 and entered into force on 26 February 1965 (CETS No 35; 529 UNTS 89). The Revised European Social Charter (CETS No 163) was opened for signature in Strasbourg on 3 May 1996, and entered into force on 1 July 1999. The Revised Charter does not bring changes to the control mechanism of the original Charter but enriches the list of the rights protected. In this chapter, the expression 'European Social Charter' refers to the 1996 version; where reference is made to the earlier instrument, the expression '1961 European Social Charter' is used.

[12] For a systematic comparison, see O De Schutter, *Future of Europe: International Human Rights in European Integration* (UN Office of the High Commissioner for Human Rights, 2020).

[13] For a more detailed examination, see O De Schutter, 'The European Social Charter as the Social Constitution of Europe' in N Bruun, K Lörcher, I Schömann and S Clauwaert (eds), *The European Social Charter and the Employment Relation* (Oxford, Hart, 2017) 11–51.

than guaranteeing claimable entitlements.[14] The result was, however, that some major gaps remain in the catalogue of rights they adopted.

The most notorious example is the right to work. The EU Treaty lists full employment as part of the objectives of the Union (Article 3(3)), and Article 9 TFEU provides that 'the Union shall take into account requirements linked to the promotion of a high level of employment' in defining and implementing its policies and activities. Nevertheless, whereas Article 1(1) ESC commits States Parties to achieve and maintain 'as high and stable a level of employment as possible, with a view to the attainment of full employment', the equivalent provision in the CFREU refers only to the freedom of all to engage in work (replicating Article 1(2) ESC), without implying a duty of the state to aim to provide employment to all. Although other provisions of the EU Charter refer to the right of access to placement services free of charge (Article 29) or to the right to protection against unjustified dismissal (Article 31), these are only specific dimensions of the broader set of duties that correspond to the fulfilment of the right to work as a human right.[15]

Secondly, the status of certain social provisions in the Charter of Fundamental Rights remains debated. In part because certain employers' organisations opposed the incorporation of social rights in the Charter, arguing that social rights required positive action from governments,[16] and in part because of the scepticism towards such rights expressed by some members of the Convention in charge of drafting the Charter. The members of the Convention who were in favour of an ambitious approach to social rights sought to convince the other members that social rights could be more than purely 'programmatic' provisions, even where the objectives they were setting were too vague to be expressed as self-standing 'rights' that courts could guarantee in the absence of any implementation measure. The idea of 'normative justiciability' emerged from this debate. According to this doctrine, although a right such as the right to housing or the right to a healthy environment could require implementation measures to be given concrete meaning, such rights are not purely programmatic. Instead, they can be invoked in judicial contexts because they can 'be opposed to an action that would directly run counter [to such a right]'; they can be relied on by a court 'when it must combine different fundamental rights between them'. Finally, 'when concrete implementation measures have been adopted, the right can be opposed to acts that would challenge the core content of such measures'.[17]

[14] Conclusions of the Cologne European Council, 3–4 June 1999, Annex IV.

[15] The right of access to placement services free of charge reflects Art 1(3) ESC, which commits States Parties to 'establish or maintain free employment services for all workers'. Art 24 of the European Social Charter recognises the right of workers to protection in cases of termination of employment; and protection against unjustified dismissal is considered by the UN Committee on Economic, Social and Cultural Rights as part of the right to work mentioned in Art 6 of the International Covenant on Economic, Social and Cultural Rights (see General Comment No 18: The right to work (Art 6 of the Covenant), UN doc E/C.12/GC/18 (6 February 2006), paras 34–35).

[16] CBI submission to the Convention on the Charter (12 April 2000), CHARTE 4226/00 CONTRIB 101.

[17] See the contributions of Guy Braibant, the representative of the French executive to the Convention, presented in May 2000 (CHARTE 4280/00, CONTRIB 153 (2 May 2000), CHARTE 4322/00, CONTRIB 188 (19 May 2000)).

This later led to the drawing of a distinction between social guarantees that constitute 'rights', when others are considered to be mere 'principles'. This distinction was reinforced when, in 2007, the horizontal provisions of the Charter were revised in order to allow for the integration of the Charter in the European treaties.[18] The distinction between 'rights' and 'principles' may explain some of the hesitations in the case-law of the CJEU.[19] It sometimes may have discouraged the Court from imposing on the EU institutions positive duties to promote the guarantees listed in the Charter, or may have provided the Court with a justification for refusing to assess the validity of EU secondary legislation against the requirements of the Charter.[20] This is of course regrettable, because it deprives the Charter of its full enforceability through courts.[21]

Thirdly, the EU has been highly selective in defining its relationship to international human rights instruments ratified by the EU Member States, and this selectivity has particularly problematic consequences for the status of fundamental social rights. The EU recognises a 'special significance' to the European Convention on Human Rights (ECHR). The CJEU has also sought inspiration, in developing the general principles of Union law which it ensures respect for, from the International Covenant on Civil and Political Rights[22] and from the Convention on the Rights of the Child.[23] In contrast, the provisions of the ESC that do not correspond to guarantees listed in the CFREU are not considered to constitute an authoritative reference point:[24] the use of expressions such as 'particularly important principle of European Union social law' to designate social rights listed in the ESC betrays the hesitation of the Court in this regard.[25] Moreover, in contrast to the status of the jurisprudence of the European Court of Human Rights (which the Court of Justice of the European Union in general treats as authoritative), the interpretation by the European Committee of Social Rights (ECSR) of the ESC is not considered binding or even persuasive. This unbalanced approach persists despite the fact that a number of provisions of the Charter of Fundamental Rights have been inspired by (and replicate some of the wording of) provisions of the ESC.

[18] Art 52(3) of the Charter of Fundamental Rights.

[19] For an illustration, see Case C-176/12 *Association de mediation sociale*, judgment of 15 January 2014 (EU:C:2014:2), paras 45 and 47.

[20] See, for instance, Case C-356/12 *Wolfgang Glatzel v Freistaat Bayern*, judgment of 22 May 2014 (EU:C:2014:350), para 74.

[21] This infirmity may be compensated in part, however, by reference to the right to an effective judicial remedy, as stipulated in Art 47 CFREU: see eg, Case C-414/16 *Egenberger*, judgment of 17 April 2018 (EU:C:2018:257).

[22] See, eg, Case 374/87 Orkem v Commission [1989] ECR 3283, para 31, and Joined Cases C-297/88 and C-197/89 Dzodzi v Belgian State [1990] ECR I-3763, para 68.

[23] Case C-540/03 *European Parliament v Council of the European Union*, judgment of 27 June 2006, para 37.

[24] Case C-116/06 *Sari Kiiski*, judgment of 20 September 2007; Case C-268/06 *Impact*, judgment of 15 April 2008.

[25] See, eg, Case C-579/12 RX-II *European Commission v Strack*, judgment of 19 September 2013, para 26. For a more systematic review, see S Robin-Olivier, 'The contribution of the Charter of Fundamental Rights to the protection of social rights in the European Union: a first assessment after Lisbon' (2013) 1 *European Journal of Human Rights* 109–34 (in French).

2.2. Social Rights in the Socioeconomic Governance of the EU

The limitations listed above are too well known to bear repeating here. The more significant limitation, however, and the most relevant to understanding the intentions underlying the adoption of the EPSR, results from the failure to take into account social rights in the new architecture of the Economic and Monetary Union (EMU). This new architecture was established following the financial and economic crisis of 2009–10, which was followed by the public debt crisis of 2010–13. These episodes brought to light the many structural deficiencies of economic governance in the EU, and they led to the introduction of fundamental reforms. Social rights, however, were for the most part ignored in that reform process.

The general diagnosis following the critical months of 2010–11, during which the single currency was put to the test, was that in the eurozone, fiscal discipline was too weak, and tools to ensure macroeconomic convergence too few, leading to an imbalance between monetary and economic integration. What was called for therefore was a profound revision of the Stability and Growth Pact (SGP) and of the mechanism of fiscal and socioeconomic surveillance and coordination. This is now ensured mainly by the so-called 'Two-Pack' and the establishment of the European Semester. In parallel, the Member States' internalisation of the Union's new budgetary discipline was achieved by the Treaty on Stability, Coordination and Governance in the Economic and Monetary Union (TSCG), known colloquially as the 'Fiscal Compact'. On top of the European Semester, a special, 'enhanced surveillance' procedure was also established for states facing, or threatened by, serious economic and budgetary difficulties. Finally, the lack of a permanent firewall for the eurozone, which would be able to provide swift financial assistance to Member States in need, was made up for through the setting up of the European Stability Mechanism. The following paragraphs describe the main components of the new architecture of socioeconomic and fiscal governance of the European Union, systematically examining the extent to which fundamental social rights play a role in their design or implementation.[26]

[26] For extensive analyses of the new governance framework of the EMU, see, among others, F Allemand and F Martucci, 'La nouvelle gouvernance économique européenne' (2012) 48(1) *CDE* 17–99; F Fabbrini, E Hirsch Ballin and H Somsen (eds), *What Form of Government for the European Union and the Eurozone?* (Oxford, Hart, 2015); A Hinarejos, *The Euro Area Crisis in Constitutional Perspective* (Oxford, OUP, 2015) 15–50; P De Grauwe, *Economics of Monetary Union* (Oxford, OUP, 2012) 105–18; see also, for a critical description of the basic assumptions of the Maastricht macroeconomic constitution, K Tuori and K Tuori, *The Eurozone Crisis – A Constitutional Analysis* (Cambridge, CUP, 2014) 105–16.

2.2.1. European Semester

At the core of the new socioeconomic governance of the EU now lies the European Semester,[27] designed to enhance macroeconomic and systemic convergence across the eurozone and the Union.[28] The European Semester is intended to strengthen the ability of European institutions to 'monitor, coordinate and sanction the economic and budgetary policies of Member States',[29] thus fixing the structural deficiencies of the initial European system of economic and monetary governance. It brings under one regulatory and institutional umbrella various policy coordination mechanisms: the Europe 2020 Strategy,[30] the Stability and Growth Pact,[31] the EuroPlus Pact,[32] the Macroeconomic Imbalance Procedure[33] and the requirement (introduced in May 2013) imposed on the Member States of the eurozone to submit draft budgetary plans for review by the Commission.[34]

The Semester is in essence a timeline, which provides for both ex ante orientation and ex post correction and assessment. While there is no space here to describe its stages in any detail, it is fair to summarise the process as one that strengthens the policy-steering capacity of the European institutions (and mainly that of the European Commission[35]), enabling them to supervise and monitor, with various levels of constraint, a very wide set of national policies – from social security to health care and from taxation to education, to name but the most significant – all in the name of macroeconomic and budgetary convergence.

[27] The European Semester is established under Art 2a(2) of Council Regulation (EC) No 1466/97 on the strengthening of the surveillance of budgetary positions and the surveillance and coordination of economic policies, as amended by Regulation (EU) 1175/2011 of the European Parliament and of the Council of 16 November 2011 ([2011] OJ L 306/12).

[28] For an extended overview of the working of the European Semester, see K Armstrong, 'The New Governance of EU Fiscal Discipline' (2013) 38 *European Law Review* 601ff.

[29] B Van Hercke and J Zeitlin, 'Socializing the European Semester ? Economic Governance and Social Policy Coordination in Europe 2020', *SIEPS*, Report No 2014:7, 23.

[30] A soft law coordination cycle, centred on growth and competitiveness.

[31] Both in its preventive (soft law reporting through Stability or Convergence programmes) and corrective (the Excessive Deficit Procedure) arms, as amended and strengthened by the 'Six-Pack' (in this regard, see K Tuori and K Tuori, n 26 above at 105–11).

[32] A new coordination mechanism launched in 2011 as an international agreement among Member States, mainly focusing on competitiveness, financial stability and fiscal strength. See Conclusions of the European Council of 24–25 March 2011, EUCO 10/1/11, 20 April 2011.

[33] A coordination cycle initiated by the Six-Pack in 2011 designed to prevent and correct dangerous macroeconomic developments: see Regulation (EU) No 1176/2011 of the European Parliament and of the Council of 16 November 2011 on the prevention and correction of macroeconomic imbalances ([2011] OJ L 306/25).

[34] This is one of the elements of the 'Two-Pack': Regulation (EU) No 473/2013 of the European Parliament and of the Council on common provisions for monitoring and assessing draft budgetary plans and ensuring the correction of excessive deficit of the Member States in the euro area ([2013] OJ L 140/11).

[35] In this regard, see M Bauer and S Becker, 'The unexpected winner of the crisis: the European Commission's strengthened role in economic governance' (2014) 36(3) *Journal of European Integration* 213–229.

Neither EU primary law (Articles 121, 126 and 148 TFEU, Protocol No 12 on the Excessive Deficit Procedure), however, nor secondary legislation (Regulation No 1466/97, Regulation No 1173/2011, Regulation No 1176/2011, Regulation No 1174/2011 and Regulation No 473/2013) organising the European Semester refer explicitly to a duty to take into account fundamental rights. This is not to say that fundamental rights (and social rights in particular) are irrelevant to the European Semester's workings. Regulation (EU) No 1176/2011 and Regulation (EU) No 473/2013, parts respectively of the 'Six-Pack' and of the 'Two-Pack' packages, adopted under Article 126 TFEU in order to monitor macroeconomic imbalances or to strengthen the surveillance of budgetary and economic policies in euro area Member States – with closer monitoring of Member States that are subject to an excessive deficit procedures – provide that '[i]n accordance with Article 28 of the Charter of Fundamental Rights of the European Union, [they] shall not affect the right to negotiate, conclude or enforce collective agreements or to take collective action in accordance with national law and practice'.[36] Many instruments also encourage a strong involvement of all relevant stakeholders, with a specific emphasis on the social partners, and civil society organisations.[37] Some instruments also explicitly refer to Article 152 TFEU (which recognises and promotes the role of social partners at EU level) or emphasise the need for the European Semester to respect national practice and institutions for wage formation.[38] Regulation No 473/2011 specifies, in its Recital 8 and Article 2(3), that the budgetary monitoring mechanisms it sets up should be applied without prejudice to Article 9 TFEU, the so-called 'horizontal social clause', which provides that 'in defining and implementing its policies and activities, the Union shall take into account requirements linked to the promotion of a high level of employment, the guarantee of adequate social protection, the fight against social exclusion, and a high level of education, training and protection of human health'. Moreover, when acting in the framework of the European Semester, EU institutions remain bound not only by the horizontal social clause of Article 9 TFEU,[39] but also by the CFREU.

If, however, there indeed exists such a duty to comply with fundamental rights in the new socioeconomic governance architecture, and in the framework of the European Semester, on the part of the EU institutions, it appears to be 'more

[36] Preamble, Recital No 7, and Art 1(2) of Regulation No 473/2013; Preamble, Recital No 20, and Art 1(3) and 6(3) of Regulation No 1176/2011.

[37] Art 2a Regulation No 1466/97.

[38] See, for example, Art 1(2) of Regulation No 473/2013.

[39] From a constitutional perspective, this clause has a crucial function: it seeks to rebalance the relationship between the 'social' and the 'economic' in the European Union. It has been described as 'a potentially strong anchor that can induce and support all EU institutions … in the task of finding an adequate (and more stable) balance between economic and social objectives' (M Ferrera, 'Modest Beginnings, Timid Progresses: What's Next for Social Europe?' in B Cantillon, H Verschueren and P Ploscar (eds), *Social Inclusion and Social Protection in the EU: Interactions between Law and Policy* (Cambridge, Intersentia, 2012) 29).

honoured in the breach than in the observance' (to borrow from Shakespeare's phrase).[40] First, despite increased attention being paid in recent years to employment, social fairness and inclusion issues,[41] the European Semester remains focused primarily on fiscal consolidation and budgetary discipline. Insofar as social considerations enter into the picture, they appear as side constraints, rather than as ends that macroeconomic governance should pursue for their own sake. Second, the involvement of the European Parliament and its national counterparts, the social partners and civil society is still kept to a strict minimum. Rather, what emerged is what observers labelled a 'new intergovernmentalism'.[42] The only serious 'external' partner the EU institutions rely on when acting within the framework of the Semester seems so far to be the national executives, with which they regularly engage in bilateral dialogues. The European Parliament[43] and the European Trade Union Confederation (ETUC) have voiced concerns in that regard.[44] Thirdly, at the supranational level, the Commission mainly has the upper hand: in practice, the Council of the EU generally defers to the assessments of the Commission, particularly as regards the country-specific recommendations.[45]

[40] See for detailed examinations of this point, B Van Hercke and J Zeitlin, 'Socializing the European Semester? Economic Governance and Social Policy Coordination in Europe 2020', n 29 above; F Costamagna, 'The European Semester in Action: Strengthening Economic Policy Coordination while Weakening the Social Dimension?', Centro Einaudi Working Papers, 2013/5; S Bekker, 'The EU's stricter economic governance: a step towards more binding coordination of social policies?', WZB Discussion Papers, No 2013-501, January 2013; R Coman and F Ponjaert, 'From One Semester to the Next: Towards the Hybridization of New Modes of Governance in EU Policy', CEVIPOL Brussels Working Papers, 5/2016, 32–57; S Bekker and I Palinkas, 'The Impact of the Financial Crisis on EU Economic Governance: A Struggle between Hard and Soft Law and Expansion of the EU Competences?' (2012) 17(2) *Tilburg Law Review* 360–66; D Chalmers, 'The European Redistributive State and a European Law of Struggle' (2012) 18(5) *European Law Journal* 667–93; M Dawson, 'The Legal and Political Accountability Structure of Post-Crisis EU Economic Governance' (2015) 53(5) *Journal of Common Market Studies* 976–93.

[41] In that regard, see B Van Hercke and J Zeitlin, 'Socializing the European Semester? Economic Governance and Social Policy Coordination in Europe 2020', n 29 above. More generally, on the political will of the EU institutions to strengthen the social dimension of the EMU, see Conclusions of the European Council from 13–14 December 2012, EUCO 205:12; Conclusions of the European Council from 27–28 June 2013, EUCO 104/2/13; European Parliament Report with recommendations to the Commission on the report of the Presidents of the European Council, the European Commission, the ECB and the Eurogroup, 'Towards a genuine Economic and Monetary Union', 24 October 2012 (2012/2151 INI); Communication from the Commission to the European Parliament and the Council, 'Strengthening the Social Dimension of the EMU', COM(2013)690.

[42] See, among others, U Puetter, 'Europe's Deliberative Intergovernmentalism – The Role of the Council and European Council in EU Economic Governance' (2012) 2(19) *Journal of European Public Policy* 161–78; U Puetter, 'New Intergovernmentalism: The European Council and its President' in E Ballin, F Fabbrini and H Somsen (eds), *What Form of Government for the European Union and the Eurozone?* (Oxford, Hart Publishing, 2015) 253ff; C Bickerton, D Hodson and U Puetter, *The New Intergovernmentalism* (Oxford, OUP, 2015); S Fabbrini, 'From Consensus to Domination: The Intergovernmental Union in a Crisis Situation' (2016) 38(5) *Journal of European Integration* 587–99.

[43] European Parliament, 'Country-Specific Recommendations need national owners and social partners', Press Release, 23.06.2015.

[44] See, for example, ETUC Statement on the 2014 CSR's concerning wages and collective bargaining systems, 4 June 2014.

[45] This is because of the combined effect of the reverse qualified majority voting procedure (which has become common for the Council in the field of economic governance) and the 'comply or explain' rule. As a result, the ability of the Council to exercise its discretion is very much reduced.

Because of the lack of transparency of the Commission's methodology in the framework of the European Semester, particularly in the preparation of the AGS or the CSRs, it is difficult to assess the extent to which such assessments take into account fundamental rights. Until the adoption of the EPSR, however, nowhere did the methodology used by the Commission to produce the key instruments of the Semester – such as the Annual Growth Surveys or the CSRs – refer to fundamental rights concerns. And the procedural guarantees included in the instruments organising the European Semester (such as the duty to involve the social partners or civil society representatives in the process, or the promotion of an active role of the European Parliament and of national parliaments) could not be seen as a substitute for ensuring that fundamental rights be taken into account in the design of national reform programmes or of convergence/stability programmes, in part because of their poor implementation, which is highly uneven across EU Member States.

2.2.2. *Fiscal Compact*

Although the initial reaction to the public debt crisis of 2009–10 led to the revision of the Stability and Growth Pact, as well as to the adoption of a set of regulations and Directives (the 'Six-Pack') that significantly strengthened the coordination of national budgetary and macroeconomic policies within the EMU, it was considered desirable to enshrine the new budgetary discipline within the European Treaties themselves. Because this proposal faced the opposition of the British government, soon joined by the Czech government, an intergovernmental agreement was concluded formally outside the Treaties.[46] On 2 March 2012, the Treaty on Stability, Coordination and Governance within the Economic and Monetary Union (TSCG) was thus signed by the representatives of 25 EU Member States (all Member States with the exceptions of the United Kingdom and the Czech Republic[47]) in the margins of the European Council convened in Brussels. The TSCG entered into force on 1 January 2013.

The general purpose of the TSCG is to

> strengthen the economic pillar of the economic and monetary union by adopting a set of rules intended to foster budgetary discipline through a fiscal compact, to strengthen the coordination of [the] economic policies [of the EU Member States] and to improve the governance of the euro area, thereby supporting the achievement of the European Union's objectives for sustainable growth, employment, competitiveness and social cohesion (Article 1).

The TSCG has a number of provisions on the coordination and convergence of economic policies in its Title IV, and on the governance of the euro area in its

[46] However, consistency and connection with EU law are guaranteed in the Treaty (Art 2).

[47] In the meantime, the Czech Republic decided to join the Treaty in March 2014. Since its accession to the EU on 1 July 2013, Croatia has been eligible to become part to the Treaty but has so far failed to do so.

Title V. But its most crucial provisions are certainly to be found in its Title III, entitled 'Fiscal Compact'.[48] The 22 states bound by this part of the TSCG (the 19 euro area states plus Bulgaria, Denmark and Romania) commit to seek to maintain 'balanced budgets', or even to strive for a 'surplus' (Article 3(1) a)). To this end, they must ensure swift convergence towards their country-specific medium-term objective (Article 3(1), b) and c)), from which they may deviate only if faced with exceptional circumstances. Finally, in case of significant deviations from the medium-term objective or the adjustment path towards it, a correction mechanism, managed by a national independent authority, will be triggered automatically (Article 3(1), e)). The main innovation of the TSCG certainly lies in the requirement Article 3(2) imposes on the States Parties to internalise the rules of the Fiscal Compact (including the balanced-budget rule and the automatic correction mechanism) in rules of constitutional rank in the domestic legal order.[49] Such internalisation was considered by the Treaty makers as locking-in budgetary discipline.

The TSCG pays little heed to fundamental rights and their preservation within the framework of applying the rules set out in the Fiscal Compact, although here again the social partners' role is acknowledged in its Preamble. In particular, although Article 3(3)(b) of the TSCG allows for certain deviations from budgetary commitments in the presence of 'exceptional circumstances … provided that the temporary deviation of the Contracting Party concerned does not endanger fiscal sustainability in the medium-term', an 'exceptional circumstance' is defined as 'an unusual event outside the control of the Contracting Party concerned which has a major impact on the financial position of the general government or to periods of severe economic downturn as set out in the revised Stability and Growth Pact'. The notion of 'exceptional circumstance' thus does not encompass a situation in which the requirement to balance public budgets might be incompatible with the fulfilment of economic and social rights.

2.2.3. Enhanced Budgetary and Economic Surveillance Framework

Formally located outside the European Semester, the second branch of the Two-Pack, Regulation No 472/2013,[50] sets up an 'enhanced surveillance' mechanism for countries of the eurozone facing, or threatened by, serious financial

[48] For more comprehensive analyses of the TSCG, see, among others, P Craig, 'The Stability, Coordination and Governance Treaty: Principles, Politics and Pragmatism' (2012) 37 *European Law Review* 3, 231–48; F Martucci, 'Traité sur la stabilité, la coordination et la Gouvernance, Traité instituant le mécanisme européen de stabilité. Le droit international au secours de l'UEM' (2012) 4 *Revue d'Affaires Européennes* 716–31.

[49] Such internalisation is to be carried out, following Art 3(2), 'through provisions of binding force and permanent character, preferably constitutional, or otherwise guaranteed to be fully respected and adhered to throughout the national budgetary processes'.

[50] Regulation (EU) No 472/2013 of the European Parliament and of the Council on the strengthening of economic and budgetary surveillance of Member States in the euro area experiencing or threatened with serious difficulties with respect to their financial stability ([2013] OJ L 140/1).

and budgetary difficulties. The mechanism applies automatically to those that requested or received financial assistance.[51] Regulation No 472/2013 places such countries under closer macroeconomic and budgetary scrutiny than that normally applied to Member States within the framework of the European Semester,[52] in order to ensure that the macroeconomic structural adjustment programmes, imposed as a condition for the provision of financial assistance, are implemented effectively.[53] The objective, as stated in the Regulation, is to allow for the 'swift return to a normal situation' and to '[protect] the other euro area Member States against potential adverse spill-over effects' (Recital 5).

The decision to subject a Member State to enhanced surveillance falls to the Commission, which is supposed to reassess its decision every six months (Article 2). The country under scrutiny is subject to a general duty to adopt structural measures 'aimed at addressing the sources or potential sources of difficulties' its economy and public finances may encounter (Article 3(1)). The procedure includes, inter alia, intensive information exchanges with, and review missions by, the Commission. The Council (acting with a qualified majority) may also recommend to the Member State concerned the adoption of precautionary corrective measures or the preparation of a draft macroeconomic adjustment programme,[54] if no such programme has yet been adopted (Article 3(7)). Article 18 also specifies that the European Parliament may seek to trigger an informative dialogue with the Council and the Commission on the application of enhanced surveillance.[55]

As in many of the other instruments organising the European Semester, Regulation No 472/2013 requires that any measure adopted as part of economic

[51] For an extensive analysis of Regulation No 472/2013, see M Ioannidis, 'EU Financial Assistance Conditionality after the Two Pack' (2014) 74 *ZaöRV* 61–104.

[52] For countries falling within the scope of application of Regulation No 472/2013, the application of the European Semester is as such suspended (Arts 10, 11, 12, 13), mainly in order to avoid duplication of efforts.

[53] In that regard, Regulation No 472/2013 helps to clarify the relationship between EU law and ESM/EFSF/EFSM assistance following the adoption of Memoranda of Understanding with the borrowing state (A Hinarejos, n 26 above, at 32, 135 and 162). Indeed, by requiring of the state requesting financial assistance that it prepare a macroeconomic adjustment programme, to be later approved through a Council implementing decision (Art 7), Regulation No 472/2103 brings the conditionalities linked to such assistance back within the EU legal order, thus lifting the ambiguity that used to exist around the status of such agreements and the attached conditionalities under EU law. It remains to be seen, however, whether this will make a difference in terms of judicial review. We return to this point below.

[54] The macroeconomic adjustment programme 'shall address the specific risks emanating from that Member State for the financial stability in the euro area and shall aim at rapidly re-establishing a sound and sustainable economic and financial situation and restoring the Member State's capacity to finance itself fully on the financial markets' (Art 7(1)). The programme is prepared by the relevant Member State, proposed by the Commission and approved by the Council (Art 7(2)). Its implementation is monitored by the Commission, acting in liaison with the ECB and, where appropriate, with the IMF (Art 7(4)). Significant deviations from the programme may lead to more thorough monitoring and supervision (Art 7(7)). A system of post-programme surveillance is also provided for (Art 14).

[55] According to Art 18 (Informing the European Parliament), 'the European Parliament may invite representatives of the Council and of the Commission to enter into a dialogue on the application of this Regulation'. See also Art 7(10); and for national parliaments, see Art 7(11).

adjustment programmes comply with the right of collective bargaining and action recognised in Article 28 of the EU Charter of Fundamental Rights (CFREU) (Article 1(4), Article 7(1)). Likewise, the Regulation recalls the duty to observe Article 152 TFEU and to involve social partners and civil society (Recital 11 of the Preamble, Article 1(4), Article 7(1), Article 8). The Preamble (Recital 2) also mentions the Horizontal Social Clause of Article 9 TFEU. Article 7(7) moreover specifies that the budgetary consolidation efforts required following the macroeconomic adjustment programme must 'take into account the need to ensure sufficient means for fundamental policies, such as education and health care'. As in the case of the European Semester, however, nowhere is it explicitly confirmed that fundamental social rights will be duly taken into account in the preparation, and implementation, of such programmes.

An examination of the macroeconomic adjustment programmes adopted under Regulation No 472/2013 confirms that fundamental social rights are barely considered in the design and implementation of such programmes. This is illustrated for instance by the third Greek Rescue Package[56] adopted in the summer of 2015, and the 2013 Cyprus bail-out programme.[57] Some reference is made, of course, to the need to minimise harmful social impacts of adjustment programmes (Article 1(3) of Decision 2013/463, Article 1(3) of Decision 2015/1411), especially as regards impacts on disadvantaged people and vulnerable groups (Article 2(2) of Decision 2013/463, Article 2(2) of Decision 2015/1411). The third rescue package for Greece also emphasises its ambition to promote growth, employment and social fairness (Recital 7 of Decision 2015/1411), as well as to involve social partners and civil society in all the phases of the adoption and implementation of the adjustment programme (Recital 16 of Decision 2015/1411). Analysis of the political background against which these programmes were adopted, however, especially the resistance they encountered from workers' unions and from public opinion in both Cyprus and Greece, brings to light the limited 'inclusiveness' of the processes by means of which such programmes were designed. More fundamentally, the policy reforms required under those programmes in the sectors of health care, education, social security, pensions or public administration, have barely taken into account fundamental social rights; on the contrary, measures adopted within the framework of Regulation No 472/2013 seem to have been driven mainly by financial consolidation and competitiveness concerns. Fundamental social rights have not been relied on as a tool to guide budgetary choices. Instead, on issues such as the reform of public administrations, health care or the energy sector, policy choices reflected through the conditionalities rest almost exclusively on considerations of cost-effectiveness and long-term financial sustainability, at the

[56] See Council Implementing Decision (EU) No 2015/1411 of 19 August 2015 approving the macroeconomic adjustment programme of Greece ([2015] OJ L 219/12).

[57] See Council Implementing Decision (EU) No 2013/463 of 13 September 2013 on approving the macroeconomic adjustment programme for Cyprus and repealing Decision 2013/236/EU ([2013] OJ L 250/40).

expense of other 'non-efficiency' factors, such as the guarantee of a certain level of quality, accessibility and equity in the provision of public services. Moreover, whether on the expenditure or the revenue side, most of the burden falls on the middle class (which are the main beneficiaries of the social programmes affected), an unfair allocation that is particularly blatant in the case of Cyprus.[58]

2.2.4. *European Stability Mechanism*

As the sovereign debt crisis initially unfolded, threatening the stability of the eurozone, two emergency mechanisms were set up to provide financial assistance to Member States facing serious difficulties financing themselves on the capital markets: the European Financial Stability Facility (EFSF) and the European Financial Stabilisation Mechanism (EFSM). They were conceived as temporary tools, and their lending capacities remained limited. They were later replaced by the more ambitious European Stability Mechanism (ESM), a permanent financial assistance mechanism, tasked with preserving financial stability within the EU, and endowed with a maximum lending capacity of 500 billion euros. The ESM is sometimes described as the 'IMF of the EU'. Its design relies extensively on IMF practice, and it is intended to cooperate closely with the IMF.[59] The ESM was not established as an EU institution, but as a distinct international organisation, with its own legal personality, headquartered in Luxemburg. As a consequence, its founding act was not adopted within the framework of the EU Treaties, but has the status of an international treaty.[60] As the creation of this more stable and effective arrangement raised doubts concerning its compatibility with the Treaties, and more specifically with the so-called 'no bail-out' clause (Article 125 TFEU) which prohibits the debts of the EU Member States from being assumed either by the Union itself or by any other Member State,[61] it was deemed wise and necessary to explicitly affirm in the EU Treaties the Member States' power to establish a permanent crisis management mechanism that would safeguard the euro area's stability. The European Council thus revised Article 136 TFEU, adding a new paragraph 3 that created such an explicit basis,[62] following the simplified amendment

[58] See Decision No 2013/463, Art 2(8) to (14).

[59] See Recitals 8, 12, 13 of the ESM Treaty, Arts 13 and 38.

[60] The ESM Treaty was signed on 2 March 2012, and entered into force on 1 May 2013.

[61] Art 125(1) TFEU reads: 'The Union shall not be liable for or assume the commitments of central governments, regional, local or other public authorities, other bodies governed by public law, or public undertakings of any Member State, without prejudice to mutual financial guarantees for the joint execution of a specific project. A Member State shall not be liable for or assume the commitments of central governments, regional, local or other public authorities, other bodies governed by public law, or public undertakings of another Member State, without prejudice to mutual financial guarantees for the joint execution of a specific project.' For commentary, see J-V Louis, 'The No-Bailout Clause and Rescue Packages' (2010) 47(4) *Common Market Law Review* 971–86.

[62] Art 136(3) is worded as follows: 'The Member States whose currency is the euro may establish a stability mechanism to be activated if indispensable to safeguard the stability of the euro area as a whole. The granting of any required financial assistance under the mechanism will be made subject to strict conditionality.'

procedure provided for in Article 48(6) TEU.[63] The validity of this much contested amendment was later confirmed by the Court of Justice in the *Pringle* case.[64]

The general purpose of the ESM is 'to mobilise funding and provide stability support under strict conditionality, appropriate to the financial assistance instrument chosen, to the benefit of ESM Members which are experiencing, or are threatened by, severe financing problems, if indispensable to safeguard the financial stability of the euro area as a whole and of its Member States'.[65] The granting of stability support follows a four-step procedure (Article 13): (i) a request from the ESM Member; (ii) a principled decision of the ESM on the granting of stability support; (iii) the negotiation and signature by the European Commission, on behalf of the ESM, of a Memorandum of Understanding detailing the conditionalities attached to the financial assistance facility; and (iv) compliance monitoring by the Commission.[66] ESM financial assistance can be granted through various stability support instruments: loans (Article 16), purchase of bonds on the primary market (Article 17), interventions on the secondary market (Article 18), precautionary financial assistance (Article 14) or bank recapitalisation programmes (Article 15). Like any other financial institution, the ESM has its own pricing policy, which includes achieving an appropriate profit margin (Article 20). For the performance of its purpose, it borrows on capital markets (Article 21), and in order to guarantee its creditworthiness, it designs its own investment policy (Article 22). When the capital stock exceeds its maximum lending capacity, the ESM distributes dividends to its members (Article 23).

Central to the ESM's financial assistance policy is the principle of conditionality. Conditionality is negotiated by the European Commission (in liaison with the ECB and the IMF), and detailed in the MoUs signed with the ESM member requesting assistance. It ranges from compliance with the pre-established eligibility conditions to the adoption of a macroeconomic adjustment programme. Although this conditionality is defined as strict (Recital 6, Article 3, Article 12(1)), there is room for flexibility, as conditionality should remain appropriate to the financial assistance instrument chosen (Article 12(1)).

[63] European Council Decision 2011/199/EU of 25 March 2011 amending Art 136 of the TFEU with regard to a stability mechanism for Member States whose currency is the euro ([2011] OJ L 91/1).

[64] Judgment of 27 November 2012, C-370/12 *Thomas Pringle v Government of Ireland*, EU:C:2012:756. On this decision, see, among others, P Craig, 'Pringle: Legal Reasoning, Text, Purpose and Teleology' (2013) 20(1) *Maastricht Journal of European and Comparative Law* 3–11.

[65] Art 3 of the ESM Treaty.

[66] The ESM being an international organisation as such, the MoUs negotiated and concluded by the European Commission on behalf of the ESM lie outside the scope of EU law. A clear connection is established with the existing EU law framework, however, and more specifically with Regulation No 472/2013, in Art 13(3): the Commission must guarantee the consistency of the MoU's it negotiates and concludes within the framework of the ESM Treaty, with the macroeconomic adjustment programme adopted under Regulation No 472/2013. While not an act of EU law, the MoU's content is to be reflected in the macroeconomic adjustment programme adopted under Regulation No 472/2013, and subsequently endorsed in a decision of the Council (see above).

The ESM Treaty does not make any reference to fundamental social rights. However, although the Court of Justice of the European Union took the view in its *Pringle* ruling of 27 November 2012 that EU Member States, when they established the ESM as a separate international organisation,[67] were not implementing EU law, within the meaning of Article 51(1) CFREU, the Court later confirmed that the institutions of the EU acting within the framework of the ESM remained bound to comply with EU law, including with the CFREU. In a judgment of 20 September 2016 delivered in Joined Cases C-8/15 P to C-10/15 P – which concerned the impacts of measures adopted following the conclusion of the Memorandum of Understanding between Cyprus and the ESM and the possibility for the persons affected to file claims for compensation of alleged violations of the right to property – the Court considered that 'the tasks allocated to the Commission by the ESM Treaty oblige it, as provided in Article 13(3) and (4) thereof, to ensure that the memoranda of understanding concluded by the ESM are consistent with EU law',[68] and that the Commission 'retains, within the framework of the ESM Treaty, its role of guardian of the Treaties as resulting from Article 17(1) TEU, so that it should refrain from signing a memorandum of understanding whose consistency with EU law it doubts'.[69] The EU institutions, the Court noted, remain at all times under a duty to comply with the Charter of Fundamental Rights. The Charter, the Court noted,

> is addressed to the EU institutions, including … when they act outside the EU legal framework. Moreover, in the context of the adoption of a memorandum of understanding such as that of 26 April 2013 [signed by the Minister for Finance of the Republic of Cyprus, the Governor of the Central Bank of Cyprus and the Commission, before being approved on 8 May 2013 by the ESM Board of Directors], the Commission is bound, under both Article 17(1) TEU, which confers upon it the general task of overseeing the application of EU law, and Article 13(3) and (4) of the ESM Treaty, which requires it to ensure that the memoranda of understanding concluded by the ESM are consistent with EU law (see, to that effect, judgment of 27 November 2012, *Pringle*, C-370/12, EU:C:2012:756, paragraphs 163 and 164), to ensure that such a memorandum of understanding is consistent with the fundamental rights guaranteed by the Charter.[70]

Thus, if a Memorandum deprives a state of its ability to uphold the right to education (Article 14 of the Charter) or the right to social security (Article 34), or to

[67] *Thomas Pringle v Government of Ireland*, cited in n 64 above, para 180. The Court, answering the argument that the establishment of the ESM is not accompanied by effective judicial protection, and thus potentially in violation of Art 47 of the Charter, states that: 'the Member States are not implementing Union law, within the meaning of Art 51(1) of the Charter, when they establish a stability mechanism such as the ESM where … the EU and FEU Treaties do not confer any specific competence on the Union to establish such a mechanism'.

[68] Joined Cases C-8/15 P to C-10/15 P *Ledra Advertising Ltd et al*, EU:C:2016:701, para 58. On this decision, see P Dermine, 'ESM and Protection of Fundamental Rights: Towards the End of Impunity?', *Verfassungsblog*, 21 September 2016; A Hinarejos, 'Bail-outs, Borrowed Institutions and Judicial Review: Ledra Advertising', *EU Law Analysis*, 25 September 2016.

[69] Ibid, para 59.

[70] Ibid, para 67.

maintain high levels of health care provision (Article 35) or access to services of general interest (Article 36), the non-contractual liability of the Commission could in principle be engaged.[71] The CJEU moreover takes into account, when assessing measures adopted to remove excessive budget deficits, whether the sacrifices imposed on the population are shared equally.[72] It is therefore disappointing that, although the ESM Treaty was recently revised, neither the ESM, nor the Commission itself, have adopted the tools that would allow them to effectively discharge the duties to ensure that reforms will further not undermine social rights and contribute to the reduction of inequalities.

2.2.5. Conclusion

These various components of the new economic and social governance of the EU are entirely blind to the requirements of fundamental social rights in general and of the ESC in particular. This explains why, in the case of Greece, the first wave of fiscal consolidation measures, adopted following the conclusion of the 2010 Memorandum of Understanding between Greece and its creditors,[73] led to a number of ECSR decisions identifying various instances of non-conformity with the ESC.[74] These decisions illustrate the problems associated with the failure to take into account the ESC's requirements in the design and implementation of adjustment programmes adopted within the framework of the 'enhanced surveillance' mechanism provided for under Regulation No 472/2013, which places countries receiving financial support under closer macroeconomic and budgetary scrutiny. A preventive approach, in which any impacts on social rights are assessed before the adoption of fiscal consolidation measures, would be the only effective means of avoiding potential conflicts between the disciplines imposed on the eurozone Member States and the requirements of the ESC. The Political Guidelines for the next European Commission presented in July 2014 by President Juncker included a commitment to ensure that future support and reform programmes would be

[71] Actions for annulment of the actions taken by the Commission within the framework of the ESM, however, remain excluded, because these actions fall outside the EU legal order: see *Ledra Advertising*, judgment of 20 September 2016, para 54.

[72] Case C-49/18 *Escribano Vindel v Ministerio de Justicia*, judgment of 7 February 2019, para 67.

[73] For an excellent summary of the background, see L Papadopoulou, 'Can Constitutional Rules, even if "Golden", Tame Greek Public Debt?' in M Adams, F Fabbrini and P Larouche (eds), *The Constitutionalization of European Budget Constraints* (Oxford, Hart Publishing, 2014) 223–47.

[74] *European Committee of Social Rights, General Federation of employees of the national electric power corporation (GENOP-DEI) and Confederation of Greek Civil Servants' Trade Unions (ADEDY) v Greece*, Complaint No 65/2011, decision on the merits of 23 May 2012; and four decisions adopted on 7 December 2012 concerning pensioners' rights: *European Committee of Social Rights, Federation of employed pensioners of Greece (IKA-ETAM) v Greece*, Complaint No 76/2012; *Panhellenic Federation of Public Service Pensioners v Greece*, Complaint No 77/2012; *Pensioners' Union of the Athen-Piraeus Electric Railways (ISAP) v Greece*, Complaint No 78/2012; *Panhellenic Federation of Pensioners of the Public Electricity Corporation (PAS-DEI) v Greece*, Complaint No 79/2012; *Pensioners' Union of the Agricultural Bank of Greece (ATE) v Greece*, Complaint No 80/2012.

subjected to social impact assessments to feed into the public discussion.[75] As a follow-up to this commitment, in October 2015 the European Commission announced its intention to pay greater attention to 'the social fairness of new macroeconomic adjustment programmes to ensure that the adjustment is spread equitably and to protect the most vulnerable in society'.[76] But 'social fairness' is not quite as powerful as a reference to binding fundamental social rights, and the promise to bring about further improvements has not been kept.

3. The European Pillar of Social Rights

3.1. Contribution of the European Pillar of Social Rights

The EPSR is ostensibly based on the need to ensure that, in addition to being monitored for budgetary discipline, the performances of the euro area Member States in the employment and social domains are assessed, with a view to ensuring a greater degree of convergence within the EMU. Indeed, as explained by the International Labour Office in an early contribution on the future EPSR, the EU27 (then EU28) have been either diverging, or converging towards lower standards of protection in a number of areas (or sliding towards higher poverty levels) since the economic and financial crisis of 2009–10. The implication is that unless affirmative action is taken to improve convergence towards improved standards, the macroeconomic disciplines imposed on the EU Member States may threatened part of the social *acquis* within the EU.[77] Referring to the 'soft' mechanisms put in place in the EU since the European Employment Strategy was launched in 1997 to favour convergence in social policies (now streamlined under the Europe 2020 strategy), the ILO noted that the 'disappointing results (at least in terms of convergence in social and employment outcomes) seem to indicate that divergence cannot be addressed by assuming individual policies will converge towards common goals. Soft convergence might not be effective unless it is built upon a social floor applicable in all Member States.'[78]

[75] 'A New Start for Europe: My Agenda for Jobs, Growth, Fairness and Democratic Change, Political Guidelines for the next European Commission', 15 July 2014.

[76] European Commission, Communication from the Commission to the European Parliament, the Council and the European Central Bank: On Steps Towards Completing Economic and Monetary Union, COM(2015) 600 final of 21.10.2015, 5.

[77] See ILO, *Building a Social Pillar for European Convergence* (Geneva, 2016) 23 (noting that 'an examination of the trends over time indicates that there has been either considerable divergence between countries (eg unemployment) or, worse, convergence towards undesirable outcomes (eg higher income inequality) … [While] these developments are very much a function of national policies and country-specific circumstances … the distributional consequences of policy inaction at national and EU-wide levels could be large').

[78] ILO, Building a Social Pillar for European Convergence, n 77, at 31. On this issue, see already O De Schutter and S Deakin (eds), *Social Rights and Market Forces. Is the open method of coordination of social and employment policies the future of social Europe?* (Brussels, Bruylant, 2005).

The Pillar, the Commission explained early on, should provide a safeguard against these risks of divergence in social standards or of a race to the bottom across the EU. The Pillar thus 'should become a reference framework to screen the employment and social performance of participating Member States, to drive reforms at national level and, more specifically, to serve as a compass for renewed convergence within the euro area'.[79] It therefore could contribute to a rebalancing between the economic and the social in the constitution of the European Union. In particular, in the European Semester of policy coordination, described above, the EPSR should lead the Commission to put greater focus on social priorities and put them on a par with economic objectives at the core of the annual cycle of economic governance.[80] Thus, in its March 2018 Communication assessing progress on structural reforms, prevention and correction of macroeconomic imbalances, and results of in-depth reviews,[81] the Commission notes, referring to the adoption of the EPSR, that:

> A key message of the 2018 Annual Growth Survey is the need to implement the Pillar for a renewed convergence towards better working and living conditions across the EU. This requires fair and well-functioning labour markets, as well as modern education and training systems that equip people with skills that match labour market needs. This should be supported by sustainable and adequate social protection systems. The country reports published [in March 2018] look at how Member States deliver on the three dimensions of the Pillar: equal opportunities and access to the labour market, fair working conditions, and social protection and inclusion. The provision of adequate skills and persistent gender employment gap, high labour market segmentation and the risk of in-work poverty, the low impact of social transfers on poverty reduction, sluggish wage growth, and ineffective social dialogue are areas of particular concern in some Member States. In order to analyse Member States' performances in a comparative perspective, the country reports also build on the benchmarking exercises conducted on unemployment benefits and active labour market policies and on minimum income.[82]

An examination of both the 2018 AGS and the assessment provided by the Commission of the country reports demonstrates the strong influence of the EPSR on the analysis proposed. The Commission thus seeks to ensure that 'convergence towards better socioeconomic outcomes, social resilience and fairness, as promoted by the European Pillar of Social Rights, [shall become] an essential part of the efforts to strengthen and complete the Economic and Monetary Union'.[83] If

[79] First preliminary outline for a European Pillar of Social Rights, Annex to the Communication from the Commission, *Launching a consultation on a European Pillar of Social Rights*, cited above.

[80] Communication from the Commission to the European Parliament, the Council, the European Economic and Social Committee and the Committee of the Regions, Monitoring the implementation of the European Pillar of Social Rights, COM(2018) 130 final of 13.3.2018, 3.

[81] Communication on the assessment of progress on structural reforms, prevention and correction of macroeconomic imbalances, and results of in-depth reviews (COM(2018) 120 of 7.3.2018).

[82] Ibid, 3.

[83] Communication from the Commission to the European Parliament, the Council, the European Economic and Social Committee and the Committee of the Regions, Monitoring the implementation of the European Pillar of Social Rights, COM(2018) 130 final of 13.3.2018, 5.

this effort is pursued further, the Pillar could gradually lead the EU to set binding targets for the reduction of poverty and inequality, to be enforced through mechanisms similar to those already agreed to enforce macroeconomic prescriptions concerning annual deficits and the size of the public debt.

In addition, the EPSR could result in the identification of necessary new legislative initiatives for the European Union. Indeed, this was one of the professed intentions of the Action Plan adopted at the Porto Social Summit. The EPSR is limited in what it can achieve in this regard within the EU's current constitutional framework, however. The debate on minimum income schemes in the EU is typical in this regard. Minimum income schemes across the Union are woefully inadequate, almost all of them proving to be ineffective in lifting people out of poverty. They also vary wildly among the Member States. The Council of the EU itself deplored their stark discrepancies in terms of adequacy and coverage, as well as beneficiaries' access to enabling services, and requested that the Commission make proposals to 'effectively support and complement the policies of Member States on national minimum income protection'.[84] Providing support to families is also consistent with the pledge made in Principle 14 of the Pillar, on minimum income. Regrettably, the Action Plan relegates action on minimum income to a Council recommendation, instead of the framework Directive advocated by the European Parliament, national governments including Germany and Portugal, and numerous civil society organisations. Such a framework Directive on minimum income schemes in the EU[85] could establish a set of common human rights principles referring to the adequacy, universal unlimited access and coverage, and enabling character of minimum income schemes.[86] Relying on a human rights framework could help, because the criteria following from the International Covenant on Economic, Social and Cultural Rights,[87] the ILO Social Security (Minimum Standards) Convention, 1952 (No 102), and ILO Recommendation (No 202) on Social Protection Floors, could be taken as minimum requirements. The choice for a recommendation rather than a new legislative instrument is based on institutional and legal considerations. These are perhaps understandable, but they do show clearly that, without a reassessment of the background constitutional structure of the EU, which still condones social competition between the

[84] Council Conclusions on Strengthening Minimum Income Protection to Combat Poverty and Social Exclusion in the COVID-19 Pandemic and Beyond, 9 October 2020, para 22.

[85] Based on a combination of Arts 153(1)(c) (social security and social protection for workers), 153(1)(h) (integration of people excluded from the labour market) and 175 (strengthening of economic, social and territorial cohesion) TFEU.

[86] The ILO noted that, while an adequate level of minimum income guarantee should at least protect beneficiaries from being at risk of poverty, in some Member States – such as Bulgaria, Latvia, Poland and Romania – 'the minimum income guarantee for a single person amounts to less than 30 per cent of the national median income, far below the at-risk-of-poverty threshold [defined in the EU as 60 per cent of the national median income]' (ILO, *Building a Social Pillar for European Convergence*, see n 77 above, at 41).

[87] Committee on Economic, Social and Cultural Rights, *General Comment No 19 (2008): The right to social security (Art 9)* (E/C.12/GC/19).

EU Member States, the impacts of proclaiming social rights at EU level will remain limited.

This is not to say that the EPSR is purely cosmetic. In some cases, the consensus it has led to on the need to strengthen the social dimension of the EU's socio-economic governance has encouraged the Commission to take bold action to encourage reform. The definition of the conditions under which the level of the statutory minimum wage should be set provides an example: implicitly acknowledging that the failure of certain Member States (particularly Germany) to raise wages in line with productivity increases has been a major cause of macroeconomic imbalances within the EU – and the risks implicit in divergences between the EU Member States[88] – the Commission proposed that one of the principles of the Pillar should be that:

> All employment shall be fairly remunerated, enabling a decent standard of living. Minimum wages shall be set through a transparent and predictable mechanism in a way that safeguards access to employment and the motivation to seek work. Wages shall evolve in line with productivity developments, in consultation with the social partners and in accordance with national practices.[89]

In the EPSR, Principle 6 (Wages) reflects this concern:

> Adequate minimum wages shall be ensured, in a way that provides for the satisfaction of the needs of the worker and his/her family in the light of national economic and social conditions, whilst safeguarding access to employment and incentives to seek work. In-work poverty shall be prevented.

In order to implement this Principle, the Commission proposed in October 2020 a new Directive on adequate minimum wages in the EU, requiring that Member States set minimum wages 'guided by criteria set to promote adequacy with the aim of achieving decent working and living conditions, social cohesion and upward convergence'.[90]

These are important benefits associated with the adoption of the European Pillar of Social Rights. However, further progress could be made in three areas. First, the EPSR could be incorporated in a revised version of the impact assessments that are currently being prepared by the European Commission, while ensuring that such strengthened impact assessments are also prepared to assess the impacts of structural reform measures prescribed to EU Member States receiving financial support. Secondly, the implementation of the EPSR could be more explicitly rights-based, and take into account the ESC. Thirdly, to further affirm the need to promote upward social convergence, social imbalances in the internal

[88] ILO, *Building a Social Pillar for European Convergence*, see n 77 above at 35–39.

[89] Communication from the Commission to the European Parliament, the Council, the European Economic and Social Committee and the Committee of the Regions, *Launching a consultation on a European Pillar of Social Rights*, COM(2016) 127final, 8 March 2016.

[90] COM(2020)682 final, 28.10.2020 (Art 5(1)).

market and in the EMU should be scrutinised with the same care as are macroeconomic imbalances. These three areas are explored in turn.

3.2. Moving Forward

3.2.1. The Role of Fundamental Social Rights in Impact Assessments

In 2011–15, there was no systematic assessment of the impacts on social rights of the various measures adopted in response to the so-called 'sovereign debt crisis'. In fact, the guidance published by the European Commission concerning Impact Assessments (IAs) still suggests that in the field of economic governance, including 'recommendations, opinions and adjustment programmes', impact assessments are not a priori necessary, because (it is said) such 'specific processes are supported by country specific analyses'.[91] This is a mistake. In the future, the EPSR should provide a framework to assess the impacts of Stability or Convergence Programmes presented by the EU Member States and of the country-specific recommendations addressed to states (both adopted under the European Semester framework), as well as the impacts of adjustment programmes negotiated with countries that have been provided with financial support. The political consensus on a set of objectives identified as desirable in the EPSR could allow such impact assessments to be prepared, in order to ensure that these measures support the attainment of such objectives. While impact assessments are not an end in themselves, they can favour accountability and ensure that greater attention will be paid to social rights in the adoption of such measures.

The role of impact assessments in the EU law- and policy-making process has regularly been strengthened since they became systematic in 2002 for legislative measures,[92] and they were generalised for other initiatives within the 'Better Regulation' agenda. Since 2015, the quality of impact assessments has been examined by an independent body, the Regulatory Scrutiny Board, which includes members external to the EU institutions, and whose role it is to 'check major evaluations and "fitness checks" of existing legislation' by delivering an 'impartial opinion on the basis of comprehensive know-how of the relevant analytical methods'.[93]

Fundamental rights have gradually played a greater role in such impact assessments. The guidelines for the preparation of impact assessments presented in 2005 already referred to the potential effects of different policy options on the guarantees

[91] See the Better Regulation Toolbox, Tool #5: When is an IA necessary?; http://ec.europa.eu/smart-regulation/guidelines/tool_5_en.htm.

[92] European Commission, Communication on Impact Assessment, 5 June 2002, COM(2002)276 final.

[93] Replies of the European Union to the list of issues raised in regard to the initial report submitted in accordance with Art 35 of the Convention on the Rights of Persons with Disabilities (CRPD/C/EU/Q/1/Add 1, 8 July 2015), para 26.

listed in the Charter.[94] In 2009 and 2011, successive Staff Working Papers of the Commission made the role of fundamental rights in impact assessments increasingly more explicit.[95] The guidance these documents provided to Commission Services applies only to legislative proposals submitted by the Commission. In contrast, the tools developed as part of the 'Better Regulation' agenda apply to all initiatives, whether legislative or regulatory or whether they consist of the introduction of new policies or amendments to existing policies. Fundamental rights and (for the external dimension of EU action) human rights are now better integrated in these tools.

Despite this significant progress, a number of deficiencies remain, as well as a gap between the shift towards the inclusion of 'social fairness' considerations in reform programmes, and a social rights-based assessment of their impact. First, the inclusion of fundamental rights in impact assessments has not led to modification of the basic structure of such assessments, which still rely on a division between economic, social and environmental impacts. Despite requests from the Parliament,[96] the Commission has repeatedly stated that it was unwilling to perform *separate* human rights impact assessments, distinct from the assessment of economic, social and environmental impacts. This so-called 'integrated' approach allows fundamental rights impacts to be factored into a broader set of considerations. This makes it possible to compensate certain negative impacts (such as a curtailing of civil liberties or of the provision of certain public services) by means of positive impacts at other levels (including on economic growth and social cohesion), in the overall assessment presented to decision-makers.[97]

Secondly, impact assessments as they are currently performed still insufficiently provide that the fundamental rights concerned are mainstreamed in the EU's decision-making process. An empirical study assessing how impact assessments serve the various horizontal 'mainstreaming agendas' concluded that they were not giving

[94] See SEC(2005)791, 15.6.2005.

[95] See, respectively, SEC(2009) 92 of 15.1.2009 and SEC(2011) 567 final of 6.5.2011.

[96] European Parliament resolution of 15 March 2007 on compliance with the Charter of Fundamental Rights in the Commission's legislative proposals: methodology for systematic and rigorous monitoring (2005/2169(INI)), OP 11 (where the Parliament 'Calls on the Commission to think over its decision to divide its considerations on fundamental rights into the current three categories in its impact assessment – economic, social and environmental effects – and to create a specific category entitled "Effects on fundamental rights", to ensure that all aspects of fundamental rights are considered').

[97] This is a defensible position, but also represents a strong argument for not allowing impact assessments, thus understood, to become a substitute for rigorous compatibility checks based on legal analysis. The Commission notes in this regard – correctly, in the view of this author – that an 'Impact Assessment does not, and cannot, operate as the fundamental rights check. It cannot be a substitute for legal control. In the end result, fundamental rights proofing can only be performed via a legal assessment based on a crystallised draft legislative text. However, while not being, in itself, the legal control for fundamental rights compliance, the Commission recognises that the Impact Assessment can do some of the groundwork to prepare for the fundamental rights proofing of legislative proposals' (Communication from the Commission, *Report on the practical operation of the methodology for a systematic and rigorous monitoring of compliance with the Charter of Fundamental Rights*, cited above, 6).

equal attention to the six mainstreaming objectives referred to by the TFEU.[98] 'While social and environmental concerns are primary objectives of assessment of the IIA system', this study notes, 'fundamental rights constitute a more ad hoc horizontal category'.[99] Of the 35 impact assessments examined (covering the period 2011–14), fundamental rights were taken into account in 19 cases. In the cases in which they were ignored, no justification was provided. The relatively marginal role of fundamental rights in impact assessments (certainly compared with economic considerations about regulatory burdens on businesses, but also compared with the other 'mainstreaming objectives' listed in the TFEU, with the exception of gender and non-discrimination) is further illustrated by the findings of the Impact Assessment Board (IAB), which since 2007 has been tracking which issues are addressed in impact assessments and adopts recommendations to improve the process. It would appear that, whereas 80 per cent of IAB reports included comments on the consideration of economic impacts in an average year, recommendations related to fundamental rights were found in only 10 per cent.[100]

Thirdly, the Guidance provided to Commission Services concerning the preparation of the fundamental rights component of impact assessments[101] refers almost exclusively to the CFREU, as if the rights, freedoms and principles codified in the Charter were the only fundamental rights recognised in the EU legal order. In the future, impact assessments should move beyond references to the CFREU alone, to integrate the full range of social rights guaranteed in international human rights law, including in particular the ESC.[102] The preparation of such social rights

[98] In addition to fundamental rights, these objectives are: gender equality (Art 8 TFEU); the promotion of a high level of employment, adequate social protection, the fight against social exclusion, and a high level of education, training, and protection of human health (as stipulated in the so-called 'horizontal social clause' of Art 9 TFEU); non-discrimination on the basis of gender, racial or ethnic origin, religion or belief, disability, age or sexual orientation (Art 10 TFEU); environmental policy integration for sustainable development (Art 11 TFEU); and consumer protection (Art 12 TFEU).

[99] S Smismans and R Minto, 'Are integrated impact assessments the way forward for mainstreaming in the European Union?' (2017) 11(3) *Regulation & Governance* 2. The study also notes that 'while the six mainstreaming objectives receive attention in the IIA [integrated impact assessments] institutional set-up, other objectives receive at least as much attention. Indeed, both the assessment of economic impacts and of regulatory burdens are predominant in the set-up of the IIA system, although neither of these are set out in the treaties as constitutional horizontal objectives' (ibid).

[100] Ibid, 15. The authors of this study attribute this state of affairs to the fact that 'the EU's fundamental rights regime is mainly conceived as a negative guarantee, intended to ensure that the EU should not negatively impact on fundamental rights, rather than as a positive regime promoting these values in a proactive way at policy level. The operational guidelines on fundamental rights in the IA are, thus, steered to set off a warning light whenever policy intervention would negatively impact on fundamental rights, while failing to use IAs actively to define the objectives of new policy initiatives that positively promote fundamental rights': ibid, 13 (citing O De Schutter, 'Mainstreaming Human Rights in the European Union", in P Alston and O De Schutter (eds), *Monitoring Fundamental Rights in the EU. The Contribution of the Fundamental Rights Agency* (Oxford, Hart, 2005) 37–72).

[101] Operational Guidance on taking account of Fundamental Rights in Commission Impact Assessments, SEC(2011) 567 final of 6.5.2011.

[102] See, for a detailed analysis, O De Schutter, *The European Social Charter in the context of the implementation of the Charter of Fundamental Rights of the EU*. Study prepared at the request of the European Parliament's Committee on Constitutional Affairs (AFCO) (PE 536.488, 2016).

impact assessments taking into account the ESC would also appear to be in line with the position of the European Commission, according to which (as stated by Commissioner M Thijssen on its behalf in response to a parliamentary question) it is 'important that Member States comply with the European Social Charter also when implementing reform measures'.[103]

Fourthly, no procedures have been established to ensure meaningful participation of trade unions and other components of civil society in the design and implementation of such programmes, and for a re-examination of the draft programmes if negative impacts on social rights are found to occur. Regulation (EU) No 472/2013 already establishes certain procedural requirements linked to the assessment of the impacts of the measures to be adopted: Article 6 provides that the European Commission must evaluate the sustainability of sovereign debt, and Article 8 imposes on the country placed under enhanced surveillance that it 'seek the views of social partners as well as relevant civil society organisations when preparing its draft macroeconomic adjustment programmes, with a view to contributing to building consensus over its content'. To date, these requirements have generally been ignored.

The Action Plan for the implementation of the EPSR endorsed in May 2021 at the Porto Social Summit provides that '[in] planning the allocation of financial resources, Member States should make greater use of distributional impact assessments in order to better take account of the impact of reforms and investments on the income of different groups and to increase transparency on the social impact of budgets and policies'. The European Commission pledges to '[p]resent in 2022 guidance to enhance Member States' use of ex-ante distributional impact assessments in budgeting and planning of reforms'.[104] This would be an important step forward. It would only partly fill the gap, however, because even if the EPSR were taken as a departure point to provide the analytical grid for the preparation of social impact assessments, this still would not lead to a genuinely rights-based approach in the area of impact assessments.

3.2.2. The European Pillar of Social Rights and Social 'Rights'

For the most part, the EPSR develops existing rights, that are already part of the EU *acquis*, in order to further clarify their implications (and thus increase their relevance) in the current economic context, or in order to define as a 'principle' a guarantee already stipulated in secondary EU legislation. The updating of existing rights, or the attempt to define new principles for a changing economy, are

[103] Statement made by Commissioner M Thijssen on behalf of the European Commission on 30 April 2015, in response to a parliamentary question on the social rights impacts of reform programmes (more specifically, on wage decline in Spain) (question from P Iglesias (GUE/NGL) of 6 March 2015, P-003762-15).

[104] Action Plan, 35.

generally progressive. For some of the principles of the EPSR, moreover, Member State ratification of relevant international instruments features among the tools that the Commission considers for the implementation of the principles of the European Pillar of Social Rights.[105]

It is important, however, that the proclamation of the European Pillar of Social Rights be seen as a means of supporting, and not as a substitute for, the recognition of social rights. The March 2016 communication formally announcing the initiative referred to 'common values and principles' that 'feature prominently in reference documents', such as the CFREU or international instruments such as the ESC adopted within the Council of Europe and recommendations from the ILO.[106] The Pillar, the communication suggested, should support the further implementation of social rights that are part of the *acquis* of the European Union: the principles that shall be attached to the 20 policy domains concerned by the initiative, it is said, 'take as a starting point a number of rights already inscribed in EU and other relevant sources of law, and set out in greater detail possible ways to operationalise them'.[107]

The EPSR should therefore not be confused with a new catalogue of rights, complementing the rights of the CFREU in the areas insufficiently covered by this instrument. As stated again in March 2018 in the Commission Staff Working Document accompanying the Communication 'Monitoring the Implementation of the European Pillar of Social Rights', '[g]iven the legal nature of the Pillar, for these principles and rights [listed in the EPSR] to be legally enforceable, they first require dedicated measures or legislation to be adopted at the appropriate level.'[108]

It is therefore incorrect to state, as the Commission does in its presentation of the Principles included in the EPSR, that the added value of the Pillar is to define as a right what was merely an advantage granted, in the absence of any legal obligation, to the individual.[109] The Pillar remains for now a policy instrument: it

[105] As regards Principle 6 for instance, it refers to ILO Convention No 131 on minimum-wage fixing and to ILO Convention No 154 on the promotion of collective bargaining (SWD(2018) 67 final of 13.3.2018, 33). Similarly, while Principle 7 refers to the protection of workers in case of dismissal (including the right to be informed of the reasons and be granted a reasonable period of notice), reference is made to the fact that EU Member States are encouraged to ratify relevant ILO conventions, such as Convention No 122 on Employment Policy, Convention No 144 on Tripartite Consultations, Convention No 135 on Workers' Representatives, or Convention No 154 on Promotion of Collective Bargaining. While most references in this regard are to ILO conventions, the commentary of Principle 12 of the EPSR (Social Protection) includes a reference to the contribution to EPSR implementation that could result from the ratification of the European Social Charter and from the extension of the list of accepted provisions by Member States (SWD(2018) 67 final of 13.3.2018, 60).

[106] Communication from the Commission, *Launching a consultation on a European Pillar of Social Rights*, see n 2 above, para 2.4.

[107] Ibid, para 3.1.

[108] SWD(2018) 67 final of 13.3.2018, 4.

[109] For instance, the Commission notes, concerning Principle 11, that 'the Pillar establishes that *all* children *have the right to* good quality early childhood education and care (ECEC)' (SWD(2018) 67 final of 13.3.2018, 55). As regards Principle 12 (Social Protection), the Commission states: 'The Pillar transforms the call for a replacement income which will maintain the workers' standard of living

provides useful guidance, but does not create legal guarantees enforceable before courts of other independent bodies. Efforts developed within the EU legal order to strengthen the protection of social rights as enforceable entitlements should therefore be pursued, and this concerns in particular the strengthening of the relationship with the ESC.[110]

3.2.3. *The 'Social Imbalances' Procedure*

In advance of the Porto Social Summit, the Belgian and Spanish governments submitted a proposal (in the form of a 'non-paper') to establish, alongside the Macroeconomic Imbalances Procedure (MIP) set up in 2011, a 'Social Imbalances Procedure (SIP)' 'to identify, prevent and address the emergence of potentially harmful social imbalances that could adversely affect the employment situation and living conditions in a particular EU Member State, the euro area, or the EU as a whole'.[111] This would enhance the role of the EPSCO Council position in the European Semester process. It would also clarify the role of the indicators in the Social Scoreboard, as revised following the adoption of the EPSR: rather than these social indicators being included in the MIP, as what appears to be a rather artificial 'add-on', the social indicators would feed into a specific and parallel procedure, making visible the need for a balanced approach across both macroeconomic and social convergence processes.

An additional benefit is that, when implementing the country-specific recommendations addressed to them, which focus on fiscal sustainability (and avoiding the increase of public deficits), the Member States would be made fully aware that they cannot do so at the expense of social rights. This is key, considering the role that CSRs have played in the past. A study commissioned in 2019 by a Member of the European Parliament calculated that between 2011 and 2018 there were 63 CSRs recommending cuts in or privatisation of health care, 50 recommending suppression of wage growth, 38 reducing job security, and 45 reducing support for unemployed, vulnerable or people with disabilities.[112] Trade unions have

in [Council Recommendation 92/442/EEC of 27 July 1992 on the convergence of social protection objectives and policies, [1992] OJ L 245/49] *into a right*.' But such statements are incorrect, or purely rhetorical, as long as the guarantees listed in the Pillar are enforceable in the absence of further legislative action, at EU or Member State level. It would be more accurate to state that the reference to such 'rights' in the Pillar expresses an intention to transform such objectives into claimable entitlements.

[110] A number of proposals have been made elsewhere concerning how to strengthen such synergies with the European Social Charter. There is therefore no need to repeat this exercise here: see O De Schutter, *The European Pillar of Social Rights and the Role of the European Social Charter in the EU Legal Order* (Council of Europe, November 2018), https://rm.coe.int/study-on-the-european-pillar-of-social-rights-and-the-role-of-the-esc-/1680903132.

[111] Introducing a 'Social Imbalances Alert Mechanism' in the European Semester, Non-paper presented by the Belgian and Spanish governments in advance of the Porto Social Summit, May 2021.

[112] E Clancy, 'Discipline and Punish' (February 2020) 28; https://emmaclancy.files.wordpress.com/2020/02/discipline-and-punish-eu-stability-and-growth-pact.pdf.

also found many instances of CSRs recommending reforms of health systems to increase fiscal sustainability and cost-efficiency, with no references to allocating further investments in this sector.[113] Academics have made similar findings.[114] The introduction of the SIP would be a powerful antidote to this.

The 'non-paper' does not take a position on the precise criteria or indicators that should feed into the 'alert mechanism' to be put in place. It suggests, however, that such a mechanism should present two characteristics. First, rather than addressing failures to fully uphold social rights as such (which could lead the least wealthy Member States to be targeted disproportionately), the mechanism should focus on trends, taking into account Member States' different starting positions. What the mechanism should alert us to is a lack of progress, or regression, rather than simply a failure to conform to certain floors. The consequences of this approach are rather ambiguous. On one hand, it encourages further progress in the implementation of social rights, to the maximum available resources of each state, in line with the status of economic and social rights in international human rights law. This implies that even the wealthiest countries, boasting the most advanced systems of social protection, should pursue their efforts, in particular by adopting fiscal policies and public budgets in line with the objective of the progressive realisation of rights.[115] On the other hand, it may perpetuate the idea that social rights are not 'real rights' after all, but rather policy objectives that each state should be allowed to pursue at its own pace. This may underestimate the importance of 'treating economic and social rights as human rights, rather than as desirable goals, development challenges, social justice concerns or any of the other formulations that are invariably preferred', as expressed in a report of the former UN Special Rapporteur on extreme poverty and human rights, which provides a strong plea for taking social rights more seriously. This implies legal recognition, institutionalisation and accountability.[116]

Secondly, beyond the focus on specific states, the 'non-paper' from the Belgian and Spanish governments suggests that the mechanism should make it possible to identify diverging trends across states, which could tilt the economic and monetary union off balance, or lead to unfair competition within the internal market. As such, the alert mechanism could provide an impetus to the further deepening of European integration in the area of social rights by identifying the need for new legislative initiatives.

[113] ETUC, 'COVID19: the impact of health care cuts' (May 2020); www.etuc.org/en/document/covid19-impact-health-care-cuts.

[114] N Azzopardi-Muscat et al, 'EU Country Specific Recommendations for health systems in the European Semester process: Trends, discourse and predictors' (2015) 119 *Health Policy* 3; www.sciencedirect.com/science/article/pii/S016885101500010X.

[115] See O De Schutter, *The rights-based welfare state: Public budgets and economic and social rights* (Geneva, Friedrich-Ebert-Stiftung, November 2018).

[116] Report of the Special Rapporteur on extreme poverty and human rights to the thirty-second session of the Human Rights Council (A/HRC/32/31 (28 April 2016)), para 8.

4. Conclusion

The European Pillar of Social Rights has created new momentum. If the opportunity is to be seized, however, it is important to move beyond the current tools that were designed to ensure its implementation. Neither the revised Social Scoreboard, nor the Action Plan implementing the EPSR, are truly transformative. This contribution has proposed three directions forward. It has suggested the need to strengthen the role of social rights in impact assessments, whether these concern EU policy or legislative initiatives, or whether they accompany the use of EU funds at domestic level. It has emphasised the need to recognise the specificity of social rights as human rights: rather than being degraded to the rank of principles guiding policy, they should be firmly linked to existing human rights standards, such as those listed in the European Social Charter. Finally, it has referred to the proposal to establish a 'Social Imbalances Procedure' alongside the 'Macroeconomic Imbalances Procedure', to ensure that social convergence makes progress as effectively as macroeconomic convergence. What is at stake, ultimately, is the EU's ability to deliver to its population, and thus to reignite enthusiasm for the European integration project.

21

Enforcing EU Labour Law in the Context of EU Economic and Monetary Policy

MÉLANIE SCHMITT AND MARCO ROCCA

1. Introduction

The European Union's (EU) 'New Economic Governance' (NEG) encompasses a series of reforms enacted during the economic crisis of the 2010s. These changes were aimed at reinforcing the power of EU institutions to coordinate economic policies across Member States, with the objective of avoiding similar crises in the future. Because of this, their approach and ideological framing were deeply influenced by the narrative of the crisis accepted by EU institutions, and in particular by the (at the time) EU Commission. Such a narrative is underpinned by the idea that the crisis was brought about by the 'fiscal profligacy' of the Member States of the EU periphery and would thus be solved through what have become known as austerity policies.[1] Interestingly, the introduction of New Economic Governance in turn marks an implicit shift from the belief that the simple unfettered action of 'the market' would bring about such coordination.[2]

Although at first sight they might appear to be 'soft' instruments, devoid of binding effect, and directed mainly at budgetary aspects, in fact they cover a broad array of areas belonging within the scope of labour law. Therefore, this chapter considers whether and to what extent the instruments of New Economic Governance can, or should, be used to improve the enforcement of EU labour law, defined as the contents of the EU legislative *acquis* in this area. To this end, the chapter is structured as follows. Section 2 presents the instruments of New

[1] See in general M Blyth, *Austerity: The History of a Dangerous Idea* (Oxford, Oxford University Press, 2013); P Krugman, *End This Depression Now!* (New York, WW Norton & Company, 2012).

[2] J Jordan, V Macarrone and R Erne, 'Towards a Socialization of the EU's New Economic Governance Regime? EU Labour Policy Interventions in Germany, Ireland, Italy and Romania (2009–2019)' (2020) 1(2) *British Journal of Industrial Relations*.

Economic Governance (2.1), as well as their relationship to labour law in general (2.2) and EU labour law in particular (2.3). Section 3 considers the potential benefits (3.1) and the risks (3.2) of using the instruments of New Economic Governance to ensure better application of EU labour law.

2. EU Economic Governance and its 'Socialisation'

2.1. New Economic Governance

New Economic Governance includes several instruments, some of which are presently being phased out. The most infamous of these instruments, falling within the aforementioned 'phasing out' category, is the Memorandum of Understanding (MoU), examples of which have been signed between the so-called Troika[3] and individual Member States requesting financial assistance during the crisis. These documents include an extensive list of conditionalities, that is, conditions to be fulfilled by the recipient to obtain or maintain access to financial assistance.[4] The last MoU expired with the end of the Greek adjustment programme.[5]

A second set of instruments, by contrast, outlived the crisis and is now deeply embedded in EU economic governance thanks to the process known as the 'European Semester', an annual cycle of surveillance and enforcement of economic policies.[6] Several instruments contribute to the cycle, namely the Country Specific Recommendations (CSRs), the Stability and Growth Pact (SGP), the Macroeconomic Imbalances Procedure (MIP),[7] and the Europe 2020 strategy.

In this chapter, we will focus mainly on Country Specific Recommendations (CSRs), which are annual recommendations drafted by the Commission (in May) and adopted by the Council (in July).[8] The term 'Recommendation' is used somewhat loosely in this context, given that failure to comply can lead to sanctions, at least in some instances. While this has not yet occurred, CSRs related to compliance with the budgetary criteria established by the Stability and Growth Pact or to the Macroeconomic Imbalances Procedure can lead to financial sanctions, which,

[3] Comprising the International Monetary Fund, the European Commission and the European Central Bank.

[4] See S Babb and B Carruthers, 'Conditionality: Forms, Function, and History' (2008) 4(13) *Annual Review of Law and Social Science*.

[5] The third (and last) economic adjustment programme for Greece ended on 20 August 2018.

[6] C Degryse, 'The new European economic governance' (2012) 14(1) ETUI Working Paper 36.

[7] Art 2 of Regulation (EU) No 1176/2011 of the European Parliament and of the Council on the prevention and correction of macroeconomic imbalances: '"excessive imbalances" mean severe imbalances, including imbalances that jeopardise or risk jeopardising the proper functioning of economic and monetary union'.

[8] See further A Verdun and J Zeitlin, 'The European Semester as a new architecture of EU socioeconomic governance in theory and practice' (2017) 1(3) *Journal of European Public Policy*.

having been proposed by the Commission, can only be rejected by a qualified majority in the Council.[9] Notably, Member States that are part of the eurozone risk fines equal to 0.2 per cent (SGP) or 0.1 per cent of GDP (MIP). Furthermore, since 2014 a Member State risks losing access to EU structural funds if they fail to comply with CSRs.[10] One can also discern an appetite to further strengthen the link between 'EU money' and compliance with CSRs, further reinforcing sanctions arsenal, in a recent report by the EU Court of Auditors.[11]

2.2. The 'Social Dimension' of New Economic Governance

2.2.1. The Socialisation of New Economic Governance?

It is worth noting that an important number of CSRs are related to labour rights, employment and social policies. This comes as no surprise if one considers that Memoranda of Understanding, too, were focused especially on labour and social security reforms.[12] In particular, research from the European Trade Union Institute (ETUI) shows how between 40 and 63 per cent of CSRs adopted over the past decade (2011–19) have focused on social aspects.[13]

Areas covered by these 'social' CSRs vary widely so that it would be impossible to provide a full account here.[14] Focusing on CSRs in the areas of labour law and employment policy, several groups of recommendations can be identified. The first deals with wages. Recommendations in this area, particularly in the first years of the European Semester (up until 2014), focused on the revision of wage indexation mechanisms, with the aim of reducing or eliminating such mechanisms.[15] The following years marked a shift, with CSRs now encouraging

[9] C De la Porte and E Heins, 'A new era of European Integration? Governance of labour market and social policy since the sovereign debt crisis' (2015) 13(8) *Comparative European Politics* 12.

[10] Jordan, Macarrone, and Erne, n 2 at 6; V Vita, 'Revisiting the Dominant Discourse on Conditionality in the EU: The Case of EU Spending Conditionality' (2017) 4(1) *Cambridge Yearbook of European Legal Studies*.

[11] European Court of Auditors, 'The European Semester – Country Specific Recommendations address important issues but need better implementation', 2020, 35: 'The Commission should strengthen the link between EU funds supporting reform processes in Member States and Country Specific Recommendations. CSRs should be taken into consideration in the different stages of budgetary processes.'

[12] A Sapir, G Wolff, C De Sousa and A Terzi, *The Troika and Financial Assistance in the Euro Area: Successes and Failures* (Brussels, Bruegel, 2014).

[13] S Clauwaert, 'The country-specific recommendations (CSRs) in the social field. An overview and comparison. Update including the CSRs 2019–2020' (2019) 3(1) *ETUI Background Analysis* 11; S Clauwaert, 'The country-specific recommendations (CSRs) in the social field. An overview and comparison. Update including the CSRs 2017–2018' (2017) 2(1) *ETUI Background Analysis* 12.

[14] See for analysis of the latest round of recommendations S Rainone, 'An overview of the 2020–2021 country-specific recommendations (CSRs) in the social field' (2020) 1(1) ETUI Background Analysis. When referring to CSRs in this chapter we will use the country code (AT for Austria) and the year to identify a specific recommendation.

[15] See for instance 2011 and 2012 (BE, CY, ES, LU, MT), 2013 (BE, LU).

Member States to 'ensure that wages can evolve in line with productivity'.[16] In this same group we also include CSRs aimed at the decentralisation of collective bargaining systems, that is, requesting a shift from sectoral to company collective bargaining,[17] which were particularly visible in the first years of the CSRs (up to 2014).[18]

A second group of CSRs revolves around employment protection legislation, focusing on rules on dismissal. The relaxation of dismissal rules for open-ended contracts is often the focus of these recommendations, justified either as a measure to combat segmentation of the labour market[19] or to encourage the hiring of workers with open-ended contracts.[20] The third group of CSRs covers areas related to employment policies, with a specific focus on improving the labour market participation of women,[21] older[22] and younger[23] workers.

This focus represents a new challenge for labour lawyers in the EU. To an extent, the challenge is similar to the one experienced during the application of MoUs. Indeed, large and important areas of labour regulations and practices, such as, to cite just the most obvious example, collective bargaining and wage policies, are directly influenced (sometimes to an important extent) by instruments whose legal nature escapes the usual classifications leading to difficulties in exerting judicial control, for instance when it comes to respecting fundamental social rights.[24] The same can be said for social actors, such as national trade unions, who can find it difficult to mobilise their power resources, often anchored in national practices and institutions, to challenge the outcomes of New Economic Governance and its impact on national labour laws.[25]

Evidently, this is not the first time labour lawyers have been confronted with 'soft law' instruments in relation to EU social policy. Indeed, the Open Method of Coordination (OMC) received significant attention in the first decade of the

[16] For instance, in the CSRs rounds between 2016 and 2018, these kinds of CSRs were addressed to 12 to 14 Member States each year.

[17] See T Schulten and T Müller, 'A new European interventionism? The impact of the new European economic governance on wages and collective bargaining' in D Natali and B Vanhercke (eds), *Social Developments in the European Union 2012* (Bruxelles, ETUI-OSE Publications) 186.

[18] See for instance BE (2011–2013), ES (2011), IT (2011).

[19] See for instance FR (2016), SI (2011), IT (2011, 2012).

[20] See for instance ES (2017), NL (2017).

[21] These cover measures concerning the expansion of childcare and long-term care, and improving employment services. See for instance HU (2011), SK (2012), IE (2015), AT (2017), IT (2019).

[22] These cover measures concerning lifelong learning, active labour market policies, and vocational education. See for instance BE (2012), LT (2014), FI (2016), DE (2018).

[23] Covering measures such as the improvement of apprenticeship and vocational education, the introduction of a youth guarantee, and the improvement of the quality of education. See for instance DK (2011), PL (2014), CY (2017).

[24] C Kilpatrick, 'Are the bailouts immune to EU social challenge because they are not EU law?' (2014) 10 *European Constitutional Law Review* 393.

[25] P Copeland and M Daly, 'The European Semester and EU Social Policy' (2018) 1 *Journal of Common Market Studies* 13.

new millennium.[26] The integration of these aspects in the much more penetrating machinery of economic governance, however, and the ever present (if so far theoretical) threat of sanctions, constitute a marked difference with existing instruments. At the same time, this also underpins the point of view from which we approach the topic in the present chapter. If indeed New Economic Governance can give soft law instruments some teeth, this might help bridge the gap between them and traditional hard law instruments. Moreover, enforcing labour standards through the NEG instruments offers also the promise of a relatively easy procedure, because, as we saw in the previous section, CSRs are drafted by the Commission and then adopted by the Council, therefore circumventing the European Parliament.

Labour lawyers, particularly those at the international level, can appreciate the importance of having enforcement tools that go beyond solving individual disputes. This kind of monitoring system based on periodic reporting immediately brings to the mind those put in place in the context of the International Labour Organisation (ILO) or the European Social Charter. Although these systems operate without the threat of sanctions, they are able to tackle violations of labour standards which are not easily addressed by individual litigation. A good example of this would be the gender pay gap arising from differences in wage levels between male- and female-dominated sectors (vertical segregation),[27] where non-discriminatory approaches would struggle to succeed in the absence of a comparator.[28]

The increased focus on social aspects has led some authors to conclude that we are witnessing a 'socialisation' of New Economic Governance, balancing social retrenchment with social investment, and rediscovering the 'flexicurity' approach.[29] In purely quantitative terms, the number and scope of socially orientated CSRs have been reinforced from 2011 to 2014, while during the period 2017–20, CSRs dedicated to, or at least linked with, social aspects represent more than the half of all CSRs addressed to Member States.[30] This was saluted by the European Trade Union Confederation (ETUC) which, in its Action Programme 2019–23, asserted that 'a process of making the European Semester more social has started', all the while lamenting the enduring primacy of 'restrictive macroeconomic policy' and the 'liberal market bias' of New Economic Governance.[31]

[26] D Ashiagbor, 'Soft Harmonisation: The Open Method of Coordination in the European Employment Strategy' (2004) 10 *European Public Law* 305.

[27] ILO, *Global Wage Report 2018/19. What lies behind gender pay gaps* (Geneva, International Labour Office, 2018) 74.

[28] Advisory Committee on Equal Opportunities for Women and Men, *Opinion on the effectiveness of the current legal framework on Equal pay for equal work or work of equal value in tackling the gender pay gap* (Brussels, 2009) 10.

[29] S Bekker, 'Flexicurity in the European Semester: still a relevant policy concept?' (2017) 25 *Journal of European Public Policy* 175; J Zeitlin and B Vanhercke, 'Socializing the European Semester: EU social and economic policy co-ordination in crisis and beyond' (2017) 25 *Journal of European Public Policy* 149.

[30] See also B Hacker, 'A European Social Semester? The European Pillar of Social Rights in practice' (2019) 5(1) ETUI Working Paper.

[31] ETUC, *ETUC Action Programme 2019–2023* (Vienna, 2019) 23.

Indeed, this re-orientation was accompanied by a reductionist vision of social objectives and rights, henceforth centred on the idea of a floor of rights for the most vulnerable categories of workers (and citizens).

These parallel trends are confirmed by studies dealing with more recent cycles of the Semester.[32] It is clear that improving the protection of all workers is not the objective guiding Economic and Monetary Policy. In this context, establishing a harmonisation of social legislation by means of EU (social) Directives has been supplanted by a search for convergence of social policies, including labour market and social security policies, as elements of economic convergence broadly understood. Other authors have criticised the 'socialisation' conclusion, reaffirming the need to go beyond the simple categorisation of CSRs as 'social' on the basis of their literal context, to read them in light of their accompanying documents, different level of (potential) sanctions, and impact on the national environment.[33] In one example, this approach made it possible to determine that a seemingly 'neutral' prescription on the need to improve 'transparency' in the setting of minimum wages was instead meant to create obstacles to the unilateral increase of the minimum wage proposed by a centre-left government.[34] Another important element to keep in mind when considering the 'socialisation' of the semester is that, even in the face of an unprecedented economic and social crisis, the 2020 CSRs maintained that Member States would still be expected to implement the recommendations adopted in 2019.[35] As such, it is difficult to shake the feeling that the markedly 'social' direction of the 2020 CSRs (which will possibly extend to 2021) is conceived, first of all by the Commission and the Council, as an exception.

Finally, the 'socialisation' of New Economic Governance also covers the increased participation of social partners in the process.[36] In 2016, a quadripartite statement on a 'New Start for Social Dialogue' was signed, with the aim of improving said participation.[37] This included a commitment of EU institutions (notably, the Council and the Commission) to enhance the involvement of Union level social partners in New Economic Governance, as well as the involvement of social partners at national level in the relevant steps of the European Semester, such as the process of drafting national reform plans and implementing CSRs. This followed a period (2011–13) in which said participation was considered to be inadequate by social partners and academic observers.[38] A more recent study by Eurofound,

[32] 'The country-specific recommendations (CSRs) in the social field. An overview and comparison. Update including the CSRs 2019–2020'.

[33] Jordan, Macarrone, and Erne, n 2 at 9.

[34] Ibid.

[35] In 2020, CSRs all featured a common recital stating that 2019 CSRS 'remain pertinent and will continue to be monitored throughout next year's European Semester annual cycle'. See Rainone, n 14 at 9.

[36] Zeitlin and Vanhercke, n 29 at 19.

[37] 'A New Start for Social Dialogue', Statement of the Presidency of Council of the European Union, the European Commission and the European Social Partners, 2016.

[38] For an overview of these criticisms see S Sabato, B Vanhercke, S Spasova, 'Listened to, but not heard? Social Partners' multilevel involvement in the European Semester' (2017) 35(1) OSE Paper Series 9.

however, focusing on participation in the 2017 round of CSRs, found that social partners in a large number of Member States still lamented insufficient involvement in the implementation of policy reforms at national level in the context of the Semester.[39] These criticisms generally point to a merely formal process of consultation, so that claims of 'socialisation' based on the mere 'involvement' of social partners at some point of the process should be considered carefully.

That being said, some measure of a more 'social' approach can be found when looking at social security and social assistance. Although these areas fall outside the scope of the present Chapter, we will touch upon them briefly to complete the picture. These CSRs often focus on the establishment/improvement of a minimum level of protection aimed at poverty alleviation.[40] Specific attention to these instruments is to be found in the 2020 round of CSRs.[41]

2.2.2. The European Pillar of Social Rights, Instrument for the Integration of Social Policy into New Economic Governance

Elaborated by the Commission during a year-long consultation phase, and officially launched on 26 April 2017 via a Recommendation,[42] the EPSR was endorsed by the Commission, the Parliament and the Council in an Institutional Proclamation on 17 November 2017. While characterised by an unclear legal nature and effects,[43] the instrument nevertheless reflects a shared view that the EU's social dimension needs to be strengthened. In that perspective, the EPSR consists of a set of 20 social rights and principles inspired by existing European and international instruments, including those emanating from the European Semester as 'initiatives to strengthen efforts on pressing priorities and to update the EU "acquis"'.[44]

The EPSR rights and principles are structured around three chapters: 'equal opportunities and access to the labour market' (chapter 1);[45] 'fair working conditions' (chapter 2);[46] 'social protection and inclusion' (chapter 3).[47] In this

[39] Eurofound, *Involvement of the national social partners in the European Semester 2017: Social dialogue practices* (Luxembourg, Eurofound, 2018).

[40] See for instance HR (2018, 2019), LT (2018–20).

[41] Rainone, n 14 at 8.

[42] Commission Recommendation to the European Parliament, the Council, the European and Social Committee and the Committee of the Regions on the European Pillar of Social Rights, Brussels, 26 April 2017.

[43] Z Rasnača, 'Bridging the gaps or falling short? The European Pillar of Social Rights and what it can bring to EU-level policymaking' (2017) 5(1) ETUI Working Paper 14.

[44] European Commission, Communication Launching a consultation on a European Pillar of Social Rights, COM (2016) 127 final, 6.

[45] Chapter 1 comprises the rights to education, gender equality, equal opportunities, and active support to employment.

[46] Covering secure and adaptable employment, wages, information about employment conditions and protection in case of dismissals, social dialogue and involvement of workers, work-life balance, health and safety and data protection.

[47] Covering childcare and child support, social protection, unemployment benefits, minimum income, pensions, health care, inclusion of people with disabilities, long-term care, housing, and access to essential services.

section, we focus on the first two chapters, combining labour law and employment policy. The rights and principles briefly set forth in this tripartite structure form a skeleton, which is complemented with staff working documents[48] giving flesh to the bones.

Primarily addressed to Member States, the aim of the Pillar is 'to serve as a guide towards efficient employment and social outcomes'.[49] The Commission puts special emphasis on the idea that 'most of the competences and tools required to deliver on the European Pillar of Social Rights are in the hands of local, regional and national authorities, social partners as well as civil society'.[50] Nonetheless, for each right or principle, the accompanying documents also put forward proposals of pre-existing and new pieces of EU legislation and soft law measures. However, the EPSR does not entail an extension of the Union's powers and tasks,[51] which is not surprising in the absence of a revision of the Treaty. The new legislative initiatives that are mentioned therefore rely on social policy legal bases, namely Article 153 TFEU, reinforced by a reference to relevant provisions of the Charter of Fundamental Rights of the EU. In that respect, the Pillar can be conceptualised as a 'Social Agenda' identifying priorities and orientations for further social policy (legislative) developments,[52] rather than a new institutional framework for social policy, which remains formally determined by the provisions of title X of the TFEU. This notwithstanding, Directives adopted in 2019[53] as direct follow-up to the EPSR showcase that the Pillar is an instrument able to boost the EU's (employment-related) social policy legislation.[54]

Soft law initiatives are also mentioned as possible implementation avenues for the EPSR, where the EU has no legislative powers. For instance, in the first preliminary outline of a European Pillar of Social Rights, Articles 165 and 166 TFEU are mentioned as bases for strengthening access to education and professional training in order to preserve their entry and participation in the labour market.[55]

[48] Commission Staff Working Document Accompanying the document Communication from the Commission to the European Parliament, the Council, the European and Social Committee and the Committee of the Regions Establishing a European Pillar of Social Rights, Brussels, 26 April 2017 SWD(2017) 201 final.

[49] EPSR, Preamble, recital 12.

[50] Communication from the Commission to the European Parliament, the Council and the European Economic and Social Committee, Monitoring the implementation of the European Pillar of Social Rights, Strasbourg, 13 March 2018, COM(2018) 130 final.

[51] EPSR, Preamble, Recital 18.

[52] S Sabato, D Ghailani, R Peña-Casas, S Spasova, F Corti, and B Vanhercke, *Implementing the European Pillar of Social Rights: what is needed to guarantee a positive social impact* (Brussels, European Economic and Social Committee, 2018).

[53] See section 2.3.2 below.

[54] S Garben, 'The European Pillar of Social Rights: Effectively Addressing Displacement?' (2018) 14(210) *European Constitutional Law Review* 221.

[55] Arts 165 and 166 TFEU set out that the Union shall implement a vocational training policy and shall contribute to the development of quality education by encouraging cooperation between the Member States, supporting and supplementing their action.

Although reinforcing the status of employment and social considerations as 'an essential feature of the process of economic policy coordination at EU level',[56] the formal preservation of social policy appears unable to safeguard its 'philosophy' and very objective, that is workers' protection. One should not underestimate the extent to which social policy has been deeply transformed by its economic objectives under the EPSR: to 'deepen the Economic and Monetary Union'[57] and contribute to 'fair and well-functioning labour markets and welfare systems in 21st century Europe'.[58] In the first preliminary outline, the Commission further developed the philosophy underlying the Pillar: 'social policy should also be conceived as a productive factor' which plays a prominent role in growth and job creation. In the same vein, social rights and principles of the Pillar are more in line with employment policy objectives, as set out in Article 145 TFEU, than with the 'social' objective of improving working conditions. In that conceptual framework, the 'social goals' (protection of workers) pursued by social policy and its instruments are now in competition with (possibly) contradictory and (more) powerful economic goals.

Moreover, the Pillar not only sets new economic goals for the social rights and principles it (re)affirms. Following the abovementioned first preliminary outline, 'the principle proposed here … offers a way to assess and, in future, approximate for the better the performance of national employment and social policies'[59] and 'should become a reference framework to screen the employment and social performance of participating Member States, to drive reforms at national level and, more specifically, to serve as a compass for renewed convergence within the euro area'.[60] Social principles are then transformed from 'protection shields' into objectives to be achieved in order to comply with EU economic requirements.[61]

Monitoring of the implementation of the Pillar within the European Semester is entirely consistent with this new functionalisation of social rights and principles, as well as with the emphasis put on Member States' responsibility in the implementation process. For the Commission, the European Semester provides the most appropriate tool for monitoring progress in key areas covered by the European Pillar of Social Rights. The reasons are twofold: it is

> specific to the situation of each country: it acknowledges the diversity of challenges and the need to prioritise in the light of different starting points and available means across countries. The European Semester is also the way to structure collective efforts over time: it builds on in-depth dialogue and reporting throughout the year, which is

[56] First preliminary outline of a European Pillar of Social Rights, Annex 1 to the Communication from the Commission to the European Parliament, the Council and the European Economic and Social Committee, Launching a consultation on a European Pillar of Social Rights, 8 March 2016, COM(2016) 127 final.

[57] EPSR, Preamble, Recital 13.

[58] EPSR, Preamble, Recital 14.

[59] First preliminary outline of the European Pillar of Social Rights, March 2016, 8.

[60] Ibid, 7.

[61] K Chatzilaou, 'Vers un socle européen des droits sociaux: quelles inspirations?' (2017) 3 *Revue de Droit du Travail* 175.

> transparent and open to all actors, and it is used in particular to structure peer reviews and benchmarking among Member States.[62]

This subsequent 'socialisation' of the European Semester, particularly visible in the growing number of 'social CSRs' as mentioned in the previous section, is a direct consequence of the integration of the Pillar into the same process. Another development with a potentially important impact on the enforcement of EU Labour Law resides in the statistical approach of monitoring via the Social Scoreboard (see section 3.1 below). The whole monitoring process reflects the notion of convergence calling for renewed relationships between economic and social considerations and their respective institutional frameworks.

The European Pillar of Social Rights Action Plan, published by the Commission on 4 March 2021,[63] complements and further develops these essential orientations. To make the Pillar concrete, social policy initiatives, including Directives, are combined with employment policy actions in the same programme. The major achievement of the Action Plan indeed resides in the dilution of this new framework for social policy within New Economic Governance: based on the employment policy model, social policy initiatives are intended as an element of economic policy coordination with the aim of achieving goals of inclusive and sustainable growth. The three new 'EU targets to set ambitions for 2030' set out in the first section of the Action Plan[64] further exacerbate this dilution. The Action Plan also constitutes an OMC tool within the framework of the European Semester, in which national implementation measures that would have to be decided will be monitored. To that end, the Commission presents a revised Social Scoreboard which 'will track Member States' trends and performances'. New headline and secondary indicators are added to the initial ones, but again, none of them deals with 'fair working conditions', thus confirming that workers' protection is not an objective of economic policy coordination.

2.3. Focus on EU Labour Law within New Economic Governance

2.3.1. EU Labour Law in the CSRs

Having taken stock of the main areas of labour law and employment policy covered by CSRs, one should then consider which areas of EU labour law have

[62] Communication from the Commission, Monitoring the implementation of the European Pillar of Social Rights.

[63] The EPSR Action Plan consists legally of a Communication but the formal reference cannot be found, even in the document itself, see: https://op.europa.eu/webpub/empl/european-pillar-of-social-rights/en/.

[64] The three targets are as follows: at least 78 per cent of the population aged 20 to 64 should be in employment by 2030; at least 60 per cent of all adults should participate in training every year; the number of people at risk of poverty or social exclusion should be reduced by at least 15 million by 2030.

been touched by these instruments so far. At first blush, and in light of the main categories of CSRs we outlined in the previous sections, the answer would be: not many. Indeed, CSRs seem to be related more to employment policy than to labour law. To an extent, this is reassuring, as the Commission, which drafts CSRs, has other instruments at its disposal to ensure the correct application of EU Labour Law Directives and Regulations, such as the opening of infringement proceedings.

That said, if one goes beyond the text of CSRs themselves and considers the explanations which accompany them, some areas of overlap can be identified.

The first of these areas relates to non-discrimination Directives, related to equality between women and men[65] and to other protected grounds.[66] As we have seen in section 2.2, several CSRs have dealt with improving the labour market participation of 'disadvantaged' groups, such as women, young and old workers, and workers with a migrant background.[67] Hence, these areas are covered mainly in terms of employment policy, only very partially overlapping with labour law issues. In the case of women, this was addressed mostly by recommending the expansion of childcare services,[68] but also by pointing to the existence of a gender pay-gap or gender segregation in low-paid or part-time employment.[69] Similarly in the case of workers with a migrant background, CSRs focused on the importance of fostering equal opportunities in terms of labour market access, as well as addressing unequal access and outcomes in the context of education.[70] Again, issues related to the low employment rate of older and younger workers, as well as people not in employment, education or training (NEETs) are addressed through the lens of labour market participation. This leads to CSRs aimed at improving active labour market policies for these groups, as well as their access to vocational training and/or lifelong learning.[71]

A second area, emerging from CSRs related to employment protection legislation, as well as from some related to younger workers' participation in the labour market, concerns atypical employment. A good example of this is the 2017 CSR for Germany, which stressed the need to avoid abuses of temporary agency work and fixed-term contracts. More specifically, the same document lamented the

[65] Directive 2006/54/EC of the European Parliament and of the Council of 5 July 2006 on the implementation of the principle of equal opportunities and equal treatment of men and women in matters of employment and occupation (recast).

[66] Council Directive 2000/78/EC of 27 November 2000 establishing a general framework for equal treatment in employment and occupation; Council Directive 2000/43/EC of 29 June 2000 implementing the principle of equal treatment between persons irrespective of racial or ethnic origin.

[67] This trend appears to be bound to continue, as these groups' labour market access is the main element mentioned under the heading of 'fairness' in the 2021 Annual Sustainable Growth Strategy presented by the Commission. See Communication from the Commission to the European Parliament, the European Council, the Council, the European Central Bank, the European Economic and Social Committee, the Committee of the Regions and the European Investment Bank, Annual Sustainable Growth Strategy 2021, COM/2020/575 final, 7–8.

[68] See for instance, AT (2012), CZ (2015), FI (2018).

[69] See for instance, AT (2014), CY (2014), EE (2019), IT (2019).

[70] See for instance, DK (2013), AT (2014), BE (2017), NL (2019).

[71] See for instance, EE (2011), ES (2014), PL (2015), BE (2016).

wage gap between fixed-term and permanent contracts,[72] echoing the protection against discrimination established by clause 4 of the Fixed-term Work Directive.[73] The importance of allowing workers to access permanent contracts, which is also put forward in the Preamble of the Directive,[74] also comes up in certain CSRs.[75] Some Recommendations also highlighted the existence of a wage gap, in connection with the gender pay gap, in the context of part-time employment.[76] Again, this can be seen as an attempt to concretise the right to non-discrimination guaranteed by Clause 4 of the Directive on part-time work.[77] In 2013 France also received a CSR aimed at improving the situation of temporary agency workers, though the link with a provision of the corresponding Directive[78] cannot be established clearly.

A third area, notably collective bargaining, is only loosely connected to EU labour law. Article 28 of the EU Charter of Fundamental Rights recognises the fundamental right to collective bargaining, but, leaving aside the limited impact of this recognition,[79] no specific legislative intervention in this area can be identified in EU labour law. However, the issue of wages, which, as we have seen before, is strictly interrelated with that of collective bargaining in the context of CSRs, could soon fall within the scope we are currently exploring. Indeed, this would apply to the proposed Directive on adequate minimum wages, if adopted.[80] Although we will not consider the challenges and legal issues raised by the proposal itself, the ultimate adoption of this Directive remains uncertain. As such, we will consider its potential impact and interest for the topic at stake in the next section, devoted to future prospects. It is also worth noting that the issue of adequate minimum wages, as well as the previous two areas, are addressed in the EPSR, which contributed significantly to the socialisation of New Economic Governance.

[72] '[F]ixed-term contracts appear to have a comparatively high wage gap of 27 per cent compared to permanent contracts'.

[73] Council Directive 1999/70/EC of 28 June 1999 concerning the framework agreement on fixed-term work concluded by ETUC, UNICE and CEEP.

[74] CY (2017): 'recruitment [of young people and long-term unemployed] is likely to occur on temporary contracts, therefore not addressing the challenge in structural terms'; PL (2013 and 2014): 'Combat in-work poverty and labour market segmentation including through better transition from fixed-term to permanent employment and by reducing the excessive use of civil law contracts'.

[75] See PL (2014).

[76] See AT (2019): 'Female part-time employment also explains an important share of the unadjusted gender pay gap'.

[77] Council Directive 97/81/EC of 15 December 1997 concerning the Framework Agreement on part-time work concluded by UNICE, CEEP and the ETUC – Annex: Framework agreement on part-time work.

[78] Directive 2008/104/EC of the European Parliament and of the Council of 19 November 2008 on temporary agency work.

[79] F Dorssemont and M Rocca, 'Article 28 – Right of collective bargaining and action', in F Dorssemont, K Lörcher, S Clauwaert and M Schmitt (eds), *The Charter of Fundamental Rights of the European Union and the Employment Relation* (Oxford, Hart Publishing, 2020).

[80] Proposal for a Directive of the European Parliament and of the Council on adequate minimum wages in the European Union, COM/2020/682 final.

2.3.2. EU Labour Law in the EPSR

While economic and employment objectives remain predominant, the social CSRs adopted since 2019 demonstrate that the Pillar has played a role in the substantive socialisation of New Economic Governance. The strong anchoring of the Pillar in the EMU and the European Semester is criticised precisely regarding its (in)ability to improve workers' rights and (legal) protection.[81] The adoption of several social policy Directives (on the basis of Article 153 TFEU) to deliver the Pillar is not sufficient to remove all doubts about this concern. As regards enforcement, the question raised above all deals with the linking and combination of the two enforcement processes, ie enforcement by (national and/or European) judges and inspectorates, on one hand, and (soft) enforcement within the framework of the European Semester, on the other.

Insofar as the EPSR is dedicated to social rights, it obviously deals with areas directly linked with EU labour law. Thus, half of the Pillar's rights and principles refer to employment and working conditions. In line with the CSRs, chapter 1 of the Pillar covers rights and principles focused on 'equal access to the labour market'. Not surprisingly, the first area of the EPSR overlapping EU labour law is non-discrimination: besides the general right to equal opportunities regarding employment regardless of gender, racial or ethnic origin, religion or belief, disability, age or sexual orientation (point 3), the Pillar puts special emphasis on gender equality (point 2). These provisions are consistent with the abovementioned non-discrimination Directives. In the same vein, the EPSR Action Plan 'encourages Member States to implement the reinforced Youth Guarantee with a particular focus on quality offers that support a stable labour market integration'. In addition, special attention is paid to the right to professional training and to active support in that perspective (points 1, 3 and 4). This focus is particularly visible in the Action Plan because, following the second target set out for 2030, 'at least 60 per cent of all adults should participate in training every year'. Progress made by Member States will be monitored by two new secondary indicators introduced in the revised Social Scoreboard.[82] All these rights and principles (and now also targets) are consistent with a market-oriented approach, which is also characteristic of the 'flexicurity' policy and objectives. The aim of the Pillar is not to improve workers' personal fulfilment and their dignity and freedom in employment, but resides in the efficient functioning of the labour market. As a consequence, protection afforded by labour law devices should reside primarily in, and result from, access for everyone to the labour market.

[81] P Rodière, 'Le dévissement de l'Europe sociale – sur les "explications" du socle européen des droits sociaux par la Commission' (2018) 1 *Revue trimestrielle de droit européen* 45; S Garben, n 54 at 221; K Lörcher and I Schömann, 'The European pillar of social rights: critical legal analysis and proposals', 139 *ETUI Report* 1, 18–19.

[82] Participation of low-qualified adults in learning and share of unemployed adults with recent learning experience.

Such an essential link with employment policy also infuses rights and principles set out in chapter 2 'fair working conditions', addressing both working conditions strictly speaking (for instance, the right to health and safety at work[83]) and employment protection. Beyond this, the wording of the rights and principles further incorporates economic considerations in their very definitions. This is particularly visible in Point 5 entitled 'Secure and adaptable employment': while stating that 'Employment relationships that lead to precarious working conditions shall be prevented, including by prohibiting abuse of atypical contract' (point 5, d) – which, again, is in line with the Directive on fixed-term work – the Pillar insists on 'the necessary flexibility for employers to adapt swiftly to changes in the economic context [that] shall be ensured' (point 5, b). However, point 5, d) enshrines a new principle in that '[a]ny probation period should be of reasonable duration'. The individual right to information, already protected by the so-called Written Statement Directive no 91/533, provides another example of how social rights are formulated in light of an economic conceptual framework. As stated in Point 7, a) of the Pillar, '[w]orkers have the right to be informed in writing at the start of employment about their rights and obligations resulting from the employment relationship, including on probation period'. Here, the requirement of fairness resides exclusively in access to information, which corresponds to mainstream neoliberal economic thought, following which transparency and predictability of information for all economic agents is the key requirement for well-functioning (labour) markets. Points 5 and 7 of the Pillar have both boosted the adoption of Directive no 2019/1152 on transparent and predictable working conditions in the European Union,[84] which combines the revision of the Written Statement Directive and new provisions setting 'minimum requirements relating to working conditions'. In a similar vein, workers' right to a working environment adapted to their professional needs should 'enable … them to prolong their participation in the labour market'.[85]

The legislative route has also led to a new Directive on work–life balance (Point 9), which improves parents' and carers' rights.[86] As regards the enforcement issue, the Social Scoreboard could be complementary and bring added value to the usual enforcement routes of Directive implementation in the Member States, via the possible incorporation of new indicators (such as the percentage of workers benefiting from parental leave). Besides the Member States' duty to implement the minimum requirements of social Directives, such indicators could be useful to assess and improve the effective enjoyment of rights enshrined in these Directives. Work–life balance also implies that workers are entitled to a right to disconnect,

[83] EPSR, Point 10, a).

[84] Directive (EU) 2019/1152 of the European Parliament and of the Council of 20 June 2019 on transparent and predictable working conditions in the European Union, [2019] OJ L 186/105–21.

[85] EPSR, Point 10, b).

[86] Directive (EU) 2019/1158 of the European Parliament and of the Council of 20 June 2019 on work-life balance for parents and carers and repealing Council Directive 2010/18/EU.

following a European Parliament Resolution.[87] In the EPSR Action Plan, the Commission officially takes this initiative into account but its initiative will be limited to 'ensur(ing) an appropriate follow-up'. More generally, when it comes to occupational safety and health, the Action Plan confirms that this area remains neglected by the Pillar, particularly in the Social Scoreboard, as it is in the context of New Economic Governance. Public authorities and social partners are simply encouraged to 'ensure the application and enforcement of existing rules'. The same applies to working time: the Commission will present a report on the implementation of Directive 2003/88 only in 2022. However, the Action Plan announces new initiatives in respect of working conditions. More important in terms of commitment is a legislative proposal on the working conditions of platform workers, which will be presented in Q4 2021 following the ongoing consultation of social partners. This proposal of a new social policy Directive should be preceded by another proposal of an EU regulation on Artificial Intelligence in Q2 2021, for the uptake of trustworthy AI in the EU economy, including in the workplace for all forms of work.

In two other labour law areas, the Pillar goes further than the EU social *acquis*. One area is addressed in Point 7 b) affirming the right to protection in case of dismissal, whereas there is no EU general minimum requirement on this important element. This situation can be explained by the fact that the adoption of a Directive would require unanimity under Article 153, para 2, TFEU. Moreover, the right to be informed of the reasons for dismissal and be granted a reasonable period of notice, which is part of employment protection following the Pillar, goes further than Article 30 CFREU. Concretising this right at national level would necessarily imply enforcement outside the social policy framework. The question is then raised of the (ir)relevance of NEG processes and tools.

Wages (Point 6) are the second area in which the EPSR goes beyond the EU *acquis* by establishing the 'right to fair wages' and to 'minimum adequate wages' and stating that '[a]ll wages shall be set in a transparent and predictable way according to national practices and respecting the autonomy of the social partners'. These provisions provide the direct inspiration for the Commission's initiative for a Directive on adequate minimum wages in the EU, already mentioned. While recognising that '[a] common framework at EU level would reinforce trust both among Member States and social partners [and that w]ithout it, individual countries may be little inclined to improve their minimum wage setting because of the perception that this could negatively affect their external cost competitiveness',[88] the Commission perpetuates and even sharpens policy guidance already issued

[87] European Parliament resolution of 21 January 2021 with recommendations to the Commission on the right to disconnect (2019/2181(INL).

[88] Commission Staff Working Document, Analytical Document Accompanying the Document Consultation document Second phase consultation of Social Partners under 154 TFEU on a possible action addressing the challenges related to fair minimum wages, Brussels, 3 June 2020 SWD(2020) 105 final, 47.

within the European Semester by incorporating monitoring tools inspired by New Economic Governance. The major stakes of EU labour law enforcement could not have been more clearly introduced, as we will discuss now in section 3.

3. EU Economic Governance as an Avenue for (Better) Enforcement of EU Labour Law?

Is New Economic Governance an appropriate framework for enforcing EU labour law, notably in the perspective of ensuring and improving the application of workers' rights and protection? In this final section we wish to draw attention not just to the feasibility and potential of such a 'repurposing' of New Economic Governance instruments, but also to the potential and sometimes elusive dangers that such a strategy might entail.

3.1. The Possibility of a Social 'Re-instrumentalisation' of EU Economic Governance

As we have seen in the previous chapter, New Economic Governance already covers areas related to EU labour law. The following step, if one wants to pursue such an agenda, is then to consider if and how this form of enforcement might be expanded to other areas. Therefore, in this section we will consider areas that appear to be 'adjacent' to those already (partially) covered by CSRs in the past. An important starting point is that New Economic Governance should not aim at replacing existing instruments for enforcing EU labour law. As such, for those rights and obligations that stem from Directives and Regulations, the ultimate enforcement through the EU Court of Justice, activated either by national judges through preliminary questions or by the Commission through an infringement procedure, should not be supplanted by the instruments we are presently considering. This is not just because new instruments should naturally complete and expand the already existing legal arsenal, but also to avoid the hollowing out of the fundamental tool of judicial enforcement. In particular, enforcement by the Court of Justice provides an authoritative interpretation of EU labour law, which simply could not be replaced by the instruments of New Economic Governance. Thus formulated, the question of the potential repurposing of New Economic Governance to improve the enforcement of EU labour law becomes one of added value.

Non-discrimination is a perfect example of this potential. As we have seen before, CSRs in this area have sometimes targeted the existence of a gender pay gap in Member States. This is an area in which individual action based on a fundamental rights approach might not be the instrument best suited to tackle the issue, for instance, because of the lack of a comparator when inequalities are caused by vertical segregation, with female-dominated sectors being characterised by lower wages. Considering its pre-existing inclusion in CSRs, this represents somewhat low-hanging fruit. Attention to this aspect is also shown by the inclusion of the fight against the employment gap in the European Social Pillar Action Plan,[89] which specifically mentions the European Semester as a tool to monitor Member State policies in this area.[90] The gender pay gap is included in the Social Scoreboard, accompanying the EPSR.[91] Better enforcement in this area could be achieved by elevating the gender pay gap to a 'proper' indicator, such as those included in the scoreboard for the Macroeconomic Imbalance Procedure.[92] This would open the way to the existence of a threat, albeit theoretical, for Member States failing to take into account CSRs in this area. This would also be linked to the existing activities of the EU Commission on fighting the gender pay gap.[93] Such an approach – that is, the inclusion of 'social' indicators among those instruments which allow for the threat of sanctions – could constitute the blueprint for similar interventions in other areas, such as youth unemployment (in its turn, already addressed in the EPSR and included in the Social Scoreboard), transformation of temporary contracts into permanent ones, or (ab)use of agency workers. To facilitate this process, most of these indicators could be construed as part of the economic rationale,[94] fostering equal access to the labour market and the structural reduction of unemployment.

A more difficult test for the 'socialisation' of New Economic Governance could emerge from the enforcement of certain aspects of the proposal on adequate minimum wages, recently put forward by the Commission. It goes without saying that these brief considerations stem from the present text and envisage a future scenario in which such a text would be adopted. Now, to the dismay of many,[95] the proposal does not include, in its legal text, any 'hard' threshold for assessing the adequacy of a minimum wage. Indeed, such indicators – notably 60 per cent of the gross median wage and/or 50 per cent of the gross average wage – are included only in the recitals of the proposal.[96] This is easily explained by the attempt to

[89] Communication from the Commission to the European Parliament, the Council, the European Economic and Social Committee and the Committee Of The Regions, The European Pillar of Social Rights Action Plan, Brussels, 4 March 2021, COM(2021) 102 final, 6.

[90] Ibid, 8.

[91] EU Commission, Social Scoreboard, https://composite-indicators.jrc.ec.europa.eu/social-scoreboard/. See Rasnača, n 43 at 13.

[92] For an analysis of the need to improve the indicator itself see ETUI, 'The Social Scoreboard revisited' (2017) 3 ETUI Background Analysis 1.

[93] See for instance the Communication from the Commission to the European Parliament, the Council and the European Economic and Social Committee, EU Action Plan 2017–2019 Tackling the gender pay gap.

[94] See M Dawson, 'New governance and the displacement of Social Europe: the case of the European Semester' (2018) 14 *European Constitutional Law Review* 191, 192.

[95] A Lo Faro, 'Al andar se hace camino: la Proposta di Direttiva sul salario minimo tra ottimismo della volontà e …' (2021) *Eticaeconomia*, www.eticaeconomia.it/al-andar-se-hace-camino-la-proposta-di-direttiva-sul-salario-minimo-tra-ottimismo-della-vo-lonta-e.

[96] Proposal for a Directive on adequate minimum wages in the European Union, Recital 21.

minimise potential legal challenges based on the conflict with the exclusion of legislative competences in the area of wages which stems from Article 153(5) TFEU. It goes without saying that the inclusion of these thresholds as real 'indicators' would constitute a major step forward in the socialisation of the NEG. However, as already mentioned, here we will proceed on the basis of the existing text of the proposal. Keeping to this, the *only* actual numerical threshold included in the legal text is to be found under Article 4 and concerns the level of collective bargaining coverage that Member States should ensure. This is fixed at 70 per cent of workers and is presently met by only 10 Member States.[97] The proposal itself provides for the establishment of an action plan to 'promote collective bargaining' for those Member States that do not meet the threshold. As such, it is not unthinkable for such a quantified indicator to be integrated into New Economic Governance. Indeed, the objective of reducing inequalities is already present in the Social Scoreboard, which we have already mentioned, and research from the International Monetary Fund has highlighted the link between trade union presence and inequality.[98]

Moreover, besides the usual form of enforcement as regards Directives – that is, the judicial route[99] – the Commission has already proposed a follow-up to the (possible) Directive, which is directly and broadly inspired by the process and timescale of New Economic Governance. In that perspective, Article 10 of the proposal is dedicated to data collection tools that Members States would have to put in place and report on to the Commission. To ensure the effectiveness of the Directive, the Commission will report every year to the European Parliament and to the Council its assessment of developments in the adequacy and coverage of minimum wage protection on the basis of these data and information. In addition, progress should be monitored within the framework of the process of economic and employment policy coordination at EU level (European Semester). In this context, the Employment Committee will every year examine the situation with regard to collective bargaining on wage setting, as well as the adequacy of minimum wage protection in the Member States, based on the Commission's reports.

Of course, it would be somewhat ironic if CSRs were addressed to Member States asking for reinforcement of collective bargaining coverage, not even a decade after MoUs led to a drastic reduction of such coverage.[100] However, this is

[97] Data from the ICTWSS Database of the Amsterdam Institute for Advanced Labour Studies (AIAS), elaborated by the European Trade Union Institute, see: www.etuc.org/en/pressrelease/eu-countries-weak-collective-bargaining-have-lowest-wages.

[98] F Jaumotte and C Osorio Buitron, 'Inequality and Labor Market Institutions' (2015) IMF Staff Discussion Note 1.

[99] Proposal for a Directive on adequate minimum wages in the European Union, Article 11 (right to access to effective and impartial dispute resolution and right to redress, including adequate compensation, in the case of infringements).

[100] See M d R Palma Ramalho, 'Portuguese labour law and industrial relations during the Crisis' (2013) 54 ILO Working Paper 1, 3; ILO, *Report on the high level Mission to Greece* (Athens, 2011), §§304–307; ILO, *Report of the Committee of Experts on the Application of Conventions and Recommendations*

precisely why the inclusion of such an indicator under the 'strong' New Economic Governance regime represents a real test of the socialisation hypothesis.

3.2. Dangers of a Social 'Re-instrumentalisation' of EU Economic Governance

The idea of repurposing the powerful and seemingly malleable tool of New Economic Governance to further the enforcement of EU labour law appears particularly attractive. At the end of our analysis, we wish to highlight a number of caveats that should be borne in mind by anyone embarking on such a strategy.

Research on New Economic Governance shows the difficulties trade unions and social movements might face in trying to politicise this area,[101] as well as in trying to advance their demands vis-à-vis the actors representing the 'economic rationale' of New Economic Governance.[102] As such, social objectives might be difficult to defend, let alone advance, in a procedure in which recommendations are ultimately adopted by the Council in its Economic and Financial Affairs configuration.[103] Of course one might postulate that in the 'repurposing' scenario these actors would also have embraced the value of enforcing labour rights through New Economic Governance. Even in such a case, however, actors interested in advancing a social agenda for the EU should carefully consider whether this might be easier to advance in an arena less susceptible to political pressure.

A second risk comes from the potential hollowing-out of classical legal instruments, such as the Directive, and their enforcement mechanisms (labour inspections, judicial action). After all, CSRs can be adopted to, for instance, recommend that Member States close the gender pay gap or to facilitate the transformation of temporary contracts into permanent ones. Why should EU institutions go through the much more cumbersome and uncertain legislative procedure to adopt a Directive in this area? This is all the more true regarding protection against dismissal, a domain in which Directives would be subject to a unanimity vote in the Council (Article 153, para 2, TFEU). However, the instruments of New Economic Governance are ill-suited to the language of rights, and therefore lack any clear pathway to the creation and enforcement of individual situations. Even more problematically the tailored nature of CSRs would take away the very idea of an EU floor of rights embodied by labour law Directives. For that reason, it would necessarily renationalise social and political struggles, as

(International Labour Conference 103rd Session, 2014), 112. The reduction was around 90 per cent. See V Delteil and M Bănărescu, 'Roumanie – le modèle social sous la pression des bailleurs de fonds: les syndicats à la recherche de nouvelles "tutelles"' (2013) 143–44 *Chronique Internationale de L'IRES* 133, 142.

[101] R Erne, 'A supranational regime that nationalizes social conflict: explaining European trade unions' difficulties in politicizing European economic governance' (2015) 56 *Labor History* 345, 347.

[102] Copeland and Daly, n 25 at 13.

[103] Dawson, n 94 at 202.

different Member States are shown different faces of New Economic Governance, a problem highlighted perfectly by Roland Erne.[104] Because of this, developments in the social aspects of New Economic Governance might end up being counter-productive for transnational solidarity and the Europeanisation of social struggles.

In light of these dangers, one should also assess the actual added value and effectiveness of taking the 'NEG path to enforcement'. The most important limitation of effectiveness comes from the fact – highlighted in section 2.1 – that the threat of sanctions is directly connected to the context of the recommendation. Those which are relevant to attaining the SGP or MIP objectives can lead to sanctions, an unlikely scenario to start with, when addressed to Member States facing an excessive deficit or macroeconomic imbalances procedure. The non-respect of CSRs falling outside the SGP or MIP – that is, those related to Europe 2020 targets – cannot constitute the basis for a sanction.

The focus of CSRs on poverty alleviation and on disadvantaged groups, which we have already highlighted,[105] gives the impression of a mechanism better suited to addressing minimal protection floors. The third target set out in the EPSR Action Plan ('The number of people at risk of poverty or social exclusion should be reduced by at least 15 million by 2030') confirms that impression. More significantly, the only new indicator introduced in the chapter dedicated to working conditions is limited to fatal accidents at work per 100,000 workers, which is far from sufficient to monitor the concretisation of the broad notion of health and safety promoted by Directive 89/391[106] and of the 'high level of protection' granted by Point 10 of the Pillar. In this sense, from the perspective of labour rights, the issue of minimum wages might be best suited to being monitored and enforced through the instruments of New Economic Governance. This is also plausible in light of its more 'quantifiable' nature. Still, the fact that the proposal put forward by the Commission does not include any reference to an actual threshold for minimum wages, like those which are instead included in the explanatory memorandum,[107] would probably undermine this potential use.

Even when promoting this fairly basic level of enforcement of social rights through New Economic Governance one should keep in mind the caveats we put forward in opening our conclusions. Once absorbed by New Economic Governance, there is no guarantee that the social logic of minimum wages will survive, let alone prevail, in the encounter with economic logic. Indeed, during the last economic crisis, so-called 'internal devaluation'[108] – that is, the relative

[104] Erne, n 101 at 353–55.

[105] See section 2.2.1.

[106] See Chapter 14 in this volume.

[107] Proposal for a Directive of the European Parliament and of the Council on adequate minimum wages in the European Union, 10.

[108] P Pochet and C Degryse, 'The programmed dismantling of the "European Social Model"' (2012) 47 *Intereconomics* 200, 216.

reduction of wages vis-à-vis trading partners – was the flagship strategy used to tackle macroeconomic imbalances in the absence of exchange rate flexibility (because of the euro).[109] What is more, the so-called Five Presidents Report of 2015,[110] a blueprint for 'better economic governance in the euro area', included a proposal to establish so-called 'Competitiveness Authorities', that is, 'independent entities with a mandate to assess whether wages are evolving in line with productivity and compare with developments in other euro area countries and in the main comparable trading partners'.[111] Any strategy aimed at repurposing the instruments of New Economic Governance to advance a 'social' agenda should thus be wary of playing into the hands of those who would like to see labour standards completely subsumed by the logic of competitiveness and budgetary rules.

[109] N Roubini, 'Eurozone Crisis: Here are the Options, Now Choose' (2011), *EconoMonitor*, www.economonitor.com/nouriel/2011/11/09/eurozone-crisiswell-at-least-we-have-options/; R Janssen, 'Internal Wage Devaluation – The IMF Admits It Does Not Work' (2013) *Social Europe*, www.social-europe.eu/2013/12/internal-wage-devaluation/.

[110] JC Juncker, *Completing Europe's Economic and Monetary Union* (Brussels, European Commission, 2015).

[111] Ibid, 8.

22

Proposal for a Directive on Effective Enforcement

ZANE RASNAČA, ARISTEA KOUKIADAKI,
KLAUS LÖRCHER AND NIKLAS BRUUN

1. Introduction

Without effective enforcement, EU labour law's ability to protect workers would be seriously blunted. The degree of effectiveness very much depends on the respective legislative framework. This is the main reason for proposing a specific Directive on effective enforcement of EU labour law.

2. Context of the Proposal

To address several of the enforcement gaps identified in this book at least partially, in this chapter we propose a horizontal (effective) enforcement Directive for the area of EU labour law. It is of course a work-in-progress, but our aim is to trigger a wider discussion focusing on how to improve the enforcement of EU-based workers' rights across the EU.

2.1. Reasons for and Objectives of the Proposal

A common thread throughout the chapters of this book is that the enforcement of EU labour law could and should be further improved. We present concrete proposals in multiple chapters, ranging from the need to broaden access to courts, not only for individuals but especially and primarily for collective actors such as trade unions,[1] to the need to ensure that workers' representatives have a say regarding employers' decisions[2] and making sure that labour inspectorates have

[1] See Chapter 3 in this volume.
[2] See Chapters 11 and 14 in this volume.

the resources they need to work effectively (Aude Cefaliello) and many other inspiring ideas. This chapter aims to turn at least some of these ideas into a more concrete proposal for enhancing the enforcement of EU labour law in the Member States. All in all, there are several regulatory options for improving the enforcement architecture.

One option could be to broaden the possibilities at the EU level (EU-level enforcement) by, for example, giving broader enforcement powers to the European Commission, extending the possibilities to bring cases (directly) before the CJEU and expanding the enforcement-related competences of the European Labour Authority (ELA).[3] Another option would be to specialise and to create more intricate and even specifically tailored enforcement tools for specific areas of EU labour law (such as occupational safety and health, information and consultation rights, or migrant workers).[4] In fact, this approach has been the dominant one in the EU so far. Examples of existing enforcement measures that were intended to cover only a specific area are the Posted Workers Enforcement Directive[5] and Directive 1999/95/EC concerning the enforcement of provisions in respect of seafarers' hours of work on board ships calling at Community ports. One can also imagine focusing on specific types of enforcement (such as enforcement by administrative means, via criminal, civil or even soft law separately). Such an approach was taken by the European legislator in the case of the European Labour Authority. This new institution has competence to act only within the scope of a closed list of EU secondary law measures. Its main role is to provide assistance with administrative enforcement in the EU. Such a specialised approach has its merits because it can consider the specific features of a particular setting. One could imagine that in occupational safety and health the emphasis is on prevention first and enforcement second. Likewise, in areas in which workers are especially disadvantaged or atypical, enforcement should be tailored to their needs and the usual reliance on private enforcement might not work.

Nevertheless, what the EU is currently missing most, at least in our humble opinion, is improvement of the enforcement system available for workers at large. There is currently no horizontal measure focusing exclusively on enforcement in all of its diversity that would correspond to the specific needs of workers in a holistic way. We are not the first to make this point. Garben et al have already argued that a new Directive to cover a broad set of factors enhancing compliance with EU rules is necessary.[6] Instead, at least in practice enforcement is almost entirely left

[3] The regulatory framework in respect of competition law enforcement is a prime example.

[4] See Chapters 11, 12 and 14 in this volume.

[5] Directive 2014/67/EU on the enforcement of Directive 96/71/EC concerning the posting of workers in the framework of the provision of services and amending Regulation (EU) No 1024/2012 on administrative cooperation through the Internal Market Information System.

[6] S Garben, C Kilpatrick and E Muir, 'Towards a European Pillar of Social Rights: upgrading the EU social acquis', CEPOB – College of Europe Policy Brief Series (2017), No 1.17, 6.

to the individual Member States and incorporated in their national systems, even though there is meaningful body of EU-level substantive law that one can describe as EU labour law.

Our starting point in proposing this effective enforcement Directive is the idea that there are commonalities in the enforcement-related situations faced by the EU workers that need to be uniformly addressed. Moreover, the national level enforcement structures are not usually constructed with enforcement of EU law in mind, hence, they might lack the ability to address the need for effective enforcement of EU labour law. By and large, other than the general duty to provide effective protection of EU rights equivalent to national rights, Member States have remained free to regulate procedural law on access to justice, legal costs and other matters.[7] At the same time, EU law is certainly distinguishable from national law and plays a different (including a unifying) role and thus, we believe, it merits a special set of enforcement rules or principles.

For this reason, a Directive on effective enforcement of EU labour law is proposed here. It is meant to enhance and broaden enforcement possibilities in a way that is not generic but is tailored to EU labour law, as well as to broaden the opportunities for actors already active in the enforcement process whose options are at times curtailed by national law. In this way we hope to reduce fragmentation in terms of workers' rights, and also to address the general issues with enforcement by constructing certain general principles vital for dealing with enforcement gaps. At the same time, the proposal attempts to address some issues faced by certain groups of workers (for example, by extending liability in subcontracting and by requiring more tailor-made solutions for more disadvantaged workers, such as seasonal workers).

2.2. Consistency with Existing Policy Provisions in the Policy Area

As already mentioned, some EU secondary law measures deal with certain aspects of enforcement. In addition, a set of enforcement-oriented provisions can be found in many secondary law measures adopted under either free movement of workers rules (eg Directive 2014/54/EU on facilitating exercise of rights conferred on workers in the context of free movement for workers) or the Social Policy title in the TFEU (eg Recast Gender Directive (2006/54/EC)). Our proposal is not meant to replace them in any way but either to underpin them by offering underlying principles to be obeyed by the Member States in ensuring adequate enforcement tools for the workers concerned or to complement them and empower workers by offering new enforcement tools for their rights where or if they previously did not exist (see eg the proposal to introduce collective redress).

[7] Ibid, 5.

In the manner of *lex specialis derogat legi generali* the pre-existing and more specialised EU enforcement rules are not replaced; however, at times they are complemented by new, more advantageous rules intended to aid workers in their enforcement efforts (see also rules on liability below).

3. Legal Basis, Subsidiarity and Proportionality

3.1. Legal Basis

In its most recent Opinion, the CJEU's Grand Chamber compiled the principles for properly defining the legal basis for an EU act in the following terms:

> In accordance with settled case-law of the Court, the choice of the legal basis for an EU act, including one adopted in order to conclude an international agreement, must rest on objective factors amenable to judicial review, which include the aim and the content of that measure …
>
> If the examination of an EU act reveals that it pursues two aims or that it has two components and if one of those aims or components is identifiable as the main one, whereas the other is merely incidental, the act must be founded on a single legal basis, namely, that required by the main or predominant aim or component. Exceptionally, if it is established, however, that the act simultaneously pursues a number of objectives, or has several components, which are inextricably linked without one being incidental to the other, such that various provisions of the Treaties are applicable, such a measure will have to be founded on the various corresponding legal bases …[8]

According to these principles, the proposal, as laid out below, is based on Article 153(2)(b) TFEU, which provides for the adoption of Directives setting minimum requirements with respect to, in particular, 'working conditions', as set out in Article 153(1)(b) TFEU. This is the same legal basis as for the majority of substantive rules for whose effective enforcement the Directive set out below is proposed.

There are also other elements in the proposal which refer, for example, to the 'protection of representation and collective defence of the interests of workers' (Article 153(1)(f) TFEU). Compared to the content as a whole, however, they do not form such an important part[9] that they would require a specific reference in the legal bases. This is demonstrated in a number of Directives in the social policy field regulating also 'social dialogue' or workers' representatives. According to the more incidental nature of these provisions in relation to the context of the whole Directive, there is also no problem with the exclusion of legislative competence provided for by Article 153(5) TFEU.

[8] Opinion of the Court 1/19 (Istanbul Convention), 6 October 2021, ECLI:EU:C:2021:198, paras 284 and 285.

[9] See ibid, para 187 ('the criteria in respect of which the incidental nature of a purpose or component of an act may be determined include the number of provisions devoted to it, in comparison with the act's provisions as a whole, and the nature and scope of those provisions').

Even though the instrument's centre of gravity lies in the enforcement of workers' and not only migrant workers' rights, rules on free movement of workers might need to be referred to as well when considering the legal basis. In this case Articles 46 and 48(1)(b) TFEU seem like an appropriate additional legal basis to be invoked.[10]

Although 'enforcement' is not mentioned in Article 153 TFEU it is obvious that it forms an indispensable addition to the substantive rules. This is demonstrated, first, by the fact that most (if not all) Directives on EU labour law contain provisions on enforcement. Second, there are several examples in which Directives (only) on enforcement have been adopted despite the fact that the respective legal basis did not explicitly contain a provision on enforcement.[11]

This legal basis ensures that social partners are properly involved in the adoption process and duly consulted (Article 154 TFEU). This consultation could lead to an agreement between them according to Article 155 TFEU. Otherwise, the ordinary legislative procedure would apply.

3.2. Subsidiarity and Proportionality

In putting forward a proposal on a horizontal Directive on effective enforcement of EU labour law, it is acknowledged that this would cut across the boundary between EU and national competence. Given that the objective of this Directive, namely to strengthen enforcement of EU Labour Law and as regards acts where breaches of Union law can cause serious harm to the public interest, through effective worker protection, cannot be sufficiently achieved by the Member States acting alone or in an uncoordinated manner, but can rather be better achieved at Union level by laying down common minimum standards for worker protection, and given that only Union action can provide coherence and align the existing Union rules on worker protection, the Union may adopt measures, in accordance with the principle of subsidiarity as set out in Article 5 TEU. In accordance with the principle of proportionality, as set out in that Article, this Directive does not go beyond what is necessary to achieve that objective.

In particular it should be taken into account that this Directive is aimed at improving the realisation of fundamental rights. In substantive terms, in particular the enjoyment of workers' individual rights to fair and just working conditions (Article 31 CFREU), as well as collective rights (Articles 12, 27 and 28 CFREU) will be improved if a transparent, coherent and effective enforcement system is ensured throughout the territory of the EU. The same applies for the procedural rights mainly under Article 47 CFREU.

[10] These provisions were, among others, the legal basis for Regulation (EU) 2019/1149 establishing a European Labour Authority. Another option would be to resort to Art 114 TFEU as an additional legal basis if the link to enforcement in Art 46 and 48(1) TFEU (material scope) is found to be insufficient.

[11] See eg Directive 2014/67/EU of 15 May 2014 on the enforcement of Directive 96/71/EC concerning the posting of workers in the framework of the provision of services and Directive 2004/48/EC of 29 April 2004 on the enforcement of intellectual property rights.

4. Other Elements

The final point to consider is the scope of the measure. There are several ways in which EU instruments typically address this issue: a very general definition of the scope, a closed list of measures (Regulation on the European Labour Authority) or a very specific definition of scope (Enforcement Directive for posted work). Here we suggest a broad approach. Even though the EU legislator so far has chosen mainly to focus on enforcement in specific measures with very specific scope or by establishing enforcement mechanisms for a certain group of measures (eg the ELA), a horizontal measure that would facilitate enforcement across the area of EU labour law is proposed here. Hence, this instrument would concern enforcement of work-based rights in a broad sense comprising both EU rights arising from the Treaties, measures adopted under Article 153 TFEU, rights of EU migrant workers (Articles 45–48 TFEU), but also rights of migrant workers from third countries and thus work-related EU rules adopted under the area of freedom, security and justice for immigration with the purpose of work (Part 3, Title V TFEU) (like seasonal work). While such an approach might be controversial and it might not be easy to get the qualified majority vote necessary for its adoption across the line, this approach appears absolutely necessary to avoid further fragmentation of EU workers' rights and to underpin the existing EU-based substantive rights with adequate tools for enforcement in a comprehensive way.

5. General Observations on the Structure of the Draft Proposal

5.1. General Explanations

The Draft Proposal is divided into different chapters. Besides the usual 'General Provisions' in Chapter I, the two following chapters deal with the main substance: Chapter II contains the core provisions because it addresses 'Judicial enforcement'. Because of its importance, it is further divided into sections. The different sections mainly follow the course of judicial proceedings: Section 1 treats 'Access to Court' as starting point, while Section 2 addresses the procedures themselves. Section 3 looks at the (possible) outcome of the procedures, whereas the final Section 4 ensures the enforcement of judgments.

In contrast to Chapter II, Chapter III addresses 'Non-judicial enforcement'. It is also divided into sections, the first of which highlights the roles of trade unions and social partners (Section 1). Section 2 looks into the wider field of administrative and criminal enforcement. The final Section 3 deals with 'Alternative dispute resolution' mechanisms.

Chapters IV and V contain 'Horizontal' and 'Final provisions', respectively. The latter are largely based on the provisions incorporated in similar instruments.

5.2. Text of the Draft Proposal for a Directive

Preamble

Having regard to the Treaty on the Functioning of the European Union, and in particular point (b) of Article 153(2), in conjunction with point (b) of Article 153(1) thereof,

Whereas:

[1] Globalisation and digitalisation have increased the risk of a large number of workers being harmed by unlawful practices. Infringements of Union law can cause workers' detriment. Without effective means to bring unlawful practices to an end and to obtain redress for workers, workers' confidence in the internal market is reduced.[12]

[2] The lack of effective means for the enforcement of Union law protecting workers could also result in the distortion of fair competition between infringing and compliant employers that operate domestically or across borders.[13]

[3] The improvement of living and working conditions and harmonisation upwards are fundamental objectives of social policy enshrined in the Treaty on the Functioning of the European Union (TFEU). The implementation and enforcement of those objectives are further developed by the Union and aim to guarantee a level playing field for businesses and respect for the rights of workers.[14]

[4] According to Article 3 of the Treaty on European Union, the Union is to promote social justice and protection. According to Article 9 TFEU, in defining and implementing its policies and activities, the Union is to take into account requirements linked to the promotion of a high level of employment, the guarantee of adequate social protection, the fight against social exclusion, and a high level of education, training and protection of human health.[15]

[5] The Charter of Fundamental Rights of the European Union guarantees fundamental social rights in several provisions such as Articles 1, 12 and 47, but in particular in its Title IV 'Solidarity'.[16]

[12] Source of inspiration: Directive (EU) 2020/1828 of 25 November 2020 on representative actions for the protection of the collective interests of consumers and repealing Directive 2009/22/EC ('Representative Action Directive'), Recital (1).

[13] Source of inspiration: ibid, Recital (2).

[14] Source of inspiration: Directive (EU) 2018/957 of 28 June 2018 amending Directive 96/71/EC concerning the posting of workers in the framework of the provision of services ('Revised Posted Workers Directive'), Recital (1).

[15] Source of inspiration: ibid, Recital (3).

[16] Source of inspiration: Directive on transparent and predictable working conditions, Recital (1).

[6] Labour law should be applied effectively throughout the Union. But comprehensive studies in specific EU labour law areas have concluded that the effectiveness of Union law is compromised by a lack of awareness among claimants, competent authorities' hesitance in enforcing effectively EU labour law, and the inability of relevant stakeholders to contribute to the improvement of enforcement of labour and social rights, as well as workers' redress.

[7] At international level, all Member States are bound by the International Covenant on Economic, Social and Cultural Rights, the International Covenant on Civil and Political Rights, the eight ILO Fundamental Rights Conventions (Nos 29, 87, 98, 100, 105, 111, 138 and 182), as well as the Labour Inspection Convention (No 81).[17]

[8] ILO Convention No 81 contains, in particular, provisions on the means of enforcing workers' rights, which are common standards applicable at international level and implemented in all Member States. This Directive should not affect Member States' international obligations.[18]

[9] Despite the international instruments ratified by all Member States, there are still major disparities as regards the means of enforcing workers' rights.[19]

[10] The current disparities also lead to a weakening of substantive labour law and to a fragmentation of the Internal Market in this field. Effective enforcement of substantive labour law should be ensured by specific action at Union level.[20]

[11] This Directive does not aim to establish harmonised rules for judicial cooperation, jurisdiction, or the recognition and enforcement of decisions in civil and commercial matters, or to deal with applicable law. There are Union instruments that govern such matters in general terms and are, in principle, equally applicable to workers' rights.[21]

[12] It is necessary to define the scope of this Directive as widely as possible in order to encompass all workers' rights covered by Union provisions in this field and/or by the national law of the Member State concerned.[22]

[13] Breaches of Union labour law, regardless of whether they are categorised under national law as civil, administrative, criminal or other types of breaches, may cause serious harm to the public interest, in that they create significant risks for the welfare of society.[23]

[17] Source of inspiration: Directive 2004/48/EC of 29 April 2004 on the enforcement of intellectual property rights, Recital (4).

[18] Source of inspiration: ibid, Recital (5).

[19] Source of inspiration: ibid, Recital (7).

[20] Source of inspiration: ibid, Recital (9).

[21] Source of inspiration: ibid, Recital (11).

[22] Source of inspiration: ibid, Recital (13).

[23] Source of inspiration: Directive (EU) 2019/1937 of 23 October 2019 on the protection of persons who report breaches of Union law ('Whistle-blower Protection Directive'), Recital (3).

[14] Enforcement of worker protection currently provided for in the Union is fragmented across Member States.[24]

[15] Common minimum standards ensuring that workers are protected effectively should apply as regards acts and policy areas where there is a need to strengthen enforcement, and breaches of Union labour law can cause serious harm to the public interest. Member States could decide to extend the application of national provisions to other areas with a view to ensuring that there is a comprehensive and coherent worker protection framework at national level.[25]

[16] Effective enforcement of Union law requires that protection should be granted to the broadest possible range of categories of persons, who, irrespective of whether they are Union citizens or third-country nationals, by virtue of their work-related activities, irrespective of the nature of those activities and of whether they are paid or not, are in need of better protection.[26]

[17] The autonomy of the social partners and their capacity as representatives of workers and employers should be respected. It should therefore be possible for the social partners to improve the level of protection of workers beyond the level guaranteed by this Directive.[27]

[18] Given that the objective of this Directive, namely to strengthen enforcement of EU Labour Law and as regards acts where breaches of Union law can cause serious harm to the public interest, through effective worker protection, cannot be sufficiently achieved by the Member States acting alone or in an uncoordinated manner, but can rather be better achieved at Union level by laying down common minimum standards for worker protection, and given that only Union action can provide coherence and align the existing Union rules on worker protection, the Union may adopt measures, in accordance with the principle of subsidiarity as set out in Article 5 of the Treaty on European Union. In accordance with the principle of proportionality, as set out in that Article, this Directive does not go beyond what is necessary in order to achieve that objective.[28]

[19] This Directive respects, protects and fulfils fundamental rights and the principles recognised in particular by the Charter, in particular the fundamental social rights enshrined in Title IV 'Solidarity' (Articles 27, 28 and especially Article 31), as well as procedural rights in Title VI 'Justice' (in particular Article 47). Accordingly, it is essential that this Directive be implemented in accordance with those rights and principles by ensuring full respect for, inter alia, fair and just working conditions, the right to information and consultation, the right to collective bargaining and collective action, as well as the right to an effective remedy.[29]

[24] Source of inspiration: ibid, Recital (4).
[25] Source of inspiration: ibid, Recital (5).
[26] Source of inspiration: ibid, Recital (37).
[27] Directive on transparent and predictable working conditions, Recital (38).
[28] Source of inspiration: Whistle-blower Protection Directive, Recital (108).
[29] Source of inspiration: ibid, Recital (109).

Chapter I – General Provisions

Article 1 – Purpose and Subject Matter

The purpose of this Directive is, through the achievement of a high level of worker protection, to ensure the effective enforcement of EU labour law. To this end, this Directive also aims to improve workers' and trade unions' access to justice and fair trial, as well as all appropriate means of non-judicial enforcement.[30]

Article 2 – Material Scope

This Directive lays down common minimum standards for the effective enforcement of Union law in relation to the employment area.

Article 3 – Definitions

For the purposes of this Directive, the following definitions apply:

(a) 'right-holder' means everyone who can rely on a right in relation to the material scope, in particular, workers;
(b) 'employer' means any natural or legal person who has an employment relationship with the worker and has responsibility for the undertaking and/or establishment;[31]
(c) 'contractor' means any natural or legal person of which the employer is a direct or indirect subcontractor;[32]
(d) 'labour inspectorate' means the national body or bodies that have an inspection function on the labour market in a Member State;[33]
(e) 'third country national' means any person who is not a citizen of the Union within the meaning of Article 20(1) TFEU;[34]
(f) 'migrant worker' means a person who is to be engaged, is engaged or has been engaged in a remunerated activity in a State of which he or she is not a national;[35]
(g) 'workers representatives' means persons who are recognised as such under national law or practice, whether they are
    (i) trade union representatives, namely, representatives designated or elected by trade unions or by members of such unions; or

[30] Source of inspiration: Art 1(1) 2nd sentence of Representative Action Directive.
[31] Source of inspiration: Council Directive 89/391 of 12 June 1989 on the introduction of measures to encourage improvements in the safety and health of workers at work.
[32] Source of inspiration: Art 12(1) of Directive 2014/67/EU of 15 May 2014 on the enforcement of Directive 96/71/EC concerning the posting of workers in the framework of the provision of services.
[33] Source of inspiration: Proposal for a Directive to strengthen the application of the principle of equal pay for equal work or work of equal value between men and women through pay transparency and enforcement measures, COM/2021/93 final.
[34] Source of inspiration: Directive 2014/36/EU of 26 February 2014 on the conditions of entry and stay of third country nationals for the purpose of employment as seasonal workers ('Seasonal work Directive').
[35] Source of inspiration: UN International Convention on Migrant Workers.

(ii) elected representatives, namely, representatives who are freely elected by the workers of the undertaking in accordance with provisions of national laws or regulations or of collective agreements and whose functions do not include activities which are recognised as the exclusive prerogative of trade unions in the country concerned;[36]

(h) 'social partners' means, on one side, individual employers and/or their organisations and, on the other side, trade unions (irrespective of their respective corresponding levels or sectors);

(i) 'alternative dispute resolution' means a mechanism in out-of-court bodies involved in the consensual resolution of labour disputes.

Chapter II – Judicial Enforcement

Section 1 – Access to Court

Article 4 – Effective Access

Member States shall ensure that every right-holder has the right to effective access to justice[37] in a fair, timely, speedy, affordable and easily accessible manner.

Article 5 – Collective Redress

Member States shall ensure that representative trade unions and other representative and qualified entities have the right to bring representative actions before courts and competent administrative authorities on behalf of right-holders. Member States may decide at which stage of the proceedings individual right-holders are able to exercise their right to opt in to or out of a representative action.[38]

Article 6 – Legal Aid and Assistance

In their own prerogative, Member States shall ensure that every right-holder without sufficient resources has the right to legal aid and assistance,[39] including free translation, to be decided upon in a speedy and easily accessible summary procedure.

Article 7 – Jurisdiction

Member States shall ensure that right-holders can always bring a claim in the court of the Member State where they carry out work, in the Member State where either employer or contractor is domiciled or in the courts of the place where an accident at work occurred.

[36] ILO Workers' Representatives Convention, 1971 (No 135), Art 3.

[37] Source of inspiration: Art 47(2) CFREU ('Everyone is entitled to a fair and public hearing within a reasonable time by an independent and impartial tribunal previously established by law') which is based on Art 6(1) ECHR; the respective jurisprudence of the ECtHR provides for ample examples in relation to 'access of justice', even to 'effective right of access' (9 October 1979, No 6289/73, *Airey v Ireland*, para 24). Moreover, para 3 of Art 47 CFREU explicitly refers to 'ensure effective access to justice'.

[38] Source of inspiration: Representative Action Directive, Art 7.

[39] Source of inspiration: Art 47(3) CFREU.

Section 2 – Court Procedures

Article 8 – Fair trial

Member States shall ensure that every right-holder has the right to a fair trial. In particular, any interpretation of a procedural provision has to ensure that the position of the worker as weaker party in the employment relationship has to be effectively compensated.[40]

Article 9 – Speedy Procedures

Member States shall ensure that every right-holder has the right to the resolution of employment disputes with particular urgency.[41] Additional urgency should be foreseen for disputes in which third-country nationals are claiming their rights.

Article 10 – Injunctions

Member States shall ensure that in the course of a judicial procedure the judicial authorities may issue against the *prima facie* infringer an injunction aimed at prohibiting the continuation of the infringement. Non-compliance with an injunction shall be subject to a recurring penalty payment, with a view to ensuring full compliance.

Member States may provide that, in appropriate cases and at the request of the person liable to be subject to the measures provided for in this section, the competent judicial authorities may order pecuniary compensation to be paid to the injured party instead of applying the measures provided for in this section if that person acted unintentionally and without negligence, if execution of the measures in question would cause them disproportionate harm and if pecuniary compensation to the injured party appears reasonably satisfactory.

Article 11 – Evidence

Member States shall ensure that, on application by a right holder, trade union, workers representative, or representative and qualified entity, which has presented reasonably available evidence sufficient to support its claims, and has, in substantiating those claims, specified evidence which lies in the control of the opposing party, the competent judicial authorities may order that such evidence be presented by the opposing party, subject to the protection of confidential information.[42]

Article 12 – Burden of Proof

Member States shall ensure that every right holder has the right that, when this person has established facts from which it may be presumed that the measure

[40] Source of inspiration: Art 47 CFREU and the Judgment by CJEU in Case C-55/18 *CCOO*, ECLI:EU:C:2019:402, para 44.

[41] Source of inspiration: Art 47(2)1st sentence CFREU and the respective ECtHR jurisprudence in relation to employment disputes in which the Court stated 'that special diligence is necessary in employment disputes and that this requirement is reinforced additionally in respect of States where the domestic law provides that such cases must be resolved with particular urgency' (ECtHR, 10 December 2013, No 26042/06, *Vilotijević v Serbia*, para 53).

[42] Source of inspiration: Directive 2004/48/EC of the European Parliament and of the Council of 29 April 2004 on the enforcement of intellectual property rights.

against this person was based on unlawful grounds, it shall be for the employer to prove that the measure was lawful.[43]

Article 13 – Third Party Interventions by Trade Unions

Any trade union has the right to intervene as a third party in a court case in which it is not party itself.[44]

Article 14 – Legal Costs

Member States shall ensure that reasonable and proportionate legal costs and other expenses incurred by the successful party shall, as a general rule, be borne by the unsuccessful party, unless equity requires otherwise, taking into account Article 8 in particular.

Section 3 – Remedies and Sanctions

Article 15 – Principle

Member States shall ensure that remedies and sanctions, provided for by national law, for infringements of Union law in relation to the employment area guarantee real and effective judicial protection.[45]

Article 16 – Compensation or Reparation

Member States shall ensure that where compensation or reparation is made available under national law, it shall be adequate in relation to the damage sustained and shall extend, if available in national law, to punitive damages in a way which is dissuasive and proportionate to the damage suffered.

Article 17 – Sanctions and Fines

1. Member States shall lay down rules on sanctions applicable in the event of infringements of EU labour law and shall take all the necessary measures to ensure that they are effectively implemented and complied with. The sanctions provided shall be effective, proportionate, dissuasive and non-discriminatory.
2. Member States shall lay down rules on sanctions against contractors for non-compliance with EU labour law in so far as it concerns breaches of rules on remuneration, working conditions and health and safety. The penalties provided shall be effective, proportionate, dissuasive and non-discriminatory.

Article 18 – Specific Sanctions in Case of Child Labour, Forced or Compulsory Labour or Serious Breach of Occupational Health and Safety Rules

1. Member States shall ensure that infringement of prohibition of child labour, forced or compulsory labour and serious breach of occupational health and

[43] Source of inspiration: Provisions on (the reversal of) the burden of proof in several Directives (developed mainly in respect of anti-discrimination), in particular as a recent example Art 18(3) of the Directive on transparent and predictable working conditions.

[44] Source of inspiration: Rule 44 of the Rules of Procedure of the ECtHR.

[45] Source of inspiration: Art 47 CFREU and CJEU case-law (eg Judgment CJEU in Case C-14/83 *Sabine von Colson and Elisabeth Kamann v Land Nordrhein-Westfalen*, ECLI:EU:C:1984:153).

safety rules constitutes a criminal offence when committed intentionally, and natural persons who commit such an offence are punishable by effective, proportionate and dissuasive criminal penalties. Such criminal penalties should be applied without prejudice to other sanctions or measures of a non-criminal nature.

2. In respect of each infringement of this prohibition, Member States shall ensure that the employer shall be liable to pay any outstanding remuneration, taxes and social security contributions.
3. Member States shall ensure that legal persons may be held liable for any offence referred to in paragraph 1 where such an offence has been committed for their benefit by any person who has a leading position within the legal person and where the lack of supervision or control by such a person has made possible the commission of the offence referred to in paragraph 1 for the benefit of that legal person by a person under its authority. Liability of a legal person shall not exclude criminal proceedings against natural persons who are perpetrators, inciters or accessories in the offence referred to in paragraph 1.

Section 4 – Enforcement of Judgments

Article 19 – Principle

Member states shall ensure speedy and effective enforcement of judgments. Where a right holder has a right to compensation or any other follow-up right stemming from a final judgment, there should be no need for separate procedures for workers to assert and enjoy these rights and/or compensation.

Article 20 – Specific Protection for Migrant Workers

Member States shall ensure that judgments in favour of migrant workers, in particular concerning compensation due to them, are enforced independently of whether or not the worker has already left the territory of the Member State. To achieve this objective Member States should make sure that courts and administrative authorities have the necessary means, including available cooperation procedures, to reach migrant workers who could benefit from the judgment. Member States should adopt rules in order to ensure that where a worker who is a third country national has already left the Member State, they still can benefit from enforcement of a judgment in their favour, at the very least by receiving just compensation.

Chapter III – Non-judicial Enforcement

Section 1 – Role of Trade Unions and Social Partners

Article 21 – Trade Unions and Workers' Representatives

Legal provisions shall recognise the legitimate interest for trade unions and workers' representatives to combat non-compliance with EU labour and social law. To this end, Member States shall ensure that the respective means shall include:

(a) the right of access to continuous information on implementation and realisation of rights;

(b) the right to be consulted in relation to any improvement of enforcement;
(c) the right to act on behalf or in support of a right holder or a group of right holders who is the alleged victim of an infringement of any right or obligation related to social or labour law.

Article 22 – Social Partners

Member States shall ensure that the respective means for effective enforcement shall include

(a) the right of associations, organisations and workers' representatives or other legal entities which have, in accordance with adequate criteria laid down by national law, a legitimate interest in ensuring enforcement of workers' rights, to engage in any negotiations and/or, following judicial or administrative procedure, to enforce any of the rights or obligations related to labour or social law;
(b) the recognition of bodies or entities or practices established by social partners in order to promote enforcement of social and labour law;
(c) procedures for collective settlements aimed at providing redress to workers, but courts or administrative bodies should be given the power to set aside unfair settlements.

Article 23 – Social Dialogue

1. Member States shall, in accordance with their national traditions and practice, take adequate measures to promote dialogue between the social partners with a view to fostering effective enforcement of EU labour law, including through the monitoring of workplace practices, collective agreements, codes of conduct and through research or exchange of experiences and good practices.
2. Where consistent with their national traditions and practice, Member States shall encourage the social partners, without prejudice to their autonomy, to conclude at the appropriate level agreements laying down rules to promote enforcement in the fields referred to in Article 1, which fall within the scope of collective bargaining. These agreements shall respect the minimum requirements laid down by this Directive and by the relevant national implementing measures.[46]

Section 2 – Administrative and Criminal Enforcement

Article 24 – Labour Inspection

1. Member States shall ensure that appropriate mechanisms are in place for monitoring of employers, and where applicable, contractors, and that effective and adequate inspections are carried out in their respective territories to

[46] Source of inspiration: Directive 2006/54/EC of 5 July 2006 on the implementation of the principle of equal opportunities and equal treatment of men and women in matters of employment and occupation (recast).

ensure compliance with and enforcement of EU labour law.[47] The requirements provided for in the ILO Labour Inspection Convention, 1947 (No. 81) shall apply.

2. The number of labour inspectors shall be sufficient to secure effective enforcement of EU labour law[48] but not less than 1 inspector per 10,000 persons who work[49] and Member States shall ensure that an adequate number of experts and specialists with due knowledge of EU labour law are working in labour inspection.
3. With a view to increasing the effectiveness of inspections, Member States shall, on the basis of a risk assessment, regularly identify sectors or activities in which there is a heightened risk of infringements of EU labour law and use this information in planning inspections. In respect of each of those sectors, Member States shall, before 1 July of each year, communicate to the Commission the inspections, both in absolute numbers and as a percentage of the employers for each sector, carried out in the previous year, as well as their results.

Article 25 – Facilitation of Complaints

1. Member States shall ensure that there are effective administrative mechanisms through which workers may lodge complaints against their employers, directly or through third parties designated by Member States such as trade unions or other associations or a competent authority of the Member State when provided for by national legislation.
2. Member States shall ensure that migrant workers and third country nationals working in their territory have suitable mechanisms for lodging complaints against their employers. Complaint mechanisms should be accessible in multiple languages and personal assistance should be available upon request for completing and submitting complaints.
3. Member States shall ensure that there is a possibility to submit complaints anonymously.
4. Member States shall ensure that entities representing workers' interests, such as trade unions, works councils and other workers' representatives, have the right to request information on behalf of workers concerning working conditions, working time, remuneration, and reasons for dismissal. In any case the individual worker also has a right to request such information from the employer or the contractor.

[47] Source of inspiration: Seasonal work Directive.

[48] Source of inspiration: ILO Convention No 81 Art 10.

[49] Source of inspiration: ILO GB GB.297/ESP/3, Governing Body 297th Session Geneva, November 2006, para 13: 'the number of labour inspectors in relation to workers should approach: 1/10,000 in industrial market economies'. But it should not be limited to 'workers but to all persons who work (even if they do not have the recognized status of a worker').

Section 3 – Alternative Dispute Resolution
Article 26 – Principle

Member States have the right to establish independent, impartial, transparent, effective, fast and fair alternative dispute resolution procedures. This Directive is without prejudice to national legislation making participation in such procedures mandatory, provided that such legislation does not prevent the parties from exercising their right of access to the judicial system.

Article 27 – Exclusion

Mandatory, non-waivable, rights should not be subject in any case to alternative dispute resolution.

Chapter IV – Horizontal Provisions
Article 28 – Right to Be Informed

Every right holder, as well as their representative, has the right to receive information about the enforcement of their rights under EU labour law. Member States shall put in place appropriate mechanisms to comply with this requirement, including provisions for adequate redress where no such information has been provided.

Article 29 – Protection against Adverse Treatment

Member States shall ensure that right holders, including those who are trade union representatives or other qualified entities, are protected against dismissal or any other adverse treatment by the employer for seeking to exercise rights under this Directive and as a reaction to a complaint or to any legal proceedings aimed at enforcing compliance with the obligations under this Directive.

Article 30 – Promotion of Effective Enforcement

Member States where enforcement coverage is below a threshold of 70 per cent shall, in addition to all other measures, provide for a framework of enabling conditions for better enforcement, either by law after consultation of the social partners or by agreement with them, and shall establish an action plan to promote enforcement. The action plan shall be made public and shall be notified to the European Commission.[50]

Chapter V – Final Provisions
Article 31 – Non-regression and More Favourable Provisions

1. This Directive shall not constitute valid grounds for reducing the level of protection already afforded to workers within Member States.
2. This Directive shall not affect Member States' prerogative to apply or to introduce laws, regulations or administrative provisions which are more favourable

[50] Source of inspiration: Proposal for a Directive of the European Parliament and of the Council on adequate minimum wages in the European Union, COM/2020/682 final, Art 4(2).

to workers or to encourage or permit the application of collective agreements which are more favourable to workers.

3. This Directive is without prejudice to any other rights conferred on workers by other legal acts of the Union.

Article 32 – Transposition and Implementation

1. Member States shall take the necessary measures to comply with this Directive by … They shall immediately inform the Commission thereof.
2. When Member States adopt the measures referred to in paragraph 1, they shall contain a reference to this Directive or shall be accompanied by such reference on the occasion of their official publication. The methods of making such reference shall be laid down by Member States.
3. Member States shall communicate to the Commission the text of the main measures of national law which they adopt in the field covered by this Directive.
4. Member States shall, in accordance with their national law and practice, take adequate measures to ensure the effective involvement of the social partners and to promote and enhance social dialogue when implementing this Directive.
5. Member States may entrust the social partners with the implementation of this Directive, where the social partners jointly request to do so and provided that Member States take all necessary steps to ensure that they can at all times guarantee the results sought under this Directive.

Article 33 – Dissemination of Information

Member States shall ensure that the national measures transposing this Directive, together with the relevant provisions already in force relating to the subject matter as set out in Article 1, are brought to the attention of workers and employers, including small and medium-sized undertakings.

Article 34 – Review by the Commission

By …, the Commission shall, after consulting the Member States and the social partners at Union level, review the implementation of this Directive and propose, where appropriate, legislative amendments.

Article 35 – Entry into Force

This Directive shall enter into force on the twentieth day following its publication in the Official Journal of the European Union.

Article 36 – Addressees

This Directive is addressed to the Member States.

Conclusion

ZANE RASNAČA, ARISTEA KOUKIADAKI, KLAUS LÖRCHER AND NIKLAS BRUUN

1. Enforcement: The Forgotten Aspect of EU Labour Law

The enforcement of labour law within national boundaries has been receiving increasing scholarly and policy attention.[1] The same cannot be said of the enforcement of EU labour law, however. With limited exceptions, no comprehensive attempt has been made hitherto to critically assess the state of affairs in this area and to put forward proposals for the development of a regulatory framework to guarantee effective enforcement of labour rights that derive from EU law.[2] A number of reasons may account for this, including the relative absence of a sectoral approach to enforcement of labour rights in the EU regulatory infrastructure, the challenges associated with the implementation of EU substantive rules, predominantly set out in Directives, in relation to a relationship between, usually, a private employer, and a worker, and the resulting complexity for litigants and related stakeholders.

In this context, the starting premise of this collective work is that there is a close relationship between EU substantive labour rights and their enforcement mechanisms.[3] On one hand, without effective enforcement, EU labour law would be deprived of much of its content aimed at protecting workers. On the other hand, the entire objective of harmonisation of minimum labour standards within the EU would become an empty shell if enforcement mechanisms were not able

[1] For recent examples, see D Weil, *The Fissured Workplace: Why Work Became So Bad for So Many and What Can Be Done to Improve It* (Harvard University Press, 2017); G Davidov, 'Compliance with and Enforcement of Labour Laws: An Overview and Some Timely Challenges' (6 June 2021) 3 *Soziales Recht* 111–27, https://ssrn.com/abstract=3861150; G Davidov, 'The Enforcement Crisis in Labour Law and the Fallacy of Volontarist Solutions' (2010) 26(1) *The International Journal of Comparative Labour Law and Industrial Relations* 61.

[2] It will soon be 20 years since the publication of the book *Effective Enforcement of EC Labour Law*, edited by J Malmberg (Iustus, 2003) and it is more than 10 years since Bercusson devoted an important part of his landmark book on EU labour law to its enforcement (B Bercusson, *European Labour Law* (Cambridge University Press, 2009) 401–518).

[3] F Hoffmann and F Kurz, 'Introduction to the "Law of Remedies"' in F Hoffmann and F Kurz (eds), *Law of Remedies: A European Perspective* (Cambridge, Intersentia, 2019) 12.

to provide effective redress in cases of EU labour law violations. Recognising, as Bercusson argued, that EU labour law 'has specific qualities of enforceability which distinguish it from domestic labour laws',[4] we considered that it was crucial to address the question of EU labour law enforcement in a systematic and comprehensive way. All the more so given the unprecedented challenges facing the European social model in recent years. The financial crisis that started in 2007–08,[5] the growing influence of the gig economy and artificial intelligence on working conditions[6] and more recently the Covid-19 crisis have drawn attention to multiple enforcement challenges that limit the effective realisation of EU labour rights.[7] Also within the trade union movement, concerns have been raised regarding lack of enforcement. In its 2019–23 Action Programme, the ETUC stated with regard to the current situation:

> All too often workers suffer reprisals when they demand their rights. They are denied the right to be represented, or wait for years for a ruling, or encounter prohibitive legal costs. Even when workers win cases, they sometimes find it impossible to obtain cross-border compensation payments. The problems of enforcement cannot go on being ignored, or EU employment rights are in danger of becoming meaningless.[8]

From an academic perspective, recent analyses have attempted to provide a more comprehensive and, simultaneously, nuanced understanding of the issue of enforcement. In the law and regulation literature, attention is increasingly being paid to the need to address the issue of enforcement in a holistic way, thus extending the focus to include the issue of prevention and compliance, the role of stakeholders as co-enforcers, and strategic enforcement in ensuring effective redress (see also the Introduction to this book).[9] In the industrial relations literature, the challenge of enforcement has recently been linked to the existence of so-called 'protective gaps'. These may be further subdivided into mechanism gaps (for example, gaps in access, process, remedies), awareness gaps (such as lack of awareness of rights and how to enforce them), power gaps (for example, fear of loss of employment) and coverage gaps (such as the extent of workplaces that are not protected).[10] From a labour law perspective, it can be argued that the

[4] Bercusson, n 2 above at 403.

[5] For evidence of this, see, among others, the chapters in the book edited by N Countouris and M Freedland, *Resocialising Europe in a Time of Crisis* (Cambridge, CUP, 2013).

[6] See, among others, A Koukiadaki and I Katsaroumpas, 'Temporary contracts, precarious employment, employees' fundamental rights and EU employment law' (Brussels, European Parliament Policy Department C: Citizens' Rights and Constitutional Affairs, 2017).

[7] See European Commission, Guidelines on Seasonal Workers in the EU in the Context of the Covid-19 Outbreak, Communication from the Commission, Brussels, 16.7.2020, C(2020) 4813 final, L Vogel, 'Work, a blind spot in the Covid-19 crisis' (2020) HesaMag 22; www.etui.org/sites/default/files/2020-11/2-Laurent_Vogel_Work%2C%20a%20blind%20spot_in_the_Covid-19_crisis_2020.pdf.

[8] ETUC Action Programme 2019–23, 69.

[9] For examples, see also the references in n 1 above.

[10] See D Grimshaw, M Johnson, A Keizer and J Rubery, *Reducing Precarious Work: Protective Gaps and the Role of Social Dialogue in the UK* (University of Manchester, EWERC, 2016), https://documents.manchester.ac.uk/display.aspx?DocID=48990, 8.

emergence and manifestation of such gaps is intrinsically linked to the role of the regulatory framework. The latter may exhibit a Janus-faced function:[11] progress in one dimension (such as laws intervening to extend the range of stakeholders involved in enforcement) may be counterbalanced by movement in the opposite direction in other dimensions (for example, regulatory mechanisms failing to adapt in a way that would respond to changes related, for instance, to the rise of the platform economy). Such gaps may be amplified in the case of EU labour law as a result of its polycentric and multi-level regulatory framework.[12] All in all, it is becoming clear that a more holistic understanding of the regulation of enforcement of EU labour law, one that considers it as a constantly moving target, is required.

2. Reframing the Question of EU Labour Law Enforcement

When assessing enforcement, it is important to distinguish it from other, related concepts. As Dorssemont discusses in his analysis in Chapter 16, a distinction should be made first between enforcement and implementation of EU labour law: enforcement concerns action that contributes to the effective application or observance of labour law standards, while implementation refers to the setting of those standards. It is also generally accepted that the notion of compliance should be distinguished from that of enforcement, as the former does not focus on detecting violations but instead prioritises voluntary adherence to the duties imposed by legislation.[13] Whereas a number of chapters in this book focus on enforcement stricto sensu – that is, in the sense of detecting ex post violations and applying appropriate remedies and sanctions – the analysis in other chapters also considers the role of ex-ante compliance mechanisms (see, for instance, the analysis of health and safety by Cefaliello in Chapter 14). In a similar vein, the concept of 'soft enforcement' may be considered something of an oxymoron. As Chapter 6 on soft law by Kollonay-Lehoczky argues, however, this is not the case. Adopting a wide definition of enforcement that goes beyond remedial or penal procedures initiated before judicial or administrative organs in response to infringements or rights violations, it is suggested that so-called 'soft' methods may even achieve more stable results in the long term than traditional forms of enforcement.

[11] JC Barbier and F Colomb, 'The Janus Face of EU Law: A Sociological Perspective on European Law Making and its Influence on Social Policy in the EU' in JC Barbier, R Rogowski and F Colomb (eds), *The Sustainability of the European Social Model: EU Governance, Social Protection and Employment Policies in Europe* (Cheltenham, Edward Elgar, 2015).

[12] On this, see Koukiadaki and Katsaroumpas, who applied the concept of enforcement gaps to the case of EU fundamental rights and labour law in respect of precarious work, n 6 above.

[13] On this, see the discussion in Davidov (2021), n 1 above.

A central theme that emerges from the analysis in the various chapters is that the regulatory landscape for the enforcement of EU labour law has traditionally been characterised by vertical and horizontal fragmentation (see, among others, Chapter 1 by Jacobs on the overall EU regulatory architecture and Chapter 2 by Koukiadaki on how this plays out in respect of remedies and sanctions). At the vertical level, fragmentation largely reflects the fact that EU labour law enforcement has long been considered an exclusive task for the EU Member States. As Jacobs explains in his chapter, the enforcement mechanisms for EU labour law have traditionally relied on those established by Member States for their own domestic legal systems. However, this presents challenges on two fronts. First of all, as the enforcement mechanisms at domestic level were not established primarily to deal with EU labour law violations, they may not be able to capture adequately the complexities of such cases and provide effective redress. Secondly, reliance on domestic regulatory solutions may increase the risk of significant discrepancies between different systems and the ways in which they deal with such violations.[14]

On the horizontal level, regulatory fragmentation is largely the outcome of the lack of a consistent and systematic approach by the EU to the question of enforcing EU labour rights. This has two dimensions. The first is external, that is, vis-à-vis other areas of EU law. It is fairly undisputed that the issue of enforcement of EU labour law has not received similar levels of policy attention as other areas of EU law. The prime example here is competition law, where the establishment and promotion of enforcement mechanisms at EU level has long characterised the regulation of this area.[15] Other examples include intellectual property law, procurement law and consumer protection, where there is increasing evidence of more systematic attempts to address issues of enforcement.[16] With very limited and specific exceptions (such as with regard to posting of workers, see Chapter 8 by Houwerzijl) this has not taken place in respect of EU labour law. A second dimension of horizontal fragmentation is internal, namely between different EU labour law instruments. While the majority of EU regulatory instruments in labour law tend to defer to national rules and procedures on

[14] For instance, the REFIT exercise on the Written Statement Directive identified varying effectiveness of enforcement mechanisms. There was strong evidence to suggest that remedy systems based only on claims for damages were less effective at ensuring protection of employees' rights and ensuring compliance with the Directive. By contrast, the use of written statements as a protection mechanism appeared to be most effective in conjunction with other protection mechanisms, for example, in countries where there are strong trade unions and/or labour inspectorates with a mandate to monitor employers' compliance with the obligation to inform (Ramboll Management Consulting, 2016).

[15] See, for instance, Directive 2014/104/EU of the European Parliament and of the Council of 26 November 2014 on certain rules governing actions for damages under national law for infringements of the competition law provisions of the Member States and of the European Union.

[16] On procurement, see Directive 2007/66/EC with regard to improving the effectiveness of review procedures concerning the award of public contracts. On consumer protection law, see Directive 2005/29/EC of the European Parliament and of the Council of 11 May 2005 concerning unfair business-to-consumer commercial practices in the internal market.

enforcement, there are still significant discrepancies between different EU labour law rights. The clearest example of a progressive approach to enforcement may be found in equality law: a more comprehensive framework for the enforcement of such rights has been developed over time at EU level (see Chapter 10 on equality by Kollonay-Lehoczky). On the other hand, a rather piecemeal and generic approach seems to have been adopted in a wide range of other EU labour law rights, which may be inadequately tailored to respond to the challenges associated with these rights (see, for instance, Rainone's analysis of information and consultation rights in Chapter 12).

In this context, the book calls for the development of a conceptual and normative framework for the evaluation of the regulatory framework for the enforcement of EU labour law that builds on the concept of effectiveness. It is true that in EU law, the question of enforcement has been traditionally framed around the principles of effective judicial protection and effectiveness. The former seeks to ensure that, in an EU based on the rule of law, individual rights are protected by the courts. The latter, on the other hand, aims at ensuring that national rules do not impede the effective application of EU law, consistent with the broader principle of *effet utile*.[17] While these principles have been of crucial importance in the EU judicial architecture, it is notable that the term 'effective enforcement' has rarely appeared in CJEU case law related to social policy.[18] At the same time, the question of enforcement of EU labour law has been approached in EU regulation largely from the perspective of judicial processes, neglecting the role of administrative intervention and the role of other actors, most notably industrial relations actors, who have traditionally played a crucial role in enforcing labour rights.[19]

Taking these issues into account, we put forward a notion of effective enforcement of EU labour law that builds on the regulatory and conceptual developments in this area to date, but also extends the debate in two specific ways. The first is through adopting, as Malmberg and his colleagues suggested in the past, a broader notion of enforcement in EU labour law that should cover, not only judicial enforcement, but also enforcement through administrative and industrial relations processes.[20] While our approach is still largely doctrinal, various chapters

[17] For a useful summary of the similarities and differences, see HK Ellingsen, 'Effective judicial protection of individual data protection rights: Puškár' (2018) 55 *Common Market Law Review* 1879–98.

[18] A basic search in the Curia database reveals that 234 documents make reference to the notion of 'effective enforcement'. Out of these, only two decisions are related to social policy (see Joined Cases C-870/19 and C-871/19 *Prefettura Ufficio territoriale del governo di Firenze v MI* (C-870/19), *TB* (C-871/19), Case C-513/17 *Baumgartner*, ECLI:EU:C:2018:772). See also Opinions of Advocate Generals in Case C-171/18 *Safeway Ltd v Andrew Richard Newton, Safeway Pension Trustees Ltd*, Case C-274/18 *Minoo Schuch-Ghannadan v Medizinische Universität Wien*, Case C-69/08 *Raffaello Visciano v Istituto nazionale della previdenza sociale (INPS)*, Case C-268/06 *Impact*, Joined Cases C-231/06 to C-233/06 *Émilienne Jonkman and Others* and C-312/86 *Commission v France*.

[19] On this, see Malmberg, n 2 above.

[20] See also discussion in Malmberg, n 2 above.

illustrate how such mechanisms and the actors involved in them are crucial in the context of EU labour law enforcement (see, for examples, the chapters by Unterschütz (Chapter 4), Orlandini (Chapter 15) and Cefaliello (Chapter 14)). At the same time, our approach extends beyond the work of Malmberg and his colleagues as we seek to assess the state of enforcement across a wide range of areas, mechanisms and actors. In doing this, we aimed to provide a state-of-the-art evaluation of recent regulatory developments, while being attentive to the evolution of these issues across a longer historical period. In this respect, the Treaty of Lisbon (particularly Article 3, but also Article 19(2) TEU) and the elevation of the CFREU into primary law had the potential to alter considerable the regulatory landscape concerning enforcement of EU labour rights. Building on these insights, the ultimate way in which our work contributes to the debates in this area is in respect of the main premise behind the concept of effective enforcement. Rather than framing the notion of effectiveness on the basis of an EU market integration rationale, our objective is to evaluate the evolution and state of the enforcement regime in EU labour law against the ideals of social justice and progress, as explicitly advocated by Article 3 TEU.[21] On one hand, the notion of social justice is sensitive to the impact of structural inequalities in the employment relationship on the ways in which EU labour rights are enforced. On the other hand, the concept of social progress itself depends, among other things, on the dynamic development and adequate functioning of enforcement mechanisms for EU substantive rights. Conceptualised in this way, the effective enforcement of EU labour law requires a theoretical reconsideration of the nature, function and extent of the regulatory mechanisms made available to provide adequate redress in cases of violations of EU labour rights.

3. Evolution of the Enforcement of EU Labour Law: Quo Vadis?

Inspired by the framework described above, this book adopts a sectoral approach to critically evaluate the state of enforcement of EU labour law. In doing so, it integrates the expertise and analysis of several labour law scholars with the intention of setting out the wider context in which enforcement takes place (Part I of the book), the most salient areas of interest when it comes to substantive labour rights (Part II of the book), and the particular mechanisms and actors involved in these processes (Part III of the book). Our cross-thematic approach enables us to examine a wide range of specific labour policy areas, mechanisms and actors and to evaluate the ways in which enforcement has evolved in a manner that reflects the criterion of effectiveness in a polycentric and multi-level regulatory framework.

[21] For similar, see also N Countouris and M Freedland, 'Epilogue: Resocialising Europe' in N Countouris and M Freedland (eds), *Resocialising Europe in a Time of Crisis* (Cambridge, CUP, 2013).

Drawing on the rich analysis provided in each chapter, we can identify a number of broad themes related to the evolution and effectiveness of EU labour law enforcement. First of all, the analysis across topics, mechanisms and actors suggests that developments in the nature and extent of enforcement of EU labour law can be distinguished on the basis of three types of responses. The first consists largely of an express recognition of substantive labour rights at EU level, but deferring the issue of enforcement to the national level, albeit within the context of application of the principles of effectiveness, equivalence and effective judicial protection. This is the case in respect of, among other things, information and consultation rights (see Rainone, Chapter 11) and non-standard workers to some extent (see Kresal, Chapter 13). In a similar vein, while the issue of incorporating social clauses in procurement has been to some extent resolved with the adoption of the 2014 Directives, enforcement gaps exist when it comes to the enforcement of such clauses calling for the development of contractual solutions to fill those gaps (see Bruun, Chapter 19). A second type of response concerns extending already existing enforcement mechanisms. The most prominent example here is the EU legislation on anti-discrimination. The analysis by Kollonay-Lehoczky (Chapter 10) aptly elucidates the ways in which the enforcement regime in respect of equality rights has been progressively reconfigured in order to respond effectively to changing norms in society and economy. While there is certainly still room for improvement, the regulatory framework for enforcement of EU equality rights can be characterised as the most progressive in the labour law sphere. Another area in which there have been considerable developments in terms of the nature and type of enforcement comprises free trade agreements and association agreements. These have been used by the EU to exercise regulatory influence in the social policy field (among other things) beyond its own borders (see Deakin and Billa, Chapter 9). The third type of response focuses on setting new enforcement standards in areas that were previously largely unregulated. The interplay between criminal law and labour law is an example of an area in which there is evidence of regulatory innovation (see Chapter 5 by Unterschütz on enforcement by means of criminal law).

Beyond this range of responses, a number of related observations may be made regarding the nature and extent of regulatory changes dealing directly with, or affecting in other ways the way EU labour law has been enforced. The nature of labour law – that is, private but with public law elements – has meant that enforcement has usually combined elements of private and public enforcement.[22] In their capacity as private rights, labour rights have traditionally been enforced by the means of civil or specific labour law proceedings. At the same time, public authorities, often including, for example, labour inspectorates, play a significant role in enforcing labour rights. The advantages of pursuing private or public enforcement are quite distinct. On one hand, private enforcement relies

[22] See also Davidov, n 1 above.

on making use of private information about infringements and as such takes advantage of the claimants' ability to identify breaches of the law efficiently, while on the other hand, public enforcement may enable more effective allocation of enforcement resources.[23] The analysis in the chapters provides some evidence of a growing hybridisation of enforcement across a wide range of areas in EU labour law, including, for example, the area of migrant workers (for example, the Employers' Sanctions Directive, as discussed by Rasnača, Chapter 12).

Secondly, there is evidence of new enforcement agencies and mechanisms that have been established to address existing enforcement gaps. The most obvious example here is the EU's youngest agency, the European Labour Authority (ELA), which is responsible for ensuring fair labour mobility in the EU. As the analysis by Van Nuffel (Chapter 17) suggests, the ELA is not only a mechanism for monitoring the enforcement activity of national authorities, but can also function as a means of reinforcing the operational capacity of national enforcement authorities involved with cross-border labour mobility. An opportunity has been missed, however, to grant the new authority more far-reaching powers, including monitoring of national authorities through binding decisions sanctioned by penalties, which would have promoted the objective of enforcement more concretely. Another missed opportunity concerns the Whistleblowing Directive. In his analysis, Cobbaut (Chapter 18) underlines the particular interest of alerts for better enforcement of EU labour law because of the importance of the duty of prevention in the field of the occupational safety and health protection and the general absence of application of alert laws in EU labour law. The adoption of Directive 2019/1937, which aims to improve and harmonise the alert rules in EU law, could have addressed these shortcomings. Disappointingly, the Directive regulates only whistleblowing and does not cover reporting of violations of EU labour law. It is increasingly being recognised, however, that the environment in which the EU labour law framework operates demands a more strategic approach to enforcement that both builds on successful policies used in the past, but also puts forward mechanisms to capture the evolving challenges in the world of work. As the chapter on strategic litigation by Lörcher (Chapter 7) suggests, legal and human rights expertise is key to creating an enabling environment to better defend and promote workers' and trade union rights, fundamental social rights and human rights.

The emergence of new actors and agencies takes place against the wider context of the involvement in enforcement of long-established actors, most notably collective ones. The involvement of collective actors, particularly in the form of trade unions, reduces the possibility of workplace violations. As Dorssemont (Chapter 16) illustrates, collective actors are able to function as

[23] JU Franck, 'Private Enforcement versus Public Enforcement' in F Hoffmann and F Kurz (eds), *Law of Remedies: A European Perspective* (Cambridge, Intersentia, 2019) 128.

actors of enforcement of EU labour law mainly because three important tools are available to them: (i) monitoring the legal exercise of the managerial prerogative, (ii) access to justice, and (iii) recourse to collective action. However, an important and overarching obstacle for the effective enforcement of EU labour law is, as Lörcher (Chapter 3) identifies, the fact that the architecture of the EU judicial system fails at present to provide 'effective access to justice', given that direct access to EU courts is still practically non-existent, especially for trade unions. Furthermore, the scope for collective actors to engage in enforcement action has not always been well-defined. As Rasnača suggests, the regulatory mechanisms concerning migrant workers have largely adopted an individualistic approach, framing workers and employers as isolated individuals and lacking specific tools to help develop collective forms of solidarity.

Finally and relatedly, there is evidence of a growing EU influence on how national implementation of EU labour laws, norms and standards should be organised and executed. This has partly been driven by the evolution of the EU regulatory mechanisms dealing more explicitly with enforcement at supranational level, leading to a so-called supranationalisation of enforcement. It is also the result of the growing focus on the protection of fundamental rights through the CFREU and other EU-level initiatives in the social policy sphere (see Chapter 3 by Lörcher on access to justice and Chapter 20 on the EPSR by De Schutter). However, EU labour law enforcement is not only affected by regulatory developments dealing directly with such issues. It may also be affected by the operation of other norms, legal or otherwise, in other spheres of EU action. The idea of repurposing the powerful and seemingly malleable tool of New Economic Governance to further the enforcement of EU labour law constitutes the focus of the analysis by Schmitt and Rocca (Chapter 21). Their concluding assessment suggests that relying on New Economic Governance to advance a 'social' agenda would probably play into the hands of those who would like to see labour standards completely subsumed by the logic of competitiveness and budgetary rules.

All in all, a lot remains to be done for the purpose of promoting the effective enforcement of EU labour law. Inspired by the rich ideas developed by the authors of the various chapters, the penultimate chapter puts forward a comprehensive proposal for a Model Directive on EU Effective Labour Law Enforcement. In doing so, it seeks to address the twin challenges identified earlier, namely those of vertical and horizontal regulatory fragmentation, which jeopardise the effective realisation of EU labour rights. In putting forward this proposal, we are aware of two possible objections. The first concerns the fact that the call for coordinated action across many interconnected domains presents particular political challenges for the EU Member States, but also the social partners. However, there is a strong argument for being attentive to the need to approach the issue of enforcement of EU labour rights in a holistic way, even more so in the present challenging circumstances. The second challenge concerns the fact that effective regulation to deal with the issue of enforcement would have to cut across the boundary between EU and national competences.[24] Rather than advocating a set of EU prescriptive rules, we are calling for the establishment and promotion of a set of principles and guidelines that are sensitive to the particular characteristics of EU labour rights enforcement, but which also respect the diverse legal traditions and institutional differences between EU Member States, in particular by referring to minimum requirements.

[24] For a discussion of these issues in different contexts, see A Davies, 'Regulating Atypical Work: Beyond Equality' in N Countouris and M Freedland (eds), *Resocialising Europe in a Time of Crisis* (Cambridge, CUP, 2013); and Koukiadaki and Katsaroumpas, n 6 above.

INDEX

www.ingramcontent.com/pod-product-compliance
Ingram Content Group UK Ltd.
Pitfield, Milton Keynes, MK11 3LW, UK
UKHW021029041026
15470UKWH00013B/374

9 781509 944415